P9-EDW-199

DATE DUE

DISCARDED BY PC LIBRARY

ELIZABETHAN DRAMA AND SHAKESPEARE'S EARLY PLAYS

Peninsula College Library
Port Angeles, Washington

ELIZABETHAN DRAMA
AND SHAKESPEARE'S
EARLY PLAYS

An Essay in Historical Criticism

by

ERNEST WILLIAM TALBERT

5893

Chapel Hill

THE UNIVERSITY OF NORTH CAROLINA PRESS

PR 2976
.T23

Copyright © *1963 by*

THE UNIVERSITY OF NORTH CAROLINA PRESS

Library of Congress Catalog Card Number 63-21080

PRINTED BY THE SEEMAN PRINTERY, DURHAM, N.C.

Manufactured in the United States of America

To my wife

Preface

BECAUSE MANY of the following pages deal with the structure of plays, with details whereby a character is portrayed, and with the reflection of ready-made concepts and current representational methods in the dramas of Shakespeare and his early contemporaries, I probably should note at the outset that the reader may find it helpful to have the text of a play before him—although I hope, of course, that the main point of any discussion will be clear without his having to turn to the drama being considered.

Since the purpose and the point of view of the present essay are expressed in the first chapter, my pleasant duty here is to record my indebtedness. I am deeply grateful to Dr. James G. McManaway for his patient criticism of the entire study. I am also indebted to Professor D. T. Starnes for reading and criticizing some of the following chapters. If I have not profited from their suggestions, the fault is mine. I also owe much to my colleagues C. Hugh Holman and George M. Harper. They graciously volunteered to lighten my departmental duties during the final stages of preparing the manuscript of this study and of the related one entitled *The Problem of Order*. I wish to acknowledge my indebtedness to the Alumni Annual Giving funds of The University of North Carolina, administered by the University Research Council, for aid in the publication of this book and to the Ford Foundation for a grant under its program for assisting American university presses in the publication of works in the humanities and social sciences.

E. W. T.

Contents

ELIZABETHAN DRAMA AND SHAKESPEARE'S EARLY PLAYS

I

Some General Considerations

THE PRESENT STUDY is concerned with Shakespeare's dramas written from about 1590 to 1595-96 and with some plays by his early contemporaries. Very few of them are negligible as dramatic art. The point of view that will be preserved in the following pages is based essentially upon a single consideration. Before these dramas could be read in quarto or folio, they were seen and heard in performance; and thus their authors must have been concerned with the likely effect of their art upon an Elizabethan audience. As a result, the intricate discussions of possible strata in the dramas and the many revealing studies of their sources are not considered in any detail. In the first place, others have pointed out the well-founded objections to the theory of continuous copy. Here it is assumed, for example, that each play by Shakespeare, as it has survived in a form other than that given by the bad quartos, represents a dramatic development that was determined by him or at least acceptable to him.[1] In the second place, it is assumed that an Elizabethan audience, however aware it might be of the result, would not be aware, in general, of the way in which the authors followed or changed their sources, even though an individual spectator might be familiar with that material. The basic point of view of the following chapters is that for drama especially, "literature exists not only in expressing a thing; it equally exists in the receiving of the thing expressed."[2] At least Shakespeare, who was an actor as well as a playwright, must have been aware of this. Certainly he, as well as some of his early contemporaries, pleased Elizabethan audiences and molded their expectations.

At the outset, then, it seems well to note a few characteristics of the age that were so general and so obviously pertinent to the drama that they need little discussion. Elizabethan patriotism and Elizabethan animosity toward Rome could be useful tools for creating enthusiasm or hatred of situations and characters; and upon such grounds some of the following discussions of particular scenes rest.[3]

The taste of the age for a nonclassical multiplicity also needs little elaboration.[4] Either explicitly, or tacitly by their practice, such a predilection was recognized by literary men. Giraldi Cinthio and others defended the maxim that there could be more variety than classical precept would allow and still be an effective unity, and Ben Jonson defended writing in accordance with the "elegancie and disposition of the times" wherein he lived.[5] Jonson combined two comedies by Plautus, the *Aulularia* and the *Captivi,* to produce *The Case is Altered;* and Shakespeare in writing *A Comedy of Errors* also turned to two plays by that classical author, constantly doubled the mistaken-identity motif, and multiplied incidents. At the same time and in a variety of ways, both Jonson and Shakespeare also attempted to achieve an appreciable unity; for one of the basic artistic problems of sixteenth-century drama, as well as of the stage itself, was "the organization of a number of divergent scenic elements into some principle of . . . unity."[6] Obviously such a problem implies the dramatists' acceptance of an audience's predilection for multiplicity and diversity.

An Elizabethan author's elaboration of scenes might also accord with the emphasis that the age put upon its academic tradition and especially upon rhetoric. Although some assertions about the nature of Shakespeare's audience may seem to separate the illiterate and the educated, with the one demanding an unlicensed mirth and the other demanding rhetorical niceties, yet there is no reason to assume that the illiterate might not be entranced by rhetoric, even though some of it would be described by Jonson as "furious vociferation." The rhetoric of the long declamatory speech, moreover, frequently marked a dramatic process; and in an Elizabethan audience there were probably many persons aurally alert to any such development. Though not formally educated, many were accustomed to listening to sermons and they apparently delighted in public spectacle, with its frequent inclusion of rhetorical greetings and explanations.[7]

Of more importance than anything so far noted, however, is the basic but simple consideration that the literature being examined is drama. Even as in the present age, a spectator's presence within a theater would testify to his anticipation of being pleasurably aroused by the performance—an anticipation that would contribute to a particular sort of temporary but willing cessation of the powers of disbelief. Aside from the fact known to every rhetorician that the minds of men are more open to impressions when many are gathered together than when they are alone, the "affections" of men, as Bacon phrased it, "carry ever an appetite to apparent good" but behold "principally the good which is present." And as the present fills "the imagination more," the reason, with its dialectical process of thought, "is commonly vanquished and overcome."[8] Thus if a dramatist successfully works with the minds of men, their consciousness will tend to be bound by the momentary action of the stage, and a thoroughly false situation will arise whereby the theatrical plane of the stage-world becomes a momentary fact for the audience. In such circumstances, the spectators are concerned with the particular case, rather than with projecting that case speculatively against elements of reality that have preceded and that will follow the performance. The more the playwright is successful, the less impulsion and means the audience will have "to correct or criticize what is given here and now," "to limit . . . objectivity by measuring it against something not given, something past or future." In a much more limited sense than the way in which Cassirer used these words, but as part of a process analogous to mythical thinking, the spectator's consciousness will proceed increasingly upon what the author and his instruments, the actors, give it. "Truth" and reality will tend to dissolve "into the mere presence of the content," and the audience's consciousness will be bound by what is seen and heard. During the successful creation of a play-world, "all phenomena are situated on a single plane," and any tendency on a spectator's part to formulate *his* recollections will be overridden by the formulation that the playwright achieves as he creates a force that momentarily binds his audience's consciousness. The "single plane," the plane of the play-world, may have levels of meaning; but their existence will be started by the playwright's directing an audience's momentary attention to those levels and by his maintaining, in some way or another, a liminal consciousness of them.[9]

This is not to say that reflections of Elizabethan life do not appear in the drama. Because they may have contributed to an impression of actuality, they probably intensified a spectator's willing cessation of his power of disbelief. The pageantic, processional beginnings of some of Shakespeare's history plays must have seemed realistically familiar to anyone who had watched, from a house or a "standing," a royal entry or any other processional display.[10] The stage might also reflect current nontheatrical mirth. Certainly its creation of the comic might be expected to strike at least a note of familiarity. In other situations, however, this cessation could be inaugurated, in part at least, by what was familiar and expected in the surroundings in which acting usually took place. And once the dramatic movement of a play is begun, it will proceed upon what has become familiar within the play-world.

As a result, a knowledge of some characteristic situations, concepts, and roles in sixteenth-century drama is helpful for understanding the art of any one dramatist. Although the concern of the modern scholar is obviously not that of an Elizabethan playwright or audience, the audience might expect certain roles, such as one for the principal comedian; and with the possible or usual fate of certain serious types of character, a theater-goer might well be familiar.[11] In other words, even though precise delineations of typical characters are not entirely pertinent to the present point of view, that which might contribute to the vague expectations of a theater-goer should be examined. With those expectations, a playwright and his actors presumably would work as they created the particular and successive forms of any one drama unfolding upon the stage.[12]

An examination of conventional situations in Elizabethan drama also provides one with relatively firm grounds upon which to consider facets of an author's artistry that might be less theatrically obvious but that, like imagery, would contribute to the particular yet total effect of any one play and perhaps bind together that which was greeted with enthusiasm or hatred and that which was multiple, diverse, and rhetorical.[13]

Consequently, although strata and sources are not within the province of this essay, certain dramatic traditions very definitely are. In an attempt to describe and establish the validity of those traditions, certain aspects of the comic and certain aspects of structure and serious character-types are considered first. In these discussions, especially in the second one, the dramatic practise of Shakespeare's early contemporaries is emphasized. Shakespeare's plays are then examined against this background that seems to illumine both his technique and his intent in writing his dramas through *Richard II*.

Some readers, of course, may consider any concern with an author's intent to be essentially fallacious; and certainly reviewers have written that it "might be amusing to work out in this twentieth-century Shakespeare the age's dearly bought distrust of the English reputation for blundering into success, and something like a resolve that the greatest English poet shall not be set down for a haphazard fluker. . . ."[14] Yet any artist must control his materials, and any successful dramatist will capture his audience. To do so, he will develop narrative and emotional focal points, and his portrayal of characters will be effected by and within his dramatic order. Technique certainly can be analyzed; and by technique, intent is achieved—and for the critic, illumined. The following pages, consequently, consist almost entirely of analyses of dramas; and those pages are written in the belief that an author's artistry and its intent can be perceived best in the light of its genre and its age.

II

Aspects of the Comic

CERTAINLY A ROLE for the principal comic actor was expected and, indeed, demanded by an Elizabethan audience and an Elizabethan acting company; and in spite of Hamlet's advice to the players, one cannot assume that a playwright found the role distasteful, at least when it was controlled. In any play, such a part was meant to capture an audience's attention, regardless of whether the character turned a table on others, furthered his master's desires, reinforced or commented upon situations and upon other characters, or filled up a moment on the stage by appearing indecorously with a king or by answering a lady and talking bawdry.[1] Of course, English critics of the sixteenth century, like Continental opponents of tragicomedy or of the romance, were predisposed usually in favor of what they considered classical practice. A gentlemanly snobbishness or puritanic censoriousness, mixed with zeal for an apparently ancient book of rules, would criticize much comedy as indecorous or meaninglessly episodic; and the popularity of the public theater, with some carelessly executed plays, undoubtedly could supply material to substantiate this critical predisposition. In this respect, the modern may be closer to the theater-goer of the age than was the literary critic who repeated dogma about decorum or who, like Jonson's Mitis, condemned scenes for violating rules that the author never intended to follow.[2]

Actually a clown's conversation with a king or his bawdry with a lady may be controlled by a structural purpose. That is a matter to be determined by analyses of individual plays. Analyses would also determine whether the role for the chief comic was dominantly akin to what at least one modern critic, relying in the main upon the *Tractatus Coislinianus,* believes to be the basic comic types: the *alazon* (the imposter, boaster, or hypocrite), the *eiron* (the one who deprecates himself and thereby deflates or exposes the *alazon*), the *bomolochus* (the buffoon, the character who amuses by his mannerisms or power of rhetoric), the *agroikos* (the rustic and the gull).[3] From the point of view of an Elizabethan audience, however, any predisposition to classify probably would be overridden by laughter if the role were successful.

A kindred consideration holds true for the rhetorical doctrine of character-types. Literary men, actors, and at least some theater-goers might well have encountered those academic precepts based upon classical ones that were repeated *ad nauseam*: "a man of good years is counted sober, wise, and circumspect; a young man wild and careless; a woman babbling, inconstant, and ready to believe all that is told her"; "a soldier . . . a great bragger, and a vaunter of himself; a scholar simple; a russet coat sad, and sometimes crafty; a courtier, flattering; a citizen gentle." In addition to age, sex, and vocation, characters might be classified by nationality and an Englishman would be noted "for feeding" and varying his apparel, a Dutchman for drinking, a Frenchman "for pride and inconstance," a Spaniard "for nimbleness of body and much disdain," an Italian "for great wit and policy," a Scot "for boldness."[4] For what is appropriate to comedy, however, unless they were used to display a character's wit (as in Portia's description of her suitors), the general characteristics of rhetorical decorum when developed in the theater would fall in the main into such a classification as that based upon the *Tractatus Coislinianus,* and hence would be valid for the critic rather than for the Elizabethan watching the development upon a stage of an author's artistry.

To proceed upon relatively firm grounds in this instance means viewing scenes as far as possible in the light of the common comic experiences of sixteenth-century spectators; for one would assume that an author's attempt to produce laughter would proceed along the lines of whatever were the age's comic expectations and proclivities. At first glance, features of contemporary life like "naturals," bumpkins, and court-fools might seem particularly appropriate for any consideration of roles for the principal comedian; and a number of these individuals are described by the comic actor Robert Armin in his *Foole vpon Foole, or, Sixe sortes of Sottes* and his *Nest of Ninnies*. The range therein is certainly great. Armin's "sots" extend from harmless idiots to the violently insane. Treated with a laughing tolerance, an occasional or a frequent whipping—to which some were comically impervious or weepingly glad—their antics, necessarily parasitical, were those of a meaningless or a bungling stupidity, an apt shrewdness, or a ridiculous lunacy. Certainly the attributes just noted were constant on the sixteenth- and seventeenth-century stage. Witness Redford's Ignorance and Armin's own John i' the Hospital, the madmen used as vaudeville entertainers, and Middleton's attempt to represent classifications of madness in the late Jacobean play *The Changeling* (*ca.* 1622).[5] Yet in another sense, the range is small. Regardless of the probable derivation of Armin's pamphlet from a minor literary genre rather than from observation, it quite naturally does no more than describe some ridiculous figures. Like the existence of the court-fool,[6] it provides no background for any relationship between comic figures themselves; nor does it, naturally enough, indicate much in the way of motifs, both large and small, that normally might be associated with any principal figure causing laughter. Ideally, a much more appropriate background would be matter that probably was known to the regular theater-goer, that could have been known also to one never inside a theater, and that was dramatic. Fortunately, a considerable body of information exists that does fill in such a background in contemporary life and that can be of considerable use to the historically minded critic who frequently must be concerned with both comic intent and form.

The nature of some Elizabethan merriment, dramatic but not necessarily theatrical, can be fairly well outlined; and against such a background, for example, the comic reception of a "sot's" punishment—a situation similar to matter noted in Armin's treatise—and even of a character's unsuccessful attempt to hang himself can be fairly established. For it seems likely that such situations on the stage might well have been associated for audiences in general, not with instances of idiocy, madness, or man's inhumanity to man, but with the antic actions and confessions of a figure in the retinue of a Lord of Misrule or with that figure's death and resurrection as part of a larger sequence conventional to merriment.[7]

A wider but equally popular background is provided by the ballads and antics of minstrels and players, by songs hawked on the streets, and by revelry at taverns. From such a background the professional jig emerged as "a fad of the London populace when Elizabethan drama was at the peak," and the probability is great that "general allusions to ballad singing among the people cover many actual jig performances" and that "in their use of the ballad jig the comedians were merely giving a professional turn to what was common enough in everyday life."[8] The ballad singer appeared often enough in the contemporary scene to be attacked by Chettle in 1592 as one who had infected all of London and the neighboring shires; and when Butler published his *Principles of Musik* (1636), he attacked the influence on "unstable yunkers" of ballad makers and dance makers. The latter taught filthy practises and "immodest and shameless gestures"; but the former were even more guilty, for they spread their merchandise not only at "publik Merriments" but in private homes and on streets, where their "Factors" vented filthy songs "boldly without any blushing."[9] To Breton, ballads were "most in vse with Players, and Musitians, for else they goe downe the world for imployment."[10]

Obviously the nature and milieu of such merriment was both varied and wide. Lodge's character sketch of *"Immoderate* and *Disordinate Ioye"* in 1596 also indicates this. In *Wits Miserie* such unrestrained mirth is "incorporate in the bodie of a ieaster," whose "studie is to coine bitter ieasts, or to show antique motions, or to sing baudie sonnets and ballads." When given a little wine, he "hath all the feats of a Lord of misrule in the countrie."[11]

As one might expect, like their ancestors and their descendants, Elizabethans and Jacobeans of all degrees apparently delighted in song and dance, in spite of the disdain with which some might view it. Elizabethans and Jacobeans also seem to have enjoyed satiric rimes and the relatively formalized, though perhaps still disorderly, merriment that stretched from city tavern to the country. Like riddle songs or trick songs with verbal gymnastics that became bawdy when performed as a three- or four-man round,[12] the appeal of this balladry and mirth was not restricted to the vulgar and the uneducated. We are indebted to Peacham for the name of one who around 1620 was noted for what Lodge calls *"Immoderate* and *Disordinate Ioye"*—as Charles Chester, the Elizabethan, was, or as the Pastons' retainer Woode may have been in the years 1470-73 when he was not performing "Seynt Jorge, and Robin Hod and the Sheryff off Notyngham."[13] Although Godfrey Colton, as described in Peacham's *Worth of a Penny,* was a tailor by trade, he was also "a merry companion with his tabour and pipe, and for singing of all manner of *Northern Songs* [satirical pieces, or "bitter ieasts"] before Nobles and Gentlemen, who much delighted in his company; besides he was Lord of Stourbridge Fair and all the misorders there."[14] Obviously, both before and after 1663—when the Office of the Revels wished jurisdiction over such occasions—at rural feasts and wakes, revelling and music would occur constantly; and there would be minstrelsy, singing, and dancing at nocturnal feasts and banquets in public houses.[15]

In tavern-revelling an Elizabethan undoubtedly would encounter much merriment; and as part of the boisterousness, constant in any generation, this revelry might be expected to include the song and dance of the era as well as its mockery. As a result, the similarity between a passage in Heywood's *2 Edward IV* and Shakespeare's *1 Henry IV,* although it may result from borrowing, may also be explained by the fact that both passages seem to be rooted in current mirth. In Heywood's play, the French scorn of the English invaders is reported as being shown even in the drunken revelry of the French leaders. Jigs are made of the

English, and it is told in jests how they lie in the fields like rogues. One of the "drunken sottes," with a mock supplication and mock-heroic garments, impersonates an English herald, asks that a dog kennel be given his king for lodging, and with other like foolery causes all to burst out laughing:

> My Lord he [the Constable of France] lies, and reuelles at S.
>   Quintens,
> And laughes at *Edwardes* comming into France,
> There Dominering with his drunken crue,
> Make Jiggs of vs, and in their slauering Jestes,
> Tell how like Rogues we lie here in the field,
> Then comes a slaue one of those drunken sottes,
> In with a Tauerne reckoning for a supplication,
> Disguised with a cushion on his head,
> A Drawers Apron for a Heraldes Coate,
> And tels the Count, the king of England craues
> One of his worthy honors Dog-kennels,
> To be his lodging for a day or two.
> With some such other Tauerne foolerie:
> With that this filthy rascal greasie rout,
> Brast out in laughter at this worthy iest,
> Neighing like horses.[16]

With such a description, written by 1599 at least, should be noted the authorities' concern over ephemeral "seditious" matter that was performed "in hostels and taverns" and connected with songs and holiday games;[17] the bawdy ballads, "bitter ieasts," and "antique motions" of *"Immoderate* and *Disordinate Ioye,"* who with a little wine has "all the feats of a Lord of misrule in the countrie"; Chester's and Colton's comparable actions; and Colton's singing of satiric matter before nobles and gentlemen. At taverns and hostels one would normally expect the ballad singer or minstrel; and thus there might be established a milieu for the age's song, dance, and witty improvisation or for a theatrical jig, which could always be mimicked for impromptu merriment.

When in more sophisticated circumstances Ben Jonson and his friends established rules for their meeting in the Apollo chamber of the Old Devil Tavern, they seem to have had in mind features of the immoderate joy just indicated. Characteristically enough, they wished to restrain rather than abolish it. No minstrel, consequently, could enter the chamber while they were revelling unless he had been summoned: "15. Fidicen, nisi accersitus, non venito." Only when a person had been admitted (or only when he had been initiated) would feasts be celebrated with "laughing, leaping, dancing, jests and songs/And what ere else to grateful mirth belongs": "16. Admisso; risu, tripudiis, choreis, cantu, salibus, omni gratiarum festivitate, sacra celebrantor."[18] Bitter jests are banned; and the banalities of generalized satire as it might be extemporized or developed from set "improvisations" may have been part of the background condemned by rules 18 and 19: "18. Insipida Poëmata nulla recitantor"; "19. Versus scribere, nullus cogitor."[19]

With popular merriment in mind, one may not need to take refuge in a polite doctrine of scholarly despair and say that we are ultimately helpless to analyze comedy because of the greatly different effect it would have upon a London footman, a Gabriel Harvey, and a witty Nashe.[20] A variation in appreciation will always exist. The literary and academic antecedents of much Renaissance comedy would be quite unknown to a footman or a lord's rustic retainer in a London theater for the first time. Yet the likelihood is great that both retainer and footman would bring to their experience in a theater the comic anticipations and the proclivity for laughter that would be derived from what they had encountered in the vaguely dramatic circumstances of popular song, dance, and merriment, both extemporaneous and formalized. Thereby at least a part of the variation between the reactions of an academically trained spectator and of a muddy "gaper" in the pit could be one of degree rather than of kind. The pamphlets of Harvey and Nashe —to preserve the example—show a familiarity and an effective use of comic motifs and phrases that were conventional to folk merriment. As a result, against this background of current mirth, the artistry of Elizabethan playwrights sometimes can be analyzed more fully and their comic intent determined more objectively than may have been realized. A concern with such a background also agrees with conclusions of writers who are interested in the general nature of comedy and the comic: "Comedy is an art form that arises naturally whenever people are gathered to celebrate life, in spring festivals, triumphs, birthdays, weddings, or initiations. For it expresses the elementary strains and resolutions of animate nature, the animal drives that persist even in human nature, the delight man takes in his special mental gifts. . . . What justifies the term 'Comedy' is not the ancient ritual procession, the Comus, honoring the god of that name . . . but that the Comus was a fertility rite and the god it celebrated a fertility god, a symbol of perpetual rebirth, eternal life."[21]

Although one may wish to avoid too great an extension of the remarks just quoted, the matter to be considered here is concerned very much with what arose when Elizabethans gathered together in a holiday mood, when they took delight in their mental gifts, and when that holiday mood would be created. When elections to the House of

Commons could cause duels and feuds, when bullbaiting and bearbaiting were popular sports, it should not be surprising that Shakespeare and his contemporaries showed a red-bloodedness that did not exclude mental dexterity but that also utilized the laughter and merriment of the "vulgar." Such a statement need not be construed as an assumption derived by a modern in sentimental retrospect.[22] Elizabethan thought, however subtle, might always be close to the mythical; and Elizabethan living, however magnificent, close to the "crude." However much his comedy might be concerned with correcting values and manners, Ben Jonson never forgot its roots in the common fertile soil. The following discussion, consequently, proceeds upon the assumption that in a society wherein situations, motifs, and typical characters appear constantly in contexts of merriment, an author can draw upon that association when he wishes to produce laughter. Indeed, laughter always demands some element of familiarity, as well as some distortion to produce a modified shock. Moreover, when those situations, motifs, and characters are reflected in any one play, they can be used to produce a dramatic process that verges upon a comic automatism, as the figures involved may be risibly inadequate or sympathetically laughable in a vigorous adequacy.

At any rate, when one turns to a more detailed consideration of Elizabethan merriment, the nature and the popularity of which have been indicated briefly, a logical beginning would be to examine some aspects of comic wooing. No motif was more widespread—so much so that it had some conventional enlargements in its usual representation. A basic one provided the central wooer with rivals; and thus the Lord of the Induction in Shakespeare's early "native" farce can say to an actor about a role which turns out to be that of "Soto,"[23]

> This fellow I remember,
> Since once he play'd a farmer's eldest son.
> 'Twas where you woo'd the gentlewoman so well.
> I have forgot your name; but, sure, that part
> Was aptly fitted and naturally performed.
> *Sincklo.* I think 'twas Soto that your honour means.
> *Lord.* 'Tis very true; thou didst it excellent.

> (ll. 83-89)

That the fool, or "sot," won the maid was characteristic of rival wooing in the dance drama of the folk; and also characteristic was the inclusion in the wooing group of a figure like the farmer's eldest son, developed with varying effectiveness, but usually with the intent of ridicule. Such a figure might be associated quite naturally with the actor Sincklo, or Sincler, because of the Elizabethans' apparent reaction to his skinniness. The locale, before an alehouse in the country, is noticeably congruent; for these Shakespearian characters, including the one portrayed by Sincklo, are meant to represent traveling players, whose performances for a country audience might well have paralleled in a sophisticated manner the antics of May Day on the village green.[24]

Much earlier in the century, in the "Proclamation" to his *Satire of the Three Estates,* Lyndsay introduced with a dance a scene that treated farcically the rival-wooing motif. Therein a courtier, a merchant, a clerk, and a fool wooed an old man's wife.[25] The basic situation, including the success of the fool, parallels, for example, the Revesby Play; and the motif of rival wooing can be connected with a great variety of corresponding literary phenomena that are not necessarily comic, though related to folk entertainment: with, for example, the many wooing songs and ballads having at least two interlocutors; with the survival into the Renaissance of the medieval *demande d'amour* and the *pastourelle* tradition; and, indeed, with all forms of song and dance dramas and singing games in which groups of rivals appear.[26] Variations on the stage akin to wooing dance and song, serious or comic, range from a mocking dance directed at the cuckold Mars[27] to Peele's inversion of the basic situation being considered here. Handled in part by pantomime in his courtly *Arraignment of Paris,* Peele's punishment of Thestylis shows the scornful "faire lasse" wooing a "foul, croked Churle." She sings an old song called the "Wooing of Colman," is "crabedly" refused, and then tarries behind to sing a complaint and farewell replied to by a shepherds' chorus.[28]

That the maid might be won by the fool or the country clown agrees not only with many comic wooing songs but also with the fact that in his association with folk play or game, the fool is commonly the cleverest dancer;[29] and strikingly appropriate for our purpose are the fool's associates in these dramatic pieces. Although the old man is usually the major rival of the fool-clown, as in the mummers' play, he may be surrounded by other wooers who reflect the society concerned, as Lyndsay's "Proclamation" indicates. This is especially true for plays of the Lincolnshire region. There one finds the eldest son, the farming man, and the lawyer (the Bassingham Play), or the knight, the lawyer, the eldest son, the husbandman (the Broughton Play).[30] In one scene of the Revesby Play appear the "Lord of Pool," the "Knight of Lee," the beggar man or man of "poor estate," and the money lender. In another scene, two of the "Britches" are a "youth of jollitree" and an "eldest son"; while in the preceding situation the fool had driven out the dancers of the sword dance "Nelley's Jig" and had posed as "a valiant knight just come from [over] the seas," one who would not have shown his valour "had it not been in this country." During the later contest in love addresses to Cicely, a soldier says his part, although the emphasis falls conventionally upon the old wealthy wooer against the lusty wooer (the fool); and it is this last figure, of course, who can make the wench "laugh in a secret place."[31]

In jigs and ballads current during Elizabeth's reign, such characters as those just enumerated, as well as the cobbler and the miller, appear in the simplest of situations and also in situations with a varying farcical emphasis and with a varied blending of popular and sophisticated comic material—a variety achieved also by plot devices that may have close analogues in Boccaccio's *Decameron,* for example.[32] There is little need to specify Guilpin's "Satire V" as a sign of the popularity of such material;[33] the utilization of it on stage can be seen at the end of the century in such varying groups of rival wooers as the student, lawyer, and clownish son of a farmer in *Wily Beguiled* (1596-1606); the parson, miller, and cobbler in *Grim the Collier* (1600); and the rivals pursuing the country girl in Jonson's *A Tale of a Tub* (*ca.* 1596)— eldest son and squire, justice, and husbandman, with the maid crudely desirous of a mate.[34] With this group, who are placed in Queen Mary's reign, Jonson associates a rural priest disguised as a soldier. Although he is not a rival wooer, he is involved intricately in the complications. Here, and elsewhere in this portion of the discussion, the question, of course, is not one of indebtedness, but of motifs and figures to which an audience was comically accustomed and out of which might arise, relatively easily, the hilarity of Elizabethan comic artists, embroidering such matter with their particular variations.

After the fool, the old man was usually the most prominent member of a comic group concerned with wooing. In the *Mirrour of Good Manners,* when he describes such a figure, Barclay adds details to "non benè saltantis personam sustiner [*sic*] ille":

> Not well presenteth he the wower in a daunce,
> But very ill he playeth the volage amorous,
> Which fetered in a gine would gambalde leape
>   and praunce,
> Attached to a chayne of linkes ponderous.[35]

Whatever kinship may exist between Pantalone and particular representatives of this figure, the ridiculous old man must have been almost as familiar to an Elizabethan as the fool-clown; and to create laughter he probably needed relatively little development. He appears not only in mummers' plays but in jigs and in singing games, and in such ballads as that entitled "The Complaint of a widdow against an old man." The ballad began "Shall I wed an aged man" and probably continued in a manner that accorded with the grotesque capers in dancing which the old wooer might perform.[36] Similarly connected with this figure, for example, is one of Squartacantino's songs in *The Bugbears* (III, i, 1-18), a song on his master who is ridiculed as a lover and who, in spite of his "gray beard," "daunceth, praunceth, *and* skippeth, *and* playeth friskoioly, *and* singeth" as if he had colt's teeth in his head instead of the "fayre payre of hornes" he will undoubtedly get from one "sick of two left heeles" (ll. 22-53).[37]

As part of the comic development of the wooing motif, the girl herself may be bold, as with Jonson's Audrey in *A Tale of a Tub* or Porter's Moll in *The Two Angry Women* (1596-98). Sidney created the ugly but love-sick Mopsa in the nondramatic and polite circumstances of his *Arcadia*. In an entirely different context, but with a definite sureness of touch, Shakespeare has Beatrice describe Benedick as an omnivorous swaggerer (*Much Ado about Nothing,* I, i, 48 ff.); and when she sees the future marriage of hero and heroine, Shakespeare has her remark, with memory of songs given the bold or foul girl, "Thus goes everyone to the world but I, and I am sunburnt. I may sit in a corner and cry 'Heigh-ho for a husband!' " (II, i, 330-32). When Celia reproves Rosalind for her bold conduct that has betrayed her sex, one realizes that Shakespeare's heroine is a gentle parody of this type (*As You Like It,* IV, i, 205-8). Young, naïve, and lusty, or old and repulsive, or with any combination of those attributes, the bold female was undoubtedly familiar to the most uneducated spectator in the pit through ephemeral and semidramatic literature[38]—just as she also might be familiar to the best educated spectator in the gallery through her possible Italian prototypes.[39] Only a step removed in one direction were shrewish women and, in another direction, roistering females, imagined or real, who, like Meg of Westminster, were celebrated in popular song.[40]

More general in nature, but appearing likewise on the stage, in ballads and in jigs, were parodies of terms of endearment, prayers for kisses, sufferings of the lover, laments at parting, and other aspects of wooing.[41] The association between cries against Cupid and their comic utilization by Tarlton is neatly illustrated, well after the comedian's death, by a passage in *Greenes News both from Heauen and Hell.* Therein an assembly called by Lucifer is broken up when Tarlton enters "apparrelled like a Clowne, and singing this peece of an olde song":

> *If this be trewe as true it is*
> *Ladie Ladie:*
> *God send her life may mende the misse,*
> *Most deare Ladie.*[42]

The song is a parody of the famous Elderton ballad "Pangs of Love" (1559); and the constant mocking of this matter can also be illustrated by such a song as "It fell upon a sollem holledaye," with the lover's bombastic narrative of being shot by Cupid and a boy's mocking refrain.[43] Such matter provides a "vulgar" parallel for a favorite comic device underlying dialogue in even Lyly's sophisticated plays. Witness Sir Thopas, Epiton, and others (*Endymion,* V, ii), or dialogue between Shakespeare's Armado and Moth; while Strumbo's love-sickness in *Locrine,* and that of his kin, is the full theatrical equivalent of Tarlton's parody in Hades.[44] On a higher scale, when the transmuted Benedick sings four love-sick lines of another Elderton ballad of *ca.* 1562-63, the merriment of the last act of *Much Ado* is briefly, but realistically and surely, heightened.[45]

Parodies of wooing and marriage usually emphasized shrewish wives and the noisy bawdry of brawling females. About the latter group in contemporary life such ordinances as an Edinburgh one were bound to be ineffective: "na maner of wemen within this burgh speciallie the frute sellares [shall] be fund on the hie gaitt flyting with others or with the officeris of the burgh or using of ony maner of bairdrie."[46] Such scolding and bawdiness—the realistic accompaniment of a literary "flyting"—was apparently a common form of merriment. When fish-women "haue done their Faire, they meet in mirth, singing, dancing, and in the middle as a *Parenthesis,* they vse scolding, but they doe vse to take and put vp words, and end not till either their money or wit, or credit be cleane spent out." From the days of Dunbar and Skelton to those of the Pepys collection of ballads or D'Urfey's *Wit and Mirth, or Pills to purge Melancholy,* this exercise of wit and scurrility continued to be reflected in popular literature. So did railing between the sexes, as did ballads and songs of the *mal mariée* type.[47] On an actual holiday level were the Easter Smacks and Hocktide abuse between the sexes and perhaps the quarrelling lovers Jonson would exclude from the Apollo Chamber; while upon the academic stage, Ralph Roister Doister called for a dance to accompany a comic song on the duty of the husband to be subservient to his wife, and Delia and Iniquity of *Nice Wanton* sang a mocking *mal mariée* dialogue.[48]

Ballads constantly celebrated the shrew, as did the following piece that represents what possibly may have been sung and danced by Kemp, who in its performance may consequently have appeared as a cobbler, one of the conventional associates or guises of the clown-fool: "A merry new Song. Wherein is shewed the sorowful Cudgelling of the Cobler of Colchester, and the great fault he committed against his wife, for the which he suffered hard penance. To a pleasant new tune called Trill lill."[49] The existence in literature of many variations upon the major motif of shrewish wives needs no elaboration. It is doubtful that anyone escaped it. Domestic brawls, lusty interviews and intervals, and other comic features of both wooing and marriage were celebrated consistently in ballads, song, and dance; and thus there was established an ephemeral parallel to theatrical performances, if not from the days of "goodman Adam," at least from the days of Noah and his wife. Against such a background should be placed Heywood's adaptation of French farce, a portion of Lyndsay's proclamation in his *Satire of the Three Estates,* or a scene in Ingelend's adaptation of I. Ravisius Textor. Here belongs the shrewish wife of John Cobbler, who is associated with Derricke in *The Famous Victories;* and here too Strumbo in *Locrine* would appear, with his vigorously lusty means of controlling his shrewish consort.[50] In such a wide and noisy tradition of hilarity, *The Taming of a Shrew* and Shakespeare's *The Taming of the Shrew* were written; while a generation of clown-fools upon the stage were married to shrews of varying virtue. Witness Ralph in the *Cobbler's Prophecy,* Bullithrumble in *Selimus,* as well as John Cobbler and Strumbo mentioned above.[51]

In ephemeral literature, with both shrew and roisteress, but usually divorced from a wooing motif, might appear a crew of tavern-haunters, cutting-dicks, roarers, robbers, and prostitutes, or such figures as the miller, cobbler, and collier—groups that surrounded or dominated female boldness in city or country.[52] Such comic matter swirled from Elizabethan street and country to singing jig and stage jest and back again. Of the preceding groups only bawd, prostitute, or sharper might object—a possibility seized upon by Chettle, who in his *Kindheart's Dream* (1592) has a bawd complain to the comedian Tarlton that players "open our crosse-biting, our conny-catching, our traines, our traps, our gins, our snares, our subtilties: for no sooner haue we a tricke of deceipt, but they make it common, singing Iigs, and making ieasts of vs, that euerie boy can point out our houses as they passe by."[53]

Meretrix, Vice, and the two swaggering soldiers of *Cambises* should be placed against such a background, as well as against the constant parodies of wooing and marriage. Also appropriate here would have been that lost play by Dekker and others written in 1624 and called *Keep the Widow Waking.* Its comic plot was woven into the serious one of a contemporary murder by one Nathaniel Trindall, and both stories had been sung on the streets. The authors also developed the natural affinity between low-life cozenage practiced upon the old and wealthy Mrs. Elsdon and the comedy of mock wooing, tavern-revelry, and farcical interlude in which a sharper takes part. That affinity would certainly contribute to a comic view of the duping of an old woman in an alcoholic stupor; and it might well seem to demand the addition of such a rival-wooing motif as is indicated by the ballad that refers to the play. According to that song, not only does a sharp youth woo the old widow in the play at the Red Bull but so do a broker, a horse courser, and a comfit maker. Although it could have been true for the first two figures as well, only about the comfit maker is there any indication of the possible satire that might have caused the author's choice of wooers:

> The third would wyn with sweete words,
>   he practiz't Comfit makeing,
> But all his wit noe tricke affords
>   to keepe the widowe waking.

In that lost play, a "Lawyer with a nimble tongue" also appeared, probably on the basis of the actual event.[54]

Similar satire occurs in many other plays when a comic actor apes his betters and thereby parodies those derisible persons who pretended to be accomplished in the ways of a sixteenth-century gentility. The pose of the fool in the Revesby Play as "a valiant knight" from over the seas corresponds with the fact that ridicule of the pretentious dolt and upstart was strikingly apparent in some of Kemp's jigs and must have occurred in much nontheatrical mimicry and burlesque.[55] In ballad and song, the clown would boast of rustic wealth as an inducement to his love; or in rivalry with a knight, he would make a show of boldness to cover his cowardice.[56] Thus when Kemp as the sham gallant wished to be called "Monsieur" and "Cavalier," he was continuing a comic motif in ephemeral mirth and one that had been developed more fully in formal drama since, at least, the first pose of Mak in the Towneley mystery cycle. Apparently the comic actor Tarlton sometimes developed his off-stage antics with a ridiculous bravery,[57] and upon the stage as Derricke in *The Famous Victories* he may have spoken such lines as the following: "Am I a clown? Sownes, maisters, Do clownes go in silk apparell? I am sure all we gentlemen Clownes in Kent scant go so well: Sownes! you know clownes very well: Heare you, are you maister Constable? And you be, speake, for I will not take it [the word "clown"] at his [Robin Pewterer's] hands" (ii, 136-41).

Although the comedian usually backs down from such a pose, comparable lines appear in the *Cobbler's Prophecy*;[58] while in *Selimus,* Bullithrumble, with the clown's great "slops," would nevertheless imitate the Constable and a well-educated man's metaphorical language. Thus he comments on his phrase "society of puddings": " . . . did you marke that well vsed metaphor? Another would haue said, a company of puddings: if you dwel with me long, sirs, I shall make you as eloquent as our parson himself" (ll. 1983-87). This provincial clown, lusty for food and posing as one of his betters, also is convinced that the emperor's son is a conycatcher: "Good Lord, Sir, you are deceived, my names master *Bullithrumble:* this is some cousoning conicatching crosbiter, that would faine perswade me he knowes me, and so vnder a tense of familiaritie and acquaintance, vncle me of victuals" (ll. 1949-52). With a different variation, this comic attitude is reflected in *The Three Ladies of London.* Simplicity would no longer be a miller because girls call him "Dusty-poll" and strike him on neck and "noll"; yet he, too, thinks he is a fine fellow.[59] The continuity of such ridicule is attested also by *Edmond Ironside,* when one Stitch assumes the manners of gentility and enters "in his lord*is* attire with Blewcoates after him" (ll. 1243-56, 1261-70).[60]

In a comparable manner, but with derision pointed at the characters themselves rather than at those whose manners the principal comedian might be aping, Robert Wilson elaborated the general social satire that also appeared in ephemeral song and dance.[61] In this respect, his comedies might be related also to the rival wooers in folk drama, who represented the organization of rural society and who would become faintly derisible even as they were worsted by the fool-clown. In contrast with Simplicity, the rustic man of false importance in *The Three Ladies of London* is Dissimulation, a farmer with a long coat, a cap, and a "party-colour'd" poll and beard. Although townsfolk may believe him honest, in the country he did "nothing but cog, lie, and foist with Hypocrisy."[62] Akin to Dissimulation is the fawning, wealthy country gentleman in the *Cobbler's Prophecy*; but when, for example, he would buy the soldier to be a captain for him, he is duped into the ranks instead.[63] Although the soldier is at times an honest and outspoken individual, he too represents an appropriate roguery and ridiculousness.[64] By such characters, as well as by the disdainful courtier,[65] Wilson develops one of his favorite points. Only a herald can "decipher a Gentleman from a knave"; but with times as they are, heralds wait to see who "grows to wealth, / And comes to beare some office in a towne" before they help anyone to a coat-of-arms (ll. 750-72). These characters certainly could have had overtones of familiarity for even a footman or a rustic retainer, who might well have encountered in folk play or in ballad the farming man, the husbandman, the eldest son, and the knight, as well as ridiculous but more citified types approaching gentility. Wilson's Fraud is especially interesting. When given a sword and buckler, he cares not whom he serves—even the devil himself. He promises to "flaunt it and brave it after the lusty swash," and such a development reminds one of a speech, with its appropriate action, that is given the fool at one point in the Revesby Play:

> I can kill you a man for an ounce of mustard,
> Or I can kill you ten thousand for a good custard.
> I have an old sheep skin,
> And I lap it well in,
> Sword and buckler by my side, all ready for to fight![66]

In another derisive direction appeared the Spaniard, both lusty and wooing, both in jig and ballad.[67]

Certain minor themes in the popular comic tradition were also well-known, although they were not so widely dispersed as the motifs and figures sometimes connected with wooing and marriage. The country-man's wonder at the city, the world-upside-down theme, and news from a variety of places could be used for social and religious satire.[68] Especially the last of these motifs seems to have been popular in the latter half of the sixteenth century.[69] We hear of it in connection with religion in the second year of Mary's reign, when an apprentice of a minstrel at Colchester was tortured for a song "called Newes out of London, which tended agaynst the Masse and against the Queenes mis-proceedinges." Roy and Barlow of *Rede me and be nott wrothe* give an account of the death of the Mass in a news dialogue; and in 1557, players were arrested for a "Sacke full of Newes." In 1574, Fenton added to his source a condemnation of magistrates who do not suppress "these Players, whether they bee Minstrels, or Enterludours, who, on a scaffold" babble "vaine news to the sclander of the world, put there in scoffing the vertues of honest men." This motif could be used for merry edification, as in the conversation between Robin Goodfellow, just come from Hell, and Tom Tell Troth, a clown—a dialogue that appeared under the title of *Tell-Trothes New-yeares Gift* in 1593. Robin Good-fellow, who elsewhere might preside over folk merriment, also was advertised as Tarlton's companion in *Tarlton's Jests, and Newes out of Purgatorie*.[70] Shakespeare's use of the motif in *Titus Andronicus* will be discussed later.

Like the news motif, the recantation was capable of accommodating a great variety of attitudes and subject matter; so was the related testa-ment, as well as the repentance. In the *Cobbler's Prophecy,* Ralph's open-ing song about a nut-brown maid is described by him not as a love song but as "my own recantation" (1. 64); while a mock repentance, testament, or confession might also appear in relatively unsophisticated circumstances. Witness the recantations, confessions, and testaments connected with Jack-o-Lent in ephemeral literature[71] or the lecherous friar in *Edward I,* who enters with a rope about his neck, delivers his repentance, and sings a song of farewell to Richard, his pikestaff (xviii).[72]

These last situations reflect folk merriment, of course; for the lusty fool, as in the Revesby Play, sometimes would deliver a burlesque testament before he was executed. With a more definite satiric purpose, the London stage would cudgel Martin Marprelate. By "Jigges and Rimes," he was "nipt in the head" and "kild . . . cleane." In "sundrie waies," he was "curstlie handled"—*"drie beaten,"* his bones broken, "whipt that made him winse," "wormd and launced." All of this, Martin "tooke verie grieuouslie, to be made a *Maygame* vpon the *Stage,* and so bangd, both with prose and rime on euerie side, as he knewe not which way to turne himselfe, and at length cleane *Marde."* "*Vetus Comœdia"* called in "a counsell of Phisitians," who found that "hee would spit out his lunges within one yere." These are theatrical situations, or Nashe-like witticisms, or both, that have unmistakable overtones both of the mock death of the central figure in folk plays and of the appearance of Jack-o-Lent in Machyn's report of the retinue of a London Lord of Misrule.[73]

In contrast, Greene's *Repentance* (1592) represents, and may have inaugurated, a vogue in pamphleteering that used the repentance motif, frequently combined it with dream materials, and ornamented it with Latin tags. These sensational pamphlets were meant to disclose prison life, topical atrocities, robberies, and conycatching tricks.[74] In an equally different manner, Shakespeare utilized the mock testament when he wrote the Epilogue of *Troilus and Cressida.* At the same time, by lines given to Pandarus he also effected an apparent improvisation upon a theme, a witty development that was conventionally associated with a central comic figure:[75]

> O world! world! world! thus is the poor agent despis'd! O traders and bawds, how earnestly are you set a-work, and how ill requited! Why should our endeavour be so desir'd and the performance so loath'd? *What verse for it? What instance for it? Let me see:*
>
>> "Full merrily the humble-bee doth sing,
>> Till he hath lost his honey and his sting;
>> And being once subdu'd in armed tail,
>> Sweet honey and sweet notes together fail."
>
> Good traders in flesh, set this in your painted cloths:
>> As many as be here of Pandar's hall,
>> Your eyes, half out, weep at Pandar's fall;

> Or if you cannot weep, yet give some groans,
> Though not for me, yet for your aching bones.
> Brethren and sisters of the hold-door trade,
> Some two months hence *my will shall here be made.*
> *It should be now,* but that my fear is this
> Some galled goose of Winchester would hiss.
> Till then I'll sweat and seek about for eases,
> And *at that time bequeath you my diseases.*[76]

The ephemeral contention between classes or professions was also capable of being adapted to a variety of purposes and provided a rough, "vulgar" parallel to what had been embodied in the English dramatic tradition since at least the days of John Heywood.[77] It would also be utilized in prose works by Dekker and others.[78] In less sophisticated circumstances, like the other motifs noted here, it was undoubtedly useful for improvising upon themes, whether they might be developed offstage as part of revelling and merriment or elaborated from a statement given the comedian by a member of his audience.

As a result, since Elizabethans of all sorts were probably familiar with a situation wherein the fool-clown was victorious, or was the cleverest of the company, a repetition of such a development in a drama would have a strong element of familiarity, as the principal comedian directed laughter or derision at ranks or classes. In such a situation, the widely circulated theme of "all's fool but the fool" would also emerge, at least implicitly. Witness, then, the disputation in the *Cobbler's Prophecy.* At first Ralph, the cobbler and fool, insists that he will take part; but he is persuaded by Contempt to render judgement on the contention between soldier, courtier, scholar, and countryman. Ralph promises to speak his mind; and by doing so, he satirizes each of the disputants, who brag of their estate and criticize one another.[79] In mocking the combatants, Ralph also utilizes a short mock prophecy, another motif in ephemeral literature, although a minor one:[80]

> The time shall come not long before the doome,
> That in despite of Roome
> Latin shall lacke,
> And Greeke shall beg with a wallet at his backe.
> For all are not sober that goes in blacke.
> Goe too scholler, theres a learning for your knacke.
>
> (ll. 309-14)

> But for all this ill and wrong,
> Marke the Coblers song.

The hie hill and the deepe ditch,
Which ye digd to make your selues rich,
The chimnies so manie,
And almes not anie,
The widowes wofull cries,
And babes in streete that lies,
The bitter sweate and paine
That tenants poore sustaine,
Will turne to your bane I tell ye plaine,
When burning fire shall raine,
And fill with botch and blaine
The sinew and each vaine.
Then these poore that crie,
Being lifted vp on hie,
When you are all forlorne,
Shall laugh you lowd to scorne.
Then where will be the schollers allegories,
Where the Lawier with his dilatories,
Where the Courtier with his brauerie,
And the money monging mate with all his knauerie.
Bethinke me can I no where els,
But in hell where Diues dwels.
But I see ye care not yet,
And thinke these words for me vnfit,
And gesse I speake for lacke of wit:
Stand aside, stand aside, for I am disposed to spit.

            (ll. 319-45)

  The preceding situation roughly repeats a basic device of the entire play, whereby Ralph constantly demonstrates two functions likely to appear in any role for the principal comedian, whether he be fool, clown, or cobbler. By the wise, witty remark, Ralph acts as a choric character; and the author's use in this cobbler's role of comic and satiric speeches that are relatively long creates the impression, at times, of Ralph's being not simply a choric character but also a presider and even a presenter. *Summers Last Will and Testament* (1592-93), which shows affinities with folk merriment and was written by Nashe to be performed before a courtly audience, provides an excellent illustration of the more formal use of the latter technique.[81] And early in the next century, upon the popular stage, when the newly organized Worcester's Men were establishing their repertory, the comedian Kemp certainly presided in the role of Nicholas in *A Woman Killed with Kindness* (1603). This is actually true of the dancing scene (I, ii) and figuratively true of Nicholas' discovery of villainy and his revelation of it to Frankford (II, iii, 170-86; III, ii, 25-97).[82]

What has just been noted agrees, moreover, with a fairly constant feature of Elizabethan merriment. Much of the ephemeral satire and mirth of the period was connected with revelry in which a particular person, like Woode or Colton, would dominate the merriment momentarily or continually. Certainly this would be true when mockery and burlesque were being performed; and even by bitter jests or a news song, a minstrel or ballad singer would give the impression, perhaps only momentarily, of excelling others in wit and shrewdness. As a result, the theater-goer probably would not find it unusual that the principal comedian, even as a bumpkin, might be the wittiest character on the stage. In Robert Wilson's part for Simplicity, a stupid corruption of words appears with witty choric comments that mock character, incident, and even audience.[83] Here, too, appear lines that remind one of comic improvisations on themes and of satiric quips found in comic pieces developed from a recantation, testament, or news motif, as well as some that approach the nonsense verse of folk entertainment.[84] Similarly, even though Miles in *Friar Bacon* has trouble defining *nomen substantivo* and in general is represented as "the greatest blockhead in all Oxford" (v, 40, 32), yet his quips on the jealously sceptical Burden show a wit that is both pointed and apposite. Along with their comic applicability to Burden's "book," that is, to the hostess of the Bel Inn, Miles's comments imply that the Oxford doctor knows only fables, "mystical" meanings (as, for example, those of mythology), and the gender of nouns—matter elementary in even the grammar school curriculum.[85] Especially in scenes with Ralph, when that court fool is in disguise, do the lines of Miles show an intelligence usually associated by literary critics with the sophisticated fool. When Ralph mistakes "reparrel" for "apparel," it is Miles, for example, who comments upon the ridiculous "master fool and a covey of coxcombs" (v, 59-69). During this masquerade wherein Ralph impersonates his master but appears to others as a ridiculous fop who is one of "the hare-brained courtiers" (vii, 114, 117), Greene also gives his comically stupid servant neat improvisations in Skeletonics, which include lines about a topsy-turvy Ship of Fools (ll. 102-13).

As late as *ca.* 1594, the clownish nature of Shakespeare's Costard does not preclude his pointed satirical comments or his use of the word *honorificabilitudinitatibus*. That word, incidentally, also demonstrates Shakespeare's effective use of the *lazzo* of mock-Latin; for the word does not need to be translated to make comic sense. That rustic Costard is given such "copy", however, accords with other situations in the drama, wherein, for example, his "store and furniture" of words used wittily becomes a basic element in representing the principal comedian's conventional lustiness:

> *King.* It was proclaimed a year's imprisonment, to be taken with a wench.
> *Cost.* I was taken with none, sir; I was taken with a damsel.
> *King.* Well, it was proclaimed damsel.
> *Cost.* This was no damsel neither, sir; she was a virgin.
> *King.* It is so varied too; for it was proclaimed virgin.
> *Cost.* If it were, I deny her virginity: I was taken with a maid.
> *King.* This maid will not serve your turn, sir.
> *Cost.* This maid will serve my turn, sir.
>
> (*Love's Labour's Lost,* I, i, 289-301)

From the point of view of generic classification, Simplicity, Miles, and Costard have at times attributes, not of the ignorant "mistaker" of words, but of the sophisticated "corrupter of words," as Feste was to describe himself. Be that as it may, laughter probably developed along the lines of what was familiar to all and conventionally associated with merriment—even though the educated in the audience, upon reflection, might recognize also that Shakespeare was using for a comic effect a material fallacy resulting from the ambiguity of language.[86]

The effective use of popular merriment for satire on current events has been referred to briefly, especially when it touched on religion, received official censure, and hence might be noted for subsequent generations. Well-known comic motifs associated with folk merriment, which have been noted as being connected with the Marprelate controversy, also were used in the seventeenth century, both on stage and off, as a means of ridiculing Puritans.[87] Tarlton, the famous comic actor, apparently engaged in satire directed at the ecclesiastical order when he took part in the discovery of Simony "in Don John of London's cellar."[88] Henslowe's *Diary* notes the performance by Strange's Men in 1592 of what may have been an earlier play that from its title, "pope Jone," might have ridiculed Catholicism vigorously with the old anti-papal story of a female pope.[89] In *The Troublesome Reign of King John* (1587-91), Faulconbridge clears away the dissolute nest of Alice the Nun in scenes that are written in jig meter and that have, like some of the fuller jigs, analogues in *novelle*.[90] A similar situation, but with more emphasis on merriment only, can be found in the songs and incidents between the friar, the wench, and the man in *Edward I* (ii, 46-100). Later in the 1590's, then, but with a glance in the direction of ignorant priests,

Shakespeare also would utilize briefly this comic association between religion and ballad or jig when he developed a situation including Touchstone, Audrey, Sir Oliver Martext, and Jacques. Not only does Shakespeare have his melancholy commentator remark on the warping nature of a hedge-priest's work but also in Touchstone's mocking song, Shakespeare turns to popular merriment. The result is the burlesque farewell and lament of "O sweet Oliver," as with suitable personal mockery Touchstone improvises neatly upon a popular song. Again Shakespeare's laughter utilizes overtones from real, though ephemeral, mirth—even though this fantastical knave is unable to flout this Oliver, this Martext, out of his calling, as others are said to have "marde" Martin Marprelate.[91]

In addition, reflections of the *pastourelle* support Touchstone's role. With a magnificent comic variation upon the aristocratic, condescending figure who woos a shepherdess, Shakespeare's dizzard rings sophisticated changes of a burlesque and "capricious" Ovid, both lusty and wooing, upon the country-wide merriment implicit in goat-girl, foul wench, honesty, and feigning (*As You Like It,* III, iii, 1-64). Thus in accordance with his mock aristocratic air, by his learning about wise men and fools, by a learned *ipse* and other aspects of rhetorical "copy," Touchstone frightens away his rival with a brave, courtly pose (V, i, 1-65).[92] The merriment of an age of Maypoles, of laughter on St. George's day, and of the kindred mirth of ballad singer and tavern would support this development.

Against the background here considered, a dominant feature of Shakespeare's artistry in *A Midsummer Night's Dream* would unfold with comic sureness for a contemporary audience. Therein a stage-world begins and ends in a festive time at court, and in the woods it is presided over by an agent of a supernatural ruler. Robin Goodfellow manipulates, comments upon, and enjoys with the audience the fantastic course of events that through his mistake persists in becoming rival wooing. He was a figure, of course, in nursery tales; and as has been noted, he also appeared sometimes as the presiding grotesque in folk merriment. Hence it is not surprising that he should be connected, in more sophisticated surroundings, with the merry edification of a Tom Tell Truth and with the laughter that Tarlton produced. That comic actor's news out of purgatory was advertised as having been published by Robin Goodfellow, "an old companion" of the comedian; and at least one ballad presented this folk figure in dialogue with the dead actor: "a pleasant Dyttye Dialogue wise betwene Tarltons ghost and Robyn Good Fellow" (1590).[93] Later in the century, Robin would be joined with a third figure of contemporary fun when he was represented as saying,

"Why, see you not how cranke the Cobler is, that will forsooth correct *Dick Tarltons* doings, a man famous in his life for merrie conceites, and especially for a book of my publishing?"[94] Anything approaching a complete discussion of *A Midsummer Night's Dream* would be inappropriate at this time, but the fact that Shakespeare utilized as a basic feature of his drama a presiding figure of folk lore and current mirth indicates that a good deal of the laughter created by his play—in a manner not at all discordant with Thalia's evanescence and luxuriance— was rooted firmly in an audience's nontheatrical merriment.

Also close to a background of current mirth are aspects of *The Old Wives' Tale*. It probably was performed during the plague years of the early 1590's by some of the actors who had performed in Wilson's plays; and if the form in which it survives represents the drama as it was given in the provinces, it may have been designed consciously to be close to the current but relatively naïve mirth of the era. Whether that be true or not, it has been noted that reflections of the pretentious exquisite and the braggart, who are found in full flower in sophisticated literature, also appear in folk drama and in ballad. Portrayed in earlier Tudor days, those figures were given pretensions of all sorts, both to wealth and to gentility, to learning and bravery, as well as to features of "the body of compliment" thought necessary for a Renaissance gentleman.[95] Although there might be a differentiation in dominant emphasis between *miles gloriosus* and *caballarius gloriosus,* in such figures as Iniquity or Hickscorner and in the fuller portrayals of some later dramas, comic aspects of both related types were constantly merged into one role. To separate them, of course, would be easy and natural, nor would one lose thereby the familiar echoes of current merriment.

The Old Wives' Tale, then, shows such a differentiation along the lines of fustian-speaking braggart and ridiculously attired rustic, proud of his dress. Perhaps Peele did this as part of an attempt to satirize Harvey; but if so, certainly not all in an audience could be expected to be aware of his purpose or even of the literary gossip upon which it perhaps was based. In contrast, the basic invention is relatively simple, and it may be revealing that Huanebango and Booby are kept together during their first appearance. As a result, the "merged" type bifurcates from a stock comic pose as rival wooing is mentioned. Huanebango's genealogy is part of his self-conceived superiority, as is Booby's ridiculous precedence in dress; while "cousin Bustagusteceridis" affords brief satire on the conventionally derisible subject of courtiers.

> *Huan.* Now, by Mars and Mercury, Jupiter and Janus, Sol
> and Saturnus, Venus and Vesta, Pallas and Proserpina, and by

the honour of my house, Polimackeroeplacidus, it is a wonder
to see what this love will make silly fellows adventure. . . .
Beauty, I tell thee, is peerless, and she precious whom thou
affectest. Do off these desires, good countryman; good friend,
run away from thyself; and so soon as thou canst, forget her,
whom none must inherit but he that can monsters tame,
labours achieve, riddles absolve, loose enchantments, murther
magic, and kill conjuring,—and that is the great and mighty
Huanebango.

Booby. Hark you, sir, hark you. First know I have here the
flurting feather, and have given the parish the start for the
long stock. . . .

Huan. If she be mine . . . she shall . . . be invested in the
most famous stock of Huanebango,—Polimackeroeplacidus
my grandfather, my father Pergopolineo, my mother Dionora
de Sardinia, famously descended.

Booby. Do you hear, sir? Had not you a cousin that was
called Gusteceridis?

Huan. Indeed, I had a cousin that sometime followed the
court infortunately, and his name Bustegusteceridis.

Booby. O Lord, I know him well! He is the knight of the
neat's-feet.

(*Old Wives' Tale,* ll. 303-53)

When rival wooing is later dropped, although the bifurcation continues, the double portrayal runs along conventional lines. Huanebango
claims Zantippa, "a little fair" but the "curstest quean." He will
"royalize" her and her progeny with his pedigree; and he offers her, in a
manner reminiscent of the successfully wooing Fool, not simply a
"thousand pounds in possibility" but also "things fitting thy desire in
possession." Quite naturally from this "curst daughter" comes the line

Lob be your comfort, and cuckold be your destiny!

(ll. 788-89)

As this pairing-off of male and female is being developed, Corebus, or
Booby, is linked with Celanta, "the foul wench," but no shrew. From her
and the head, Booby wins gold that can mend his wit (ll. 923-24). In
other words, as was true for Huanebango and Booby, Zantippa and
Celanta might seem to an unlearned Elizabethan to diverge from a
conventional comic type. A pretentious stupidity is matched thereby with
a cuckolding, shrewish ugliness; and as Booby's precedence in dress is
related only to the parish, so the portrayal of the four figures might seem

to rest upon conventional types that were widespread and quite unsophisticated.

The preceding development accords with other features of the
drama, which shows an abundance of folk motifs. In the provinces, for
that matter, the likelihood would be increased that the comedy of Huanebango, Booby, and their loves would be associated with the same background Peele drew upon if he were the author of *Edward I*. Yet
comparable matter for a courtly audience appears, for example, in Lyly's
Endymion (1588), where it provides an antic accompaniment to a
partial Neo-Platonic *schema*.[96] In this play, Sir Thopas is concerned both
with "learning," that is, the Latin that has saved his inferiors' lives (I,
iii, 125) and with "honor," or hunger, that "inciteth" him (II, ii, 114).
He also suffers from a love that makes him feel "all Ovid" for the old
enchantress Dipsas, who has cheeks that "hang down to her breasts like
dugs and . . . paps to her waist like bags" (III, iii, 69-70).

In later plays for a full company, the treatment of such ridiculous
male and female characters might lead to further variety. When a boy
actor received a comic female role that was relatively full but avoided
an emphasis on shrewishness for one upon pretentions to the "body of
compliment," he might well expect to find himself linked not only with
a timorous husband but also with a male companion all "exquisite," or
nearly so. Witness Fallace, Deliro, and Fastidious Briske, as well as
other characters like Saviolina (that lady of genteel perception).[97] Even
without an emphasis upon wooing, and without a pairing-off of male and
female characters, such a bifurcation as that made by Peele might have
seemed a trifurcation to the theatrically uneducated. Thus in *Every Man
in his Humour,* Jonson would display three "zanies" (II, iii, 53):
Bobadilla, city braggart or "Paulesman"; Matheo, the town gull; and
Stephano, the country gull. All are ridiculously pretentious, but Jonson
effects a neat differentiation by his emphases and portrays thereby
"masters" of sword-play, of poesy, and of the body of compliment. In
such circumstances, Cob remains at the social level of the conventional
clown, beats his wife, comments on Matheo and Thorello, is duped by
Bobadilla, and is without pretentions—except for oaths learned from
Bobadilla and an antic concern over the Cobs's genealogy found in
names conventional to folk merriment. In this way too, as well as in the
many ways that Baskervill pointed out, Jonsonian humor-comedy builds
upon the familiar.[98]

One must grant, of course, that a basic feature of the sociology of
the era might be utilized in any portrayal of braggart and exquisite.
Certainly the rivalry between those who would rise in society by intelligence and those who would rise by wealth reinforced the vitality of

ridicule directed at the appearance, wit, and pseudogentlemanly conduct of a bragging "water-fly," "spacious in the possession of dirt."[99] No doubt the dramatic tradition of merged *miles gloriosus* and *caballarius gloriosus* would accord with the scornful attitude both of contemporary intellectuals and of members of the older gentry. In addition, however, for those who had little or no learning or theatrical experience, elements congruent with ridicule of the exquisite and braggart might well have been encountered in the merriment of the age. Like the bravery and self-admiration found in the comic mélange of Kemp, such matter needed only to appear on a higher level in order to be ripe for an exposure that would develop in accordance with the expectations of anyone familiar with the unsophisticated treatment of some conventional comic figures.

As a result, the wide pattern of rival wooing and of conventional comic types might well have created equally wide comic anticipations for all classes of spectators. It could have created also a proclivity for laughter that might serve as a sounding board for the artistry of author and actor; and it may have determined, in part at least, a playwright's choice of characters. Placed against such a background, the comic artistry of *The Two Gentlemen of Verona* appears more effective than it might otherwise; for in creating Thurio, Shakespeare elaborates the motif of rival wooing instead of developing any complication of the transvestite motif that he found in *Diana* or one of its analogues. In his first scene (II, iv), Sir Thurio is clad in a jerkin or doublet and appears as an angry, stupid, ugly rival of the hero. The stupidity that makes him the fit butt of Valentine's puns would agree neatly with what has been noted, especially when Thurio is referred to as "My foolish rival, that her father likes / Only for his possessions are so huge" (ll. 174-75). As the play develops, subsequent scenes intensify the ridiculous portrait; and scene two of the last act sums up Thurio's attributes as he would have appeared throughout the play—quarrelsome but cowardly (ll. 19-21), "spacious" in possessions (ll. 25-28), and foolishly in need of lessons in courtship (ll. 15-18 and III, ii). Descended "from a gentleman to a fool" (V, ii, 22-24), he is a thoroughly ridiculous rival wooer with clownish overtones of the favored "eldest son" and of the satirical variation provided more pointedly by Wilson's Dissimulation and country gentleman (ll. 25-26, 29). Indeed, Thurio's spindle-shanks, not mentioned specifically until the last act (V, ii, 3-7), could have intensified the possibly ludicrous appearance of a doublet, so stuffed, as Stubbes describes some, that they had to be worn loose to allow the wearer to move (II, iv, 10-20).[100] Given such an appearance, an audience might well have been laughing at Thurio before he spoke a word. But be the stage appearance of that particular coat as it may, when this rival wooer is placed against the sounding board sketched here, he probably did not need much development to emerge for both courtly and noncourtly spectators as a clearly laughable creation.

To summarize from another point of view the appropriateness of what has been sketched, consider its pertinence for any examination of an author's comic intent and technique. Obviously derision might be part of any rival-wooing situation, especially when satire was effected by the use of the fool-clown's rivals. As regards the fool-clown there might also be present an element of comic familiarity in which not derision but a laughing acceptance, closely approaching sympathy, would pre-dominate. Consider, then, Shakespeare's introduction of Faulconbridge in *King John*. The source for this character would not be known to the uneducated; and even in a group of regular theater-goers there certainly might be some who had not seen *The Troublesome Reign*. In contrast, what could be comically familiar in Faulconbridge's first appearance is strong. Here is a rustic gentleman or soldier with a heavily modified ridiculousness—with, for example, a gauche outspokenness on the one hand and an apt, witty gleeking on the other. Thus a dominant emphasis in Faulconbridge's role—especially his outspokenness and his satirical comments (e.g., I, i, 71)—probably would create that rapport between dramatic figure and audience that lead to the sympathy accorded the principal comedian, even though this particular figure now happens to be raised in the social scale to a position that in other circumstances would make the rustic eldest son (ll. 50 ff.) an object of satire as part of a conventional representation of rural society. The derision in such satire, however, is utilized in Philip's favor; for Shakespeare has provided him with a rival who insists that he is the eldest son, who is mocked, and who is risible in his Thurio-like appearance (ll. 138-47). Though the motif of rival wooing be absent, notes of familiarity that could be derived from its popular and widespread development seem to be there. At the same time, the honest gleeking of Philip, who is revealed to be a regal bastard and not a rural "gentleman" or a knight's eldest son, would separate him distinctly from another theatrically recognizable character-type. This latter type, who might appear with the bar sinister, also scoffed at the individuals and the society of the play-world but did this as he performed or planned villainy.[101] After performing a miming satire against pretension, Philip, however, would learn deceit to avoid deceit, which shall "strew the footsteps" of his rising (ll. 181-216). From such a beginning, one clearly delimited in two directions, a "new" and thoroughly attractive figure for creating merriment would seem to emerge from the play-world—a figure whose appearance starts its growth, nevertheless, from a situation having the widest of comic affinities, and when viewed in this light, a figure created with a sureness of touch that is striking.

On the social level of a legitimate Faulconbridge, there might appear around 1588-89 heroes and their witty companions who were engaged in wooing the fair and gentle countrymaid of low degree, as in *Friar Bacon* and *George a Greene*—with their chapbook affinities and their age-old king-commoner motif. In such instances, the witty companion may also be a witty commentator, although of high degree; and in later drama such a character may be provided with a comparable lady. Just as the derisible, lecherous braggart when born a prince was to be given a libidinous court lady (e.g., *Philaster*), so the nonderisible, truly witty companion of the hero was to be given, especially in Shakespeare's comedies, a female counterpart for a combat of wit and for resolved or unresolved debate. Thereby an exuberant wit and rhetoric would be exercised constantly upon the stage situation. In this respect, and in the light of what has been noted elsewhere, consider the role of Berowne in Shakespeare's *Love's Labour's Lost*. At one point in the play, the device of harmless eavesdropping, with its comic censure of forsworn king and lords, places Berowne in the position of a dizzard of high degree—a jester, comic observer, and, to a degree, a presenter or presider as well:[102]

> *King.* Ay me!
> *Bir.* Shot, by heaven! Proceed, sweet Cupid; thou hast *thump'd* him with thy *bird-bolt under the left pap.* In faith, secrets!
>
> > (IV, iii, 22-25)
>
> *King.* . . . Who is he comes here?
> What Longaville! and reading! Listen, ear.
> *Bir.* Now, *in thy likeness, one more fool appear!*
> *Long.* Ay me, I am forsworn!
> *Bir.* Why, *he comes in like a perjure, wearing papers.*
> *King.* In love, I hope; sweet fellowship in shame.
> *Bir.* One *drunkard* loves another of the name.
> *Long.* Am I the first that have been perjur'd so?
> *Bir.* I could put thee in comfort. Not by two that I know.
> Thou makest the triumviry, the corner-cap of society,
> The shape of *Love's Tyburn that hangs up simplicity.*
>
> > (ll. 43-54)
>
> *Bir.* This is the *liver-vein,* which makes flesh a deity,
> A *green goose* a goddess; pure, pure idolatry . . . .
> *Long.* By whom shall I send this?—Company! stay.

Bir. "All hid, all hid"; an old infant play.
Like a demigod here sit I in the sky,
And wretched fools' secrets heedfully o'er-eye.
More sacks to the mill! O heavens, I have my wish!
Dumaine transform'd! *four woodcocks in a dish!*

(ll. 74-82)

In this particular scene, all eavesdroppers become mockers; but such a role has been constant for Berowne, and here it is appropriately dominant as he is given lines that create the effect of his introducing the other lovers ("in thy likeness, one more fool appear," "I have my wish"), and even of his judging or punishing them:

King. What will Biron say when he shall hear
Faith infringed, which such zeal did swear?
How will he scorn! how will he spred his wit!
How will he triumph, leap, and laugh at it!
For all the wealth that ever I did see,
I would not have him know so much by me.
Bir. Now step I forth to whip hypocrisy

(ll. 145-51)

Although he is no thoroughgoing companion of Robin Goodfellow—for Berowne himself is engaged seriously in wooing—yet one aspect of his role is developed in a manner that would have familiar overtones and specific comic associations for all in an audience, especially for those who because of their lowly position would never be found at court to witness a Jacobean performance of *Love's Labour's Lost*.[103] Even more than Faulconbridge's introduction, Berowne's mocking position might well have seemed familiar to a spectator of 1594 or earlier as a result of the background constantly referred to here. Certainly such words and phrases as those italicized in the preceding lines have direct affinities with matter already noted, especially with parodies of wooing and its mockery, which might be effected or sung by one who momentarily dominated or presided over the merriment.

There can be do doubt that the wit and rhetoric of Berowne's first long speech, wherein in a form reminiscent of the schools he opposes the theme of academic retirement, point to courtly antecedents in Lyly's plays, in earlier drama with a debate technique, in Castiglione's *Courtier* and other courtesy books;[104] but as has been noted, that direction by the mid-1590's need not be incompatible with the one just indicated. As regards the form of Berowne's first speech, a theater-going audience had been exposed increasingly to effective rhetoric; and the age's ear

had been attuned to its display. As regards its content, this initial opposition to a theme is enlarged so that two major wooing patterns
emerge. On the higher level, the wooing is developed in a debate-like
manner, but with connotations that constantly recall Elizabethan merriment and that are reinforced by the low comedy. Unresolved by the
nature of the catastrophe, this wooing is also paralleled by an intellectual
Grobianism that provides an antic accompaniment to the wit and
rhetoric of high degree and mocks the pedantry of the age. By such a
development of both wooing patterns, comic cohesion is effected; and
as scene succeeded scene, even members of Shakespeare's audience with
no formal education may well have encountered familiar mirth in the
courtly and sophisticated matter of the play. As earlier noted, the italicized words and phrases in the preceding quotations are illustrative; and
a few more details from individual scenes are illuminating.

To preserve the previous example, notice Berowne's pose of being
impervious to the Promethean fire of ladies' eyes, of being neither loved
nor loving; and when this comic railer rails at himself, the anti-Petrar-
chan soliloquy that results might also seem to have a basic comic affinity
with the omnipresent satire against marriage and women found in ballad,
popular song, and jig:

> What! I love! I sue! I seek a wife!
> *A woman, that is like a German clock,*
> *Still a repairing, ever out of frame,*
> *And never going aright, being a watch,*[105]
> *But being watch'd that it may still go right!*
> Nay, to be perjur'd, which is worst of all;
> And, among three, *to love the worst of all,*
> A whitely wanton with a velvet brow,
> *With two pitch-balls stuck in her face for eyes;*
> *Ay, and, by heaven, one that will do the deed*
> *Though Argus were her eunuch and her guard.*
> And I to sigh for her! to watch for her!
> To pray for her! Go to; *it is a plague*
> *That Cupid will impose for my neglect*
> *Of his almighty dreadful little might.*
> Well, I will love, write, sigh, pray, sue, groan:
> *Some men must love my lady, and some Joan.*
>
> (III, i, 191-207)

This speaker, certainly, would seem to preserve the theatrically intel-
ligible position of a mocking central figure, who in addition is wooing the
"black" Joan of his level, the tartest female among the ladies, the one

who is reproved with the line, "A pox of that jest! and I beshrew all shrews" (V, ii, 46). Granted the courtly background and derivations of the play, yet here a dizzard, though of high degree, is wooing; and wooing one whose attributes are said to be comparable to those of a shrewish, ugly female in current merriment.

A similar consideration holds true for mockery of Armado by Moth, as already has been noted. Whatever the literary genetics of the last figure may be, for at least some of the uneducated in the audience, his manner may well have been illuminated by such popular songs as "It fell upon a sollem holledaye" with its mocking refrains.[106] Mockery of the lords as lovers, which agrees with the more limited and more derisive mockery of Armado, is carried on by the ladies when they assume the conventional position of the scornful loved ones. This is especially true, of course, for Berowne's opponent, "black" Rosalynde; and the ladies also engage in flyting-like jests at one another's expense.

When the ladies mock Boyet, the situation ends on a note that might have seemed close to the familiar one of comic improvisation on a theme with the purpose of putting down one of the participants. The theme, moreover, looks in two directions: toward courtly sonneteering about "shooters" and "suitors" and the hitting of "harts"-"hearts," and toward bawdy improvising upon "pricks" and "pins" (IV, i). In fact, this putting down of a participant is noted for the audience by Costard's speech:

> By my soul, a swain! a most simple clown!
> Lord, Lord, how the ladies and I have put him down!
> O' my troth, most sweet jests! Most incony vulgar wit!
> When it comes so smoothly off, so obscenely, as it were, so fit.
>
> (ll. 142-45)

Quite meaningfully, then, Costard's next lines speak of Armado and Moth; for earlier the three had engaged in a scene that even more definitely emphasized riming improvisation. There the riddling "moral,"

> The fox, the ape, and the humble-bee,
> Were still at odds, being but three,

had been augmented by a comparable "l'envoy,"

> Until the goose came out of door
> And stay'd the odds by adding four.

It was also augmented by Costard's riming summation:

> The boy hath sold him a bargain, a goose, that's flat.
> Sir, your pennyworth is good, and your goose be fat.

> To sell a bargain well is as cunning as fast and loose.
> Let me see; a fat l'envoy; ay, that's a fat goose.
>
> (III, i, 102-5)

That Armado was put down is obvious from his "Come hither, come hither. How did this argument begin?" (ll. 106-7). Both scenes, consequently, might well have appeared to some in the audience to be an amplification of what had been Tarlton's comic forte, that is, his excellence at improvisation, a device he apparently utilized both on stage and off.[107] The scenes might also seem to be an amplification of the jesting wit of a leader in revelry and merriment.

This closeness of situations, as well as the closeness of words and phrases, to conventional matter associated with Elizabethan merriment was probably sufficient to start the laughter in scenes or to cap scenes with laughter; and even closer to a familiar comic background would be the figure of Costard and his appearance with Jaquenetta and Armado. Although this rival wooing is never developed fully in incident or in the portrayal of Jaquenetta, it is well developed in the portrayal of the two other characters; and in view of its conventional nature, neither the incidents nor the figure of the rustic maid may have needed much emphasis.

Costard's defense of being taken with Jaquenetta has been mentioned. With puns on "mutton" (that is, sheep's flesh–woman's flesh), this clown with the "great limb or joint"—which makes him suitable to "pass as Pompey the Great"[108]—insists that Jaquenetta will serve his turn, she who is adored by the Spaniard, both lusty and wooing. Like all such wenches, however, she apparently prefers the chief dizzard of low degree—an impression that would be solidified by the fact that she is always in Costard's company during her brief appearances. Though her Spanish wooer calls her a "most immaculate white and red," Moth makes it clear that "Most maculate thoughts . . . are mask'd under such colours" (I, ii, 95-97). As the fool-clown of folk plays can please a maid "in a secret place," so in a context of bawdy word-play, and in accordance with Elizabethan pronunciation, Costard was taken "following"-*fallowing* Jaquenetta in the park.[109] Although loved by Armado, she briefly mocks him (I, ii, 145); and Costard's announcement that she is two months with child—for the Spaniard has quickened her with an offspring that "brags in her belly already"—serves to mock Hector-Armado out of his part and to provide an approach to mock combat between the clown and this worthy (V, ii, 677 ff.). In the comic parallelism of the catastrophe, Armado vows "to hold the plough" "three year" for Jaquenetta's "sweet love." In view of what has been sketched here, this rustic wench and the references to her probably needed little development for laughter, in spite of the fact that Shakespeare has thrown his emphasis elsewhere. In this line of action, his subsidiary touches may well have been enlarged by their stage clarity, by Elizabethan pronunciation, and by their roots in contemporary merriment.

Even as Shakespeare develops his main emphasis, which is upon wit and rhetoric, he draws upon current nontheatrical mirth. Costard's wit has already been noted; and his comic logic, his mock Latin, his mistaking of words and intent effect in part the antic accompaniment to the wit of the lords and ladies. Shakespeare also stresses the ridiculous intellectual discipline of Armado; and it is interesting to note that at the very beginning of the next century Jonson developed his braggart Tucca with a similar emphasis as part of a dramatic *ars poetica*.[110] Like Tucca and others of his breed, braggart Armado runs true to type.[111] He escapes the combat with Costard by the genteel excuse that he will not fight in his shirt; and when it is disclosed that he has none, he is ready again with the excuse of penance for this lack of apparel. Likewise in accordance with his type, he comforts himself that other heroic figures have been in love, "O well-knit Samson! strong-jointed Samson! I do excel thee in my rapier as much as thou dost me in carrying gates. I am in love too" (I, ii, 77-79). Quite revealingly, though, Armado would have the ballad of "the King and the Beggar" "newly writ o'er" as a "mighty precedent." A "vulgar" context is effected also by lines that refer to French brawls, jigging "off a tune," and the refrain of "the hobby-horse is forgot" (III, i, 8-34).[112] It seems quite possible, therefore, that such lines would also stir up associations in merriment not limited to the stage. All of this, moreover, develops the situation of a ridiculous soldier and Spaniard worsted by a clown-fool.

In such a familiar comic development involving a country wench, a rustic dizzard, and a bragging soldier who is a foreigner, there also appear a pedant and a curate; and since a relationship between a curate and elementary pedagogy would be natural to the age, it seems doubly pertinent to note that into the milieu of folk merriment, the pedant and schoolmaster seems to have found his way with dancing antics comparable, apparently, to those of the grotesque old lover (e.g., "Pickelherring Dill, dill, dill").[113] Divorced from a wooing motif, this figure in more formal drama afforded the means of such generalized satire as that in the *Cobbler's Prophecy*. There the scholar would obviously be delighted to creep into credit at court, and his Latin is mocked by the principal comedian.[114] Although Shakespeare effects a bifurcation of the type, and although Holofernes and Nathaniel are not members of a group of rival wooers, yet both figures appear where they might be expected. Like Robert Wilson and Peele, Shakespeare is elaborating familiar figures for a particular purpose. The schoolmaster's comment on the braggart is applicable to both himself and his companion: "He draweth out the thread of his verbosity finer than the staple of his argument" (V, i, 18-19); and their ridiculous pedantry reinforces Armado's ill-digested rhetoric. Like Boyet and Armado, however, both pedant and curate, especially Holofernes, are "put down" by both Moth and Costard (e.g., V, i, 33-83). Thereby the central situation of much folk merriment might seem to be transferred to another milieu, but with an identical result: Moth, with his witty quips, and the rustic dizzard are triumphant; and though pedant and curate are not defeated in wooing, they are defeated in wit.

Even in the most Lylyesque of his dramas, consequently, Shakespeare's comic artistry is close to Elizabethan merriment and hence, for a popular audience, much surer and firmer than is sometimes realized. This consideration may go far toward explaining how as late as January, 1604-5, the play was apparently in the repertory of Shakespeare's company. Though perhaps it had not been performed regularly for some time, it could be given before Queen Anne, presumably on short notice. There at court the polite antecedents of the drama might be appreciated; but there, too, at a court that became interested in the Cotswold games, the elaborate figures of fun with strong overtones of folk merriment probably would be appreciated as well. Certainly Jonson capitalized upon such a tradition when he developed his antimasques for presentation at James's court.

In examining the artistry of any play, in addition to what might have overtones of familiarity even for those who had never before been in a theater, there should be considered matter that had been established on the stage by at least the early 1590's. As part of the heritage of Elizabethan merriment that could have been derived from plays and interludes, one finds, for example, the comic use of broad dialect; malapropisms and the corruption of characters' names; satire of the proud gentry, fine clothing, and taxes; as well as satire effected by the portrayal of courtly knaves, strutting gallants, and other figures that reflect the *caballarius gloriosus*.[115] In earlier plays, as in ephemeral literature and revelry, there appeared parody and burlesque. Witness the heather priest's and choirboy's parody of divine service (the Digby *Mary Magdalene*) or the burlesque representation of a manorial court *(Mankind)*.[116] With song in the earlier drama went vigorous dance; and even without song, the antics and miming of vice and devil must have been close at times to the nondramatic vigor of peasant brawl and

of the song, dance, and banquet-revelling that form a background for
the later theatrical jig.[117] Indeed, there probably was enough comic
horsemanship in the old farcical action of one character carrying another
off on his back so that there would not stand alone such a bit of comedy
as the elaborate bridling of Inclination in the *Trial of Treasure* (before
1567).[118]

Later examples of stage comedy can be illustrated by scenes and
stage-groupings in *The Famous Victories* (1583-88), *Selimus* (1586-
93), *A Looking Glass for London and England* (1587-91), *The
Wounds of Civil War* (1587-92), *Solimon and Perseda* (1589-92),
Locrine (1591-95), and the earlier but well-known *Cambises* (1558-
70). Although one finds in those plays a crude handling of comic matter,
it would be material to which a theater-going audience of the early
1590's would have been accustomed, so much so that the serious
Cambises' vein could be parodied around the year 1597. From such
plays, both actor and audience might well think of the theatrically comic
as involving a number of characteristic antics that were not modified
along any other line than the most obvious one of their being associated
with the appearance of comedians—although among those antics there
might appear incidents that literary geneticists, quite understandably,
would associate with the roarer, the knavish servant, or a Grobianus.[119]
The same consideration is true for matter reminiscent of the literary
braggart or for the portrayal of the much earlier, cowardly Watkyn in
the Digby *Slaughter of the Innocents*. A comic mélange might always
have seemed valid in all of its literary heterogeneity.

As a result, a brawling preparation of a king's banquet *(Cambises)*
might seem congruent to a regular theater-goer with the gormandizing of
a Strumbo *(Locrine)*, a Bullithrumble *(Selimus)*, or an Adam *(Looking
Glass)*.[120] Similarly, the monologue of the servant who unwittingly
betrayed his master, though it demonstrated the charms of drink
(Wounds of Civil War), could seem in its manner to be akin to any
elaboration of a theme, even to one that pointed out the virtues of a
cow or the vices of a wife *(Looking Glass)*.[121] The antics of Ambidexter
at a banquet *(Cambises)* would be comically harmonious with any brawling mischief-making, including one that ended with the witty resolution
of cowardice into wisdom *(Cambises)*. Whether or not the comedian was
represented as thirsting for honor and knighthood "Basiliscolike"
(Solimon and Perseda), these antics might include on the field of battle
the mock death of a Strumbo *(Locrine)* or the brave trickery of a
Derricke in the capture and escape of an enemy *(Famous Victories)*. In
these situations, the comic trick of a foreign patter might appear or the
tickling of one's nose to make one bleed valiantly.[122] Given the ap-

pearance of warfare in the play-world, comic recruiting or pressing
scenes would provide an antic accompaniment to the serious matter;[123]
and in times of peace, a libidinous brawling, with or without the cuckold
motif or clownish chop-logic, might parallel any wooing or pairing-off
of characters.[124] In combination with serious matter or by itself, comic
actors appeared as a comic crew; and constantly a comic bravery
mingled with a social bumptiousness in the principal comedian's
role[125]—the artistic crudeness of which is sometimes apparent by the
way an actor's laughter and cries seem to have been used simply to
arouse laughter in the audience.[126]

When this comedy was connected with warfare or revolt or courtly surroundings, its familiarity was derived probably for the stage
itself, although it might have had overtones from common life and current merriment. For the regular theater-goer, then, there would appear in
1 Henry VI a familiar association between a group of lesser actors and
comments on a brawling course of action—comments that reflect the
"better part of valor," spoils won by words on the field of battle, and
drinking in the tavern (I, iii, 89-91; II, i, 78-81; III, i, 147-48).
Similarly corresponding to familiar comedy would be the brief turn of
the innkeeper, in a grim context, during the Queen's play of *The True
Tragedy of Richard III*.[127]

When comedy of this sort was developed in a number of scenes, by
the simple fact that there probably would be a principal comedian, the
impression would be created once more of a presiding or dominant
figure. In *2 Henry VI* this situation is merged with the comic's pride in
himself, his aping of his betters, and his social bumptiousness; and
Shakespeare thereby produces a strikingly original sequence. On his first
appearance, to the accompaniment of mocking, punning, and sometimes bawdy comments, Cade is given an oration, wherein he proclaims
a mock genealogy and notes his admirable "places" of character as part
of his praise of himself as a leader:

> *Cade.* We Jack Cade, so term'd of our supposed father,—
> *Dick.* Or rather, of stealing a cade of herrings.
> *Cade.* For our enemies shall fall before us, inspired with
> the spirit of putting down kings and princes,—Command silence.
> *Dick.* Silence!
> *Cade.* My father was a Mortimer,—
> *Dick.* He was an honest man, and a good bricklayer.
> *Cade.* My mother a Plantagenet,—
> *Dick.* I knew her well; she was a midwife.
> *Cade.* My wife descended of the Lacies,—

Dick. She was indeed, a pedler's daughter, and sold many laces.

Smith. But now of late, not able to travel with her furr'd pack, she washes bucks here at home.

Cade. Therefore am I of an honourable house.

Dick. Ay, by my faith, the field is honourable; and there was he born, under a hedge, for his father had never a house but the cage.

Cade. Valiant I am.

Smith. 'A must needs; for beggary is valiant.

Cade. I am able to endure much.

Dick. No question of that; for I have seen him whipp'd three market-days together.

Cade. I fear neither sword nor fire.

Smith. He need not fear the sword; for his coat is of proof.

Dick. But methinks he should stand in fear of fire, being burnt i'th' hand for stealing of sheep.

Cade. Be brave, then; for your captain is brave, and vows reformation.

(*2 Henry VI*, IV, ii, 33-70)

In this scene there also appear age-old objects of mocking laughter: knighthood (ll. 122-29), gentility (ll. 5-32), learning and lawyers (ll. 84-117). Here, too, is derision of the many-headed multitude, deriders in turn derided by their leader's comment (ll. 198-200). In such a way, a conventional comic mélange is developed admirably and centered about a presiding comedian when he first appears to move into a role based on history.

Equally important, however, is the way in which this comedy of revolt, like that connected with warfare, probably built upon a familiarity that was of the theater alone. Certainly its relationship to what is serious in the play was necessarily of the theater; and consequently that relationship demands some attention here, for it involves not only the effect of roles for the principal comedian but also some consideration of the derision in laughter. By its burlesque genealogy, the scene of Cade's introduction provides a comic variation upon what is treated seriously elsewhere in the drama. But in spite of that burlesque, the serious matter that is comparable to Cade's mock oration is not derided. Cade's descent is made ridiculous within the confines of the scene itself; York's is in no way ridiculed thereby. Similarly, the serious and relatively serious rhetoric of the lords and ladies in *Love's Labour's Lost* is not derided by the burlesque rhetoric of the lower line of action. The same consideration holds true for the relationship between the comic and the relatively serious wooing scenes that appeared in many dramas since the days of *Fulgens and Lucres*. The matter is important; for such a technique appears constantly in Elizabethan drama and may effect a variety in unity that extends from a single interlude to a consistent series of scenes.

A most obvious illustration from the fifteenth century is afforded by the "Second Play of the Shepherds" in the Towneley mystery cycle; and the earliness of the example also serves to illustrate the vitality on the English stage of the comic attitudes and materials already noted. Over a hundred years before the formation of Queen Elizabeth's Men, the comic parallel of the *præsepe*-kernel in the Towneley cycle was elaborated with an assumption of superiority by the principal comic actor; with complaints about the weather, taxgatherers, and shrewish wives; with a representation of the latter; with false Latin and a mock conjuration; and, finally, with the trickster tricked. In this development, folk lore was handled comically and ended with Mak's being tossed in a blanket.[128] The author developed his comic scene, however, so that the duper was caught in his own invention by the sympathy of man and by the undeniable fact that a sheep is a sheep even though a lamb. Thus laughter doubled back upon itself so that nothing outside the comic antics was explicitly, or even implicitly, ridiculed; and certainly not the actual miracle of the true paschal lamb nor the serious *Officium Pastorum* that was introduced by this comic parallel. Whether any doctrinal consideration about the true, miraculous lamb was intended by contrast, or even liminal in this treatment of Mak's story, cannot be demonstrated with certainty, even when one allows for medieval predilections both homologous and symbolic. The effect of cohesion and unity in the whole playlet, however, cannot be denied,[129] nor can one deny the structural existence of a comic variation that in no way implies any critical or rational qualification of that which is paralleled.

In a later age, the same effect is true for Dametus' martial and chivalric action in Sidney's *Arcadia*.[130] Dametus himself is ridiculed thereby; no knightly or chivalric action is questioned by this burlesque that embroiders with a comic variation matter that was important to Sidney. In the mature artistry of Shakespeare such an effect also exists in the speech beginning "On, on, on, on, on! to the breach, to the breach!"—the antic accompaniment in no way derisive of Henry V's martial lines of patriotic rhetoric: "Once more unto the breach, dear friends, once more."[131] Such a technique needs little discussion. That which is treated seriously, or relatively seriously, is sufficiently dominant to make the parallel risible, and usually the comedy of the parallel also is elaborated by at least one deriding emphasis within the scene.

More complex, and in some respects more interesting, is a technique that within the comic scene produces almost the contrary effect. In such instances, laughter related to the immediate situation may dissipate antipathy, derision, or ridicule[132] and hence may have a good deal of effect upon the impression created by the role for the principal comedian. The technique whereby this is done is especially interesting and pertinent in Shakespeare's artistry; and to arrive at an appreciation of it, a beginning can be made by considering some situations the results of which probably were appreciable to author, actor, and audience.

Obviously, immediate situations are paramount in determining the emphasis or effect of any speech and hence in determining ultimately the total impression of any role. Ambidexter as a malicious character, for example, appears only briefly; he is given only a few lines by which he can be said to influence in any way the villainous actions of King Cambises. Otherwise, his antics in their immediate theatrical circumstance are usually separated from the horrific deeds and ranting of Cambises and from the lamentations of that tyrant's victims. As a result, Ambidexter is essentially a comic figure.[133] The same is true when "vice-like" characters manipulate figures in a course of action that has, at best, only a slightly serious implication. They appear primarily to be interesting and amusing mischief-makers of the stamp of Diccon in *Gammer Gurton's Needle*.[134]

Even when a dominant, serious context has been established and preserved, and when a mocking speech upon a situation runs counter to this main emphasis, a comic effect may result because of the sharp disjunction between the speech and its context; but that which is ridiculed is not made derisible thereby. In such instances because the speaker has produced such an effect, he may have a theatrical appeal, but it probably will not be a sympathetic one. The mocks of Shakespeare's Aaron appear with his blackness and his deviltry, attributes that accord with his appearance in the succession of scenes as a vicious antagonist of the hero; and the continuing dominant emphasis created thereby probably was especially strong for an audience close to the morality play and thoroughly familiar with representations, both pictorial and verbal, of the Devil's actual and figurative blackness. Thus in the immediate theatrical situation of the nurse's murder, for example, any laughter resulting from Aaron's "Weke, weke! so cries a pig prepared to the spit" (*Titus Andronicus,* IV, ii, 146) probably would be the result of its sharp disjunction with its context, rather than the result of any wit in this mock *qua* mock.

When that which is mocked is not horrific or pitiable, however, and is neither treated seriously nor made appealing, any sharpness of disjunction will be mitigated and the appeal of the instigator of laughter will increase. If any truism about laughter holds good, it is that he who causes laughter by effectively pointing the merriment at a person or a situation has an appeal for an audience, at least temporarily. As commentator or as inciting cause, he directs the audience's emotions; or by his wit, and perhaps by his manipulating antics as well, he attracts an audience whose emotions the playwright has not aroused otherwise. As a result, his appeal is a sympathetic one; and because of his unbridled tongue or his witty manipulations, in the immediate situation of the stage-world he may seem a wise fool—in Gossip Tattle's words, "the finest man i' the company" with "all the wit." For that matter, even a previous ridiculousness predicated of such a figure may be lost thereby, at least momentarily.[135]

It is this last effect that is especially interesting in Shakespeare's artistry. It is achieved sometimes by witty comments that are applicable to situations which are outside the scene, which are relatively serious, and with which the comedian has not so far been involved. In *A Midsummer's Night's Dream,* the bumptious stupidity of the principal comedian is intensified by his sudden acquisition of an ass's head and by his comically ironic lines,

> What do you see? You see an ass-head of your own, do you?
> I see their knavery; this is to make an ass of me. . . .
> (III, i, 119-20, 123)

Congruent with such a derisive emphasis is Bottom's song with its running commentary (ll. 125-31, 133-39).

Into this scene, however, Shakespeare has inserted short, witty speeches that show relatively little disjunction with their context. Titania's statement that the "fair virtue" of Bottom makes her love him on "first view" is answered with the words, "Methinks, mistress, you should have little reason for that: and yet, to say the truth, reason and love keep little company together now-a-days; the more the pity that some honest neighbours will not make them friends. Nay, I can gleek upon occasion" (ll. 145-50). This declaration by Bottom that he, too, can gleek is then followed by his denying that he is as wise as he is beautiful; and he confirms his lack of wisdom by referring to the immediate play-world: ". . . if I had wit enough to get out of this wood, I have enough to serve mine own turn" (ll. 152-54). Acting like many principal comic characters and like all choric characters, Bottom indicates a point of view that is applicable to a relatively large situation.

That situation, moreover, is not essentially serious, for the conventional incompatibility of reason and love has been demonstrated farcically by the actions of all the major characters in this wood, with the exception of Puck and Oberon. Bottom's wit then is applied to a comparable immediate situation. In brief, Shakespeare places Bottom in the theatrical position that Puck maintains; and the laughter, momentarily, is not pointed at Bottom in spite of his ass-headed ridiculousness.[136]

Even when no rough parallel exists, a wit that dissipates ridicule or derision may appear. The technique whereby this is done can be illustrated even in the playwriting of Jonson; and of all playwrights during the English Renaissance, Jonson probably was most concerned with creating derisive contexts, whereby laughter would be pointed at characters embodying the fatuous vices of the age in order to "fright their pride and laugh their folly hence."[137] Yet in the banquet scene of *Poetaster,* for example, or in the final scene of *Volpone,* Jonson sometimes will have leading characters comment wittily upon immediate situations in a manner that mitigates any derision or censure that may be directed at them. The last example can be treated briefly, for it does not become involved with Jonson's view of Roman history.[138] Thus at the end of Jonson's first "great" comedy, Volpone's final line blunts his censurability, as it also shows an imperviousness to punishment characteristic of some roles for the principal comedian:

> Avoc. i. Deliver him to the *Saffi.* Thou, VOLPONE,
> By bloud, and ranke a gentleman, canst not fall
> Vnder like censure; but our iudgement on thee
> Is, that thy substance all be straight confiscate
> To the hospitall, of the *Incurabili:*
> And, since the most was gotten by imposture,
> By faining lame, gout, palsey, and such diseases,
> Thou art to lie in prison, crampt with irons,
> Till thou bee'st sicke and lame indeed. Remoue him.
>   VOLP. This is call'd mortifying of a FOXE.

$$(V, xii, 116-25)$$

The reference to "mortifying," that is, to making fowl or other game "tender, by hanging it vp, or (otherwise) keeping it some while after it is killed,"[139] varies from its context primarily in tone. Its undeniable applicability saves it from complete disjunction; and its manner, in that it moves the punished one toward the position of final commentator, accords with Volpone's earlier position of being the central figure in manipulating and duping the butts. Such a vice-like comment upon severe punishment, in that it is directed by Volpone at himself, tends to divorce the speaker, but not the speech, from the immediate situation; while it places Volpone in the familiar position of directing the merriment.[140] Any derisive ridicule of Volpone is thereby mitigated.[141]

Sometimes, in contrast with Volpone's comment and Bottom's gleeking, the result of dissipating or blunting derision may not be choric in its applicability to an immediate situation or a sequence of scenes. The laughter resulting, consequently, is "free";[142] and since at the moment a general consideration is being discussed, it seems fair to turn to a later drama by Shakespeare in which there is an explicit statement illustrating this fact. At a crucial moment in the role for the principal comedian of *All's Well that Ends Well,* a witty personal satire momentarily balances, and even dominates, a scene developing derision for such a conventional object of ridicule as the braggart and exquisite. When Parolles' cowardly revelations have laid the groundwork for his predetermined unmasking, however, Shakespeare begins to create a different situation within this major context. To do this, he utilizes the hero of the play, part of whose education is to be effected by this scene, and balances him against the second Lord Dumaine. About this second lord, a nearly nameless character, the audience has heard little; nor has he appeared frequently upon the stage. In this respect, he is potentially a choric character; and in this scene he does perform such a function. Although at first he has to be stopped by Bertram from striking Parolles (IV, iii, 209-17), when Bertram becomes angry at Parolles' wit, Dumaine speaks lines that emphasize this comic variation that Shakespeare effects within a conventionally derisive context:

> *1. Sold.* . . . once more to this Captain Dumaine. You have answer'd to his reputation with the Duke, and to his valor; what is his honesty?
> *Par.* He will steal, sir, an egg out of a cloister. For rapes and ravishments he parallels Nessus. He professes not keeping of oaths; in breaking 'em he is stronger than Hercules; he will lie, sir, with such volubility, that you would think Truth were a fool. Drunkenness is his best virtue, for he will be swine drunk, and in his sleep he does little harm, save to his bedclothes about him; but they know his condition and lay him in straw. I have but little to say, sir, of his honesty. He has everything that an honest man should not have; what an honest man should have, he has nothing.
> *2. Lord. I begin to love him for this.*
> *Ber.* For his description of thine honesty? A pox upon him for me, he's more and more a cat.

1. Sold. What say you to his expertness in war?

Par. Faith sir, he has led the drum before the English tra-
gedians. To belie him, I will not, and more of his soldiership
I know not; except, in that country he had the honour to be
the officer at a place there called Mile-End, to instruct for the
doubling of files. I would do the man what honour I can, but
of this I am not certain.

*2. Lord. He hath out-villain'd villany so far, that the rarity
redeems him.*

Ber. A pox on him, he's a cat still.

(ll. 276-307)

Momentarily, Parolles controls the scene in spite of the derisive irony
directed at him and underlying the entire sequence. Yet the object of
his wit is not made ridiculous. Dumaine's comments, and such a detail
as the reference to Mile-end,[143] allow a critic to be relatively sure of his
ground. Here Bertram's lines run athwart the immediate comic
emphasis, although he, as well as Dumaine, is not ridiculed; the force
of the total, derisively ironic context prohibits that. In brief, wit as wit
momentarily becomes dominant, with its amusing personal satire blunted
by the attitude of Dumaine—by an appreciative audience on stage, and
one can assume off stage as well. At the same time, derision of Parolles
is dissipated briefly as laughter or amusement rewards his rare ingenuity
and, with no fit object, becomes necessarily free.

Such a technique is developed most effectively in some of the scenes
centered about Falstaff, wherein Shakespeare also utilizes material that
in the theater was associated conventionally with the chief comic actor.
That these scenes create the laughter here called "free" has been commented upon, in different words, by previous critics.[144] Infrequently,
however, have individual episodes been analyzed with emphasis upon
this point or upon the relationship between the type of laughter under
discussion and the comic mélange spoken of earlier, that is, the comic
atypicality that was thoroughly familiar to regular theater-goers when
Shakespeare began his career as a playwright. Especially suitable for
analysis, then, would be a scene wherein the age-old comic device
mentioned above, that of having the duper duped, also appears in the
development of the action; for with that motif, a variation in laughter
might appear within the bounds of the comic scene—as it does not in
the "Second Play of the Shepherds" but as it does, momentarily, in the
confession of Parolles. In such a category, of course, falls Act II, scene
iv, of *1 Henry IV*. Certainly one of the ideas expressed most frequently
in Shakespearian criticism is that in this scene Falstaff escapes the trap

laid for him by a magnificent display of the wit upon which he can always rely. The idea can be expressed generally in terms of different types of laughter by saying that the situation develops toward making Falstaff an object of derision through his persistence in a series of egregious lies. The scene then turns from the Bergsonian rigidity of an individual so that a free laughter results from a wit that makes rigid for its own logical purposes those features of society's beliefs that had been used for that ridicule.

When one considers the scene in some detail, it is obvious that as far as a first audience is concerned, the brief general anticipation that Falstaff's lies will cause merriment (I, ii, 205 ff.) could have been satisfied adequately by the lines that begin with Falstaff's entrance and culminate in the revelation of the truth. It is here that the basic device of trapping the braggart in his pose of bravery is developed originally, to be sure, but along conventional lines that include a number of tricks usually given to the boaster. There is the braggart's criticism of the puny times (e.g., the refrain of "A plague of all cowards," "villainous coward"). There is his account of a mighty action and his insistence upon his veracity by repetition ("What, art thou mad? art thou mad? Is not the truth the truth?"). Falstaff is given evasive oaths and vituperations ("S'blood, you starveling, you elf-skin, you dried neat's tongue, you bull's pizzle, you stock-fish! O for breath to utter what is like thee! you tailor's-yard, you sheath, you bowcase, you vile standing tuck," etc.). There is his first attempt to explain away valorously his revealed ignominy: "What, upon compulsion? 'Zounds, and I were at the strappado, or all the racks in the world, I would not tell you on compulsion. Give you a reason on cumpulsion! If reasons were as plentiful as blackberries, I would give no man a reason upon compulsion, I." To move ahead briefly in the sequence of the scene, as Stoll and others have pointed out, here there also appears the braggart's conventional whining ("Ah, no more of that, Hal, and thou lovest me!"); and his quick acceptance of anything, in addition to vituperation, that will allow him to evade the issue:

> "What doth Gravity out of his bed at midnight? Shall I give him his answer?" (ll. 325-26)

> *Prince.* Yes, Jack, upon instinct.
> *Fal.* I grant ye, upon instinct. Well, he [Douglas] is there too, and one Mordrake, and a thousand blue-caps more. . . . (ll. 389-92)

> *Fal.* . . . Art thou not horribly afraid? Doth not thy blood thrill at it?

Prince. Not a whit, i'faith; I lack some of thy instinct.
Fal. Well, thou wilt be horribly chid tomorrow when thou
comest to thy father. If thou love me, practise an answer.

(ll. 405-12)

But such matter—conventional devices in the technique of exhibiting
a braggart—is subordinate, both by position and by emphasis, to a
true wit and to the continuation of a complex witty combat that might
be associated traditionally with a stage hero and his companion and that
began with the first appearance of Hal and Falstaff.[145] A major part of
the effect for an Elizabethan audience, moreover, would reside in the
fact that one of the participants is a regal figure, an heir apparent, who
should be concerned with good counsel and conduct. At least one other
basic element of familiarity is also obvious. Limited in no way by
conventional types *qua* types, the pertinent wit of the principal comedian
frequently coexisted with his oafish attributes, and certainly it would
be compatible with any revelling in a tavern.

In this particular instance, then, when the inventor of deceits has
been "hoist with his own petar" through the invention of others, the
scene moves from a derisive context to one consistent with Falstaff's
previous display of wit in company with the prince. It is then that Poins'
duping trick, the invention itself, is turned back upon itself. Neither
the duper who would dupe nor the inventors of the trick that would turn
the tables are laughed at—save, perhaps, as Hal and Poins partially base
their invention on a generally accepted scale of values that they would
apply to the comic world of tavern-haunting and noisy robbery. Falstaff
of the true wit, a character who in that sense is a traditional companion
of a hero, accepts their invention and, with it, their basis for ridicule.
He also affirms, however, the incomplete application of their invention:
the fact that they have forgotten the nature of one of the participants,
the true prince. Thus they fallaciously reprove one who, even on instinct,
was aware of that fact, a fact that the age agreed should be uppermost
always in any speech or action by a good counselor.

In this scene, consequently, valor and cowardice are equated with
the lion's instinct around a *true* prince; and the pertinent puzzle of
descent (a question of great weight to Elizabethans) is resolved thereby—as it will be resolved in the play extempore on the basis of a wise
father who knows his son, chiefly by the foolish hanging of his nether
lip. As a result, the most elementary mythical thinking of the age,
joined with political thought and with the most commonplace of comic
adages, appears at a time when Shakespeare's comic effect is heightened
uniquely—when a duper who would dupe by hacked sword and by

pierced and bloodied clothing, but who himself has been duped, would turn ridicule away from himself by merging ideals of society with superstitions and common jests, uncommonly expressed. In the first situation, Falstaff also turns to the great Hercules: "Was it for me to kill the heir-apparent? Should I turn upon the true prince? Why, thou knowest I am as valiant as Hercules; but beware instinct; the lion will not touch the true prince. Instinct is a great matter; I was now a coward on instinct. I shall think the better of myself and *thee* during my life; I for a valiant lion, and *thou* for a true prince."[146]

This central figure in merriment then develops the theme, not of his instinct, but of the more important, related idea of Hal's royal face, descent, and conduct (e.g., ll. 443-49). Indeed, the continuity throughout the scene, as well as its shift from a pointed derisive context, is especially apparent when its resolution is considered. At that time, since Elizabethan pronunciation made homophones of *made* and *mad*, a theatrical performance would allow both meanings to be applicable to Falstaff's statement that the prince is "essentially" *made-mad* "without seeming so" (ll. 540-41).[147] Thus the thought of that line goes back, with a magnificent sureness, to the idea just mentioned, an idea expressed by Falstaff as he began to escape derision ("I shall think the better of myself and *thee* during my life. . .").

Between Falstaff's excuse and the end of the mock interview, moreover, the witty consequences of Falstaff's "logical" acceptance of Hal's trick is also developed in a manner that involves the popular topic of appearance and reality and the general idea that men should be what they seem. Such a development appears when tavern burlesque gets under way and the appearance of Hal's nether lip is cited as proof of his descent. It is continued as those ideas can be applied to Falstaff: "If then the tree may be known by the fruit, as the fruit by the tree, then, peremptorily I speak it, there is virtue in that Falstaff. . . " (ll. 470-73).

Yet Falstaff, to others, undeniably appears as "that trunk of humours, that bolting-hutch of beastliness, that swollen parcel of dropsies, that huge bombard of sack. . . ." As a consequence, his final display of wit on Hal's nature and appearance applies a kindred line of argument to the prince—an argument based, however, on the way in which Hal's habitual actions (an important "place" in any character description)[148] deny his essential nature. Previously in the play-world, in spite of his mother's word and this mock king's own opinion, Hal apparently had shown that "virtue" and "manhood, good manhood" had almost been "forgot upon the face of the earth." A valiant man like Falstaff could beat Hal out of his kingdom with a "dagger of lath" and drive all his subjects "like a flock of wild geese." Previously also, an incident and related lines had appeared that are to be utilized finally by Falstaff and that had linked the idea of appearance with figures about a ruler and with a king's coinage of nobles and royals (6*s* 8*d*. and 10*s*. respectively). In answer to the hostess' announcement that "a nobleman of the Court" had come from Hal's father, an audience would have heard, "Give him as much as will make him a royal man, and send him back to my mother." Thus when Falstaff still has "much to say in behalf of that Falstaff" and when a sheriff and "a monstrous watch" are at the door, if Falstaff's excuse from derision is to continue and embody also the admonitory overtones suitable to a counselor of royalty, the further elaboration of these ideas and of such a figure is most apt. Falstaff also can begin to make the point again that he, too, is not to be judged only by unfavorable appearances:

> *Host.* The sheriff and all the watch are at the door; they are come to search the house. Shall I let them in?
> *Fal.* Dost thou hear, Hal? Never call a true piece of gold a counterfeit.

The wit combat, however, is still continuing; for Hal ignores Falstaff's statement that the prince's appearance also denies the prince's nature. To Hal, Falstaff's appearance had represented reality accurately, and men are what they seem: "And thou a natural coward, without instinct." Falstaff, nevertheless, unswervingly perseveres. He had disproved Hal's major premise by instictive action. Now, it is Hal's turn; and in spite of Hal's misunderstood appearance, but in accordance with valor's instinct *et al.,* this prince *can* demonstrate indisputably that he *is* essentially regal ("essentially made") by denying the sheriff: "I deny your major. If you will deny the sheriff, so; if not, let him enter." Should the worst befall, the courageous Falstaff, well brought up in valor and manhood, and now perhaps to be "brought up" by a hanging, knows that his ingrained fortitude, even in the greatest adversity, will allow him to become "a cart as well as another man"—but only if his instinct had been fallible.

With a world of unreality wittily established as logically real, upon a premise that was given him by those who would dupe him and upon which could be developed appropriate similitudes, Falstaff can relax—though the image of a king's coinage with its levels of meaning lingers on in a degenerate and counterfeit age:

> *Prince.* Go, hide thee behind the arras; the rest walk up above. Now, my masters, for a *true face* and good conscience.

    Fal. Both which I have had; but their *date* is out, and
therefore I'll hide me.

(ll. 549-53)

Within the scene, in contrast with the technique of the "Second Play
of the Shepherds," the duping of a duper, as well developed as it is,
moves into a nonderisive context that is achieved essentially by an
elaboration upon well-known themes. Thereby the shifting burden of wit
is carried lightly but alternately by Hal and by Falstaff in a manner that
corresponds to that of the unresolved debate or of the wit combat *per se,*
wherein any derisive pointing of laughter is diminished by the mutual
skill of the combatants.[149]

The dexterity of the accomplishment given the principal comedian
must have produced a laughter that transcended in its freedom—and
almost transformed into a new creation—any world that might believe
in unnatural natural science. At the same time, it accepted a world
concerned about regal descent and about debased or counterfeit coinage,
both actual and figurative. Shakespeare's audience had read, or at least
heard, some of those serious precepts about conduct that fascinated the
age, especially when they were concerned with the conduct of princes.[150]
A major feature of those precepts, Shakespeare has Falstaff accept, as
the situation of a duper duped is woven into that of the mock interview.
Thus part of the mental dexterity given this principal comedian not only
is tied into the witty excuse of a revelling braggart but also develops out
of that which is used to make him derisible and out of Hal's importance
as a prince. As a consequence, in its relationship to that which is
treated seriously, the scene agrees with the rest of the drama. Falstaff's
witty theme elaborates Hal's comment on his own actions in his first
soliloquy. In this respect, the corollary to Falstaff's escape from derision
accords with the serious interview and the progress of the drama
toward Shrewsbury.

As far as Falstaff is concerned, the scene also agrees with the
development of the play. The laughter is centered about him as
Shakespeare's technique elaborates a feature of the current comic milieu
that could be part of a vulgar theater-goer's expectations. The comedy is
close to the probable predilections of even a thoughtless spectator who
might feel strongly about the way in which rulers and their principal
subalterns should act but who, at the same time, expected a witty,
central figure in his merriment.[151] Even before he saw Falstaff, such a
one probably remembered with pleasure the actions of Tarlton and
Kemp upon the stage, or the mock bravery and cowardice of clowns in

song and central figures in revelry and "immoderate joy"; and he probably felt kindly toward the actions of even an earlier Bullithrumble:

> *Cali.* Well there is no remedie.
> > *Exeunt* all, but Bullithrumble stealing from them closely away.
> *Bulli.* The mores the pitie. Go with you quoth he, marrie that had bene the way to preferment, downe *Holburne* vp *Tiburne:* well ile keepe my best ioynt from the strappado as well as I can hereafter. . . .
> > > > > > (*Selimus,* ll. 2078-85)

Obviously no such analysis as that which has just been given took place in the theater. If what has been written is correct, however, Shakespeare's technique in handling the relationship between the serious and the comic reminds one of that shown in the "Second Play of the Shepherds." The laughter of the scene in relationship to the rest of the drama is free. This representation of extempore revelling—which in itself seems close to the merriment of the tavern, of singer-comedian and farcical jig or interlude[152]—is a hilarious anticipation of serious matter and includes a comic parallel that neither mocks the true interview nor qualifies it in any way. In this respect also, it elaborates a feature of Shakespeare's earlier artistry, although Cade's genealogy, for example, was mocked within its own scene.

Finally, when one turns from a general consideration concerned with types of laughter to the era of Bullithrumble, some attention should be given to the artistic use upon the Elizabethan stage of at least one other strand in the complex noted in earlier pages of this chapter, namely, the way in which the punishment or death of a dizzard might be treated risibly. Avarice in *Respublica* exits to his death with a jest long before Volpone is given a similar action.[153] Indeed, the death of a dizzard sometimes seems to have been used simply because it was conventional, especially in folk drama. In such a light one probably should view the scenes in which the clown appears in *Titus Andronicus.* They begin with an echo of the news motif, "News, news from heaven!" (IV, iii, 77); and in accordance, perhaps, with the danger in singing a news song, the sequence ends with the clown on his way to be hanged. Otherwise, this comic development shows conventional tricks used briefly and baldly: a corruption of words (IV, iii, 79-80, 93; IV, iv, 40); a reference to drinking and carriers and brawling (IV, iii, 84-85, 86-87, 92-94); a worn pun on "grace" (IV, iii, 90-91); and a comic desclaimer of presumption:

> *Tit.* Why, dost thou not come from heaven?
> *Clo.* From heaven! alas, sir, I never came there. God forbid
> I should be so bold to press to heaven in my young days.
>
> (IV, iii, 88-91)

The bit part then ends with the clown's final jest:

> *Sat.* Go, take him away, and hang him presently.
> *Clo.* How much money must I have?
> *Tam.* Come, sirrah, you must be hang'd.
> *Clo.* Hang'd! by'r lady, then I have brought up a neck to
> a fair end.
>
> (IV, iv, 45-49)

Although it was not to be realized, the possibility of a subsequent scene with a mock repentance or testament, comparable, for example, to that of the friar's last appearance in *Edward I,* may have mitigated any element of grimness in the preceding situation. Be that as it may, the same result probably would be achieved by an audience's awareness of the mock death of the dizzard, which was conventional in the drama of the folk. This clown's exit, consequently, undoubtedly stood by itself as matter that was conventionally comic, however naïve it might be.[154] Certainly it lacks the neat motivation of an imperviousness to execution that Kyd effected for grim humor in *The Spanish Tragedy.* Falsely secure in thinking his pardon at hand, Pedringano also jests at his hanging.[155]

Surprising as comic artistry at first glance is Jonson's representation of Farmer Sordido. He enters "with a halter about his necke," curses the "star-monger knaves" who make almanacs, and reads a letter about a father's "benevolence" and about revels. He then tests his halter for comfort as he leaves his possessions to no one: "Stay; I'le trie the paine thus a little, ô, nothing, nothing. Well now! shall my sonne gaine a beneuolence by my death? or any body be the better for my gold, or so forth? No. Aliue, I kept it from 'hem, and (dead) my ghost shall walke about it, and preserue it; my son and daughter shall starue ere they touch it: I haue hid it as deep as hel, from the sight of heauen, and to it I goe now" (*Every Man Out,* III, vii, 60-67).

Probably the literary genetics of the incident are to be found in Hoby's translation of *The Courtier* (1561). It was to be repeated in *Macbeth* (II, iii, 4), in *The Curse of Corne-horders* (1631), in Peacham's *The Truth of our Times* (1638) and *The Worth of a Penny* (1647), and in John Taylor's *Part of this Summers Travels, Or News from Hell, Hull, and Hallifax* (ca. 1640).[156] Yet for the purpose of social satire, Jonson's method may have seemed to an audience of 1599 to effect a neat variation upon the conventions of that *Vetus Comœdia* that *"Marde"* Martin Marprelate "cleane."[157] That Jonson in his first "Grex," which is probably addressed to readers, applies the term *Vetus Comœdia* to the genre before Menander (ll. 230-70) reflects Jonson's humanism; but the scene in the drama may not have been at all incompatible with his actor's knowledge of an Elizabethan audience.[158]

The artistry of Shakespeare in representing the death of Cade is also especially firm; for Cade's comedy, which is at first essentially antic, becomes loathsome, and then strikes a unique comic note before Iden's censure closes that line of action. Before the scenes began, and hence before Cade's being "whipp'd three market-days together" would appear in a strong comic context (*2 Henry VI,* IV, ii, 61), an audience had heard of "a headstrong Kentishman," a "stubborn" Cade, whom York had seen "Oppose himself against a troop of kerns" and fight

> . . . so long, till that his thighs with darts
> Were almost like a sharp-quill'd porpentine. . . .

Being rescued, he would

> . . . caper upright like a wild Morisco,
> Shaking the bloody darts as he his bells.
>
> (III, i, 360-66)

The promise of such a description, with its overtones of folk merriment ("Morisco"-morris dancer), would be realized in Cade's first scene. His central position among a comic crew, his burlesque oration and ridiculous genealogy, the reappearance of age-old objects of mocking laughter—knighthood, gentility, learning, lawyers—and Cade's derisive quip about the many-headed multitude have all been mentioned. In such a manner, Shakespeare develops a conventional comic mélange. Indeed, the attitude of Cade and his followers toward the loss of the dukedom of Maine supports such an emphasis. Although that loss is attributed incorrectly to Say, Cade's attitude is that of patriotic Englishmen when they had spoken of England's humiliation (I, i, 104-31). In other words, although it is motivated by the ambitious York, Cade's first appearance is not divorced from the strong comic appeal of the principal comedian and his crew, here performing a villainous, but nonetheless antic, sequence. Thus after Cade quips that he himself has invented his mock genealogy, he refers to gallant Henry V; and the loss of Maine appears, when the ridiculing of learning continues, with a comic logic that is amusing *per se:*

> *Cade.* Go to, sirrah, tell the King from me, that for his
> father's sake, Henry the Fifth, in whose time boys went to

span-counter for French crowns, I am content he shall reign;
but I'll be Protector over him.

Dick. And furthermore, we'll have the Lord Say's head for
selling the dukedom of Maine.

Cade. And good reason; for thereby is England main'd, and
fain to go with a staff, but that my puissance holds it up.
Fellow kings, I tell you that the Lord Say hath gelded the commonwealth, and made it an eunuch; and more than that, he
can speak French, and therefore he is a traitor.

Staf. O gross and miserable ignorance!

Cade. Nay, answer if you can. The Frenchmen are our
enemies. Go to, then, I ask but this: can he that speaks with
the tongue of an enemy be a good counsellor, or no?

All. No, no; and therefore we'll have his head.

(IV, ii, 164-83)

The bloody and impervious dangerousness of this scene, along
with some bragging heroics, will be used, however, to move Cade's
punishment and death, not into the area of Sordido's social satire,
but into that of a political sin which, however ridiculous, is nonetheless damnable. Although that which is comic is at first dominant (IV, ii,
1-129), even before the preceding reference to Maine had appeared, this
eruption in the order of the state began to be represented as an abhorrent commonality. Not only did the Staffords refer to the comedian
and his crew as "Rebellious hinds, the filth and scum of Kent, / Mark'd
for the gallows" (ll. 130-31) but Cade's mock oration ended with the
risible promise that there would be "reformation" and that food and
drink and all things would be held in common: ". . . your captain is
brave, and vows reformation. There shall be in England seven halfpenny
loaves sold for a penny; the three-hoop'd pot shall have ten hoops, and
I will make it a felony to drink small beer. All the realm shall be in
common, and in Cheapside shall my palfrey go to grass. . ." (ll. 69-76).
Yet as Sebastian was later to remark about Gonzalo and his commonwealth, Cade would be king in this land of commonality:

> . . . and when I am king, as king I will be,—
> *All.* God save your Majesty!
> *Cade.* I thank you, good people,—there shall be no money
> All shall eat and drink on my score; and I will apparel them
> all in one livery, that they may agree like brothers and worship
> me their lord.

(ll. 76-82)

Lawyers and law then became the center of attention (ll. 83-90). But for the educated in the audience, one aspect of these last speeches might have been capable of stirring up a momentary fear and disgust inculcated by contemporary concepts about the viciousness of Cade's doctrine, in spite of its Platonic echoes. The concept of "reformation" with "All the realm . . . in common" and the levelling of the lines last quoted might be associated easily with an earlier Anabaptism and its fiasco at Münster, for that event of relatively recent history frequently was used as a concrete instance of the barbaric consequences of religious radicalism and its attack upon order and degree.[159] At the moment, in this first appearance of Cade, that which is comic in these statements, even by their context, is undoubtedly dominant. A lusty hunger and thirst had been associated with the principal comic figure since the days of Aristophanes and, much more meaningfully, was being embodied in the current theatrical scene by such clowns as Bullithrumble and Strumbo.

In contrast, during the long scene wherein the rebels are triumphant, the thought of the Stafford's speeches and the viciousness of Cade's command that all lords and gentlemen be killed (IV, ii, 192-97) begin to bear the emphasis, and the scene increasingly represents the bloody imperviousness of the many-headed. Although the brave, effective rhetoric of Say causes remorse even in Cade, he will "bridle it" (IV, vii, 111-12). Thus when Say is lead off stage to be beheaded, the ridiculous levelling of communism and the lust of the comedian reappear; but the context is changed. Noblemen will be treated as Say has been; and what might be the most comic of attributes—the principal comedian's lusty vigor, embracing both gluttony and lechery—is now treated more fully than before and phrased in a manner close to that conception of a community of wives which was said to have been practiced by abominable radicals:

> *Cade.* Away with him! and do as I command ye. [*Exeunt some with Lord Say.*] The proudest peer in the realm shall not wear a head on his shoulders, unless he pay me tribute. There shall not a maid be married, but she shall pay me her maidenhead ere they have it. Men shall hold of me *in capite;* and we charge and command that their wives be as free as heart can wish or tongue can tell.
>
> (IV, vii, 125-33)

Confirming such a shift in emphasis is the fact that with Cade's next long speech there appears a bloody spectacle, centering about the kissing heads of Say and Cromer:

Re-enter one with the heads.

Cade. But is not this braver? Let them kiss one another, for they lov'd well when they were alive. Now part them again, lest they consult about the giving up of some more towns in France. Soldiers, defer the spoil of the city until night; for with these borne before us, instead of maces, will we ride through the streets; and at every corner have them kiss. Away!

(ll. 138-45)

To this spectacle, the giving up of French towns is now subordinate, as it is subordinate also to the sacking of London and Cade's disordered order. Even the most iron-nerved of London spectators might have been opposed to the continuation of Cade's rule with an emotional strength capable of overriding any penchant for laughing at the antics of a presiding comedian; and Shakespeare skillfully achieves such an effect by repeating aspects of Cade's first scene but varying their context.[160]

The same consideration holds true for Shakespeare's treatment of Cade's final scene, before Iden's last speech would turn the ignorant gaper, excessively fond of the principal comedian and his tricks, toward an attitude more easily predicated of his educated neighbor (IV, x, 82-90). Cade's burlesque oration had lead into a mock heroism that had been emphasized especially in the short scenes leading up to his triumph (IV, iii, vi). Never divorced from a dangerous vigor (e.g., IV, viii, 57-67), this feature of Cade's portrayal is obviously capable of wide variations; and to its comic aspects Shakespeare returns for Cade's final speeches. At that time, Shakespeare also enlarges upon the principal comedian's conventional gluttony. Although it is realistically motivated, its result is comic (IV, x, 7-17, 26-28),[161] especially since it is linked now with Cade's burlesque heroism: "Brave thee [Iden]? Ay, by the best blood that ever was broach'd, and beard thee too! Look on me well. I have eat no meat these five days; yet, come thou and thy five men, and if I do not leave you all as dead as a doornail, I pray God I may never eat grass more" (ll. 39-44). When Cade is defeated by Iden, and as Cade delivers a mock curse and an exhortation that all be cowards, this incongruity is intensified by his insistence that "Famine and no other" has slain him (ll. 65-68, 79-81). As a result, the death of this principal comedian is accompanied by a mock heroic imperviousness, rather than by a conventional jest. With a unique effect that builds, nevertheless, upon the familiar, Shakespeare displays the comic antics and the heroics of a lusty countryman who with his crew embodies a vicious disorder. In an abhorrent revolt, no less than in an Irish battle, Cade capers "upright like a wild Morisco" to the danger of his associates and opponents.

What has been written is obviously no complete treatment of the comic in the English Renaissance or even of the comic on the Elizabethan stage during the late 1580's and the early 1590's. There is no consideration of the miming tradition; but like bawdry and puns of all sorts, since it demands a more minute discussion than is appropriate here, the probable miming of actors can be considered when necessary in the discussion of individual plays. Parody and burlesque have been mentioned only briefly; but less defensible, perhaps, is the little attention paid to the grotesque, which in its widest manifestation can be seen constantly in Renaissance art and literature. As it may involve tension between the comic and the terrifying, it can be seen, for example, in a portion of *The True Tragedy of Richard III*,[162] in Pedringano's hanging, perhaps in the clown incidents of *Titus,* certainly in some of Aaron's scenes in that drama, and possibly in the Sordido incident. In the sequence of scenes devoted to Cade, although the comic and the terrifying are emphasized successively, those emphases overlap. The more obvious features of this characteristic of Renaissance literature certainly should be viewed in historical perspective. But because of the diversity of emotions that the grotesque might arouse and because of the fact that it might thereby shape a character and engrave it in the memory of a regular theater-goer, it, too, can be treated best as it may arise within the development of particular plays. This portion of the discussion, consequently, can end fittingly with a final reference to the merriment of Maypoles, morris dances, and tavern-revelry. The members of an Elizabethan audience were probably familiar with those features of current life, with the rival wooing of jigs and ballads, and with other situations that appeared in the song and dance of the era. For dramatists to write with an awareness of this and with an awareness of comic traditions familiar to theater-goers would be only natural. As the preceding examples indicate, to do so shows good comic, as well as common, sense.

III

Aspects of Structure and Serious Character-Types

WHEN IN SERIOUS circumstances a relatively few types of character appear, dramatic patterns may emerge in a portion of a drama or throughout an entire play. Although one should assume that an audience's conscious awareness of these patterns might be slight, yet ideas about rulers could accord easily with certain narrative developments. So, too, could concepts of honor, ambition, fortitude, the nature of law, and the law of nature. Developments resulting from situations that appeared frequently upon the stage might also lead to a portrayal capable of being typed simply because of that recurrence. As a consequence, the relationship between certain types of characters and recurring dramatic movements, especially when it can be indicated by logical and historical considerations alone, indicates formative elements in the dramatic artistry of the period. Both actor and theater-goer might come to expect these developments, and for the author they might constitute one of the means whereby he controlled at least a portion of his material.

As was true for the discussion in the preceding chapter, what is pointed out here seems to illumine features of Shakespeare's artistry and that of other Elizabethan playwrights. In contrast with the previous discussion, however, Shakespeare's plays will be considered in subsequent chapters; for here we are concerned usually with entire dramas, a number of which will be examined in some detail after the nature of the preceding relationship between types of character and structure has been outlined. What is written here, of course, is not meant to be a complete survey of serious types of character. Attention will be focused, instead, upon certain typical figures who appear in tragedies and histories and whose representation might involve some five to seven developments that could accord with concepts about rule or about the actions of individuals of high degree. In some instances, those patterns also correspond with the structural processes found in earlier dramatic traditions, but this aspect of the literary scene will be considered here only briefly.

Certainly similar to the development of some moralities might be an author's representation of a passive protagonist attacked by a vicious antagonist,[1] and thoroughly memorable might be the lamentation of the protagonist as he became enmeshed in vicious designs. If the playwright had his eye on Seneca, the form and nature of the protagonist's speeches also might have antecedents in the two plays about Hercules. Long rhetorical speeches were the essence of "Senecanism," and according to contemporary testimony, those bravura passages were appealing and memorable, arising as they did from understandable passions and perturbations of mankind.[2]

When placed in a worldly, rhetorical milieu, the hero's lamentation would be even more noticeable if it were embroidered with a franticness that expressed thwarted impulses arising from honor and a desire for revenge. In these circumstances, a dramatist might insert appropriate *sententiæ,* as Seneca did, and utilize ideas that had sprung up around "honor," "justice," "ambition," and kindred springs of conduct. When one considers that to the sixteenth-century "Stoutnesse, both to withstand and reuenge" could be a manifestation of the law of nature,[3] the appearance in such a situation of the ambiguous ethos of vengeance seems eminently logical. So, too, does the fact that there might appear in these dramas the stamp of Seneca's *Thyestes.* As a result, in a variety of ways and at different times in the course of the drama, the protagonist may cease being essentially a passive figure and become an active one who by himself or with the help of others attempts to retaliate.

The figures involved in this dramatic process might include those in the large category of historical rulers who were not viciously censurable but equivocally human. What has been written here would be applicable in varying degrees to any character who suffers from the actions of an antagonist, who inaugurates at least a slight retaliatory action, and who is represented as being relatively worthy of an audience's sympathy, be the play tragedy, history, or tragicomedy, melodramatic in varying degrees.[4]

Although involved in plots of the greatest diversity, this protagonist, especially in a tragedy, might express his suffering in soliloquy, dialogue, or frantic action so intensely that he would be called "mad." As the additions to *The Spanish Tragedy* show, the representation of this emotional state was also theatrically appealing. It was varied in length; it was real or feigned; and it might cause laughter, but never to the extent that this major character would become essentially derisible. His madness might be associated, instead, with appeals to a supraterrestial law or with censure or ridicule directed at others. With the appearance of a revenge motif, the protagonist's madness probably would be associated also with his alert though equivocal statements and with his subsequent or concomitant designs.[5] When this happens, especially as the protagonist seizes or attempts to seize the initiative, his speeches may verge toward the intellectual attitude characteristic of the plotting antagonist and be controlled by a more logical oratorical manner than they would be otherwise. The more logical the manner of speech, of course, the more obvious the protagonist's counteractions.

Whether or not an audience were aware of the protagonist's plans, the shift in dramatic emphasis, whereby an essentially passive figure becomes active, probably would be appreciable to the spectators through their own fear and grief, or their desire and joy,[6] especially when the playwright utilized a relatively few ideas or situations with a strong emotional appeal to channel his course of events to a tragic outcome. The nature of the dramatic scene during the plague years, when dramas might be shortened for provincial acting or through degenerate hackwork, could have stressed this turning movement. In any circumstance—even if it showed little regard for the ethics of the conflict—it might have been watched by Elizabethans as avidly as they watched bullbaiting and bearbaiting. Details must be filled in from individual plays; but a thoroughly logical dramatic method and some rhetorical consequences, rather than any specific, relatively detailed attributes of character, could be associated quite naturally with this protagonist and with comparable figures who are acted upon and then react against their opponent.

The attributes of the vicious antagonist, however, are relatively easy to enumerate. As has been indicated in part, this figure might be expected to show qualities characteristic of the Machiavellian or of a Senecan Atreus or Aegisthus.[7] Although in a strict sense one would expect the former type to be grasping for a throne, in the Elizabethan theater—as with the figure whom Marlowe's Machiavelli introduced—political power may not be his primary objective. Revenge, or self-protection, or even a private viciousness may motivate his actions. Hypocrisy, ambition, allegiance to the doctrine of might, as well as a virtuosity in plotting, also belong to him. Although the concept of the more specific Machiavellian may well have helped to embed these villainous figures in a courtly milieu, yet that background itself would be suitable to any Renaissance individual of high degree; and at times such a realistic circumstance alone seems to motivate the villain's conventional secrecy—which would be another theatrically inescapable attribute. Witness one of Lorenzo's speeches at the Spanish court:

> I list not trust the air
> With utterance of our pretence therein,
> For fear the privy whisp'ring of the wind
> Convey our words amongst unfriendly ears,
> That lie too open to advantages.
> *E quel che voglio io, nessun lo sa;*
> *Intendo io: quel mi basterà.*
>
> (*The Spanish Tragedy,* III, iv, 78-84)

Obviously such a figure might appear not only as the opponent of a suffering protagonist but also as a rising Machiavel in the body politic. In both instances, a repetitive development is liable to occur, for the type will manipulate events and may perform concatenated villainies or instigate concatenated plots wherein the consequences or loose ends of one action lead to the next or make the next necessary. The relationship between this development and the character's soliloquies is obvious. An audience would perceive by the character's speeches that a series of small plots or horrific incidents was being developed within a larger dramatic process:

> Now to confirm the complot . . . cast
> Of all these practices, I'll spread the watch,
> Upon precise commandment from the king,
> Strongly to guard the place where Pedringano
> This night shall murder hapless Serberine.
> Thus must we work that will avoid distrust;
> Thus must we practise to prevent mishap,
> And thus one ill another must expulse.
> This sly enquiry of Hieronimo
> For Bel-imperia breeds suspicion.
> And this suspician bodes a further ill.
> As for my self, I know my secret fault,
> And so do they; but I have dealt for them.
>
> (*The Spanish Tragedy,* III, ii, 109-21)

This feature of a drama also would give to the play an air of intellectuality.

Especially when the principal villain was portrayed as one rising in the body politic and when he was not opposed to one figure essentially, his secrecy and his repetitious plotting might be elaborated by having him abjure current ideas about the foundation and bonds of society:

> I have no brother, I am like no brother;
> And this word "love," which greybeards call divine,
> Be resident in men like one another
> And not in me. I am myself alone.
>
> (*3 Henry VI,* V, vii, 80-84)

In accordance with a resolve to "set the murderous Machiavel to school," this villain expresses his conventional attitude of vicious secrecy and isolation in a manner that places him in opposition to humanity itself.

Attributes that belong to the Machiavel, in accordance with Gentillet's perversion of *The Prince,* also may complement those of the tyrant.[8] Tyranny sometimes was conceived of as trifurcating into the acquisition of rule, its exercise, and its aim.[9] The complete villainy of a tyrant, quite naturally, might be represented from these three points of view. Thus there may be only a tenuous line between the tyrant and the Machiavel when a viciously aspiring and plotting figure appears in a drama that represents his rise to power and his continuation in power, with or without a retributive fall. In *Selimus* (1586-93), for example, the "perfect picture" of complete tyranny is called to an audience's attention:

> Some men will say I am too impious,
> Thus to laie siege against my fathers life,
> And that I ought to follow vertuous
> And godly sonnes: that vertue is a glasse
> Wherein I may my errant life beholde,
> And frame my selfe by it in auncient mould.
> Good sir, your wisedomes ouerflowing wit,
> Digs deepe with learnings wonder-working spade:
> Perhaps you thinke that now forsooth you sit
> With some graue wisard in a pratling shade.
> Auant such glasses: let them view in me,
> The perfect picture of right tyrannie.
>
> (ll. 273-84)

Before the play is finished, Selimus acquires "empiry" by his villainous deeds and the drama closes with this tyrant regnant.

As a consequence, during the time that the stage-world represents a Machiavel's or a tyrant's accession to power, and during the time that it represents a tyrant's exercise of rule, repetitious villainies or horrors attendant upon a Nero, a Lycus, or an Eteocles may hold the stage and perhaps be mixed with revenge and lust, as well as with the ranting irascibility of a Herod. When commanding a nation, the type frequently appears in dramatizations of ancient legend or in representations of Eastern rule, although the emperors of Asia, and especially of Turkey, were thought to violate the nature of a true commonwealth more than did the rulers of pre-Christian times.[10] Accordingly, the vicious ruler might be expected to exhibit the antithesis of kingly action and thereby illustrate such a passage as Lucan's ironic index of tyranny: "The power of kings is utterly destroyed, once they begin to weigh considerations of justice; and regard for virtue levels the strongholds of tyrants. It is boundless wickedness and unlimited slaughter that protects the unpopularity of a sovereign. If all your deeds are cruel, you will suffer for it the moment you cease from cruelty. If a man would be righteous, let him depart from a court. Virtue is incompatible with absolute power. He who is ashamed to commit cruelty must always fear it."[11]

Obviously this type, as in the crude *Cambyses,* will have none—or at the best only a few—of the attributes of the traditional king, even as they were embodied, for example, in John of Salisbury's twelfth-century treatise. The tyrant, consequently, may be arrogant, not humble; lecherous, not chaste; concerned with his own not his subject's good; heedless of wise counsel; unlearned; and wholly subject to the affections of flesh and blood. Surrounded by actors, mimes, buffoons, harlots, and an unrestrained soldiery, he may be given an outstanding theatrical sign in his quick, angry recourse to the sword—an action that in the words of Lucan's Pothinus shows no fear of cruelty.[12] In these circumstances, a ruler's viciousness probably will be shown by repetitive incidents that could capitalize upon the theatrical appeal inherent in the complete absence of ethics.[13]

In contrast with the final appearance of a tyrant like Selimus, the end of a drama that displayed this type might accord with concepts about retributive justice and with a tradition that had been elaborated as far back as the twelfth century. At that time, versions of the *Officium Stellæ* looked forward to a Slaughter of the Innocents and to the horrifying death of Herod. Accordingly, an audience might find satisfaction in a tyrant's death and in the representation of the human instrument whereby his reign was terminated. The pyramidal structure of rise and fall and the simpler structure of horrors and a fall would be connected thereby with this villainous figure.[14] In connection with the first pattern, a spectator's memory of pictures of Fortune's Wheel would accord with the process of the drama, especially if one had that concept called to his attention. Witness a speech given the page in *The True Tragedy of Richard III* (1588-94): "I see my Lord is fully resolued to climbe, but how hee climbes, ile leaue that to your iudgements, but what his fall will be thats hard to say" (ll. 475-76). Educated spectators could also project this development, as well as that of horrors and a fall, against the background of contemporary thought that found expression in Cinthio's tragedies with a "happy" ending.[15]

The same tyrannical vein may appear also in tragicomedies. In these circumstances, however, there may be reflected the double conflict that was characteristic of the most popular type of moralities, namely those that dramatized the struggle between virtues and vices. The central figure's fall into vice—his giving way to his affections and passions, his failure to heed good counsel, his neglect of the commonwealth, and his recourse to the sword—would then be concluded by a second redemptive conflict or situation.[16] In a play of this sort, the protagonist's actions may be sufficiently vicious so that at least a portion of the drama represents the suffering and lamentation of those under his control.

In all three instances, consequently, whether the play closed with the tyrant regnant, the tyrant dead, or the ruler redeemed, there probably would be impressed upon an audience's consciousness the fact that an essentially vicious rise or reign, with or without a retributive fall or a final redemption, embraces pathetic interludes, the misfortunes of minor figures, and minor falls from power. Part of Richard's fortune in *The True Tragedy* involves, for example, the misfortune of Hastings, of Lord Rivers, of the princes, of George Stanley, and of Buckingham; and the tangential, pathetic fall of Jane Shore (scene xi) would reinforce an awareness of these consequences of the turning Wheel of Fortune and the rise and reign of a tyrant. In these dramas, the principal that the limbs and the rest of the body politic suffer from the head's misrule would be emphasized also by admonitory precepts, narratives of similar past occurrences, and other choric features. In all of this, the lamentation of both principal and subsidiary characters might be projected, of course, against the relationship between fall and lament that was established firmly in England by such a continuing compilation as *The Mirror for Magistrates*.

This last consideration, however, points much more directly to situations wherein pathos is applicable to a ruler as he is moved away from tyranny and placed in the broad area between black vice and glowing virtue. In these circumstances, when the fall of one who has not been a complete tyrant is shown, there may emerge another simple but basic structural pattern. As tyranny recedes through something more than a redemptive ending, a workable pattern results from representing a ruler's errors, sins, or qualified viciousness before his separation from power and then elaborating upon the pity of his fall.[17] Appropriate scenic groupings concomitant with an emphasis upon the ruler's attributes that are relatively commendable, or concomitant with rhetorical preparations for pity, actually may constitute a mid-portion of the drama. Into this development, dramatists also may introduce a rising figure who is not necessarily a vicious antagonist; and thereby they would work out a pattern of fall and concomitant rise. This structural movement may embrace a number of minor falls or minor rises and falls. Worked out in accordance with a taste for multiplicity, these plays could exhibit some complex ramifications but yet repeat, or be based upon, this logical, simple, and theatrically obvious development: the misfortune, error, or viciousness before the fall from power; the pity after it.

If the illustrious one who rises or reigns is essentially virtuous and does not fall from power—as with his direct opposite, the rising Machiavel or the successful tyrant—the structural pattern probably will be repetitive and show the successive overthrow or disappearance of threatening or opposing forces. The course of events may then illustrate the effectiveness of Elizabethan patriotism, of chivalry, or of vigorous Virgilian ethics. Indeed, heroic attributes of all sorts, including those of medieval and sixteenth-century romance, may be given to this virtuous character—both for their own sake and as attributes that effect Christian rule and make a state prosper. The political and religious position of Protestant England also might confirm the repetitive action connected with such a character, just as it could be seen, for example, in the imagery of the contestants who took part in the anually enacted romance of chivalry during Elizabeth's Accession Day Tilts.[18]

The theatrical heroism displayed by this typical character would be most noticeable and effective, perhaps, when a playwright was concerned once more with distant lands. In such a drama, what might be true for the dominant vicious figure as a type probably would be especially true for the "hero." He would be given an overriding force that constantly surpassed ordinary, human conduct. When portrayed by conscientious dramatists, however, this type may move from an improbable realm—in this instance, perhaps, from one of "*scenicall* strutting and furious vociferation"[19]—to one grounded upon a conceptual basis. Although the validity of the idea of *virtù* has been overemphasized at times, what Burckhardt writes of it certainly can be considered an attitude of the age when the theater is in question.[20] Such an attitude, which is to a degree applicable also to the Machiavel, makes for the acceptance of the theatrical virtuosity of the "hero," especially when his purpose is expressed with convincing, though heightened, rhetoric. Upon the stage, there was a true glory in achievement—the more difficult the better. Accordingly, this type might be given a surprisingly strong tenacity of purpose and an unconquerable belief in himself and in the virtue of accomplishment *per se*. In such circumstances, the portrayal can capitalize also upon an audience's delight in titanism and magnificence.[21] As a result, the portrayal of the "hero" may also utilize, in part, the theatrical appeal of the absence of ethics; for the playwright dealing with him may not attempt to arouse ethical prejudgments. They would be applicable to lesser individuals. As regards this indomitable figure, the dramatist may dismiss the theatrical norm otherwise appropriate to persons of the highest degree.[22]

A representation of a vigorous rising figure in recent history and Western lands, however, may move easily toward a representation of ambition. When this is true, both author and audience may well be concerned with that which is equivocal and ambivalent. Although portrayals of a rising figure inclined toward ambition might have associations for a regular theater-goer with portrayals of the Machiavel, yet those associations could be qualified by an ambiguous relationship between ambition and honor as it might be seen, for example, in the actions of martially inclined noblemen, especially if they were young.[23] Even when the question of revolt appears in a drama, the theatrical earmark of this type may be the "mounting" spirit and the contempt for fortune given to the man of *virtù* or the man of honor. In conjunction with vigorous rhetoric and deeds, that characteristic would have at least a strong theatrical appeal. Thus the audience's taste for the heroic and their reaction to the manner conventionally associated with the "hero" might well carry over to closely related concepts and a similar manner when they were used to portray a rising, though ambitious, figure in Western history.

Also related to the "hero" may be the rising figure, as major or minor character, who achieves his rightful position as heir to a throne. The variations in representing such a one are many, and sometimes his rise may be essentially a figurative one.[24] Sometimes, of course, his rightful position is not achieved. In that event, his fortune may contribute to the elaboration of a structural movement associated with one of the preceding types. Associated also with those types may be good counselors, loyal followers, bad counselors, time-serving parasites, and, of course, related women—all of whom may be used to produce a variety that elaborates the major structural movements just considered.

To review those structural movements briefly. In the first, that of protagonist versus vicious antagonist, the hero's change from a passive to an active figure is likely to be theatrically appreciable. There, too, successive, repetitive incidents probably will occur in the representation of the antagonist. This repetition, whether concatenated or not, probably will constitute the major feature of a development showing the rise of a dominant vicious figure. A third basic movement displays the characteristic actions or the characteristic rule of a censurable figure and his retributive fall or death. Although its combination with the second movement would result in a drama showing both the rise and the fall of the central figure, the tradition in back of representations of Fortune's Wheel make it more accurate, historically, to consider such a combination a fourth structural development. Indeed, it is a dominant one in sixteenth-century drama.[25] Associated with the third movement, but varying from it strikingly as the drama closes, is a fifth structural pattern that shows a redemptive, instead of a retributive, ending and thereby reflects the double conflict that had been characteristic of the structure of some moralities. The third structural development noted here can also bifurcate in accordance with the nature of the falling figure so that a welcome retributive justice does not overtake an essentially culpable protagonist; scenic groupings and the lament tradition may be used, instead, to create pathos for one whose actions contributed to his downfall. In this last instance, the merging of a fall with a related rise gives added point to designating this development a sixth structural pattern. The seventh development, like the second, is repetitious; but it dramatizes the success or the rise of a virtuous or a heroic figure. Its repetition, the outcome of its line of action, and the nature of the character involved may be varied, however, so that it verges toward the second movement or falls into the pattern of the fourth.

As has been indicated, these five to seven processes may merge with one another, or attributes of a character-type clearly associated with one structural movement may be used to portray figures in another one of these basic patterns or in one of their combinations. Conversely, there may be a separation by emphasis in the treatment of these processes; and thus if a fall and a rise are not represented as being concurrent, successive emphases may effect a linear multiplicity reminiscent of cyclical drama.[26]

Finally, the practice of constructing a drama so that it might be divided into three parts may be reflected in all of these developments.[27] The first part, frequently corresponding to Acts I and II, would reflect definitions of a protasis (an introduction of the characters and an indication of what is to follow). The second, frequently corresponding to Acts III and IV, would accord with definitions of an epitasis (the busy part of the play that culminates in the point of greatest complication). Act V would then represent the catastrophe. The practice is especially noticeable in academic dramas, although this five-act structure also appears with varying degrees of clarity in plays written for the popular stage. Except for educated persons interested in writing drama, however, the playwright's control of his materials in this respect would not be as

appreciable in the theater, or even in retrospect, as the structural movements outlined above.

The analyses that follow are meant to supplement the preceding remarks by pointing out some serious, usually tragic, developments related
to the basic dramatic movements just noted. The plays considered are
arranged so that the analyses will coincide in general with the order of
the preceding discussion prior to its summarizing paragraphs. All of
the dramas were written by Shakespeare's early contemporaries. Most
of the plays he probably knew or had heard of at one time or another.
All of the dramas that will receive special attention show a conscientious
artistry. Indeed, one of the purposes of the present study is to demonstrate this fact. When one considers that an Elizabethan audience of the
late 1580's and the early 1590's might also be satisfied by inexpert
dramas, the purposeful control that these playwrights show is all the
more commendable. This is true both for their writing of an entire play
and for their portrayal of characters in a manner that was probably
meaningful to all in an audience.

At any rate, regardless of their artistry, most of the dramas were
memorable ones. Thus they indicate what was, or what might become,
familiar in serious character-types, structure, context, or emphasis to
anyone in touch with the dramatic scene. Even the fact that the dating
of these plays usually can be determined only within a span of three to
five years does not diminish their illustrative value. This study is not
concerned with specific indebtedness. Whether or not the influence of
Marlowe upon Shakespeare can ever be established to the satisfaction of
all, any such investigation must proceed upon the assumption that two
writers can work with similar situations or with the same literary
traditions and achieve comparable but thoroughly independent results,
regardless of any particular date at which they wrote within a brief,
though in the strictest sense, an indeterminate, period of time. The
present study is concerned with representational methods and with concepts available to all authors during the late 1580's and early 1590's—
especially with what might constitute an awareness of the contemporary
theater that could belong to both authors and regular theater-goers
during Shakespeare's early years as a playwright. Although his work
was as instrumental as that of any other dramatist in perpetuating and
shaping what was theatrically familiar, the development of his artistry
will be considered elsewhere.

When later playwrights began to show within the theater an explicit,
critical awareness of earlier drama—and indicated thereby a background
familiar to at least some in their audiences—a scrivener appeared upon
the stage in 1614 to tell the spectators that the playwright will "pass

vnexcepted at, heere," anyone who swears that *"Ieronimo,* or *Androni-cus* are the best playes, yet." Such a person is "constant" and has been so for the past "fiue and twentie, or thirtie yeeres." Though his opinion is a bad one, "it is a vertuous and stay'd ignorance . . . such a one, the *Author* knowes where to finde him."[28] The popularity of Kyd's *Hieronimo,* that is, *The Spanish Tragedy,* certainly makes it fit for the present purpose.

Although Kyd's play (*ca.* 1584-88) does not mark the introduction of sensationalism to the English stage,[29] no previous Elizabethan drama had so emphasized the horrific character of events while preserving a Senecan effect and an over-all control of melodramatic materials. In writing *The Spanish Tragedy,* Kyd obviously remembered *Agamemnon* and *Thyestes;* indeed, it has been demonstrated that he also knew the eight other tragedies assigned to Seneca.[30] Although both of the plays to which he seems particularly indebted would confirm the popular revenge motif, Kyd modifies his representation of a conflict between protagonist and antagonist so that only the antagonist is vicious—in contrast, for example, with *Thyestes.* With the eight deaths that occur throughout the play, as well as other sensational events, with both Horatio and Hieronimo suffering from the designs of Lorenzo and Balthazar, with a minor congruous movement turning upon the viciously plotting Villuppo,[31] Kyd also shows his acceptance of a Renaissance multiplicity as he develops the major movement of suffering protagonist becoming active and effecting his revenge against a viciously intriguing opponent.

This major movement points to an interesting division that seems to control Kyd's multiplicity and that is underlined by the choruses. Throughout the first 856 lines, the revenge motif arises in a naïve context of chivalry and courtly love. Its culmination in the murder of Horatio leads to a development double in length (some 1746 lines). The first portion of this later development represents the vicious antagonist and the suffering hero and might well be called the mid-portion of the play (some 1218 lines). The latter portion represents the effectively plotting hero (some 528 lines).[32] The long mid-portion at first emphasizes the plotting of the antagonist and then the resulting passion of the protagonist. Such a shift in emphasis, consequently, makes its parts correspond more nearly in length to the introductory and the final portions of the drama. Although the introductory unit, usually printed as the first two acts, effects a tangential beginning in that Hieronimo appears therein only as a subsidiary figure, it nevertheless clearly indicates the nature of what is to come. As it closes, Hieronimo emerges as the protagonist, and the course of the action has been developed by a brief plot and counterplot.[33]

There is structural precision in the play. Indeed, the main features of the preceding development are signalled by what must have impressed itself on any spectator. In what is usually printed as Act II, scene ii, Kyd effects upon the stage three concentric circles of attention: Bel-imperia and Horatio, with their stichomythia and love-rhetoric; the watching Balthazar and Lorenzo, with their despairing love and villain-ous foreboding; the hovering ghost of Andrea and Revenge. Such a theatrical situation is then represented even more strikingly in the different circumstances of the catastrophe: the play-within-the-play; the main play-world; and Andrea and Revenge. One theatrical feature of the approach to the ending of a dramatic introduction is thus repeated in the aproach to the ending of the play. Similarly, Hieronimo's reading of two letters (III, ii, 24 ff.; III, vii, 19 ff.) frames Kyd's emphasis upon Lorenzo's concatenated plots and may well have been conceived of as a structural device.

In the introductory development, however, Kyd avoids some poten-tial thematic conflicts. When, for example, Balthazar learns that his captor is Bel-imperia's lover, no chivalric regard for Horatio (e.g., I, ii, 192-94) is balanced against Balthazar's thwarted love. In answer to Lorenzo's question as to how pleased he is with the revelation, Balthazar replys:

> Both well and ill; it makes me glad and sad:
> Glad, that I know the hinderer of my love;
> Sad, that I fear she hates me whom I love:
> Glad, that I know on whom to be reveng'd;
> Sad, that she'll fly me, if I take revenge.
> Yet must I take revenge, or die myself,
> For love resisted grows inpatient.
> I think Horatio be my destin'd plague:
> First, in his hand he brandished a sword,
> And with that sword he fiercely waged war,
> And in that war he gave me dangerous wounds,
> And by those wounds he forced me to yield,
> And by my yielding I became his slave.
> Now in his mouth he carries pleasing words,
> Which pleasing words do harbour sweet conceits,
> Which sweet conceits are lim'd with sly deceits,
> Which sly deceits smooth Bel-imperia's ears,
> And through her ears dive down into her heart,

And in her heart set him, where I should stand.
Thus hath he ta'en my body by his force,
And now by sleight would captivate my soul. . . .

                                        (II, i, 111-31)

Like the use of *gradatio* in the preceding speech (a word at the end of
one line reappearing early in the next), the theatrical effectiveness of revenge is its own excuse. "They reck no laws that meditate revenge" (I, iii,
48).[34] Yet even though the motif is not developed as part of an explicit
thematic nexus, such an attitude is censured; for by embodying it in the
figures of Lorenzo and Balthazar, the major and the minor villains, Kyd
develops a situation at the end of the second act that makes Hieronimo,
the father of the murdered Horatio, a character worthy of pathos. As it
has been noted, this feature of the drama departs from Seneca's portrayal
of Thyestes. Seen in the light of moralities, it moves Hieronimo toward
the position of Mankind. This favorable aspect of the protagonist's
portrayal will be stressed subsequently by the king's regard for
Hieronimo and by lines about his public justice.[35] This last development,
consequently, builds upon the horrific representation of Horatio's death
at the hands of Lorenzo and Balthazar.

At the same time, the emergence of Hieronimo as the protagonist
would arouse anticipations of further bloodshed. In Act II, scene iv,
when a repetition of love-rhetoric is broken by the seizure, hanging, and
stabbing of Horatio, and as the cries of Bel-imperia introduce the
lamenting passion of Hieronimo and his wife, an audience would witness
the cutting down of Horatio's body and the display of a handkerchief
smeared with blood. They would hear a vow that the handkerchief shall
remain with Hieronimo until the murder is avenged, and they would see
the bloody body of Horatio carried off stage. Thereby the spectators
would be prepared for the larger sequence of plotting and counterplotting
that also will involve the hero's tragic passion and his turn from an
essentially passive figure to an active one.

Although the later additions quickly move the representation of the
tragic hero to a frantic, even laughing, madness (II, v, 70 ff.), Kyd
moves much more gradually in that direction.[36] With Hieronimo's first
appearance in the third act, Kyd strikes only the note, conventional
since at least the days of Seneca, that the heavens cannot be called just
if a villainous deed, such as the murder of Horatio, goes unpunished
(III, ii, 1-23). The appearance of the first letter then motivates the
further plots of the antagonist; and although that letter also motivates
the hero's search for confirmation, Hieronimo is given only some slightly
distraught action (ll. 54-66). The idea of justice is returned to with

relative restraint on his next appearance (III, vi). At that time, Hieronimo balances his public justice against the fact that "neither gods nor men be just" to him (ll. 10). His subsequent appearance follows logically (III, vii): his introductory lines (1-18) develop the idea just mentioned; the remaining lines are concerned with the fact that the second letter confirms the first and with some rhetorical, but still relatively restrained, vituperation of Lorenzo and Balthazar.

Frantic speech and action are emphasized, however, during the last 634 of the 1218 lines in the long mid-portion of the drama (III, viii, through the final scene of Act III). And the popularity of this franticness is attested by the fact that it was elaborated in all of the additions. Isabella's madness (III, viii) is reinforced by the rhetoric of Belimperia's lamenting speech (III, ix, 1-14) and anticipates the scene of Hieronimo with the Portuguese, who laugh at this man they believe to be "passing lunatic" or doting from the "imperfection of his age" (III, xi). The emphasis is continued in Hieronimo's next scene but intensified. Witness, for example, the business with the halter and especially with the dagger (III, xii, 16-20, 70 ff.). Frustrated by the villain in attempting to secure justice from the ruler, the hero shows a "fury" (l. 79) that is falsely interpreted, first by Lorenzo, as resulting from extreme pride and covetousness, and then, quite sympathetically, by the king, as a melancholy to be cured (ll. 84-100). This portrayal of a pathetic distraction is then enlarged by the madness of the parallelism between Hieronimo and Don Bazulto (III, xiii, 46-173).

In spite of his emphasis upon the passion of his hero, and immediately before the parallelism just noted, Kyd, nevertheless, gives to Hieronimo a speech that is once more relatively restrained (III, xiii, 1-45). From the Latin tags of a book, Hieronimo weighs alternate lines of action, defends the one chosen, and emphasizes patience. This last thought agrees, for example, with lines in earlier scenes between the appearance of the two letters (III, ii, to III, vii). The topic also had been stated explicitly in Bel-imperia's speech of Act III, scene ix (ll. 1-14); and in the varying circumstances of the Portuguese court, patience had been referred to as the only remedy against the wrongs of an infected earth until justice be achieved (III, i, 31-37). By giving such a speech to Hieronimo, Kyd reinforces the relationship between the latter part of Act III and its earlier portions; but he also adumbrates the resolution of the drama. Relatively restrained rhetoric in a soliloquy is what one might expect of a figure who, in spite of a present emphasis upon his "madness," will become effectively active.

Kyd's emphasis, however, almost obscures the first movement of

Hieronimo from a passive to an active figure, even though that development had been called explicitly to an audience's attention:

> But wherefore waste I mine unfruitful words,
> When naught but blood will satisfy my woes?
> I will go plain me to my lord the king,
> And cry aloud for justice through the court,
> Wearing the flints with these my wither'd feet;
> And either purchase justice by entreats,
> Or tire them all with my revenging threats.
>
> (III, vii, 69-75)

As has been indicated, the antagonist's success in stopping Hieronimo's complaints to the king led to the protagonist's intensified distraction and to a line both famous and infamous to Elizabethans:

> *Lor.* Back! see'st thou not the king is busy?
> *Hier.*   O, is he so?
> *King.* Who is he that interrupts our business?
> *Hier.* Not I. Hieronimo, beware! go by, go by!
>
> (III, xii, 28-30)

The situation was then repeated:

> *Hier.* Justice, O, justice! O my son, my son!
> My son, whom naught can ransom or redeem!
>   *Lor.* Hieronimo, you are not well-advis'd.
>   *Hier.* Away, Lorenzo, hinder me no more;
> For thou hast made me bankrupt of my bliss.
> Give me my son! you shall not ransom him!
> Away! I'll rip the bowels of the earth,
>   *He diggeth with his dagger.*
> And ferry over to th' Elysian plains,
> And bring my son to show his deadly wounds.
> Stand from about me!
> I'll make a pickaxe of my poniard,
> And here surrender up my marshalship;
> For I'll go marshal up the fiends in hell,
> To be avenged on you all for this.
>   *King.* What means this outrage?
> Will none of you restrain his fury?
>   *Hier.* Nay, soft and fair! you shall not need to strive.
> Needs must he go that the devils drive.
>
>   *Exit.*
>   (ll. 64-81)

Granted that these incidents were memorable in the theater, their franticness probably overrode any realization that Hieronimo was becoming an active figure. Although he is more nearly successful in his second attempt than in his first, the consequence of this digging episode is that any effective action by the hero is left for the catastrophe.

For that matter, Kyd's theatrical emphases, achieved in part by his multiplicity—by such incidents as those involving Don Bazulto, the Portuguese, and the women connected with the hero—obscure the appearance of *sententiæ* even more easily than they obscure the first representation of retaliatory action by the protagonist.[37] And again, the ideas expressed by those maxims are not developed thematically. In the middle, as in the first, portion of the drama, what is melodramatic dominates any thematic interest a situation might have had in the theater.[38] Kyd has created, however, a memorable protagonist, with a minor parallel in Bazulto and pathetic women.

Certain features of the portrayal of Lorenzo, who is the vicious antagonist, have been noted already. Although he is connected with the court and with important events, political power is not the objective of his villainy; nor is his plotting motivated explicitly by any desire to clear a touchy "honor," blemished, for example, by the rivalry of Horatio.[39] Only Lorenzo's association with Balthazar and his position as confidant to the rejected lover explicitly motivate the action that causes Hieronimo to become a suffering hero. Even then, there is no mention, let alone any development, of the idea of friendship, that exceedingly popular Renaissance topic. The situation accords with what has just been noted. In this portrayal, Kyd apparently considered a villainous secrecy and melodramatic actions to be a theatrically sufficient point of interest.

The soliloquies given Lorenzo and their repetitive pattern, however, may well have engraved upon a theater-goer's memory the impression that he was a man of intellectual virtuosity. The quick, skillful, and successful way in which he knits up the loose ends from an initial deed of villainy must have been theatrically obvious. Hieronimo's question about Bel-imperia leads to Lorenzo's plot with Pedringano against Serberine. This is followed by Lorenzo's soliloquy about his plans for Pedringano (III, ii, 53-129). The successful execution of the plot against Serberine follows immediately (III, iii). It leads to Lorenzo's fear of betrayal and to his plot with Balthazar against Pedringano (III, iv, 1-34). This leads to another soliloquy (ll. 35-46). The appearance of a messenger then leads to the plot using the page. Lorenzo is then given his third soliloquy (ll. 74-84). The accomplishment of the last plot follows immediately and is developed, as it has been noted in the

Peninsula College Library
Port Angeles, Washington

previous chapter, with a grim ironic humor that shows Kyd's variation upon a conventionally comic development (III, v, vi). With increasing complexity, in the two deaths following from the murder of Horatio, there has appeared a triple representation of cause, plotting dialogue, and soliloquy, and a double representation of the plotter's success.[40] Such a development is clearly capable of visual, repetitive stage-groupings; while the concatenation of incidents would be pointed out constantly, and the successful duping "policy" of the villain's manipulating secrecy would be constantly apparent:

> Why so, this fits our former policy,
> And thus experience bids the wise to deal.
> I lay the plot; he prosecutes the point:
> I set the trap; he breaks the worthless twigs,
> And sees not that wherewith the bird was lim'd.
> Thus hopeful men, that mean to hold their own,
> Must look like fowlers to their dearest friends.
> He runs to kill whom I have holp to catch,
> And no man knows it was my reaching fatch.
>
> (III, iv, 35-43)

Another situation characteristic of the vicious plotter should also be noted. It appears when Lorenzo protests that all he has done to Belimperia has been to protect her honor (III, x). This aspect of a witty hypocrisy that with rhetoric would effect its purpose with a woman is thoroughly compatible with the Elizabethan's belief in the power of the spoken word and with the intellectual aura given to Lorenzo. Similarly, in accordance with Lorenzo's earlier virtuosity, and even as Hieronimo's franticness and Isabella's madness dominate the stage, this villain continues to exhibit a quick ingenuity. He stops Hieronimo's approach to the king and then capitalizes upon it; and in Lorenzo's next scene, Kyd represents his villain as again seizing upon the immediate to suggest, with the pose of an honest man, that

> 'Twere good, my lord, that Hieronimo and I
> Were reconcil'd, if he misconster me.
>
> (III, xiv, 91-92)

The success of this last stratagem of Lorenzo's is handled, however, with a dramatic irony that makes the catastrophe possible.[41]

In brief, Kyd skillfully elaborates with a Renaissance fullness, but with precision, the old motif of protagonist and vicious antagonist. Lorenzo's clever but fearsome villainy makes the world one in which patience is man's only remedy—unless he is willing to sacrifice himself and achieve a just vengeance by an equally clever and bloody stratagem (IV, iv). The melodrama of *The Spanish Tragedy,* however, overpowers even this reflective consideration as theatrically memorable figures perform their parts in a conventional structural movement, the elaboration of which provided the age with its conventions for the tragedy of blood.

In view of what has been noted about *The Spanish Tragedy,* it is revealing of Marlowe's artistry to see how traditions apparent in that play are utilized also in *The Jew of Malta* (1589-91). One is confronted, however, with the belief that the text of the drama, which survives only in a 1633 quarto, has suffered as a result of the manipulation of the play on the stage and that this corruption is apparent toward the end of the second act and especially in Acts III and IV. Should one invoke the Jesuit doctrine of probable opinions in considering this belief about the corruption of the drama, the weight of opinion by frequency of statement would substantiate the sentiment of those unwilling to give to Marlowe a "crude" series of melodramatic plots elaborating the motif of revenge.[42] Yet the Barabas of this portion of the drama shows a specific, though intensified, aspect of an attribute given his portrayal in the first scene of the play. In addition, the portrayal of Barabas during the latter part of Act II and throughout Acts III and IV shows a theatrical virtuosity not discordant with Marlowe's abilities—if one grants that the effect of a grotesque horribleness was purposeful. An adumbration of this effect also appears early in the drama when Marlowe represents his protagonist's immediate reaction to the confiscation of his wealth (I, ii, 161 ff.), and it is repeated in Barabas' gleeful recovery of his bags crammed with treasure (II, i). Because of such considerations, it seems a fair assumption that at least the structure of the play as it is printed in the 1633 quarto varies little, if at all, from its original design.[43]

As a result, the basic dramatic movement of *The Jew of Malta* seems quite original with Marlowe, although that originality apparently results from an unusual development of what was conventional. A passive figure, that is, one who is acted upon, recovers his wealth; his vengeance then leads to a concatenated series of vicious plots until he is destroyed through his final stratagem. Although the artistic development of the play after Barabas recovers his wealth is different from that in the preceding portion of the drama, such a difference is concomitant with the central figure's turn to an active counterdesign in order to avenge an injury. In the light of the Elizabethan theater and a conventional representational method, this change in emphasis, with a variation in effect, is thoroughly natural and logical.

As a result, concatenated plots to hide a villainous deed dominate the major portion of the drama. Because of Barabas' revenge, directed at Ferneze and effected by the deaths of his son and of Mathias (II, iii; III, ii), four plots result: that of the rice pottage (III, iii, 20 ff., iv, vi; IV, i, 1-21), the dead friar (III, vi; IV, i, 22 ff.), the poisoned flowers (IV, ii, iii, iv), and the feigned death (V, i, ii, 1-23). There are appropriate soliloquies for each (II, iii, 248-56, and III, iv, 1-13; IV, i, 117-31; IV, iii, 1-17, 61-70; V, ii, 1-8).

Because of the last of the preceding stratagems, however, Barabas is left without his wealth. The final plots, consequently, appear in circumstances partially similar to those at the beginning of the drama. Revenge reappears to motivate the stratagem of the hollow rock (V, ii, 26-34):

> I'll be reveng'd on this accursed town;
> For by my means Calymath shall enter in.
> I'll help to slay their children and their wives,
> To fire the churches, pull their houses down.
> Take my goods too, and seize upon my lands!
> I hope to see the governor a slave,
> And, rowing in a galley, whipp'd to death.
>
> (V, ii, 2-8)

With the success of this stratagem and with Barabas triumphant, the motive of villainous secrecy for self-preservation is repeated briefly (V, iii, 27-33); but this motive for the plot of the feast and the trick balcony is modified immediately by a Machiavellian virtuosity in forceful, profitable, and obviously vicious accomplishment:

> And since by wrong thou gott'st authority,
> Maintain it bravely by firm policy.
> At least unprofitably lose it not:
> For he that liveth in authority,
> And neither gets him friends, nor fills his bags,
> Lives like the ass, that Æsop speaketh of,
> That labours with a load of bread and wine,
> And leaves it off to snap on thistle-tops:
> But Barabas will be more circumspect.
> Begin betimes; occasion's bald behind;
> Slip not thine opportunity, for fear too late
> Thou seek'st for much, but canst not compass it.
>
> (ll. 35-46)

Such a final emphasis accords with the introduction of the play by Machiavelli, who at that time advocated plotting hypocrisy and the doctrine that might makes right. Certainly the process of the drama seems to be well controlled.

Since the portrayal of Barabas must have been a memorable part of the theatrical scene *ca.* 1589-91, its artistry and its effect deserve attention. When the play begins, Barabas is given a Machiavellian *virtù* by Machiavelli himself when he speaks of how he has come, not

> To read a lecture here in Britain,
> But to present the tragedy of a Jew,
> Who smiles to see how full his bags are cramm'd,
> Which money was not got without my means.
>
> ("Prologue," ll. 29-32)

When everything but the final stratagem has been represented, Barabas' trade has been heightened so viciously that it can be said to be of "a kingly kind":

> Why, is not this
> A kingly kind of trade to purchase towns
> By treachery and sell 'em by deceit?
> Now tell me, worldlings, underneath the sun
> If greater falsehood ever has been done.
>
> (V, vi, 46-50)

To effect this final vicious emphasis, Marlowe also has been representing Barabas' "kingly" trade in terms that might well have evoked anti-Semitic feelings. Although Barabas has attributed his Machiavellian "policy" to Christians, he says it is a life characteristic of Jews (V, iii, 109-14). Elsewhere in this portion of the play, Barabas is referred to as an "unhallow'd Jew," a "villain," a "slave," "accursed," a "base Jew," whose actions are "the unhallow'd deeds of Jews" and "a Jewish courtesy" (V, iii, 13, 25, vi, 55, 69, 88, 104). Such a turn of thought within a Machiavellian villainy is congruent, for example, with Abigail's earlier lament that there is "no love on earth, / Pity in Jews, nor piety in Turks" (III, iii, 53-56).[44]

As the drama opened, however, the godless *virtù* of a Machiavel had been subordinated to the romantic appeal in stories about the immense wealth of merchant princes. Thus the villainy explicitly anticipated in the "Prologue" was overpowered initially by Marlowe's poetic fire in representing Barabas' riches:

> So that of thus much that return was made:
> And of the third part of the Persian ships,
> There was the venture summ'd and satisfied.
> As for those Samiotes, and the men of Uz,

That bought my Spanish oils and wines of Greece,
Here have I purs'd their paltry silverlings.
Fie, what a trouble 't is to count this trash!
Well fare the Arabians, who so richly pay
The things they traffic for with wedge of gold,
Whereof a man may easily in a day
Tell that which may maintain him all his life.
. . . .
Give me the merchants of the Indian mines,
That trade in metal of the purest mold;
The wealthy Moor, that in the eastern rocks
Without control can pick his riches up,
And in his house heap pearl like pebble-stones,
Receive them free, and sell them by the weight;
Bags of fiery opals, sapphires, amethysts,
Jacinths, hard topaz, grass-green emeralds,
Beauteous rubies, sparkling diamonds,
And seld-seen costly stones of so great price
As one of them indifferently rated,
And of a carat of this quantity,
May serve in peril of calamity
To ransom great kings from captivity.
This is the ware wherein consists my wealth;
And thus methinks should men of judgement frame
Their means of traffic from the vulgar trade,
And as their wealth increaseth, so enclose
Infinite riches in a little room.

                                        (I, i, 1-37)

Although there are references in the opening scene to the doctrine that godless might and intellectual virtuosity alone succeed, they are expressed, for example, by the satirical comment that hatred or fear suit the powerful because a Christian conduct is either hypocritical or conducive to beggary. Indeed, in a context of glamorous, almost mythical, wealth, the usual violence of the Machiavel is unnecessary, even useless. Thus the variation between Barabas' trade and actually being a king is explained by the fact that quiet times are practical if one would achieve the power that belongs to this Jew and a relatively few merchant-princes (ll. 111-38).[45]

In the incidents that follow, however, conventional features of the Machiavel begin to emerge more clearly. Barabas' shrewd intelligence is emphasized—"he can counsel best" (l. 141). So, too, is his perceptive cleverness. He alone judges the reason for the Jews being summoned to the senate house and makes an appropriate provision for preserving his wealth. It is from this wealth that the Machiavel's conventional attitude of isolation arises, modified only by Barabas' concern for his daughter (I, i, 151-52):

> How'er the world go, I'll make sure for one,
> And seek in time to intercept the worst,
> Warily guarding that which I ha' got.
> *Ego mihimet sum semper proximus.*
> Why, let 'em enter, let 'em take the town.[46]
>
> (ll. 185-89)

Into this antisocial attitude is woven the fact of Barabas' race; and thus in the next scene, Barabas balances some Jews against all Christians and, if necessary, all Jews against righteous Barabas:

> Some Jews are wicked, as all Christians are;
> But say the tribe that I descended of
> Were all in general cast away for sin,
> Shall I be tried by their transgressions?
> The man that dealeth righteously shall live;
> And which of you can charge me otherwise?
>
> (I, ii, 113-18)

Both the "honesty" and the scorn of the villainous plotter as a type are apparent in the preceding speech, which also derides the doctrine of original sin and of salvation through faith alone. The Machiavel's conventional scorn had been apparent also when Marlowe's Jew spoke contemptuously both of silver and of other Jews:

> Fie, what a trouble 't is to count this trash!
>
> (I, i, 7)
>
> These silly men mistake the matter clean.
>
> (I, i, 178)

In the confiscation scene, however, the attitude in these asides is emphasized strongly when it appears as a part of Barabas' "ireful mood" (I, ii, 171, 202-3, 211 ff.).

In other words, the Machiavel's mocking and clever viciousness is so channelled into a representation of Barabas' great wealth and shrewdness that this protagonist emerges as an essentially dangerous force in the play-world only after the confiscation of the Jews' wealth has been dramatized—that is, only after Barabas has been represented as one acted upon. The curse he lays upon the officials of Malta is magnificent in its concentrated rhetoric and venom (I, ii, 163-69); and such an emphasis in Barabas' portrayal increases as the Jew learns of his further losses.

At the same time that he begins to emphasize the dangerousness of his protagonist, Marlowe also achieves another interesting variation in this portrayal of a Machiavel. Although the viciousness of Barabas is clear, it begins to appear in serio-comic contexts. For that matter, even in the scene of the confiscation, when it was a "misery" to behold him, the passion of Barabas was not a pathetic frenzy but an anger caused by the loss of some of his wealth. And that wealth, like the money of the Renaissance usurer under attack, was so strongly personified as to create the impression of its being animate.[47] Barabas was a leader in battle. His riches were not only his arms but also his soldiers, whom he saw slain in a field amidst his enemies (I, ii, 202-10). After this display of an ireful "ecstacy," which was exaggerated both in its concept of wealth and in its statement of hoplessness, there followed a soliloquy that began in dangerous scorn but that ended in Barabas' consolation of himself (ll. 215-25). Abigail then consoled this man resigned to "sufferance" (l. 240)—a man who knew, however, that he had at hand the means for "sufferance." The situation, consequently, verged upon a fearsome parody of the suffering, frantic, but patient protagonist attacked by the vicious antagonist.

It is then that an unexpected turn of events occurs. Barabas, who has fooled his opponents by hiding a valuable kernel of his wealth, is now fooled in turn. Because of the sudden confiscation of his house, he cannot retrieve his hidden treasure (I, ii, 249-69). As a consequence, the plot of Abigail's feigned conversion follows (ll. 346-49, 353-63). It is carried out with anxious asides mixed with vituperation that may well have produced the mechanistic effect that Bergson writes of in his analysis of laughter. The effect exists, moreover, within the counter comic motif of a trick successfully played on nuns and friars. In Barabas' next scene, lines compatible with a fearsome horror are qualified by reminders of the cause of Barabas' lamentation and are exorcised by his exaggerated glee upon receiving his treasure:

> Thus, like the sad presaging raven, that tolls
> The sick man's passport in her hollow beak,
> And in the shadow of the silent night
> Doth shake contagion from her sable wings,
> Vex'd and tormented runs poor Barabas
> With fatal curses towards these Christians.
> The incertain pleasures of swift-footed Time

> Have ta'en their flight, and left me in despair;
> And of my former riches rests no more
> But bare remembrance, like a soldier's scar,
> That has no further comfort for his maim.
>
> (II, i, 1-11)
>
> Now I remember those old women's words,
> Who in my wealth would tell me winter's tales,
> And speak of spirits and ghosts that glide by night
> About the place where treasure hath been hid:
> And now methinks that I am one of those;
> For, whilst I live, here lives my soul's sole hope,
> And when I die, here shall my spirit walk.
>
> (ll. 24-30)
>
> *Abig.* Then, father, here receive thy happiness.
> *Bar.* Has thou't?
> *Abig.*   Here!
>
> *Throws down bags*
>   Has thou't?
> There's more, and more, and more.
>   *Bar.*   O my girl!
> My gold, my fortune, my felicity!
> Strength to my soul, death to mine enemy!
> Welcome, the first beginner of my bliss!
> O Abigail, Abigail, that I had thee here too!
> Then my desires were fully satisfied:
> But I will practise thy enlargement thence.
> O girl! O gold! O beauty! O my bliss!
>
> *Hugs his bags.*
> (II, i, 44-53)

This juxtaposition of the darkness of horror and anxiety with an exaggerated joy probably would create once more a serio-comic effect. Especially pertinent are Barabas' hugging of his bags and his lines that evoke the brightness of day with another personification of wealth that produces a figure of speech likening Barabas to a singing mother lark:

> Now Phœbus ope the eyelids of the day,
> And for the raven wake the morning lark,
> That I may hover with her in the air;
> Singing o'er these, as she does o'er her young
> *Heromoso placer de los dineros!*
>
> (ll. 59-63)

In a similar manner, when the motif of revenge is emphasized upon Barabas' next appearance, it is developed with *double-entendres* (e.g., II, iii, 59, 62, 65). There, too, occur asides that range from the comic mock—Lodowick looks "Like a hog's-cheek new singed" (ll. 43-44)—to treacherous villainy:

> As for the diamond, sir, I told you of,
> Come home and there's no price shall make us part,
> Even for your honourable father's sake.—
> It shall go hard but I will see your death—*Aside*.
> But now I must be gone to buy a slave.
>
> (ll. 93-97)

This combination of disparate elements from Act I, scene ii, to Act II, scene iii, certainly seems intended to produce a grotesque effect. In such a vein, the remainder of the act is played out. In the first dialogue between Barabas and Ithamore, for example, there appears the first explicit reference to Barabas' nose, as well as an exaggerated account of horrors and Ithamore's vicious glee (II, iii, 179, 180-213, 214-18). The remainder of the drama, consequently, seems to be an extension of this grotesque artistry. The normal melodrama of the revenge motif is heightened by ingenious villainies and is developed, i.a., by a courtesan (Bellamira), a bully (Philia-Borza), a lecherous, drinking servant (Ithamore), and even a French musician playing the lute for revelers (Barabas).

Although the development of *The Jew of Malta* also seems to reflect a division into protasis (I, II), epitasis (III, IV), and catastrophe (V),[48] the original artistry of the drama is not illumined as effectively by such an analysis as it is by considering the way in which a figure introduced by Machiavelli is portrayed. Marlowe uses structural patterns connected with both passive protagonist and vicious antagonist. Barabas is so portrayed that at first he appears in a relatively sympathetic light; then the introduction of a revenge motif leads to concatenated plots. The romantic appeal of great wealth thereby turns into a theatrical appeal based upon ingenious villainies. Both emphases might accord with tales of an opulent Mediterranean and Near East, where Machiavellian deeds might be performed. Marlowe's imagination certainly seems to have been fired by the first of these concepts; and from the second, serio-comic scenes develop as the drama unfolds the horrible grotesqueness of a "policy" like that of the Borgias (e.g., III, iv, 95). Both in method and in concept, Marlowe builds upon what probably had at least an element of familiarity for regular theater-goers. Their attention and imagination probably were captured most effectively. In *The Jew of Malta,* however, as in *The Spanish Tragedy,* the author seems to utilize concepts primarily for their theatrical appeal. They are not resolved, for example, into conflicting attitudes or ideas that are represented as valid for a character contemplating action.

A vicious *virtù* in a simpler vein than that shown in *The Jew of Malta* might be given an historical figure involved in the intrigues and the policy of a Western court. In *The Massacre at Paris* (1591-93), Marlowe again worked with attributes conventionally associated with the Machiavel. This time, however, he dramatized French history, probably in accordance with English propaganda and pamphleteering that resulted from the horror of St. Bartholomew's Day;[49] and his portrayal of a major villain thereby becomes involved with the portrayal of regal characters. Since the drama survives only in a degenerate text, or at least in a questionable one, the value of any analysis of its artistry may seem doubtful. Yet Marlowe's representation of his characters shows a kinship with concepts and methods developed more fully elsewhere.

Especially in the portrayal of Guise do attributes of the vicious plotter appear. As an ambitious performer of horrors and stratagems perpetrated in the name of religion, the Catholic Guise is represented as having acquired power that exceeds, or at least rivals, that of the French ruler. Anjou-Henry and Epernon liken him to a dictator, surrounded by pomp, subservient senators, and subservient citizens; and Guise's own references to the conquering "ancient Romans" and to Caesar aid in filling out the portrayal of the villainous sun-king this duke wishes to become.[50] He is surrounded, however, by a group of regal figures: a comparably vicious woman (Catherine de' Medici); a weak king (Charles IX); a rising "hero" (Henry of Navarre); and a minor villain who at first becomes a weak king, who shows signs of the tyrant, and who is murdered to avenge one whom he has had murdered (Anjou-Henry III). As a result, the portrayal of Anjou-Henry, rather than that of Guise, is more to the point as a further supplement of the general remarks in the introductory section of this chapter.[51]

At first, even though he is subordinate to Guise, Henry is a thoroughly vicious figure in the scenes that dramatize the massacre proper. Indeed, his treacherous guile and his hypocrisy remain constant. But the purpose of his villainy changes. The Machiavel's villainous isolation, for example, takes the form of Henry's discharging his council:

> Make a discharge of all my council straight,
> And I'll subscribe my name, and seal it straight.

My head shall be my council; they are false;
And, Epernon, I will be rul'd by thee.

(xvi, 78-81)

In that it constitutes a seizure of absolute power, this action might be regally evil. "My head shall be my council" might also signal a Machiavellian wittiness—as it does, in part—or a tyrannical arrogance concerned only with its own good and relying upon a favorite. But Henry's command is strongly qualified at this point in the drama by the surrounding picture of a court of Catholic viciousness. Thus Henry's discharge of his council moves the king, as an opponent of Guise, toward his final anti-Catholic position and toward his last lines about being a "faithfull freend" of Elizabeth of England. Similarly, the scoffs of Henry appear later in the play as his mockery of Guise, cuckolded by a royal minion.

Accordingly, when Guise receives his due reward and is murdered as the result of a plot by this ruler who had been a subordinate villain, the portrayal of Henry shows a juxtaposition of what otherwise might be antithetical attributes. With lines that might be given to a Cambises,[52] Henry calls Guise's son to view his dead father:

Ah, this sweet sight is physic to my soul!
Go fetch his son for to behold his death. . . .

And that youth vigorously censures such a ruler:

Art thou king, and hast done this bloody deed?
I'll be reveng'd. . . .

(xviii, 92-93, 122-23)

In this respect, Henry's subsequent death is retributive; yet before the son's appearance, the Elizabethans' hatred of Spain and their love for England and Elizabeth had been used to justify the murder:

I ne'er was king of France until this hour.
This is the traitor that hath spent my gold
In making foreign wars and civil broils.
Did he not draw a sort of English priests
From Douay to the seminary at Rheims,
To hatch forth treason 'gainst their natural queen?
Did he not cause the king of Spain's huge fleet
To threaten England, and to menace me?

(ll. 99-106)

Thus with continuity—but by such ways as the Babington conspiracy of 1586 and the Armada of 1588—the minor Machiavel is given theatrical signs of the tyrant but moved toward a final, relatively sympathetic position, before he, too, is murdered with a poisoned knife as he allies himself with the Protestant Navarre.[53]

When Henry was represented as ascending the throne, in fact, he had been marked with the additional stigma of "minions"—a vice that had been given also to Charles IX. To both the Middle Ages and the Renaissance, wanton favorites undermined a king's estate and might lead him to ruin;[54] and the structural movement connected with this situation could be akin to one that showed a central figure's fall in his magnificence.[55] Charles had been overridden by a "pleasure uncontroll'd" that had weakened his body and would "waste his realm." As a result, he was overridden also by a powerful relative's vicious ambition. Guise daily won Charles with words, executed villainy, and left the blame to the ruler, whose sorrow and repentance for the massacre make his death welcome to Catherine and the Duke. These vicious Catholics, consequently, are pleased with the way in which Henry's mind also "runs on his minions, / And all his heaven is to delight himself" (xi, 44-47). While Henry "sleeps securely thus in ease," Catherine, the Cardinal of Lorraine, and Guise hope to "plant" themselves "with such authority" that none may live without their permission (xi, 48-51).

In brief, the representation of Charles and of Henry indicates the continuing validity in the theater of such naïve descriptions of kingship and tyranny as that found in John of Salisbury's medieval treatise. For in spite of the fourth act of a later *Macbeth* (IV, iii, 44-100), one does not always find a clear dividing line between that which is private and not tyrannical and that which is public and tyrannical. John of Salisbury's definition of a tyrant, for example, which has been given in the introductory section, illustrates a basic concept that might provide a variety of theatrical emphases for establishing a relationship between a ruler's wantonness and a ruler's malfeasance or tyranny.[56] Off the stage, the necessity for a ruler to follow good advice, and thereby avoid wantonness, flatterers, minions, and favorites, had been expresed as early as the days of Plutarch and as late as the week of Elizabeth's coronation. It was repeated in writings by such diverse individuals as Sir Philip Sidney, the Jesuit Robert Parsons, the Puritan exile Dudley Fenner, and the divine-rightist James IV of Scotland. This idea also had been merged with treatments of the four cardinal virtues made applicable to rule and with precepts for restraining ambitious persons who had achieved power.[57] Upon the stage, a similar process of thought appears. This is especially true for the way in which tyranny might be linked with the counsel of lowly-born favorites. In the imitative *Edmond Ironside,* for example, there appears a Canutus who is as easily angered as Cambises and who shows the susceptibility to flattery that also had been embodied in the theatrical vein of an earlier Herod.[58] This ruler is influenced constantly by the ambitious, treacherous, and lowly-born Edricus, who can "play an Ambodexters parte" (e.g., ll. 742-96, 1040-1111, 330-31), and whose counsel easily leads to an application of the measure of the sword (e.g., ll. 566-732). The dramatization in *Edmond Ironside* of the origins of Edricus and his choice of a follower also repeats matter in *A Looking Glass for London and England* (1587-91), *James IV* (1590-91), and *Woodstock* (1591-93). In those plays, by the representation of Radagon's origins, the relationship between Ateukin and his servants, and the relationship between Tresilian and Nimble, a progressively comic variation is effected on a lower social scale than that of Henry's favorites in Marlowe's drama.[59] But in those plays also, the ruler was tyrannical when he was associated directly or indirectly with favored upstarts who fed his wantonness or his lack of emotional control.

As a consequence, although the brevity of the *Massacre* does not allow one to be sure about the total portrayal of the minions of Charles and of Henry,[60] there can be little doubt that Marlowe was working with what was conventional when he established a relationship between a ruler's wantonness and favoritism and a ruler's malfeasance. The picture of Edward IV in the opening portion of the play by that name also testifies to this fact. Heywood's drama, indeed, may be a reworking of lost plays popular during the late 1580's and early 1590's.[61] Completely unhypothetical, however, is the first structural movement in the anonymous *Edward III*, and therein the possibility that wantonness alone may become malfeasance and tyranny is dramatized.

In this last play, entered in the Stationers' Register on December 1, 1595, the two initial acts introduce the repetitive pattern connected with a hero. In them, although it obviously arises in his private world, Edward's sudden love for the Countess of Salisbury moves toward a culpable neglect of public duties. He has not heard of the good news from the Continent, for he is "in his closet, malcontent" (II, ii, 15). He receives Derby distractedly and dismisses the troops that nobleman had levied. Only the appearance of the Black Prince reminds the king that he has violated a precept basic to treatises *de regimine principum*:

> Shall the large limmit of faire Brittayné
> By me be ouerthrowne, and shall I not
> Master this little mansion of my selfe?
>
> . . . .
>
> I go to conquer kings; and shall I not then
> Subdue my selfe?
>
> (II, ii, 95-100)

In all probability, with a preceding line, "Away, loose silkes of wauering vanitie!" the actor of Edward's role threw off a sign of his wantonness.[62]

Edward's failure to be constant in his resolve, however, leads immediately to a forceful swing in the opposite direction when he hears that the countess approaches (ll. 103-17). There then follows a tentative movement toward an act characteristic of a tyrannical Cambises:

> No more; thy husband and the Queene shall dye.
> Fairer thou art by farre then Hero was,
> Beardles Leander not so strong as I:
> He swome an easie curraunt for his loue,
> But I will through a Hellespont of bloud,
> To arryue at Cestus where my Hero lyes.
>
> (ll. 152-57)

In a manner comparable to Edward's resolution to master the "little mansion" of himself, his contrary emotion also had been justified by a moral tag, unconvincingly expressed, however, and thoroughly un-fitting for any concept of regal "honor":

> The sin is more to hacke and hew poore men,
> Then to embrace in a vnlawfull bed
> The register of all rarieties
> Since Letherne Adam till this youngest howre.
>
> (ll. 114-17)

This representation of Edward's love as an affection that leads to a villainous recourse to the sword and a neglect of the commonwealth and its heroic affairs agrees with the melodramatic ending of the episode, which was drawn in part from Bandello's Novel XLVI (tr., Painter, *Palace of Pleasure*). The countess' noble virtue stops any further neglect of public honor and duty, any vicious anger, "humourousness," or bloody stage tyranny; but the possibility of this last development was certainly obvious.[63]

One should also remember that the derivation of this story about a ruler's "doting," and its potential tyranny, was not specified until the source studies of modern critics appeared. Certainly at least some in an Elizabethan audience would have accepted it as history. If one inclined to literature had remembered the *Palace of Pleasure* while the drama was being performed, there is just as great a possibility that a similarly inclined member of the audience would recognize that one source of the drama was Holinshed's *Chronicle of Scotland*.[64] If associated with any-thing else, however, Edward's passion in the immediate circumstances of the theater probably would be viewed in the light of other dramatic representations of the way in which the wantonness of a ruler might affect adversely the entire realm; for a court was the center of a kingdom.[65]

Indeed, by the time that *Edward III* was entered in the Stationers' Register and probably before it was performed, the vicious consequences of a regal lasciviousness as it affected a commonwealth had been portrayed by Greene, who also capitalized upon any audience's susceptibility to romance in their annals. Although the course of the action in *James IV* (1591-92) had a redemptive ending, the passion of Greene's king actually became a regal malfeasance. Greene's unconscientiousness in making history out of one of Giraldi Cinthio's *novelle* cannot be denied,[66] but certainly the performance of *James IV* might emphasize any impression that a ruler's private vice might easily become a public one.

In *James IV,* three major developments fill out a morality-pattern. In Acts I and II, a vice-like figure named Ateukin overhears the wanton love of James for Ida, and since Ateukin encourages this wantonness, he is favored by the ruler. Virtue thereupon departs from James's conduct and from his court as well. In the next two acts, vice reigns. Virtuous counselors have left the court, and from it the queen flees. She is attacked, the king welcomes the supposed murderer, and death is decreed for all murmurers. At this time, a minor villain appears. He plans to intrigue against the dominant vice-like figure and thereby anticipates the ensuing struggle with England. By the beginning of the last act, a nadir in the affairs of Scotland has been reached. The nobility have left James, the commons are afraid, the land is being despoiled by an invader. The murderer flees, however, as the principal vice despairs (ll. 2074-93);[67] and with the aid of the good counselors, the queen stops the great battle between Scotland and England. James repents and makes amends for the injuries he has committed (ll. 2366-402, 2544-61). Structurally, therefore, the drama fills out the framework of moralities in which virtues and vices struggled for the control of a central figure, and virtue's losing conflict at the beginning of the play was righted by a final conflict or situation. By such a development, for example, Magnyfycence had been displayed. Vices intruded into his court during prosperity; he became enmeshed in sin and despaired in adversity; but ultimately he returned to virtue. The appearances of the "stoical," or misanthropic, Bohan, who with Oberon introduces the drama, stress this triple movement in Greene's play.

Although Greene first represents his principal vice as an astrologer (ll. 314-17), Ateukin is given attributes conventional to both the Machiavel and the flatterer who gives vicious counsel.[68] "Matchauell" is an author Ateukin has annotated (l. 1303); and when his counsel is based on precept, it is one of absolutism and force:

> Tut, pacifie your grace,
> You haue the sword and scepter in your hand,
> You are the King, the state depends on you:
> Your will is law. . . .
>
> (ll. 375-78)

As he elaborates this counsel with Machiavellian shrewdness, Ateukin wrests out of their context words by Aristotle and uses the conventional analogy between body and state to justify a "pollicie" of murder (ll. 1858-72). Finally, he briefly sums up his vicious stratagems for an audience (ll. 934-35, 2082 ff.).

After his initial eavesdropping, however, Ateukin rises by the vice of flattery. Just as he gives most vicious counsel when he insists upon its virtue, so he flatters most when he says he is no flatterer (ll. 1136-39, 349-55, 399-405). Throughout the play, there are running comments on the public danger of sycophancy (e.g., 1274-75); and the viciousness of the situation at James's court is underlined by a variety of incidents ranging from robbery and the sale of court-favor to the representation of Ateukin's servant as being more powerful than the king's purveyor—as hated as purveyors were during these years (ll. 1246-94).[69] The "scourge that waits on bad aduice" is the fear of Andrew, the minor Machiavel, who sees flatterers and murderers "grow big" (ll. 1904-21). Ateukin himself calls attention to the shameful evils of flattery when he briefly recounts the major sequence of his plots (ll. 2078-93).

Before the resolution of the drama, signs of the stage tyrant also appear. Witness the titles that Ateukin and Andrew give James and that had adhered to angry tyrants and the tyranically inclined since at least the days of Herod:

> Good Lord how rage gainsayeth reasons power,
> My deare, my gracious, and beloued Prince,
> The essence of my sute, my God on earth,
> Sit downe and rest your selfe. . . .
>
> (ll. 1110-13)

Another obvious sign of tyranny is this ruler's anger on being given good advice and his banishment of a virtuous counselor on pain of death. With its pageantic entrance and its subsequent stage directions, this scene obviously was contrived from its beginning to impress an audience with the public evils that result from wantonness and favoritism:

> *Enter the Bishop of S. Andrewes, Earle Douglas,*
> *Morton, with others, one way, the Queene with*
> *Dwarfes an other way.*
>   *B. S. Andre.* Oh wrack of Common-weal! Oh
> wretched state!
>   *Doug.* Oh haplesse flocke whereas the guide is
> blinde!
> *They all are in a muse.*
>   *Mort.* Oh heedlesse youth, where counsaile is
> dispis'd.
>
> (ll. 936-42)

The bishop especially laments the woeful state of James's commonwealth and fears the overthrow of this ruler, whose unkingly attributes are specified (ll. 955-1018).

Although a fall from power and a retributive death might have awaited James, Greene's romantic emphasis upon Queen Dorothea, who constantly expresses her affection for her husband, involves censure of the vicious counselor rather than of the ruler. Such an emphasis adumbrates James's mild punishment and his admission of guilt, wherein the viciousness of the flatterer is emphasized once more (ll. 2501-66). But aside from the fact that the king must atone for his misdeeds to his queen and his father-in-law, James must "Embrace and reconcile" his nobles. They are his "hands," whereby he "ought to worke"; and they for a long time have been banished from the court. The king, consequently, admits to his lords and princes that he has wronged both them and theirs (ll. 2544-61).

Greene's representation of the virtue of Dorothea needs no comment, nor does his emphasis upon the melodramatic aspects of her story, whereby he brings in some relatively sophisticated motifs of Renaissance romance. By constantly relating the queen to virtue in the commonwealth, however, Greene preserves her position in a dramatic movement that affects public as well as private affairs. Concomitant with her flight in disguise is Greene's picture of a "trim world" of flattery, lust, murder, and a death penalty for all who complain about the major vice and the minor Machiavel (ll. 1888-92).

With the other material noted here, Greene's protagonist and the development of his story would become part of a background that might be familiar to authors, actors, and regular theater-goers. *The Tragedy of Thomas of Woodstock* (1591-95), for example, shows that its very competent author was aware of the preceding concepts that might be related to tyranny. Not only may this author have known plays by Marlowe and Shakespeare but he also utilized the morality pattern that Greene filled out.[70] At one point in his drama he, too, represented a rule that would crush murmurers. In addition, he displayed a new-fangledness that accompanied courtly vice and sycophancy, and he thereby reflected not only some current theatrical situations but also a conventional satiric attitude that scoffed at new fashions and treated the upstart with contempt.

Probably before *Woodstock* was written, however, Marlowe also had utilized comparable concepts and representational methods, and not only to dramatize French history. His *Edward II* develops from a ruler's fondness for a flattering minion. In it, signs of a tyrant appear, and there is a conflict between noble counselors and vice. A queen is once more wronged, and a rising Machiavel is again portrayed. This drama progresses, however, to the fall from power and the death of the protagonist; and at that time, Marlowe turns to the poetic lament that for decades had been considered appropriate to tragedy and that had been associated with the fall of princes. As a result, the final development in *Edward II* displays a ruler who has become a sympathetic figure. The basic structural movement, expressed crudely but simply, is that of errors or viciousness before the fall from power, pity after it.

The general sweep of *Edward II* is surprisingly simple in its unadorned outline, when, for example, its major narrative developments are considered in the light of the usual act-division of editors. Strife between king and nobles because of the recall of a base-born minion and an apparent resolution of the strife (Act I) are followed by a representation of the falsity of that solution and a dramatization of the nobles' success (Act II). Edward's success in pitched battle is the next obvious development (Act III); then follows the nobles' success in pitched battle (Act IV). The tragic catastrophe is then developed and the play ends with the establishment of kingly rule by Edward's son. Yet any such indication of the process of the play—a development that once more is not discordant with concepts about the "parts" of a drama—is unrealistic in that it grossly fails to do justice to Marlowe's artistry.

Even in a survey of the obvious, for example, the younger Spencer and the figures connected with him demand notice. They appear at the beginning of the second act (II, i); and immediately after Gaveston has been lead to his death by Warwick (III, i), they counsel Edward to use the greatest severity. In young Spencer is represented the nobles' motive for continuing the struggle with a king who favors "smooth dissembling flatterers" and a parasite who is a "putrefying branch, / That deads the royal vine" (III, ii, 163-64, 170). Having incited the despairing king to vengeance (ll. 124-28), the Spencers are with him when he defeats the nobles—when his "bloody colours" suggest "Remembrance of revenge immortally" upon the nobles' "accursed traitorous progeny" (III, ii, 140-42, iii). They continue at Edward's side until they disappear at the end of the fourth act (IV, v, 82, vi, 112). The Spencer matter thereby spans, or overlaps, the second, third, and fourth of the preceding developments, just as the Gaveston matter, because of the queen's success with Mortimer, had spanned the first and the second.

A later development between the queen and Mortimer then overlaps the fourth and the fifth acts. Just after the nobles have been successful a second time, an illicit love between Isabella and Mortimer is mentioned. Although it has been anticipated skillfully—by, for example, the queen's innocent relationship with Mortimer that leads to Act II—only after Edward has been defeated a second time (Act IV) does the audience have called to its attention that now

> . . . Mortimer
> And Isabel do kiss, while they conspire;
> And yet she bears a face of love forsooth.
> Fie on that love that hatcheth death and hate!
>
> (IV, v, 21-23)

With emphasis upon Isabella's hypocrisy and upon Mortimer's ambition and his Machiavellian cleverness, this relationship carries over to the catastrophe. It motivates the murder of Edward and thereby causes its own destruction. In brief, an innocent relationship spanning Acts I and II has developed into a vicious relationship that spans Acts IV and V; while the Spenser matter overlaps Acts II, III, and IV.

A similar structural feature of the drama is connected with young Edward. He first appears after Gaveston has been led to execution and immediately before the news of the minion's death will be given to Edward. In such a manner, a later emphasis is anticipated; for the representation of Edward's affection for Gaveston through Acts I and II will be balanced by the progressive concern of king and prince for one another in Acts IV and V (IV, ii, 43, v, 70; V, ii, 93, 96; IV, iii, 52-53; V, i, 40-42, 115-17). Thereby Edward's love for another figure, that is, his placing Gaveston above kingly regiment (e.g., II, ii, 220-23), is repeated but sympathetically intensified when Edward resigns the crown to preserve his son's right (V, i, 91-93, 115-17, 121-23). From a point of view focused upon Edward, a vicious relationship that spans Acts I and II has become a virtuous one that spans Acts IV and V. That this last development occurs as the relationship between Mortimer and

Isabella is darkened is one of the clear indications that Marlowe intended to create pathos for Edward in the latter part of the drama.

This linking of major bodies of material shows a remarkable precision. It also shows an effective use of repetition, and this is true of other features of the drama. Witness the two scenes between Edward and Gaveston (I, i, 140 ff., iv, 106-69), the latter of which is developed with greater intensity; or the two scenes between those characters and the nobles (I, iii, 8-105; II, ii, 50-111), with the action of the last, the wounding of Gaveston, being much more serious than that of the former.[71] A different sort of repetition and variation appears also in the rising figures of Gaveston, the younger Spencer, and Mortimer. The play-world moves thereby from a flattering minion, to a political flatterer who argues that an oath-breaking severity is a necessary "haut resolve," to an ambitious Machiavel.

When one considers the portrayal of individual characters only, another sort of intensification, as well as a similar precision, appears. Since Mortimer is Edward's constant opponent, Marlowe represents an increasing viciousness not simply in his triple portrayal of rising figures but in one figure alone. This development is balanced by an opposite movement in the portrayal of Edward; and between Mortimer and Edward, Marlowe places the figure of Edmund, Earl of Kent. His remonstrance of Edward in Act I precedes his change of allegiance in Act II, when Kent turns to the nobles. His censure of Mortimer and Isabella in Act IV precedes his change of allegiance in Act V, when Kent turns back to Edward. In both instances, those from whom this nobleman turns are the cause of evils in the commonwealth. As a result, Edmund is an effective choric character, whose speeches and actions both affect and accord with the succession of contexts and the over-all pattern that emerges when the play is viewed in the light of its emotional focal points.

Rather than any of the spanning or balancing relationships, it is this emotional development of the play and its connection with public vice that must have stood out within the confines of a theater. Indeed, it is revealing to note that in order to produce his first emotional focal point in the portrayal of his protagonist, Marlowe builds upon a familiar structural movement that showed two forces struggling for control of a central figure, with the force that loses the first struggle winning the second one. As will be indicated, this pattern, characteristic of moralities, clearly underlies the development of the initial act. Marlowe's intensified repetition of the first portion of that pattern in the second act (II, ii) then involves his emphasis upon the public ills that result from a ruler's wanton favoritism. At that time also, the good advice of the loyal Kent leads only to his being banished. Since this situation in the second act represents an England on the verge of ruin and a court bereft of good counsel because of a ruler's favoritism and angry absolutism, Marlowe's technique is strikingly sure. He builds upon a pattern that conventionally showed a descent into vice, and he repeats its initial development, which conventionally led to vice's rule, as he emphasizes the public evils that have resulted from Edward's preoccupation with his minion. With such an emphasis, of course, one would expect the normal reaction to Edward to be an unsympathetic one. The matter, at any rate, demands further attention.

Obviously, the second act in *Edward II* builds upon emphases established in the first. As the drama begins, two brief developments dramatize a situation that all in an audience might have considered alarming for a commonwealth. The first of these centers on Gaveston only. Its opening soliloquy identifies him as a regal favorite and a wanton, with the last characteristic dominant; and the conventional scorn of a viciously rising figure is a note that Marlowe also strikes—first briefly and then twice with relative fullness (I, i, 12, 18-23, 39-42). Immediately thereafter Gaveston becomes an eavesdropper upon the second development. He speaks of his hatred of those nobles who are opposing his return in accordance with their promise to Edward's father, and he speaks approvingly of Edward's insistence upon having his way (l. 98). The last comment reflects the conventional association between headstrong absolutism and sycophancy;[72] and that last attribute is soon emphasized:

> My lord, these titles far exceed my worth.
>
> (l. 157)

> It shall suffice me to enjoy your love,
> Which whiles I have, I think myself as great
> As Cæsar riding in the Roman street,
> With captive kings at his triumphant car.
>
> (ll. 171-74)

This develops after an audience has heard of Gaveston's plans to "draw the pliant king which way" this wanton favorite pleases (l. 53). Clearly Gaveston would be one of those individuals who encourage a ruler in his vices[73] and who may even destroy his regality.[74]

In the second development, moreover, Edward's insistence upon his absolutism involves the threat of a quick recourse to the sword. This is true of his reaction to the Mortimers' words (ll. 91-92) and of his reaction to Lancaster's frown:

> Frown'st thou thereat, aspiring Lancaster?
> The sword shall plane the furrows of thy brows,
> And hew these knees that now are grown so stiff.
> I will have Gaveston; and you shall know
> What danger 't is to stand against your king.
>
> (ll. 93-97)

When Warwick joins the dispute, he is threatened with death (ll. 119-20). When the angry nobles leave, Edward moves to an immediate open war in fulfillment of his angry promises, with a fourth insistence upon the absoluteness of his office (ll. 79, 92, 97, 135).

Quite congruently, then, Edward's joy on embracing Gaveston is represented by the exaggerated statement that the ruler subordinates his realm to this particular manifestation of his own affections and appetites:

> Now let the treacherous Mortimers conspire,
> And that high-minded Earl of Lancaster:
> I have my wish, in that I joy thy [Gaveston's] sight;
> And sooner shall the sea o'erwhelm my land
> Than bear the ship that shall transport thee hence.
>
> (ll. 149-53)

The ruler immediately bestows powerful offices on his minion:

> Lord High Chamberlain,
> Chief Secretary to the state and me,
> Earl of Cornwall, King and Lord of Man.
>
> (ll. 154-56)

In spite of Kent's objection, further powers are granted to this favorite: a private guard, access to the royal treasury, and the regal power to "Save or condemn" (ll. 164-70). With this last power especially, a manifestation of the relationship between private and public vice probably would be obvious. Inescapable, however, would be the impression that a reprehensible figure has won his coveted position and become extremely powerful in spite of the opposition of the nobles.

In the next conflict (I, iv), the nobles are joined with the church and are successful. Gaveston is seized, and Edward is forced to sign the order for his banishment. By the end of the act, however, through the intercession of a wronged queen, the figures of a public world (king-minions-nobles) and of a private world (king-minion-queen) are reconciled with each other and within those relationships. As the elder Mortimer phrases it,

The mightiest kings have had their minions:
Great Alexander loved Hephestion;
The conquering Hercules for Hylas wept;
And for Patroclus stern Achilles droop'd.
And not kings only but the wisest men:
The Roman Tully lov'd Octavius;
Grave Socrates, wild Alcibiades.
Then let his grace, whose youth is flexible,
And promiseth as much as we can wish,
Freely enjoy that vain, light-headed earl;
For riper years will wean him from such toys.

(I, iv, 391-401)

It seems fairly obvious, then, that Marlowe's first act proceeds in a manner that might well have been familiar to an audience of the early 1590's. The action develops around a central figure who in the initial conflict embraced a vicious one. By the removal of the latter figure through vigorous opposition by both church and state, the consequence of the successful intrusion of vice was stopped. The central figure apparently repents, and he and those who should support him are reconciled by the persuasive force of a queen and by the acceptance of a youthful vice if it remain private. Except for this last development, Greene utilized such a pattern for an entire play; so did the author of *Woodstock* and so had writers of late as well as early moralities, some of which apparently were being performed still.[75]

As has been noted, Marlowe then repeats a portion of this pattern in Act II. He intensifies the situation, however, as he already had intensified smaller ones. An audience would learn that Edward has not perceived the error of his ways; and they would hear, at some length, of the grievous ills in the commonwealth that have resulted from the relationship between Edward and Gaveston. The treasury is dry from the wantonness of their displays and from the "prodigal gifts" given to the minion. The commons are mumuring and "overstretched." English garrisons have been beaten out of France. The "lame and poor lie groaning at the gates." The Irish have invaded successfully "the English pale." The Scotch have driven south to York. The Danes control the Channel. Foreign princes scorn the king. The court

. . . is naked, being bereft of those
That make a king seem glorious to the world;
I mean the peers, whom thou should'st dearly love.

(II, ii, 174-76)

Libels against the king are thrown in the streets. Ballads and rimes predict his fall. The English of the North curse the names of Edward and Gaveston as they see "their houses burnt, / Their wives and children slain. . . ." (ll. 179-80). In brief, Edward II's kingdom is in much worse straits than Edward III's or than James IV's. His England is that of an Elizabethan's nightmare.[76] But Edward's soldiers are decked in pomp and kept idle (ll. 182-87).

Refusing the "broad seal," by which he could "gather" throughout the realm, Montimer vows to sell his birthright to ransom his uncle, the English warrior who has fought in the North. Lancaster promises to seize possessions with the sword when that is gone (ll. 147-53, 196-99). Thereby civil strife will provide the horrible, though logical, climax to the preceding picture of a wasted realm.

As the king determines to "be cruel and grow tyrannous" because of the noblemen's angry criticism and promise (1. 206), Kent speaks. In the first act he had admonished Edward, though he remained at his side; and previously in the present scene, he had admonished Mortimer when that baron angrily argued that his uncle who had been captured in Edward's wars should be ransomed by the king (ll. 145-46). The picture of ruined England followed, however; and the breach between king and nobles became even greater than before. As a result, Kent now advances the only solution to the approaching nadir in England's affairs.

> My lord, I see your love to Gaveston
> Will be the ruin of the realm and you,
> For now the wrathful nobles threaten wars,
> And therefore, brother, banish him for ever.
>
> (ll. 208-11)

Persisting in his advice, Kent receives an angry, tyrannical sentence of banishment:

> *K. Edw.* Art thou an enemy to my Gaveston?
> *Kent.* Ay, and it grieves me that I favour'd him.
> *K. Edw.* Traitor, begone! whine thou with Mortimer.
> *Kent.* So will I, rather than with Gaveston.
> *K. Edw.* Out of my sight, and trouble me no more!
> *Kent.* No marvel though thou scorn thy noble peers,
> When I thy brother am rejected thus.
>
> *Exit.*
>
> *K. Edw.* Away!
>
> (ll. 212-19)

Though the queen remains, the power and counsel of principal leaders have left the court; and Marlowe has effected a portrayal of his ruler that redounds in favor of the nobles and their concern for the ills of the realm. Indeed, the king's lines that immediately follow Kent's exit repeat what has been indicated before: namely, Edward's willing subordination of kingly rule to his love for Gaveston:

> Do what they can, we'll live in Tynemouth here;
> And, so I walk with him about the walls,
> What care I though the earls begirt us round?
>
> (ll. 221-23)

From such a development, there will be no repetition of a peaceful solution. Instead, the motif of Edward's revenge will appear and be carried through Act III especially. By the previous development, however, Marlowe has created a picture of a culpable ruler ripe for chastisement.[77]

As he has been moving toward this emotional focal point, Marlowe also has been laying a groundwork for a countermovement; and this second aspect of his technique deserves attention. In spite of the unfavorable emphases in the portrayal of Edward II, he is a ruler. By developing this fact, as part of a skillful qualifying artistry, Marlowe keeps alive the concept of revolt first mentioned by the younger Mortimer himself:

> For howsoever we have borne it out,
> 'Tis treason to be up against the king.
>
> (I, iv, 280-81)

As Kent had reminded the peers and the audience, a ruler should be inviolate (e.g., II, ii, 146). The point is made again when Edmund joins the nobles. At that time, the scene ends with Lancaster's lines:

> None be so hardy as to touch the king;
> But neither spare you Gaveston nor his friends.
>
> (II, iii, 27-28)

Furthermore, even as the second act begins, Marlowe alternates emphases against Edward with this emphasis upon his rulership.[78] In other words, Marlowe begins to establish an emphasis that will bear directly upon the ultimate development of sympathy for his protagonist even as he moves toward a most unfavorable representation of his central figure.[79]

Subsequently, after the nobles have been successful in capturing Gavestion, Marlowe introduces the elder Spencer, who shows a forceful loyalty to Edward.[80] At this time, Marlowe also turns his ruler's headstrong anger toward the field of battle, where it will appear as the vigorous attribute of a warrior king. This shifting of emphasis, which qualifies the earlier emotional focal point in the play, appears especially in the latter part of the second act, in all of the third act, and in the early portion of the fourth act.

Any simple separation of dramatic components, that is, any specifying of (1) the fact of Edward's rulership, (2) the effect of the elder Spencer's appearance, (3) the turning of Edward's anger to the field of battle, is as unrealistic as must be expected when effective artistry is being discussed. The effect of all this can be demonstrated, however, by the other point that has just been made, namely, that Marlowe alternates emphases that can be called pro-Edward with those that can be called anti-Edward. For example, in Act III, scenes ii and iii, the counsel of self-seeking parasites—a theme conducive to a lack of sympathy for Edward—proceeds upon the note that the ruler has been too merciful and has been treated like "a schoolboy still" (III, ii, 1-31). This leads to Edward's vow of vengeance. But the immediate context of that vow is Gaveston's death, which has resulted from Warwick's vow-breaking (III, i, ii, 116-43)—a context that would give a degree of substance to the king's reaction and hence to such lines as "Unnatural wars, where subjects brave their kings . . ." (1. 87). Marlowe then returns immediately to his unfavorable emphasis in the portrayal of Edward. Young Spencer is adopted and "merely" because of the king's love given the earldom of Gloucester and the office of Lord Chamberlain (ll. 145-48). Accordingly, the next long speech, that of the herald, expresses the loyalty of the barons and appeals to the age's dislike of flattering upstarts. It also appeals to the Elizabethans' belief that a ruler should heed good advice, foster virtue, and listen to a wisdom that, like Kent's, would spare the shedding of English blood by Englishmen:[81]

> The barons, up in arms, by me salute
> Your highnes with long life and happiness;
> And bid me say, as plainer to your grace,
> That if without effusion of blood
> You will this grief have ease and remedy,
> That from your princely person you remove
> This Spencer, as a putrefying branch,
> That deads the royal vine, whose golden leaves
> Empale your princely head, your diadem,
> Whose brightness such pernicious upstarts dim,
> Say they; and lovingly advise your grace,
> To cherish virtue and nobility,
> And have old servitors in high esteem,

And shake off smooth dissembling flatterers.
This granted, they, their honors, and their lives,
Are to your highness vow'd and consecrate.

(III, ii, 157-72)

At the conclusion of the scene, however, Edward's lines appeal to English loyalty:

My lords, perceive you how these rebels swell?
Soldiers, good hearts, defend your sovereign's right,
For now, even now, we march to make them stoop.
Away!

(ll. 182-85)

The stage is filled with *"Alarums, excursions, a great fight, and a retreat";* and then Marlowe gives to Edward vigorous lines that within the confines of a theater could be associated easily with the attitude of indomitable warrior kings:

Why do we sound retreat? Upon them, lords!
This day I shall pour vengeance with my sword
On those proud rebels that are up in arms
And do confront and countermand their king.

(III, iii, 1-4)

The younger Spencer's lines are topped consistently by those given the elder Spencer, and the last line before the renewal of the battle is given to Edward:

War. St. George for England, and the barons' right!
K. Edw. Saint George for England, and Edward's right!

(ll. 34-35)

Yet between the two encounters, Edward insists that he will "Make England's civil towns huge heaps of stones, / And ploughs to go around our palace-gates" rather than banish his favorites (ll. 30-31); and this vow is called a "desperate and unnatural resolution" (l. 32). Granted that revenge might be its own theatrical excuse, yet such fury toward one's native soil was characteristic of the tyrant, not the king.

The technique continues in the dramatization of Kent's second banishment. Although Edward expresses joy at avenging the death of "Good Pierce of Gaveston, my sweet favorite," his speech begins by noting that the rebels are conquered "not by chance of war, / But by justice of the quarrel and the cause" (III, iii, 36-37). Edward's vengeance is expressed, however, with the full force of tyrannical fury—e.g.,

> Away with them, my lord of Winchester!
> These lusty leaders, Warwick and Lancaster,
> I charge you roundly—off with both their heads!

(ll. 60-62)

Yet in two surrounding and theatrically obvious actions, Kent is banished only and Mortimer simply imprisoned.

Marlowe's technique in this portion of the drama, consequently, is both an alternating and a qualifying one. The portrayal of young Spencer and the representation of Edward's favoritism and fury are sufficient to give validity to Kent's soliloquy which follows immediately and in which Edward is called an "unnatural" king (IV, i, 1-10). At the same time, this unfavorable emphasis is qualified by the loyalty due a ruler, by Edward's own battlefield vigor, and even by the relatively mild punishment of Edmund and Mortimer. Similarly, Mortimer's reference to Edward as England's "scourge" (l. 73) appears in the same speech in which Mortimer refers to his own aspiring "virtue" (ll. 71-72)[82]—an attribute that could be theatrically characteristic of both an heroic figure and a Machiavel.

In the scenes that follow, this qualifying artistry is continued. With its bases now established, however, a pro-Edward emphasis emerges that is stronger than before. Loyalty to Edward and the fact of his father's rulership are constant in the young prince's speeches from the time that he is represented as being on the Continent (IV, ii, 3-7, 21-25, 43-44, 68). At the same time, Edward's pleasure that he triumphs "with his friends uncontroll'd" is modified forcefully by his warlike vigor at the approach of battle and is joined with regard for the young prince:

> Gallop apace, bright Phœbus, thorough the sky,
> And dusky night, in rusty iron car:
> Between you both shorten the time, I pray,
> That I may see that most desired day
> When we may meet these traitors in the field.
> Ah, nothing grieves me but my little boy
> Is thus misled to countenance their ills.
> Come, friends, to Bristow, there to make us strong;
> And, winds, as equal be to bring them in,
> As you injurious were to bear them forth!

(IV, iii, 48-56)

Marlowe then represents Edward's heroism even in defeat. Such an attribute, with its strong theatrical appeal, although it can be construed as a variation upon his earlier anger, has become by this time a major aspect of this ruler's portrayal.

> What! was I born to fly and run away,
> And leave the Mortimers conquerors behind?
> Give me my horse, and let's reinforce our troops:
> And in this bed of honour die with fame.
>
> (IV, v, 4-7)

After the king's exit, Marlowe clinches his present emphasis, now pro-Edward and anti-Mortimer, with Kent's second soliloquy. Mortimer and Isabella now "do kiss"; and Edmund sorrows, not for England under an unnatural king, but for defeated Edward:

> This way he fled, but I come too late.
> Edward, alas! my heart relents for thee.
> Proud traitor, Mortimer, why dost thou chase
> Thy lawful king, thy sovereign, with thy sword?
> Vild wretch! and why hast thou, of all unkind,
> Borne arms against thy brother and thy king?
> Rain showers of vengeance on my cursed head,
> Thou God, to whom in justice it belongs
> To punish this unnatural revolt!
> Edward, this Mortimer aims at thy life!
> O fly him, then!
>
> (IV, v, 10-20)

In the remainder of the drama, only in the thought expressed by Rice ap Howell (IV, vi, 112-15) and, briefly, in one of the king's last speeches (V, iii, 41-45) do earlier anti-Edward emphases appear. Instead, in the last scene of the fourth act and throughout the fifth, Marlowe brings to bear upon his portrayal of Edward the force of a pathos that was inherent in the strong literary tradition of the fall of illustrious men and that was expressed, for example, in current mirrors for magistrates:[83]

> O! hadst thou ever been a king, thy heart,
> Pierced deeply with sense of my distress,
> Could not but take compassion of my state.
> Stately and proud, in riches and in train,
> Whilom I was, powerful, and full of pomp:
> But what is he whom rule and empery
> Have not in life or death made miserable?
>
> (IV, vi, 9-15)

Marlowe, moreover, is not satisfied with any Stoic reaction one might have upon perceiving the fall of one whom the rising sun saw proud (*Thyestes,* 613-14). Although he uses Seneca's line in the Earl of Leicester's speech, it leads to no statement about a stronger power controlling all human power.[84] It appears, instead, in a context that involves the antipathy now connected with Isabella and Mortimer and the "passionate" pity of Leicester:

> The queen's commission, urg'd by Mortimer;
> What cannot gallant Mortimer with the queen?
> Alas, see where he [Edward] sits, and hopes unseen
> T' escape their hands that seek to reave his life.
> Too true it is, *Quem dies vidit veniens superbum,*
> *Hunc dies vidit fugiens jacentem.*
> But, Leicester, leave to grow so passionate.
>
> (IV, vi, 49-55)

From a reference to Isabella, Edward's lament in the central portion of this scene calls forth the abbot's choric speech: "My heart with pity earns to see this sight— / A king to bear these words and proud commands!" (ll. 70-72). The lines italicize Leicester's "Alas! see where he sits" and add a note of protest stronger than that in the earl's last speech. In addition, the relationship between Edward, young Spencer, and Baldock is now called friendship, surviving alone for an otherwise deserted Edward (ll. 67, 90, 91, 98). As a result, the spectacle of fallen Edward probably was developed with sufficient pathos so that it would not be qualified strongly, if at all, by the fact that it is Spencer who laments Edward's exit and thereby elaborates the note struck by Leicester and the abbot:

> O! is he gone? Is noble Edward gone?
> Parted from hence, never to see us more?
> Rent, sphere of Heaven! and, fire, forsake thy orb!
> Earth, melt to air! gone is my sovereign,
> Gone, gone, alas! never to make return.[85]
>
> (IV, vi, 99-103)

The last act then increases the force of this beginning to Marlowe's final movement. As he almost states explicitly, Marlowe is aiming at a sympathy for Edward that would arouse protest and find its resolution in the final action of young Edward. Witness the lines given to attendant noblemen and to King Edward himself as he speaks of the torment that martyrs his thoughts and of the anger that stems from a grief which makes him "lunatic" (V, i, 75-82, 111-14). As a result, the actions of the stage direction *"The King rageth"* (1. 85) and of the speech during which Edward tears Mortimer's decree (ll. 139-40) probably would have an audience's sympathy. For the king's concern that "England's vine" not perish and that Edward's name survive "though Edward dies" contrasts with references to "unnatural," "false" Isabella and to "proud," "usurping" Mortimer, who "spots" a king's "nuptial bed with infamy" (ll. 17, 31, 38-48, 51-57, 86-94, 102-07, 115-22). Those lines, indeed, are part of a poetic elaboration upon the fact of kingship, which had been inculcated in all Elizabethans with the conventional figures of brightness and the "celestial sun" that Marlowe uses here, as well as with the opposing figures of foul bestiality that are represented as attacking it (ll. 59-70, 71-72, 87-89, 98-101, 115-17). In such circumstances, Edward's hesitant and defiant resignation of the crown probably aroused an increasing protest that would be based also on the political villainy of rising Mortimer, who boasts that he now "makes Fortune's Wheel turn as he please" (V, ii, 53, iv, 1-20, 48-72).[86]

The puddle-water incident dramatizes the literal defilement of an English king (V, iii). Kent's unsuccessful attempt to rescue Edward allows the scene to end with the choric line: "O miserable is that commonweal, / Where lords keep court, and kings are lock'd in prison!" (ll. 63-64). The subsequent description of Edward's physical and mental torture and of his surprising endurance (V, v, 1-13) would build upon what had preceded.

In the next and final scene, Fortune's Wheel is mentioned again; and in a characteristic manner, it causes the sharp falling off and casting away of one who purposefully had mounted it. At that time, Mortimer's speech shows attributes of a *virtù* that verges upon a Renaissance "titanism":

> Base Fortune, now I see, that in thy wheel
> There is a point, to which when men aspire,
> They tumble headlong down: that point I touch'd
> And, seeing there was no place to mount up higher
> Why should I grieve at my declining fall?—
> Farewell, fair queen; weep not for Mortimer,
> That scorns the world, and, as a traveller,
> Goes to discover countries yet unknown.
>
> (V, vi, 59-66)

But in spite of this brief development, the portrayal of Mortimer's Machiavellianism and the force of lamentation and of the successive contexts have been so turned upon the king's side that the pathos of Edward's tragedy probably became quiescent in the retributive vigor and justness effected by a new ruler who is supported by his noblemen and who is firm also in the pageantic, though blooody, circumstances of his grief:

> *King.* . . . Accursed head [Mortimer's]
> Could I have rul'd thee then, as I do now,
> Thou had'st not hatched this monstrous treachery!—
> Here comes the hearse; help me to mourn, my lords.
> [*Enter Attendants with the hearse and funeral robes.*]
> Sweet father, here unto thy murdered ghost
> I offer up this wicked traitor's head;
> And let these tears, distilling from mine eyes,
> Be witness of my grief and innocency.
>
> (V, vi, 95-102)[87]

Although all of the preceding details would not be consciously appreciable in a theater, their total effect in producing a dominant structural movement from vice in rule to pity in fall undoubtedly would be. The Elizabethans' belief in the necessity for good counsel and for loyalty to the crown would support the entire play, although emphases upon those concepts appear successively. To effect this change in emphasis Marlowe develops a countermovement even as he portrays the culpability of his ruler, and he then turns the anger of a tyrannically inclined king into a forceful English vigor on the field of battle. Thereby a groundwork is laid in the middle portion of the play for Edward's sympathetic representation as the drama closes. Once more, a unique artistry builds upon that which probably had an element of familiarity for all Elizabethans. That Marlowe's method and its conceptual basis are rooted in the literature and thought of his time is a sure sign of his dramatic genius.

It is equally interesting to note, however, that Marlowe fails to develop a political crux that is reflected in Kent's first soliloquy:

> Fair blows the wind for France; blow, gentle gale,
> Till Edmund be arriv'd for England's good!
> Nature, yield to my country's cause in this.
> A brother? No, a butcher of thy friends!
>
> . . . .
>
> Unnatural king! to slaughter noblemen
> And cherish flatterers!
>
> (IV, i, 1-9)

On the one hand, love of kindred and obedience to the ruler constitute "Nature"; on the other, a ruler's love of noblemen and his hatred of

flattery. Yet in the political thought of the sixteenth century, the superiority of a "country's cause," that is, of "England's good," also
could be drawn from natural law; for the whole was superior to the
part. Marlowe, consequently, avoids the difficult application of this last
aspect of nature's law when a ruler was considered to be a part of the
whole, even though the superior part. Or a ruler might be placed not
only under God but under the law, because the law made him a king.[88]
In other words, as the play develops from this soliloquy, instead of
continuing with Edward's public sins, or the consequences of those sins
as they involved the English at large, Marlowe changes the emphases in
his portrayal of characters. Mortimer and Isabella become thoroughly
vicious; and Marlowe achieves thereby an ethical, and theatrical, dichotomy. This is not to criticize his artistry adversely. Marlowe simply
chose to represent Mortimer as a theatrically memorable Machiavel and
to elaborate skillfully the tradition of the lament, rather than to work
with a more difficult, but more intellectual, dramatic problem. Certainly,
in the light of its genre and its age, *Edward II* is well conceived and well
executed.

As has been noted, an audience's liking for vigor on the battlefield is
reflected in the portrayal of Edward II. Achieving fame and glory
through battle (e.g., *Edward II*, IV, v, 4-7) also lent itself upon the
Elizabethan stage to rhetorical displays that range from speeches before
battle to narratives by messengers. A concern for glory and honor might
be expressed also by a rhetorical bravura that showed a sure instinct
and a strong will for victory, as well as a defiance of Fortune, fear, and
death. The last three acts of *Edward III* are developed in this heroic
vein. In spite of its beginning, as an audience watched this drama, they
would come to know "King Edward for no wantonesse, / No loue sicke
cockney, nor his souldiers iades" (III, v, 101-2). The spectators also
would see the pageantic arming of Edward's son and witness how the
French were conquered by the force of the Black Prince's "noble vnre-
lenting heart / Wald in with flint of matchlesse fortitude" (III, iii, 181-
82). With or without the virtue of a true religion—which was given to
the rising figure of Navarre in Marlowe's *Massacre*[89]—the heroic play
would be melodramatic and probably reminiscent of chivalric romance.
Sometimes, as in the portrayal of Edmond Ironside, the protagonist also
shows an intuitive cleverness reminiscent of the folk-hero.

As has been indicated, when the "hero" was the central figure, even
if a particular conflict dominated a series of events, there probably would
result a basic repetitive pattern of victory over a "world of odds"
(*Edward III*, III, v, 19-63).[90] Consider, for example, Marlowe's *1
Tamburlaine* (1587-88). In Acts I and II, Tamburlaine's spell and

might overcome Theridamas, Persian military leader; Mycetes, king of Persia; and Cosroe, who with Tamburlaine's aid has seized the Persian crown. In Acts III and IV, Bajazeth is conquered, as are the kings of Fez, Morocco, and Argier. At that time, the movement to Act V also begins; and in the last act Tamburlaine conquers the Governor of Damascus, the Sultan of Egypt, and the allied King of Arabia. To these, one should add the beautiful Zenocrate.

1 Tamburlaine, of course, was written before *Edward II, Edward III, The Massacre at Paris,* or *Edmond Ironside;* and in writing it, Marlowe immortalized the naïve vein of stage heroism found in such plays as *Sir Clyomon and Sir Clamydes* or *Common Conditions.* To do so, he chose a hero from the fabulous East, where the limits of "empiry" might be measured by "east and west, as Phœbus doth his course." There other playwrights also found a suitable background for fabulous and infamous deeds that were their own theatrical excuse;[91] and there the figure of Tamburlaine seemed outstanding to some of Marlowe's contemporaries.

Although all in an Elizabethan audience probably were not aware of the fact, in nondramatic and relatively learned circumstances Tamburlaine was associated sometimes with primal conditions throughout a wide geographic area. When Louis Le Roy wrote his popular commentary on Aristotle's *Politics,* for example, he referred to Tamburlaine in his gloss on the definition of a city and its contraries. In this discussion, which is made up of Renaissance commonplaces, Le Roy notes that all things terrestrial, aquatic, and aerial live in communities. The first society of man is that of husband and wife, and from this association appear at length groups of people gathering in "Towne-houses" to "conferre togither of the Common-wealth." Yet there will be variations resulting from a community's geographical position. Extremes of heat and cold produce a barter society and a nomadic existence. This was the life of the barbarous Scythians in ancient times, and they were succeeded by the Tartars. This last "companie" "vnder the conduction of Cynkys their Prophet and first Emperour" occupied a great part of the North, East, and South when their appearance around 1211 followed the phenomenon "of a great blasing starre by the space of six moneths before." Then "came the great Tamerlane, in the yeare 1400, who ledde an armie of twelue hundred thousand fighting men, terrifying all the whole earth that is inhabited, with this incredible multitude, and the feare of his own valiancie."[92] These words about a barbarous society, a star, a prophet, a first emperor, and a terrifying Tamburlaine appear as Le Roy moves into a discussion of "masterly" rule, which is still preserved by the Persians, the Turks, the Muscovites, and Prester John. It is a rule that can be unconcerned with "equitie."[93]

On the basis of such commonplaces, an Eastern hero's fearsome "valiancie" might be expected to vary from the heroism of a Christian ruler. When Edward III's wrath is aroused by the inhabitants of Calais, it is controlled not only by his queen but also by his knowledge that peace, not conquest, establishes a true rule. Edward also would have it

> ... knowne that we
> As well can master our affections
> As conquer other by the dynt of sword. ...

As a result, the inhabitants of Calais, and especially the six wealthiest merchants delivered for execution, "shall liue to boast of clemencie, / And, tyrannie, strike terror to thy selfe" (V, i, 50-55). In contrast, when Tamburlaine's settled and known method of conquest is disregarded, this conqueror overcomes even the force of his consort's beauty and orders the slaughter of the virgins of Damascus; for he will persevere in his "martial observations," which are purposefully terrifying (V, ii, 58-65, 72-93).

The Elizabethans' attraction to such a picture as that indicated by Le Roy—and, for that matter, by aspects of Marlowe's later *Jew of Malta*—probably was the result of tales that had filtered into England from the East; while the terrifying force of the Turks, of a Suleiman the Magnificent or a Selim II, might evoke thoughts of the scourge of God, numenous beings, and the absence of conventional ethics. Upon such emotions, Marlowe bases, in part, his portrayal of a mighty hero who conquers not only the Turkish Emperor and other distant rulers but also the force of heavenly beauty when it would blunt his purpose. If such a context for Tamburlaine were established successfully, any ethical prejudgments grounded upon principles *de regimine principum,* or even upon Christian common sense, might well have been exorcised; and this, in brief, seems to have been one aspect of Marlowe's purpose.

When, for example, he utilizes Christian sentiments, Marlowe does so to support the portrayal of his hero. When the Turkish Emperor is conquered by this "sturdy Scythian" shepherd, then will be avenged the havoc made of "Christian blood" by "cruel pirates of Argier," the "scum of Africa." The pitiable Christian captives—chained, starved, and beaten in galleys—will be freed. At Bajazeth's overthrow, Christians will make bonfires and ring their bells for joy. In these circumstances, Tamburlaine refers to himself as "the scourge and wrath of God" (III, iii, 44). The emphasis appears both before and after the battle that decides the fate of the Turkish potentate (III, iii, 46-60, 236-43).

Within the sweep of the "great and mighty" Tamburlaine's victories, however, this levying upon Christian sympathies is only an eddy of retributive force that converges upon Bajazeth. With its second appearance, it is overborne immediately by an expression of the wonder and vastness in Renaissance geography and in Tamburlaine's will. The "walled garrisons" of "Afric and Greece," by which Bajazeth hopes to rewin his glory, will be subdued by Tamburlaine. He will write himself "great lord of Africa," and "from the East unto the furthest West" he will "extend his puissant arm":

> The galleys and those pilling brigandines,
> That yearly sail to the Venetian gulf,
> And hover in the Straits for Christians' wrack,
> Shall lie at anchor in the isle Asant,
> Until the Persian fleet and men of war,
> Sailing along the oriental sea,
> Have fetch'd about the Indian continent,
> Even from Persepolis to Mexico,
> And thence unto the straits of Jubalter;
> Where they shall meet and join their force in one,
> Keeping in awe the bay of Portingale,
> And all the ocean by the British shore;
> And by this means I'll win the world at last.
>
> (III, iii, 245-60)

By such speeches, grandeur, awe, and fearsomeness are established as the aura of Tamburlaine. Indeed, as Marlowe immortalizes the heroic vein, he also intellectualizes this most theatrical of dramatic traditions; and he does this by drawing upon attitudes and beliefs so generally known and so widely held that both learned and unlearned probably followed his dominant emphasis with conviction.

One can specify easily a combination of circumstances during the performance of this drama that would be conducive to an acceptance of the theatrical moment. Some of them, of course, are obvious: the artistry of the actor Allen, the movement from battle to battle typical of the hero, and Marlowe's blank verse and rhetoric that probably entranced even "ignorant gapers." Reinforcing those theatrical considerations, however, is a probable knowledgeableness even on the part of a water-carrier from the streets. For this was an age in which folk, who might fix their eyes on the heavens for the time of day, might also know that both terrifying and propitious omens could exist in the clouds or in the reaches above the clouds, where comets, eclipses, bright or fading stars appeared. Even the uneducated probably had heard, at least, of horoscopes, of astrological charms that warded off evil or gave men power, and of a definite relationship between physiognomy and celestial configurations. From such knowledgeableness, sparks of credibility and of familiarity probably would be struck when Tamburlaine spoke of what the "gracious stars" had promised at his birth, or when he was described as

> . . . valiant Tamburlaine, the man of fame,
> The man that in the forehead of his fortune
> Bears figures of renown and miracle.

The face and personage of this hero is that of a "wondrous man":

> Nature doth strive with Fortune and his stars
> To make him famous in accomplish'd worth.
>
> (II, i, 2-34)

As generations of critics have noted, comparable lines appear throughout the drama as Marlowe elaborates Tamburlaine's good fortune—a fact that he could have found in his sources.[94] At the same time, an awareness of the fact that some men seemed blessed by Fortune would accord with Marlowe's dominant emphasis and thereby enlarge for the educated the knowledgeable attitude of even an "ignorant gaper." This concept could be derived, of course, from even a general awareness of history, or it could be derived from such an idea as that of the *fortunati*. According to Pontano, since God assigns some of his duties to Fortune, certain men seem to be driven by her superior power; and in order to meet the objections of Egidio da Viterbo, he reconciled this theory with the idea of providence and linked it with the power of the stars. These *fortunati* are always confident; they grasp every occasion; they never delay. They follow their appetites, impulses, and inclinations and act without caution, advice, or counsel. They are never deterred by odds; and even if they violate the dictates of reason, they never fail. Unlike the virtuous ones, they do not need a code of conduct; for if they follow their impulses, they will be carried to the highest goals.[95]

Removed from its Christian framework in accordance with Marlowe's locale, Pontano's concept seems especially applicable to Tamburlaine when statements about his fortune and confidence are intensified by the way in which he turns against Cosroe. Struck by the thought that it is "passing brave to be a king, / And ride in triumph through Persepolis" (II, v, 53-54), Tamburlaine suddenly follows his impulse and inclination:

> . . . shall we wish for aught
> The world affords in greatest novelty,
> And rest attemptless, faint, and destitute?
> Methinks we should not: *I am strongly mov'd,*

> *That if I should desire the Persian crown,*
> *I could attain it with a wondrous ease.*

> . . . .

> 'T will prove a pretty jest, in faith, my friends.

> . . . .

> Then shalt thou see the Scythian Tamburlaine
> Make but a jest to win the Persian crown.
>
> (II, v, 72-98)

Like the *fortunati,* he is confident, undeterred by odds, unconcerned with the dictates of reason or of a code of conduct, and yet he does not fail. The situation accords also with the resolve, confidence, and sensing of success given to the "hero" as a type, just as it accords with the power of the stars ranged on Tamburlaine's side.

In addition, when the achievement of this play-world has become the acquisition of empire, and an "earthly crown" is "perfect bliss and sole felicity" (II, vii, 27-29), Marlowe begins to emphasize man's laudable striving for achievement as one of his hero's attributes:[96]

> Nature that fram'd us of four elements,
> Warring within our breasts for regiment,
> Doth teach us all to have aspiring minds:
> Our souls, whose faculties can comprehend
> The wondrous architecture of the world,
> And measure every wand'ring planet's course,
> Still climbing after knowledge infinite,
> And always moving as the restless spheres,
> Wills us to wear ourselves, and never rest,
> Until we reach the ripest fruit of all. . . .
>
> (II, vii, 18-27)

The idea expressed in the preceding lines is obviously akin to that of *virtù* and need have been in no way esoteric.[97] Probably the majority in any one audience knew that "virtue" might mean the distinguishing force characteristic of anything. That meaning they undoubtedly gave the word when they heard about the attractions of kingship and of wearing "a crown enchas'd with pearl and gold, / Whose *virtues* carry with it life and death" (II, v, 60-61). The meaning would also be singularly opposite when Tamburlaine refers to poets' "restless heads," in which will "hover" always

> One thought, one grace, one wonder, at the least,
> Which into words no *virtue* can digest.
>
> (V, ii, 109-110)

Thus the meaning would persist and be merged with that of *virtù* when an audience heard in the same soliloquy that in spite of his birth, Tamburlaine would give the world to note

> That *virtue* solely is the sum of glory,
> And fashions men with true nobility.

(ll. 126-27)

In other words, as the play developed from the time that the protagonist attacked Cosroe, it probably would become increasingly apparent that the "virtue" of Tamburlaine was a martial *virtù*. Displaying a tenacious purpose and an overwhelming success in gigantic achievement, he constantly demonstrated the value in accomplishment *per se*. Thereby new monarchs and a new nobility were established by this leader of a "companie" that approximated primitive societies and moved from a life of shepherds and sturdy Scythian thieves to control a "most puissant and mightye" empire. Witness, for example, the "course of crowns" at Tamburlaine's banquet as the fourth act closes (IV, iv, 122 ff.).

In such a manner, the wonders and the fearsomeness of the East, ideas about the influence of the stars, the origins of societies, the *fortunati,* and a restless "virtue"-*virtù* may have merged with one another but constantly filled out and intellectualized the heroic vein, even as it appeared in the equally theatrical East. By such speculative concepts, expressed with striking dramatic poetry, Tamburlaine is placed outside the normal framework of society. Awesome and terrifying images are associated with him and his followers; but the preceding aspects of Marlowe's artistry constitute the answer to the wonder of Tamburlaine's opponents when they are defeated by this "god, or fiend, or spirit of the earth" or "monster turned to manly shape," a figure "from earth, or hell, or Heaven," leader also of the "strangest men that nature ever made" (II, vi, 15-23, vii, 40).

Upon the preceding bases, Marlowe also creates a climactic effect within the repetitive pattern associated with the heroic play—an effect that is more conscientious and artistic than one produced by any temporary variation or melodramatic heightening of single situations. Edmond Ironside, for example, fights four times and is defeated only once, and then through treachery; while the first victory of the Black Prince overshadows the immediately preceding one at Crécy and his success at Poitiers overshadows his father's capture of Calais. But in Marlowe's drama the movement from foolish Mycetes, to usurping Cosroe, to Bajazeth is an obvious theatrical progression. The last scene in which Mycetes appears is comic; and the portrayal of that weak-witted Persian king is part of the dramatization of Cosroe's rise.[98] In dramatizing Cosroe's fall, Marlowe develops the anger, wonder, and awe produced by Tamburlaine's *virtù;* but the incident is only a preparation for the fall of Bajazeth,

> ... the Turkish Emperor,
> Dread Lord of Afric, Europe, and Asia,
> Great King and conqueror of Græcia,
> The ocean, Terrene, and the Coal-black sea,
> The high and highest monarch of the world. . . .

> (III, i, 22-26)

Not only does Marlowe utilize a Christian sympathy to strike a retributive note in his dramatization of Bajazeth's fall but, when the emperor's request for ransom is denied, Marlowe briefly develops a disjunction between Bajazeth's insistence upon his sacredness and the course of events:

> *Baj.* Ah, villains!—dare ye touch my sacred arms?
> O Mahomet!—O sleepy Mahomet!

> (III, iii, 268-69)

This movement toward retributive ridicule (see also ll. 225-26) is then elaborated in subsequent scenes when the caged and ranting Turk affords sport for Tamburlaine as a "goodly show at a banquet" (IV, ii, 1-100, iv, 1-77). It is then that Marlowe develops a mixture of the derisible, the stupendous, the strange, and the terrifying that he elaborated further in the *Jew of Malta.*

From such a situation, a horrifying death for Bajazeth might have been developed in a manner not discordant with the Herod-strain of earlier drama.[99] Marlowe, however, utilizes Bajazeth's death to intensify the approach to Tamburlaine's final battle. At that time, both hero and heroine encounter their greatest difficulty; for Zenocrate's father, the Sultan of Egypt, and her former love, the King of Arabia, are now Tamburlaine's opponents. Zenocrate, consequently, has asked that mercy be extended to her country (IV, ii, 123-24, iv, 78-85); and Tamburlaine has granted safety to her father and her friends, although he has insisted that he will maintain the force of his "virtue" (IV, ii, 125-26, iv, 86-103). Thus on his next appearance (V, ii, 1-65), even though the city is a part of Zenocrate's country, he turns a deaf ear to the virgins of Damascus, whose pleas have been unheeded by their own erring ruler (V, i, 23-33). But Tamburlaine appears at this time *"all in black and very melancholy"* (V, ii, S-D). The sorrows of Zenocrate lay "more siege unto" his soul than anything so far dramatized. He then calls to an audience's attention that his perception and praise of beauty are no weaknesses. Beauty touches the soul of any man and affects the "conceits" of any warrior (ll. 72-119). Feeling strongly the force of beauty, Tamburlaine, nevertheless, has conquered what the gods themselves did not. He thereby has made it known that nobility and glory reside in "virtue" alone, that is, in his amoral force (V, ii, 120-27).

After this trial of the hero, Marlowe turns to the trial of the heroine as he develops those sorrows that have laid siege to Tamburlaine's soul. To do this, he utilizes the deaths of Bajazeth and his empress, as well as the tradition of lament associated with the fall of the illustrious:

> *Zab.* Why live we, Bajazeth, and build up nests
> So high within the region of the air
> By living long in this oppression,
> That all the world will see and laugh to scorn
> The former triumphs of our mightiness
> In this obscure infernal servitude?
> *Baj.* . . .
> O dreary engines of my loathed sight,
> That sees my crown, my honour, and my name
> Thrust under yoke and thraldom of a thief,
> Why feed ye still on day's accursed beams
> And sink not quite into my tortur'd soul?
> You see my wife, my queen and emperess,
> Brought up and propped by the hand of fame,
> Queen of fifteen contributory queens,
> Now thrown to rooms of black adjection,
> Smear'd with blots of basest drudgery,
> And villeiness to shame, disdain, and misery.
>
> (V, ii, 186-91, 196-206)

These "words of ruth" (l. 207) have their horrific development in the rulers' braining of themselves and even in the brief but conventionally "frantic" passion of Zabina, the woman connected with this suffering figure (ll. 242-59). But Marlowe then uses this horrific spectacle to continue with the lament tradition and to bring into the scene the admonition conventionally associated with it. The sorrow of Zenocrate at seeing "Damascus' walls dy'd with Egyptian blood" (ll. 260-79) is intensified by this "bloody spectacle." She also sees it as a warning to Tamburlaine and his contempt of "earthly fortune" and as a warning to herself and her failure to be moved with pity:

> Those that are proud of fickle empery
> And place their chiefest good in earthly pomp,
> Behold the Turk and his great Emperess!
> Ah, Tamburlaine! My love! sweet Tamburlaine!
> That fight'st for sceptres and for slippery crowns,
> Behold the Turk and his great Emperess!
> Thou, that in conduct of thy happy stars
> Sleep'st every night with conquest on thy brows,
> And yet would'st shun the wavering turns of war,
> In fear and feeling of the like distress
> Behold the Turk and his great Emperess!
> Ah, mighty Jove and holy Mahomet,
> Pardon my love!—O, pardon his contempt
> Of earthly fortune and respect of pity,
> And let not conquest, ruthlessly pursu'd,
> Be equally against his life incens'd
> In this great Turk and hapless Emperess!
> And pardon me that was not mov'd with ruth
> To see them live so long in misery!
> Ah, what may chance to thee, Zenocrate?
>
> (ll. 293-312)

Just as Zenocrate's beauty—that is, her distinctive "virtue"—has been the only force to affect Tamburlaine, so the hero's "virtue" here affects the heroine.[100] In spite of this development, however, Marlowe keeps the scene within the context of this Eastern play and his portrayal of a Tamburlaine whose sword is guided by a star that "rules the skies and countermands the gods" (e.g., l. 170). The dominant emphasis of the entire play returns in Anippe's speech:

> Madam, content yourself, and be resolv'd.
> Your love hath Fortune so at his command,
> That she shall stay and turn her wheels no more,
> As long as life maintain his mighty arm
> That fights for honour to adorn your head.[101]
>
> (ll. 313-17)

Yet the heroine's sorrow continues through the death of Arabia and is not allayed until the final grouping of characters. At that time, by Tamburlaine's conduct, Zenocrate's father is doubly won, inasmuch as Zenocrate has been used "with honour" (V, ii, 420-50). Thus Marlowe's play ends with the heroine's sorrow banished and the hero's "virtue" triumphant, as Tamburlaine "takes truce with all the world."

Quite understandably *1 Tamburlaine* was a resounding success. Although its repetitive pattern is intensified, Marlowe does not capitalize upon the terrifying simply for the sake of such a vicious and sensational emphasis as that found in *Selimus,* or for the sake of such a retributive force as that found in *The Looking Glass,* with its picture of Rasni's court. He creates an entirely different world, one that is more intellectualized and much more poetic than those of the preceding dramas or of such heroic and Turkish plays as *Alphonsus King of Aragon* (1587-88), *The Battle of Alcazar* (1588-89), *Alphonsus Emperour of Germany* (1587-99), and probably the lost *Turkish Mahomet and Hiren the Fair Greek* (1581-94).

To understand the appeal of the dramas just mentioned one must take into account the nerveless acceptance of an active, primitive ruthlessness. In contemporary life, it was apparent in the use of torture, the impaling of heads, the methods of execution; and it is reflected not simply in the hardened sensibilities of the ignorant but also in kindred reactions springing from the quiet discipline of a Fulke Greville.[102] All of the plays so far considered reflect this primitive violence so obviously that its occurrence needs little comment. It can be seen in the flaying of a Sisamnes in *Cambises;* the bloody course of events in the widely different contexts both within and between *The Spanish Tragedy* and *Edward II;* the murders of Guise and of Henry III and of the Huguenots; the mutilation of noble hostages by Canutus; the loud insensateness of the derision of Bajazeth; the braining of this emperor and his consort; the derision both by and of Barabas; the murder of Edward II, who is crushed to death beneath a table.

An acceptance of the pitiless "virtue" of Tamburlaine perhaps can be seen when a Platonizing Le Roy wrote that what this conqueror lacked most was an effective historian.[103] Although Marlowe is not that historian, his *1 Tamburlaine* does provide a conceptual treatment of this primitive ruthlessness, for which his poetry creates a numenous aura. Drawing speculative motifs from history, from current thought, and from conventional laments, this play dramatizes a "virtue" by which empires were created;[104] and it interprets that "virtue" in astrological terms and in the terms of one who belonged to the *fortunati.* In doing this, Marlowe's drama expresses an attitude found also in the refined natural magic of the era. For behind both—behind this representation of a type that by its very nature was heroic and behind the cultivated mythical thinking of the period—stands not too far off the primitive "omnipotence of thought and desire" through which men would build up the reality of things and from which they would distill legend, horror, and sophisticated concept. Small wonder, then, that Tamburlaine took an unforgettable place in the Elizabethans' theatrical memories.[105]

As with the male figures that might compare and contrast with Tamburlaine, so female figures on the stage of the late eighties and early nineties when compared with Zenocrate would produce memories of some relatively simple character-types that, nevertheless, ran a gamut from Tamburlaine's consort, James IV's Queen, and his virtuous love Ida to vicious Remilia, who was the consort of Rasni. There, too, would appear the proud, vengeful female Machiavel, represented here only by the portrayal of Catherine de' Medici[106]—a portrayal that balances a feminine tenderness that sometimes was raised to the ruling mercy of Edward III's queen.[107] With both virtuous and vicious females might be associated rhetorical pyrotechnics; and with the virtuous ones, situations of rival wooing might also emerge. This last motif is developed faintly even in *1 Tamburlaine;*[108] but it is handled with tragic irony when Marlowe brings upon the stage the heroic Dido wooed by her "historical" suitor, as well as by Æneas, her poetic and heroic one.[109]

In the dramas so far considered, the most skillful use of current concepts to substantiate theatrical developments is found, obviously, in Marlowe's plays. In addition to what has been noted, witness the way in which the concept of fortitude is expressed in Faustus' boast, "learn thou of Faustus manly fortitude" (*Dr. Faustus,* iii, 89). That boast then becomes ironically applicable to the protagonist himself, who in contrast with the old man is terrified by the threat of physical pain but entranced by the sensual shows that "feed his soul" (xiii, 89-90, 100-2, 135 ff., vi, 88 ff., 110-11, 194, xiii, 115). Thus repentance becomes impossible.[110]

In this connection, thematic developments connected with Edward III's control of himself should be mentioned, and two other plays also should be considered. Both develop themes, one effectively and one woodenly. Neither approaches Marlowe's flamboyant artistry; but since both deal with the history of Richard II's reign, they should be considered on that score alone. The first play, *Woodstock,* is remarkably workmanlike in its dichotomous use of ideas. Remarkably immature, however, is the dramatized sermon on obedience that was entitled *The Life and Death of Jack Straw.*

The Tragedy of Thomas of Woodstock shows once more a contention between vice and virtue over a ruling figure, and it displays again the consequences of vice's rule. In contrast with *James IV,* the play is based on history; and as it portrays a culpable English ruler, it also represents, in different circumstances than Shakespeare's *2 Henry VI,* the fall from power and the death of an illustrious nobleman. Although the beginning of *Woodstock* is comparable to that of *Edward II*, this anonymous work lacks the final tragic movement in Marlowe's drama, as well as its anticipation in the mid-portion of the play. The relationship between these two dramas has been debated,[111] but there is little doubt that Shakespeare was familiar with *Woodstock* before he wrote his *Tragedie of King Richard the Second*. The problem of indebtedness and even the exact sequence of playwriting, however, is of less importance for the purpose of this chapter than is the fact that the preceding dramas show an awareness of similar ideas and methods.

Certainly it would be clear to all who saw, read, or acted in *Woodstock* that a neglect of government through wantonness and favoritism leads to a villainous recourse to the sword, to great public evils, and to retribution. Richard's failure to rule as a king leads most obviously to the murder of Thomas of Woodstock, Duke of Gloucester; but it also leads to a realm where "rancorous weeds" have "choked the ground" and left England's "pleasant meads like barren hills" (V, vi, 1-5).[112] After Gloucester is murdered, Richard is defeated in battle and at least humbled by his own subjects. In such a manner, the body politic is cured.

Throughout the drama, Virtue is embodied in Woodstock, in his serving-man Cheyney, and in four noblemen. Vice is embodied in Tresilian, in his serving-man Nimble, and in Richard's four favorites. As a result, Virtue is represented as "bearded age, concern for the country (with veneration for its glorious past, under Edward III), plaindealing, frankness." It also is represented as antipathy to France and "the wish to be loyal to the son of the Black Prince, if only he will shake off the upstarts." Vice is represented as "beardless youth, political recklessness, luxury, contempt of tradition and respect." It also is represented as "oppression of the people, with crooked law and scheming, treachery even among the upstarts, and a preparedness to back bad with worse, in seeking help from the traditional enemy across the Channel." In Woodstock is embodied "English straight-dealing," "true-born nobility," and plainness both in speech and a coat of frieze. In Tresilian is embodied the unscrupulousness that farms the realm, destroys Woodstock, and supports the lavish newfangledness of the upstarts by an unconscientious cleverness. This viciousness appears even in the "jocularities of the demon lawyers"—a mirth that contrasts with Gloucester's "Thomas-More-like" humor.[113]

In addition to what the most recent editor of *Woodstock* has pointed out, some vestiges of the double conflict seem to appear as the author develops his action from the previous alignment, which clearly is reminiscent of the morality. Like the earlier *Mundus et Infans*—though

without its triple conflict and its consequent emphasis on original sin—
Woodstock begins as does *Edward II* with the central figure's wantonness
established. In contrast to the initial situation in Marlowe's drama,
however, Richard's favorites already exercise power in the realm and
are capable of poisoning the opposed noblemen.[114] As a result, during
the first two acts of *Woodstock,* only the possibility of Virtue's success
exists. It is hoped that Richard and his favorites will be controlled by the
king's marriage to Anne and by a Parliament of the estates. These hopes
are blasted even as they are dramatized—with one for each act (I, i, ii;
II, i, ii). Virtue, consequently, leaves the court and only the queen
remains—as in *James IV.* Richard has ended the protectorship of
Woodstock and made Tresilian lord chief justice; the four favorites have
replaced virtuous noblemen in their important offices; and the center of
the commonwealth appears "As if the world were topsy-turvy turned!"
(II, ii, 142). Thus the defeat of Virtue is achieved with relative ease.

Richard wavers, however, as the fourth act closes and good Queen
Anne is dead (IV, iii). Her death, he fears is

> . . . but chorus to some tragic scene
> That shortly will confound our state and realm.
> Such sad events black mischiefs still attend,
> And bloody acts, I fear, must crown the end.
>
> (ll. 148-51)

He believes that he has "too much provoked the powers divine," repents
his wrongs to "good" Woodstock, and is suffering from "inward"
wounds (ll. 173-82). Although it is too late to stop Gloucester's murder
and although Richard is no longer repentant when he next appears
(V, iii), he once more laments and recognizes his guilt when Greene is
dead and the revolt is successful (V, iv, 47-54). As a result, two lamenting speeches, the second of which is clearly connected with Virtue's
triumph as the play closes, appear at the end of the fourth and fifth acts.
Though relatively brief, they seem to balance those hopes in the first
and second acts that had been blasted as Virtue was defeated. Taken
together, they may reflect the central figure's final redemption as it is
dramatized in earlier moralities, as well as in *James IV* and at the end
of the first act in *Edward II.*[115] Unfortunately we do not know whether
Richard acted upon his second perception of guilt, as he had, briefly but
unsuccessfully, upon his first. The ending of the drama in Egerton Manuscript 1994 is missing.

Be that as it may, the morality-like process of the drama is obvious.
When Virtue is driven from Richard's court at the end of the second act
and Vice is established firmly, Vice's rule is dramatized. A king's body-

guard appears, and plans go forward to raise excessive amounts by blank charters and to deal with "treasonable" whisperers (III, i). Although Gloucester, Lancaster, and York hope to quiet them (III, ii), the commons are rebellious. Their burden is heavy and their discontent justifiable (III, iii). Richard and his favorites also realize that the commons are restive, but they divide the realm and plan to farm the revenue. The dukes will be proclaimed traitors and help will be sought from France (IV, i). Gloucester is abducted by the trickery of Richard and his men (IV, ii); and in accordance with Richard's directions, he is murdered at Calais (V, i). In all of this, except for the first scene of Richard's lamentation (IV, iii), there is no shading of right and wrong, as there is in *Edward II*. One does not need the lines before battle in the last act to realize that the author's emphasis is constant throughout the drama:

> *Kings Men.* Let our drums thunder begin the fight.
> *Lords Men.* Just Heaven protect us; and defend the Right.
>
> (V, iii, 125-26)

From what has been written, one can judge that the portrayal of Richard does not need much comment. Even more than Greene's James IV, Richard is represented, except for two moments, as a vicious prince. A "wanton king," "degenerate from his noble father," he is "wounded with a wanton humour, / Lulled and secured by flattering sycophants" (I, i, 29, 45, 144-45). Preoccupied with his own desires, he will not accept good counsel; and his headstrongness can become anger or a tyrannical vindictiveness, the cruelty of which he hides because of the love all the realm gives to Gloucester (e.g., I, iii, 151-54, 160-61, 167, 196; IV, i, 72-82; IV, ii, 125 ff.; V, iii, 108-9). As one might expect, Richard's insistence upon the absoluteness of his office appears with these theatrical signs of a tyrant. It is most noticeable, perhaps, in connection with his lavishness and his order to rack the commons soundly:

> *King.* . . . . rack them soundly and we'll maintain it.
> Remember ye not the proviso enacted in our last
> parliament, that no statute, were it ne'er so prof-
> itable for the commonwealth, should stand in force
> against our proceeding?
> *Green.* Tis true, my lord: then what should hinder
> ye to accomplish anything that may best please your
> kingly spirit to determine?
> *King.* True, Greene, and we will do it in spite of
> them. . . . Is't just, Tresilian?
> *Tres.* Most just, my liege.
>
> (IV, i, 170-80)

Such a rule destroys the fact of Richard's kingship and the allegiance that goes with it. It is the rule of a "wanton tyrant" "not English born" (V, iii, 3-5, 100). In the conventional speeches preceding a conflict, this ruler condemns the rebels who draw their swords

> . . . against our sacred person,
> The highest God's anointed deputy,
> Breaking . . . holy oaths to heaven and us. . . .
>
> (V, iii, 57-59)

But Richard is no king, nor is he simply a "landord." His condemnation by the ghost of Edward III is repeated to deny even Richard's Englishness. This ruler is "Richard of Bordeaux," who has racked his subjects and lost the hearts of Englishmen (V, iii, 94-107). In this respect, Woodstock's fidelity, which is an integral part of his portrayal, runs counter to the impetus of the drama. Gloucester is greatly upset about the ills of the realm, but he insists upon remaining loyal; and from that loyalty the cruelly ironic scenes of his capture and his murder result.[116]

The total effect of *Woodstock,* consequently, is one in which the contrasting figures stand out so strongly that the viciousness of favoritism and of flattery and the concomitant necessity for good subaltern rulers are illustrated clearly. As has been pointed out, Elizabethans believed in this doctrine strongly. It is comparable to the premise of an heroic Black Prince and an heroic Edward III, or comparable to an Elizabethans' chauvinism—matter that is used also in the scene of Woodstock's murder.

Even the comic elements in the drama show this emphasis upon the portrayal of the opposing forces. Because of Woodstock's plain clothing, the horse of an officious courtly exquisite is left with the duke, who is mistaken for a "rude swain." Gloucester's words to the animal then establish the proposition that the beast's wit is as great as its master's (III, ii, 162-63, 168-70). The exquisite returns, exhibits himself, and proceeds to the proof of Woodstock's proposition (ll. 199-223). At the conclusion of this literate stupidity, "Plain Thomas" returns to the concerns of a true subaltern ruler, who will keep the peace in the portion of the country under his control, although he will not go to court (ll. 238-39). Woodstock's humor, in both the modern and the Elizabethan sense, demonstrates the vapidity of an exquisite thriving at court and the sound wit of an unpretentious nobility.

In the next scene, Master Ignorance, stupid rustics, a mistaking of words, and a comic *non sequitur* about hanging appear. The author also draws upon the fact that folk merriment sometimes had been considered seditious. As it might be expected with Vice dominant, a song becomes "treason in the ninth degree"; and even whistling is made out to be seditious by the fool's logic of Nimble (III, iii, 233-57).[117] In other words, although they are ignorant, the commons are virtuous. They do not show the riotous many-headedness that was their conventional vice in the political commonplaces of the age.[118] In contrast, the comic actions of Tresilian's imitative servant redound upon himself and are a dissonance and an evil in the body politic. Thus the basis for the comic scene accords with the emphasis of the drama and is far from being comic.[119]

One aspect of the comedy, accordingly, culminates in the scene of Woodstock's murder, wherein the past glories of England are placed in grotesque juxtaposition with the tidiness of an expert in murder (V, i). On the other hand, the comic process of the drama leads to the rogue comedy of Tresilian's capture—effected when this chief justice is out-witted by his own servant, whose training in the law burlesques his master's (V, v, vi).[120]

In contrast with the favorites, the noblemen act for the common good; and when they are concerned with their honor, they are righteous-ly indignant. When Woodstock breaks his council staff, the action is part of his plainness and is linked specifically with the virtue this duke had shown in public affairs (II, ii, 155-57). Lancaster's anger is as-sociated with his age and is restrained almost immediately. As in *Edward II,* this theatrical attribute of great persons is emphasized when sycophants and upstarts are granted power; and such an attribute prob-ably corresponded to the actual touchiness of Elizabethan noblemen. By Gloucester's action, for example, the world shall never "report an upstart groom / Did glory in the honours Woodstock lost" (ll. 159-60). But just as the common people do not show their conventional vice, so the noblemen never show the vice of the powerful few. They demonstrate neither ambition nor factiousness.[121]

The evil in this body politic emanates from a ruler who violates the reason for rule, namely, the good of the commonwealth. As has been indicated, then, this drama demonstrates that when favoritism and wantonness run their course, public evils result, as does a vicious re-course to the sword. In this instance, these vices are countered by a successful revolt.

The Life and Death of Jack Straw (1590-93), however, is concerned with inculcating the righteous simplicity of obedience. In this fortunately anonymous play, the cause of revolt is the gathering of a "taske," or "beneuolence," for the king; and in this instance the collection of revenue in Richard II's reign is represented as legal. Only in the initial situation is right on the side of the rebels and then simply because the collector is exceeding his power. Otherwise, the point is made constantly that there has been no overstepping of bounds on the king's part or on that of his councilors, who are nevertheless worried about the slowness of the payment.

When the secretary makes the point that the commons are unhappy and also insists that the unhappiness of the land resides in the "unnatural" revolt of the many, the author's lack of skill, even in his wooden treatment of ideas, is obvious (sig. B2). Yet his purpose is clear. This playwright sets up a situation that ignores any conflict in a divine-rightist's ideal. The "taske," for example, was granted to the king by Parliament; it was "given at high court of Parliament" and is a result of an "Act of Parliament" (sigs. Blv, B2r, Clv). Richard is a "true succeeding Prince" and a "true annointed" one (Blv, B2v, B3v); and his actions substantiate such titles. As the revolt is dramatized, he shows the characteristics of a good ruler. He will meet the commons and redress any evil they may have sustained (sig. Clr). He refuses to have any guard when meeting them because he will not run the chance of shedding "a world of blood." He more accounts "the blood of Englishmen than so" (sig. Dlv). He is constantly merciful and just. Richard is willing to give Jack Straw the sword that this rebel first demands, that is, the one worn for Newton's "owne defense." Straw's demand that Newton surrender his sword of office, that is, the one that belongs to the king, results, however, in Walworth's going to the aid of Newton and mortally stabbing the rebel leader (sigs. E1v-E2v). The king, nevertheless, mercifully pardons even those who have persevered in rebellion, with the exception of the two remaining leaders, who are

> . . . two vnnaturell Englishmen,
> O might I say no English nor men.
>
> (sig. F2r)

Not only is there no question as to where right resides and no complexity in determining that right, but the commonwealth is the king's:

> . . . the Noble and the slave,
> And all doo liue but for a Common weale,
> Which Common weale in other termes, is the Kings.
>
> (sig. B2r)

The point is made early in the play. The situation is as simple as that: when a prince's decree is "set down," it should be "irreuocable" (sig. Clv).

From such a point of view, it is no wonder that among the rebels there are no men "of any worth"; and had there been, the bishop could not "choose but pittie them" (sigs. B4v-C1r). The rebels are only "poore" souls, "simple inough." When given an ineffective repetition of old comic tricks—such as miming with a staff and mistaking of words —the principal comedian seems "a starke nidiot" (sigs. D3v-D4r). As a group, however, the multitude are terrifying (sigs. B2v-B4r, C3v-C4r). Their "barbarous mindes" have lead them not only to the "unnatural" act of revolt but to despoiling their own countrymen, as well as the Flemish (sig. C4v). In spite of their refrain that they will be lords every-one, their doctrine abolishes differences in degree and involves hatred of rich men, gentlemen, and lawyers. Their leaders, of course, like Shakespeare's Cade, assume supreme rule (sig. C3r). Their ideas are said to be those of John Ball, but to an Elizabethan they also might seem to repeat those Anabaptist beliefs that advocated a "communitie":

> But when *Adam* delued, and *Eue* span,
> Who was then a gentleman.
> Brethren brethren, it were better to haue this communitie,
> Than to haue this difference in degrees.
> But follow the counsell of *John Ball*
> I promise you I loue yee all:
> And make diuision equally,
> Of each mans goods indifferently. . . .
>
> (sig. A4r-v)

This dramatic exercise that would commemorate the heinousness of revolt is so uninspired that the inherited doggerel just quoted is the unhappy best of the play. By its premises, it anticipates such a composi-tion as Heywood's *Royal King and Loyal Subject* (1602-8), a play cited by modern students interested in the theory of divine right;[122] but Hey-wood also works with emphases derived from concepts of honor and justice. The treatment of history in *Jack Straw* would complement that in *Woodstock,* especially in the portrayal of Richard II, if the work had any dramatic value.

Of the structural movements noted in the introductory portion of this discussion, that which involves the rise and fall of a vicious individ-ual in the body politic has been mentioned only in passing. As it has been indicated, it appears frequently in Elizabethan drama and underlies the over-all development of the anonymous *True Tragedy of Richard III.* It also can be seen, for example, in the short dramatization of the final rise and fall of Mortimer in the last two acts of *Edward II.* As one might expect, in both instances the Wheel of Fortune is called to an audience's attention. Given the age's awareness of this concept, it would be especially suitable for the present discussion to consider the variation of the pyramidal pattern of rise and fall that might be effected when the story of a virtuous person was dramatized. As a result, *Sir Thomas More* would be most suitable—if one could be sure that this play was ever performed on the Elizabethan stage.[123] The emphasis of the drama, as well as its basic structural development, is specified clearly:

> *No, wife, be merie;—and be merie, all:*
> *You smilde at rising, weepe not at my fall.*
> Let's in, and heere ioy like to priuate freends,
> Since dayes of pleasure haue repentant ends:
> The light of greatness is with triumph borne:
> It sets at midday oft with publique scorne.
>
> (IV, iii, 90-95)

More, of course, is no villain; and given the "merie" conception of his character, his fall is so dramatized that it illustrates his fortitude and thereby avoids the sharp descent conventional to the pyramidal pattern. Three units roughly comparable in length appear in the manuscript as it has survived. More's rise results from his services to the commonwealth as they are focused upon his suppression of the ill May-day riot and are dramatized in some 890 lines.[124] More's fall, focused upon his fortitude and his refusal to retreat from the position he has taken, is dramatized in some 839 lines (IV, ii, until the end of the drama).[125] A third portion of comparable length involves humorous scenes, the majority of which appear after the dramatization of the result of the riot (III, ii, through IV, i).[126] Consequently, a symmetrical variation upon a conventional pattern seems to have been the basic design of the drama as the authors would represent the rise, the merry "rule," and the fall of a virtuous, though erring, subaltern in the body politic.

The artistry of individual scenes also shows a variation from what might be associated conventionally with the height of tragedy. This is specially true in the portion of the drama that shows More cast off from Fortune's Wheel. He gracefully puns upon his name during one of his farewells (IV, v, 176-89); and his kindness, as well as his sorrow at leaving his loved ones (V, ii, iii), is balanced with a wit whereby the old comic trick of imperviousness to punishment and execution is raised to a controlled tragic level:

> *Hang.* I beseech ye, my lord, forgiue me!
> *Moore.* Forgiue thee, honest fellowe! Why?
> *Hang.* For your death, my lord.

Moore. O, my death? I had rather it were in thy power of forgiue me, for thou hast the sharpest action against me; the lawe, my honest freend, lyes in thy hands now; hers thy fee [*His pursse*]; and, my good fellowe, let my suite be dispachte presently; for tis all one payne, to dye a lingering death, and to liue in the continuall mill of a lawe suite. But I can tell thee, my neck is so short, that, if thou shouldst behead an hundred noblemen like myselfe, thou wouldst nere get credit by it; therefore (looke ye, sir), doo it hansome-ly, or, of my woord, thou shalt neuer deale with me heerafter.

(V, iv, 94-110)

Although this development may remind one of the comedy in saints' lives that were elaborated so that the martyr's jests or his scorn toward his persecutor produced laughter,[127] in this instance a mean is struck and neither persecutor nor protagonist becomes ludicrous. Instead, the quiet humor of the scene accords with the final emphasis upon a quiet sorrow:

> . . . be it spoken without offence to any,
> A wiser or more vertuous gentleman
> Was never bred in England.
>
> (V, i, 9-11)

> A very learned woorthie gentleman
> Seales errour with his blood.
>
> (V, iv, 135-36)

> Lets sadly hence to perfect vnknowne fates,
> Whilste he tends prograce to the state of states.
>
> (V, iv, 137-38)

In other words, the author or authors apparently would arouse no satisfaction at More's death. His fall is retributive only because of his silent "errour,"[128] and, perhaps, implicitly, because More had chosen to mount Fortune's Wheel.[129] On the other hand, because of this error and because More was only a subaltern, he who wrote the scene apparently would avoid developing that combination of pathos and protest suitable to an illustrious one who had not been a thoroughgoing tyrant. In brief, even in a manuscript showing alterations, additions, and collaboration, there seem to be clear signs of a conscientious artistry;[130] and thus a brief notice of that artistry seems appropriate here, especially because of the Shakespearean Hand D.

The preceding analyses indicate how the structural movements that were described in the first portion of this chapter and that were related to certain types of character can be supplemented and illustrated by the artistry of Kyd, Marlowe, Greene, the anonymous author of *Woodstock,* and other playwrights. The emphasis has fallen, quite naturally, on Marlowe; and all of his dramas, with the exception of *2 Tamburlaine,* have been considered in greater or less detail. The precision underlying Kyd's *Spanish Tragedy,* as well as features of its structural pattern, is found in the portrayal of grotesque and fearsome Barabas. In a different vein, Marlowe develops the scenes of Bajazeth in captivity, but still with a mixture of that which is terrifying and comic. In *Edward II,* Marlowe's architectonic strength is especially noticeable, as is his effective use of the tradition of the lament that was associated with the fall of illustrious men. There one also finds the use of a morality pattern, the vitality of which is attested by both *James IV* and *Woodstock.* The technique, intent, and original artistry of this playwright are illumined also when one considers how he worked with current methods and concepts in writing the first part of *Tamburlaine.* Of the other plays considered here, *Woodstock* shows effective workmanship, and its author's ability to write comic scenes is striking. As its most recent editor has remarked, this drama is unusual in its representation of a revolt that was successful, unequivocally beneficent, and directed at a ruler who held the English throne by succession. Its process of thought is akin, however, to what can be found in *The Massacre at Paris, James IV,* and related plays, as well as in *Edward II.* In this last historical drama, Marlowe emphasizes successively two concepts in current political thought, each of which is developed separately in *Woodstock* and *Jack Straw.* Finally, Shakespeare's early plays also supplement what has been written in the introductory portion of this chapter. But inasmuch as all of his dramas through *Richard II* will be examined and attention will be focused at times upon his use of comedy, his early work is arranged in an order that is roughly chronological; thereby aspects of his development as a dramatist may also be illumined.

IV

Titus and the Earliest Comedies

PERHAPS THE MOST ordinary of critical commonplaces is the statement that when one turns from Shakespeare's dramas written after 1595-96 to his earlier plays, one is struck by the author's relative immaturity. Yet equally commonplace is the statement that from Shakespeare's earliest playwriting emerged the unique artistry of the later dramas. From this last point of view alone, a detailed study of his early work should be worthwhile. One can not assume, however, that immaturity from a modern point of view or from the point of view of the entire Shakespearean corpus would be considered immaturity in the early 1590's. In the late sixteenth century, criticism probably would be based upon the way in which an artist reflected the external objects of his day and the representational methods of his era; and as the preceding chapters have indicated, any reflection of external objects in the drama seems to be subordinate to the playwright's use of popular motifs, current concepts, and structural developments.[1] From this point of view, Shakespeare's plays through *Richard II* show such a skillful use of Elizabethan attitudes, ideas, and theatrical traditions that it would be difficult, if not impossible, to name any dramatist writing before 1596 who shows a greater skill and variety.

The preceding discussions established the nature of some methods used in creating laughter and the nature of some serious characters and structural movements that probably were familiar to author, actor, and regular theater-goer. The immediately preceding chapter also indicated the technique of some of Shakespeare's early contemporaries and the control that they exercised over their material. In the following pages, consequently, Shakespeare's use and control of the comic within the confines of the individual play will be examined. In addition, as *Titus Andronicus* and the early history plays are analyzed, it will be seen how Shakespeare also utilized the serious types of character and the structural patterns that have been noticed in the artistry of his contemporaries. So effectively does Shakespeare develop what was conventionally comic and serious that if he had stopped writing after 1593, his dramatic work still would have to be studied by anyone interested in the formative elements of Elizabethan drama. From about 1594 to about 1595-96, Shakespeare also wrote five plays, at least three of which are "for all time" rather than "of an age"; and in doing this he continued to work with concepts and methods that he had used already. Obviously, he developed his dramatic technique with a skill equal to the best of his contemporaries and with an equal originality.

One always should remember, moreover, that Shakespeare's plays were business ventures. If one feels sure of nothing else, one probably can believe that "the players praised Shakespeare"; and it is only logical to assume that the vast majority of his dramas were popular with contemporary audiences. For that matter, one might expect a dramatist's varied and skillful use of current traditions, both dramatic and non-dramatic, to be successful in the theater. Well after it was composed, *Titus Andronicus* was popular enough to be reflected in a sixteenth-century pen and ink drawing, and it probably was remembered by the audience of Jonson's *Bartholomew Fair*.[2] Neither the players nor Shakespeare, presumably, would have had it otherwise, even though Jonson would ridicule *Titus* along with Kyd's *The Spanish Tragedy*.

Certainly the beginning of *Titus* must have been interesting to Elizabethans. It develops a situation that may have had an element of familiarity, and soon thereafter the fact would have emerged clearly that the drama probably would show a theatrical vein of sophisticated brutality more striking than that of *The Spanish Tragedy*.[3] The argumentative conflict of the initial situation is handled pageantically to utilize the upper stage and opposite entrances, and such a beginning was probably appealing and familiar to any spectator who had watched open-air pageantry.[4] Emerging from this development, and startlingly noticeable, would be the killing and burial of Mutius. So too would have been the earlier sacrifice of Alarbus.[5] Vigorous action and bloodshed is well under way. At the same time, the death of Mutius, and possibly Titus' deafness to Tamora's plea that mercy be granted Alarbus, would be an early indication of the "Roman" honor that Shakespeare gives his protagonist, whose concern for public religion and for his public integrity smothers any softer instinct. In this respect, too, a sophisticated though naïve brutality would be apparent.[6]

Six bloody spectacles and the sorrowing speeches of the Andronici develop from the opening situation;[7] and equally characteristic of the horrifying nature of the play is Lavinia's revelation (IV, i) and the four "mad" incidents that follow (IV, ii, 1-28; iii; iv, 1-60; V, ii, 10 ff.). Also characteristic are the two foiled stratagems that are designed by the antagonists for their own safety and that lead to a nurse's sudden murder (IV, ii, 52 ff.), a near hanging (V, i), and a pseudo-allegorical episode of Revenge, Murder, and Rape (V, ii). This last development is merged with the fourth "mad" episode and leads to two throats cut by the mutilated Titus and blood caught in a basin by the mutilated Lavinia. All this, then, before the horrible banquet and the close of the play, which shows four corpses littering the stage. Obviously this dramatist was capitalizing upon the popularity of the tragedy of blood.

To a modern, if the players praised Shakespeare for this horror, they might seem as injudicious as Jonson felt them to be when they praised Shakespeare for never blotting a line. Yet when one considers this tragedy somewhat more closely, one can perceive that it is not uncontrolled. There also may have been other reasons for its popularity aside from the fact that its melodramatic and bloody spectacles reflect the primitive ruthlessness noted in the previous chapter.

Although its elaboration is naïve and devoted to the display of a bloody multiplicity, a basic structural precision and a unifying control is at work in *Titus Andronicus*. Lucius' going to the Goths (III, i, 284-301) signals the subsequent change in the direction of the play. With Lavinia's revelation (IV, i), it seems to accord with the development of an epitasis. Even more noticeable structurally is the pattern of passive protagonist and vicious antagonist, apparent also in *The Spanish Tragedy*. After Shakespeare's first act, the next major development comprises successful plots against Titus, including a representation of his tragic passion (Act III). There then follows the counter movement of a "distraught" Titus before the final scene is dramatized. Both developments are almost exactly equal in length (some 910 lines for the six scenes of Acts II and III; some 914 for the six scenes of Act IV, scene i, through Act V, scene ii). The result is a precise and original variation from Kyd's emphases.

The treatment of the protagonist is also interesting. Since the introductory development is controlled by Titus or focused upon him, Shakespeare avoids Kyd's tangential introduction of Hieronimo. Shakespeare's protagonist is not a relatively minor fingure at first. He is dominant and active. Because of this, and also in contrast with the treatment of Hieronimo, Shakespeare's play moves toward the ethical position of Seneca's *Thyestes*.[8] Although *Titus* is wronged by Saturninus, Titus' insistence upon the sacrifice of Alarbus wrongs Tamora. Like Kyd, however, Shakespeare achieves a differentiation between the opposed forces by the end of the first act. By means of the second spectacle of entombment in particular, Titus' "Roman" honor (e.g., ll. 341-86) contrasts with the concern for public "honour" and revenge given to

Saturninus (ll. 432-33) and with the secret villainy of Tamora's "honour" that effects a false resolution to the "honourable" conflicts just dramatized (ll. 436, 466, 476, 477).

Subsequently, although the tragic passion of Shakespeare's hero is shared with his brother Marcus (e.g., II, iv, 11-57), it appears less frequently than does Hieronimo's. In accordance with Titus' initial dominance and his Roman attributes, this franticness is also more controlled than that of Kyd's hero. Except for lines about the fly (III, ii, 52 ff.), it shows a florid development of figures of speech rather than a mad inconsequence.[9] Accordingly, even as they seem most illogical, Titus' "lunacy" and his "brain-sick humours," with considerable dramatic irony, become the means of entrapping his enemies (V, ii, 70-71, 21, 64-65, 84-85, 142-44).

Within its tradition, this treatment of the protagonist is not unskillful, although it carries with it the submergence of the efficient, vicious antagonist until the beginning of the second act. At that time, Aaron's first vicious stratagem begins the dramatization of what is to be avenged; and in accordance with Shakespeare's emphasis in the portrayal of Aaron, the plot is not linked causally with subsequent ones.[10] Yet although the vicious plots are not concatenated, they are balanced precisely against the subsequent events whereby the nature of the initial plot is revealed and Titus becomes an active figure once more.

Although in the portrayal of Aaron and in the development of certain episodic effects, Shakespeare's artistry seems to be closer to earlier dramatic traditions than does Kyd's,[11] yet this "crudest" of Shakespeare's plays also shows some noticeable affinities with the current academic tradition. In the latter part of the years 1589-92,[12] this learned feature of a horrific thriller might well have seemed a sign of excellence to players thirsty for popularity, for this aspect of the drama just might appeal to "the wiser sort," who otherwise might view playwriting with complete condescension.

In the initial development of the play, for example, the dialogue may have given the impression of classical speech that comes to rest upon sententious statements appropriate both to the Senecan concept of tragedy and to the present course of events.

> Fair lords, your fortunes are alike in all,
> That in your country's service drew your swords;
> But safer triumph is this funeral pomp,
> That hath aspir'd to Solon's happiness
> And triumphs over chance in honour's bed.

> (ll. 174-78)

... and thanks to men
Of noble minds is honourable meed.

(ll. 215-16)

... when I do forget
The least of these unspeakable deserts,
Romans, forget your fealty to me.

(ll. 255-57)

He lives in fame that died in virtue's cause.

(l. 390)

... ingratitude
Which Rome reputes to be a heinous sin. . . .

(ll. 447-48)

Though the scene emphasizes startling action, such lines bow, at least slightly, in the direction of Jonson's "fulnesse and frequencie of Sentence."[13]

Just as this introductory movement turns toward the ethical situation of Seneca's *Thyestes,* from which Shakespeare derived the device of the banquet, so Ovid's influence is constantly apparent in this play. *Titus* also shows Shakespeare's largest number of references to classical myth and legend.[14] Indeed, an educated spectator may have recognized that this play exaggerates both Seneca's controlled horror and Ovid's condensation of a heroic bloodiness in the later books of the *Metamorphoses*.[15] Equally interesting, moreover, is the way in which the Horatian verse that is used to indicate how Andronicus will revenge "worse than Progne" (V, ii, 196) is identified as one read "in grammar long ago" (IV, ii, 23). Indeed, the theatrical revelation of Aaron's first horrific invention, taken in part from classical myth, is based upon the fact that Ovid's *Metamorphoses* was an integral part of the English academic curriculum and read by schoolboys like young Lucius (IV, i, S-D).[16] Not without reason might these "learned" features of the play seem a notable part of a dramatic artistry that appears injudicious to a modern but that probably was attractive to an audience early in the 1590's. At least once, even vulgar spectators would have been reminded that they were hearing echoes of the current academic tradition, which differentiated the learned from the unlearned.

It is interesting to note, consequently, that while the Horation verse is derived explicitly from a "learned" background, the closeness between Titus' lying on the ground when overlooked in his plea and Hieronimo's digging the ground with his dagger is left to the regular theater-goer's memory (III, i, 1-22). So too is the closeness between Aaron's revela-

tion of his horrific deeds and the gleeful villainies of Barabas and Ithamore (V, i, 111-20, 125-44).[17]

Other aspects of the play also show a skill that is compatible with
what has been noted. In the first bloody stratagem against Titus, there
appears a technique that again may reflect current academic training.
When the linked plots against Lavinia and Bassianus and against
Quintus and Martius are to develop, one of the two speeches in the
introductory dialogue is soon balanced by a contrary development. As a
result, one is reminded of the current rhetorical tradition and even of
grammar-school exercises, which included the "thesis" with its description or praise of such contrary things as day and night.[18]

> My lovely Aaron, wherefore look'st thou sad
> When everything doth make a gleeful boast?
> The birds chant melody on every bush,
> The snake lies rolled in the cheerful sun;
> The green leaves quiver with the cooling wind
> And make a chequer'd shadow on the ground.
> Under their sweet shade, Aaron, let us sit,
> And, whilst the babbling echo mocks the hounds,
> Replying shrilly to the well-tun'd horns
> As if a double hunt were heard at once,
> Let us sit down and mark their yelping noise;
> And, after conflict such as was suppos'd
> The wand'ring prince and Dido once enjoy'd,
> When with a happy storm they were surpris'd
> And curtain'd with a counsel-keeping cave,
> We may, each wreathed in the other's arms,
> Our pastimes done, possess a golden slumber;
> Whiles hounds and horns and sweet melodious birds
> Be unto us as is a nurse's song
> Of lullaby to bring her babe asleep.
>
> (II, iii, 10-29)
>
> Have I not reason, think you, to look pale?
> These two have 'tic'd me hither to this place;
> A barren detested vale you see it is;
> The trees, though summer, yet forlorn and lean,
> O'ercome with moss and baleful mistletoe.
> Here never shines the sun; here nothing breeds,
> Unless the nightly owl or fatal raven;
> And when they show'd me this abhorred pit,
> They told me, here, at dead time of the night,

> A thousand swelling toads, as many urchins,
> Would make such fearful and confused cries
> As any mortal body hearing it
> Should straight fall mad, or else die suddenly.
> No sooner had they told this hellish tale
> But straight they told me they would bind me here
> Unto the body of a dismal yew,
> And leave me to this miserable death.
>
>   (ll. 91-108)

A vulgar audience probably would not be aware of the nature of rhetorical exercises, but the author undoubtedly was. Perhaps one is justified in again seeing an attempt to write in a manner that the educated spectator might relate to a tradition that included, once more, both Seneca and Ovid.

In addition, Shakespeare's development of particular situations is not at all unskillful—granted their horrific bases. Like other plays of the era, *The Spanish Tragedy* shows a constant awareness of the age's predilection for rhetoric; but *Titus* also shows poetic developments within its rhetorical process that are of interest even to one concerned with an unhistorical imagery. Consider the episode of the hand and the heads (III, i). The words and images of Titus' lying upon the ground (ll. 6-47) are carried over and intensified with appropriate variations in his first encounter with the mutilated Lavinia (ll. 59-135).[19] After another Kydian echo has been preceded by a thought that is dramatized fully with Aaron's entrance,[20] images of weeping and of water are intensified further with Aaron's exit[21]—until two heads and Titus' hand are brought on stage to be carried off in a gruesome but spectacular manner (ll. 280-83).

The two aspects of Shakespeare's artistry that have just been noted can be connected with the fact that throughout the drama the imagery is developed from a "like to" or an "as" so that it creates the effect of momentarily stopping the action by its elaboration,[22] just as the contrasting descriptions had. The lines when Martius is in the pit with the murdered Bassianus illustrate this:

> Upon his bloody finger he doth wear
> A precious ring that lightens all this hole,
> Which, *like a taper in some monument,*
> *Doth shine upon the dead man's earthy cheeks*
> *And shows the ragged entrails of this pit.*

> So pale did shine the moon on Pyramus
> When he by night lay bath'd in maiden blood.
>
> (II, iii, 226-32)

Marcus' astonishment at the sight of the mutilated Lavinia also involves images that are developed briefly, but almost for their own sake:

> Alas, a crimson river of warm blood,
> Like to a bubbling fountain stirr'd with wind,
> Doth rise and fall between thy rosed lips. . . .
> And, notwithstanding all this loss of blood,
> As from a conduit with three issuing spouts,
> Yet do thy cheeks look red as Titan's face
> Blushing to be encount'red with a cloud.
>
> (II, iv, 22-32)

This imagery reinforces the more noticeable effect of such speeches as the sensuous dialogue between Tamora and Aaron (II, iii, 10-50); Tamora's description of a "barren detested vale"; or even the tableau-like situation in the stage groupings of the first vicious plot, when an audience also was reminded of a similar picture earlier in the play (II, iii, 163-65). Since *Titus* shows a greater emphasis on bloody spectacles than does *The Spanish Tragedy* or *The Jew of Malta,* such halting flowers of rhetoric seem to accord with the relatively static effect of successive tableau-like scenes of horror. For that matter, this aspect of the imagery is also in harmony with obvious features of Shakespeare's portrayal of Aaron.

In comparison with *The Spanish Tragedy, Titus Andronicus* has a tangential beginning as far as the efficient, vicious antagonist is concerned. In spite of the few introductory lines about revenge (I, i, 449-55; II, i, 23-24, 121), that motif and the basic pattern of the drama begin to emerge only with Aaron's appearance in the second act. At the same time, in spite of Saturninus' sudden passion for Tamora, the motif of lust is developed explicitly for the first time; and since it is tangential to that of revenge, it seems compatible, on a larger scale, with those rhetorical flowers that are tangential to the main thought of the speeches in which they occur. Even more to the immediate point, perhaps, is the lack of concatenation in Aaron's villainies; for, as a result, they are essentially unexpected and thereby congruent in a structural sense with the imagistic effect noted above.

Also because of this last fact, because of Aaron's loose causal connection with revenge, and because of his blackness and his short mocking lines, the appearance of Shakespeare's villain probably stirred up memories of the devilish vice, who, in Jonson's words, had appeared "t'aduance the cause of *Hell*."[23] The role of Aaron, indeed, must have seemed a good deal closer to an earlier dramatic tradition than did that of the courtly Lorenzo or of the wealthy, Machiavellian Barabas. The need for secrecy, which motivated Lorenzo's series of plots, for example, is expressed by Aaron only in the most general of considerations about "an Emperor's court" and "the house of Fame," and then it is related simply to the "squaring" of Demetrius and Chiron over their lust for Lavinia (II, i, 126 ff.). Not until the birth of Aaron's child, that is, not until Shakespeare develops a seventh bloody spectacle, is a need for secrecy about the major lust of Tamora and Aaron emphasized (e.g., IV, ii, 144-45, iv, 37-38). In a similar manner, although an audience knows that villainy is being prepared, the nature of the first double plot, that of the pit and the mutilation, becomes clear only as it is dramatized. The same is essentially true, and certainly dramatically so, for the second scheme of the hand and heads. It is anticipated only in four words of a brief aside (III, i, 203). The murder of the nurse is almost entirely unexpected (IV, ii). Only Aaron's plan to use Muli and his wife is mentioned, and then it is not represented (IV, ii, 150 ff.). As a result, Aaron's motivation throughout the play is essentially that of diabolical-ness *per se;* and no soliloquy specifies concatenated stratagems. For any summation of villainies, one waits for the speeches of Aaron that remind one of dialogue between Barabas and Ithamore. At that time, in contrast to the motivation of Barabas' plots that are dramatized, deviltry is its own excuse:

> I pried me through the crevice of a wall
> When, for his hand, he had his two son's heads;
> Beheld his tears, and laugh'd so heartily
> That both mine eyes were rainy like to his. . . .
>
> (V, i, 114-17)

The concluding lines of the speech, indeed, depart completely from the events of the play:

> Even now I curse the day—and yet, I think,
> Few come within the compass of my curse—
> Wherein I did not some notorious ill,
> As kill a man, or else devise his death,
> Ravish a maid, or plot the way to do it,
> Accuse some innocent and forswear myself,
> Set deadly enmity between two friends,
> Make poor men's cattle break their necks,

Set fire on barns and hay-stacks in the night,
And bid the owners quench them with their tears.
Oft have I digg'd up dead men from their graves
And set them upright at their dear friends' door,
Even when their sorrow almost was forgot;
And on their skins, as on the bark of trees,
Have with my knife carved in Roman letters,
"Let not your sorrow die, though I am dead."
Tut, I have done a thousand dreadful things
As willing as one would kill a fly,
And nothing grieves me heartily indeed
But that I cannot do ten thousand more.

(ll. 125-44)

Certainly this vicious antagonist is an "incarnate devil" (V, i, 40); and his theatrical appeal, including the disjunction of his mocks, may well have exceeded the appeal of a Lorenzo simply because of Aaron's exaggerated emergence from a popular tradition.[24] But the result, as has been indicated, is generally that of startling episodic spectacles, congruent, in a structural sense, with what can be noticed constantly in the drama.

In addition, other situations in *Titus* are essentially episodic or tangential to the main line of action. The braving between Demetrius and Chiron is caused by lust, not revenge. Although the baiting of Tamora, with comments on her gift of "horning" (II, iii, 51-88), starts the murder of Bassianus, it nevertheless halts the development of the immediate stratagem. A similar effect is produced by the hunting scene (II, ii), by Titus' lying upon the ground (III, i, 1-48), and by the episodes involving the clown.[25] In the last stratagem of the vicious antagonists, not only is the form of Tamora's "enchantment" unknown before it is dramatized (IV, iv, 88 ff.), but it is developed into a little episode of disguise and then is defeated by the spectacle of throats being cut on stage.

Although firmly embedded in the basic movement of protagonist versus vicious antagonist, these halting, episodic, and digressive effects appear throughout *Titus*—from images, speeches, and brief groupings of characters to the larger sequence of horrors. In this respect, the artistry of the play seems purposeful in its consistency, especially since Shakespeare exercised the greatest freedom in choosing material to dramatize. Indeed, the basic pattern of the drama exists within two relatively brief emphases that accord with the preceding effect but at the same time reinforce the unifying impression produced by that same basic pattern.

The initial situation was concerned with the rule of Rome, and the problem was carried over to develop Act I after funeral pomp first held the stage. In the remainder of the drama, Tamora's revenge was related briefly to Rome, Rome was censured briefly by Titus as "a wilderness of tigers," and public considerations alternated with the clown scenes and the near-hanging of Aaron as the fourth act ended and the fifth began.[26] An emphasis comparable to the initial one appears, however, after Saturninus has been killed. Then Shakespeare returns to the concerns of "sad-fac'd men, people and sons of Rome, / By uproars sever'd" (V, iii, 67-68). This speech and the following ones probably were delivered from the upper stage; and this account of the preceding course of events leads to "Lucius, all hail, Rome's royal Emperor!"—whereupon Lucius promises to rule beneficently, "To heal Rome's harms and wipe away her woe" (ll. 141, 147-48). A pathetic incident (some 27 lines) and a villainous one (some 25 lines) return to the major emphasis of the drama. But the preceding lines with their oratorical process (some 82 in all) have returned to the matter and the manner of the initial situation. Thereby Shakespeare delimits his play. Two kindred emphases, and probably a return to a stage picture reminiscent of the earliest one, produce a brief framing effect for the major succession of horrors. Such an effect, presumably, was noticeable. At any rate, if Shakespeare did not, another person "tagged" this fact for the closing lines of the drama:

> See justice done on Aaron, that dam'd Moore,
> By whom our heavy haps had their beginning.
> Then, afterwards, to order well the state,
> That like events may ne'er it ruinate.
>
> (ll. 201-4)

By these brief emphases at the beginning and the end of the drama, there is effected a judgement or a rectifying conclusion in a context wider than that of the struggle itself.[27] The effect is comparable to conclusions in both the miracle and the morality.[28] Between those similar emphases an audience would see a succession of scenes developed in an Elizabethan vein of sophisticated brutality but showing, in their episodic effects and in their principal antagonist, dramatic features that also were close to those same earlier traditions. In doing so, *The Most Lamentable Tragedie of Titus Andronicus* might well have satisfied a taste for multiplicity in unity.

As a result, one can perceive some good reasons for the popularity of this drama. The glaring horrors of a Kydian tradition are merged with aspects of the current scene and an earlier drama. Not all of those reasons, however, are devoid of artistic considerations. *Titus* reflects the age's interest in its academic discipline. Precision in the construction of the play is noticeable. A cohesive artistry appears both within and between the development of its episodic emphases.

Even more noticeable features of a dramatic artistry that would effect both unity and multiplicity are apparent in Shakespeare's earliest histories and in the framing device of his *Comedy of Errors*. This last drama also shows the vitality that the academic tradition had for a beginning playwright. In *Titus,* this vitality is apparent in the frequent use of classical myth and legend, in the closeness of incidents to Seneca's *Thyestes,* and in the intermittent echoes of the manner and the curriculum of Elizabethan schools; but in the first of Shakespeare's comedies, the academic discipline of the age provides the design for the entire play, both as *The Comedy of Errors* is derived from classical drama and as its development is controlled by precepts about five-act structure. Furthermore, to the well-educated spectator, this comedy might seem to effect a pleasing Terentian variation upon a multiple Plautine source; for Shakespeare matches each Antipholus with a woman.[29]

In contrast with *Titus Andronicus,* however, there are no situations and no lines in *The Comedy of Errors* that specifically indicate for uneducated spectators that they are encountering in the vulgar theater matter that could be found in the schools. Yet such a difference should not be emphasized, for a classical note appears intermittently throughout the comedy from the time that the duke and hapless Ægeon set the milieu and Shakespeare writes a *narratio* about two converging ships "making amain," "Of Corinth that, of Epidaurus this" (I, i, 93-94).

In addition, the mystery and glamour of the world from "farthest Greece" "through the bounds of Asia" comes to rest with increasing emphasis upon Ephesus, a town of "nimble jugglers that deceive the eye," "Dark-working sorcerers," "Soul-killing witches" (I, i, 133-35, ii, 97-102). With memories of the New Testament, and with the Elizabethans' belief in possession and witchcraft, this aura of mystery would heighten at first the dramatic irony in what will become a comic repetitive pattern that achieves multiplicity primarily by heaping up incidents of the same mistaken identities.[30] For this motif and the general course of the action, Shakespeare was indebted, of course, to Plautus' *Menæchmi.*

The preceding remarks obviously lead to a closer examination of Shakespeare's artistry, and a suitable beginning can be made by noticing how the structure of this play is derived from concepts about the parts of a comedy as they were elucidated by Renaissance scholars. Getting the Syracusans into the house of Antipholus of Ephesus is the narrative focal point of the protasis (Acts I and II). The development of the complications then follows in the epitasis (Acts III and IV). Its narrative focal point is the binding of "mad" Antipholus of Ephesus. Out of this last incident develops the forward movement to the catastrophe. By a detailed use of the *Andria* formula, Shakespeare controls his non-classical multiplicity.[31]

The appearances of Ægeon at the beginning and the end of the play also give unity to the drama. In contrast with the political emphasis of *Titus,* the fate of Ægeon is not woven into the latter part of the main action; and thus Shakespeare's use of that brief narrative appears to be an even more obvious structural device than does his development of opening and closing emphases in his tragedy. This feature of the artistry of *The Comedy of Errors* gives added point to similar developments in other plays by Shakespeare and seems to confirm the unifying intent of the initial and final situations in *Titus.* On this score alone, one would like to know whether *The Comedy of Errors* preceded or followed the tragedy, but one can not be sure of the priority of the dramas even if one ascribes to the attractive date of 1589 for the composition of the comedy.[32]

In this respect, however, attention should be given to the change in tone between the farcical emphasis of *The Comedy of Errors* and its serious framing device that involves a perilous circumstance. Too great an emphasis upon the latter might well mitigate the comedy of mistaken identity. Thus it is pertinent to note that Ægeon is not called to an audience's attention after the opening lines of Act II (i, 1-8). Although the clock ticks in this drama, it ticks explicitly toward dinner, five o'clock, supper, and night—not explicitly toward the fact and hour of Ægeon's possible death.[33] Even the two sequences on time arise from the comic jesting and lead into farcical action. The first sequence is resolved by a series of puns that ends with "a bald conclusion" and with the appearance of angry women (II, ii, 65-111). The second sequence is resolved by puns about a sergeant turning back an "hour [pronounced as was "whore"] in a day" and is followed by a hasty exit (IV, ii, 51-63). With crowded action building repetitiously upon an audience's expectation of another mistake, the return to seriousness when a "five o'clock" finally is joined to a "melancholy" "place of death" must have been largely unexpected (V, i, 118-22). The "great thing forgot" in a welter of puns and compounded confusion must have been only faintly liminal at the best. The skill of a beginning playwright is obvious, however. Without mitigating the comic for an audience, he has delimited a play neatly; and his apparent desire to achieve an impression of unity through the use of Ægeon is certainly justifiable in the light of the multiplicity from Act I through Act V.

By Shakespeare's treatment of his mistakes, the comic intent of the drama would be realized during performance, and his skill in developing this aspect of the multiplicity in Elizabethan drama is especially worthy of attention.[34] Antipholus and Dromio of Syracuse are the first twins to appear, and thus a confusion centering about this Antipholus is developed immediately in some 65 lines that close the first act. That confusion is enlarged in the latter part of the next scene, when Dromio of Ephesus reports to Adriana and Luciana (II, i, 44-116). It is repeated, with Dromio of Syracuse, in the entire subsequent scene. The first part of the third act then dramatizes a confusion centering about Antipholus of Ephesus (III, i). The second part of this act, however, dramatizes a triple confusion centering about Antipholus of Syracuse (III, ii). There is first the wooing of Luciana (ll. 1-70), then Dromio of Syracuse's report about his being mistaken (ll. 71-169), and then the delivery of the chain by Angelo (ll. 170-90). After that, there follows a confusion centering about Antipholus of Ephesus once more (IV, i). After another scene involving the women and a Dromio (this time of Syracuse), Shakespeare continues to dramatize alternating confusions. One centering about Antipholus of Syracuse (IV, iii) is followed by one centering about Antipholus of Ephesus (IV, iv, 1-146). As this last situation is concluded, another confusion is begun by the appearance of Antipholus of Syracuse. This carries over into the next two groupings of characters in the fifth act: that involvnig Angelo and the second merchant, and that involving the women and the supernumeraries (V, i, 1-32, 33-37). An interlude is effected by Adriana's appeal to the abbess and to the duke (ll. 38-167). This is stopped by the appearance of the messenger and then by a confusion caused by Antipholus and Dromio of Ephesus. The duke attempts to discern the facts with only one Antipholus and Dromio before him. After three false starts,[35] the two pairs of twins appear face to face.

When the duke attempts to straighten out the situation, the basic confusion centered about the Antipholi have been eight (counting as one that which extends from Act I to Act II, as well as that which extends from Act IV to Act V): Antipholus of Syracuse (I, ii)—Antipholus of Syracuse (II, i, ii)—Antipholus of Ephesus, Antipholus of Syracuse (III, i, ii)—Antipholus of Ephesus, Antipholus of Syracuse, Antipholus of Ephesus, Antipholus of Syracuse (IV, i, iii, iv, 1-46, 147-162)— Antipholus of Syracuse, Antipholus of Ephesus (V, i, 1-37, 190-255). While each incident tends to become more complicated, the first stretches through the protasis, two confusions appear within the third act, and three within the fourth act, plus another sequence begun as the fourth act closes and continued as the last act opens. Obviously Shakespeare wished to increase progressively the confusion that he also has compounded by twin servants until its greatest complication would be developed in the fourth act and lead into the catastrophe.[36] An audience's anticipation of comic confusion would be realized fully, even as an awareness of the probability of its resolution might increase.

Especially at the end of Act IV and in Act V, Shakespeare also elaborates the basic dramatic irony by developing situations wherein one character's account of events is confirmed at first by another character but then denied by the same figure. The technique is anticipated briefly at the end of the second act, becomes especially noticeable as the third confusion in the fourth act is dramatized, appears at the beginning of the fifth act, and is developed fully as the duke attempts to discover the truth.[37] As a consequence, this aspect of mistaken identity also is elaborated progressively as the confrontation of twin with twin approaches.

During this comic process, word-play is emphasized, although it is, in general, subordinate to the increasing confusion. Probably Shakespeare derived this aspect of the comic from his classical sources, although Elizabethans delighted in verbal ingenuity and in the way a sentence could be "but a chev'ril glove to a good wit." In his *Nine Days Wonder,* Kemp imitated the punning of dramatists with a result that to the modern seems as wooden as the majority of the jests that Manningham noted in his diary.[38] Although the punning in *The Comedy of Errors* may seem barren, the drama certainly would capitalize upon the fact that in equivocating word-play the "toe of the peasant" came "near the heels of our courtier."

Although punning may be emphasized, Shakespeare also reflects the popular merriment of his era. As the protasis is developed, a shrewish wife appears. So do complaints about marriage and a profligate husband (II, i, 32-41, 87-101, etc.). At this time, there occurs a miming speech, which is given to the character who at the moment is the chief comic.[39] Both before and after Dromio of Ephesus is on the stage, the speeches of Luciana and Adriana are developed so that the scene might appear to carry on an argument between patience and jealousy in a "pleasant manner dialogue wise." Adriana's shrewishness, which is here most noticeable during the sequence with Dromio, is then mitigated (II, i, 58, 78, 81-85, ii, 112 ff.). Nevertheless, these scenes are closer than is anything in Plautus' *Menæchmi* to the noisy representation of that female attribute in one of the most widespread of comic motifs. In the later scene, Shakespeare also develops another dialogue so that it approaches the wit-combat (II, ii, 66-110). In it, the comedian maintains a statement with jests against an interrogator who would resolve the theme to naught. One is reminded of what was said to be Tarleton's forte, not simply in the elaboration of a theme but also in trading jests with his audience. In both of the conversations with the Dromios, Luciana begins to take part in the merriment (II, i, 69, ii, 195-96, 201). This tendency will be emphasized in the succeeding scene (III, i), and thereby the witty maid of Shakespeare's later plays is adumbrated faintly.

When viewed against current Elizabethan merriment, this last scene is especially interesting. The central situation is taken from Plautus' *Amphitruo* and dramatizes the exclusion of a husband and a servant because a "husband" and a "servant" are already at home. The incident is preceded by sententious dialogue between Balthazar and Antipholus of Ephesus and is followed by a similar dialogue that continues Luciana's theme of patience (III, i, 22-29, 85 ff.). In this contrasting setting, the episode from *Amphitruo* is developed so that overtones of the jig must have been noticeable to any spectator. Witness the rhyming and the anapestic and dipodic meter that accords with a rollicking situation:

> But, soft! my door is lock'd. Go bid them let us in.
> *Dro. E.* Maude, Bridget, Marian, Cicely, Gillian, Ginn!
> *Dro. S.* [*Within*] Mome, malt-horse, capon, coxcomb,
>   idiot, patch!
> Either get thee from the door or sit down at the hatch.
>
> (ll. 30-33)

Including word-play, especially on "ass,"—matter picked up from Luciana's last speech with a Dromio—the episode is complicated progressively. With the line given Antipholus of Ephesus (l. 38), dialogue between Dromio of Ephesus and his twin is enlarged for three participants. With that given Luciana (l. 48), it is enlarged for four. Then it is enlarged for six, with Luciana excluded but Adriana, Balthazar, and Angelo included (l. 61 ff.). As part of the word-play, a reflection of the conventional lechery of the principal comic figure develops with mistaken and purposeful name-calling (ll. 31-35). Proverbs, which Dromio of Syracuse had been using in the second act, develop bawdily and are exchanged between Luciana and the servants (ll. 51-53).[40] Laughter at scurrility, comparable to some in older comedy, breaks out briefly (ll. 75-76).[41] Finally, in five instances, choric comments on the humor of the situation are given to the doubled role for the principal comic actor (ll. 50, 53, 56, 62, 65). Here certainly, although the basic *inventio* is classical, the comic manner is compatible with constant features of Elizabethan merriment.

This reflection of current mirth, which had been anticipated in the second act, continues through the rest of the third act and into the fourth. A gentleman's wooing that is mistaken by a maid and ends with her doubly ironic comment (III, ii, 70) is followed by a servant's report of his being wooed by a mistaken foul wench, and her ugliness is anatomized. With this parallelism in wooing, the emphasis falls upon what was embedded firmly in the laughter and hilarity of the era.[42] As a result, Nell and her actions, even by report, are conceived with a surer comic touch than sometimes has been credited to the beginning Shakespeare. In the fourth act, although the emphasis declines, conventional matter in ephemeral songs is reflected in the lament and in the cursing of love during the dialogue between the women (IV, ii, 1-28). Current mirth is reflected also in the derisive puns on buff jerkins (IV, ii, 32-45, iii, 13-33)—one of whom has appeared already. Punning on "hours"-"whores" continues (IV, ii, 55-62); and a whore will appear in the focal point of the epitasis (IV, iii, 45 ff.). Like the "sergeant of the band," she then becomes the subject for a brief witty theme by the chief comic (IV, iii, 51-58, 61 ff.).

Except for humor at the expense of Doctor Pinch, probably acted by Sincklo (e.g., V, i, 168-77, 237-45),[43] and except for the abbess' turn of the tables to condemn Adriana's shrewishness (V, i, 44-86), in the latter part of the drama beatings and word-play again make up the principal incidental comedy. It is revealing, indeed, that after the confusions have been resolved and even as the play closes, instead of utilizing matter akin to Elizabethan merriment, Shakespeare extends once more his Plautine mistakings by having Dromio of Syracuse and Antipholus of Ephesus momentarily mistaken all over again (V, i, 408-11). Although the device is well conceived as a brief echo of previous confusions now solvable and as a lingering, repetitive trick for laughter, it indicates what the total artistry of the play also indicates, namely, that Shakespeare here relies heavily upon his classical sources. Even when the epitasis was being developed in the third act, word-play, which accords with Plautus' practice, was rampant; and in spite of what has just been noted, Tudor merriment is not developed as fully in this comedy as it had been in the earlier, and much simpler, academic comedies by Udall and by "Mr. S."[44]

Nevertheless, within its academic skill and within its emphasis upon mistaken identities, the comic intent and touch of *The Comedy of Errors* is sure, knowledgeable, and at times similar to what has been noted about the portrayal of Thurio. Thereby the precision of academic comedies and of Lyly's plays is attuned vigorously to the public acting of an adult comedy.

By Shakespeare's use of the story of Ægeon and Æmilia, moreover, the scope of his play becomes wider than that of his classical sources. In this respect, *The Comedy of Errors* shows a slight kinship with Lyly's comedies, which constantly develop a thematic interest. After all identities have been established, the duke forgives the ransom necessary to save Ægeon's life. This contrasts with the fact that when the play began, even though the duke's "soul" would "sue as advocate" for Ægeon, this ruler was convinced that "passed sentence" could not be recalled but to his "honour's great disparagement" (I, i, 146, 148-49). To the reunion of a family and the consequent readjustment of the society of the play-world, Shakespeare adds the ruler's readjustment to retaliation in kind upon all merchants from Syracuse—an action the duke had considered essential because of his "laws," "crown," "oath," and "dignity" (I, i, 143-44).

One should do no more than note this oblique comment on the conduct of rulers. Just as the occasional didacticism of the play is subordinate to its laughter, so the duke's remission of the ransom is but part of the alignment of the play-world as it ought to be. This act of mercy, moreover, is followed by Shakespeare's final extension of his comic confusions. The thematic lines in *The Comedy of Errors* are interesting, nevertheless—especially the final ones.[45] Such a tendency is developed fully in *The Two Gentlemen of Verona.*

In this second comedy to be considered here, there is neither the framing emphasis of *Titus Andronicus* nor the framing device of *The Comedy of Errors.* Instead, the circumvention of faithless or stultified figures and the circumvention of a ruler's rigid dignity are effected by what has been spoken of throughout the drama. In this respect, *The Two Gentlement of Verona* is much closer to Lyly's thematic dramas than is *The Comedy of Errors;* but closer, for example, to his *Alexander and Campaspe* than to his *Endymion* or his *Midas.*[46]

The thematic interest of *The Two Gentlemen* deserves initial attention; for that feature of the comedy indicates, once more, how Shakespeare's dramas, or portions of his dramas, are animated by relatively sophisticated concepts derived from what was considered to be worthwhile. Instead of reflecting aspects of the academic curriculum, however, in *The Two Gentlemen* Shakespeare turned to a widespread belief in the virtue of a true gentility and in the discipline by which it could be achieved. This concept had appeared in earlier interludes, in academic dramas, and in plays written for boy companies;[47] and it was thoroughly conventional to nondramatic literature of the sixteenth century. That the play never has had its sources delineated completely can probably be attributed to the fact that this concept and the narrative motifs of the drama were so widespread that they were almost universal.[48]

As many critics have pointed out, one of the ideas in the play, namely, the importance of friendship, is used so blatantly in the catastrophe that the "unhappy" happy ending seems to be a sign of the experimental nature of *The Two Gentlemen* and hence of its early date.[49] No one can quarrel with those conclusions. Certainly here, if anywhere in Shakespeare's work, is apparent the reflection, rather than the interpretation, of a current concept. Yet such criticism emphasizes Valentine's relinquishment of his love Sylvia rather than Shakespeare's larger emphasis upon the worth of a true discipline that alone can validate the importance of friendship.[50] In this broader light, the last act of the drama may have been viewed by Shakespeare's contemporaries, with as much attention being given to the duke's conviction that Valentine is "worthy of an empress' love" (V, iv, 141) as to the hero's relinquishment of Sylvia.

In other words, from a true "vertue" springs Valentine's repudiation of a false friend, Julia's denunciation of inconstancy, their acceptance of repentence, and the renewal of friendship. This virtue motivates not simply the emphasis upon constancy in this portion of the drama (V, iv, 110-15) but also the duke's conviction, which finally resolves all difficulties. Even the motif of repentence and its potential melodrama is controlled by the sophisticated concept embodied in Valentine's actions. The hero shows an "unrival'd merit." He is a "gentleman and well deriv'd" (ll. 144-46). When one remembers that the origins of gentility were said to reside in the noble acts of one's ancestors, the duke's oath by which he expresses his conviction is, quite fittingly, by "the honour" of his "ancestry" (l. 139). Belief in the worth of a Renaissance gentility also underlies the duke's recall of the other outlaws (ll. 150-59). And although it is at first naïvely expressed by the question, "Have you the tongues" (IV, i, 33), the same consideration, that is, the power of Valentine's good parts and discipline, had led the outlaws to make him their captain. He is

> . . . beautified
> With goodly shape . . .
> A linguist and a man of such perfection
> As we [the outlaws] do in our quality much want. . . .
>
> (IV, i, 55-58)

One needs only to remember Sidney's constant emphasis, Elyot's *Governor,* or Lyly's *Euphues* to realize that Shakespeare is utilizing the contemporary humanists' belief in the worth of a disciplined gentility.[51]

Facets of this concept appear elsewhere in the play, especially in speeches at the beginning of the protasis and in the later development of the epitasis.[52] As the play begins, the idea is enunciated that travel to "see the wonders of the world abroad" will keep youth from "shapeless idleness" and from "living dully sluggardiz'd at home" (II, i, 1-10). By travel, one "hunts" honor (I, i, 63), particularly if he is attached to an important court. The idea is returned to in Panthino's counsel about Proteus. Some sons, even of parents who have but a "slender reputation," seek "preferment" abroad:

> Some to the wars, to try their fortune there;
> Some to discover islands far away;
> Some to the studious universities.   (I, iii, 8-10)

At Milan, Proteus, like his friend Valentine, will

> . . . practice tilts and tournaments,
> Hear sweet discourse, converse with noblemen,
> And be in eye of every exercise
> Worthy his youth and nobleness of birth.[53]
>
> (I, iii, 30-33)

Although friendship and love overshadow these accomplishments in Milan, the value of foreign residence, which was included usually in discussions of a desirable discipline, has been used to inaugurate a development from which conventional motifs suitable to comedy will emerge.

Shakespeare, nevertheless, continues to remind his audience about the larger concept of gentility. Although the irony of the situation will become apparent as the play develops, in the second act Valentine enunciates this courtly ideal in his discription of Proteus as one who is young in years but old in experience. With "head unmellow'd" but with "judgement ripe," he is an individual who has made "use and fair advantage of his days." He is "complete" not only "in feature" but also "in mind" and already has "all good grace to grace a gentleman" (II, iv, 62-74). This praise confirms the duke's acceptance of Valentine's friend as one "worthy for an empress' love" and "meet to be an emperor's counsellor" (ll. 76-77). Also with considerable irony directed at Proteus, Shakespeare has this faithless character accept the disguised Julia as a servant chiefly because her face and behavior "Witness good bringing up, fortune, and truth" (IV, iv, 72-74). Quite fittingly Valentine is to be slandered

With falsehood, cowardice, and poor descent,
Three things that women highly hold in hate.

(III, ii, 32-33)

In such a light, Proteus' faithlessness is adumbrated by his admission that
love has made him neglect his studies, lose his time, "War with good
counsel, set the world at naught" (I, i, 63-69).

As the epitasis moves toward its focal point, both Sylvia and the
outlaws, like the spectators, are aware of what constitutes true worth.
Sylvia condemns Proteus (e.g., IV, ii), while the outlaws accept Valentine and value his "honourable mind" (IV, i, 55-58; V, iii, 13). This
heroine also turns to Sir Eglamour because he is "a gentleman," "valiant,
wise, remorseful, well accomplish'd." As such a one, he also knows
that Sylvia's love and grievance "virtuously are placed" (IV, iii, 38).
Sylvia, too, is a "virtuous gentlewoman, mild and beautiful," as even
the jealous Julia admits (IV, iv, 185).

In other words, Shakespeare once more gives to a drama for the
popular stage the color of what was considered to be a worthwhile
sophistication. The constant brief reminders of a Sidneyesque gentility
accord with the beginning and the ending of the play and also with the
third form that the basic concept takes here. Not only is the "gentle"
Valentine successful in courtship, but his advice apparently is sought
in such a matter by the duke himself (III, i). The duke believes in the
true ability of Proteus and wishes him to coach Thurio in courtly conduct so that Thurio can win Sylvia's love (III, ii). The conventional
nature of this development, in the milieu of honor learned and won by
intercourse with foreigners and by counseling a ruler (II, iv, 77), needs
little comment. Although wooing obviously was not as important as
serving a state, counseling a prince, entertaining ambassadors, or being
constant in friendship, it, too, could demonstrate a disciplined gentility.
As might be expected in a comedy, it is part of the essential matter of
the play.[54] As a result, what Panthino has called "sweet discourse"
takes the particular form of courtship during the second and third acts.
Viewing the drama in such a light, the sophisticated spectator may well
have admired the author's "pregnant dexteritie of wit" and his felicitous
"invention."

In the beginning of the drama, then, love has been balanced against
a sixteenth-century discipline, and then is placed in tension with friendship; and from this latter situation arises the motif of the swearing and
forswearing of undisciplined individuals when the "mighty lord" Love
holds sway (II, iv, 136). The power of love and the value of friendship
were conventional topics. Witness Elizabethan sonneteering, including

Shakespeare's, and the fact that Cooper considered the theme of friendship and love to be suitable in England's academies. When the future Bishop of Winchester advertised his Latin-English *Thesaurus,* he pointed out that if the studious young man wished to write on love and friendship, he could choose two or three words—*amicus, amo, amor*—and by considering the words derived from them and the phrases belonging to them, he would find nothing "partaining to the matter, but that he shall be able copiously to vtter it."[55]

In view of the basic concept with which Shakespeare is working, it is not surprising that Proteus' violation of his oaths of friendship is represented in a manner conventional to the vicious plotter or the rising villain, although his soliloquies are modified, by position and content, to accord with the lesser matter of comedy (II, iv, 191-214; II, vi). In a similar manner, Valentine's banishment is phrased in language suitable to the duke's important court:

> Why Phaëthon—for thou art Merop's son,—
> Wilt thou aspire to guide the heavenly car
> And with thy daring folly burn the world?
> Wilt thou reach stars, because they shine on thee?
> Go, base intruder! overweening slave!
> Bestow thy fawning smiles on equal mates,
> And think my patience, more than thy desert,
> Is privilege for thy departure hence.[56]

> (III, i, 153-60)

The soundness of Shakespeare's conception also can be illustrated by noticing another obvious feature of this drama. Because of Proteus' faithlessness, he becomes involved in rival wooing; and that motif is elaborated also by the fact that the duke and Thurio are another pair of friends (III, i, 62). Indeed, the ruler's pose of being an old, incompetent wooer (III, i, 81-88) agrees with the actions of Thurio, whose protrayal reflects a comic feature of current rival wooing. Shakespeare then joins this motif with the transvestite theme (III, ii; IV, ii).[57] Thereby two pairs of thwarted lovers appear, with one woman unloved but loving the man who is unloved but loving. When this last wooer (Proteus) verges in manner toward the rising villain, the third character who is unloved but loving (Thurio) becomes thoroughly ridiculous. Finally, the unloved-loving sequence is resolved when outlaws who liken themselves to Robin Hood's men control the action (IV, i, 36-37). In other words, although it is developed about a sophisticated, well-known concept, the drama also has overtones akin to elaborated folk play and ballad; and constantly a comedian holds the stage with sequences that in every instance show comic elements probably familiar to all theater-going Elizabethans.

Just as the first dialogue that puns on musical terms recalls for an audience the popular tune "Light o'love" (I, ii, 83), so in scenes involving Launce and Speed, Shakespeare's artistry is close to the probable expectations of his spectators, whether or not they realized that these servants were drawn from the witty slave of Roman comedy. At the same time, those comic sequences, with one exception, parallel the affairs of Valentine and Proteus or provide an antic variation upon aspects of their scenes.

Even the exception is a consequence of Proteus' wooing and shows a loose causal relationship with the affairs of the masters. Because of Launce's stupidity and negligence, Proteus engages the disguised Julia: "'tis no trusting to yond foolish lout" (IV, iv, 71). The sequence apparently explains Launce's specific stupidity (ll. 1-42). Although it is not related closely to what has just been dramatized, by its use of an animal and of other conventionally comic devices, it probably was the most hilarious of the servants' episodes.[58] Kemp undoubtedly seized upon its artistic scurrility and the opportunities it offered for the exaggerated miming sometimes characteristic of jigs.[59] The other comic episodes involving Launce and Speed, however, include familiar comic devices and also are integrated smoothly with the actions of Valentine and Proteus. This can be illustrated by considering two examples.

The scene involving Valentine, Sylvia, and a letter (II, i) balances an earlier one involving Proteus, Julia, and a letter (I, i, 70 ff.). Aside from punning, the later scene includes familiar comic developments: the exaggerated *non sequitur* of a comic cry (ll. 5 ff.), a brief thesis-like description that makes fun of a lover (ll. 18-32), witty scurrility on that topic ((ll. 33-42), equivocating lines on the lover's praise of his mistress (e.g., ll. 43-76), and Speed's comments upon the dialogue. As a result of this comedian's mocking lines and his two riming conclusions, Speed moves into the familiar and conventional position of one who directs the merriment, comments upon it, or explains it (ll. 105, 109, 126, 139-46, 165-74). Among other things, he refers to Valentine's earlier criticism of Proteus (ll. 76-79, 81-84); and the comedian even comments on his own explanation: "All this I speak in print, for in print I found it" (l. 175). Since reference has been made to his conventional laziness (ll. 85-89), the scene ends fittingly with mention of his conventional hunger. This last feature of the comic's role is developed, moreover, so that it includes brief mockery both of Love and of Valentine's love and thereby accords with the presiding position into which Speed has moved:

> *Speed.* Why muse you, sir? 'Tis dinner time.
> *Val.* I have din'd.
> *Speed.* Ay, but harken, sir; though the chameleon
> Love can feed on the air, I am one that am nourish'd by my
> victuals and would fain have meat. O, be not like your mis-
> tress; be moved, be moved.
>
> (ll. 176-81)

Although the boisterousness and riming of jig-like merriment is qualified strongly by the courtly dialogue between gentleman master and noble maid (ll. 102-40), the effect of a central figure pointing to the total comic effect is much more obvious than anything in the *Amphitruo*-episode of *The Comedy of Errors;* and any restraint in boisterousness is more than made up for elsewhere in this drama by Launce's miming interludes.

When the preceding scene has completed the groundwork for a double course of love, the next two appearances of the comic actors, instead of being witty dialogue about situations of relative seriousness, represent, in part at least, comic parallels to what has been dramatized (II, iii, v).[60] This process culminates in the later part of Act III, scene i. After Launce enters with probably the loudest of the comic cries yet heard (l. 189), the lover's conventional complaint that he is nothing when separated from his love enables Launce to ask if he may reverse the usual situation between master and man and strike "nothing" (ll. 199-204). As that jest is continued, an effectively mocking meaning is given to the "old vice" of mistaking words; for when Launce refers to the fact that Valentine is banished, one hears that this lover has "vanished" (l. 216). When the servants read Launce's inventory of his love, the previous mockery of the lover's hyperboles becomes a comic parallel to the master's worship of Sylvia. At that time, jests on a woman's pride and shrewishness constitute part of the description of Launce's milkmaid, who in a manner reminiscent of other wenches in current mirth is "not a maid," but her master's maid. Quite appropriate-ly, Launce has commented also on the major conflict: "I am but a fool, look you, and yet I have the wit to think my master is a kind of knave. . ." (ll. 261-62). Reinforcing the integration of this sequence with what has just been dramatized are the closing lines. Although they are directed at Speed and in themselves a comic *non sequitur,* they echo, nevertheless, one aspect of the thought in the duke's words of banishment. Like aspiring Phaëthon-Valentine, Speed is "an unmannerly slave that will thrust himself into secrets."

After this scene, only Launce appears again, when he talks to his dog; and by that time, Shakespeare has begun to turn his comic process toward the derisive development it finally takes. To do this, he utilizes his transvestite motif so that it elaborates the conventional situation wherein a witty figure comments upon what is developing on the stage. Julia's position sometimes was represented as pathetic. Witness Sidney's story of the way in which Plexirtus' daughter disguised herself as a page to serve her love.[61] But when Julia appears as a boy in *The Two Gentlemen of Verona,* Shakespeare merges his representation of Julia's loyalty with the tradition of the witty page—a motif that also was reflected in ephemeral literature.[62] As a result, learned punning succeeds the comedians' antics (IV, ii, 57-72); and were it not true that her subsequent asides also underline the trueness of Julia, those comments would be derisively mocking (ll. 107-8, 119, 127-28). The technique is continued in the dialogue between Julia and Sylvia, as the lines of the transvestite heroine also stress the dramatic irony of the scene (IV, iv, e.g., 143). As a result, except for Launce's last sequence, ridicule of Thurio in the last act[63] is separated from the parallel antics of a relatively free laughter by a witty and ironic movement involving the disguised Julia. This succession of comic tones corresponds with the thematic resolution of the play and is both logically and effectively executed; for as the drama closes, the duke denounces his former "friend," the ridiculous rival wooer, and speaks in repetitious phraseology of Valentine's, not Proteus', true gentility.

Even this most "experimental" of dramas shows a skill in playwriting that may explain, in part, how Shakespeare was known by 1592 for a "facetious grace in writting, that aprooues his Art."[64] Dramatic irony lightens the relatively serious matter of *The Two Gentlemen*[65] and the comic sequences are integrated firmly with the rest of the play. At the same time, the comic process of the entire drama, as well as the development of the comic scenes, shows a mastery of merriment that parallels conventional aspects of Elizabethan mirth. This last feature of Shakespeare's artistry will be developed strongly in *The Taming of the Shrew,* a drama in which Shakespeare derived support from an earlier academic play as he derived it here from a conventional Renaissance concept.

It seems likely that by 1594 Shakespeare had turned to the writing of a play about a shrew and hence to the noisy tradition of one of the most widespread of comic motifs. At that time, he once more developed a rival-wooing motif, found also in Gascoigne's *Supposes,* the academic drama that supplied Shakespeare with his subplot. Should it be necessary, the popularity of such a combination of motifs could be indicated by the fact that the same materials are used in *A Pleasant Conceited*

Historie, Called the Taming of a Shrew (pb. 1594), a short anonymous comedy presumably acted by Lord Pembroke's Men during the plague years. The most striking feature of this anonymous play, however, is the monotony of its end-stopped lines, which also show a botched patchwork of Marlowesque language.[66]

As might be expected, in *The Taming of the Shrew* Shakespeare again controls his multiplicity in a recognizable manner. The focal point of the narrative in the third act, for example, is the wedding of Petruchio and the shrew; but since that mad occurrence is only described by Gremio (III, ii, 151-84), the immediately following dramatization of Kate's removal to the country stands as an anticipation of the farcical emphasis in the remainder of the "busy part" of the drama (Act IV). This structural intent is underlined clearly by dialogue ending in a rime:

> *Gre.* Went they not quickly, I should die with laughing.
> *Tra.* Of all mad matches never was the like.
> *Luc.* Mistress, what's your opinion of your sister?
> *Bian. That, being mad herself, she's madly mated.*
> *Gre. I warrant him, Petruchio is kated.*
>
> (III, ii, 243-47)

By the end of the fourth act, however, Petruchio is not kated; Kate is petruchioed as a result of the noisy farce and slapstick that has dominated the play-world but alternated with the progress of the plot drawn from Gascoigne (IV, ii, iv). This derived plot here ends with an enunciation of the way in which Lucentio will marry Bianca (IV, iv, 87 ff.). The demonstration of the validity of Petruchio's stratagem to tame Kate is then joined with the appearance of Lucentio's father, Vincentio (IV, v, 27 ff.). From such a situation, the appearance of Vincentio in the last act breaks out to make good the conclusion of the alternating plot (V, i).[67] By that situation at the end of Act IV, a groundwork also is laid for the former shrew's appearance as a dutiful wife, who reproves the other brides of the play (V, ii).

In view of what has just been noted, and in accordance with the lines of intrigue started in the first act, the logical focal point of the narrative in the second act is the agreement with Baptista about the marriage of his daughters (II, i, 115-333, 334-400). The line of action involving Petruchio had arisen from the agreement between Hortensio and Gremio, who are rival wooers of Bianca. By this agreement, they planned to provide a suitor for Kate is accordance with Baptista's resolve that his curst elder daughter be married before his younger one. It is this intrigue that is uncomplicated in its forward movement though fully developed in its farcical scenes.

The other line of action is quite complicated. In addition to Hortensio and Gremio, it involves Lucentio and his plan to disguise as a schoolmaster in order to woo Bianca. This results in Tranio's disguise as Lucentio and in Lucentio's command that this servant of his "make one among these wooers" (I, i, 250-53). Before developing that complication any further, however, Shakespeare establishes a subordinate line of action connected with Hortensio. Disguised as a music master, he will be presented to Baptista by Petruchio. As a consequence, a foundation is laid in the first two acts for rival wooing in disguise between Lucentio and Hortensio (II, i, 54-60, 77-84), and both of those individuals are left out of the agreement with Baptista. Nevertheless, for the three disguises started in Act I (Lucentio-schoolmaster, Tranio-Lucentio, Hortensio-musician), a forward movement is effected in the second act. The movement arises from and elaborates a rival-wooing motif and draws together the first disguise and the subordinate third. In such a manner, the complicated intrigue focused on Bianca and the simple one focused on Kate progress to the agreement about their marriage. From this, the "busy" part of the plays develops.

Acts I and II, consequently, constitute what might be called a double protasis for a double and a partially redoubled epitasis. The redoubling is the result of Hortensio's disguise, which fills out the third act with a rivalry between apparent tutors (III, i)—a development that balances the immediately preceding rivalry between Gremio and Tranio. That redoubling is only partial, however, because just as Hortensio was left out of the agreement at the end of the second act, so he drops from the rival wooing in the fourth act (IV, ii, 1-43). His leaving Bianca for a "lusty widow," of course, furthers Lucentio's plan; but it also brings Hortensio on stage to observe the taming of Kate in preparation for his taming of his wife (IV, ii, 54-58; IV, iii, 36 ff.; IV, v). Acts III and IV, consequently, show a partial redoubling of rival wooing and of taming a shrew. They also develop a double process that dramatizes the farcical story of Kate and Petruchio and the advancing complication of Lucentio's plot. As has been indicated, both lines of action are joined temporarily at the end of the fourth act, when the real Vincentio appears on his way to Padua and meets Petruchio, Hortensio, and a tamed Kate, and the fifth act develops from this situation.

The five-act structure of this farce obviously reflects academic precepts that have been apparent in the other early comedies. Two lines of action that cross one another and that are elaborated by scenes in which Gremio and Hortensio appear are controlled with striking precision. In this respect, *The Shrew* contrasts with the simpler *Comedy of Errors* and its repetitive confusions, as well as with *The Two Gentlemen of*

Verona and its relatively uncomplicated narrative. Because of this control of complicated materials, indeed, it seems likely that if Shakespeare had a collaborator, both authors knew the way in which *The Taming of the Shrew* was going to be developed. Such a conclusion need not be qualified by either the acceptance or the rejection of the argument that *The Shrew* represents Shakespeare's reworking, and possibly his completion, of an earlier version of the drama that he had written *ca.* 1592 or 1593—a version used by an anonymous author for the much simpler and much less effective *A Shrew*.[68]

Although there seems little need to analyze the way in which laughter must have been constant during the performance of *The Shrew*— especially in view of the uncertainty in dating the drama—some similarities between it, *The Two Gentlemen,* and other plays considered here, may be pertinent. In the first place, probably as a result of Shakespeare's regard for Aphthonian places of character, the play-world of *The Taming of the Shrew* is momentarily similar to that of *The Two Gentlemen of Verona*. A "course of learning and ingenious studies" is to be undertaken in Padua by a youth from Lombardy, for Lucentio would "deck his fortune with virtuous deeds" (I, i, 9, 16).[69] With a turn that reminds one of the initial development of *Love's Labour's Lost,* Tranio then argues that youth must not be stultified nor learning divorced from pleasure. A regard for a Renaissance discipline is picked up by Bianca's and Baptista's lines about books, music, instruments, and poetry—all of which are taught by "cunning men" who bring up the children of "kind" and "liberal" parents (ll. 82-83, 92-95, 97-99). Although this thematic start is dropped for intrigue and farce, its sententiousness is akin to other didactic lines. Witness the reflection on drink given to the Lord of the Induction and even the ridicule of fashion given Petruchio ("Induction," i, 34-35; IV, iii, 87-91).

Also similar to a feature of *The Two Gentlemen* is the portrayal of Gremio. Although this wealthy old wooer is derived probably from Gascoigne's *Supposes,* he is close to a conventional, derisible figure in rival-wooing motifs. Not only lines given to the Lord of the Induction but also lines given to Petruchio specify such a comic milieu for an audience that probably was unaware of any literary indebtedness and probably uninterested in such matters. Wealth is the accompaniment of Petruchio's "wooing dance," be the maid

> . . . as foul as was Florentius' love
> As old as Sibyl, and as curst and shrewd
> As Socrates' Xantippe, or a worse. . . .
>
> (I, ii, 68-71)

Petruchio's speech also builds upon such conventionally comic situations as an equivocating servant, a knocking at a door, and corporeal punishment—matter that had been utilized with a vengeance in *The Comedy of Errors* (*The Taming of the Shrew*, I, ii, 1-19)[70]. Fully developed as the second act closes is the display of rivals flouting each other. At that time, Gremio, the old wooer, contends with the disguised Tranio, posing as a wealthy father's only son (II, i, 334-43, 348-93, 401-6).

The concentric circles of attention that Kyd utilized in *The Spanish Tragedy* also appear in *The Taming of the Shrew,* for individuals are constantly being watched by other individuals on the stage.[71] Perhaps Shakespeare derived this feature of his drama from Gascoigne's representation of eavesdropping.[72] It is interesting to note, however, that the plotting intriguer of the Elizabethan stage here appears as the noisy instigator of farce and starts his soliloquy explaining his plan for the taming of Kate with words reminiscent of serious "politic" milieus:

> Thus have I politicly begun my reign;
> And 'tis my hope to end successfully.
>
> (IV, i, 191-92)

Indeed, a supporting figure appears with this deviser of a stratagem, after a frantic woman, but one now comically so, has held the stage (IV, iii, 36 ff.). As a result, for some in an audience, these appurtenances of an intriguer, regardless of their derivation, may have seemed to burlesque briefly the current stage tradition.

Finally, an interesting speculation is afforded by the argument that Shakespeare turned to writing a drama about a shrew before the publication of the anonymous play. Granted that Shakespeare's Sly and his companions might have dropped unnoticed from *The Shrew* during its performance, yet if the continuation of that action in *A Shrew* indicates the original intent of Shakespeare, then he may have planned once more to return to an initial situation for the conclusion of a drama.[73] The consideration need not be emphasized, however; for one is also aware of Shakespeare's desire to unify his dramas by his control of the complexities of *Titus* and of his earliest comedies. In them, Shakespeare achieved an Elizabethan multiplicity within a unity provided by a popular dramatic pattern and an academically derived five-act structure. As will be indicated in the next chapter, that fact can give meaning to the artistry of his earliest history plays, in which Shakespeare intensified the episodic effects noted in *Titus* and again widened the scope of his dramas.

V

The Henry VI Trilogy and Richard III

IN CONTRAST TO a feature of the artistry that has been discussed in the previous chapter, when Shakespeare wrote his earliest histories he does not seem to have been concerned with effecting a sixteenth-century multiplicity within a five-act structure. He seems rather to have been interested in producing effects that accord with current theatrical and rhetorical practices and with a tradition that for all practical purposes died out with the end of the mystery cycles. For that matter, the following examination of the Henry VI trilogy supports the normal assumption that when an author capable of effecting a particular kind of unity does not do so, he quite possibly has another artistic purpose in mind.

A failure to view the dramas about Henry VI in the light just indicated may have lead modern critics to become preoccupied with advancing theories about collaboration or revision and with underlining reflections in those plays of a current "policy" or of a simplified scale of being. Unfortunately, this latter approach leaves one with the impression that the three parts of *Henry VI* are essentially dramatic treatises meant to mirror current propaganda, or dramatized sermons on unity and obedience that have England as their hero. Granted that Shakespeare, who used current histories as his sources, might be expected to show propagandistic aspects of Tudor historiography, yet by emphasizing that fact, no less than by focusing one's attention on signs of "revision," Shakespeare as an effective popular dramatist languishes, even as he gains sureness in his art and develops a skill in delineating a great variety of characters.[1]

Although the *Henry VI* trilogy stands in striking contrast to the histories of Queen Elizabeth's Men[2]—the company that before Shakespeare's time had shown the greatest interest in England's annals—it seems logical to begin a consideration of the preceding statements by turning directly to Shakespeare's plays and noticing what seems inescapable when each play is viewed in its entirety and in its relationship to the others. But as in all art, so here. The line between technique and subject matter is liable to become tenuous, at the least, if one is concerned in any way with an artist's purpose.

As generations of critics have pointed out, *1 Henry VI* shows English faction ruining a national unity. In addition, there is a noticeable cohesion throughout the drama in the way in which prophecies emphasizing cause and effect and operating like Nemesis appear in all parts of the play, even when they are given to Greene, Peele, Lodge, Nash, and Shakespeare.[3] Thus it is again a fair assumption that if there were collaboration, each author knew the general course of the development of the drama. Even if Shakespeare were only one of the authors— and not the only or the principal one who shows occasional flashes of what is to become his mature style—he probably was aware of the end result of *1 Henry VI*. To him is usually given the scene dramatizing the way in which the white rose and the red came to designate factious parties, and the same is true for at least one of the scenes dramatizing Talbot's last battle.[4]

In accordance with what has just been indicated, and in contrast to what has been noted about Kent as Marlowe's chorus in *Edward II,* a political moral that would attack faction not only appears at crucial points in the drama but is expressed by more than one character. As the play opens, the ruinous effect of dissension is stated by the first messenger (I, i, 69-81). It is also implicit in the comic comment of the mayor that closes the third scene, though that comment is directed at the stage situation that has just been dramatized (I, iii, 90-91). Quite inescapable is the expression of the moral by Exeter in the third act (i, 187-201). In the fourth act, he again attacks discord among the nobles in another soliloquy occurring just before the author dramatizes the occasion of Talbot's death (i, 182-94). During those six scenes, the moral also appears in pleas for aid to Talbot: Lucy enunciates the idea after his dialogue with York, and at that time a reference to Henry V probably reminded an audience of the beginning of the play; Lucy also repeats the idea when speaking with Somerset:

> Thus, while the vulture of sedition
> Feeds in the bosom of such great commanders,
> Sleeping neglection doth betray to loss
> The conquest of our scarce cold conqueror,
> That ever living man of memory,
> Henry the Fifth. Whiles they each other cross,
> Lives, honours, lands, and all hurry to loss.
>
> (IV, iii, 47-53)

> The fraud of England, not the force of France,
> Hath now entrapp'd the noble-minded Talbot.
> Never to England shall he bear his life,
> But dies, betray'd to fortune by your strife.
>
> . . . .
>
> His fame lives in the world, his shame in you.
>
> (IV, iv, 36-39, 46)

The effectiveness of this fourth act, which focuses on Talbot's death, is witnessed by Nashe in a publication of 1592. According to him, the "teares of ten thousand spectators at least (at seuerall times)" have "newe embalmed" Talbot, as Elizabethans "in the Tragedian that represents his person, imagine they behold him fresh bleeding."[5] One could not hope for a better nondramatic comment to corroborate an artistic emphasis in the very early 1590's. One also is struck by the fact that this representation of the death of Talbot occurs when, by academic precept, the author would be developing the focal point of the epitasis. A general political precept thereby seems to accord with a conventional structural development.

Yet upon second thought it becomes obvious that the artistry of *1 Henry VI* is not illumined completely by what has just been pointed out. For that matter, this precept against faction, which was one of the most commonplace of political ideas, rather than expressing the basic reason for dramatic artistry, might well have been conceived of as a major means of heightening the emotional appeal of what was appearing upon the stage in the early 1590's. Another Armada might appear in the none too distant future; and so with worry, as well as with jubilant memories, the truth underlying Lucy's references to the "vulture of sedition" and the "fraud of England" could have been in men's minds and could have substantiated their emotional protest at what they were witnessing in the theater.

The same consideration holds true for the very sensible suggestion that events of July-August, 1591, may underlie Lucy's rejoinder to Joan la Pucelle's scornful speeches. In those lines requesting the bodies of Talbot and his son, Lucy's last turn of thought prophesies that

> . . . from their ashes shall be rear'd
> A phoenix that shall make all France afeard.
>
> (IV, vii, 92-93)

In July, 1591, as it was rumored that the queen was to accompany him to Portsmouth, Essex had been appointed Lord General of the English forces fighting France; and he landed at Dieppe on August 3.[6] In other words, not only would Lucy's speech adumbrate the just deserts that the most scornful of the Talbots' adversaries will receive, but also, by the preceding lines, the situation may have levied upon any current nontheatrical enthusiasm for defeating the French.

This use of a specific enthusiasm accords with the use of a precept against faction and with the use throughout *1 Henry VI* of anti-French and anti-Catholic emotions. An inherited Lancastrian animosity toward France had been solidified by the intervention of Elizabeth in French affairs on behalf of the Huguenots, an intervention that would end, from the English point of view, by the French playing her false. After the massacre of St. Bartholomew's Day, a dislike of the French always could be mixed with dread and hatred of Catholicism and the Pope's feigned power; and such anti-Catholicism probably would show that mixture of derision and fear that is always useful to propagandists. All "men, yea half wise women and babes can well judge" the Pope's power "worthy to be laught at: and were it not bolstred and propped vp with sweorde and fagot, it wolde (as it will notwithstanding) shortly ly in the myre. . . ."[7] Such strong emotions, with an intense patriotism, can be the very stuff of drama and can exist not as a playwright's end but as his tools, useful in this instance for developing a reaction to Talbot's death upon which Nashe, for example, would comment.

From this point of view, as has been argued elsewhere,[8] propaganda can exist for Elizabethan playwriting rather than vice versa. Propagandists will stir up current emotions and use the appeal or the odium connected with certain ideas to effect their specific purpose; but without any regard for the propagandists' end, literary men can also use those emotions to achieve an artistic purpose. When, in *Pierce Pennilesse,* Nashe referred to Talbot's death, he was arguing that contemporary plays show "the ill successe of treason" and "the fall of hastie climbers" and that no drama "encourageth any man to tumults or rebellion, but layes before such the halter and the gallowes; or praiseth or approoueth pride, lust, whoredom, prodigalitie, or drunkenness, but beates them down vtterly." The "Collian" and usurer see no good in representing the heroic success of a Henry V and are blind to the "right of Fame" "due to true Nobilitie deceased." Actually, "no immortalitie, can be giuen a man on earth like vnto Playes." By such portrayals as that of Talbot, one's "forefathers valiant acts (that haue line long buried in rustie brasse, and wormeeaten bookes) are reuiued, and they themselues raised from the Graue of Obliuion, and brought to pleade their aged Honours in open presence."[9]

With these words, aspects of a mirror tradition are evoked and so is a love of glory and its concomitant honor, both of which could be validated by any person's admiration for human achievement. One is reminded, consequently, of the heroic vein used to display glorious accomplishments in warfare. By this representational method, Talbot's portrayal is developed throughout the drama. That method is also apparent in the portrayal of lesser figures whose heroic deaths occur within the larger representation of Talbot's tragedy. The heroic vein likewise accords with the death laments that appear in *1 Henry VI* well before the major lament by Lucy (IV, vii, 60-71, 77-86, 92-93).

The preceding considerations obviously focus one's attention upon any principle of dramatic order that may be apparent in *1 Henry VI;* and when the order of the drama is considered, it becomes obvious that an artistic purposefulness is at work and is concerned with producing sequences smaller than those normally associated with protasis, epitasis, and catastrophe. Within those sequences, moreover, stage groupings seem to be handled so that repetitive effects will result. Although the skill with which this is done is sometimes wooden and almost mechanical, if these considerations be true, in *1 Henry VI* a cyclical process is started that embraces both a representation of the "vulture of sedition" and a theatrical vein of heroism. Upon the demonstration of such a proposition, of course, depends any subsequent consideration of the artistic validity of the drama and the possible reason for so dramatizing English history.

When one considers the order of *1 Henry VI* and turns once more to what is inescapable, one cannot avoid noticing that the first scene of the drama is developed precisely and purposefully and that the dominant rhetorical emphasis of that scene will be developed in a dramatic sequence comparable in length to the first three scenes. Like *Titus Andronicus,* this drama begins with honorable "funeral pomp," although its nature and its development is quite different from that in the opening situation of Shakespeare's tragedy. The pageantic entrance with "Dead March" of the funeral of Henry V is "attended on" by the Regent of France, the Protector, the earl who is special governor to the king, the Bishop of Winchester, and the Earl of Warwick. It probably was filled out also by as many supernumeraries as possible—the "Heralds, etc." of the folio text. This spectacle is continued as the uncles and grand-uncles of Henry VI speak a death lament based upon Henry V's glory. As one might expect, this beginning rhetorical process starts in a manner conventional to model academic "impersonations." An introductory apostrophe is followed by a movement from past to present and then, presumably, to future.[10] Bedford's speech stands as an exordium of apostrophe (ll. 1-7). Gloucester's is a brief general survey of a gloriously heroic past (ll. 8-16). Exeter's continues with lines about the present (ll. 17-27). Winchester's apparently would repeat the process before it moves into the future (ll. 28-32).

Winchester's giving credit for Henry's success to the church, however, breaks the lament (l. 32). Gloucester reacts angrily and mutual vituperations between the Protector and the bishop follow. This development is stopped by Bedford, whose speech picks up the interrupted rhetorical process, moves from mournful present to mournful future, and then calls upon the ghost of Henry V to protect the realm (ll. 44-56).

Again this oratorical, elegiac process that speaks of Henry V as a new star "more glorious" than Julius Caesar is interrupted—this time by the first messenger's sad news of the warlike present on the Continent. As his lines cause Bedford to swear that he will fight the French (ll. 84-88, cf. 162), so the second messenger's news causes Gloucester's resolve:

> We will not fly but to our enemies throats.
> Bedford, if thou be slack, I'll fight it out.
>
> (ll. 98-99)

This development is strengthened by the third messenger's long narration of heroic Talbot's capture.

Like the other rhetorical processes here, the classical *narratio* of the third messenger also is interrupted—in this instance by a brief beginning to another death lament: "Is Talbot slain? Then I will slay myself" (l. 141). When corrected, Bedford reaffirms his vow; and the scene ends as three great noblemen hasten to their necessary tasks in the immediate future while the nobleman of the church speaks briefly of Machiavellian plans. In brief, the normal *dispositio* of any "impersonation," moving from past to present to future, has been extended to this entire dramatization; and the haste of the secular lords to perform their duties and fulfill their oaths leaves the stage clear for the vicious plans of the Bishop:

> Each hath his place and function to attend.
> I am left out; for me nothing remains.
> But long I will not be Jack out of office.
> The King from Eltham I intend to steal
> And sit at chiefest stern of public weal.
>
> (ll. 173-77)

In spite of this last speech, however, the drama is not going to be developed by the structural movement usually connected with a vicious riser. This is indicated by the longest and most obviously rhetorical speech in the scene—that is, the third messenger's lines. The glory of

England's dead Henry has begun a grouping of characters in which the present glory of a lesser star's heroism has been described fully and vigorously. As a result, the enemies of the lesser star, Talbot, are portrayed next as they encounter an English heroism that accords with the messenger's account of Talbot's valor: e.g.,

> . . . valiant Talbot above human thought
> Enacted wonders with his sword and launce.
> Hundreds he sent to hell, and none durst stand him;
> Here, there, and everywhere, enrag'd he slew.
>
> (I, i, 121-24)

It is this speech that had established the dominant rhetorical emphasis of the first scene; and the exaggerated manner of narrations found, once more, in Senecan tragedy or in the later books of Ovid's *Metamorphoses* is obvious. In the subsequent scene, then, this heroic emphasis is preserved even as the French are introduced. When Salisbury defeats their attack, any disastrous result of the first messenger's faction is forgotten. Only praise of the heroic English appears, even from the mouths of both past and present Frenchmen:

> Froissart, a countryman of ours, records
> England all Olivers and Rolands bred
> During the time Edward the Third did reign.
> More truly now may this be verified,
> For none but Samsons and Goliases
> It sendeth forth to skirmish. One to ten!
> Lean raw-bon'd rascals! who would e'er suppose
> They had such courage and audacity?
>
> (I, ii, 29-36)

The forward movement of this heroic vein is then indicated by its qualified appearance in the introduction of Joan la Pucelle (ll. 46-150).

When the dominant rhetorical note of the first scene has been so dramatized, then faction reappears. As Gloucester proceeds with his important tasks, he is "flouted" by "dunghill grooms" at Winchester's command. A derisive anti-Catholicism is brought to bear in Gloucester's favor and is stressed by the mayor's line, "This cardinal's more haughty than the devil" (I, iii, 85). Although this faction is mentioned briefly in a subsequent scene (II, iv, 116-18), it will not be dramatized again until Act III, scene i. Instead, between Act I, scene iii, and Act II, scene iv, the fortunes of Talbot are represented heroically as they are concerned with the loss and recapture of Orleans. This last sequence, then, dramatizes fully the spirit of the longest and most obviously rhetorical speech in the opening scene and repeats the beginning action of the second scene. In other words, Act I, scene i, not only introduces the next two scenes but also leads into a dramatic sequence that is comparable in length to those first three scenes (I, i through iii, some 418 lines; I, iv through II, iii, some 404 lines).[11] Although faction is dramatized, it seems to intrude into a theatrical process in which it is not operative. In contrast, the spirit of the third messenger's *narratio* about Talbot is developed into a unit comparable to the entire introductory sequence. In it, although the valorous leader of the second scene in the play falls, he is avenged by the even more heroic Talbot.

In this second major sequence (I, iv through II, iii), just as faction has not been emphasized, so the earlier misfortune of Talbot's capture is now negated by his having been ransomed with honor. A dominant vein of heroic fortune is established in spite of Salisbury's death, and this emphasis begins with Talbot's *narratio* of the thwarted passion of his own illustrious person:

> Then broke I from the officers that led me,
> And with my nails digged stones out of the ground
> To hurl at the beholders of my shame.
>
> (I, iv, 44-46)

The sequence also includes a death lament, this time for Salisbury (I, iv, 72-99); and once more a lament is interrupted, this time by alarms and noise on earth and by "tumult" in the heavens. The groans of heroic Salisbury are added to these signs of the death of an illustrious person (l. 104); and he is then avenged after spectacular developments—after alarms, fighting, a "dead march," and a scaling operation. These deeds, of course, display Talbot's heroic virtue and show how he fulfilled his vow to "the body of old Salisbury." In the market place of Orleans, the "middle centre of this cursed town" (II, ii, 4-6), the interrupted death lament is completed; and the perpetual glory of an illustrious Englishman is assured, not simply by his place in this drama, but by Talbot's vow for the future:

> And that hereafter ages may behold
> What ruin happened in revenge of him,
> Within their chiefest temple I'll erect
> A tomb, wherein his corpse shall be interr'd;
> Upon the which, that every one may read,
> Shall be engrav'd the sack of Orleans,
> The treacherous manner of his mournful death,
> And what a terror he had been to France.
>
> (II, ii, 10-17)

The sequence about the siege of Orleans, therefore, grows directly out of the major element in the introductory sequence (some 327 lines of the 418 of Act I, scenes i-iii), a sequence that had begun with an emphasis upon the immortal and heroic deeds of a great English king. In both units, there appears a rhetorical process that is subject to interruption but concerned with death, glory, and immortal fame. Glory and fame for the warrior, the admiration of all for striking achievement, and the appeal of a noisy and crowded stage are obvious preoccupations of the author. Because of these emphases, the entire second development illustrates the heroic vein already noted in *Edward III,* although the present "hero's" connection with a noblewoman appears only when his sensing of the future is dramatized in the duping of the Countess of Auvergne (II, iii).[12] Indeed, this light scene with the favorite comic motif of the duper duped solidifies the unit-like effect of the second sequence and its development of fortunate heroism. "The Siege of Orleans, with the lamentable death of Salisbury and the heroic revenge of ever-renowned Talbot" might be its name. Even more than the episodic effects of *Titus Andronicus,* it fills up a portion of a theatrical canvas with a representation that reminds one of those narrative units in the "comprehensive" method of pictorial art to which the Elizabethans were heirs no less than their contemporaries on the Continent.

This heroic development is then repeated briefly but carefully, for the siege of Rouen (III, ii) shows the same basic movement as that apparent in the siege of Orleans. In both, the loss and recapture of a city is dramatized and linked with the death of a valiant English nobleman. Like Salisbury, brave Bedford refuses to be "dishonoured" by retreat, even though old and ill. As Salisbury's body was brought on stage and placed in the center of Orleans, so Bedford in his chair watches the defeat of the French and dies with "quiet soul" (l. 110). Just as the sequence is shorter than that of Orleans, however, so the details vary. Bedford's lines emphasize the heroic vein and England's heroic past, even in the days of Uther Pendragon, the mythical progenitor of the Tudor line:

> *Bur.* Courageous Bedford, let us now persuade you—
> *Bed.* Not to be gone from hence; for once I read
> That stout Pendragon in his litter sick
> Came to the field and vanquished his foes.
> Methinks I should revive the soldiers' hearts,
> Because I ever found them as myself.
> *Tal.* Undaunted spirit in a dying breast!
> Then be it so.

> (III, ii, 93-100)

Similarly, words about Bedford's funeral rites are brief. They end in consolatory couplets and hence noticeably close the scene. Although there are such variations, and although a brief *ubi sunt* theme is used mockingly for the fleeing French (ll. 121-25), the correspondence between the basic process of both developments probably would be emphasized in performance by the visual similarity of two valiant, fallen heroes on stage with a triumphant Talbot.

The sequel is then dramatized. As an English march is played, Talbot marches "Paris-ward" with "his colours spread"; but Burgundy, "batt'red" by Joan's "haughty" rhetoric, deserts the English hero—an act which is "Done like a Frenchman; turn and turn again!" (III, iii, 85). Thus in contrast with the scene involving the Countess of Auvergne, a duping woman here captures her prey. Yet the similarity between this sequence and the earlier process remains; and in spite of variations, the repetitive structural movement usually connected with an heroic figure is emphasized.

Before this capture of Rouen had been dramatized, scenes of a length comparable to the introductory unit and to the Orleans sequence had unfolded (II, iv, through III, i; some 454 lines). It was then that the faction of the introductory unit had reappeared and been joined with the new faction between Platagenet and Somerset. Of the participants in the first scene of this sequence, only Warwick had appeared previously; but since he had been given no lines, he too would seem to be a new character. This appearance of fresh characters and a new complication gives added point to the terminal effect of the scene involving the Countess of Auvergne, as it had developed from Talbot's victory at Orleans.

Within this third sequence, before the antagonism between York and Somerset is joined with the older faction between Gloucester and Winchester, the inauguration of the new rivalry is dramatized and then developed by a pathetic interlude (II, iv, v). Brought on stage in a chair, as Bedford will be, another new character appears in this last scene, for the author portrays the end to "the dusky torch of Mortimer, / Chok'd with ambition of the meaner sort" (II, v, 122-23). Giving counsel that the house of Lancaster is "strong-fixed" and "not to be remov'd," Mortimer requests that order be given for his funeral and dies supported by his heir, Plantagenet (ll. 102-3, 112). Then for "those wrongs, those bitter injuries" that Somerset has offered to his house, Plantagenet vows to be redressed "with honour," to be restored to his "blood," or to make his "ill" "th'advantage" of his good (ll. 124-29). Obviously, the author is concerned with representing in a different vein another death of an illustrious person and another vow of vengeance that now provides the forward movement to the Parliament scene and its continuing display of faction. At that time, Warwick and Plantagenet are aligned with Gloucester; Somerset, with Winchester (III, i, 51, 56-64, 152-56; 52, 56-60). After Plantagenet's vow to be restored to the Dukedom of York has been accomplished, the new faction reappears, most strikingly in Somerset's aside (l. 178), just as the old faction might have seemed settled were it not for Winchester's aside (l. 141). Thus by a development that is repetitive in some respects with the battlefield sequences,[13] this third major process introduces new figures and intensifies the emphasis of the last scene in the introductory unit (I, iii)—a scene that had intruded without operative force into a representation of English heroism.

Although these four sequences do not show Marlowe's shifting emphases, their author or authors seem to have aimed at a varying or intensified repetition comparable to what appears in *Edward II*. When one allows for the appearance of faction in the first sequence, two cyclically repetitive movements alternate with each other after that first scene: battlefield heroism (I, ii); faction (I, iii); battlefield heroism (I, iv–II, iii); faction (II, iv–III, i); battlefield heroism (III, ii–iii). Both movements lead to the scenes in Paris; and the drama then starts to repeat the process, which now is modified by Exeter's first soliloquy and by Joan's successful duping of Burgundy.

The siege of Rouen, however, was about half the length of the unit devoted to Orleans; and, quite appropriately, the Paris scenes, which are repetitive within their own process, constitute a unit roughly equal in length (III, ii-iii, some 228 lines; III, iv, and IV, i, some 239). When the scenes devoted to both Rouen and Paris are considered as a group, the figure of Talbot is again dominant. In each of the scenes at Paris, however, he appears only in the first grouping of characters. After that, in both instances, faction reappears—briefly at first; and then much more fully when Henry VI, for the second time in the play, attempts to reconcile opposites. Both with and within the Paris scenes, consequently, the author or authors are still concerned with repetitive effects. Now, however, the context of Talbot's appearances accentuate the divergence between the preceding Continental scenes and these at Paris. Talbot leaving the stage with faction at his heels is a striking variation from the triumphant Talbot at Orleans, followed by a duped Countess, and the triumphant Talbot at Rouen, followed by a duped Burgundy.

As a result, even though the act division of the folio might seem to emphasize the repetition of those scenes that would effect union (III, i, and IV, i), this countermovement is submerged. Before and after the tableau-like scene of Plantagenet's restoration (III, i, e.g., 169), faction had been developed by the alignment of a new antagonism with an old. The result was an ironic scene of union. Even more obviously, after Talbot has been created Earl of Shrewsbury in another tableau-like scene (III, iv, 1-27), faction reappears; and with his departure from Paris (IV, i, 77), the dramatization of this increasing strife closes the sequence. At that time, indeed, Exeter is given his second soliloquy (IV, i, 182-94). In brief, a repetitive process is apparent in the scenes of union, but faction is intensified; and the short juxtapositions of heroism and faction in the scenes at Paris look forward to the subsequent development of the drama that now focuses upon the death of Talbot.

At the same time, this use of relatively short sequences for the movement from Act III, scene ii, through Act IV, scene i, accords with the use of short scenes to represent Talbot's death and to weave the reversal of his death (the capture and derision of Joan) into new forward movements. The death of Talbot is represented by a succession of scenes that move from an introduction, through a complication, to a catastrophe (IV, ii-vii).[14] When that sad event has been dramatized, just as the new matter of Plantagenet's descent had appeared with the conclusion of a heroically fortunate emphasis, so the new matter of peace and marriage appears with the conclusion of a heroically tragic emphasis (V, i). Thus the death of Talbot is separated from the fate of his principal adversary by this new subject; while the representation of the fate of Joan is broken by the matter of Margaret and marriage. This material involving Margaret is comparable in length to that involving Joan, and the scene introducing this new character who also caused woe for England begins with a stage situation that is a rather close parallel to the capture of la Pucelle (V, iii, 45-195, some 151 lines; V, ii and iii, 1-44, iv, 1-93, some 158 lines).[15] The final stroke in Joan's portrayal is then followed by York's protest over peace and by his and Warwick's attempt to destroy its effeminacy (V, iv, 94-175). That situation is paralleled roughly by Gloucester's protest at the new marriage and his attempt to destroy the effect of Suffolk's persuasive oratory (V, v). In brief, after the death of Talbot, as similar situations are developed, the underlying process is essentially an alternating one again: peace and marriage (V, i); Joan (V, ii-iii, 44); Margaret and marriage (V, iii, 45 ff.); Joan (V, ii, 1-93); peace (V, iv, 94 ff.); marriage (V, v). This alternation and weaving together of subjects in what might be called the last unit in the drama is also similar to that of new faction, death, old faction, new faction in the third sequence (II, iv-III, i), and to the simpler process of defeat, success, and epilogue in the developments concerned with Orleans and Rouen.

Within these movements other repetitions of various sorts have appeared. Most interesting, perhaps, is the fact that the author used a comparable concept and a comparable pictorial effect in milieus as vastly different as a prison and a battlefield. On Plantagenet's appearance after "Just Death, kind umpire of men's miseries" had been evoked, Mortimer embraced Richard and "in his bosom" Mortimer would spend his "latter gasp." This pitiable picture was specified by the lines, "O, tell me when my lips do touch his cheeks,/That I may kindly give one fainting kiss." It was indicated also by Plantagenet's lines, "First, lean thine aged back against mine arm;/And in that ease I'll tell thee my dis-ease" (II, v, 39-40, 43-44). When pathos reappeared in the fuller representation of Talbot's death, visual outlines of this earlier situation were repeated and intensified, even though the younger and older figures changed positions. This later scene, moreover, began with lines that continued the earlier death laments and evoked once more the Gothic figure of Death—this time by using echoes of an *ubi sunt* formula that previously had been used mockingly (III, ii, 121-25):

> Where is my other life? Mine own is gone.
> O, where's young Talbot? Where is valiant John?
> Triumphant Death, smear'd with captivity,
> Young Talbot's valour makes me smile at thee.
>
> (IV, vii, 1-4)

In such a manner, "antic Death, which laugh'st us here to scorn," "Brave Death," Death, who had he been French, "then Death had died today" (ll. 18, 25-28), presides over a situation in which lines specify a stage-picture comparable to the earlier one:

> Come, come, and lay him in his father's arms.
> My spirit can no longer bear these harms.
> Soldiers adieu! I have what I would have,
> Now my old arms are young John Talbot's grave.
>
> (ll. 29-32)

Certainly to the author, the presiding Death of earlier drama was still valid; and if Nashe is right, the author's artistry was sure, as the picture of dying Talbot built upon that of dying Mortimer.

In view of the interwoven developments already noted, as well as the repetitions within those developments, one is justified, perhaps, in pointing out that the emergence of a vicious riser to end the last scene in the drama repeats the emergence of a vicious riser to end the first scene; while between those developments the emergence of a rising York is dramatized. The combination of new faction with old in the scene of York's restoration continues the alignment of Gloucester versus Winchester, adumbrates the death of Talbot, and causes that death; whereupon that combined alignment is continued in the viciously strengthened reappearance of Winchester (V, i) and elaborated by the subsequent appearance of a villainous Suffolk. Although the ill consequences of further faction are left unspecified, a cyclical repetition is apparent even in such cohesive details.

It is primarily because of this last detail connected with Suffolk that the modern reader feels *1 Henry VI* to be incomplete. This impression has contributed strongly, perhaps, to an acceptance of the argument that the original version of the play was revised by Shakespeare to adapt it to the second and third parts. Yet in view of what has been pointed out, the ending of *1 Henry VI* seems to show a continuation of a recurring cyclical process, the components of which were shortened with the dramatization of the siege of Rouen. If Shakespeare's revision took place and was concerned primarily with the ending of the drama, it certainly seems to have been developed with notable precision out of a cyclical dramaturgy already established.

Furthermore, a movement by short interwoven steps at the end of *1 Henry VI* to the first sequence of *2 Henry VI* accords not only with other features of the first play but also with a movement by short interwoven steps between the two major developments of the second play— a movement that the title of the derivitive quarto specifies as being appreciable to at least one of Shakespeare's contemporaries (i.e., the banishment of Suffolk, the death of Winchester, the death of Suffolk).[16] The rising figure of Suffolk at the end of *1 Henry VI,* moreover, accords with the rising figure of York in open rebellion at the end of *2 Henry VI* and with the rising figure of Machiavellian Richard at the end of *3 Henry VI;* and this intensified repetition contrasts with the rising figure of Richmond at the end of *Richard III.*

It seems eminently fair to argue, then, that the preceding analysis of the dramatic movement of *1 Henry VI* and the considerations just mentioned substantiate the earlier statement that the structural intent apparent in Shakespeare's first histories was purposefully different from that in the other dramas so far examined. Pertinent, too, may be the fact that although *Titus Andronicus,* like the earliest comedies, reflects academic precepts about structure, yet it also shows episodic effects stretching from the use of images to the development of major situations in its basic dramatic pattern.

The last of the similarities in Shakespeare's early histories, however, would be appreciable only when four dramas were performed successively; and even if those plays were performed on successive afternoons, one certainly could not be sure that an identical audience witnessed all of the performances. The similarity in the endings of the four histories is certainly pertinent to any consideration of Shakespeare's artistic intent, but it is equally pertinent to consider for a moment how justifiable as Elizabethan artistry *1 Henry VI* is as it now stands. The political moral, current hostility to the French and to Catholicism, love of spectacle, admiration for outstanding achievement, and its manifestation in the theatrical heroic vein and in reminders of the glory won by past inhabitants of God's blessed isle—all these features of the play indicate that it was conceived and executed with a purpose to which Nashe incidentally testified. In such a light, *1 Henry VI* seems to be thoroughly propagandistic in its attack upon faction and in its enthusiasm for fighting the French and repeating the past glories of English arms. Those glories were as remote, yet as near, as the times of Uther Pendragon, whose blood sometimes was conceived of as having been renewed, phoenix-like, in the Tudor line. Yet the question of the probable acceptability of the author's technique and the effect of its "incomplete" ending remains.

As regards its technique, *1 Henry VI* develops in a repetitive manner to focal points of interest that build upon one another and effect a forward narrative movement. The structural features of such a movement are successive sequences that include repetitive alignments of character and repetitive theatrical situations that are visually appreciable. Since this over-all development may well be called cyclical, it seems pertinent to note that although Protestant officialdom objected to the mystery cycles, their performance probably was remembered by at least the older generation of Shakespeare's contemporaries. In those cycles, events in the Old Testament and in Jesus' ministry that for generations had been explained as types of Christ's resurrection might be treated for a repetitive climactic effect that sometimes was accented by the recurrence of noticeable stage action or stage groupings.[17] There too might appear material that was treated in a spectacular and pageantic manner; and the processional nature of some of those cycles would make such an impression a dominant one. Although a similar effect could have been obtained by emphasizing the normal repetition in any drama, the cyclical process within *1 Henry VI* could build, to an appreciable degree, upon a time-honored tradition the force of which had made itself felt in Shakespeare's own lifetime. As many writers have pointed out, his references to Herod may indicate his familiarity with the earlier mystery plays, whether or not he encountered in his youth the performance of the old Coventry cycle. Some of the patterned scenes in *1 Henry VI,* indeed, remind one of the technique apparent in some of the older playlets that were part of a cycle.[18]

Shakespeare and his fellow Elizabethans were also undoubtedly aware of similar contemporary phenomena. The pageantry of the age, as well as features of pictorial art, presumably would contribute to an acceptance of episodic effects; and events at Coventry after 1580 stand as a pertinent illustration of a relationship that could move from Biblical cycle to historical pageant.[19] There within a relatively short distance from Stratford-on-Avon, one John Smythe, an Oxford scholar, was hired in 1584 to write a semireligious, historical play on the destruction of Jerusalem as a substitute for the Coventry mystery cycle. In 1591 a substitute for Smythe's play was proposed in turn. This was to be a play on the conquest of the Danes and the history of Edward the Confessor. One is reminded of the fact that a play about Jerusalem—centering perhaps upon the heroic Godfrey of Bouillon—was revived by Henslowe's groups for the vulgar stage in 1592, that the episodic effects of heroic plays might accord with an earlier dramatic tradition, and that in the 1580's and early 1590's not only were there a number of two-part plays but sometimes a single play was called Five Plays in One, or Three Plays in One, and in these instances connected with the memorable name of Richard Tarlton.[20]

As part of an older dramatic tradition, moreover,—a tradition that some Elizabethans may have remembered when they saw Biblical stories dramatized upon the popular stage[21]—playlets sometimes had been picked out from cycles and performed as civic or academic entertainments for visiting personages. Records have also survived of cycles being performed piecemeal, perhaps annually. In such an event, references to what had preceded and to what would follow merely continued the references between playlets within a cycle.[22] Especially this last consideration may have a bearing upon an audience's willing acceptance of the forward-looking ending of *1 Henry VI*. In this respect, it also may be pertinent to note that a similar ending can be found in *Edmond Ironside*—that play about Anglo-Saxon England that is outstanding only for its inartistic utilization of conventions popular in the theater during the late 1580's and early 1590's.[23] There are some reasons to suppose, then, that the cyclical nature of *1 Henry VI* and even the "peculiarity" of its ending would be accepted almost as readily by a contemporary audience as cyclical drama and portions of cycles had been accepted by the Elizabethans' forebears.

In addition, the popularity or the acceptance of *1 Henry VI* also may have involved the nature of its political picture. Since it is only in the union scenes, in the one other scene at Paris, and in the last act that the ruler appears, his portrayal may have had a bearing upon any Elizabethan's reaction to the drama. Certainly it has a bearing upon the author's intent, for this final picture of Henry VI points to something other than the propagandistic intent indicated above. Henry's failure to follow Gloucester's advice leads to the rising villainy of Suffolk's last speech—about which an audience, conditioned to theatrical villainy, might be expected to be interested but unsympathetic. One might also expect some of the audience to be interested in the fact that this king might be described now as one who briefly illustrates a conventional excess of the ruler, just as the previous scenes illustrate both the conventional excess and the possible excellence of the nobility.

The portrayal of Henry before the final scene emphasized his excellence and his youth. In both Act III, scene i, and Act IV, scene i, this king had demonstrated one of the necessary functions of a ruler. Although it was effected only momentarily, he quieted the jarring strife of nobles. In the second instance, he also had been praised by Warwick for playing the orator "prettily," even though Warwick had chosen the white rose. All this, as Henry was called a youth and a child (III, i, 71, 133; IV, i, 149); and at the beginning of the last act, his youth was emphasized when he was told about his proposed marriage to solidify the proposed peace:

> Marriage, uncle! Alas, my years are young!
> And fitter is my study and my books
> Than wanton dalliance with a paramour.
> Yet call th'ambassadors, and, as you please,
> So let them have their answers every one.
>
> (V, i, 21-25)

As a result, the conclusion of the drama indicates further difficulties in England not only by Suffolk's ambitious speech but also by the change in Henry's submissive attitude about marriage. The king is placed briefly in the position of an erring ruler who is controlled, not by a person with public authority, but by a duping orator and by his own emotions and affections. Although Henry errs not too greatly because of his youth (V, v, 97-99), he does violate a basic political precept.[24]

Even because of the king's youth, the political picture of *1 Henry VI* illustrates another commonplace; for a state with a ruler in his minority, like a state with a king who did not exercise his power, was thought to be in perilous circumstances. A young ruler especially needed to follow good advice, for the powerful few in a body politic must be controlled by a wise, forceful, unifying restraint. In an age of honor, such a consideration could not have been esoteric. Early in the play, for that matter, the mayor had noted what all spectators had just seen: "Good God, these nobles should such stomachs bear!" (I, iii, 90). Even the best ordered of kingdoms might be beset by the evils that result from the fact that the powerful few are "exceeding apt vnto Outrages," to which "Courage, State, and Dignity maketh them prone." Thus during the youth of the excellent Euarchus, as Sidney phrased it, "those great Lords, & litle kings" in the "betweene-times of raigning (by vnjust favouring those that were partially theirs, & oppressing them that woulde defende their libertie against them) had brought in (by a more felt then seene maner of proceeding) the worst kind of *Oligarchie.*"[25] Indeed, the lines that complete Exeter's second soliloquy clearly express this concept:

> But howsoe'er, no simple man that sees
> This jarring discord of nobility,
> This shouldering of each other in the court,
> This factious bandying of their favourites,
> But that it doth presage some ill event.
> 'Tis much when sceptres are in children's hands;
> But more when envy breeds unkind division,
> There comes the ruin, there begins confusion.
>
> (IV, i, 187-94)

The consequences for heroism when Exeter's "more" is true is then dramatized, but his "much" is not forgotten. Nor could it have been with a boy actor for Henry. That "much," consequently, is dramatized briefly for a terminal emphasis as it involves Margaret, a plotting Suffolk, and a king who now follows his emotions instead of good advice. It completes the present picture of England under Henry VI, just as it illustrates a common political phenomenon, the process of which, "more felt than seene," could be of the greatest danger unless it were controlled.

As a result, the cyclical manner apparent throughout the drama and the Janus-like function of its conclusion—one aspect of which is repeated at the end of the other histories in the tetralogy—point to a basic concept that animates *1 Henry VI* and that is essentially intellectual in nature and wider than any propagandistic intent. Sometimes a cyclical change was predicated of states. Their mutability was demonstrated constantly. In the history of Rome, educated Elizabethans found a great variety of governments.[26] To some of Shakespeare's contemporaries, then, the drama might illustrate the beginnings of a vicissitude comparable, at the least, to that described by Sidney when he wrote of young Euarchus' fictional kingdom. The nature of the English state under Henry VI is such that it can be wrested from a kingly rule to the worst sort of oligarchy or to some other form of government. It is difficult not to accept this as a purposeful effect; and a cyclical technique would be a thoroughly natural corollary as it builds upon an older dramatic method, now revitalized in accordance with Elizabethan political commonplaces. When such a concept is then extended over three more plays, each varying in the development of its basic process but all progressing to a renewal of a glorious English rule, the result need not be explained in terms of the emotional Tudor myth alone. However naïve minor aspects of Shakespeare's technique may be, the result can also be looked upon as an accomplishment that is intellectual, objective, and, in its main design, artistically original.

Before considering the second and third parts of *Henry VI,* however, one should note that a large number of characterizations were demanded of the author or authors of *1 Henry VI.* Although those portrayals are not complex, a beginning playwright must have learned something by being conected with their composition and with their presentation in the theater. About the principal character, Talbot, little need be said. Although his portrayal in an heroic vein is too naïve and rhetorical for modern taste, its probable success with Elizabethans has been noted already. Arranged about Talbot are old and valiant Salisbury, brave Bedford, heroic young Talbot, cowardly Fastolfe, and wise, commenting Exeter.

Jarring noblemen are differentiated along conventional lines. In this respect, it is interesting to note that in spite of the sharp differentiation between Gloucester and Winchester, the portrayal of the former may seem somewhat more complex to the modern critic than it might seem to an Elizabethan. Both in literature and life Shakespeare's contemporaries were close to the angry "honor" of illustrious or would-be illustrious persons—an attribute probably accepted in such circumstances as a normal generic one rather than an individualizing feature. The point has been made already by comments on the Gloucester and the noblemen of *Woodstock,* and it can be substantiated by the generic characteristics of a state's conventional components.[27] Portrayals of the French within a strong anti-French sentiment are even more obvious. As they are related to the comic process of the drama, they will be discussed later. They, too, fill up the canvas with variety.

As can be seen, in contrast with the concept that may have animated the development of *1 Henry VI,* the characterizations, in general, illustrate a somewhat naïve reflection of ready-made concepts and conventional representational methods. Only in the portrayal of York is the promise of character complexity noticeable. Although successive emphases dominate his portrayal, as they do Henry's, one can perceive a tendency on the author's part to unify that which is disparate.

In the scene of York's first appearance, the scales are weighted in his favor rather than in Somerset's.[28] Moreover, the scene of Mortimer's death follows immediately. Therein the force of pathos and of genealogical considerations continues the favorable emphasis in York's role. Plantagenet certainly is no base-born upstart, and counsel that he accept the firm establishment of a ruling house is in no way rejected (II, v, 102-3). The force of pathos is turned against "those wrongs, those bitter injuries / Which Somerset hath offer'd to the house of York" (ll. 124-25). Plantagenet probably would seem "politic" in this respect only (l. 101), for the word occurs only once and then before Mortimer speaks his final lines. As he is introduced, this rising figure varies greatly from Winchester, the later Suffolk, and other "politic" risers in the current theatrical scene.

Warwick is joined with Gloucester, and Somerset with Winchester, in the quarrel that follows immediately. Plantagenet also sides with Gloucester (III, i, 61-64). Here, certainly, he is with an audience against plotting Catholicism, which has just been associated derisively with Rome (l. 51).[29] In the scenes at Paris, York displays an anger comparable to Somerset's only after Talbot's second exit. Yet he restrains himself, and his "rancorous spite" is expressed only as a probability in the first part of Exeter's soliloquy:

> *War.* My Lord of York, I promise you, the King
> Prettily, methought, did play the orator.
> *York.* And so he did; but yet I like it not,
> In that he wears the badge of Somerset.
> *War.* Tush, that was but his fancy, blame him not.
> I dare presume, sweet prince, he thought no harm.
> *York.* And if I wist he did,—but let it rest;
> Other affairs must now be managed.
> *Exe.* Well didst thou, Richard, to suppress thy voice;
> For, had the passions of thy heart burst out,
> I fear we should have seen decipher'd there
> More rancorous spite, more furious raging broils,
> Than yet can be imagin'd or suppos'd.
>
> (IV, i, 174-86)

In the subsequent sequence, York, as well as Somerset, is represented as being guilty of Talbot's death. Similarly variable, though in an opposite direction, is York's appearance in the last portion of the drama. In contrast with Warwick, York speaks with angry protest at Winchester's entrance with news of peace (V, v, 102-12). York's reference to the Englishmen's "great progenitors" accords with the heroism in the drama and is firmly cohesive with the opening death lament for Henry V.[30] York's next lines show the frustrated passion that had been used to introduce Talbot (ll. 120-22). It is York also who answers "Insulting

Charles" and who promises, with an echo of the thought in Lucy's prophecy about a phoenix, that the French ruler shall

> Either accept the title thou [Charles] usurp'st,
> Of benefit proceeding from our king
> And not of any challenge of desert,
> Or we will plague thee with incessant wars.
>
> (ll. 151-54)

York's vigor then gives a strong terminal note to the warfare of the
play:

> Then swear allegiance to his Majesty,
> As thou art knight, never to disobey
> Nor be rebellious to the crown of England,
> Thou, nor thy nobles, to the crown of England.
> So, now dismiss your army when ye please;
> Hang up your ensigns, let your drums be still,
> For here we entertain a solemn peace.
>
> (ll. 169-75)

Clearly, York emerges in the last act as the figure who succeeds to
Talbot's heroic vigor.[31]

It might seem, consequently, that the author's unit-like dramaturgy
and his desire to create protest at the death of Talbot determined the
unfavorable features in York's portrayal, that, in brief, the process of
varying sequences within the play was primary for the author. Critics of
modern painting and sculpture could justify such an emphasis and such
a result. But there is a tipping of the scales in York's favor even in the
scenes involving York, Lucy, and Somerset. It is Somerset who violates
the king's specific command (IV, i, 164-65). Although he and York
blame each other, it is York who praises Talbot consistently, who
frantically weeps for Talbot with "Mad ire and wrathful fury," whose
breath is almost stopped with vexation that father and son "greet in the
hour of death (IV, iii, 25-26, 28, 39-42). In contrast, it is Somerset who
criticizes Talbot as being "over-daring" and, in denial of the dominant
emotion of the play at this point, asserts that that heroic figure
> Hath sullied all his gloss of former honour
> By this unheedful, desperate, wild adventure.[32]
>
> (IV, iv, 5-7)

One is reminded of the qualifying and overlapping dramaturgy that
would appear, or was appearing, in *Edward II*. Here, certainly, emphases
in the portrayal of York are, in general, successive; but they are unified

partially by the variation in representing a culpable York and a culpable Somerset; and that variation continues an earlier one. From this tipping of the scales, the subsequent portrayal of York in an heroic vein develops. Although one cannot deny the variation effected by successive emphases, the character of York turns thereby in the direction of those ambivalent portraits that will be outstanding in Shakespeare's subsequent plays. It is especially interesting to note, consequently, that when the vigorous, anti-French York emerges in Act V, the portrayal of Henry also turns in an ambivalent, but unsympathetic, direction. At the same time, Margaret appears, and she will have a more disastrous effect on the English state than did Joan.

Only two aspects of the play remain to be considered. Both are connected with what has been noted already. Both show a reflection of current ideas and of current theatrical techniques modified for an immediate purpose. The first—namely, the appearance in the drama of a naïve concept of honor—may well have contributed to an impression of unity within the cyclical recurrences of the drama.

One of the current manifestations of "honor" as it involved vengeance for a lack of success on the battlefield had been used in its bare simplicity to inaugurate the basic movement of *The Spanish Tragedy*. Elaborated sometimes in a manner that might have had classical overtones for the educated, the constant emphasis upon this concept makes it more noticeable in *1 Henry VI* than in Kyd's drama. Not simply does Talbot speak of avenging Salisbury's death, but, in the siege of Rouen, the French, as well as Talbot, speak of the fortunes of war in terms of revenge and treachery (I, iv, 93-94, 105, v, 35; II, i, 35-37; III, ii, 30-40). In the scenes between Talbot and his son, this concept of martial honor and revenge is constant (e.g., IV, v, 13-18, vi, 20-24, 30, 39). Indeed, as the author shifts to stichomythia, this last dramatization of heroism on the field of battle has strong classical overtones (IV, v, 34 ff.). In view, for example, of the later books of the *Metamorphoses,* it also is interesting to note that the "proud" and fearsome ghost of Talbot is referred to as the capture of Joan approaches (IV, vii, 87-88; V, ii, 16).

A concern for honor in warfare results in Talbot's being created Earl of Shrewsbury, and it also is apparent in Bedford's fidelity to his vow made in the first scene of the drama. The antithesis of this honor is embodied in Fastolfe, whose actions also might have contributed to an impression of unity between the opening scene and the scenes of Talbot's success (I, i, 131, iv, 35-37; III, ii, 104-9; IV, i, 9-47). In an aura of honor, and just before the scenes at Rouen, Plantagenet had been restored; thereby his father's wrongs were "recompens'd" (III, i, 161).

As this last situation indicates, aspects of a Renaissance honor also cause and contribute to dissension. The challenges and blows of "the law of arms" and of vengeance appear in the scenes at Paris (e.g., III, iv, 38). Those words and actions continue the challenges in the garden scene, the rhetorical manner of which had been extended into the speeches of Gloucester and Winchester during the scene in Parliament (e.g., II, iv, 88-95; III, i, 8-13).

Because of these two concepts of honor, a liminal but unifying cohesion runs through the episodic emphases of the play; and one's attention is focused again on York,[33] who appears in a favorable, or relatively favorable, light during scenes that show both a martial and a factious honor. Instead of being intellectually purposeful, however, instead of constituting a dramatic definition of "honor," the appearance of these concepts and the sharp divergence between them seem to be only the result of giving a generic attribute to the noblemen engaged in the two major developments that alternate with each other. A thematic development almost appears, and perhaps would have, had there been some explicit merging or mitigation of both exaggerated attitudes.

Be that as it may, if it were not unique at the time of its "original" composition, the total artistry of *1 Henry VI* was definitely unique when that play was made one of a trilogy. For that matter, the last point to be considered looks forward to a feature of *2 Henry VI*. As in the scenes devoted to Cade, the comic process of *1 Henry VI* moves into a derisive emphasis. It also shows the theatrical supernaturalism found in the later drama and in other plays of the period.[34]

The comic process of *1 Henry VI* is centered about Joan, and overtones of the comic occur when she first appears. The love rhetoric of Charles is amusing in its absurdity. It also agrees with a comic conception that will place Charles and Joan in situations reminiscent of the braggart and of the prostitute, as well as the ugly, rustic, brawling wench.[35] Muted at its beginning, that basic conception is indicated clearly by the characteristic trick of the braggart that is given to Charles:

> Him I forgive my death that killeth me
> When he sees me go back one foot or fly.
>
> (I, ii, 20-21)
>
> Dogs! cowards! dastards! I would ne'er have fled
> But that they left me 'midst my enemies.
>
> (I, ii, 23-24)

Later in the scene, the asides of Reignier and Alençon about shriving Joan "to her smock" (ll. 117-23) seem to confirm a comic intent in giving to Joan such lines as the following:

And while I live, I'll ne'er fly from a man.

(l. 103)

Now am I like that proud insulting ship
Which Caesar and his fortune bare at once.

(ll. 138-39)

Charles's ridiculously courtly speech (ll. 140-45) would accord thereby with his brief rodomontade earlier in the scene.

Later in the play, Talbot's perception that Joan is a "strumpet" (I, v, 10-12) agrees with Burgundy's account of how he

> . . . scar'd the Dauphin and his trull,
> When arm in arm they both came swiftly running,
> Like to a pair of loving turtle-doves
> That could not live asunder day or night.

(II, ii, 28-31)

Such speeches—like the asides of the French nobles on her first appearance, and the bastard's line that "holy Joan" was Charles's "defensive guard" (II, i, 49)—seem to confirm a derisively bawdy intent in Joan's portrayal, though that emphasis is restrained at first. In the preceding instance, however, laughter may have been aroused at the *double-entendre* of Charles's defense of his watch at Orleans:

> And, for myself, most part of all this night,
> Within her quarter and mine own precinct
> I was employ'd in passing to and fro,
> About relieving of the sentinels.

(II, i, 67-70)

In such a manner, the conventional libidinous appetite of the foul rustic wench may have been reflected relatively early in this chauvinistic portrayal, wherein Joan's chastity and the "clear rays" of her holy beauty will ultimately be treated with derision.

Just as Joan's description of herself as one "black and swart before" but now beautiful (I, ii, 84) will be denied by York's "See, how the ugly wench doth bend her brows" (V, iii, 34), so her qualified heroism will be denied finally by her rustic origins and her portrayal as a witch. The fiends whom she has fed with her blood forsake her; she is "a collop" of shepherd's flesh (V, iv, 18); and her chastity is made ridiculous even before she preaches a "precise" sermon on the force of virginity (V, iv, 67, 36-53)—only to deny it by pleading that she is with child by a father she is unable to name.

> *York.* Why here's a girl! I think she knows not well,
> There are so many, whom she may accuse.
>
> (ll. 80-81)

Obviously the final derision in Joan's portrayal is part of the deserts that English spectators must have felt the scoffer of the dead Talbots deserved (IV, vii, 72-76, 87-90). Similarly, her earlier, lighter treatment accords with the note of fortunate heroism upon which the Orleans sequence ends and from which develops the interlude of Talbot duping a female duper. At that resting point in this play, as Burgundy jestingly remarks, the war seems to have turned "unto a peaceful comic sport, / When ladies crave to be encount'red with" (II, ii, 45-46).

In addition to the treatment of Joan, the comic process includes incidental comment early in the play about quarreling nobles and about brawling. This has been noted elsewhere.[36] Its brief but conventional nature also accords with a fortunate vein of heroism, and a transition to contemptuous seriousness is illustrated neatly by some of Warwick's speeches in the Temple garden. His first speech ends with a tag:

> But in these nice sharp quillets of the law,
> Good faith, I am no wiser than a daw.
>
> (II, iv, 17-18)

Quite similar is his punning choice of a white rose (ll. 34-36). This anticipates, however, the angry punning of Somerset and Plantagenet (e.g., ll. 50, 61, 62, 66, 68-72); and when wit is given to Warwick again, it is scornful, as he breaks into the quarrel between Gloucester and Winchester:

> *Win.* Rome shall remedy this.
> *War.*　　　　　　Roam thither then.[37]
>
> (III, i, 51)

With the scenes in Paris, however, any comic development connected with faction disappears; and after the death of Talbot the comedy connected with Joan becomes heavily derisive. One is reminded not only of the varying comic effects of the scenes devoted to Cade but also of the purposefulness of the comic process in *The Two Gentlemen of Verona.*

As regards structure, characterization, and the creation of the comic, Shakespeare's experience with *1 Henry VI,* whatever its details may have been, seems to lead directly into the way in which he dramatized later events in Henry VI's reign; and both the second and the third parts of this trilogy usually are given to Shakespeare in their entirety. In *2*

Henry VI, two main structural developments appear. A repetitive, cyclical movement is used in the first, which dramatizes the fall of Gloucester (I, i, to III, ii). A successive, unit-like dramaturgy is apparent in the other, which depicts Cade's revolt and York's return from Ireland (IV, ii, to V, iii).[38]

The unifying force in what is the second major process, however, is emphasized strongly almost as soon as the drama begins. When in the third act a soliloquy by the plotting York specifies the later episodic developments, the speech builds upon lines that have appeared constantly. The result is that during the first portion of *2 Henry VI,* this unifying force of the later episodes obscures the nature of the earlier repetitive process and, to a degree, the fact that it is repetitive. In addition, a Renaissance fullness that brings in the comic and the supernatural contributes to the same effect. Yet the cyclical nature of the first structural movement is established clearly; and since it reflects features of the morality tradition, it might well have had a strong element of familiarity for regular theater-goers.[39]

Another development devoted to the fall and death of illustrious persons appears between the two structural processes just noted (III, ii, through IV, i). By its nature, it complements the fall of Gloucester; but it is used for those short interwoven steps mentioned above as occurring between Gloucester's death and the appearance of Cade. Once established with a competence that in all probability also created an impression of both familiarity and newness, its dominant note of horror continues throughout the drama. As a result, *2 Henry VI* does not elaborate spectacles of a Gothic death, just or antic, brave or kind—"For that's the end of human misery" (*1 Henry VI,* III, ii, 137). From what has been indicated, nevertheless, one can see that this second drama in the trilogy is an excellent example of the fusion of the old with the new, a fusion that in the early work of Shakespeare and in dramas by Greene, Marlowe, and others heralded the florescence of later Elizabethan and Jacobean drama.

The preceding statements, as usual, demand elucidation. As the play starts, Shakespeare develops a complex of vicious plots and begins a repetitive pattern. In general, the intriguers in the first two scenes bifurcate. Winchester, Somerset, and Buckingham focus their plotting on an attempt to rid themselves of Gloucester; and thus they are involved in the repetitive pattern to be discussed later. York, the Duchess of Gloucester, and Hume have their own designs; and as a result, it is hard to see how any spectator could have missed the way in which the three soliloquies of the first two scenes firmly engrave a movement of intrigue upon the beginning of this drama.

Those three soliloquies share most of the features conventional to a display of the vicious figure rising in a body politic.[40] Regardless of the fact that the total impression of York's first soliloquy probably was modified by what had just been dramatized, his speech shows the hypocrisy, secrecy, and scorn of the type just mentioned:

> . . . I will take the Nevils' parts
> And make a show of love to proud Duke Humphrey;
> And when I spy occasion claim the crown,
> For that's the golden mark I seek to hit.
> Nor shall proud Lancaster usurp my right,
> Nor hold the sceptre in his childish fist,
> Nor wear the diadem upon his head,
> Whose church-like humours fits not for a crown.
>
> (I, i, 240-47)

The scope of the drama is posited, of course, and its concluding action stated clearly, but the manner of the preceding lines is essentially that of the Machiavel. Henry is also described as "surfeiting in joys of love / With his new bride and England's dear-brought queen" (ll. 251-52); and his "bookish rule" is referred to contemptuously (l. 259). In contrast, York will raise "aloft the milk white rose," "grapple" with the house of Lancaster, and force Henry to "yield the crown" (ll. 254-58). Until then, a wakeful, prying virtuosity will be the weapon of this rising figure:

> Then, York, be still awhile, till time do serve.
> Watch thou and wake when others be asleep,
> To pry into the secrets of the state. . . .
>
> (ll. 248-50)

A cruel pride and devilishness is apparent in the Duchess of Gloucester's association with witch and conjuror (I, ii, 75-76) and in her soliloquy:

> Were I a man, a duke, and next of blood,
> I would remove these tedious stumbling-blocks
> And smooth my way upon their headless necks. . . .
>
> (ll. 63-65)

A gleeful, vice-like ingenuity appears in the soliloquy of the minor villain Hume, during which a biting humor is apparent and a need for silence enunciated even as a covetous craftiness is emphasized:

> Hume must make merry with the Duchess' gold;
> Marry, and shall. But, how now, Sir John Hume!

Seal up your lips, and give no words but mum;
The business asketh silent secrecy.

. . . .

They [the Cardinal and Suffolk], knowing Dame Elinor's
  aspiring humor,
Have hired me to undermine the Duchess
And buzz these conjurations in her brain.
They say, "A crafty knave does need no broker;"
Yet am I Suffolk and the Cardinal's broker.
Hume, if you take not heed, you shall go near
To call them both a pair of crafty knaves.

. . . .

Sort how it will, I shall have gold for all.

(ll. 87-107)

For any spectator, especially for a regular theater-goer, a "politic"
viciousness would seem to be at work during the opening movements of
the drama; and at the same time Shakespeare also develops a situation
having overtones of the morality. In the first scene, after a pageantic
entrance has been made, the ignoble terms of peace read, and the "first
Duke of Suffolk" created, Shakespeare removes the king, the queen, and
the new duke from the stage. Thereupon Gloucester, Salisbury, Warwick,
and the Duke of York are aligned against Suffolk, Winchester, Somerset, and Buckingham. Gloucester's censure of the peace, the marriage,
and Suffolk is halted by a divine-rightist sentiment given to Winchester:

My lord of Gloucester, now ye grow too hot.
It was the pleasure of my lord the King.

(I, i, 137-38)

Gloucester insists upon the hypocrisy of that statement with a rage that
enables his enemy to attack him as an ambitious villain with "smooth-
ing words," one whose favor with the common people is only a "flattering gloss" (ll. 147, 156, 163). As soon as Gloucester has left the
stage, Winchester starts a plot against him; and with it the Duke of
Suffolk is associated (ll. 168, 170-71). Although distrustful of the
cardinal's "haughty" "intolerable" insolence, Somerset joins the churchman (ll. 172-77). So does Buckingham, who expresses his and Somerset's ambition to replace Gloucester as protector (ll. 165-66, 178-79).
Upon their exit, old Salisbury addresses a heroically lamenting Warwick
and the Duke of York, both of whom had been aligned with Gloucester
in their vituperation of Suffolk and their anger at the marriage.
By Salisbury's speech, an audience would learn that Gloucester

always has conducted himself "like a noble gentleman"; while the cardinal has been more "a soldier than a man o'the church" and has demeaned "himself / Unlike the ruler of a commonweal" (ll. 183-89). Because of his deeds, plainness, and "housekeeping," Warwick has won more favor from the people than has anyone save Gloucester (ll. 190-93). The French exploits of York have made him "fear'd and honour'd of the people" (ll. 194-98). Consequently, Salisbury urges the two noblemen to "labour for the realm" and not to act, like Winchester's faction, for "their own preferment" (ll. 181-82). He would have them join with him

> . . . for the public good,
> In what we can to bridle and suppress
> The pride of Suffolk and the Cardinal,
> With Somerset's and Buckingham's ambition;
> And, as we may, cherish Duke Humphrey's deeds
> While they do tend the profit of the land.
>
> (ll. 199-204)

Clearly, Right and Wrong are being differentiated on a basis widely held in the thought of the era. The English kingdom is a commonwealth. Rule is for the good of the whole. "Conscience" is being required "especially in gouernors," who "appear more near to God's likeness" if they can effect "not only good but can act also for the good" of others.[41] Such an impression, resulting from the first dramatization to grow out of the pageantic opening, probably would be as inescapable as the subsequent one of villainous, secret plotting.

For that matter, some of the lines just quoted accentuate a comment that was made in true morality fashion on the exit of Somerset and Buckingham. Their exit occurred soon after Winchester had left in haste to see Suffolk; and at that time Salisbury, the oldest "pillar of the state," allegorically identified those who had just departed: "Pride went before, ambition follows him" (l. 180). The situation and the comment would be inescapable in the theater. The line also agrees with the preceding dialogue between Somerset and Buckingham; and in the speech developed from that comment, the related vices of pride and ambition were used to characterize Suffolk and the cardinal on the one hand, and Somerset and Buckingham on the other. Also pertinent in this respect would have been the cardinal's lines as he left the stage:

> This weighty business will not brook delay.
> I'll to the Duke of Suffolk presently.
>
> (ll. 170-71)

Like comparable developments in earlier moralities, a vicious figure hastens to join one of his kind who already has gained entrance into a coveted objective, as Suffolk's advancement to a duke and his exit with the king and queen had indicated.[42]

The entire development probably would have overtones of familiarity for a generation close to the morality; and Salisbury's comment would increase those overtones for an audience of the early 1590's. Conflict moralities were still performed; and Greene, Marlowe, the author of *Woodstock,* and others also utilized a morality pattern in new surroundings. Although York's expression of his secret motives qualifies the alignment that has been effected, Right (Gloucester, Salisbury, Warwick, and York) is differentiated from Wrong (Suffolk, Winchester, Somerset, and Buckingham) before York's soliloquy is heard.

The relationship between Suffolk and the queen is then dramatized. Utilizing in part a minor device found in other dramas that portray the upstart and favorite, Shakespeare has Suffolk appear with individuals of low degree. They ignorantly intrude upon the duke and in turn are intruded upon by Suffolk and the queen (I, iii, 9-17). With comic irony, Suffolk finds that the petition of a whole township is against himself for enclosing the commons, but he seizes upon Peter's petition as matter that can be used against York. The "base cullions," who had been waiting for the good lord protector, are dismissed and must start their suits anew. Suffolk's contempt for poor folk and his use of the situation only for his own advantage would be obvious.[43]

In the dialogue that follows, plotting is emphasized again as Suffolk's relationship with the queen is developed so that both a public and a private viciousness appear. Gloucester will be attacked through his duchess, and York through Peter's petition (ll. 91-99, 100-1). The intent is to clear away all opposition—to weed all "one by one"—until Margaret shall "steer the happy helm" of state (l. 103). In the political commonplaces of the era, such a process was a conventional one that would destroy any commonwealth; and thereby the queen also appears as one of Sidney's "Heroicall minded" ladies.[44] The scene also indicates the queen's love for Suffolk (ll. 53-67); and thus Shakespeare weaves an unwarranted royal favor, a vicious objective, and a vicious affection into a dramatic tapestry that shows both a minor situation frequently connected with the favorite and a larger morality schema.[45]

When the king appears, the earlier alignment is preserved and Wrong will take the initiative. Although it is ironic that the regency of France is to be given to either Somerset or York, the ruler must choose between contending forces. Gloucester's insistence that "the King is old enough himself / To give his censure" italicizes that fact (ll. 119-20); and one is reminded again of a situation basic to conflict moralities, although Henry's lack of interest is part of his present portrayal (ll. 104-5). With the queen's entrance into this struggle, an insistence upon a ruler's absolutism again appears. Just as the process of the first scene had been turned to an attack on Gloucester by a divine-rightest line, so the process of this scene is turned in the same direction by the queen's line. In this respect and in view of earlier lines (ll. 46-48), not only is one reminded of the Elizabethans' belief that French rulers will become absolute if given "once a footing," but one also recalls the conventional disparity between an insistence upon a ruler's absolutism and good advice.[46] Clearly, the scene raises the question of whether Virtue will be driven from this court (ll. 121-40, 151-54).

As the situation is concluded, however, the king turns to Right, now almost solely embodied in the figure of Gloucester (l. 207). This duke has controlled his emotions before indicating his preference for York, he has submitted himself to the law, he has expressed his love "in duty" for "king and country," and he has reversed his advocacy of York when Peter's petition "breeds suspicion" (ll. 155-64, 210). Apparent to all in any audience would be the fact that when the king and Gloucester act together, at least a temporary solution to the quarreling of nobles is achieved. Granted that York is a secret villain and that a part of Suffolk's plot has been successful—with the result that one in the earlier alignment of Wrong has acquired power—yet the concentration of Right in Gloucester is clear; and so is the king's alignment with him in spite of the attack made by a Wrong strengthened by the queen. With overtones surviving from the first alignment and from the introduction of Suffolk and the queen, it is this relationship between a ruler and loyal advice which will be repeated in the St. Alban's hawking (II, i), in the London trial (II, iii), and in the Bury St. Edmond's Parliament (III, i, 1-222). This repetitive process stretches from Act I, scene iii, into Act III, scene i, and Wrong triumphs progressively.

At the same time, Act I, scene iii, is related to its immediately preceding scene as Act III, scene i, is to the scene that precedes it. Both of the preceding scenes, moreover, are short (I, ii; II, iv). Both consist of dialogue between virtuous Gloucester and his wife. Both show dialogue interrupted by anonymous messengers, who indicate the locale for the succeeding action. Both conclude with dialogue between the duchess and another figure. In the first, Gloucester's speeches are admonitory, except for that devoted to his fearsome dream. In the second, they are lamenting. Both scenes, consequently, accord with the process of Gloucester's fall and with the development of the repetitive situations in I, iii; II, i; II, iii; and III, i.

In such a manner, the cyclical artistry of *1 Henry VI* is condensed. It is refined by such details as the repetitious results of the cardinal's and the queen's divine-rightist lines. It emerges from an alignment that utilizes the tradition of the morality play, and it produces repetitive situations reminiscent of that same tradition. One is reminded of an earlier cyclical manner that sometimes had appeared within the morality tradition and sometimes had been elaborated by it.[47]

As a consequence, York's plotting does not obscure entirely the morality overtones in the first portion of *2 Henry VI*. Indeed, this last feature of the drama has not been specified completely. In the last scene just mentioned (III, i), news of the loss of France precedes the appearance of Gloucester without his staff of office and in disgrace as a result of his wife's actions. When his virtuous person is under arrest and departs from Henry, murder is planned and sworn to in a tableau-like joining of hands (ll. 93-194, 223-81). One hears that insurrection has broken out in Ireland (ll. 282 ff.); and an insurrection in England is planned by York, who now has acquired military power. The conventional nature of such a development *per se* is attested by *James IV, Woodstock,* and *Edward II.* Moreover, in early moralities when virtue departed and the decay of the central figure's state was being dramatized, the protagonist might be expected to slip into a grief that ended in despair, even to the point of his being assaulted by "mischief," that is, by the temptation of suicide.[48] So in Act III, scene i, when Gloucester exits overpowered by the plot against him, not only are signs of an increasing villainy and decay apparent, but it is called to an audience's attention that Henry has thrown "away his crutch / Before his legs be firm to bear his body" (ll. 189-90). "Thus is the shepherd beaten from" Henry's side, "wolves are gnarling who shall gnaw" the king, and Henry's "decay" is imminent (ll. 191-94). The king resigns his position in Parliament, which according to Elizabethan thought could be animated only by his call and in which he stood "most high" in times of peace (ll. 195-97).[49] He is overcome with grief and he exits lamenting (ll. 197-222).

Although one cannot assume that Elizabethans consciously remembered the morality-like processes just indicated, it is a fair assumption that they must have perceived the truth of Gloucester's fearful lines about his being the ruler's crutch. As they did, the course of events that they might have encountered elsewhere when central figures had been separated from Right would support the meaning of the immediate situation and might arouse anticipations of further misfortune for Henry, of the consequent disruption of his state, and of his own progress toward destruction.

Strongly continuing that development is the appearance of Henry in a central position once more when he enters to sit in judgment on Gloucester (III, ii, 15). Not only does the situation start to repeat that of I, iii; II, i; II, iii; and III, i, but on news of Gloucester's murder the king falls into a deathlike swoon. Thus with a political moral almost specified, and with a meaning that substantiates Gloucester's warning and Henry's departure from Parliament, the stage is in confusion:

> *Queen.* . . . Help, lords! the King is dead.
> *Som.* Rear up his body; wring him by the nose.
> *Queen.* Run, go, help, help! O Henry, ope thine eyes!
>
> (ll. 33-35)

Certainly in this representation of misfortune in the reign of Henry VI, a sureness of technique, which probably was comprehensible to both educated and uneducated, old theater-goers and new, seems again to be demonstrable as it arises in this instance from a condensed and refined cyclical movement that involves emphases of the morality. The ease and skill with which Shakespeare's later dramas can become symbolic seems to be adumbrated here by the normal closeness between the morality and symbolism.

With Henry's deathlike swoon, the first major movement of this drama is completed. When the king revives, those short interwoven steps that progress to Cade's revolt take over; and in them the two initial plotters of Gloucester's overthrow die. After the banishment of Suffolk, the parting lines between that duke and the queen are broken by the grouping of characters that includes Vaux, bringing news of the cardinal's "grievous sickness" (III, ii, 367-79). Then the second, pathetic dialogue of parting is separated from the scene of Suffolk's death by a brief dramatization of the cardinal's death (III, iii). Although this development centering upon Suffolk stretches back to the beginning of the drama, it is tied firmly into what immediately precedes and follows. By form, the parting of Margaret and Suffolk reflects that of Gloucester and Elinor (II, iv). By content, the second speech given the lieutenant in the scene of Suffolk's death ends by repeating matter in York's last soliloquy (IV, i, 70-103; III, i, 331-82). The lieutenant, consequently, specifies the developments that will appear subsequently; and the brief lament for Suffolk in his death scene (IV, i, 144-47) is carried into the sequence devoted to Cade (the queen's lines in IV, iv). Balance, precision, and cohesion are apparent in this interweaving of minor lines of action. At the same time, Act IV, scene i, completes a minor transitional process devoted to the fall and death of illustrious persons, just as Act

III, scene i, and the opening of scene ii, had completed a major process representing the fall and death of Gloucester.

In this manipulation of structural movements, one perhaps may see vague outlines of an academically derived pattern. Acts I and II indicate York's rise and Gloucester's fall. There follows a "busy" epitasis in Acts III and IV: Gloucester's fall and death, Suffolk's fall and death, Winchester's death, Cade's revolt and death, which is preceded by mention of York's return. Act V, then, would be left for York in open revolt. This development may be underlined by a new start to the play when the king banishes Suffolk and the Cliffords appear (III, ii; V, i). Yet the unit-like, successive emphases of the drama would be theatrically inescapable: first, the fall and death of Gloucester; then, the rise of York, an action that embraces Cade's revolt and the duke's return; and between those two developments, the deaths of Gloucester's initial opponents.[50]

Indeed, Shakespeare's rhetorical and political emphases, especially as they are related to his portrayal of both minor and major characters, accord with the development just noted. In this respect, *2 Henry VI* is a good deal more complex than *1 Henry VI*. This also can be demonstrated by considering the comedy and the supernaturalism in the first portion of the play. The comedy is embedded firmly into the process of the drama and is related to Shakespeare's characterization; while the serious treatment of the supernatural, aside from giving rise to prophecies that come true, is indicative of the tone of the transitional movement and that of subsequent episodes in the rise of York.

By the comic scene devoted to the conflict between Peter and Horner, for example, Shakespeare effects some relationships between York and Gloucester that accord with the dominant position of those characters in the entire play. Gloucester had presided over an earlier comic scene; York's lines introduce and comment on this one (II, iii, 47-51, 56-58, 94-95, 98-99). The episode takes place after the king has requested Gloucester's staff of office; and by the line, "Lords, let him go," York shifts attention from the exit of duteous and just Humphrey to the comedy of Peter. Later, York's long aside will precede Humphrey's final entrance, and York's subsequent soliloquy will precede Gloucester's murder (III, i, 87-91; 331-83). By its relationship to York's claim to the throne, Peter's combat also provides a comic element not otherwise apparent in the treatment of that topic; and in this respect the sequence is also related to the portrayal of Henry.

The scene undoubtedly provided an amusing interlude for Elizabethans. It is developed with a mistaking of words, a drinking crew, a cowardly servant's ridiculous name, and even his brief, though unsatirical, testament (II, iii, 88, 81-86, 72-79). As a result, not York's comment ("Fellow, thank God, and the good wine in thy master's way," ll. 98-99), but the king's seriousness runs athwart the laughter:

> And God in justice hath reveal'd to us
> The truth and innocence of this poor fellow,
> Which he [Horner] had thought to have murder'd
> wrongfully.
> Come, fellow, follow us for thy reward.

(ll. 105-8)

This last development continues the pious credulity given to Henry in the earlier St. Albans miracle. There Gloucester saw through the mock miracle and duped a duper. That jig-like episode also mocked papistical matter and allowed the noise and horseplay of punishing a comedian to hold the stage. At its conclusion, in a manner similar to Shakespeare's treatment of the episode involving Peter, the king piously denied the merriment of this uproar: "O God, seest Thou this, and bearest so long?" (II, i, 154).

Repetitious in part, both situations aid in establishing the character of Henry. The first accords also with the characterization of Gloucester and the second with the devious actions of York. Both develop comically matter treated seriously elsewhere. As laughter culminated in the whipping of Simpcox and lingered upon the stage (II, i, S-D, ll. 155, 161-62), the incident was turned by Gloucester to attack Suffolk (ll. 163-64). Even more to the point is the fact that Henry's comment on this mock supernaturalism—"O God, what mischiefs work the wicked ones, / Heaping confusion on their own heads thereby!" (ll. 186-87)—had its serious dramatization in the incantations, prophecies, and seizure of Gloucester's wife.

This comedy, nevertheless, is essentially episodic, even though it is related to characterization and to action being developed in a serious vein. In no respect is it so blended with the serious that a grotesque artistry comparable to that in *Woodstock* results. From a serious treatment of the supernatural, however, elements of fear and horror are developed and run from the first structural movement, through the transitional one, and into the final episode, where they are joined with the motif of revenge.

To an age with attitudes impregnated with mythical thinking, any prophecy might be fearsome; and in the first portion of *2 Henry VI*, spirits are conjured and prophecies result at a time "when screech-owls cry and ban-dogs howl / And spirits walk and ghosts break up their graves." The magic circle is drawn and "Conjuro te" is read. *"It Thunders and Lightens terribly,"* and *"the Spirit riseth."* In these circumstances of Act I, scene iv, prophecies would be fearsome and memorable. Indeed, the situation is so contrived that they are repeated after the startling action of breaking onto a stage has followed the Spirit's exit (ll. 61 ff.). In such a manner, Humphrey's wife is exposed and the groundwork laid for Gloucester's fall.

Although a considerable portion of the drama will elapse before any one of the prophecies comes true and Suffolk's fate is dramatized, Shakespeare also develops another sort of fearsomeness in the first portion of his play. When Henry recovers from his swoon (III, ii, 46-54), his figures of speech pick up the fearful, rhetorical note in Gloucester's account of his dream (I, ii, 25-31); and this aspect of rhetorical horror is continued in Margaret's speeches (e.g., III, ii, 60-63, 75-77, 82 ff.). It then culminates in the description of Humphrey's body (ll. 160-76), appears in invective given to Suffolk (ll. 309-28), and corresponds with the representation of the cardinal's death (III, ii, 24). In the transitional movement, indeed, it constitutes Shakespeare's dominant emphasis. The scene of Suffolk's death, for example, begins with lines of Elizabethan Senecanism:

> The gaudy, blabbing, and remorseful day
> Is crept into the bosom of the sea;
> And now loud-howling wolves arouse the jades
> That drag the tragic melancholy night. . . .
>
> (IV, i, 1-4)

As this nobleman is confronted with pirates, cutthroats, and a misunderstood prophecy now come true, Suffolk's pride—noted in the morality-like beginning of the drama—conquers a fear that has seized his limbs (*"Gelidus timor occupat artus,"* ll. 117 ff.). His head and "lifeless body" are then brought on stage for a bloody spectacle. That Shakespeare is here concerned with creating fear and horror is obvious.

This fearful vein, with its horrific accompaniment, also effects cohesion between the transitional movement and later portions of *2 Henry VI*. The bloody spectacle of dead Suffolk reappears when the queen grieves over his head and places it on her "throbbing breast" (IV, i, 142; iv, 5). Before the drama ends, to the bodies of Gloucester, Winchester, and Suffolk are added those of the two Staffords, Goffe, Cade, the elder Clifford, and Somerset—not to mention those of lesser figures. Not simply the head of Suffolk but the heads of Say, Crommer, and Cade appear; and those of Say and Crommer are used for the spectacle of their kissing, an incident that has been considered in a previous chapter. This last situation is integral to the mixture of comedy and revulsion that Shakespeare creates in the scenes in which the rebel leader appears.[51] Their effect contrasts with that of the comedy in the earlier movement, builds upon a dominant note in the transitional development, and leads into one of the emphases in the last portion of the drama.

In the final development of *2 Henry VI,* when the consequences of York's return from Ireland are being dramatized, Shakespeare returns to the rhetorical horror of Suffolk's death and embodies it especially in the lines given to young Clifford. Thereby a Senecan revenge is let loose upon the field of battle. The lieutenant's political comment that Suffolk "like ambitious Sylla" was "overgorg'd" with "gobbets" of his "mother's bleeding heart" is echoed in young Clifford's hatred and his resolve to cut any "infant of the house of York" into "as many gobbets" as "wild Medea young Absyrtus did" (IV, i, 83-85; V, ii, 57-59). In contrast with the way in which revenge upon the field of battle had been linked with glory and honor in *1 Henry VI,* Shakespeare now turns from the theatrical atrocities of Cade's revolt to an academic rhetoric. A more recent literary tradition thereby replaces the brief spectacles of Gothic tragedy in *1 Henry VI* and builds upon the dominant note in the transitional movement and its anticipation in the first portion of the drama.

As will have been noticed, the varying emphases in treating these cohesive elements in *2 Henry VI* accord, in general, with its structural movements, as do the political aspects of the drama that have been noted only in passing. Throughout the first portion of *2 Henry VI,* decisions were made by king and nobles. The powerful few were factious and ambitious; the king, weak and pious. A public virtue was embodied only in Gloucester. The morality overtones of that fact had led, among other things, to Henry's reference to his deep grave and his "life in death" (III, ii, 149-52). When Henry recovered from his swoon, Wrong still seemed triumphant. The queen's rhetorical virtuosity overrode Henry's vituperation of Suffolk and stopped Henry's lament for Gloucester (ll. 56-121). Although Warwick would "do some service to Duke Humphrey's ghost" by fighting Suffolk, the king still failed to act. In contrast with the vigor of other successful stage rulers, Henry's generalized and pious comment upon the duel may well have seemed as ineffective as his immediately preceding vituperation and lament had been:

> What stronger breastplate than a heart untainted!
> Thrice is he arm'd that hath his quarrel just,
> And he but naked, though locked up in steel,
> Whose conscience with injustice is corrupted.

> (ll. 232-35)

In this scene, however, the third conventional component of a state makes itself felt. Earlier, the commons had been mentioned as favoring Warwick and York; their reliance upon Gloucester had been dramatized in the scene of their petitioning Suffolk by mistake; and the scene immediately preceding the present one had been connected with a Parliament. Now this third element in a state acts in an effective manner. It is the commons who have forced the revelation of Gloucester's murder, and it is they who force the banishment of Suffolk. Thus they temporarily supply the virtuous support that their beloved Gloucester had given the king. Suffolk's pride remains constant in his conventional censure of the ignorant many-headed (ll. 271-77). But these commoners do not show their conventional vice. Calmed by Warwick and Salisbury,[52] they are concerned with the good of the ruler and of the commonwealth and their insistence upon Suffolk's banishment is delivered as a petition. Not simply does the manner of their approach to Henry conform to Elizabethan practice but the petition itself contains Elizabethan thoughts. It also repeats the imagery in Henry's earlier vituperation, as well as an idea congruent with his perception of his "life in death" now Humphrey is gone:

> They say in him [Suffolk] they fear your Highness' death;
> And mere instinct of love and loyalty,
> Free from a stubborn opposite intent,
> As being thought to contradict your liking,
> Makes them forward in his banishment.
> They say, in care of your most royal person,
> That if your Highness should intend to sleep,
> And charge that no man should disturb your rest
> In pain of your dislike or pain of death,
> Yet, notwithstanding such a strait edict,
> Were there a serpent seen, with forked tongue,
> That slily glided towards your Majesty,
> It were but necessary you were wak'd,
> Lest, being suffer'd in that harmful slumber,
> The mortal worm might make the sleep eternal;
> And therefore do they cry, though you forbid,
> That they will guard you, whe'er you will or no,
> From such fell serpents as false Suffolk is,
> With whose envenomed and fatal sting,
> Your loving uncle, twenty times his worth,
> They say, is shamefully bereft of life.[53]

(ll. 249-69)

One might refer to petitions by Elizabeth's Commons, and by the Lords as well, against Mary Queen of Scots. One might also note that the slight role of the nameless commons in Shakespeare's early histories is nevertheless greater than their role in the later ones and that the zeal of Elizabeth's Commons diminished appreciably from the late 1580's through the remainder of her reign.[54] But much more pertinent is the fact that at this point in the drama, the spectators must have perceived that with the support of the many, Henry now acts in accordance with his preceding speeches (ll. 39-55, 281-84). For the first time, he also speaks with consistent regal force and vigorously reproves his queen (ll. 285-99).

Given the conventional manner of describing a state as a body made up of the one, the few, and the many, the preceding situation dramatizes an obvious development. When the few in any stage-world are corrupt and the one is incapable of action, or corrupt also, hope for righting a vicious condition would reside either in outside forces or in the force of the many, be the drama a Shakespearean history or a later tragicomedy by Beaumont and Fletcher.[55] The force for good in *Woodstock* results from the many led by the virtuous few. Here, when the virtue of the few has been concentrated in Gloucester, the many are the natural inciting cause; and since Henry, in spite of his piety and weakness, has shown none of the regal malfeasance that the Richard of *Woodstock* will show, the action of the commons momentarily results in an effective union between the conventional components of a state. Only one development in the drama might qualify such an impression. Warwick and Salisbury plan to support York's claim to the throne (II, ii). Yet that possible qualification need not have impaired a reaction to the effect that when the commons make their force felt, retribution for the opponents of good Duke Humphrey begins. It is difficult to see, consequently, how any Elizabethan could have escaped an impression that Henry shows the vigor he has lacked when a new force in the body politic makes itself felt—a force quieted but represented by some of the powerful few and supported by the action of a willing ruler, hence a force that momentarily brings about an approximation of the ideal commonwealth acting as a single body to effect justice and rid itself of an evil. In this respect, too, overtones of a political morality may have been perceptible, especially in the light of the earlier situation leading to the king's apparent death.

This "new" start to the drama would then accent for an Elizabethan audience two of the subsequent developments in the play. The conventional vice of the many as it is embodied in Cade's revolt provides an implicit contrast to the virtue of the many as it appears in these commons of Bury St. Edmonds, and the beneficent force of this group reappears in the rural gentleman Iden. At about the same time, the loyal strength of the powerful few is embodied in the Cliffords. In brief, political emphases effected by Shakespeare's treatment of minor figures also accord with the episodic structure of the drama.

As has been indicated, the same consideration holds true, in general, for Shakespeare's representation of his major characters. This can be illustrated sufficiently by considering aspects of the portrayals of Gloucester, Suffolk, Henry, and York. From this discussion, a consideration of the character contrasts in the last portion of *2 Henry VI* arises naturally.

The concentration of excellent attributes of character in Gloucester, with, perhaps, the humanizing touch of his honorable choler, has developed more fully his portrayal in *1 Henry VI*. Such a characterization is essential to the repetitive process of the first structural movement, and it serves to blacken the figures opposed to Humphrey. In this respect, York's portrayal is affected, and those of Suffolk, Winchester, Buckingham, and Somerset. A variation in the characterizations of Warwick and Salisbury results from their being persuaded of the justice of York's claim to the throne after both have appeared firmly on the side of Gloucester (II, ii).

The portrayal of Suffolk is more interesting. He is a vicious figure in the body politic and the fearful representation of his death has been noted. But when his constant pride controls his fear, he momentarily becomes worthy of the first gentleman's sympathy (IV, i, 144-47). Indeed, this note of pathos builds upon Suffolk's parting with Margaret[56] and thereby testifies briefly to the conventional association between pathos and the fall of the illustrious. Such a development also produces a brief ambivalence, which is interesting not only for its own sake but because a strong ambivalence is now developed in the characterizations of Henry and of York.

In his first soliloquy, York characterized Henry before the audience could have seen that ruler in any appreciable action, aside from his creating Suffolk a duke. Gloucester's patriotic zeal, his anger over the marriage terms, the alignment of the peers, and the exit of "Pride" and "Ambition" would give substance to York's description of Henry as one who holds "the sceptre in his childish fist" (I, i, 244-45). This duke's criticism of Henry's "church-like humours" would then be repeated more fully by the queen, as she specified the Romish attributes of the king's religious zeal (I, iii, 45-67). York's description also would be substantiated by Henry's appearance when his "childish fist" acted unwillingly in the choice of a regent of France; and the effect of the king's speeches in the St. Albans "miracle" and the Peter-Horner episode would contribute to an impression of Henry's excessive piety.[57]

Just before this last episode, the king sentenced Elinor—an act consistent with sixteenth-century justice and Henry's religious zeal.[58] Contrary to the portrayal of Humphrey's excellence, however, the king also had taken Gloucester's staff of office, since "Henry will to himself / Protector be" (II, iii, 23-24). Yet upon his next appearance, an independence compatible with these actions led to his defense of Gloucester against the accusations of the queen and the peers (III, i, 66-73). Nothing approaching the majesty of competent stage rulers was developed, however. The accusations of Margaret and Suffolk dominated the king's brief speeches both by their rhetorical force and their length. Just as Henry returned to a theatrically unsatisfactory piety on hearing of the loss of France ("Cold news, Lord Somerset; but God's will be done!" l. 86), so the king failed to act upon his conviction and even resigned his position in Parliament (ll. 195-201). In brief, in the latter part of the second act and the beginning of the third, Shakespeare's technique in portraying Henry approaches that alternation between relatively favorable and unfavorable emphases that can be found in the characterizations of Edward II and Richard II[59]—although the cohesive attribute of Henry's "childish fist" is intensified both in the matter of France and in the fall of Gloucester. The result is that Henry appears as one "cold in great affairs" (l. 224). This is true even though the great affairs of France and especially of Gloucester are not those of the queen, who with considerable irony is given the immediately preceding phrase to describe the king (ll. 223-34). Such a qualifying and ironic artistry, like the development of Henry's swoon, adumbrates characteristic features of Shakespeare's later plays.

Also pertinent to the portrayal of Henry is the characterization of Margaret. In its most serious aspect, the relationship among Henry, Margaret, and Suffolk might be called a weakened representation of that between Saturnine, Tamora, and Aaron. Instead of belonging to a complex of viciousness, however, Henry's portrayal within this relationship emphasizes his inability, or his unwillingness, to control his spouse. Without strong indications of a comic intent, the traditional figures of shrewish wife and meek husband may seem far away; but the dominance of Margaret's rhetoric may have been constant enough to provide a faint overtone of derisibility in the portrayal of her husband. Conversely, when Shakespeare places the queen's argumentative laments in defense of Suffolk close to her being silenced by Henry, an audience's reaction could partake of the pleasure inherent in the old device of the tables turned. Again one seems justified in seeing a technique at work that would produce an ambivalent effect—one that in this instance ends with a relatively favorable reaction to Henry and also accords with the "new" political start to the drama.

In the transitional movement and during Cade's revolt, the piety of the king does not run athwart the dominant emphases of the scenes in which he appears. At one point, it confirms the cardinal's viciousness, and its tendency to return to its earlier use is cut short (III, iii, 27-29, 31-33). When he next appears, Henry is concerned with affairs of state. His queen mourns over the head of Suffolk and is thereby removed from the impetus of the drama, which now is concerned with Cade's rebellion (IV, iv). Although Henry's piety appears in this scene, his bravery and his concern for the common good do too; and Margaret's hypocrisy in no way diminishes the king's dominance upon receiving news of the revolt (ll. 11-14, 25, 26). As a result, except for one scene to be discussed later (IV, ix), Henry at his regal best moves into the final sequence of the drama. There he is confronted by a York who is given attributes of a battlefield heroism stronger than any that have appeared in this play. Once more, as the structure of the drama shifts, so do emphases in Shakespeare's portrayal of characters.

As far as the portrayal of York is concerned, his actions in accordance with his initial plot had appeared at first to be essentially directed against Suffolk and Somerset (e.g., I, i, 124-31, iii, 106-17). His villainy was also qualified by a phraseology that might strike a note congenial to Elizabethans and that built upon his first speech. Not even the phrase *ceteris paribus* need be used in referring to the nationalism apparent in his vituperation of Suffolk: England's kings always have had "Large sums of gold and dowries with their wives" (I, i, 129). Similarly, York's criticism of Henry (ll. 130-31) was submerged in the note that "For Suffolk's duke, may he be suffocate, / That dims the honour of this warlike isle!" (ll. 124-25). Gloucester's lines returned strongly to this emphasis. York's soliloquy, accordingly, showed a concern for "fertile England's soil" and ended with a phrase of affection: Henry's "bookish rule hath pull'd fair England down" (I, i, 258). Although Shakespeare qualified this attitude by York's hypocritical love for Gloucester (l. 241), by the villain's watchful secrecy, and his conventional concern for himself—here phrased, for example, by an emphasis upon York's "rightful" possessions (ll. 220-21)—this rising, plotting figure nevertheless spoke of the disgraceful loss of Anjou, Maine, Paris, and Normandy in a rhetorically appealing manner. Thereby Suffolk, the "peers agreed," Henry, and Margaret were placed in a position that could be described nationalistically, as well as personally, with the words "Pirates," "cheap pennyworths," "pillage," "purchase," "courtezans," "revelling like lords" (ll. 222-24). In contrast, the realms of England, France, and Ireland were a determining and living part of York's "flesh and blood." His concern for "fertile England's soil," consequently, is part and parcel of the genealogical considerations of the first and major portion of Act II, scene ii.

Before those considerations were emphasized, however, York appeared with Buckingham to close the trap on Elinor. In accordance with the fact that York now acts with someone in the initial alignment of Wrong, Shakespeare gives a strong Machiavellian cast to the duke's portrayal. Witness his ironic line, "A pretty plot, well chosen to build upon!" (I, iv, 59); and his mocking comment that "My Lord Protector will, I doubt it not, / See you well guerdon'd for these good deserts" (ll. 48-49). Here, too, appears the scoffing promise of "A sorry breakfast for my Lord Protector" (l. 79); and York reads the prophecies with a classical, ambiguous comment, *"Aio te, Æacida, Romanos vincere posse"* (l. 65). This emphasis in York's portrayal is stressed later by the most Machiavellian of his soliloquies. After banishing "misdoubt" and fear, York then speaks in the vicious riser's characteristic vein of mocking glee:

> My brain more busy than the labouring spider
> Weaves tedious snares to trap mine enemies.
> Well, nobles, well, 'tis politicly done,
> To send me packing with an host of men.
> I fear me you but warm the starved snake,
> Who, cherish'd in your hands, will sting your hearts.
> 'Twas men I lack'd and you will give them me.
> I take it kindly. . . .
>
> (III, i, 339-46)

Between those two scenes showing a strong Machiavellian emphasis, this duke elucidates his genealogy for Warwick and Salisbury. At that time (II, ii), those considerations carry conviction; and that conviction is turned against Suffolk, Winchester, and Buckingham, as York prophesies that they will find their deaths in seeking to destroy Gloucester. Yet this treatment of the principle of descent, which might always carry conviction in the arguments of propagandists,[60] is also qualified. At the close of the scene when Warwick is promised greatness, an audience is reminded, for example, of York's scheming (ll. 80-82).

In other words, Shakespeare attaches qualifying and even counter-qualifying emphases to this figure who shows characteristics of the conventional rising villain. This can be illustrated also when one considers the way in which York's portrayal is interlocked with Henry's.

Even as he appears in open opposition to Gloucester, York objects vigorously to the loss of English possessions in France. He will remedy England's humiliation or sell his "title for a glorious grave" (III, i, 91-92). This appears as Henry's "coldness" in great affairs is being dramatized. Here as elsewhere, Shakespeare reflects the heroic vein in York's Machiavellian representation.

When York appears in the second major structural development of *2 Henry VI,* however, Shakespeare drops an emphasis upon his character's Machiavellian aspects. Only in York's conversation with Buckingham is there a continuation of his dissembling (V, i, 23-31). Before the duke reappears, moreover, Shakespeare has returned to the king's contrasting weakness. In Act IV, scene ix, Henry's lines deny the cardinal precept—violated, for example, in a different manner by Sidney's Basilius[61]—that a king should act and seem like a king:

> Was ever king that joy'd an earthly throne
> And could command, no more content than I?
> No sooner was I crept out of my cradle
> But I was made a king, at nine months old.
> Was never subject long'd to be a king
> As I do long and wish to be a subject.
>
> (ll. 1-6)

Similarly, in Henry's address of thanksgiving to his soldiers, the constant public reminders by the Tudors that they acted successfully for the good of their subjects is qualifield in this king's portrayal by Henry's description of himself as "infortunate" (ll. 17-19). Finally, the king's reception of the news that York has returned from Ireland leads Henry to admit that he has not governed well. Although common sense considerations might seem to underlie the king's command that York be treated gently and that Somerset be imprisoned until York's army be dismissed, any theatrical impression of wisdom is denied immediately by Henry's speech closing the scene:

> Come, wife, let's in, and learn to govern better;
> For yet may England curse my wretched reign.
>
> (ll. 48-49)

As a result, although Henry's commanding position that has survived from the exile of Suffolk is preserved in creating Iden a knight (V, i, 64-82), its present qualification, especially Henry's wish to be a subject, contrasts strikingly with York's *"sancta majestas,* who would not buy thee dear?" (V, i, 5). That contrast is then continued when Shakespeare brings Henry and York face to face. Henry's new vigor is dominated not only by the previous display of York's "fierceness" but also by the return of a termagant Margaret; and the king's long and vigorous censure of gray-haired Salisbury's violation of his loyalty and duty is smothered by the rush of faction (ll. 58-60, 83-86, 114-21, 161-81). In continuation of this regal retrograde movement, the next and last appearance of Henry shows him to be pious, weak, and irresolute once more. Again, with an interesting irony, his queen's censure that he is slow stands as a pertinent comment on the entire development of Henry's regal character. As a consequence, when the king leaves this play he appears as one who is vigorously and somewhat shrewishly beset and as one who shows a lingering piety only:

> *Queen.* Away, my lord! you are slow; for shame away!
> *King.* Can we outrun the heavens? Good Margaret, stay.
> *Queen.* What are you made of? You'll nor fight nor fly
> Now is it manhood, wisdom, and defense
> To give the enemy way, and to secure us
> By what we can, which can no more but fly.
> If you be ta'en, we then should see the bottom
> Of all our fortunes; but if we haply scape,
> As well we may, if not through your neglect,
> We shall to London get, where you are lov'd,
> And where this breach now in our fortunes made
> May readily be stopp'd.
>
> (V, ii, 72-83)

In the rush of important conflict, the portrayal of Henry has returned to its earlier position of lying athwart the impetus of the action, which now is demonstrating, on the field of battle and elsewhere, the validity of the "rule of vertue" that one never abandon oneself.[62]

In the meantime, the contrast between Henry's wish to be a subject and York's *"sancta majestas,* who would not buy thee dear?" has been developed also in the portrayal of York; and the theatrical milieu is again helpful in understanding Shakespeare's technique and intent. In this instance, it seems essential to remember that in the early 1590's the heroic vein of a Tamburlaine was popular and memorable. In a familiar historical milieu, it might well be merged with the manner of a Talbot for a result that moved in the direction of a later theatrical titanism.[63] The "kingly joys in earth," just specified as tasteless to Henry, had been a sweet fruition for Tamburlaine and his followers, and so they are for York. If he has a soul, he will wield a scepter and rewin the loss of France:

> From Ireland thus comes York to claim his right
> And pluck the crown from feeble Henry's head.
> Ring, bells, aloud! burn, bonfires, clear and bright
> To entertain great England's lawful king!
> . . . .
> Let them obey that knows not how to rule;
> This hand was made to handle nought but gold.
> I cannot give due action to my words
> Except a sword or sceptre balance it.
> A sceptre shall it have, have I a soul,
> On which I'll toss the flower-de-luce of France.
>
> (V, i, 1-11)

Even the brief Machiavellian glance that York must dissemble is preceded by a crescendo of rhetorical lines showing a frustrated, heroic passion, apparent also in Talbot's role:

> Scarce can I speak, my choler is so great.
> O, I could hew up rocks and fight with flint,
> I am so angry at these abject terms;
> And now, like Ajax Telamonius,
> On sheep or oxen could I spend my fury.
> I am far better born than is the King
> More like a king, more kingly in my thoughts;
> But I must make fair weather yet a while,
> Till Henry be more weak and I more strong. . . .
>
> (ll. 23-31)

York's dissembling leads to his demand that "proud Somerset" be removed from the king and to Buckingham's assurance on his honor that that duke is imprisoned. When York finds that this is not so, his sweeping theatrical appeal is started again. Although it is placed by his enemy Somerset in the context of treason, York's forceful speech again repeats the thought in Henry's own criticism of his ruling conduct:

> That head of thine [Henry's] doth not become a crown,
> Thy hand is made to grasp a palmer's staff
> And not to grace an awful princely sceptre.
> That gold must round engirt these brows of mine,
> Whose smile and frown, like to Achilles' spear,
> Is able with the change to kill and cure.
> Here is a hand to hold a sceptre up
> And with the same to act controlling laws.
>
> (V, i, 96-103)

In the final portion of the drama, the ambivalence of York's portrayal is solidified in this nascent titanism. In his speeches, the convincing amorality of a Tamburlaine lingers and one is reminded of the passion to manifest one's greatness that is found in a later Bussy or Byron. In striking contrast to Henry's piety and resignation, York is resolved for "death or dignity" (V, i, 194), an attitude that is underlined when Warwick grants York the right to fight the elder Clifford: "Then, nobly, York; 'tis for a crown thou fight'st" (V, ii, 16). Only briefly in Clifford's speech does there appear the *infamia* that the *grandezza* of the elder Richard would override (ll. 22-23); whereas York's victorious lines over Clifford's body give to that *grandezza* the admirable tinct of chivalry:

> Thus war has given thee peace, for thou art still.
> Peace with his soul, Heaven, if it be thy will!
>
> (ll. 29-30)

York's theatrically appealing manner, consequently, surrounds Henry's retrograde movement; and the portrayal of this aspiring duke is completed by his soldierly and heroic concern for that "winter lion" old Salisbury,

> . . . who in rage forgets
> Aged contusions and all brush of time,
> And, like a gallant in the brow of youth,
> Repairs him with occasion. . . .[64]
>
> (V, iii, 1-7)

At the same time, Shakespeare establishes another dramatic contrast. The normal rhetorical heightening of a scene before battle had been animated upon the king's side by the Cliffords. In them and in York's sons, a fighting alignment had been developed; and the approaching conflict was heralded by figures of speech drawn from bearbaiting and from "old Nevil's crest, / The rampant bear chain'd to the ragged staff" (V, i, 202-3). The thought of such images applied to young Richard during the verbal conflict of this alignment (e.g., V, i, 157-58) is then dramatized in the death of Somerset. At that time, misshapen Richard leaves his opponent's body "under an alehouse' paltry sign" and rushes to further strife with the words, "Priests pray for enemies, but princes kill" (V, ii, 71). By such an action, Shakespeare not only dramatizes the final truth of the prophecies (l. 69) but also establishes a contrast to the ending of the encounter between the elder Richard and the elder Clifford. By this last consideration also, some of the *infamia* in the rise of York becomes embodied in another figure. Certainly the intensity of fury per se is shown upon the battlefield, not by the duke, but by his younger son.

Moreover, this representation of young Richard is paralleled by that of young Clifford. Shakespeare thereby underlines a differentiation between the admirable and the odious on the field of battle during this heroic revolt or treasonable heroism; for young Clifford's Senecan lament and vow of vengeance, whereby he will seek out his fame "in cruelty," also contrasts with the encounter between his father and York. The final episode in *2 Henry VI*, consequently, seems to be centered very definitely about contrasting characterizations. At the moment, though, this play closes with mention of another parliament, with Warwick's triumphant note, and with the consequent promise of more theatrically interesting days to come.

As a result, there is apparent in this drama a terminal emphasis that enlarges the political aspects of the play, although it is not as obvious, perhaps, as that in *1 Henry VI*. The second part of Shakespeare's trilogy ends with the theatrical appeal of victorious battle dominant. As this happens, York's conduct is linked with the retrograde development in the portrayal of Henry. Aside from moving toward the compact purposefulness of Shakespeare's later artistry, this conclusion also underlines two attributes considered necessary for effective rule, a controlling vigor and a Christian beneficence. When both were not united in a single person, misfortune was the likely fate of a kingdom.

When a pious beneficence lacked vigor, an excess of virtue might seem as bad as an excess of vice. For the educated, echoes of this generality, expressed by Montaigne, Charron, and others and agreeing with the concept of the Aristotelian mean, could have played about the action.[65] For the uneducated, the manifestations of that precept in Henry's bookish rule and church-like humors, especially when they were contrasted with York's passion for a controlling greatness, would effect something conceptually less but not greatly different. The idea is not simply apparent in the difference between Henry and York but also implicit in the relationship between the king and his factious nobles, and between Henry and his queen. Even Margaret's rhetorical virtuosity exhibits a vigor that her husband lacks.

As a consequence, it seems revealing that within the premises of this drama, unlike Selimus and the younger Richard, York never denies the validity of family bonds, which conventionally might be conceived of as leading to the origin of states. Under his control, the kingdom will show no "half-fac'd sun." His is a theatrically effective "hand to hold a sceptre up / And with the same to act controlling laws." As his force emerges in the last act from a familiar heroic note, not simply does it show an explicit concern for those "controlling laws" but in two instances—in York's concern for Salisbury and in his fight with Clifford—it also shows a chivalric, even a religious, attitude that is beneficent within its context. In this respect, and in contrast to the ending of *1 Henry VI*, an element necessary for the redemption of England becomes dominant as the play closes, although in the figures of young Richard and Clifford something approaching the author's awareness of a downward movement in the fortunes of England probably was perceptible also to an audience.

In *2 Henry VI*, consequently, one can see a development of a cyclical movement that utilizes a tradition stemming from the moralities. Elaborated by interludes of mirth that draw upon an Elizabethan's predisposition to laughter, this morality pattern is also qualified to accord with Elizabethan political commonplaces and leads directly into a repetitive transitional movement. The fearsome vein of this last development then leads into the laughter and revulsion of an abhorrent uprising, to be followed by another uprising lead by a heroic and nobly born duke. Instead of the factious honor and indomitable heroism of *1 Henry VI*, character begins to emerge as the equivocal cause of events. Witness the ambivalent portrayal of York, as it accords with the different structural developments in the drama and is represented as causing, or contributing to, this change. Witness also the no less interesting portrayal of Henry, wherein Shakespeare shows brief touches of an irony that points toward the future.[66] Although it was unfortunate for England that the vigor of York was involved with a vicious fury and a Senecan horror, the outcome of this drama performed on a single afternoon, like the outcome of all mankind's fate in the incomplete performance of mystery cycles, would be left for other dramatic episodes.

In continuing his dramatization of history in *3 Henry VI*, Shakespeare concentrates upon representing the fall and death of illustrious persons and the rise and fall of conflicting parties. These revolutions of fortune continue the cyclical process already begun and constitute the basic movement of the drama. Of special interest is the fact that with the third act, the fortunes of the houses of York and Lancaster are represented as growing out of the *habitus* or *naturæ* of some of Shakespeare's principal characters.[67] At the same time, Shakespeare's thematic concern is subordinate to theatrical ones, and variations in political thought correspond to the immediate momentum of the drama and its progress toward the deaths of York and Henry.

Possibly in line with Shakespeare's emphasis upon "places" of character is the fact that the development of *3 Henry VI* approaches the academically derived unity of his earliest comedies. Acts I and II focus respectively upon the death of York (I, iv) and the death of Clifford (II, vi). This process introduces the subsequent variations in the fortunes of rival houses. Lamentation and a description of the consequences attendant upon the deaths of these illustrious individuals are carried over into the first scene of each succeeding act (II, i; III, i). As a result, the relationship between Acts II and III seems especially close at first glance. The representation of a lamenting Henry in Act III, scene i, continues his earlier representation before the scene of Clifford's death (II, v); and both of these situations that develop around the king are similiar in their lyricism, in their tableau-like artistry, and in the fact that they contrast with the surrounding episodes. Yet a variation between them that is equally striking results from a shift in emphasis in the portrayal of Henry. This variation is apparent also in the dramatization of the *natura* of Edward and of Richard. As this portion of the play develops, moreover, a dramatic process involving Fortune becomes dominant. Instead of progressing to death scenes, Act III shows Edward regnant, Act IV shows Edward in eclipse, and Act V shows Edward regnant again, with the last two scenes of the fourth act indicating clearly the subsequent rise in the fortunes of the house of York. An opposite movement is effected, of course, for the house of Lancaster; but the characterization of Henry gives to its variations a static quality.[68] Only in the fifth act are the deaths of illustrious persons represented again. As a result, the reflection of structural principles that are apparent in the comedies of this period is much more noticeable in *3 Henry VI* than in the other histories so far examined.

At least four developments within this basic movement, however, accord with Shakespeare's cyclical process rather than with the niceties of academic precepts about five-act structure. In the first place, one again can see a repetition and combination of minor situations: e.g., the persuasion of a leader to revolt (I, ii); the stage setting of city walls and another persuasion of a leader to revolt (IV, vii); the setting of city walls and the termination of Clarence's shifting allegiance (V, i). More interesting and pertinent, however, are three inescapable features in Shakespeare's elaboration of his basic design. As one might expect, the focal point of the second act shows Henry's eclipse with Clifford's fall; and that revolution in the Lancastrians' fortunes obviously leads into the subsequent acts. But the ending of what might be called the epitatical process (IV, vii, viii) is essentially transitional to Warwick's fall and death (V, ii). Since this leads to the final defeat of the Lancastrians and to their king's murder (V, vi), it agrees with Henry's earlier eclipse upon the death of Clifford, and hence it accords with a repetitive, culminating pattern rather than with any concept that the last of the fourth act should show the height of the plot's complexity. Moreover, at the point immediately preceding this forward movement to Warwick's death and Edward's final rise, Henry's prophecy about young Richmond and the plan to send that youth to the Continent is dramatized (IV, vi, 65-102). Since nothing more is made here of this brief prophetic interlude, its appearance at a point that by academic precept was crucial for effective structure is obviously pertinent, much less to the development of *3 Henry VI,* than to the culmination of Shakespeare's larger cycle. Finally, although this prophetic incident concludes the contrasting dramatization within the third and fourth acts of the *habitus* of Henry and the *natura* of Edward, the dramatization of Richard's *natura* (III, ii, 124 ff.) progresses until this Duke of Gloucester emerges as a murdering Machiavel at the close of the drama. This last situation, as has been noted, parallels comparable developments at the close of both *1 Henry VI* and *2 Henry VI;* and all three endings contrast with the vigorous and beneficent emergence of Richmond at the end of *Richard III.* The course of *3 Henry VI,* consequently, shows a cyclical recurrence of illustrious falls and of the revolutions of Fortune's Wheel; and as its position in a tetralogy ends with the emergence of Machiavellian Richard (and thereby dramatizes the beginning of the final process in England's despair) so it also dramatizes briefly the particular form of England's salvation as it will be represented in the catastrophe of *Richard III.* By both major and minor features of the drama, consequently, one is struck again by the way in which Shakespeare utilizes current literary traditions and an earlier cyclical manner.

In view of what has been noted in other plays, one hardly needs the choric lines in the scene of York's death to realize that Shakespeare would evoke the pathos usually apparent in some way or another when an illustrious person who has not been a complete villain falls from power:

> *Q. Mar.* Alas, poor York! but that I hate thee deadly,
> I should lament thy miserable state.
>
> (I, iv, 84-85)
>
> *North.* Beshrew me, but his passion moves me so
> That hardly can I check my eyes from tears.
>
> (ll. 150-51)
>
> *North.* Had he been slaughter-man to all my kin,
> I should not for my life but weep with him,
> To see how inly sorrow gripes his soul
>
> (ll. 169-71)

Indeed, it is revealing that from the beginning of *3 Henry VI,* Shakespeare adjusts his theatrical scales to coincide with his progress to this passionate scene. Only by two mocks is the theatrical manner of the Machiavel apparent in York's first appearance, and one of those speeches refers to Margaret in a manner similar to both Exeter's and Henry's reaction to the queen (I, i, 18, 36, 211-12). In his initial appearance also, York's reliance upon force appears with his chivalric praise of his opponents, with his command over his advocates who would fight the issue out, and with, consequently, an overt confidence in his title to the crown (ll. 4-6, 119). In contrast, Shakespeare represents the Lancastrians as being those who "whisper" and "mutter" (ll. 149, 165). To Henry himself is given the aside, "I know not what to say; my title's weak" (l. 134). Exeter becomes convinced of the weakness of the Lancastrian claim to the throne (ll. 77, 79, 145, 147). "Honour" and "revenge" agitate the Lancastrians who do not accept the terms of the reconciliation between York and Henry (ll. 178-90). For spectators who had recently seen *2 Henry VI* or *1 Henry VI,* Henry's blaming Gloucester for the loss of France would further, perhaps, such a pro-Yorkist and anti-Lancastrian emphasis (ll. 111-12). As far as the portrayal of York goes, interlocked as it is with that of the Lancastrians, Shakespeare preserves the favorable emphasis in the duke's final portrayal in *2 Henry VI* in order to begin the theatrical entertainment of another afternoon. As he does this, political thought about the validity of descent is represented as favoring Richard. Obviously this beginning accords with the movement of the play toward the pathos of York's death.

Although the attributes of bashfulness and cowardice that Warwick had given the king were not apparent on Henry's entrance, yet his desire for "patience" and his attempt to use "frowns, words, and threats" probably created an impression not discordant with Warwick's characterization (I, i, 41, 61-62, 70-73). When the king accepted a conciliatory compromise, he was called "Base, fearful, and despairing," "fainthearted and degenerate," even "unmanly" (ll. 178, 183, 186). Although that criticism emanated from those whom Exeter criticized in turn as being intent on revenge "and therefore would not yield," yet this potentially unsympathetic representation of Henry is increased in the next grouping of characters. For that matter, when Margaret appears, the second situation in the drama begins with echoes of the shrewish wife and subservient husband:

Exe. Here comes the Queen, whose looks bewray her anger.
I'll steal away.

K. Hen.   Exeter, so will I.
Q. Mar. Nay, go not from me; I will follow thee.

(ll. 211-13)

Margaret's anger then emphasizes the concept that a king should maintain his office forcefully (ll. 215-25, 230-56). It also develops a thought
previously submerged in the Lancastrians' censure of Henry—"What
wrong is this unto the Prince your son!" (l. 176). As the situation
develops, the young prince's insistence upon his right and this youth's
heroic resolution, in contrast with Henry's pleadings, increase the unfavorable effect of the king's portrayal (ll. 226-27, 261-62, 228-29,
257-59). Finally, a comic disjunction plays about the beginning of
Henry's last speech in the scene:

> Poor queen! *how love to me* and to her son
> Hath made her break out into terms of rage!

(ll. 264-65)

From these developments, York moves to his death. A willingness to
preserve the peace is given to him, no less than to Exeter and Henry
(I, i, 201-6). It reappears upon York's next entrance (I, ii, 4 ff.); but
"witty" Richard plays "the orator" and persuades his father to "be
King, or die" (ll. 2, 35). York's resolution to violate the agreement,
however, occurs only after Margaret has mustered superior forces
under the "northern earls." As a consequence, the scene ends with a
heroic speech by the duke:

> Five men to twenty! Though the odds be great,
> I doubt not, uncle, of our victory.
> Many a battle have I won in France
> Whenas the enemy hath been ten to one;
> Why should I not now have the like success?

(ll. 71-75)

Not content with this development, Shakespeare then adds the pathos of
the slaughter of young Rutland to the progress toward the dramatization of York's death; and at that time it is indicated that God's justice
will punish the bloody vengeance of Lancastrian Clifford (I, iii, e.g.,
35-52).

Accented by the choric lines already noted, the rhetorical appeal
of a heroic *descriptio* is drawn upon in the death scene proper as York
refuses to shun the fury of his enemies (I, iv, 1-26). To his defiance is
added a heroic prophecy (ll. 35-36); and thereupon Shakespeare

develops a visually provocative situation centered upon a baited York, who is mockingly crowned with a paper crown and whose tears

> . . . are sweet Rutland's obsequies;
> And every drop cries vengeance for his death
> 'Gainst thee, fell Clifford, and thee, false Frenchwoman.
>
> (ll. 147-49)

Obviously Shakespeare's intent, both by preparation and by immediate dramatization, is vastly different from Marlowe's in his spectacles of a baited Bajazeth. Margaret's "sport," her mockery of York, and especially her mockery of Northumberland's choric lines place her in disjunction with a dominant context. Even in the lines with which York's role closes, Shakespeare's intent is clear. In contrast to the revenge and vindictiveness of his opponents, and in continuation of the emphasis in the preceding scenes, York's final speech must have been received sympathetically by an audience:

> Open Thy gate of mercy, gracious God!
> My soul flies through these wounds to seek out Thee.
>
> (ll. 177-78)

In this play, consequently, York still embodies those features of heroism that were associated in the theater with controlling majesty and that Henry lacks. Upon his death, degrees of inadequacy and viciousness dominate the remaining portions of *3 Henry VI*. As might be expected, protest, grief, and lamentation at his death are developed immediately; and the mythical thought of the period finds expression in the marvellous phenomenon of three suns linked with the fall of the duke but with the rise of his house (II, i, 1-40). A messenger's heroic and pathetic *descriptio* builds upon the earlier spectacle of York's death (ll. 50-67). York is likened to Hercules and to Hector, who "environed" with many foes stood in defense of the Britons' mythical home. These emotions that would substantiate any feeling that a just retribution should be visited upon the Lancastrians are then carried over into lines given to Henry when he sees the head of York:

> Withhold revenge, dear God! 'tis not my fault,
> Nor wittingly have I infring'd my vow.
>
> (II, ii, 7-8)

At the same time, Shakespeare has been developing a differentiation between Edward and Richard as he represents their reaction to the news of their father's death. Edward's lament, even by being thoroughly conventional, probably was meant to represent his despair (II, i, 48, 68-78).

But in accordance with the portrayal of a "witty" Richard in earlier scenes, and in accordance with a recognized method of consolation, Richard's fierce avenging grief is expressed in terms of Elizabethan psychology and is meant to arouse his brother to claim the throne (ll. 79-88, 91-94). With the appearance of Warwick, a heroic *descriptio*, lamentation, and vengeance appear again; and Edward accepts Warwick as the "shoulder" upon which he will lean, while Richard vows vengeance upon Clifford.

Shakespeare then turns to a portrayal of the Lancastrians. As has just been noted, Henry expresses grief upon seeing York's head; but when he repeats that sentiment his lines again begin to run counter to the vigorous impetus of the drama. He is censured as showing a "soft courage" that makes his followers faint (II, ii, 57)—an attribute reinforced once more by the contrast between this king and the young prince (ll. 56-80). In such a contrast, there may have been potential condemnation of this ruler who lacks an animating "virtue"; but as he is beginning to be separated from the warfare that will ravage England, a potential exculpation of him also seems to be emerging. Henry is kept out of the conventional bravings before battle, in which the angry fury of Richard against Clifford and the vituperation of Margaret are dominant. Pitied by the Yorkists, the "gentle" king is silenced by his own Lancastrians; and thereby, somewhat paradoxically, Henry's regality is denied more forcefully by Clifford and by Henry's queen than it is by the house of York (ll. 117-22, 159-62, 172). The remainder of the act, of course, is devoted principally to battle; and the lines given to Henry become, in part, a lyrical chorus. A son and a father mourn over the bodies of a father and a son; while a ruler, who should be a father to his country, sits "more woefull" than either (II, v, 112-13, 123-24).

As the vigorous emphasis of this play indicates, however, Henry's England is no state to be controlled simply by precepts about regality or obedience. When applied to an ideal ruler, the image of the shepherd that Henry develops would imply a beneficent control; but here Shakespeare uses that image to fill out the vehicle for the uncertain course of battle. He then continues it in Henry's wish to be a "homely swain":

> So many hours must I tend my flock,
> So many hours must I take my rest.
> So many hours must I contemplate,
> So many hours must I sport myself;
> So many days my ewes have been with young,

So many weeks ere the poor fools will ean,
So many years ere I shall shear the fleece.

(II, v, 31-37)

However lyrically it may be expressed, the thought of Henry implies an aggravated, Basilius-like desire to avoid the "duetie in that state of lyfe, unto which" it had pleased God to call him.[69]

As a result, it is revealing to note that although Henry is being moved toward the position in which he will prophesy of young Richmond, Shakespeare still continues an unfavorable aspect of the king's portrayal even in the scene that includes his choric lines. Before that scene closes, the king's criticism of himself—"How will the country for these woeful chances / Misthink the King and not be satisfied" (ll. 107-8)—is strengthened by an incident that must have been theatrically appreciable to all in an audience. As the Lancastrians are routed and as Henry's lamentation is interrupted by this rush of events—as the prince, the queen, and Exeter flee—Henry again is stopped from speaking by his supporters and only takes action when he cries,

Nay, take me with thee, good sweet Exeter;
Not that I fear to stay, but love to go
Wither the Queen intends.

(ll. 137-39)

With the queen as an insistent cause of this warfare, Henry's lines contradict his separation from civil strife. In other ways, too, this incident probably marred any sympathy for Henry, while in no way denying the pathos of the commonweal. Granted that the risible nature of Henry's and Exeter's first encounter with Margaret had been over-ridden by subsequent events, yet from the present development memories of a subservient husband matched with a vigorous mate may have been stirred once more. For learned and ignorant alike, aside from Elizabeth's queenly dominance, this was an age of feminine subservience. Futhermore, an excuse for flight after an avoidance of conflict had strong derisive potentialities by itself alone. Although Henry probably would not seem as risible as Mycetes to spectators who had seen that foolish and cowardly king trying to hide his crown during battle,[70] yet in a similar direction, if not to a similar extent, Henry's lyrical adequacy has expressed his regal inadequacy. His lyricism has been divorced from theatrically valid attributes of rule. Now, in conjunction with his love of going whither the contentious queen "intends," and after his desire to "expostulate" has almost resulted in his being left alone, Henry speaks his only martial line in a martial play-world. He thereby commands, paradoxically but comically, a forward retreat already begun. Not that Henry fears "to stay, but . . . Forward; away!" (l. 139).

That Shakespeare intended to arouse at least some censure of the king is also apparent from lines that follow immediately. They repeat, also paradoxically, part of the thought in Edward's speech when he pitied the "gentle king" (II, ii, 156-57). Now that thought is embodied in dying Clifford's lines. His speech comments seriously upon the previous lamentable scene and makes the Phaëthon image censurably applicable to Henry, whose actions have contrasted with the masterful skill of Henry's ancestors:

> O Phœbus, hadst thou never given consent
> That Phaëthon should check thy fiery steeds,
> Thy burning car never had scorch'd the earth!
> And, Henry, hadst thou sway'd as kings should do,
> Or as thy father and his father did,
> Giving no ground unto the house of York,
> They never then had sprung like summer flies;
> I and ten thousand in this luckless realm
> Had left no mourning widows for our death;
> And thou this day hadst kept thy chair in peace.
> For what doth cherish weeds but gentle air?
> And what makes robbers bold but too much lenity?
>
> (II, vi, 11-22)

As a result, the pathos of the preceding sons and fathers is now underlined by the mourning widows of a luckless realm; and it is the king who is condemned, almost in his own words, for these "woefull chances."[71]

At this point in the drama, moreover, pathos for dying Clifford is not completely absent, in spite of his earlier, cruel fury. In this respect, the thought of his lines probably would seem increasingly valid. In Clifford's speech, Shakespeare emphasizes a sound political precept that recognized the necessity of fear and force, as well as love, in controlling a body politic, and especially the powerful few. He also links that precept with an emphasis on Clifford's loyalty:

> Here burns my candle out; ay, here it dies,
> Which, whiles it lasted, gave King Henry light.
> O Lancaster, I fear thy overthrow
> More than my body's parting with my soul!
>
> (II, vi, 1-4)

In brief, this second focal point in the fortunes of battle rounds out the introductory development of *3 Henry VI;* and one may be justified in seeing an intent to unify this portion of the drama, not simply in its representation of two deaths, but also in Shakespeare's return to censurable aspects of Henry's portrayal—an intent signalled by the balanced, yet contrasting, spectacles of a heroic York and a lamenting Henry on molehills (I, iv, 67; II, v, 14).

Clifford's death lament also indicates the future course of the drama, for his speech looks forward to "mourning widows" and to a dominant house of York. For that matter, lines given to Clifford as the play began have now come true:

> In dreadful war mayst thou [Henry] be overcome,
> Or live in peace abandon'd and despis'd.
>
> (I, i, 187-88)

Accordingly, Henry enters alone and in disguise at the beginning of the third act and starts his second scene of lamentation. As he is watched by two subjects, he speaks of his "balm wash'd off wherewith" he "was anointed" (III, i, 13-21). In line with this dialectal process of the scene, he then abandons his attempt to persuade the keepers that life and their former oaths alone give him kingship. He "humbly yields" unto "what God will."

The actions of Edward, however, will nullify the unfortunate probabilities that Henry forsees (III, i, 28-54), and the Christian patience of this ruler will emerge as a laudable characteristic; for Shakespeare begins to work with new emphases. Henry's actions are now based on a devoutness visually apparent when he enters *"with a prayer-book."* This aspect of his portrayal had been emphasized in *2 Henry VI* but not in the present drama. If one may judge by the preceding artistry of the play and by that of *2 Henry VI,* this variation is meant to agree with the course of the action to be developed. As has been noted, the fate of Henry is moving toward his prophetic connection with the future savior of England. It is also moving toward his final appearance when Henry will be murdered by the Machiavel Richard. Henry's devoutness will be emphasized in the only political action that he takes; and from Act III on, his ineffectiveness will never be joined, as it was previously, with those overtones of the ridiculous apparent in his relationship with Margaret. In the present scene, accordingly, there is no criticism of Henry, explicit in his own words or strikingly implicit in a closing action, as there had been in the scene preceding that of Clifford's death. An audience would see a king commanded by commoner "kings," a ruler with "no bending knee" to call him "Caesar now," no "humble suitors" pressing "to speak for right," no man coming for redress to him (III, i, 18-20, 92-93). This representation of Henry and his Christian patience clearly reflects the lamentation and pathos suitable to a ruler fallen from power. It also accords with Skakespeare's alleviation of antipathy connected with one whose death will mark the focal point of a narrative process. If the study of literature be primarily a study of emphases, then to an audience watching this play only, a new and a constant attribute of the king's character appears as the third act begins.

As a result, Henry's piety from Act III through Act V might well be described as a Ciceronian *habitus,* the rhetorician's settled, stable attribute of character. Henry shows it in misfortune as the third act begins and in the grievous circumstances of the fifth act. He shows it also in the fourth act, when he once more becomes a ruler. At that time, when Henry transfers regal power to Warwick and Clarence, the king's piety is even represented as a *consilium,* as the reason for doing or not doing a thing (IV, vi, 16-17, 42-44). It is also linked with references to "thwarting stars," "spying and avoiding Fortune's malice," and the fact that "few men rightly temper with the stars" (ll. 22, 28-29). It is true that implicit censure might emerge from this ruler's transfer and division of regal power. It is also true that an irony may have been apparent to some in the theater—since with little regard for a strict Christian logic, Henry names God as his deliverer and Fortune as his nemesis. Yet in view of the patriotism that Henry expresses, this censure and irony probably would be less apparent to an audience than would the fact that Henry's resignation of power bows to force and fortune, which have become the impetuses of the play-world. His resignation also is represented as an action taken for the good of the whole body politic:

> He [God] was the author, thou [Warwick] the instrument.
> Therefore that I may conquer Fortune's spite
> By living low, where Fortune cannot hurt me,
> And *that the people of this blessed land*
> *May not be punish'd* with my thwarting stars,
> Warwick, although my head still wear the crown,
> I here resign my government to thee,
> For thou art fortunate in all thy deeds.[72]

(ll. 18-25)

Moreover, an audience would soon hear of the Christian excellence of Henry's rule (IV, viii, 33-50). As a consequence, throughout the last three acts of the play, although implicit criticism might emerge from the king's transfer and division of regal power, yet from his constant and basic piety there also emerges, much more clearly, his prophetic connection with Richmond, the Christian excellence of his rule, and the pathos of the final scene in the tower. Henry's Christian resignation thereby balances Edward's fortitude during the downward course of his fortune (IV, iii, 41-47, 58-59). Such an artistry is obviously well conceived,[73] especially since it will underline the viciousness of Gloucester.

Also when the third act begins, the theatrical, even visual, clarity of Shakespeare's shift in the portrayal of Henry is reinforced by the contrasting characterization of Edward and then by a contrasting characterization of Richard. Edward's lust had been referred to earlier in the play in a brief mock by Richard ("You love the breeder better than the male," II, i, 42). But it receives no emphasis until an audience hears Edward's dialogue with Lady Grey and its mocking accompaniment by both Richard and Clarence (III, ii, 1-117). As piety characterizes Henry's subsequent actions, so this attribute of Edward's character causes both Warwick and Clarence to desert the Yorkist king and fight for the Lancastrian cause. In this sense also, the third act of *3 Henry VI* begins a new dramatization, based this time upon the *natura* of a principal character.

Richard's passion for the crown then follows—a passion that his description of himself defends as a necessarily durable one, as, indeed, his *natura*. It thus provides the *consilium* for his subsequent actions that "set the murderous Machiavel to school" (III, ii, 193). Although the cleverness and vindictive fury of Richard has been constant, it is only with the third act that the images of bestiality which have been applied to him take the form of a causative thought. Since love forswore him in his mother's womb and corrupted frail nature to misshape his body, Richard's actions "to command, to check, to o'erbear" those who are his betters are a necessary consequence (III, ii, 153-71).[74] This soliloquy in which Richard describes himself is a carefully balanced moral impersonation; and the result sets off the preceding mild and pious portrayal of Henry even as it contrasts with the dramatization of Edward's lustful nature.

This triple display of dominant attributes of character seems to be an intensification, both in quantity and quality, of the way in which the last act of *2 Henry VI* developed around some character contrasts. Here the *habitus* and the *naturæ* of three principal characters set the subsequent action in motion or substantiate that action. By a theatrically appreciable manner, then, a manner that utilizes a method new to this play, the third act of *3 Henry VI* starts a new dramatic unit; and even Henry's introductory summary of events in progress reminds one strongly of characteristically introductory exposition (III, i, 28-54).

The third act is completed by a scene at the French court. There

Warwick argues for the justness of York's title to the crown, and there he turns from Edward because of that king's marriage to Lady Grey. Both aspects of the scene demand attention and both accord with what has just been noted. In the first scene of the play, it will be remembered, York's genealogical right to the crown had been represented as stronger than Henry's. Now, right by descent seems to be on Henry's side as the Lancastrians argue against Warwick (III, iii, 65-99). Warwick speaks scornfully of buckling "falsehood with a pedigree" and turns, instead, to the doctrine of possession and "gracious" rule (III, iii, 117-18). The French king then summarizes his support of Edward by emphasizing force, that is, Edward's "good success."[75] In other words, as the play progresses to Henry's murder, a dichotomy between force and the right of descent might seem to emerge—with right, in this sense of the word, being on the Lancastrian side, as it had not been when the play began. Pretty clearly, Shakespeare is concerned less with an undeviating uniformity in characterization or with consistency in political thought than with consistency in approaching the death scenes of his illustrious figures.

Shakespeare's concentration upon the *habitus* and the *naturæ* of his principal characters also carries over into his emphasis upon Warwick's "honor."[76] Previously, Warwick had been characterized as "a subtle orator" and a "great commanding" figure (III, i, 28-54). His was the "shoulder" upon which Edward would lean and build his "seat" (II, i, 189-91; vi, 100); and his anger at any reflection upon his glory had appeared only briefly in potentially contentious dialogue with Richard (II, i, 148-58). Now Shakespeare emphasizes the fact that because Edward has violated his agreement to marry the French princess, Edward has shamed Warwick; for, as that Earl says,

> . . . my desert is honour;
> And to repair my honour lost for him [Edward],
> I here renounce him and return to Henry.
>
> (III, iii, 192-94)
>
> I will revenge his wrong to Lady Bona. . . .
>
> (l. 197)
>
> Not that I pity Henry's misery,
> But seek revenge on Edward's mockery.
>
> (ll. 264-65)

Thereby a force motivated by revenge and honor reappears in the trilogy and is concentrated in this earl (e.g., III, iii, 177-78, 212, 255, 256-60). From a number of points of view, consequently, Acts IV and V develop from bases first emphasized in Act III; and since Warwick has become the principal supporter of Henry, by Clarence's changes of allegiance

(IV, i; V, i) Shakespeare signals the eclipse of Edward in Act IV and his success in Act V.

Beginning as they do with Warwick's reversal at the end of the third act, swift changes in fortune might well have seemed to be constant during the performance of the last two acts. References at the end of every scene in the fourth act to what is to be dramatized, probably would create an impression of the rush of events.[77] As one might expect in these circumstances, words about fortune and fortitude appear fairly constantly;[78] and ironies, traditionally associated with the Goddess Fortune, are rife, although they are developed briefly.[79]

The theatrical appeal of heroism on the field of battle also emerges in this portion of *3 Henry VI*, especially in the portrayals of Edward and Warwick.[80] Yet a full elaboration of English heroism never develops. Warwick's is subordinate to Edward's (V, ii, S-D, ll, 1-4), and Edward's is marred by its context. Although this Yorkist king and his court hear and accept Hastings' anti-French sentiments and his expression of the political moral of the Armada years, those lines are qualified by quarrelling, by disdain for Edward's queen, and by Richard's ambitious asides and comments (IV, i, 39 ff., 51-55, 61-64, 83, 124-26). The heroic characteristics of Edward's speeches are blunted in an equally theatrical manner by displays of Richard's vicious *natura*. This is especially true when Edward expresses remorse at bloodshed after battle (V, v, 42).

With Warwick's defeat, of course, death scenes reappear in *3 Henry VI*. At that time, concepts about honor, fortitude, fortune, and heroism are channelled into the pathos of another heroic *descriptio* that also reflects the *ubi sunt* motif and the Gothic levelling of Death (V, ii, 5-28). With two lamenting figures about the dying earl, Shakespeare also plays upon the love of brothers (ll. 33-48)—a development that contrasts sharply with Richard's thought after he has murdered Henry:

> I have no brother, I am like no brother;
> And this word "love," which greybeards call divine,
> Be resident in men like one another
> And not in me. I am myself alone.
>
>   (V, vii, 80-83)

In view of what has been considered, there should be little need to comment further upon the catastrophe, save to indicate some other noticeable balances related to the portrayal of Richard. After the young Prince's heroic resolution has inflamed Richard's murderous choler, Henry's devoutness encounters Richard's villainy with a similar courage (V, vi, 2-5). Henry's classically derived speeches also turn this villain's mocking reference to Icarus, that is, to the young prince, back upon Richard, the envious gulf (ll. 18-25). This turn of thought agrees perfectly with Richard's nature, which would command, check, and overbear his betters. Finally, just as Margaret had struck the note that nemesis hangs over the head of Edward's newborn son (V, v, 51-67), so Henry finally prophecies that many thousands will rue the hour Richard was born, as will

> . . . many an old man's sigh and many a widow's,
> And many an orphan's water-standing eye,—
> Men for their sons, wives for their husbands,
> And orphans for their parents' timeless death. . . .
>
> (V, vi, 39-42)

Mythical thought of the period and the horror that might accompany tragedy are also turned upon the misshapen body of this Machiavel (V, vi, 44-51). Accordingly, the resolution of *3 Henry VI* is marred by two of Richard's asides (V, vii, 21-25, 33-34). They give substance to Margaret's prediction and reflect Richard's ultimate aim of achieving the crown—even as the Yorkists' drums and trumpets sound to the hope of "Farewell sour annoy! / For here . . . begins our lasting joy" (ll. 45-46). Although the irony of this ending is more superficial than that implicit in other situations,[81] its effect must have been inescapable as it would arouse further interest in seeing Shakespeare's continuing dramatization of the annals of England.

All three parts of *Henry VI*, consequently, show Shakespeare's control of a cyclical process and his concern for creating climactic scenes of theatrical effectiveness. His use of a cyclical intensification is sure, purposeful, and at times noticeably precise. As he represents the varying "estate of the time then present,"[82] Shakespeare also develops his basic process by an equally precise use of situations that reflect the moralities, of comic scenes that accord with his dominant emphases, and of episodes that dramatize his characters' *habitus* or *naturæ*. Except for the concept of the vicissitude of states, the three parts of *Henry VI* show a relative freedom from the complexities and cruxes that might result from the political commonplaces of the age. Although a conflict between the validity of descent and the validity of possession is constantly apparent, Shakespeare's emphasis falls upon a disjunction within the belief that a ruler should exercise a dominant Christian force for the good of his kingdom. The essential conflict is between an ineffective virtue and a vigorous "vertue." Aside from his use of a tumultuous stage, Shakespeare's representation of this vigor is derived primarily from methods used to display the Machiavel and the "hero." In this respect, however, his emphasis falls upon heroism and revenge on the field of battle and runs a gamut from a nascent titanism to a Senecan horror and a vicious bestiality. Shakespeare also focuses his attention constantly on the deaths of illustrious persons. In those scenes, he may utilize the Senecan tradition, political precepts, a display of courageous vigor, or reflections of the motif of the coming of Death with related echoes of *ubi sunt* formulae and earlier death laments. Usually he creates pathos in these spectacles, and for their sake he subordinates even the genealogical considerations of *3 Henry VI*.

In contrast, the irony that might result from the use of some ready-made concepts—about factious nobles, fortitude, fate, or Fortune's Wheel—generally needs a slightly fuller development to be unmistakably and theatrically appreciable.[83] From the use of a morality-process in *2 Henry VI*, however, and from the qualification, ambivalence, and irony in his interlocking characterizations, Shakespeare foreshadows features of his later artistry. Finally, as the second and third parts of *Henry VI* move toward their conclusions, Shakespeare's characters emerge as figures who shape their fortune and the fate of England.

Quite in accordance with what has been noted about the concluding scene of *3 Henry VI* is the fact that *Richard III*—with the possible exception of a situation centered upon the passive Anne[84]—elaborates only the obvious irony that results from hypocrisy known to an audience and the theatrical appeal of the Machiavel. Hastings' fall and death is developed in such a manner. Although his confidence overrides mythical thought and thereby heightens the suddenness of his condemnation (III, ii), yet that effect exists within a display of Richard's villainous virtuosity. Lamentation for Hastings, for example, becomes but another instance of Richard's and Buckingham's vicious wit, as Richard speaks sorrowfully of the death of this dear one whom he took to be "the plainest harmless creature / That breath'd upon the earth a Christian" (III, v, 25-26). Then the helplessness of all in this world of vicious and triumphant hypocrisy is emphasized by a nameless scrivener (III, vi). Irony is directed at Richard only as the drama moves toward its fortunate catastrophe effected by Richmond. At that time, Shakespeare solidifies the effect of curses, lamentations, and similar speeches stretching back to the beginning of the play;[85] and he briefly elaborates this anticipatory irony by ironic developments connected with the debate between Richard and Elizabeth.[86] But until then, nothing effectively mitigates the apparently indomitable force of the witty, hypocritical, and vicious figure whose rise and reign is being dramatized.

As the last remark indicates, *Richard III* shows once more Shakespeare's grasp of an effective five-act structure that reflects current academic precepts and is focused upon the rise and fall of the protagonist. In the first act, two stratagems are accomplished. Anne is won by Richard's virtuosity in debate, and Clarence is murdered. Between those two accomplishments, faction within the house of York is dramatized (I, iii). It is controlled momentarily by the appearance of Margaret, whose maledictions indicate how the course of English history is being controlled by a vendetta. Yet even in this episode, Shakespeare preserves Richard's central position. It is he who first turns on Margaret (ll. 163-64). It is he who unites the wranglers by seeing in Margaret's sufferings the effect of his father's curse and who by that action starts her maledictions (ll. 174-214). It is he who becomes the principal object of these curses and who, with an appreciable comic effect, apparently turns them upon Margaret (ll. 233-36). After the horrific effect of her lines has been specified—

> *Buck.* My hair doth stand on end to hear her curses.
> *Riv.* And so doth mine

(ll. 304-5)

—it is Richard, in a virtuous pose, who starts the wrangling again (ll. 306 ff.) and who in his soliloquy commenting upon that action refers to a third subordinate stratagem (the arousing of Derby, Hastings, and Buckingham against the queen's kindred).

In accordance with this third stratagem, the conclusion of Act II, scene i, is dramatized. The union of Buckingham and Richard then takes the specific form of what might be called the fourth stratagem: separating the queen's kindred from the prince and imprisoning Rivers, Grey, and Vaughan in Pomfret Castle (II, ii, 146 ff.; II, iv, 42-45). Although Richard has not caused the death of King Edward—which, with Clarence's death in the first act, establishes the process of the death of an illustrious person per act[87]—Acts I and II have introduced the characters and are a "handsome" indication of what is to follow as a result of Richard's villainy. Four plots have been accomplished, with the third shifting into the fourth and being effected by Richard and the minor villain Buckingham.

In Act III, as the conclusion of this fourth stratagem is dramatized (III, iii), the major and minor villains are effecting a fifth (the winning of Hastings or his death, III, i, 151 ff., ii, iv, vi). Then they turn to the sixth stratagem (proclaiming Richard king, III, v, vii). In the meantime, Richard alone posits a seventh (the removal of his brother's offspring, III, v, 106-9). In Act IV, a major feature of the seventh, the murder of the young princes, is completed; and marriage with young Elizabeth becomes the eighth stratagem. It, too, seems to be accomplished.

In contrast with the plotting in *The Spanish Tragedy* and *The Jew of*

Malta, these vicious plans are not concatenated in the sense that the inauguration of one is necessary to escape the consequences of the preceding one. Only the eighth bears such a relationship to the fourth and sixth. Inaugurated on news of Dorset's flight to Richmond, this eighth stratagem also appears in circumstances that specify and further motivate the seventh (IV, ii, 46-66). Yet from this point of view alone, one can perceive an increasing complexity now that Richard has risen to the top of his fortune, and such a development accords with precepts about the nature of an epitasis.[88] Elizabeth's reversal of her decision, which was the result of the apparent success of the eighth plot (IV, iv, 426-30; IV, v, 7-8), then indicates the nature of the ensuing catastrophe and makes ironic the line given to Richard about a "Relenting fool, and shallow changing woman" (IV, iv, 431).

This indication of the nature of the catastrophe underlines other signs of the retributive fall awaiting Richard. There was a theatrically obvious reference to Richmond at the beginning of the fourth act—a reference that had increased the faintest of previous counteractions and that had been linked with the figures of Dorset and Stanley.[89] When the break with Buckingham adumbrated Richard's final lack of success, Richmond was mentioned again, the last time as Richard's nemesis (IV, ii, 48-49, 88, 106-10). In the second reference to the eighth stratagem, Richmond was named as the inciting cause (IV, iii, 40-42). Accordingly, his power was referred to as being a greater threat to Richard than the revolt of Buckingham (IV, iii, 46-50). Immediately after those forces opposed to Richard were mentioned in juxtaposition, the reappearance of Margaret looked back to the beginning of the drama and underscored the working out of her earlier curses. Elizabeth's fortunes, for example, bear out the fact that she was called "The flattering index of a direful pageant; / One heav'd a-high, to be hurl'd down below" (IV, iv, 85-86).[90] Since the "course of justice" now has "whirl'd about" and left Elizabeth "but a very prey to time" (ll. 105-6), this development also looks forward to the death of the central figure, whose villainous rise was dramatized during the first three acts and who was the principal person cursed by Margaret.

Shakespeare effects an increasing complexity as the fourth act closes in two other ways. The debate between Richard and Elizabeth has been referred to already, but it is pertinent to note that this intricate argument represents the height of the rhetorical complexity in the drama and hence accords with the conventional nature of the narrative development in the epitasis. At first, Richard seems to win this debate, and his apparent success is then represented in another way. An outcome favorable for him is effected by the repetitive scene that shows four messengers and Catesby bringing news of Buckingham, Richmond, and others who oppose Richard (IV, iv, 500-40). Taken together, both situations provide a false resolution before the spectators would hear of Elizabeth's reversal and have their attention turned toward the approaching warfare. The true resolution, of course, is then produced in Act V by Shakespeare's representation of the contrast and conflict between this villain and the savior of England.

The preceding movement by stratagems also involves episodes that dramatize the fate of minor illustrious persons and that extend to more than one act. Lamentation for the death of Clarence, which occurred in the first act, constitutes the last speech of Edward in the second act. That expression of sorrow is continued in the subsequent scene, where is is joined with lamentation for Edward. There then follows the forward movement of the fourth stratagem (II, ii, 120 ff.), which is partially completed in the third act by the death scene of Rivers, Grey, and Vaughn (III, iii). By this time, the emergence of Buckingham has begun. It started in the second act; and as it involves the fall and death of Hastings, it becomes strikingly apparent in the third act. It culminates in the fourth act when Buckingham turns from Richard; and in that act also, the sharp reversal of Buckingham's fortune is achieved. His death scene then introduces the last act.

Although his five-act structure is developed with a sixteenth-century multiplicity that includes antiphonal scenes of lamentation, Shakespeare simplifies this last major development in a panorama of twenty acts by relating all of his episodes to the rise and fall of his protagonist. To an appreciable degree, *Richard III* stands to the dramatization of preceding historical events as one aspect of the development of any last act stands to the preceding ones. England fell from a victorious kingly rule to a state controlled by a jarring nobility, by the "worst kind of *Oligarchie*," by the momentary dominance of the many-headed multitude, and by warfare that degenerated into a vendetta. Upon the death of Edward IV, a choric scene in *Richard III* reminds an audience of the beginning of this woe (II, iii, 34-88). After the death of York, a tyrant had begun his climb to the throne; and under him, England touches a nadir in her affairs. As has been indicated, the fact that this development of four plays should end in a relatively simple basic pattern coincides with the normal simplification of complexity as a resolution is effected. At the same time, the cyclically progressive evil stretching through the nineteen acts accords with the way in which vice frequently was represented as triumphing with progressive force until salvation was achieved relatively suddenly.[91]

With the exception of Richard's successful plots and his retributive fall, most of the features of this drama which have been noted so far probably would be unconsciously appreciable to an audience, appreciable progressively, or appreciable upon reflection. In contrast, the initial appearance of Richard probably inaugurated a theatrical portrayal that would be familiar to theater-goers and alluring even to newcomers. His opening soliloquy would build upon memories of the vicious plotter. As Richard scorns the present state of England and the triple meaning of the son-sun of York, he also repeats maliciously a traditional attitude of the blunt soldier, who may be quite worthy but who sees in peace only luxuriousness and effeminacy.[92] This attitude is preserved when Richard speaks with "forthrightness" to Clarence. In this dialogue, one might also perceive the humorous understatements of high-born individuals who theoretically should be accustomed to the vicissitudes of fortune and be ready when able to remedy them (I, i, 42-51, 113-16). Conventionally too, Clarence and Gloucester resent upstarts (ll. 62-75, 78-83, 95).

Richard's hypocrisy, however, would be inescapable, especially in his grim derision of brotherly love and of Clarence:

> Simple, plain Clarence! I do love thee so
> That I will shortly send thy soul to heaven,
> If heaven will take the present at our hands.
>
> (I, i, 118-20)

This mockery, with its twist upon conventional piety, would agree with Richard's quick answer to Brakenbury, with the bawdy word-play upon Brakenbury's retort, and with Richard's scornful phraseology (ll. 88-96, 98-100, 106). By these lines, elements of familiarity resulting from the conventional representation of a vice-like figure probably played about the portrayal of this duke, who is dominating the stage. The function of a mischievous, manipulating figure, regardless of Richard's present villainy, is also apparent in both of his lines that introduce dialogue:

> Dive, thoughts, down to my soul! Here Clarence comes.
>
> (l. 41)
>
> But who comes here? The new-delivered Hastings?[93]
>
> (l. 121)

As a result, an impression of both the malicious vice and the mischievous vice would accord with Richard's "honest" derision, his villainous piety, and his earlier mockery of love (ll. 12-13, 16-17). Memories of the old morality scheme of vices masquerading as virtues[94] also could provide congruent overtones to the honest pose of Richard and to his repetition of the theme that evil, ambitious upstarts congregate about a sensual ruler—a line of thought that will be dramatized later (ll. 62-83, 130-33, 138-42; I, iii, 42-110, 261-65, 311-15; II, i, 77-80). Although a modern critic may be thankful for some lines in the third act, the regular Elizabethan theater-goer probably did not need to have his theatrical memory explicitly jogged in order to react as has been indicated. When Richard remarks that "like the formal vice, Iniquity," he moralizes "two meanings in one word" (III, i, 82-83), the comment probably was meant to cause amusement in its immediate context. In Shakespeare's theater, memories of older vices probably were at work as an audience watched Richard during his first appearances.

In addition, when Richard woos Anne, Shakespeare gives to his vicious protagonist the wit of the rhetor. As he makes his first debate adhere to his premises, Richard utilizes an effective sophistic and thereby wins the widow of one of his victims. Probably few spectators were able to name the rhetorical devices that Shakespeare used in the two main parts of this dialogue in the second scene—and even in terminology there might be a justifiable divergence. But it is difficult to see how anyone, especially a spectator who relied on his ear for learning, could escape noticing either the division of the debate or the general pattern of its logic. The division would be underlined for him by the change specified in Richard's lines,

> But, gentle Lady Anne,
> To leave this keen encounter of our wits
> And fall something into a slower method. . . .
>
> (I, ii, 114-16)

The general pursuit of Richard's argument would be repetitive enough and forceful enough to make clear the trap set for Anne by the premise that "the causer" of deaths is as "blameful as the executioner" (ll. 117-19).[95] By such wit, illustrated by action, Shakespeare exploits the intellectual virtuosity conventionally given to the plotting villain and especially effective in dialogue with a woman.[96]

The first two scenes are then unified by Richard's gleeful soliloquy. In his opening speech, "sportive tricks," "an amorous looking-glass," and seeing his "shadow in the sun" had led to the conclusion that Richard must play the villain. Later, those ideas are elaborated; and this witty derider and ugly wooer, after mocking his loved one, mocks himself, even in his conclusion:

> Shine out, fair sun, till I have bought a glass,
> That I may see my shadow as I pass.
>
> (ll. 263-64)

By this merging of the manner of the old vice with the wit of the rhetor and the virtuosity of the vicious antagonist or the rising Machiavel, Shakespeare establishes Richard's dominance.

Shakespeare also has woven into the portrayal of Richard a fearsome horror that by itself might be considered appropriate to tragedy. In the scene wherein Richard woos Anne, her lament is provided with a pageantic entrance and setting (I, ii, S-D, ll. 1-4); but her pathetic *descriptio* soon turns to vituperation (ll. 1-13, 14-28). Her images of horror thereby precede the fear that the supernumeraries show of the "black magician" Richard (e.g., ll. 19-24; 34, 43). As her vituperation increases, the wounds of dead Henry VI "Open their congeal'd mouths and bleed afresh" (l. 56). Anne evokes God, the earth that "this blood drink'st," and the heavens to destroy the "dreadful minister of hell," the "foul devil" Richard. These speeches reflect once more the classical bravura of passages in Seneca and Ovid; and in this context Richard demonstrates his witty, vicious virtuosity. As a result, the risibility of the scene probably would be qualified by the pathos embodied in the figure of Anne, by constant reminders of Richard's viciousness, by the sight of his malevolence, by the impression of his fearsome vigor, and by the funereal circumstances to which Shakespeare carefully returns (ll. 226-27, 261). From this merging of pathos, fearfulness, ingenious wittiness, and "foul" ugliness, there may well have resulted a grotesque distortion akin to that of Woodstock's murder, or Kyd's hanging of Pedringano, or Marlowe's more flamboyant portrayal of Barabas. This aspect of the drama accords with the later scene of Clarence's death (I, iv).

Before comedy and murder are merged, however, Richard's second long soliloquy of glee may well have channelled this grotesque effect toward an amoral detachment, valid not simply for the character but for the spectator as well. In a comparable manner, when Richard next appears in the pose of an honest and pious man, his wit surmounts the horrific lines directed at him by Margaret:

> Thou elvish-mark'd, abortive, rooting hog!
> Thou that wast seal'd in thy nativity
> The slave of nature and the son of hell!
> Thou slander of thy heavy mother's womb!
> Thou loathed issue of thy father's loin!
> Thou rag of honour! thou detested—
>   *Glou.* Margaret.
> *Q. Mar.*   Richard!
> *Glou.*   Ha!

> *Q. Mar.*   I call thee not.
> *Glou.* I cry thee mercy then, for I did think
> That thou hadst call'd me all these bitter names.
>
> (I, iii, 228-36)

By this quick, witty trick to escape the effect of a curse, Richard would remain for the audience the detached but dramatic mocker who manipulates the figures on the stage. The comic vein of hypocritical piety is solidified thereby; and probably there would be solidified also that amoral detachment conducive to amusement at happenings within a bear pit or upon the place of Lopez' execution.[97]

The preceding technique appears constantly in the dramatization of Richard's rise and utilizes both derisive asides and the verbal ingenuity of "the formal vice, Iniquity," until Richard's "piety" culminates in the picture of his accepting the kingship (III, vii). After his appearance *"between two* Bishops," the manner of Iniquity disappears almost entirely. The noncomical wit of sudden decisions, and almost of improvisation, increases and a causally concatenated stratagem also appears (IV, ii, 28-35, 51-62, iii, 51-57, iv, 432 ff.). But before then, Shakespeare has developed a comic tone in villainous and fearsome circumstances for appreciable portions of the drama and thereby so heightened the theatrical appeal of Richard that villainy probably continued to exist within its own amoral premises. In accordance with this emphasis, except for the sorrow of Edward and of Hastings (II, i, 102-32; III, iv, 82-109), lamentation throughout the drama is expressed in terms of mythical thinking and horror rather than in those of pathos.

Aside from what has been noted, Shakespeare's artistry also builds upon other matter that could have been familiar to an Elizabethan. The pattern of Richard's villainous rise and fall was apparent in a tragedy performed by the Queen's Men and called *The True Tragedy of Richard the Third* (1588-94).[98] As countless critics have pointed out, Shakespeare's play also intensifies the historical tradition of Richard's villainy, a tradition established early in the century by More and Polydore Vergil.[99] In addition, when Shakespeare shows how his rising figure's stratagems were effected in part by a witty rhetorical virtuosity, he reflects a conception held widely enough for it to appear in works designed for those who preferred their reading in English rather than in Latin. Not only had Rainolde, for example, inserted an oration on Richard's tyranny into his adaptation of Aphthonius but he had also characterized this ruler as one "pregnaunt of witte."[100] Thus in Shakespeare's drama a portrayal of viciousness and its mocking comedy would be developed in a manner that would accord with the memory of a regular theater-goer, with the memory of one who had read his English history, and with the memory of whoever had studied a work that made available to untrained readers the rhetorical discipline admired by the age. Again, one would expect Shakespeare's artistry to be popular on the stage. It is both perceptive and sure.[101]

As has been noted, the comic emphasis in the role for Richard decreases once he has achieved his objective; but his dangerous viciousness and his "tyrannous and bloody" acts remain (IV, iii, 1). The representation of Richard's death, accordingly, varies appreciably from that of the majority of the characters who die in *Henry VI*. Yet it is interesting to note that within the major premise of Richard's black and tyrannical villainy, there is an adumbration of Shakespeare's later technique in writing *Macbeth*. Also within this major premise, Shakespeare glances at a retributive irony that, quite understandably, is not developed fully.

In the fourth act, Richard recognizes his "uncertain way of gain" and the fact that he is "So far in blood that sin will pluck on sin" (IV, ii, 63-65); and earlier Anne had spoken of his "timorous dreams" (IV, i, 85). In the fifth act, in line with this very brief development, an audience would see Richard in torment and hear his despair:

> O coward conscience, how dost thou afflict me!
> The lights burn blue. It is now dead midnight.
> Cold fearful drops stand on my trembling flesh.
> What! do I fear myself? There's none else by.
> Richard loves Richard; that is, I am I.
> Is there a murderer here? No. Yes, I am.
> Then fly. What, from myself? Great reason why,
> Lest I revenge. What, myself upon myself?
> Alack, I love myself. Wherefore? For any good
> That I myself have done unto myself?
> O, no! alas, I rather hate myself
> For hateful deeds committed by myself!
> I am a villain: yet I lie, I am not.
> Fool, of thyself speak well; fool, do not flatter.
> My conscience hath a thousand several tongues,
> And every tongue brings in a several tale,
> And every tale condemns me for a villain.
> Perjury, perjury, in the high'st degree;
> Murder, stern murder, in the dir'st degree;
> All several sins, all us'd in each degree,
> Throng to the bar, crying all, Guilty! guilty!

I shall despair. There is no creature loves me,
And if I die no soul shall pity me.
Nay, wherefore should they, since that I myself
Find in myself no pity to myself?

(V, iii, 179-203)

Paradoxically, even as Richard dismisses pity for himself, pathos faintly emerges, and one's attention is turned to the retributive irony mentioned above. In the epitatical fullness of Shakespeare's rhetorical process, that is, in Richard's debate with Elizabeth, Richard had been hard put to establish his premise and to specify it; and even then he made little headway because of Elizabeth's vigorous adherence to her premise.[102] He seemed to win only when he promised to repent with an oath that would "confound" himself if his protestations were not true (IV, iv, 397 ff.; e.g., 415). In the conventional process of repentance, sorrow for sin followed a recognition of sin; and this soul-harrowing process might involve the agony of despair and a temptation to suicide. Witness, then, the ghosts' antiphonal refrain, "Despair and die" (V, iii, 118-76); its fearful echo in Richard's thought about revenging himself upon himself; and his cry, "I shall despair"—a process of thought and emotion that if pursued might well make Richard's vow "Myself myself confound" come true.

Instead of pursuing this retributive irony, however, the drama turns from Richard's suffering to his final vice-like action. That Shakespeare should do this is eminently suitable in view of the panorama now being completed by the first of the Tudors and in view of the fact that Richard's viciousness is an inured one. Indeed, Shakespeare has re-established an emphasis that anticipates this development. When wooing reappeared at the end of the fourth act and Richard planned to approach Elizabeth, his earlier mockery returned: "To her go I, a jolly thriving wooer" (IV, iii, 43). That manner continued in Richard's answers to his mother and in his derisive comment at the end of his debate with Elizabeth (IV, iv, 155, 163, 175-76, 431). In accordance with these vestiges of an earlier manner, and as the stage is cleared for Richmond and his oration, Richard exists to "play the eaves-dropper" (V, iii, 220-22); and by this vice-like distortion of regality, the brief process of his suffering is stopped. What he hears is pleasing to him (ll. 271-75); and thereafter Richard's inured and diabolical viciousness enacts "wonders" on the battlefield before it is destroyed by Richmond. Shakespeare, nevertheless, has sustained his movement from epitasis to catastrophe by giving Richard a human despair. Even though the representation of his suffer-

ing and the development of a retributive irony are cut short, they
foreshadow a more mature artistry.

As has been indicated, this final development in the portrayal of
Richard is quite understandable; for by the time the fifth act was
performed, the central premise of his villainy and tyranny would obviate
any troublesome cleavage in an Elizabethan's ethical or political reaction
to the drama. Despite his theatrical appeal, Richard is a tyrant by accession, by rule, and by aim; and the fifth act dramatizes the way in
which England was rescued from her despair. When the beneficent force
of Richmond is to make itself felt, Elizabethan consciences must have
fallen easily upon the side of one who is opposing a "guilty homicide"
(V, ii, 17-18). By God and Elizabeth's grandfather, England is
delivered.[103]

Although *Richard III,* in general, does not show the ambivalence and
the ironies that in the second and third parts of *Henry VI* seems to foreshadow a later artistry, Shakespeare's rhetorical exuberance throughout
the drama is unmistakable. For his contemporaries, it probably increased
the appeal of the play. An outline of a thesis-like oration, for example,
is embodied in a speech and followed immediately by a fuller dramatization of that process (III, vii, 1-22, and ff.). Kindred developments are
rife (I, iv; II, ii, iii, iv, 8-35; III, i, 31-58, ii, 1-75).[104] Although the
uneducated members of an audience may not have followed with
expertise the shrewd argumentative process of the debate between
Richard and Elizabeth, the interest of the situation, like that of the
earlier debate with Anne, is heightened by the parry and thrust of stichomythia. Theatrically akin to the debate, for that matter, is the balanced
preparation for the final battle. In an aural age, an audience's appreciation of Shakespeare's rhetoric probably varied in degree rather than in
kind—especially since it was devoted primarily to the portrayal of the
rise and fall of a vice-like, witty, and terrifying tyrant, through whose
death a beneficent English polity was re-established. More relevant to
the life of Elizabethans than Barabas and more fully portrayed than
Mortimer, Shakespeare's Richard must have aroused the fascination
and fear that sustained the Machiavel as a political specter, haunting the
imagination of the age.

From the point of view of Shakespeare's development as an artist
the rhetoric of *Richard III* also accords with the witty virtuosity of
Love's Labour's Lost. When one considers that this last drama, and at
least seven of the preceding ones, probably were written by the time that
the acting companies were reorganized in 1594, it is not surprising that
Shakespeare became the principal playwright for one of the two major
companies.

VI

Love's Labour's Lost and A Midsummer Night's Dream

FROM A COMPARISON among Shakespeare's dramas so far considered and those yet to be discussed, there could have emerged some contrasts that for the Elizabethan theater-goer might have been apparent upon reflection but that for their author were probably obvious as he composed his plays. Against the brief jig-like merriment of the classically derived *Comedy of Errors,* against the comic scenes of Speed and Launce, and the varying distortions of Cade and even of mocking Richard, Shakespeare must have perceived that his comic artistry culminated in *Love's Labour's Lost* and *A Midsummer Night's Dream.* Although he was to surpass himself, that artistry was unique as the winter season of 1594-95 saw the public theaters reopened for something more than sporadic performances.[1]

The comic spirit of *Love's Labour's Lost* is unusual; for it emanates from a vigorous sophistic that is nevertheless mature enough to laugh at itself and its own absurdities. In this respect, Sir Walter Cope's note to Robert Cecil about a performance of this comedy in January of 1605 may seem to be singularly appropriate in that it specifies a sophisticated audience:

> I have sent and bene all thys morning huntyng for players Juglers & Such kinde of Creaturs, but fynde them harde to finde; wherefore Leavinge notes for them to seeke me, Burbage ys come, & Sayes there ys no new playe that the quene hath not seene, but they have Revyved an olde one, Cawled *Loves Labour lost,* which for wytt and mirthe he sayes will please her excedingly. And Thys ys apointed to be playd to Morowe night at my Lord of Sowthamptons, unless yow send a wrytt to Remove the Corpus Cum Causa to your howse in Strande. Burbage ys my messenger Ready attendyng your pleasure.[2]

As has been indicated in a preceding chapter, however, the exuberant rhetoric of *Love's Labour's Lost* need not have been entirely esoteric. Its figures of fun reflect situations and characters apparent in the ephemeral merriment of the era and thoroughly familiar to Elizabethans; and as the play develops, Shakespeare constantly builds his scenic processes upon what was comically familiar.

Since the structure of *Love's Labour's Lost,* as well as the nature of the drama, is indicated clearly in the first scene, a somewhat detailed consideration of the opening episode will prove profitable. As the play begins, Shakespeare's king and his three lords are brought down to the milieu of comedy; but in accordance with their positions in a body politic, there is established at first a scope characteristic of the beginning and the ending of *Titus Andronicus* and *The Comedy of Errors*—a scope that is wider than that emphasized by the line of action established in the protasis, complicated in the epitasis, and then concluded. Concomitant with this is the fact that these characters, who are proficient in the art to be distorted, would themselves distort a theatrical norm whereby young men in a comedy are primarily interested in young women.

The first lines that an audience would hear express the aim of Christian rule as it had been specified for generations:

> Let fame, that all hunt after in their lives,
> Live regist'red upon our brazen tombs
> And then grace us in the disgrace of death;
> When, spite of cormorant, devouring Time,
> Th'endeavour of this present breath may buy
> That honour which shall bate his scythe's keen edge
> And make us heirs of all eternity.
>
> (I, i, 1-7)

By 1594, the idea that a ruler and his subalterns should desire fame and honor, although it sometimes may be expressed naïvely, as in *1 Henry VI,* was no stranger to the stage; and its traditional force can be illustrated easily in the vast body of treaties *de regimine principum:* "The reward of the excellent king, which he should expect for his just acts from those whom he rules, is glory alone, and becoming honor, which, after it has been sung by a multitude of men and by diverse peoples, first increases to rumor and then grows to that fame which Homer thought never would be abolished."[3] Linked with control of the affections and "the huge army of the world's desires," a concern for honor and fame would agree with concepts about the nature of an ideal ruler and his virtuous court; and in such a manner the king's speech continues:

> Therefore, brave conquerors,—for so you are,
> That war against your own affections
> And the huge army of the world's desires,—
> Our late edict shall strongly stand in force.
> Navarre shall be the wonder of the world:
> Our court shall be a little Academe,
> Still and contemplative in living art.
>
> (ll. 8-14)

One is reminded of the tradition in back of James's opening words in his *Basilikon Doron* or of Castiglione's words that link discipline of the affections with virtue and with fame.[4] One also can turn to the four young men of Anjou mentioned in *The French Academie*.[5] Indeed, there should be a little need to gloss further the fact that the ideal of achieving fame and the related one of a courtly and philosophic discipline of the emotions were considered valid by Shakespeare's age, especially for rulers and their associates.

Equally well-known to Elizabethans might be a third idea conventionally connected with ruling conduct, namely, that a prince should not neglect his duty and retire from public affairs, like Sidney's Basilius, or, in this instance, be so concerned with establishing an "Academe" that that desire ironically becomes a preoccupying appetite. In this drama, the reception of the news that the Princess of France is coming to Navarre on public business will dispose of any such ruling distortion. Before that development appears, however, the witty turn given to the initial situation by Berowne brings up the men's violation of an equally widespread concept, one apparent in Castiglione's discourse and one especially valid for comedy, namely, that young men are expected to love.[6] The beginning of *Love's Labour's Lost,* consequently, moves from the aim of rule by a precept of rule to mention of a comic norm even as a possible political distortion is dismissed. Once this comic norm appears, however, Shakespeare concentrates upon the ideal of a polished rhetoric, not upon narrative motifs that hinder the course of true love. An approximation of this latter sort of development appears only upon Mercade's entrance in Act V.

In accordance with what will be his dominant emphasis, Shakespeare's wit would be apparent immediately. The opening lines, for example, turn upon an oxymoronic phrase, "grace us in disgrace," and develop lightly running wordplay from *breath* (i.e., *scythe's*-"sighs" and *heirs*-"airs"). Inescapable would be the protests of Berowne. His speeches are focused on the fairness of women, and by a dialectal tour de force he gives reverse English to the king's premise that the aim of study is to know "which else we should not know" (I, i, 56). The "vain delights" of the king's brief refutation are treated in a similar manner. Just as Berowne has proved that he may study to know "some mistress fine" and to know how to break the oath itself that binds him to study, so his treatment of "vain delights" emphasizes courtship—by idea, by the language of sonneteering, and even by the form of a sonnet (ll. 80-93). Berowne's method is then mocked in rime (ll. 94-96); and that mockery is itself mocked,[7] as Berowne utilizes the comic overtones of *green geese* and then puns on *follow,* which was homophonic with "fallow" (ll. 97-98). This phraseology would be associated normally with the principal figure causing merriment; and, accordingly, after Berowne has made the point that there is a time for everything, his lines develop the traditionally comic reference to a woman's talkativeness (ll. 124-129). Moreover, when the king states that "mere necessity" must allow him to confer with the princess, this dizzard of high degree immediately applies the necessity conventionally associated with ruling conduct to the norm of comedy. Thereby he indicates the development of the drama, even in his "jingling" with *last* (i.e., long *æ;* long *ę,* short *ę,* or "least"):

> If I break faith, this word shall speak for me;
> I am forsworn on "mere necessity."
>
> .   .   .   .
>
> But I believe, although I seem so loath,
> I am the last that will last keep his oath.[8]
>
> (ll. 154-61)

Through Berowne, Shakespeare has posited the direction of the play, established a witty rhetoric, touched briefly on wooing compatible with courtly sonneteering, and struck notes of Elizabethan merriment that will accord with the low comic parallel.

The drama then turns to that parallel. Costard's recent actions confirm Berowne's line that "every man with his affects is born" (I, i, 152); and thereby Costard appears as the clownish dizzard of low degree successful in accomplishing that figure's traditional way with a maid. The fact emerges as Armado's letter is read and as Shakespeare begins to develop his portrayal of this sophisticated figure of fun. The letter accusing Costard of violating the king's decree prohibiting communication with a woman exhibits a comic rhetoric not only in its *elocutio* but also in its *dispositio* and *inventio.* A stupid varying of epithets embroiders a ridiculous order of "places," and the causal place is misunderstood literally as "the ground which" (l. 241).[9] The result is a ridiculously repetitive order as absurd synonyms move in burlesque climax to the naming of Costard and Jacquenetta. Varying synonyms was a recognized rhetorical device and will be repeated—with a nonderisive appropriateness—when Costard attempts to escape punishment. By Armado's letter, consequently, the amusement inherent in his description becomes concrete; and his tales of many a knight from "tawny Spain" will be passed over for ridicule of his affectations and of the "mint of phrases" in the brain of this "refined" Spanish traveler (ll. 173-74, 166, 164).

Although the full comic effect of the letter undoubtedly would depend upon a knowledge of rhetorical precepts, laughter would have been anticipated by the comments of Berowne and Longaville; it probably would have been started by their stage laughter; and it would build upon the dialogue that had intervened between the description of Armado and the reading of his epistle (I, i, 195-202, 282-83, 184-220). Introduced by the time-honored device of a clown's mistaking words (ll. 184, 191), this dialogue had been expanded by bawdy wordplay related to the usual lechery of the clown-fool. In company with puns on *manner* and *manor* and on *form* ("shape" or "bench"), the wordplay inherent in the Elizabethan pronunciation of *follow* and *fallow* must have become increasingly apparent as Costard told an audience about the "matter" of Armado's letter:

> The matter is to me, sir, as concerning Jacquenetta. The manner of it is, I was taken with the manner.
> *Ber.* In what manner?
> *Cost.* In manner and form following, sir; all these three: I was seen with her in the manorhouse, sitting with her upon the form, and taken following her into the park; which, put together, is in manner and form following,—it is the manner of a man to speak to a woman; for the form,—in some form.
> *Ber.* For the following, sir?
> *Cost.* As it shall follow in my correction; and God defend the right!

> (ll. 203-16)

The specification of a *double-entendre* is explicit in a subsequent mistaking: "Such is the sinplicity of a man to hearken after the flesh" (l. 220).[10]

With such a beginning, the letter is read; and its sentences are accompanied by Costard's interruptions, spoken probably by Will Kemp, who here was appearing with a "great limb or joint" (V, i, 135). Some of his lines also indicate what one might expect, namely, that Kemp was adept at comic bravery or cowardice: e.g.,

> *King.* Peace!
> *Cost.* Be to me, and every man that dares not fight!
>
> (ll. 229-30)

These interruptions would continue the laughter and amusement already started. To appreciate such comedy no knowledge of grammar school matter is necessary. Costard's forthright "with a wench" (l. 265) must have been laughable to all in its juxtaposition with Armado's "child of our grandmother Eve, a female; or, for thy more sweet understanding, a woman" (ll. 266-68). All that would be required would be a predisposition to laugh at Kemp's antics, both physical and verbal; and here, as elsewhere, those antics embody conventional aspects of the principal comedian's roles.

As in his portrayal of his grotesque figures of fun,[11] Shakespeare's scenes, here and elsewhere, show a constant merging of the sophisticated and the popular. Here, Costard's quibbling to avoid punishment involves his turning from *wench,* to *damsel,* to *virgin,* and then to *maid.* This comic "copy" parallels Armado's ridiculous varying of phrases. It also leads to Costard's bawdy assertion that this "maid" will serve his turn. Thereby it confirms and repeats the thought of the earlier *follow*-"fallow" pun, even as it builds upon the traditional device of a clown's equating word with thing (I, i, 289-301). By this comic "furniture both of words and approved phrases and fashions of speaking," the lusty capability of the one who usually won the rustic maid is kept alive; and in the remainder of the drama, Costard's appearance with Jaquenetta dominates, and ridicules thereby, Armado's desire for her.

Before the immediate scene ends, however, it proceeds by way of a pun on *mutton* ("the flesh of a sheep," "the flesh of a woman," I, i, 302-5) to the concluding situation when the king and two of the lords have left the stage. At that time, the dizzards of high degree and of low are left to comment upon what has been dramatized:

> *Bir.* I'll lay my head to any good man's hat,
> These oaths and laws will prove an idle scorn.
> Sirrah, come on.
> *Cost.* I suffer for the truth, sir; for true it is, I was taken with Jaquenetta, and Jaquenetta is a true girl; and therefore welcome the sour cup of prosperity! Affliction may one day smile again; and till then, sit thee down, sorrow!

By a prediction and a hope, which continues the clown's mistakings, these speeches indicate the focal point of the protasis (the meeting of four men and four women, II) and the focal point of the epitasis (the revelation of the men's forswearing, IV, iii).

As one might expect, before Shakespeare dramatizes the first focal point, he brings Armado on stage. As this first figure embodying a derisible distortion of the rhetorical ideal is displayed, one again perceives a comic merging of the sophisticated and the popular. Just as mocking refrains might ridicule the absurd wooer in popular songs, so the witty mockery of Moth is turned upon this insipient Spaniard.[12] A dialogue of "congruent epithetons," including one with overtones of the old wooer ("tough senior," I, ii, 17), is followed by speeches that utilize the pun possible in *ace*-"ass" and prove Armado a derisible, as well as a logical, cipher, less witty than Morocco, the dancing horse (ll. 49, 27-59). Thus in addition to being barren of money, Armado is barren of "the varnish of a complete man" (ll. 35-36, 155-57, 46-47). As his complete pretentiousness in knowledge, martial endeavors, and love conceits is mocked, the bawdiness already established by Costard and Berowne may well have been reinforced by Shakespeare's juxtaposition of "base wench" with references to drawing one's sword, the humors of affection, an excellent rapier, and a strong back (ll. 62, 63, 78-79). Moth's comment upon Jaquenetta continues this sophisticated bawdry, as does his satire of a woman's "maculate" white and red (ll. 95-98, 104-13). Thoroughly fitting also is the potential pun or *hour*-"whore" and on *horse*-"whores" (ll. 39, 57), as well as the reference to the ballad of King Cophetua and the beggar maid, now to be writ "o'er" (also pronounced as was "whore"). Indeed, this song is to be in honor of one who deserves

> . . . well.
>
> *Moth.* To be whipp'd.
>
> (ll. 124-25)

As Moth preserves Shakespeare's emphasis upon derisible Armado, however, Jaquenetta is said to deserve "a better love" than this fantastic; and when the appearance of *"Clown"* and *"Wench"* reinforces comic overtones from the broad and merry tradition of rival wooing, Jaquenetta mocks Armado's face (ll. 125-26, S-D, l. 145). The closing soliloquy by Armado then builds upon his distortion of rhetoric, even as he shows a confused knowledge of the code of the duello and emerges thereby with lineaments of the braggart added to those of the Spaniard and the old man both lusty and ridiculously wooing.

King Cophetua and the beggar maid will be anatomized in the mistakes of the fourth-act complexity (IV, i, 65 ff.).[13] But at the moment, a grotesque image of the complete man, with emphasis upon his inadequate and distorted wit, holds the stage before the rhetoric of ladies and of "loving lords" appears (II, i, 37). In that succeeding episode, which is the first narrative focal point, the wooing of individuals of high degree begins; and dizzard Berowne is provided with his own "black" loved one.

In this last scene, there also appears a male figure who is given a position in the French scenes that is somewhat comparable to Berowne's in the Navarrese ones. It is Boyet who first specifies that Navarre is in love and who elsewhere acts as chorus and presenter (II, i, 234-49, 1-12, 194-214; IV, i, 55-102; V, ii, 81-86, 178-95, 256-61, 267, 286-89). Boyet also takes his place between a derided Armado and a witty Berowne, and thereby appears in some tentative but balancing relationships. After the complexity of the first scene, Berowne and Costard had remained on stage to predict and hope for a change. The second scene closed with Armado's ridiculous soliloquy. The third scene (II, i) ends with the ladies' witty attack on Boyet—an attack that nevertheless leaves Boyet with the last line, "You are too hard for me." The complexity of the fourth scene (III, i) will be followed by Berowne's soliloquy mocking himself. That of the fifth scene (IV, i) will be followed by the "putting down" of Boyet and will end with Costard's comment on that fact and on the sight of derisible Armado with his witty page. As a result, although Boyet is matched with no one woman, yet the contrast between derisible Armado and deriding Berowne soliloquizing on their loves (I, ii, 172 ff; III, i, 175 ff.) rests upon a scene that ends with a mocked Boyet (II, i, 253 ff.) A further balance is effected by Costard on stage with Berowne at the end of the first scene and on stage with Boyet at the end of the fifth. The complexity of each scene, with the exception of the middle one, begins with the entrance of Costard. From such a similarity, these closing variations that would be visually appreciable might well have underlined any impression of a purposeful forward movement. Certainly they support the slightest of narrative threads leading into the complexity of the drama and the revelation of forswearing.[14]

As has been indicated in a previous chapter, *Love's Labour's Lost* is very much of a single piece. Consider, for example, three aspects of the complication of the drama. Although that complexity is essentially rhetorical, its narrative, no less than its rhetoric, has overtones of folk merriment. What narrative complications there are in Acts III and IV arise from the fact that Costard's mistaking of words is extended to his mistaking of epistles, in a manner reminiscent of Johannes-boob, the stupid errand boy of the folk.[15] The fact that his errand consists in delivering love letters, moreover, allows for their being read in the wrong circumstances. As a result, the contrast between Armado's letter and a courtly wit is followed by the contrast between Berowne's letter and a ridiculous wit, now emanating from Holofernes and Nathaniel (IV, i, ii). In other words, when the entangled course of the letters is being developed, the entangled speech of these new characters is amplifying Armado's characteristic vein. Shakespeare also starts an additional process whereby laughter at those who are unlearned in words, but who are unpretentious as well, redounds upon the deriders. This development, which will be considered later, appears first in Act III, scene i, when Costard for a second time is on stage with Armado. It is varied in the next scene, and it is emphasized in the first grouping of characters in the subsequent scene (IV, i, 42-51, ii, 1-66). It will be reflected also in the fifth act when the figures of low degree are drawn into the entertainment of royalty.[16]

Throughout the drama, consequently, Shakespeare shows a concern for "wit" in the complete Renaissance sense of that word. Immediately before the first encounter between the men and the women is dramatized, the descriptions of Longaville, Dumain, and Berowne specify increasingly a merry wit. A cutting wit, mentioned in five of twelve lines, is the only weakness of Longaville. Wit as a balancing characteristic, mentioned in five of eight lines, is used to describe Dumaine. But wit is the outstanding characteristic of Berowne. He turns to "mirth-moving jest" every object of his eye, and these jests are delivered in "apt and gracious words" by a "fair tongue" that is "conceit's expositor." In this focal point of the protasis, as the high comedy of wooing begins to develop on the heels of its distorted counterpart, the dialogue also continues Shakespeare's emphasis in Act I, scene i, upon an amusing dialectic. Boyet's first speech praises Navarre but is aimed primarily at praising the princess (II, i, 1-12). With a comparable wit, the princess then disclaims "the painted flourish" of Boyet's praise, meant to be praised, and dispatches him to the King. The process is that of wit countering wit, of the light rhetorical debate. It appears next in the speeches between Navarre and the princess (ll. 90-113, 129-79); and it will be repeated more obviously—and, indeed, constantly—in the scenes that bring together men and women of high degree.

Furthermore, in accordance with what has been noted already, as the dialogue of the preceding scene alternates between mirth and relative seriousness, the motif of wooing is developed in both a sophisticated and a popular manner. Reflections of Elizabethan merriment overlap the conversation between the king and the princess,[17] while an effect of witty improvisation occurs as short couplets increase during the dialogue in which Berowne takes part.[18] The scene then focuses upon a situation reminiscent of song and dance as each lord asks his lady's name and exits quickly. The lines are strongly reminiscent of jigging measure, especially when Berowne reappears:

> *Bir.* What's her name in the cap?
> *Boyet.* Rosaline, by good hap.
> *Bir.* Is she wedded or no?
> *Boyet.* To her will, sir, or so.
> *Bir.* You are welcome, sir; adieu.
> *Boyet.* Farewell to me, sir, and welcome to you.
>
> (II, i, 209-14)

To any Elizabethan lover of wordplay, the sophisticated overlay that follows could not have seemed too different from this quick jig-like riming.[19]

A comparable fusion of vulgar mirth and sophisticated wit then animates Act III, scene i. The stage direction *"Enter Braggart and his Boy,"* which ends with the word *"Song,"* clearly points in the direction outlined in a previous chapter. Armado's pretentious copy then mingles with Moth's music and with his question, "Master will you win your love with a French brawl?" (ll. 8-9). Armado's misunderstanding of that reference to a vigorous dance with overtones of fertility rites leads to Moth's witty, and probably his miming, instructions in courtship.[20] The development again derides Armado (ll. 11, 48-49, 52-53); and although its conclusion is directed specifically at the Spaniard's "'Sweet smoke of rhetoric" (l. 64), it is also directed once more at Armado as the rival wooer of "hackney" Jaquenetta. This turn from ridicule of a lover to laughter at *hackney*-"prostitute" is effected by a popular refrain that mockingly completes Armado's sigh:

> *Arm.* But O, but O,—
> *Moth.* "The hobby-horse is forgot."
>
> (ll. 29-30)

A potential pun is underlined: "Callest thou my love 'hobby horse'?" And then this derision of a pretentious wit by a witty mockery is continued in lines reminiscent of the old comic horsemanship of human upon human (ll. 51-56).[21]

Even the complexity of the scene may have grown out of the clown's vigorous farcical action resulting from a broken shin. Certainly it is based upon the comic's conventional mistaking of words: "Doth the inconsiderate take salve for l'envoy, and the world l'envoy for a salve" (III, i, 79-80). The subsequent development, moreover, might have seemed to be an elaboration of the old device of the principal comedian's improvisation—an impression that would be underlined by the final invention of Costard as he runs a pun from Armado's command:

> *Arm.* We will talk no more of this matter.
> *Cost.* Until there be more matter in the shin.[22]
>
> (ll. 119-20)

Because this development is appreciated gleefully by Costard, who can follow the course of the wit, if not its sense (ll. 109-11), he appears more witty than baffled Armado, whose opinionated and "ridiculous smiling" has started the sequence (l. 78).

As a result, this scene also begins a process in Shakespeare's mirth whereby laughter at unpretentious stupidity leads to laughter at the figure who laughed first, or who in his self-conceived excellence distorts the rhetorical ideal more than an unlearned simplicity ever could. This aspect of the merriment in *Love's Labour's Lost* agrees with the tradition of the clown-fool's victory and is repeated with an appropriate variation in Act IV, scene i. Then Costard turns upon the princess herself the wit that had been displayed at his expense because of his natural question:

> *Cost.* God dig-you-den-all! Pray you which is the head lady?
> *Prin.* Thou shalt know her, fellow, by the rest that have no heads.
> *Cost.* Which is the greatest lady, the highest?
> *Prin.* The thickest and the tallest
> *Cost.* The thickest and the tallest! It is so; truth is true.
> An your waist, mistress, were as slender as my wit,
> One o' these maids' girdles for your waist should be fit.
> Are not you the chief woman? You are the thickest here.
>
> (ll. 42-51)

The derision is slight, however; for the princess had just bandied words with the forester and, conventionally enough, disclaimed her beauty. Thus Costard's speech develops, to a riming conclusion once more, the princess' earlier denial of her fairness. By that same token though, the development would heighten the monstrous rhetoric of Armado's letter, beginning as it does with exaggerated but banal praise of the beauty of wench Jaquenetta (ll. 60-64).[23]

This particular twist to Shakespeare's mirth next appears when Holofernes and Nathaniel make their entrance into the play. Embodying distorted features of academic training but preserving clear overtones of folk merriment, these new characters appear with the stupid constable Dull. Inasmuch as their speech provides a sound basis for Dull's "mistaking," this "monster Ignorance," even by the logic in the sound of a phrase, corrects an exaggerated but elementary Latinity:

> *Hol.* The deer was, as you know, *sanguis,* in blood; ripe as the pomewater, who now hangeth like a jewel in the ear of *caelo,* the sky, the welkin, the heaven; and anon falleth like a crab on the face of *terra,* the soil, the land, the earth.
>
> *Nath.* Truly, Master Holofernes, the epithets are sweetly varied, like a scholar at the least; but, sir, I assure ye, it was a buck of the first head.
>
> *Hol.* Sir Nathaniel, *haud credo.*
>
> *Dull.* 'Twas not a haud credo, 'twas a pricket.
>
> *Hol.* Most barbarous intimation! yet a kind of insinuation, as it were, *in via,* in way, of explication; *facere,* as it were, replication, or rather, *ostentare,* to show, as it were, his inclination, after his undressed, unpolished, uneducated, unpruned, untrained, or rather, unlettered, or ratherest, unconfirmed fashion, to assert again my *haud credo* a deer.
>
> *Dull.* I said the deer was not a haud credo; 'twas a pricket.
>
> *Hol.* Twice-sod simplicity, *bis coctus!*
> O thou monster Ignorance, how deformed dost thou look!
>
> (IV, ii, 3-24)

Since *haud credo* might sound to rustic, even Warwickshire, ears as "awd (old) grey doe,"[24] it is applied unerringly to the question at hand. Thereby the mistaking of a pretentious Latin mocks that aspect of an ill-digested sophistication as effectively as it ever had been ridiculed by the time-honored convention of a clown's mock Latin.[25]

In the ridiculous development that follows, Berowne's sonnet is contrasted with this pseudo-academic discipline that can only indicate such signposts on the road to rhetorical proficiency as "sweetly varied" epithets, "good old Mantuan," "Ovidius Naso," "odoriferous flowers of fancy," and *"Imitari* is nothing" (IV, ii, 9, 96, 126-28, 129).[26] When the scene ends, Holofernes, Nathaniel, and Dull leave for the repast desired by all hungry clowns; and Costard, as one might expect, exits with Jaquenetta. The entire scene introducing Holofernes and Nathaniel seems to have the same intent as the immediately preceding one, in which Armado's letter was read. By comic irony and by contrast, a *"bis coctus"* speech is ridiculed. In a rhetorical play that would mock the absurdities of rhetoric, Holofernes and Nathaniel appear fittingly in a fourth-act complexity, and they are ridiculed through Dull even as a result of their condescension.

In the next scene, a courtly wit that mocks both wit and love contrasts with this grotesque pedantry. Forswearing is revealed (IV, iii); and dizzard Berowne appears at his height, as it has been noted in a previous chapter. Once the revelation is complete, however, Berowne defends what he had foreseen as early as the beginning of the drama; and thus his subsequent tour de force of rhetoric (ll. 289-365) now agrees with the lines of love poetry and the course of the action. Just as the fullest display of Richard III's virtuosity in debate had appeared in an epitatical development, so the comic complexities of an exuberant wit, as well as those of a ridiculous verbosity, mark the fourth act here.

In contrast with *Richard III,* however, Shakespeare's rhetorical virtuosity increases its tempo during the major portion of the fifth act. Both a courtly wit and the absurdities of a pedantic speech[27] reappear as Shakespeare represents the conventional welcome due visiting royalty —a topic mentioned when the lords and the ladies first met (II, i). Inasmuch as the seriousness of the men is construed as a mirthful courtesy to be countered in kind, the masquing sequence is developed into the first unsuccessful wooing of the princess and the ladies (V, ii, 1-482). The comic irony of the situation is underlined for an audience: "There's no such sport as sport by sport o'erthrown" (l. 153).[28] Accordingly, even a declaration of love in "russet yeas and honest kersey noes" leads to mockery of the king and the lords; they are doubly forsworn because of the women's trick of exchanging favors (ll. 416 ff.). The culmination of the emphasis of the preceding scenes is then dramatized in the pageant of the nine worthies. Nathaniel, Holofernes, and Armado are baited; and as Costard helps to mock these ridiculous figures out of their parts, the clown-fool once more "proves the best Worthy." As it has been noted, *Love's Labour's Lost* is very much of a single piece.[29]

There remains to be handled, however, the result of the error that the princess and her ladies have made in considering the lovers' seriousness a sportful courtesy. Shakespeare treats this in the development brought about by Mercade's announcement of the death of the princess' father— a development that returns to the serious concerns of persons of dignity and one that also may reflect the discipline of a lover. As the women would depart, the king presses his suit, and Berowne makes the point that the cause of the courtly sonneteering by these mocked lovers is the loved one's conventional beauty. The argument that he develops elabo-

rates the eye-love psychology of the era[30] and leads to a conclusion based
on the thoroughly coventional turn of thought that the loved one is as
"guilty" as the lover:

> For your fair sakes have we neglected time,
> Play'd foul play with our oaths. Your beauty, ladies,
> Hath much deform'd us, fashioning our humours
> Even to the opposed end of our intents;
>
> .   .   .   .
>
> Which parti-coated presence of loose love
> Put on by us, if, in your heavenly eyes,
> Have misbecom'd our oaths and gravities,
> Those heavenly eyes that look into these faults,
> Suggested us to make. Therefore, ladies,
> Our love being yours, the error that love makes
> Is likewise yours. We to ourselves prove false,
> By being once false for ever to be true,
> To those that make us both,—fair ladies, you;
> And even that falsehood, in itself a sin,
> Thus purifies itself and turns to grace.
>
> (V, ii, 765-86)

Although their inconstancy to their vow might make this oath seem
little more than the exercise of a self-conscious wit, these men are no
perjured Arcadian Pamphiluses, arguing that there is no inconstancy in
a lover who changes his heart but a great constancy.[31] They have
forsworn only a vow to study; and Berowne's prognostication has come
true in circumstances that now involve, not simply the seriousness of
great persons (i.e., the "gravities" of the preceding speech), but also the
seriousness of death. The princess, indeed, would remind an audience
that the ladies, in another sense than Berowne's, have partaken of "the
error that love makes":

> We have receiv'd your letters full of love;
> Your favours, the ambassadors of love,
> And, in our maiden council, rated them
> At courtship, pleasing jest, and courtesy,
> As bombast and as lining to the time;
> But more devout than this in our respects
> Have we not been; and therefore met your loves
> In their own fashion, like a merriment.
>
> (ll. 787-94)

Primarily because of this mistake, love would have to be granted now "at the latest minute of the hour," a time "too short / To make a world-without-end bargain in" (ll. 797-99).

It is just possible that if we were sure of the nature of *Love's Labour's Won,* this countermovement to wooing and winning, effected by the entrance of Mercade, might have been another forward-looking ending.[32] In any case, the men are given penances that must be performed; and one immediately thinks of the good that might result from the despair of a lover. His rejection by his mistress could lead to the purging of all "sordid basenesse," to a "refyned" mind, and to his perception of

> . . . . a fairer forme, which now doth dwell
> In his high thought, that would it selfe excell;
> Which he behoulding still with constant sight,
> Admires the mirrour of so heavenly light.[33]

Here, however, there is no obdurate mistress. Though the prize be delayed, these ladies are won (e.g., ll. 814-17, 835, 839-40, 843-44). Yet a point not entirely incompatible with what has just been noted may have been made.[34] Just as "Honest plain words best pierce the ear of grief," so a self-conscious wit that would deny the nature of youth and a gibing wit that might become preoccupied with the hilarity of "shallow laughter" can only touch love, not achieve love's consummation. For this, a prodigal wit must be purged; and similarly one who has been concerned with displaying wit *qua* wit and with producing "shallow laughter" might also be criticized. Thus Shakespeare laughs at himself, even as the penances of the men are established. Quite fittingly, he does this through Berowne; for although that character's golden rhetoric is again valid, in part at least, the twelve-month penances are focused upon this dizzard of high degree.

It is Berowne who now is described by Rosaline as "a man replete with mocks, / Full of comparisons and wounding flouts," one whose brain needs to be purged (V, ii, 853-54).[35] Although a critic may remember the earlier favorable description of Berowne's wit, one suspects that an audience's reaction would be related, rather, to lines that they had heard more recently—to, for example, Berowne's amusing mocks that have been directed at the men in love, including himself, and at their sonneteering description of their ladies. His own sonnet, for that matter, contrasts with his mocking references to "black" Rosaline. As a consequence, in view of his trenchant comments on the feature of the drama that now is being emphasized, and within the bounds of his degree, this dizzard might have seemed to be treated in a manner that could be associated once more with a principal comedian and popular merriment—a manner apparent when other comic figures commented upon their punishment in words designed to cause laughter.[36] In writing those lines, moreover, Shakespeare uses a conventional comic device whereby the comedian refers to the actualities of a theater.[37] Earlier in the drama, the appearance of the boys who were playing the French ladies had been used for merriment. Now, apparently, this is true also for the appearance of the actors performing the roles of Dumaine and Longaville.[38] This disjunction between any play-world and theatrical reality is created once more, then, by Berowne's final witty speech, which mocks both the penances and the narrative ending of the drama:

> *Bir.* Our wooing doth not end like an old play;
> Jack hath not Jill. These ladies' courtesy
> Might well have made our sport a comedy.
> *King.* Come, sir, it wants a twelvemonth and a day
> And then 'twill end.
> *Bir.*   That's too long for a play.
>
> (ll. 884-88)

In brief, by Berowne's comment upon the penances, and in accordance with the dominant emphasis throughout the drama, wit *qua* wit remains unconquered. At the same time, since all playwrights were engaged in a "wittie" exercise, Shakespeare mocks his own wit even as his penances criticize the wit of the lovers. Like the virtuosity of Berowne, the virtuosity of Shakespeare laughs at its immediate preoccupation, which is simply dramatic artistry in general, but a comedy that had begun with a departure from the norm and now ends the same way. This is also a unique and artistic variation upon a tendency to return to an initial emphasis as a drama is concluded. A topsy-turvy ending results, as Berowne's indomitable wit points out; but it is only as momentary as the folk time of a year and a day. Then, with the laughter focused upon the author's present art, the playwright lets slip his mask, intrudes upon the fiction of a stage-world, and invites his audience to laugh at what he has created by "wytt and mirth."

What has just been written seems to be confirmed when Shakespeare immediately returns to his play-world as a world of comedy, for his wit is embodied next in the final appearance of Armado. Even in her bereavement, the princess re-establishes the mockery of this fantastic (l. 889), who now announces that he, too, is a "votary." For three solid years, and not just for a year and a day, he will "hold the plough" for the "sweet" love of wench Jaquenetta (ll. 892-93). As part of this topsy-turvydom, the "songs of Apollo," which contrast one another, solidify the many overtones that have resulted from Elizabethan mirth;

and thus distorted Armado, aided by the songs of ridiculous Holofernes and Nathaniel and by the topics of cuckoo-cuckold and greasy Joan, presides over the distorted ending. In such a manner, the "counter movement" to wooing and winning ends. A ridiculous parallel to this winning of loved ones and to the usual ending of a comedy is effected by the figure who since the first act has been a grotesque practitioner of Mercury's art. As a consequence, and in a very real sense, the god of wit and rhetoric is invoked by the playwright no less than by Armado as Shakespeare again laughs at what he has done (ll. 940-41).[39]

Whether *Love's Labour's Lost* were popular on the vulgar stage is well-nigh impossible to surmise, in spite of its constant bawdiness and its constant overtones of folk merriment.[40] Be that as it may, it is a singularly interesting drama. Because of Shakespeare's laughter at his art, one may be reminded of Theseus' statement that the "best in this kind are but shadows; and the worst are no worse, if imagination amend them" (*A Midsummer Night's Dream,* V, i, 213-14). But throughout *Love's Labour's Lost,* a wit that mocks itself and yet in no way invalidates its true virtuosity is compounded with the laughter of parallel absurdities; and thus the artistry of the play, somewhat paradoxically, indicates that there is something more in drama than Theseus' insubstantiality. This celebration of the rhetorical tradition—a celebration that mocks that tradition's aberrations (including the ending of a sophisticated comedy)—represents a critical yet enthusiastic interpretation of a vigorous sophistic that animated not simply wooing speech, amusing speech, and theater, but also grammar school, academic exercise, and public ceremony. Seen in this light, the spirit that animates *Love's Labour's Lost* is of paramount importance, even though, as in Berowne and to a lesser degree in Rosaline, its artistry also embodies a strong promise of Shakespeare's later characters.

Before that promise was fulfilled, Shakespeare partially turned from an intensified display of his witty virtuosity to write a drama having the farcical vigor of *The Comedy of Errors* and *The Taming of the Shrew.* To do this, he developed *A Midsummer Night's Dream* with remarkable precision.[41] Its general outline, for example, is indicated easily. Between a courtly beginning and a courtly ending, Shakespeare draws from contemporary mirth a suprahuman dizzard to tangle and preside over the major portion of the drama. Between that beginning and its ending—wherein aristocratic figures laugh once more at an inadequate art—Shakespeare develops, not an absurd verbosity and a contrasting true wit, but a pattern of ridiculous situations that persists in repeating the old motif of rival wooing, while the low comic parallel reinforces the theme of the play.

It is hard to see how Shakespeare's farcical intent in the major portion of the drama could be indicated more clearly than it is. In the first of the sleeping episodes when Helena comes upon the sleepers, an audience is prepared for the mechanical tripping of a predetermined situation caused by Puck's mistake; and the lines of Lysander underline the anticipatory irony of any situational farce. In answer to Hermia's wish that his "love ne'er alter" till his "sweet life end," Lysander had vowed, "Amen, amen, to that fair prayer, say I; / And then end life when I end loyalty!" (II, 60-63). But after the love juice has been squeezed in his eyes, he rushes to complete Helena's words with a transported love and anger:

> *Hel.* ...
> Lysander if you live, good sir, awake.
>   *Lys.* And run through fire I will for thy sweet sake.
> Transparent Helena! Nature shows art,
> That through thy bosom makes me see thy heart.
> Where is Demetrius? O, how fit a word
> Is that vile name to perish on my sword!
>
> (ll. 102-7)

The effect is then repeated and intensified in the next comparable situation when Lysander's line releases the catch so that Demetrius in turn can emerge as the jack-in-the-box:

> *Lys.* Demetrius loves her [Hermia], and he loves
>   not you [Helena].
> *Dem.* [*Awaking*] O Helen, goddess, nymph, perfect,
>   divine!
> To what, my love, shall I compare thine eyne?
> Crystal is muddy.
>
> (III, ii, 136-39)

Love rhetoric is obviously subordinate to the lustiness of this transported lover:

>   O how ripe in show
> Thy lips, those kissing cherries, tempting grow!
> That pure congealed white, high Taurus' snow,
> Fann'd with the eastern wind, turns to a crow
> When *thou holds't up thy hand.* O, let me kiss
> This princess of pure white, this seal of bliss.
>
> (ll. 139-44)

The italicized phrase looks very much like one of the many stage directions Shakespeare embodied in his lines. Certainly with the last line an actor would have to seize or attempt to seize Helena's hand. Clearly, Shakespeare is working to produce that laughter at an obvious automatism which Bergson describes as he begins his analysis of the comic. The preceding situations must have been contrived to develop quickly, forcefully, and probably noisily as well, in accordance with the boisterousness that might appear fairly constantly in the theaters of the era.

If Elizabethan or modern actor or critic needed anything more to confirm the farcical intent of the author, the development of the second situation just noted would surely provide it. To females' fighting each other with hands and nails (III, ii, 297-98, 303), Shakespeare adds the incongruity of the taller woman being afraid of the shorter one and being protected by quarrelling men, one of whom supplies the name-calling directed at infuriated Hermia. Boisterous antics, consequently, displace "flyting" women, although "thou painted maypole" (l. 296) and the following lines agree thoroughly with the noisy context of public scolding: "you dwarf, / You minimus, of hind'ring knot-grass made; / You bead, you acorn" (ll. 328-30). Quarreling men, a scorned, an angry, and a clinging woman then round out this noisy fun that had been anticipated by that companion of Tarlton's who was discussed in a previous chapter:

> And those things do best please me
> That befall preposterously.

> (ll. 120-21)

The scenes that develop about Bottom will be considered later, but even those concerned with the lovers alone, indicate that this drama is not meant to be simply a witty play. Shakespeare's technique points to brawny and brawling farce, and there is no reason to believe that Elizabethan actors would read the lines differently. For that matter, the mechanical but neatly articulated structure of *A Midsummer's Night's Dream* accords with such an emphasis. Indeed, Shakespeare's tendency to write patterned sequences seems to constitute his structural principle in this drama, rather than any adherence to academic precepts about protasis, epitasis, and catastrophe or any modification of structural movements derived from the tradition of the mystery or morality.

Once more, a separate line of action frames the major portion of a drama. In this respect, the structure of *A Midsummer Night's Dream* repeats what has been noted in *A Comedy of Errors*. Here the initial dialogue between Theseus and Hippolyta inaugurates its own narrative movement toward the marriage of rulers, begins a relatively long introduction of characters, and provides the central situation for the fifth act. At that time, since the reappearance of the fairies turns the emphasis from farce to marriage, the wedding of Theseus and Hippolyta also provides a smaller frame for the comical tragedy of Pyramus and Thisbe.[42] Regardless of any relationship it might have to the genesis of the drama, this framing device is artistically apt. Anticipated as the play begins, its ending reflects the actual nature of the entertainment of nobility and royalty. In conjunction with references to the weather, to regal chastity, and to stage-struck persons appearing before rulers, it may well have given a realistic aura to even this fanciful and farcical drama.[43]

Shakespeare also effects a conceptual balance in his use of this framing device. When Theseus and Hippolyta reappear and all complications in the way of love have been removed—whether that love be mortal, supernatural, comic, or a combination thereof—Theseus speaks of the fancy and the "franticness" of madman, lover, and poet (V, i, 1-22). When reason slept, fancy reigned. Not only does Theseus comment thereby upon what has just been dramatized, but he also repeats a thought expressed in soliloquy at the end of the first scene. At that time, even as her plan to tell Demetrius of the lovers' flight illustrated the fact, Helena reminded an audience that "Love's mind" has no "taste" of judgment (I, i, 232-36). In the use of a framing action alone, Shakespeare shows a structural neatness that is greater than that of *A Comedy of Errors;* for the idea expressed by Theseus and Helena, accords with Bottom's choric line enunciated in the midst of the confusions.

The rest of the drama shows a comparable precision, both in its introduction (I, i, through II, i) and in its complication (II, ii through IV, ii).[44] In the middle portion of the drama, for example, the line of action involving the lovers is developed by adapting the conventional devise of the erring errand boy again. That involving Titania is elaborated, rather than complicated, by the use of Bottom. After Oberon has squeezed the love juice in Titania's eyes and before Bottom awakes without an ass's head, the development runs as follows: the lovers, Bottom and Titania, the lovers, Bottom and Titania, the lovers. The relatively long scene devoted to the lovers (III, ii, 41-463) is enclosed by shorter scenes devoted to Bottom and Titania (III, i, through ii, 40; IV, i, 1-106), all of which is enclosed again by short scenes devoted to the lovers (II, ii, 35 ff.; IV, i, 107-203). The entire development is preceded by a dramatization devoted to Titania and is followed by one devoted to Bottom (II, ii, 1-34; IV, i, 204, through ii.[45] Between the two sleeping sequences of the mortals, as has been pointed out, an audience would hear that "reason and love keep little company together now-a-days; the more the pity that some honest neighbors will not make

them friends" (III, i, 147-49). Shakespeare's precise control of his farcical developments is obvious.

In the mid-portion of the drama, only eighteen lines devoted to
the Indian boy are not integrated immediately into the varying farce
(III, ii, 374-75; IV, i, 50-66); and agreeing with the comic force resulting from that fact is the way in which the relatively serious situations
preceding and following the complications are treated lightly or are
turned in a comic direction. Consider three incidents. In the introduction
of the characters, the fate of the lovers at its most serious is given a comic
twist by Shakespeare's underlining the ridiculousness of an angry *senex:*

> *Dem.* Relent, sweet Hermia; and, Lysander, yield
> Thy crazed title to my certain right.
> *Lys.* You have her father's love, Demetrius,
> Let me have Hermia's; do you marry him.
>
> (I, i, 91-94)

Similarly, the resolution of the lovers' difficulties is introduced by
Theseus' amused comment, after the stage direction of the folio indicates
action thoroughly compatible with the preceding farcical emphasis:

> *Shout within. Wind horns. They all start up.*
> *The.* Good morrow, friends. Saint Valentine is past;
> Begin these wood-birds but to couple now?
>
> (IV, i, S-D, 143-44)

Finally, when the quarrel between Oberon and Titania is reported, the
appearance of Robin Goodfellow as a "lob" of spirits (II, i, 16) reflects
features of Elizabethan merriment that have been sketched in a preceding
chapter; and the miming tradition in delivering comic speeches may well
have been drawn upon by the actor when he described his tricks (II, i,
42-57). This last tradition, as Shakespeare undoubtedly knew, also could
have given theatrically obvious humor to such subsequent speeches as
Puck's report of Titania's love (III, ii, 6-34).

In *A Midsummer Night's Dream,* no less than in *Love's Labour's
Lost,* Shakespeare constantly draws upon folk merriment. Witness the
startling appearance of Bottom as the ass-headed man, a possible de-
scendant of a figure in ancient mimes and one whose appearance may
well have reminded an audience of current mumming.[46] Dreams of love
on Midsummer Eve and magic flowers might also be part of an entertaining folklore.[47] During the broad farcical action of the middle of the play,
Robin Goodfellow, a grotesque in folk games, as well as a figure in
nursery tales, presides over the action. Although he is subordinate at
first to the King of Fairies, when Oberon censures Robin for his mistake

Shakespeare gives to this dizzard lines that are strongly reminiscent of the comic improvisor. At that time, the gleeking quip of generalized satire, normally associated with the presiding or principal comic, is his:

> Then fate o'er-rules, that, one man holding troth,
> A million fail, confounding oath on oath.
>
> (III, ii, 92-93)

This effect is reinforced by Puck's gleeful anticipation of the farce that will follow when Helena appears (III, ii, 110-21). With a repetition of that idea—

> And so far am I glad it so did sort,
> As this their jangling I esteem a sport—
>
> (ll. 352-53)

this figure of folklore and current merriment moves into his final controlling position. With the words, "Here comes one" (l. 400), and with mocks and mimicry, he leads the quarrelling men to their sleep on stage; and then he practically conjures up the appearance of the last mortal:

> Yet but three? Come one more;
> Two of both kinds makes up four,
> Here she comes, curst and sad.
>
> (ll. 437-39)

In these circumstances, Puck's choric comments range from a specification of knavish Cupid—an idea found, for example, in the refrains of contemporary songs—to the repetition of a country proverb that develops into a woman-mare analogy:

> And the country proverb known,
> That every man should take his own,
> In your waking shall be shown,
>   Jack shall have Jill;
>   Nought shall go ill;
> The man shall have his mare again, and all shall be well.
>
> (ll. 458-63)

The bawdy overtones of that analogy, which concludes Puck's role in the middle portion of the drama, are compatible with the next reference to the lovers as they are awakened by Theseus' horns (IV, i, 143-44). The preceding lines also enhance the vigorous roguery of Robin Goodfellow, who has moved into the position of a theatrical presenter.

All that has been noted accords with the merriment of the age, and that this merriment was evoked further is confirmed by numerous details. Especially revealing, for example, is the direction in the folio after Puck's conjuration has resulted in a stage showing four sleeping mortals. Apparently derived from a prompt copy, the direction reads, *"They sleep all the act";* and thus when the compositor gave it a separate line, presumably to help in justifying his page,[48] he also gave us a glimpse of a theatrical world concerned with music, song and dance, a comedian's exaggerated antics, and inter-acts, or, in Elizabethan theatrical parlance, "acts."[49] Very much to the point, then, is Halliwell's citation of lines from *The Fleire* (pr. 1607) that may indicate a burlesque bit of stage business in the final appearance of Bottom and his crew.[50] Other things being equal, one would expect the actor of Flute's role to work for laughs; and thus upon pronouncing Shakespeare's "sword" and then his "blade" (V, i, 350-51), this actor may well have performed the action reported in Sharpham's comedy: "Like *Thisbe* in the play, a has almost kil'd himselfe with the scabberd."

Be that last consideration as it may, an important aspect of the role of Bottom not only agrees with the neat articulation of the drama but also reflects a traditional comic technique. As the third act develops, an audience would be reminded by this clown that reason and love were keeping "little company together."[51] Just as he would preside over his fellow Athenians in spite of Quince, so at this point in the drama, Bottom would correct Titania; and by a comment comparable to those given Puck—for as Bottom tells the spectators, he, too, "can gleek upon occasion"—he would preside, even with an ass-headed bumptiousness, over the entire play-world.[52] In other words, Bottom's role constantly reflects the comic conceit of the principal comedian who would insist upon being called "Monsieur" or "Cavalier" and who would ape his betters in other ways as well.[53] Though easily analyzed, Shakespeare's artistry is well-conceived and well-executed. A conventional representational method accords once more with the artistry of a particular drama; and in this instance, as it has been pointed out in a previous chapter, it produces choric laughter as well.

What was conventionally comic is frequently transformed by Shakespeare. In Bottom's first scene, as in Cade's first scene, the principal comic actor is surrounded by a comic crew, now preparing for the celebration of a duke's wedding. Bottom runs the gamut from a burlesque of the tyrant's vein to "a monstrous little voice"; and an old, but apparently workable, joke about the loss of hair from the French disease signals a return to the familiar device of the comic's mistaking words—never more magnificently developed than here. Bottom thereby progresses from "aggravate" (I, ii, 83) to his immortal approval of that rehearsal which can be effected "most obscenely and courageously" in the woods.

The antics of a principal comedian and his crew are continued in the first portion of their next scene, when a mistaking of words becomes a misreading of lines, a harried prompter's explanation of an exit made "to see a noise," and another misreading of lines (III, i, 33, 40, 84-86, 91-100). Then Bottom returns to the scene and the ass-headed man holds the stage with an appearance that coincides precisely with Bottom's nature, as Shakespeare repeats another time-honored comic device. From a theatrically inescapable and reiterated irony ("You see an ass-head of your own do you?" ". . . this is to make an ass of me," ll. 119-20, 123-24), the comic bravery of the principal comedian is developed. Elaborated with song and with a cuckold jest upon that song, this bravery leads to the comic contrast in Titania's comment on Bottom's angelic voice (ll. 132, 140-41).

In the remainder of the scene, the fine gentlemanly fellow of comic tradition appears as Bottom's salutation of the attendant fairies merges a possessed but comic bumptiousness with the traditional literalness of a low comic's wit. This development is repeated in Bottom's next scene, where it is enlarged by the "honey-bag" lines and by Bottom's "reasonable good ear in music" (IV, i, 1-18, 30-31). It is also joined with a repetition of the earlier irony: if his hair do but tickle, Bottom is "such a tender ass" that he must scratch. Upon this premise, the traditional voraciousness of the comic is modified to "a peck of provender," "your good dry oats," "a bottle of hay," and a "handful or two of dried peas."[54]

In Bottom's first scene, Shakespeare also anatomized amateur theatricals, ridiculous aspects of an earlier drama, and, perhaps, the inexpertness of some acting companies. This could have been meaningful to Elizabethans in the mid 1590's, not simply because of amateur civic performances or performances by provincial companies, but also as a result of the printing of earlier dramas and degenerate versions of plays on the London stage. An audience would hear a ridiculous play title and a differentiation of character-types (the tyrant, the lover, the wandering knight) that would be suitable to such dramas as *Sir Clyomon and Sir Clamydes* or *Common Conditions*.[55] They would also hear of actors "slow of study," of the possibility of a dangerous reaction from an audience, and of the indisputable virtuosity of beards (I, ii, 11-98).

From the preceding aspects of Shakespeare's low comic developments, the merriment of *A Midsummer Night's Dream* culminates in the play-within-a-play. On the one hand, the earlier misreading "Ninny" is repeated twice and the mistaking in Quince's explanation of Pyramus' exit is developed fully (V, i, 205, 269, 194-95; III, i, 100, 93). On the other hand, the play begins with an example of comic "mispointing" that raises the old device of a mistaking of words to the level of academic amusement specified, for example, by both the old *Roister Doister* and the third edition of Wilson's *Rule of Reason*.[56] In view of what has been written, however, this comedy in the fifth act needs little comment. Bottom's position as the principal comic character is obvious; and twice the function of a presenting comedian is reflected in appropriate variations that make Bottom explain to Theseus the atrociously obvious course of the drama (V, i, 185-89, 355-69). The second example of this also elaborates the mock death of the principal comedian—but a mock death so integrated with the action of the play-within-a-play that its specification seems supererogatory. With such a development, at any rate, Bottom presents his audience with a choice of alternate endings (ll. 355-69)—as Shakespeare himself may have.[57]

Obviously the exuberant artistry of an educated playwright is apparent throughout *A Midsummer Night's Dream*. This seems especially true if one feels justified in considering its precision the dramatic result of a concern for a balanced *dispositio* that the formulary rhetoric of Aphthonius would inculcate. Though it has not been so commented upon in this study, a comparable dramatic tendency has been noted elsewhere: in, for example, the structural movement of *The Spanish Tragedy*, or in the developments—sometimes pageantic, usually patterned, and sometimes quantitatively so—which appear in scenes in the early histories. Such a tendency persists in *King John, Romeo and Juliet*, and *Richard II*, although in the last two of these plays, as in Shakespeare's later artistry, there are few occasions when the impression of scenes being conceived precisely is noticeable. Yet in *A Midsummer Night's Dream* this precision accords with the manipulation of puppet-like characters in anticipated situations, the development of which is thoroughly farcical.

A Midsummer Night's Dream, then, substitutes for the verbal exuberance of *Love's Labour's Lost* the farcical exuberance of patterned situations, over most of which a suprahuman dizzard presides. In the figure of ass-headed Bottom, however, and in the use of Robin Goodfellow, if he were presented as a grotesque,[58] one also sees an artistry akin to that which created Armado, Holofernes, and Nathaniel. If these features of both plays can be viewed as a varying but comic manifestation of the grotesque, their development *ca.* 1594-95 may be more noteworthy than sometimes has been realized. They would be a lighter variation of the artistry that produced a distorted Richard III and, perhaps, a Shylock.

Be that as it may, from another point of view also, the comic artistry of *Love's Labour's Lost* and that of *A Midsummer Night's Dream* seem to merge. Just as Shakespeare laughs at his dramatic inheritance in writing Bottom's tyrannical speech and in having Flute refer to a wandering knight, so in writing "Pyramus and Thisbe," with or without a nudge from Thomas Mouffet or Dunstan Gale,[59] Shakespeare again creates a laughter that is part of his vigorous acceptance of the tools of his trade and the shop in which some of them were forged. The story of Pyramus and Thisbe was cited as an example of a *narratio* in the sixteenth-century Aphthonius;[60] and the spirit that would burlesque that story and treat risibly the narrative motif of *Romeo and Juliet,* while developing farcically the foreswearing motif of *The Two Gentlemen,* is akin to the spirit that in *Love's Labour's Lost* would laugh at the current academic tradition and at the author's own art while demonstrating their validity.[61]

In other respects also, *A Midsummer Night's Dream* may have spoken meaningfully to Shakespeare's contemporaries. Though it shows a laughing detachment that is essentially critical, by that very fact it does something more than reflect current ideas and representational methods in the manner of *The Two Gentlemen of Verona.* The attitude of the Elizabethan parent who would have his children marry only as he sees fit is intensified in Egeus, the angry *senex* who thwarts the course of love. The contrary attitude is expressed by Lysander and Hermia, who would chose for themselves only as they see fit. In his treatment of those lovers, however, as well as in his treatment of his loving but unloved pair, Shakespeare modifies the eye-love psychology of the era so that the vagaries of irrational eyes are equated with a farcical course of action. The attitude of the lovers becomes as ridiculous as that of Egeon; yet in a farcical and supernatural manner, their coupling, no less than the mating of birds on St. Valentine's Day, works out satisfactorily. To a lesser degree, this is true even of those who, like Theseus, woo with the sword and win by doing injuries. Although the course of love and marriage is far from smooth and far from rational, yet it certainly is matter "for a May morning."

Such a drama would be singularly appropriate in an age when marriage generally was recognized as being a matter of social and financial convenience. Since that was especially true for those in the upper reaches of society, *A Midsummer Night's Dream* might seem particularly apt for celebrating the nuptials of important individuals. The farcical force of the play, however, would make it appropriate also for the public stage; and its theme would be equally suitable in those surroundings.[62] For that matter, Shakespeare's treatment of the lovers and of the low comic parallel centered about Bottom and Titania makes the drama pertinent to ages much later than the sixteenth century; for once the characters are in their "green world," *A Midsummer Night's Dream* becomes a comic *exempulm* on the capriciousness of love and its perpetual incompatibility with reason.

From the preceding aspects of the thematic applicability of the drama, and in view of sixteenth-century concepts about the difference between sensuality and married love, a fourth level for the appreciation of *A Midsummer Night's Dream* may have been perceptible at times to well-educated Elizabethans. In this comedy, love "looks not with the eyes but with the mind," and love's mind has not a "taste" of judgement (I, i, 232-36). Thus a philosophically inclined Elizabethan's knowledge of a Neo-Platonic love blindness that is above the intellect, and his recognition of the parody of Corinthians given to Bottom—who "has known the love of the triple goddess" in a vision, somewhat as Apuleius knew Isis (IV, i, 208-18; I Cor. 2: 9, 13)—may have suggested "that the blindness of love, the dominance of the mind over the eye, can be interpreted as a means to grace as well as to irrational animalism; that the two aspects are, perhaps, inseparable."[63]

If this be so, instead of laughing at what he has created by wit, as in *Love's Labour's Lost,* Shakespeare glances seriously at what he has created with laughter—and a spectator might have perceived that fact upon reflection. Within the confines of a theater, however, be that theater permanent or temporary, it is hard to see how the farcical force of *A Midsummer Night's Dream,* and at least its immediate applicability to love versus reason, would have allowed much time for reflection. This is not to say that Thalia, Erato, and Polyhymnia cannot coexist. In Shakespeare's day, Abraham Fraunce, for example, argued for a similar combination.[64] Like Chaucer, Shakespeare probably could view his laughter from more than one point of view, even as he was creating it. It is to say that as one allows for that coexistence, one should not be blind to the consideration that unless Shakespeare wrote with a singular lack of perception, a primary intent during his composition of the drama must have been to create the enjoyment Puck speaks of:

> And those things do best please me
> That befall preposterously.

(III, ii, 120-21)

VII

King John, Romeo and Juliet, Richard II

A Midsummer Night's Dream and *Love's Labour's Lost* show Shakespeare's controlled and laughingly detached balance in the treatment of love and in an interpretative concern with language and with his own art; but *King John, Romeo and Juliet,* and *Richard II* show a less critical and a more sympathetic interpretation not only of young love but also of emotions and ideas that might preoccupy Shakespeare's contemporaries or be of the greatest interest to them. In *King John,* for example, a tour de force of speech, in the widest sense of the word, binds together the most disparate of emphases until Shakespeare's recreation of John's story, with its clash of irreconcilables, is compounded with ironies and becomes an Elizabethan's political nightmare. With this drama, as with *Romeo and Juliet* and *Richard II,* Shakespeare uses language and spectacle less for their own sake, or for the ideas and ideals they might reflect, or for the critical amusement they might arouse, than as the means for creating a dramatic experience that might be emotionally meaningful and memorable. In these dramas, Shakespeare does not achieve his mature artistry, but he is on the border of that achievement.

As has been indicated in an earlier discussion, memories of ephemeral mirth could have given a familiar comic force to the appearance of the bastard in *King John,* just as they play about the grotesque variations of conventional types in *Love's Labour's Lost* and support the antics of a suprahuman dizzard in *A Midsummer Night's Dream.* Certainly the humor in the portrayal of Faulconbridge animates his appearance in Shakespeare's play and differentiates him strikingly from the earlier bastard in the anonymous *Troublesome Reign of King John* (*ca.* 1588).[1] In addition to what has been noted, overtones of popular merriment result from the bastard's second speech, wherein Philip elaborates the maxim that it is a wise father who knows his own son. Thereby a comic process is begun that paradoxically ridicules the legitimate Robert, whose appearance is contrasted with that of the bastard, a "good blunt fellow" and a "madcap" (I, 1, 59-71, 84). Given the artistry of Antipholus at the door and the French lords to Boyet, rime might be expected, and though at first it is brief, it is climactic:

> If old Sir Robert did beget us both
> And were our father, and this son like him,
> O old Sir Robert, father, on my knee
> I give heaven thanks I was not like to thee!
>
> (ll. 80-83)

Shakespeare then repeats the situation when he turns to the question of Sir Robert Faulconbridge's will. At that time, a punning quip (ll. 132-33) precedes lines that, with appropriate wordplay, focus attention again upon the contrasting physical appearance of the bastard and his half-brother and again end in rime (ll. 138-47). Later in the scene, after noting that Eleanor is "grandam" "by chance but not by truth," the bastard is given verse for his most extended comic riming:

> Something about, a little from the right,
>> In at the window, or else o'er the hatch.
> Who dares not stir by day must walk by night,
>> And have is have, however men do catch.
> Near or far off, well won is still well shot,
>> And I am I, howe'er I was begot.
>
> (ll. 170-75)

The miming soliloquy into which the bastard's appearance is resolved at first reflects the spirit of vulgar mirth, which was capable of verging into social satire. Therein Shakespeare moves from rustic wooing (l. 184) to laughter at a new gentility and at a favorite object of ridicule, the traveler (ll. 185-205). By a reference to an older play, the interview between Faulconbridge and his mother continues this social satire; and the comic's conventional pose of being a gentleman is raised in the social scale to the knight "Basilisco-like" that Faulconbridge has become—a knight deriding, however, not derided (ll. 244-45, 224-26). As has been noted, by the light satiric tone of both soliloquy and dialogue this rising figure is differentiated clearly from the vicious riser, who might show a theatrically effective, but maliciously trenchant, mockery.[2]

In addition, Shakespeare specifies the Plantagenet spirit of heroic Coeur-de-lion as an attribute of Faulconbridge (I, i, e.g., ll. 85, 90, 167); and to Richard I, Shakespeare returns as the scene ends. When the interview between Philip and his mother becomes relatively serious, a potentially "gleeking" comment becomes a consolatory maxim (l. 262). The bastard then speaks about the "fury and unmatched force" of Richard I, against whom "The aweless lion could not wage the fight / Nor keep his princely heart from Richard's hand" (ll. 266-67). Small wonder, then, that heroic Richard conquered Lady Faulconbridge: "He that perforce robs lions of their hearts / May easily win a woman's" (ll. 268-69). In such a manner there is evoked the courageous Richard of metrical romance and of chap-books; the English King shown in woodcut as he tore the heart from a lion; and the crusading, heroic warrior of some current chronicles.[3] The Elizabethans' heritage of a chivalric tradition, capable of having historic overtones for the educated, is merged thereby with aspects of current merriment, even as Shakespeare avoids an exaggerated display of a popular comic vein.

In time, Shakespeare will restrain completely the comedy in Faulconbridge's role. Like other figures whose theatrical appeal could have been heightened by overtones derived from Elizabethan merriment, the portrayal of this royal bastard accords with Shakespeare's development of his drama.[4] The comic aspects of the role are emphasized during the first portion of the play as the drama progresses to John's Continental success. They are dropped when Shakespeare portrays John's viciousness and the dark "indigest" of a tragic England (V, v, 15-18, vii, 26).

Since the greatest variety of approaches has been used in recent years in the criticism of *King John,* it seems best to begin an analysis of the drama, not by focusing attention upon one character portrayal, but by considering the results that probably were achieved as the play was performed. Even though the problem to be resolved in Faulconbridge's scene is the same as that in the first grouping of characters, and even though some of his lines reflect the thought of earlier ones (e.g., "And have is have, however men do catch"), yet simply because Faulconbridge is theatrically striking, his appearance turns attention away from a consideration of John's right to the English throne. It was that question Shakespeare chose to call to his audience's attention by a theatrical opening akin to the challenge and counter-challenge of opposing forces.

The "proud control of fierce and bloody war" was threatened by Chatillon (I, i, 17) and was countered vigorously by John's answers:

> Here have we war for war and blood for blood,
> Controlment for controlment: so answer France.

> (ll. 19-20)

> Be thou as lightning in the eyes of France;
> For ere thou canst report I will be there,
> The thunder of my cannon shall be heard.
> So hence! Be thou the trumpet of our wrath
> And sullen presage of your own decay.
>
>   (ll. 24-28)

As a consequence, before any exist occurred and even as John's right to kingship was questioned, Shakespeare established a situation capable of being developed by the theatrical appeal of martial heroism. Although few writers went so far as did Warner when he spoke of John's courage as being "not inferior" to that which gave Richard the name of "Lyons-hart," yet Holinshed, for example, would write about John that "Certeinelie, it should seeme the man had a princelie heart in him."[5] John's vigor will be a constant aspect of his portrayal for an appreciable portion of the drama; and the process of the play is animated at first by his movement toward warfare in defense of his right.

The questionable nature of John's right as opposed to that of Arthur, the son of John's elder brother, had been emphasized by Chatillon's "borrowed majesty," by Eleanor's repetition of the phrase, and by Chatillon's specification of John's usurpation (I, i, 4, 5, 13, 18). This development had been qualified almost immediately by associating the right of Arthur with an anti-English France and an ambitious mother (ll. 32-34, 36-38). Immediately thereafter, however, the initial emphasis was repeated and intensified. When John spoke of "Our strong possession and our right for us" (l. 39), Eleanor replied,

> Your strong possession much more than your right,
> Or else it must go wrong with you and me.
> So much my conscience whispers in your ear,
> Which none but heaven and you and I shall hear.
>
>   (ll. 40-43)

This treatment of John's right certainly makes one question any critical interpretation based on an approach that would relate Arthur's right to that of Mary Queen of Scots or that would gloss the preceding speeches of John and Eleanor by referring to Camden's *Annales* and to a statement that "the Lawes of *England* many yeares ago determined . . . that the Crowne once possessed, cleareth and purifies all manner of defaultes or imperfections. . . ."[6] To an appreciable degree, this approach to the play gives the secret wrong of John's position to Elizabeth. In such circumstances, an emphasis upon the force of possession would be hazardous unless embedded firmly within the larger context of

Elizabeth's descent and her public right to the throne as expressed, for example, at the beginning of the *Annales*.[7] In addition, the phraseology of Eleanor's last line may well have seemed to an audience to be reminiscent of conventional representations of villainous secrecy. It seems hazardous, consequently, to interpret this play-world as being contrived to refer to the problem of Elizabethan policy that had been caused by Mary Queen of Scots, wife and later widow of Francis II of France. This is true in spite of the fact that one may buttress that interpretation by referring to Elizabeth's anger and remorse at the death of Mary, and to John's anger and remorse when Arthur is reported dead. The interpretation per se is too unusual to be allowed to stand without further consideration.

The dominant idea in Camden's *Annales* has just been noted. Even more important are two other considerations. That Catholic propagandists emphasized Elizabeth's false possession of the English throne and Mary's true descent is understandable. The power of descent was a political commonplace. Along with other accepted concepts, it naturally would be utilized by a propagandist anxious to influence events. But the power of possession, as well as the power of consent, was also a political commonplace. That a dramatist would develop a conflict between commonplaces, or choose to dramatize history that had such a conflict, does not mean necessarily that he had a point of reference comparable to that of a Catholic propagandist or of any polemical writer. He may well have been concerned with creating a play-world that would be heightened by a tension between political ideas, just as he might create one that would be intensified by conflicts developed out of the idea of revenge or of honor. In the second place, Elizabeth's anger and remorse at the execution of Mary was not necessarily hypocritical, and therefore not necessarily comparable to the anger of John when he believes that Arthur has been murdered. In addition, Mary's execution took place after a trial. It also was welcomed by a nation of Protestants, thousands of whom had sworn to violate the doctrines of descent and of possession as they might be applied to anyone by whom or for whom the murder of Elizabeth had been attempted or committed. This is quite different from the supposed secret murder of Arthur, because of which the nobles turn in anger from John. Moreover, if one is to look to nondramatic considerations for current attitudes and problems with which to interpret Shakespeare's play, one should not forget John's antipapal actions that made him dear to the hearts of some Tudor Protestants.[8]

In turning to such considerations, however, one should be guided by the emphases and the development of the drama under consideration.

The conflict between John and Arthur over their rights to the English throne apparently is to produce a "fearful bloody issue" upon the battlefield. The focal point anticipated up to the appearance of the bastard is one in which there will be dramatized a conflict between a powerful possession, qualified by its secret "wrong," and a powerless "right," qualified by its foreign support. Even when one becomes preoccupied with tendencies similar to those of Jonson's "politique *Picklocke* of the *Scene*," Eleanor's lines to John, with their overtones of theatrical villainy, presumably would yield a nondramatic meaning only to a militant Catholic still emotionally aroused by Mary's execution in the year before the Armada. When one restrains any picklocking tendency —especially one meaningful to a radical Catholic angry at events that occurred some seven years past and that lead to an attempted invasion of England—the course of Shakespeare's drama seems to be moving toward a battle the outcome of which cannot be anticipated by any simple ethical dichotomy.[9]

Once more, regard for the development of the play in the theater seems essential to determine an author's intent and artistry. Indeed, a further glance at the process of the drama reveals that Shakespeare establishes his initial qualifications so firmly that at first a unique play-world emerges in which "commodity" overrides any martial attempt to break a martial deadlock. From antipapal and anti-French emotions, he then develops the first qualification of this world of commodity by portraying a victorious English John. Throughout these developments, a major note in Faulconbridge's role is comic. By turning back to John's secret wrong and intensifying it, Shakespeare then represents suddenly a villainous John. From this aspect of John's portrayal, from Arthur's French support, and from the development of a number of ironies, Shakespeare finally represents a world tragically meaningful to Elizabethans. As this happens, comedy drops from Faulconbridge's role.

In brief, even though a puzzling "political" intent may seem to be simplified by attempting to apply to *King John* the doctrine that possession clears imperfections and by interpreting Elizabeth's anger and grief at the execution of Mary as comparable to John's in slightly similar circumstances, one may well question the validity of that approach—and its simplification of the purpose of the drama. On the other hand, when one views the play as a play, one is reminded of Shakespeare's successive emphases in the earlier histories as he focused upon different aspects of a character portrayal. One is reminded also of the short alternating emphases in the Flint Castle episode of *Richard II* —a procedure already apparent in the initial situation of *King John* and one that had appeared briefly in *2 Henry VI*.[10] Shakespeare now seems to build upon and modify features of his technique in the early trilogy. Although he still works with conventional representational methods, his basic artistry is simple and straightforward as he intensifies successively aspects of the initial conflict and develops them so that a particular tragic catastrophe is reached. As a result, although this drama usually is considered to be relatively negligible when compared with the other plays of 1594-96, a somewhat detailed analysis of its development is worthwhile. From it, an intent and an artistry emerge that give to the play a meaningful position in Shakespeare's development as a dramatist.

At first glance, the process of protasis (I, II), epitasis (III, IV), and catastrophe (V) seems to illumine the structural movement of *King John*. The second act dramatizes the indecisive warfare resulting from the initial situation and the way in which that deadlock was resolved by a marriage between Lewis, the French prince, and Blanch, the niece of John. The third act shows the resumption of warfare after the scales have been tipped on John's side by the patriotic and anti-Catholic emotions aroused through Pandulph, the papal legate. At that time, the victorious English John appears, to be followed suddenly by the vicious, murdering John. From this situation, and in accordance with Pandulph's speeches at the close of Act III, the fourth act develops. Similarly, in accordance with the bastard's speech at the close of Act IV, the final act develops.

The pattern of closing speeches and subsequent acts (III-IV, IV-V) seems to indicate, however, that as in *A Midsummer Night's Dream,* Shakespeare may have been writing with other structural principles also in mind. The same consideration seems to be indicated by the fact that the longest development in the play dramatizes the way in which the English and French rulers temporized (II, i, through III, i, 134; some 732 lines). A shorter sequence then dramatizes the victory and the villainy of John and is caused and commented upon by Pandulph (III, i, 135, through III, iv; some 479 lines). Thereupon the pattern just noticed produces two sequences similar to each other in length (IV, some 562 lines; V, some 521 lines). In other words, after a short introduction (I, some 276 lines), a long development leads to an apparent resolution. As that resolution was effected by an orator, so the speeches of Pandulph then start the play upon a different direction and toward a tragic resolution. The drama then passes through three stages: the sharp variation in the portrayal of John and the two structurally similar developments that produce the tragic conclusion and that arise from the first stage.

A number of continuous processes span all of these developments and sometimes obscure them. Some features of the introduction of Faulconbridge in the first act, for example, are utilized as the play progresses to its indecisive battle. When one notes that this continuation of similarities in varying situations appears throughout the remainder of the second act and until Pandulph's speeches close the third act, one is forced to conclude that a method different from that reflecting academic precepts about a five-act structure was at times uppermost in Shakespeare's mind. The progress of the drama toward two resolutions, for that matter, reminds one of the two parts of the earlier play about John.

In *King John,* at any rate, the inauguration of each narrative focal point is embedded by appreciable scenic or poetic features into preceding situations. This involves not only the manipulation of a stage but also the use of words and images to evoke ideas that in turn become factors determining the course of the action. In this respect, one is reminded that in the Henry VI trilogy similar tableau-like groupings of characters had appeared in varying situations—in, for example, the scenes of Plantagenet with Mortimer and Talbot with his son. There, too, a continuing conceptual or rhetorical process had appeared throughout a variety of scenes. In brief, as regards the way in which spectacle, rhetoric, and imagery is used in *King John,* it is as if Shakespeare extended his use of a cohesive imagery within the particular episode— characteristic even of *Titus Andronicus*—to effect a cohesive force comparable to the vein of the startling and the horrific that had appeared during the middle and latter parts of *2 Henry VI.*

The pages that follow first illustrate what has just been noted by considering in some detail that portion of *King John* which begins with the appearance of the bastard in the first act and ends with the appearance of a murdering John in the latter part of the third act. To be considered first is the cohesion between the opening act and the subsequent portion of the play that extends to the citizen's proposal of a marriage between Lewis and Blanch. A discussion of three aspects of that cohesion will, perhaps, suffice.

In the introduction of the bastard it is hard to see how anyone in an audience could have missed the impact of a situation whereby the eyes of those on stage were focused upon Faulconbridge:

> *El.* He hath a trick of Coeur-de-lion's face;
> The accent of his tongue affecteth him.
> Do you not read some tokens of my son
> In the large composition of the man?

> *K. John.* Mine eye hath well examined his parts
> And finds them perfect Richard.
>
> (I, i, 85-90)

Throughout the first portion of that comic scene, the appearance of the bastard, Philip, as it contrasted with that of his half-brother, Robert, was constantly called to the audience's attention. Repetitious, then, is a situation that appears soon after John's entrance upon a Continental stage, when the appearance of Arthur is called to everyone's attention. This situation will be repeated twice in subsequent developments. The last time it is represented only briefly (II, i, 472-73), and the second time it appears as part of a larger tableau-like situation (ll. 236-40). But when attention is first focused upon Arthur, and the French King charges John with usurpation—with having done "a rape / Upon the maiden virtue of the crown" (ll. 97-98)—the physical appearance of John's legitimate nephew is emphasized and called to the attention of John and Eleanor especially:

> Look here upon thy brother Geoffrey's face.
> These eyes, these brows, were moulded out of his;
> This little abstract doth contain that large
> Which died in Geoffrey; and the hand of Time
> Shall draw this brief into as huge a volume.
>
> (ll. 99-103)

In other words, as the principle of linear descent is enunciated after a comic scene, a situation basic to that scene is repeated three times by a grouping of characters which focuses attention upon Arthur's appearance, just as attention had been focused on Faulconbridge's. Thereafter the word "bastard" is repeated (ll. 122, 129), and Eleanor repeats her still earlier exclamation against the charge of usurpation (l. 120). Now another mother insists upon her virtue, but this time maintains her attitude. By the word "grandam," Eleanor again would bring to her side a grandson (l. 159), and the problem of a will determining possession is again dropped with a pun (ll. 191-94). With John and Eleanor upon stage, a tableau-like effect that would be nearest in theatrical time to similar situations during the introduction of Faulconbridge is also nearest in emphasis; and other elements of the comic sequence are extended into this serious one. However Shakespeare may have phrased it, cohesion between successive but disparate scenes seems to have been intended.

The result of this cohesive element, of course, is to emphasize Arthur's right by descent to the English throne. By implication, John and Eleanor refuse to accept those premises that they had accepted in the scene centering about Faulconbridge; and by that much John's secret wrong is kept alive.

By another development, however, Shakespeare intensifies his initial qualification of Arthur's right—that is, the fact that it is supported by enemies of the English. This feature of Shakespeare's artistry also continues an aspect of the scene introducing Faulconbridge. In the comic sequence, references to Coeur-de-lion had been constant, and the scene had ended with a reference to Richard's robbing lions of their hearts (I, i, e.g., ll. 50-54, 96-104, 120-27, 136, 167, 180, 252, 265-69, 274). The next grouping of characters then brings on stage a figure wearing a lion's skin. He is introduced as "brave Austria," who by supporting Arthur's claim to the English throne would make amends for killing

> Richard, that robb'd the lion of his heart
> And fought the holy wars in Palestine. . . .
>
> (II, i, 3-4)

Austria and Arthur embrace and all move to attack Angiers. But this evocation of Richard I, constant in the very appearance of Austria,[11] is elaborated when, some hundred lines later, the bastard mocks Austria in a "braving" sequence that begins with an appropriate variation upon a maxim found, for example, in Erasmus' *Adagia* and *The Spanish Tragedy:*

> You are the hare of whom the proverb goes,
> Whose valour plucks dead lions by the beard.[12]
>
> (ll. 137-38)

Since this mockery of Austria increases as the scene progresses, it presumably would strengthen any chauvinistic antagonism toward the slayer of an heroic English king, especially since this ally of Arthur's now plans to make submissive to his cause

> . . . that pale, that white-fac'd shore,
> Whose foot spurns back the ocean's roaring tides
> And coops from other lands her islanders,
> . . . that England, hedg'd in with the main,
> That water-walled bulwark, still secure
> And confident from foreign purposes. . . .[13]
>
> (ll. 23-28)

In addition, John now bases his right to rule not simply on possession but also on service and on his English following, that is, on consent

(II, i, 206-34, 273-75).[14] Quite obviously, in contrast with the anti-John emphasis that closed the initial situation before the appearance of the bastard, Shakespeare now is emphasizing and intensifying the tenuous balance between the claims of John and Arthur.[15] This aspect of the drama at this point in its development is indicated even more clearly by the stand-off in debate and the stand-off in battle.

This inconclusiveness of battle calls attention to a third example of the cohesion between the first act and the second. Just as Arthur's right and the qualification of his right have been intensified, and John's right intensified also, so this development increases the vigorous movement toward warfare in the initial grouping of characters. In the introduction of Faulconbridge, John's initial vigor had been expressed by his riming haste to meet his opponents (I, i, 176-79). In this Continental scene it is now amplified by Chatillon's description of John's "strong" and "fiery" haste "to blood and strife" (II, i, 54-75). The first set of balanced speeches given to John and King Philip are then developed with a martial rhetoric; and when warfare results in a stand-off, the earlier vigor and haste to battle are embodied in speeches by the bastard. His lines at first override those of the citizen-orator and would turn loose upon the play-world a "mousing" Death and the cry of "havoc!"

> O, now doth Death line his dead chaps with steel;
> The swords of soldiers are his teeth, his fangs;
> And now he feasts, mousing the flesh of men,
> In undetermin'd differences of kings.
> Why stand these royal fronts amazed thus?
> Cry, havoc! kings. Back to the stained field,
> You equal potents, fiery-kindled spirits!
> Then let confusion of one part confirm
> The other's peace. Till then, blows, blood, and death!
>
> (ll. 352-60)

The God of Battles, who could establish rule as a legitimate one, has been mentioned briefly by King Philip, tangentially by John, and perhaps by the citizen-orator as well (ll. 299, 283-86, 368-72); but the preceding speech expresses a concept of warfare that is quite different. As vigor and haste to battle continue, the appeal of raging Mars and Bellona might well have been evoked by the lines of the bastard—an appeal based on an emotional thought that was sometimes characteristic of the age and that saw virtue in the purple testament of bleeding war per se.[16] Accordingly, in the bastard's next speech, "Fortune" replaces a briefly mentioned "God" and a "greater power." After a united war against the flouting "scroyles" of Angiers, it is she who

> ... shall cull forth
> Out of one side her happy minion,
> To whom in favour she shall give the day,
> And kiss him with a glorious victory.
>
> (ll. 391-94)

Although Fortune might be conceived of as God's instrument, her appearance here accords rather with those attributes of the fickle goddess conducive to an emphasis upon *occasio,* or an opportunity that should be seized vigorously.[17] In such a development one can see, perhaps, an implication of John's "strong possession." Much more obvious, however, would be the theatrical force of the bastard's speeches and the cohesion between his cry of havoc, the virtue in battle per se, and the emphasis upon an occasion to be grasped firmly. His lines thereby represent an undoubtedly audible focal point for the haste, fiery strength, strife, and blood that have appeared as far back in the drama as when John first answered Chatillon, or when with the startling accompaniment of "churlish drums" John appeared in France. As has been noted, this movement from words, images, and stage noises to an emotional force that would determine events has been continued also by a wealth of martial images in the rhetorical speeches of the debate and has just been dramatized by the action of "excursions."

Aside from emphasizing the "equal potents" of John and Arthur, the preceding reference to Fortune also indicates, perhaps, the forthcoming world of commodity. While warlike haste was being emphasized such an indication probably would not be marked in the theater. If this reference to Fortune be conceived of as anticipatory, however, it would accord with the bastard's question as he proposes a temporary union:—"Smacks it not something of the policy?" (II, i, 396). It would accord also with his vice-like glee that during the united attack, Austria and Philip will shoot at each other inadvertantly:

> O prudent discipline! From north to south,
> Austria and France shoot in each other's mouth.
> I'll stir them to it. Come, away, away!
>
> (ll. 413-15)

Not simply between the first and second acts but within the long Continental scene itself, cohesion between varying situations is effected, quite noticeably, by Shakespeare's use of word, image, and spectacle. When the force of rhetoric, so far unsuccessful, makes itself felt and restrains the reign of Death and Fortune, the warring union proposed by Faulconbridge is turned into its antithesis. To do this, the citizen-orator proposes a marriage between Lewis and Blanch, demonstrates the validity of the spoken word, and utilizes for his purpose previous aspects of the play-world. Thus, for example, when he has specified his proposition by a masterful triad of balanced questions (II, i, 426-31), some of the previous images reappear; but their present context of marriage and union gives them a different meaning. The "vexed" "current" of John's "right" and "silver water" now becomes two "silver currents" that can join to "glorify the banks," the two "controlling bounds" that are the kings of England and of France (ll. 335-40, 441-45). Similarly, the citizen's transition of his final, brief threat of stout resistance repeats fully the bastard's references to cannon, while his "match" (l. 450) shows wordplay worthy of a master of rhetoric. After Shakespeare briefly focuses attention again upon Arthur (the "yon green boy" that will have "no sun to ripe" his "bloom," ll. 472-73), other speeches continue the orator's practise. Thus the heat of combat and of blood takes on the courtly glow of a wealth and a fruition that will "gild" Blanch's bridal bed. She will be rich

> In titles, honours, and promotions,
> As she in beauty, education, *blood,*
> *Holds hands* with any princess of the world.
>
> (ll. 491-94)

When this shift to peace is resolved into Lewis' courtly rhetoric and Blanch's witty answer (ll. 496-503, 510-20), both speeches lead to their hands and lips being joined. Thereby a tableau-like situation reappears that had occurred earlier when Arthur and Austria embraced and when France held Arthur's hand as he enunciated his right to the city of Angiers (ll. 15, 20, 236-40). In other words, in this development of a peaceful resolution, imagery of joining, as well as the actual sight of joined hands and lips, keeps alive the earlier appearances of hand and arm clasping and lays a groundwork for its intensified reappearance later. At the same time, the cohesion of images in varying contexts is so tight, and the congruently varying comments of the bastard are so constant, that within a theater the satiric world of commodity must have seemed to be fused inextricably with the earlier antithetical world of haste to battle. As was indicated at the beginning of this chapter, speech in the widest sense of the word—and spectacle is an aspect of theatrical speech—binds together disparate emphases.[18] Indeed, the process of Shakespeare's play is strikingly similar to that of the citizen's oration. Even the bastard's lines that had preceded his figure of "mousing" Death—

> Ha, majesty! how high thy glory towers
> When the *rich blood* of kings is set on fire—
>
> (ll. 350-51)

is verbally congruent with the subsequent development that produces
the "richer blood" (l. 431) of Blanch and her gilded bridal bed.

From this resolution, as the clasped hands of the betrothed contrast with "sad and passionate" Constance (ll. 532-60), the bastard
turns, not to an enraged world of kings, but to the "Mad world! mad
kings! mad composition!" of his soliloquy on commodity. The speech
then ends, merrily but satirically, in a manner reminiscent of his
soliloquy in the first act; for it is focused upon the rising figure of the
bastard himself:

> And why rail I on this Commodity
> But for because he hath not woo'd me yet?
> Not that I have the power to clutch my hand
> When his fair angels would salute my palm;
> But for my hand, as unattempted yet,
> Like a poor beggar, raileth on the rich.
> Well, whiles I am a beggar, I will rail
> And say there is no sin but to be rich;
> And being rich, my virtue then shall be
> To say there is no vice but beggary.
> Since kings break faith upon Commodity,
> Gain, be my lord, for I will worship thee.[19]
>
> (ll. 587-98)

Also firmly embedded into the previous process of the drama,
however, is Constance's shrill renewal of the bastard's earlier cry for
blows, blood, and death:

> Arm, arm, you heavens, against these perjur'd kings!
> A widow cries; be husband to me, heavens!
> Let not the hours of this ungodly day
> Wear out the day in peace; but, ere sunset,
> Set armed discord 'twixt these perjur'd kings!
> Hear me, O, hear me!
> *Aust.*   Lady Constance, peace!
> *Const.* War! war! no peace!
>
> (III, i, 107-13)

Constance's earlier appearance in a lamenting tableau of grief, which, at
one point, again focused attention upon the appearance of her son,

Arthur (ll. 43-54), also shows Shakespeare's continuing use of tabeleau-like effects. Later in the scene, Blanch takes Constance's place as the grieving female figure, after both have joined in a minor tableau-like scene of kneeling (ll. 300-16, 326-36). Then, as the third act ends, Constance appears as a frantic picture of sorrow (III, iv, 17-105).[20]

Two further examples of this theatrically rhetorical process in what is now printed as Act III will, perhaps, be sufficient. The first, which is related again to Constance, shows a continuation of what has been noted already. The lamentation of Constance at the beginning of the third act picks up the meanings of *blood* (passion, descent, humor of the body) and uses the word, which had been constant throughout the second act,[21] in accordance with her display of "vex'd spirits" at France's abandonment of beautiful, pathetic Arthur:

> Gone to be married! Gone to swear a peace!
> *False blood* to *false blood* joined!
>
> (III, i, 1-2)

In such a context, King Philip is "bawd" to a "strumpet Fortune," who "adulterates *hourly* with thine uncle John," the usurper (ll. 56, 60-61). As a result, the bastard's Fortune, which had preceded a world of commodity, reappears and lingers on as "her humerous ladyship" (l. 119), after Constance's cry for "War! war! no peace!"

As part of Constance's rhetorical virtuosity, the pictorial, delaying nature of the imagery in *Titus Andronicus* is again apparent, though here it clearly accords with Shakespeare's tableau-like artistry of a "stooping" grief (III, i, e.g., ll. 43-54). This effect is then continued in Constance's lines about Fortune and in her description of Grief (ll. 69-74); and it reappears in France's speech wherein the richness and warmth of the betrothal scene is intensified as a festive brightness:

> 'Tis true, fair daughter; and this *blessed day*
> Ever in France shall be kept *festival*.
> To solemnize this day the *glorious sun*
> Stays in his course and plays the alchemist,
> Turning with *splendour of his precious eye*
> The meagre cloddy earth to *glittering gold*.
> The yearly course that brings this day about
> Shall never see it but a *holiday*.[22]
>
> (ll. 75-82)

The tendency persists in Constance's next speech, with its thesis-like, contrasting description of the present day (ll. 87-95), a description joined at first to France's imagery by her opening questions:

> What hath this day deserved? What hath it done,
> That it in *golden letters* should be set
> Among the high tides in the calendar?
>
> (ll. 84-86)

Finally, with "forsworn, forsworn!" (l. 101) and the approach to her cry for war, Constance's next speech gives both to *arms* and *blood* two separate meanings:

> You came in *arms* to spill mine enemies *blood,*
> But now in *arms* you strengthen *it* with yours.
>
> (ll. 102-3)

"Arm, arm," and "armed discord" follow (ll. 107, 111); and derision is heaped upon Austria with that reference to a "humorous" Fortune already noted. Even the semantic shift of *arms* in Constance's lines just quoted builds upon what has preceded and concurs with a visual feature of the stage that will be developed again by the theatrically obvious hand-clasping of John and King Philip.

The second feature to be commented upon concerns Shakespeare's development of a strong pro-John emphasis in the third act. This is the culmination of a movement that, after the anti-John resolution of the initial situation, emphasized the balancing claims of Arthur and John in the Angiers episode and made the soliloquy on commodity censurably applicable to both the English and the French rulers, but especially to King Philip.[23] Now Shakespeare draws upon the Protestant emotions of his age and the Elizabethans' scorn and hatred of a name "so slight, unworthy, and ridiculous" as "the Pope." Since the speeches so far given John usually have been under ten lines in length, and only once as long as twenty-nine lines, it is revealing that Shakespeare has John express fully an Elizabethan scorn of Rome while enunciating the Elizabethan doctrine of regal supremacy:

> What earthy name to interrogatories
> Can task the free breath of a sacred king?
> Thou canst not, Cardinal, devise a name
> So slight, unworthy, and ridiculous,
> To charge me to an answer, as the Pope.
> Tell him this tale; and from the mouth of England
> Add thus much more, that no Italian priest
> Shall tithe or toll in our dominions;
> But as we, under Heaven, are supreme head,
> So under Him that great supremacy,
> Where we do reign, we will alone uphold,

Without the assistance of a mortal hand.
So tell the Pope, all reverence set apart
To him and his usurp'd authority.[24]

(III, i, 147-60)

As a result, John's vigor now takes an unqualified nationalistic turn; and when this English ruler berates those who are misled by a "meddling priest," the bastard's "commodity" becomes an anti-French and anti-papal one.[25] Rulers like Philip dread

... a curse that money may buy out;
And by the merit of vile gold, dross, dust,
Purchase corrupted pardon of a man
Who in that sale sells pardon from himself. ...

(ll. 164-67)

Shakespeare then dramatizes the way in which this "juggling witch-craft" excommunicated the English ruler. Among other things, Pandulph declared that the "hand" should be called "meritorious," "Canonized and worshipp'd as a saint, / That takes away by any secret course" John's "hateful life" (III, i, 176-79). Attention is then focused upon the picture of the joined and disjoined hands of France and England (ll. 192, 195, 226-29, 234-35, 239-41, 244, 262; see also l. 103). By Pandulph's speech, Shakespeare obviously wished to draw upon emotions that had been aroused by the excommunication of Elizabeth and by attempts to assassinate her. Similarly, the representation of the falling-off of France, even more than the bastard's soliloquy on com-modity, may well have been substantiated by the emotions of those who were disgusted with Henry IV's conversion to Catholicism.[26] Thus with an Anglican dignity that builds upon anti-French and antipapal emotions, this English ruler watches the falling away of France in another theatrically noticeable stage picture that repeats a tableau-like effect established first at the beginning of the second act.

Upon this basis, John will win the victory so far denied him. With haste and heat he triumphs over the French; and the stage again is filled with "alarums" and "excursions," now doubled (III, ii, S-D, iii, S-D). Earlier images reappear in this second, intensified haste to battle and bloodshed. Now they refer to the heated passion and haste of John, and then to his surprising success in battle and his quick return to England (e.g., III, i, 339-47, ii, 1, iv, 5-14). The "rich blood" of one particular king, in the bastard's earlier words, again has been "set on fire." Before the French refer to that fact, however, this *blood* is turned from a successful warlike heat to the villainous emotions whereby Shakespeare glaringly qualifies his representation of a victorious English John.

By this shift to an antithetical emphasis, one is reminded of the artistry apparent in *Richard II* when Shakespeare alternates between Lancastrian and Richardian emphases. There the process, however, is less sharp. It is kept within the area of rule and not developed by utilizing in contrary directions the Elizabethans' public religious emotions and an audience's antipathy to secret, murderous villainy. Except for one brief use of the sun-king analogy, the characters' lines in *Richard II* also remain constant within the dramatic vein allotted each figure.[27]

In *King John*, nevertheless, Shakespeare's rhetorical artistry still appears even in this quick theatrical shift from English vigor to stage villainy. John's plan to murder Arthur is disclosed to Hubert with yet another clasping of hands (III, iii, 25). The dialogue between the two shows another thesis-like development that introduces images of darkness from references to a bright, "wanton" day. This rhetorical development changes the previous emphasis upon brightness and heat, now congruent with a "proud day," to one congruent with a "brooding" and "watchful" day. At the same time, the psychology of humors plays about the lines—a psychology that by itself might be sufficient to explain the rush of blood, that is, passion, from success in battle to villainy.[28]

> I had a thing to say, but let it go.
> The *sun* is in the heaven, and the *proud day,*
> Attended with the *pleasures of the world,*
> Is all too *wanton* and too full of *gawds*
> To give me audience. If the *midnight bell*
> Did, with his *iron tongue* and *brazen mouth,*
> Sound on into the drowsy race of *night;*
> If this same were a *churchyard* where we stand,
> And thou possessed with a thousand wrongs;
> Or if that surly spirit, *melancholy,*
> Had *bak'd* thy *blood* and made it *heavy, thick,*
> Which else runs tickling up and down the veins,
> Making that idiot, laughter, keep men's eyes,
> And strain their cheeks to idle merriment—
> A passion hateful to my purposes;
> Or if that thou could see me without eyes,
> Hear me without thine ears, and make reply
> Without a tongue, using conceit alone,

Without eyes, ears, and harmful sound of words;
Then, in despite of *brooded, watchful* day,
I would into thy bosom pour my thoughts.[29]

(ll. 33-53)

Obviously the contrast in this speech accords with the sharp, dramatic contrast in John's portrayal. At the same time, the speech adumbrates a movement toward a figurative and actual darkness that will be expressed in the bastard's soliloquy about dead Arthur and represented by the subsequent play-world (IV, iii, 139 ff.).

Shakespeare's artistry in the remainder of *King John* can be illustrated by three considerations only.[30] In the first place, his development of Pandulph's speeches at the end of Act III (that is, the speeches that specify the course of the subsequent act) may well have qualified the emotional reaction arising from John's plan to have Arthur murdered. By the treatment of John in Act IV, Shakespeare then continues this qualification but turns it into a basic irony that leads into Faulconbridge's speech closing that act. In accordance with this last speech, Shakespeare develops a vast "indigest" in which ironies are doubled and redoubled.

After John has captured Arthur and left for England, any emotional allegiance to Pandulph's attack upon John probably did not coalesce in spite of John's villainy. In the first place, Pandulph's consolation of the French involves an invasion of England. In the second place, this representative of the Pope refers to the French and to sympathetic Englishmen as many of Shakespeare's contemporaries had heard the Spanish and the English Catholics referred to when a feared invasion of Elizabeth's land was the subject of discourse:

If but a dozen French
Were there in arms, they would be as a call
To train ten thousand English to their side,
Or as a little snow, tumbled about,
Anon becomes a mountain.

(ll. 173-77)

The scene is concerned with a plan that was hated and feared by Elizabethans. The movement into Act IV thereby falls into line with what has been noted about the qualification in this drama of any simple "Right."

The development of John's vicious plan agrees with this movement. It, too, is qualified. Hubert does not carry out the murder (IV, i). John repents and perceives the truth of the maxims enunciated, ironically enough, by Pandulph at the end of the third act (IV, ii, 103-5). To a modern reader, Shakespeare's representation of the king's repentance may seem singularly undeveloped, but it is elaborated in a manner that probably was more meaningful to the sixteenth century than to the twentieth. When it takes the form of blaming Hubert, the idea is enunciated that attendants and counselors are guilty when they do not attempt to restrain the "humour" of a ruler:

> *K. John.* It is the curse of kings to be attended
> By slaves that take their humours for a warrant
> To break within the bloody house of life,
> And on the winking of authority
> To understand a law, to know the meaning
> Of dangerous majesty, when perchance it frowns
> More upon humour than advis'd respect.[31]

> (IV, ii, 208-14)

The idea is expressed even more forcefully here than it was in *Richard III,* although it lacks the power of lamenting rhetoric found in the earlier play (*Richard III,* II, i, 106-32). For Shakespeare's age such a reproach could be quite sincere, even in circumstances other than the theater.[32] Much more than in John's earlier speech to Hubert, the preceding lines also may have reminded an audience of the psychology of the era and the doctrine of a temporarily overpowering emotion. The idea of an attendant's duty is repeated, moreover, when John has to retreat from his pose of innocence:

> *K. John* Hadst thou but shook thy head or made a pause
> When I spake darkly what I purposed,
> Or turn'd an eye of doubt upon my face,
> As bid me tell my tale in express words,
> Deep shame had struck me dumb, made me break off,
> And those thy fears might have wrought fears in me.

> (ll. 231-36)

Granted that John's repentance is theologically far from complete, yet when the previous thought is joined with a recognition and admission of sin (IV, ii, 216-18), the traditional force of repentance may have qualified partially an audience's antipathy to theatrical villainy perpetrated upon pathetic innocence. Even more important than the preceding consideration is the fact that as this scene is performed, an audience knows that Arthur is living. When Hubert reveals that fact to John, the ending of the scene is apparently a fortunate one. In addition, the haste of this play-world has returned again, and the process of the

scene seems to have been contrived to underline this fact. John's reactions to his perception of guilt and to the news of Eleanor's death are
interrupted by three entrances (ll. 104, 131, 182); and three exits are
made upon the command that the messenger make great haste (ll. 174-
80, 267-69). The absence of any rhetorical display of John's emotions
is motivated thereby.[33] In these three respects, Shakespeare qualifies
John's villainy, a villainy that had in turn qualified sharply his hot and
hasty success in battle. By the first two of these considerations, Shakespeare also qualifies the politic lines of Pandulph, who had predicted
John's murder of Arthur (III, iv, 139, 162-64).

With a pathetic and tragic irony, haste continues and effects both
Arthur's death and the anger of the English nobles, who consider John
and Hubert guilty of murder and join the French (IV, iii). In the
development of this basic irony, minor ironies begin to appear. Hubert's
insistence that he is innocent, for example, intensifies the nobles' anger.
Shakespeare also has Salisbury insist upon a disjunction between appearance and reality, but only as regards Hubert (IV, iii, 107-10)—a
disjuction that earlier had been denied but applied conversely to the
same Hubert (ii, 71-73, 220-27)—whereas the truth of Hubert's
innocence now makes that disjunction applicable to the entire scene.
These tragic consequences of precipitancy build upon the death
of Arthur, whose portrayal has just been heightened by his convincing
rhetoric (IV, i); and the anger of the nobles overrides the reminder that
in the immediate course of events, dramatic irony is upon John's side
(IV, iii, 57-59).

From the nobles' anger and from the ironies just noted, Shakespeare
turns to the fearsome picture of a tableau-like effect that must have
been theatrically striking. Hubert picks up the dead Arthur, and the
bastard's long speech accompanies the action. The previous emphases
in Faulconbridge's soliloquies are preserved, however. In those speeches,
his comments on the action of princes had been subordinate to his
fuller comments upon the world in which he found himself. As a result,
the bastard's references to "proud-swelling state" and "wrested pomp,"
as they might refer to John, are overridden by the sad prospect of
England's future. Faulconbridge's mousing Death and Constance's
"carrion monster" (III, iv, 33) are extended to the "vast confusion"
that as a raven waits for "sick-fallen" England. Since "powers from
home and discontents at home" now meet in "one line," a dogged,
bristling war also reappears with this "imminent decay" and threatening
tempest. Haste is imperative, and "heaven itself doth frown upon the
land" (IV, iii, 139-59).

This tragic confusion is dramatized in the fifth act. Yet in spite of

England's being under a frowning heaven, the dramatic irony upon John's side is continued in the fact that none thought "the King so stor'd with friends" (V, iv, 1). Quite ironically, however, this development occurs after John has succumbed to Pandulph and fallen into a despair from which he never arises (V, i, 44-61, iii, 3-4).

As the catastrophe of England under a frowning heaven is elaborated, there constantly appear ironies other than the basic one from which this "vast confusion" arose. When John's anti-papal sentiments are transferred to Lewis, Pandulph fails for the first time to influence the French and stop the invasion of England (V, ii, 68-116). Earlier, an irony partially fortunate for John had occurred in the working out of the prophecy by Peter of Pomfret (V, i, 25-29). And a good deal later, Hubert's indirect service to the nobles who had condemned him is developed as they turn to their "great King John" (V, iv, 40-43, 57). At least once, the all-embracing irony is specified by Pandulph: "You look but on the outside of this work" (V, ii, 109). With a compounded artistry, however, the line is addressed to Lewis, not to the English nobles. It is quite fitting that the end of Shakespeare's qualifying, and in that respect his ironic, dramaturgy should show a concentration of ironies.

At the same time, Shakespeare continues other features of his artistry, whereby some of his images became concrete factors in the development of the play. One needs but to think of previous images of heat and of the "hot" day of John's success in their relationship to the blinding scene and its properties (IV, i) to realize that in a similar manner images connected with "water" and "currents" now reappear, until with the sinking of the sun, actual waters mar any victory (e.g., II, i, 335-40, 441-45; IV, ii, 138, 139; V, iv, 53-57; V, iii, 9-13, v, 12-13, vi, 39-41. After this last feature of the stage-world has been mentioned within an emphasis on increasing darkness, the antithetical images of blood and heat also reappear as John is shown in his final agony (e.g., V, vii, 1, 8, 30, 33, 39, 45, 48).[34] In the last act of *King John,* this tragedy of blood, passion, and precipitancy is resolved into a darkened play-world (e.g., V, iv, 33-36, v, 18, vi, 17-20). In such circumstances, England lies as an "indigest" "so shapeless and so rude" that form can be given it only by another youthful prince (V, vii, 25-27).

Thoroughly accordant with what has just been pointed out is the fact that, with the exception of Arthur and the bastard,[35] the characterization in this drama also shows a constant qualification. Austria is mocked so consistently by Faulconbridge that this figure who would make amends for the death of Coeur-de-lion is given the derisible glow

of the braggart. Conversely, Lewis speaks with Elizabethan force against
Pandulph. Upon the portrayal of Constance, though she is called
ambitious and a shrew, is loosed the force of a pathetic and frantic
rhetoric.[36] The English nobles are both right and wrong: right in their
protest as it is a protest; wrong by immediate dramatic fact and by their
siding with an invader. At the end of the third act, the papal envoy's
enunciation of maxims *qua* maxims is valid, as is his power to effect
a final quiescent ending (V, vii, 82-86); but he bears the brunt of
antipapal emotions and of Faulconbridge's vigorous patriotism (e.g., V,
vii, 87-88). Finally, the dominant irony in the portrayal of John
produces a tragic catastrophe focused upon sad events rather than upon
John's character.[37] Thus upon his death, any implication of a retributive
course of justice (V, vi, 37-38, vii, 25-27) is subordinate to theatrically
inescapable lines about the sad fall of rulers:

> What surety of the world, what hope, what stay,
> When this was now a prince, and now is clay?
>
> (V, vii, 68-69)

John's death, consequently, is but part of Shakespeare's final picture
of a darkened, though still hurried, world that is "Black, fearful, com-
fortless, and horrible" (V, vi, 20). Even the surprising stamina that
England showed when she almost was conquered by an invader has its
unfortunate consequence (V, v, 1-4, 12-13, vi, 39-42, vii, 61-64). As a
result, *King John* is not as negligible as it sometimes has been considered.
Its picture of a secret wrong and a Plantagenet vein of vigor and
comedy becoming a world of commodity and of ironic tragedy will
remain unique until an older playwright creates the totally ironic world
of *Troilus and Cressida*.[38] And to achieve this result, Shakespeare builds
upon features of his earlier dramaturgy as he now represents the clash of
irreconcilables in attributes of character, in claims to the English
throne,[39] and in imagery.

In its applicability to Elizabethans, the final effect of *King John*
probably aroused a fearful, though a thankful, reaction. A papal legate
bestows the English crown, a foreign invasion is successful, Englishmen
aid the invaders, the English ruler is poisoned by a Catholic, peace is
arranged by a prince of the Catholic church. As was true for the writers
of *Gorboduc,* but with an emotional import instead of a basic didacticism,[40] Shakespeare's primary concern in writing this drama seems to
have been to develop a rush of events toward the alarms and darkness
of a time that for Elizabethans was long past and never to be desired. In
contrast with this dark world of an Elizabethan's nightmare, the
England of Elizabeth showed no such ruler, no such revolt, no such

invasion, no such infection of the times.[41] Indeed, the closing maxim of *King John* seems designed to solidify such an impression. Applicable to the past Armada years, it promises a repetition of those years should that be necessary:[42]

> This England never did, nor never shall,
> Lie at the proud foot of a conqueror,
> But when it first did help to wound itself.
> Now these her princes are come home again,
> Come the three corners of the world in arms,
> And we shall shock them. Nought shall make us rue,
> If England to itself do rest but true.
>
> (V, vii, 112-18)

Romeo and Juliet also shows a sudden change to the darkness of tragedy, effected in this instance by an adverse fate working through the unawareness of individuals. As in *King John,* comedy is again important in the development of a play and in the portrayal of characters; but in this instance it is important also for Shakespeare's dominant tragic effect. Consider, for example, the structural outline of the drama. *Romeo and Juliet* begins with fighting, the recurrence of which provides a framing action for the protasis. The narrative focal points of that first structural unit are the meeting of hero and heroine (I, v) and their marriage (II, vi); and the dominant emphasis in this portion of the drama is one of wit, gaiety, and exuberance. With Mercutio's death and Romeo's banishment (III, i), however, the play develops with an increasing darkness; and at that time, the complications of the narrative are elaborated progressively by an emphasis upon the operation of an adverse fate.[43] With Juliet's supposed death as the fourth act closes, the drama progresses to a catastrophe that is marked in turn by a recurrence of duelling on stage. The architectonic neatness of the development just sketched reminds one of the unit-like precision that has been noticed in other plays and that can be found in other features of this drama also. In this instance, however, even more than in *King John,* Shakespeare's precision is submerged by his concentration on the rapid course of events[44] and by his continuous emphases, the most prominent of which is his creation of sympathy for the lovers. It is their destruction that produces the tragic experience of pleasure and pain with its bases in the gaiety and exuberance of the protasis and its consequent protest that such things should be.

There would be little need to elaborate the point just made were it not that a faint strain in present-day criticism may seem to question an Elizabethan audience's unqualified sympathy with Romeo and Juliet.

Certainly from sixteenth-century attitudes toward both love and marriage, a countermovement to youthful love could be developed.[45] By considering the development of the scenes, however, one can perceive how a lyrical process, as well as an attitude sympathetic with the lovers, dominates the protasis and extends into the epitasis. Any disparate or antithetical attitude is embodied within this dominant emphasis or made subordinate to it. With the third and especially the fourth acts, this process begins to give way to developments derived from some usual features of Elizabethan thought and Elizabethan tragedy. From such an examination of the drama, the unique, original, and enduring artistry of *Romeo and Juliet* emerges clearly.

In view of what has been noted about *King John* and in view of the fact that when *A Midsummer Night's Dream* begins, it expresses a sympathetic attitude toward romantic love even as it starts to mock it,[46] it would be surprising if Shakespeare did not utilize potentially contradictory attitudes as he developed his major emphasis in *Romeo and Juliet*. In *Richard II*, of course, he capitalizes upon antitheses inherent in Elizabethan political thought for his dramatization of the fall of Richard and the rise of Bolingbroke. Accordingly, as this tragedy begins, it reflects an attitude that sees in love a dangerous passion that should be controlled by man if he would live at his best in a society fit for his dignity.

Somewhat paradoxically, the reflection of this attitude is part of Shakespeare's sympathetic portrayal of Romeo, whose appearance is anticipated by a dramatic *descriptio* (I, i, 123-61). The scene had begun with bawdry and low comedy. The brawl has taken place, and the prince's public sentence has been pronounced. Then, by this description in dialogue, the play moves toward the amusement of high comedy. The description has for its body a narrative account of the kindred action of two youths, Romeo and Benvolio; and its conclusion refers to current beliefs about the way in which unusual action might indicate the existence of some overpowering emotion, potentially dangerous if not eradicated when the cause is known.[47] In connection with Romeo, *humor* is specified twice, the second time at some length as its danger is noted (ll. 135, 147-48). That danger is then repeated for the motivation of the ensuing dialogue between Romeo and Benvolio (ll. 160-63.) As in Montague's speech about Romeo's shunning "the all-cheering sun" (l. 140), contemporary meanings of light imagery would accord with the dangerousness of a "black and portentious" humor that manifests itself as an excessive sorrow, one of the conventional passions and perturbations of the soul (ll. 147, 160).[48] In such a manner, an attitude that might look askance upon love is applied to the hero.[49] But the dominant emphasis obviously is one of sympathy; for the context in which the preceding attitude appears is created by characters who are worried about Romeo.

That context continues as high comedy develops. The black and portentious nature of Romeo's humor is resolved into the "witty" speech of a young man who is in love, who expects to be laughed at, but who gains sympathy instead (ll. 189, 177-204). The oxymoron of formal rhetoric, both in phrase and in theme (ll. 177-88, 191-200, 203-4), places opposites in juxtaposition (e.g., a "brawling love" and a "loving hate") but is developed into a comic anticlimax:

> *Ben.* Tell me in sadness, who is that you love?
> *Rom.* What, shall I groan and tell thee?
> *Ben.*   Groan! why, no;
> But sadly tell me who.
> *Rom.* Bid a sick man in sadness make his will,—
> Ah, word ill urg'd to one that is so ill!
> In sadness, cousin, I do love a woman.
>
> (ll. 205-10)

Furthermore, the lover himself points to the amusement apparent in the situation.[50] Witness the line, "Dost thou not laugh," Romeo's punning, and his comment upon himself: "This is not Romeo; he's some otherwhere." The technique approaches that conventional to the witty companion, the court wit, or the dizzard of high degree. Witness also the speeches that immediately follow the preceding passage, when the humor of "In sadness, cousin, I do love a woman" is being underlined:

> *Ben.* I aim'd so near when I suppos'd you lov'd.
> *Rom.* A right good mark-man!
>
> (ll. 211-12)

As a result of the preceding considerations, it would be surprising if an audience did not sympathize with Romeo or at least follow his directions in their amusement. Later in the play, although Mercutio directs amusement at the hero's love for Rosaline, he continues a process begun by Romeo himself.

This treatment of love in a high comic vein, although it is begun by the hero, is only one aspect of his introduction. Constantly Romeo's lines reflect themes in current sonneteering; and they probably would have some of the force, or conviction, of a lyricism that was bursting into bright nondramatic vigor. Rosaline's beauty exceeds that of all other ladies; but her "severity," her vow to live chaste, cuts "beauty off from all posterity." In that vow, Romeo lives dead "to tell it now" (ll. 225-44). Although Romeo's lyricism and the concept of that lyricism are far below those of Spenser's verse published in 1595, and although high-comedy lingers in this dialogue (e.g., l. 244), yet this development lays a groundword for the actual sonneteering of Romeo's meeting with Juliet—a meeting that saves him from the despair lightly dramatized here. The poetry of the meeting then moves toward the lyrical conviction of the balcony scene and the expression of a concept akin to that in Spenser's *Amoretti and Epithalamion*. As one might expect, between that narrative focal point of the first two acts and the initial appearance of Romeo, Shakespeare has kept alive and elaborated the imagery of love. To follow that process briefly through its varied circumstances is both interesting and revealing, for one can perceive how a variety of attitudes about love and marriage are expressed as the focal point of the first act approaches and how those attitudes then merge with one another and culminate in the balcony scene.

When love imagery reappears in the second scene of the drama, Paris is asking approval of his suit for Juliet's hand. As love had been treated at first in a manner that agreed with sixteenth-century psychology, so marriage is now placed in a context that accords with the actuality of Renaissance life. In these circumstances, love imagery becomes noticeable once more when Capulet, after varying from strict parental control in matters of matrimony (I, ii, 8-19), speaks in lyrical couplets of "Earth-treading stars that make dark heaven light," of the "comfort" that "lusty young men feel / When well-apparell'd April on the heel / Of limping winter treads," and equates that sensuous exuberance with the "delight" that will be experienced "Among fresh female buds" "this night" (ll. 24-30). Introduced by a renewal of servant comedy, the reappearance of Romeo and Benvolio continues the process. Both Benvolio's consolatory maxims and Romeo's earlier riming about love are elaborated now by Rosaline's name, by love imagery that accords with contemporary psychology, and by a brief stanzaic form suitable for the ending of a sonnet (ll. 88, 90-96, 93-98).

The subsequent appearance of the nurse repeats the bawdiness of servant comedy; and thereby comic rhetoric and an earthy wit are added to the love imagery and rhetoric that reappears in Lady Capulet's lines. In her elaboration of the perfection to be achieved by the union of marriage, Lady Capulet's idea, if not her language, is thoroughly conventional. Although the ornateness of her conceits contrasts strikingly with the nurse's bawdy wit, that servant's interpolations make the erotic overtones of those conceits explicit:

Read o'er the volume of young Paris' face
And find delight writ there with beauty's pen;
Examine every married lineament
And see how one another lends content,
And what obscur'd in this fair volume lies
Find written in the margent of his eyes.
This precious book of love, this *unbound lover,*
To beautify him, only *lacks a cover.*
The fish lives in the sea, and 'tis *much pride*
For *fair without the fair within to hide.*
That book in many's eyes doth share the glory,
That *in gold clasps locks in the golden story;*
So shall you share all that he doth possess,
By having him, making yourself no less.
    Nurse. No less! nay bigger; women grow by men.

                                                    (I, iii, 81-95)

The extremes of preciousness and bawdry then move together for the riming exit of the scene:

> La. Cap.   . . . Juliet, the County stays.
> Nurse. Go, girl, seek happy nights to happy days.

                                                    (ll. 105-6)

Mercutio's first scene continues the bawdiness, now mockingly directed at love in general (I, iv, 13, 17-18, 23-24, 27-28, 40-43). Here contraries exist in dramatic manner rather than in doctrinal opposition; while Mercutio's use of masquing apparel (ll. 29-32), his exuberant rhetoric, his probable miming, the beating of a drum, and the noise of "lusty gentlemen" (a phrase repeating an idea in Capulet's speech) introduce the merriment and dancing of the next scene, when a gallant love in festive surroundings is dramatized as Romeo and Juliet meet.

In the scene of the meeting between hero and heroine, it is interesting to note how one of Shakespeare's theatrical contraries emphasizes the lovers' lines. Romeo's expression of love immediately precedes the increasing noise of angry Tybalt and angry Capulet (I, v, 42-55); and in the relative quietness that follows the quarrel, a declaration of love would burst from the stage in dialogue that has become a Shakespearian sonnet (ll. 95-108). In this lyricism, a courtly wit is joined with a "lusty" youthfulness, which already has been specified twice. Accordingly, this focal point of love imagery is clothed in phrases drawn from the tradition of courtly love. As hero and heroine meet and then kiss, an audience would hear of "blushing pilgrims" and of "prayers' sake," of a "holy shrine," a "good pilgrim," a "holy palmers' kiss," a "dear saint," and a "purg'd" sin.

In the next scene, after Mercutio's high bawdry has mocked Romeo's love for Rosaline, the conventional hyperboles of the lovers exist within a compelling lyricism in which the only valid countermovement is one of danger from feuding families (II, ii, 62-65, 70). This development obviously builds upon the theatrical contrast just effected by the representation of an angry Tybalt. Its tension relaxes, nevertheless, into the sensuousness of a "blessed moon" that "tips with silver all these fruit-tree tops." The spirit animating Juliet's speeches—

> ... the more I give to thee
> The more I have, for both are infinite—
>
> (ll. 134-35)

builds upon Lady Capulet's lines and accords with Romeo's honorable "bent" that has for its "purpose marriage." At the same time, just as a courtly preciousness and the lustiness of youth had been merged in the ballroom scene, so the earthiness of the nurse and the bawdiness of Mercutio are here transformed to an expression of a sensuous but a boundless love that includes but engulfs its erotic echoes (e.g., ll. 122-26, 177-84). After the earlier fusion of a sympathetic ornateness with an earthy wit (I, iii) and after the extended development of Capulet's festive occasion by Mercutio and by Capulet again (I, iv, v, 18-42, 67-76, 90), this scene is the direct culmination of love's poetic process here—a process that Shakespeare has taken pains to develop so that not even Capulet is placed in any theatrical opposition to it (I, ii, 1-3, 18-19, v, 66-79).[51] Tybalt by the feud and Mercutio by his mockery remain outside this continuous emphasis; but the one contributes to a theatrical impression of love's force and the other, while providing mocking references to cold and chaste Rosaline, accentuates the exuberance of youth.

Granted that the age might emphasize the danger of love or its effeminacy, yet it also joyfully included the bedding of bride and groom in its wedding celebrations, while at the same time it preserved the solemn overtones of Jonson's later *Hymenæi,* the Neo-Platonic force of Spenser's contemporary sensuousness, and the holy concept of Jan van Eyck's earlier portrait of Giovanni Arnolfini and Jeanne Cenami. It is almost as if Shakespeare would remind his audience of this—by the eroticism of the lines, by Romeo's honorable bent, and by the speech that closes the scene, anticipates the joy of love's consummation, and moves toward the next scene at the holy friar's cell (II, ii, 187-90).

Indeed, when Juliet speaks of her maidenly modesty, which, had she not been overheard, would have made her "dwell on form" and "fain, fain deny" what she had spoken, the lines validate this love by expressing and dismissing a possible Elizabethan censure of Juliet as "too fond" and "light."

Shakespeare's attitude is obvious; and the spirit of the scene must have been conveyed to an audience by the lyricism of the lines—a spirit akin to the concept expressed by Jonson when he wrote about Phanes:

> When *Loue,* at first, did mooue
> From out of *Chaos,* brightned
> So was the world, and lightned,
> As now!
>
> (*Masque of Beautie,* ll. 282-85)

Although the mythological and courtly circumstances of Jonson's lyricism vary from the human circumstances of Shakespeare's, the concept of love's benevolent brightness, which Jonson would gloss by a passage from the learned Gyraldus,[52] is Shakespeare's too, and had been evoked explicitly when love was first defined by Romeo.[53] Both the concept and its poetic expression give conviction to the conventional oxymoronic image of a "glorious" night; and such a brightening of the world by love gives substance also to an image of courtly love that, as the scene begins and ends, likens Juliet to the sun (II, ii, 3-4, 155). There should be no need to elaborate any further the fact that Shakespeare sympathetically creates the lyrical, but vigorous and sensuous, love of youth. Indeed, one of Romeo's speeches is again choric in nature:

> How silver-sweet sound lovers' tongues by night,
> Like softest music to attending ears!
>
> (ll. 166-67)

This love will be represented later as overpowering the friar's wise adages, which nevertheless do not remain in opposition to it; and the lyrical warmth of the lines looks forward to Juliet's epithalamion.[54] Much more frankly and poetically daring than any sensuous but Platonic celebration of a marriage, that later speech by its rhetorical boldness continues the process begun in the ornate oxymoron of Romeo's first long speeches. It continues, too, the erotic echoes and the lyrical beauty of this bethrothal.

Before this epithalamion would be heard, the lines that close the troth-plighting would have introduced a scene embodying the friar's criticism of Romeo's love. With Mercutio's bawdy mockery, that criticism gives to the poetic and dramatic process of the second act an intensified verbal movement that, handled differently, might have countered the intensified representation of romantic love in the balcony scene. In this development, lines in the Prologue to Act II find a place. Although subsequent lines emphasize the feud, the Prologue had begun with words about "old Desire" and a gaping "young Affection" and had ended by referring to passion and an "extreme sweet." As the play has developed, though, this "young Affection" has dismissed the unrequiting "old Desire"; and this passion and "extreme sweet" are represented neither as censurable nor as simply erotic. Because of the feud, Friar Lawrence himself will see this love as beneficent (II, iii). As a consequence, even if the lyrical force of the balcony scene had diminished sharply for an Elizabethan audience, the development of the friar's reproval to such a conclusion probably would dominate, in the theatrical moment, any criticism stirred up by the friar's earlier words. At that time, Romeo's love had been called a "doting," a foolish affection or excessive fondness that lies not in the heart but in the eye. Presumably, however, the effect of the lyricism of the troth plighting would extend, at least partially, into this scene; and the subsequent course of the drama tragically denies this criticism.[55]

In the next situation, Mercutio's mockery of Romeo and love is followed by a fuller mockery of the new style of the duello—a development that ends with climactic puns.[56] Here the exuberance of this portion of the drama returns strongly, seems to culminate in a combat of wit that begins and ends with mockery of love (II, iv, 38-106), but moves instead into a rollicking climax when the nurse and Peter appear. This comic emphasis, now abated, continues through the nurse's delay of "warm youthful blood" (II, v, 12). In the brief sequel to this scene, the friar's wise and cautious adages agree with the nature of a holy man and contribute to a tragic foreboding. But the potentially choric nature of the friar's lines—that is, their mention of "after-hours" and sorrow, their warning against "violent delights" and "violent ends" (II, vi, 1-2, 9-15)—is resolved upon Juliet's appearance only into a generally sententious statement about the lightness of lovers and of vanity (ll. 16-20). In accordance with this diminishing process, the scene ends upon a note of sympathetic high comedy; for the friar himself starts a renewal of love poetry, which he then hurriedly interrupts. As Romeo complies with the friar's line that he thank Juilet for them both, and receives her assurance of a "love grown to such excess" that she cannot "sum up sum of half" her wealth, the churchman hastens to interrupt what he himself had begun:

> Come, come with me, and we will make short work;
> For, by your leaves, you shall not stay alone
> Till Holy Church incorporate two in one.
>
> (ll. 35-37)

In the third act, this potential countermovement that has increased but that so far has been tangential to the dominant emphasis is given two focal points of its own. Mercutio's mockery and his subsequent anger at Romeo's "calm, dishonourable, vile submission" has its aftermath in Romeo's action "all for the best" and in his blaming himself for the death of his "very friend." It is then that a cry by Romeo agrees with Mercutio's attitude (II, iv, 13-17, 92-97; III, i, 76):

> O sweet Juliet,
> Thy beauty hath made me effeminate
> And in my temper soft'ned valour's steel!
>
> (III, i, 118-20)

Romeo's "submission," however, was motivated by his marriage to Juliet, about which an audience would be fully aware; and the lines just quoted are denied immediately by his "fire-eyed fury," his duel with Tybalt, and Tybalt's death. There then follows in Juliet's epithalamion a strong renewal of the dominant emphasis in this play, an emphasis maintained even by the theatricality of the way in which Juliet's curses against the slayer of Tybalt are angrily denied by Juliet herself (III, ii, 73-107).

The second focal point of this process is treated in a comparable manner. "Fearful" Romeo's mention of his "doting," his falling upon the ground, his attempt to stab himself are given an unfavorable context by the friar (III, iii, 67, 69-70, 105-7). The charge of effeminacy is repeated (ll. 88, 110, 112); and the "rude will" of the friar's first speech is made applicable to Romeo and even intensified as "wild acts" that denote the "unreasonable fury" of an "ill-beseeming" beast (II, iii, 28; III, iii, 109-14). This development, however, introduces the friar's effective consolation as he pits himself against a "desperate hand." Consolation and other sententious matter had an Elizabethan appear per se[57]—an appeal apparent in the nurse's speech (ll. 159-60). Quite appropriately, then, consolation and love here work together; for Romeo's despair, after being restrained by Friar Lawrence, is banished when Romeo hears, not of Juliet's hatred for the murderer of her kinsman, but of her constancy (ll. 94, 104-5, 162-65). Accordingly, this scene also is followed almost immediately by another expression of romantic love. In contrast with its earlier renewal after Tybalt's death and Romeo's banishment, in this later scene of some thirty-five lines Shakespeare's lyricism builds upon the tradition of the aube and heightens the conventional pathos of parting (III, v, 1-35).[58] Thereby a love now consummated has sadness added to its previous sympathy. The constancy promised in the troth-plighting and reported to a desperate Romeo also receives further emphasis. It will be progressively apparent in Juliet's vow "to love an unstain'd wife" to her "sweet love" and in her "valour" that is not abated by any "inconstant toy, nor womanish fear" (IV, i, 70, 88, 119-20, 122, 125).

Shakespeare, consequently, effects sympathy for Romeo and Juliet by his artistic constancy. Arising from a concern for Romeo, a poetic process that is ornate, sensuous, and erotic culminates in the balcony scene and expresses the lovers' honorable intent. Verbal countermovements in speeches given to Mercutio and the friar are increased when the poetic representation of love is; but they are either tangential to this poetic process or they end by confirming this love's beneficence. When in the third act, criticism of love is placed in opposition to its validity by Romeo himself, that censure is invalidated immediately by the action. When a kindred thought is repeated by the friar, its motivation has been shifted to fit the immediate context of despair versus consolation. In both instances, there follows an intensified lyrical repetition of what has been the author's dominant emphasis.[59] This love, however, is darkened by Romeo's despair; and Shakespeare then indicates that the "jaws of darkness" will "devour it up":

Jul. O, now be gone; more light and light it grows.
Rom. More light and light; more dark and dark our woes!

(III, v, 35-36)

As one might expect, when the course of the drama is developed with an emphasis upon the operation of an adverse fate, the poetic and rhetorical process of the play also moves toward a tragic end. As with the ornateness of the early love rhetoric, the force of current traditions illumines this development as it builds upon a concept emphasized in the scene showing a desperate Romeo. As the tragic hero, Romeo carries much of the rhetorical passion of the drama and also anticipates its conclusion in suicide. After the danger of the duel, this new danger appears; and the third scene in the friar's cell intensifies Romeo's faint initial despair. As Elizabethans knew, a description in which despair moved toward suicide was treated frequently as a violation of the doctrine of fortitude that the church had developed from Stoic roots into a conceptual process that might include in its introductory movement admonitory precepts about conduct in prosperity. Shakespeare perhaps reflects this fact when he develops a scene in which his churchman uses his rhetorical skill to combat the dangerous results of hopelessness and argues admonitorily that Romeo is actually fortunate.[60] In accordance with a sympathetic portrayal of the lovers, however, when despair appears again—and hence a good deal closer to the tragic catastrophe—Shakespeare avoids any condemnation of suicide. When Juliet threatens to kill herself (IV, i, 52-67), the tradition-laden word "desperate" is applied by the friar, not to Juliet's "hand," as it had been applied to Romeo's (III, iii, 108), but to the only alternative that the churchman sees for Juliet:

> Hold, daughter! I do spy a kind of hope,
> Which craves as *desperate* an execution
> As that is *desperate* which we would prevent.
>
> (IV, i, 68-70)

The last "desperate" refers to a bigamous marriage; and Juliet's "strength of will to slay" herself, her willingness to cope "with Death himself," provides an escape (ll. 71-75). Needless to say, Shakespeare chose to accept from his source the alternatives of marriage to Paris or the potion. They are his alternatives to give an audience; and it is eminently apposite to note that he does this in a scene that includes the repetition of an earlier action and the repetition of an earlier word, then used censoriously but now used sympathetically and without admonition. By such a development, Shakespeare writes not only with an awareness of possible Elizabethan predispositions but also with an artistry that would dismiss them for the tragic integrity of his drama.

Accordingly, Juliet's despair is elaborated, not with admonition, but with horrifying details that remind one of the way other dramatists would develop their tragedies. That a fearsome horror was considered an attribute of tragedy and was thought capable of being aroused in part by rhetorical speech is witnessed by the poetizing of the Hades of the *Æneid* to start Kyd's revenge play, by Shakespeare's description of dead Humphrey, by the scene of Suffolk's death, or by the classical spell apparent in young Clifford's speeches as *2 Henry VI* closes. One might also cite the speeches connected with the *visio* and its attendant grotesqueness in *Woodstock* as the anonymous author dramatized the murder of Gloucester. Rather than live stained, Juliet would "lurk / Where serpents are," be chained "with roaring bears," hide

> . . . nightly in a charnel-house,
> O'er-cover'd quite with dead men's rattling bones,
> With reeky shanks and yellow chapless skulls;

Or . . . go into a new-made grave
And hide . . . with a dead man in his shroud. . . .
(IV, i, 79-85)

These macabre details are associated explicitly with a horrifying fear (IV, i, 86).

When the process is repeated and a dagger is displayed again as a means of stopping the "desperate" marriage (IV, iii, 23), the working of "hideous fears" to the point of reason's collapse and fancy's sway accords not simply with current psychology but also with the horror being developed in this portion of the drama. At this time, Shakespeare's artistry again transforms the conventional and remains constant in its dominant emphasis. In *King John,* Constance spoke of herself as being anxious to greet an "amiable lovely death," arising from his "couch of lasting night." In her franticness, she would kiss his "detestable bones" or ring her fingers with his "household worms" and "buss" him as a wife (III, iv, 25-36). Although Juliet's speech as fancy begins its sway includes similar details, Shakespeare now transforms them by a concreteness that draws its force from the most startling event of the play-world. Death, in this situation, is "couched" in the Capulets' tomb, and there "bloody Tybalt, yet but green in earth, / Lies festering in his shroud" (IV, iii, 42-43). Instead of an evocation of Death, fancy's vision of Tybalt's ghost seeking out Romeo gives force to Juliet's desperateness; and in a similar manner, when Romeo dies "with a kiss" (V, iii, 90-120), Constance's macabre "buss" of Death is transformed with an even greater concreteness. With a magnificent fusion of contraries, Juliet and her beauty have made the tomb "a triumphant grave," "a feasting presence full of light." There an "amorous" "unsubstantial Death," a "lean abhorred monster" has kept her "in dark to be his paramour" (ll. 83-105). Thereby the age-old theme of the coming of Death is transmuted into the tragic conviction of Romeo's love and Juliet's beauty.[61] Here, certainly, no historical consideration could validate the tragedy more than its immediate artistry does, yet its lyric strength has roots in concepts and representational methods conventional to the sixteenth century.[62]

A similar realization of Shakespeare's dramatic perception and capability results when one considers two probable consequences of his representation of an adverse fate. Although Romeo and Juliet are said to be "star-cross'd" and their love "death-mark'd," the particular way in which fate will operate is not specified in the Prologue. With the beginning of the action, however, if the thumb-biting of the servants is seen as thoughtless—as intending no injury to the children of their masters—this opposed fate operates, with an inescapable irony, through the unawareness of the characters.[63] It must be granted that as the first scene was enacted, an audience's perception of this probably would be slight at the best, even when they heard Benvolio's cry, "Put up your swords; you know not what you do" (I, i, 72). At that time, the spectators would be witnessing comic and then violent action that probably engrossed their attention.

The motivation of subsequent events, however, repeats this basic situation; and after the marriage of Romeo and Juliet, this particular method of fate's operation emerges so strongly that by the time Capulet's unawareness comes into play, none could escape the conclusion that his actions are precipitating an event desperate for the love of hero and heroine and thus desperate for the daughter whom he holds most dear. Indeed, Shakespeare attempts to make it clear that Capulet's actions are the result of his concern for Juliet (e.g., IV, i, 6, 9-14; V, iii, 236-39). To him, no less than to Romeo, is applicable the line, "I thought all for the best" (III, i, 109); and the subsequent ramifications of Capulet's actions, like the counteractions of Friar Lawrence, are so elucidated in the explanatory peroration (V, iii, 223 ff.).

To an appreciable degree, as Shakespeare wrote this tragedy, the malevolent power of fate and the knowledge given his characters must have been for him two relatively separate factors; for the one operates through the other. Witness, then, the firm characterization of Friar Lawrence. It may well have resulted from an awareness of what his life probably would be if it were considered by itself, if it were distinct from a malevolent "greater power." His words to Romeo about despair might well be considered the result of his calling and his training. His specialized knowledge of herbs and potions could be derived from the events of the narrative; but his speech and actions otherwise are those that might be associated naturally with his imagined life. They would be apparent regardless of the events of any narrative. In contrast with ideas about an ideal discipline, or about gentility, or about a nobleman's honor, Friar Lawrence's religious attitudes and his process of thought appear in the play continually but almost incidentally, and not as concepts whereby the religious life might be illustrated or made to accord in certain scenes with the main outlines of the narrative. In brief, Shakespeare's portrayal of the friar seems to correspond to the way in which the twentieth century has come to conceive of characterization.

A similar consideration can be advanced for the portrayal of Mercutio. Particularly noticeable is the way in which the miming and mockery of a dizzard of high degree emerges from Mercutio's bawdy conjuration of Romeo[64] and then subsides during his next appearances into a display of wit in the description of characters (II, iv, 13-48; III, i, 5-32). This wit might well have seemed to be the result of training in rhetoric and hence appropriate to a kinsman of the prince, just as friar Lawrence's attitudes would be appropriate to him. Thoroughly congruent with those passages of satire would be Mercutio's extended wordplay with Romeo (II, iv, 49-97); his roaring out of lines from a song that probably had echoed on Elizabethan streets (II, iv, 151); his use, in song also, of the ever-ready sound of Elizabethan *whore* (II, iv, 138-46); and his ability to develop a mock conjuration that embodies the spirit of ephemeral bawdy tales.[65]

When anger is given to Capulet, although it would agree with one of the conventional characteristics of an old man as far as rhetorical decorum was concerned,[66] it also would accord with the Elizabethan parent's conventional, and probably actual, attitude when encountering disobedience (I, v, 62-90; III, v, 127-97). Shakespeare's care in indicating the advanced age of Capulet and the youth of Juliet can substantiate both considerations.[67] But those details can also substantiate the individualizing, liberal point of view that his only living child will marry "within her scope of choice" (I, ii, 14-15, 18). Capulet's anger is also represented as springing from his concern for Juliet, who seems to be grieving excessively for the death of Tybalt (IV, i, 9-15; V, iii, 236-39). This motivation could be drawn from the best of contemporary discussions about the passions and perturbations of men and the dangers liable to befall those who were dominated by an excessive grief.[68] For their own good, they must be diverted from such a passion. Here, too, a character seems to have been conceived of on the basis of probable traits applicable both to an Elizabethan world and to a specific person living in specifically conceived circumstances (e.g., the number and ages of Capulet's immediate family and his probable knowledge). Through such an individual, a "greater power" operates by means of his unawareness of events.

Similarly, the movement in Romeo's portrayal from a choleric and dangerous heat in combat to an almost overwhelming despair, a movement that avoids the intermediate villainy appearing in the similar development of King John's portrayal, is substantiated now by the precipitancy of youth. Thereby a sixteenth-century doctrine about an overpowering emotion becomes as universally valid as does the motivation of the conventional anger of an old man.

In view of all this, consequently, and in view of the fact that as *Romeo and Juliet* begins, Benvolio is placed in a situation that is unexplained but comparable to Romeo's (I, i, 125-36), one's attention is called to a related consideration. Just as Friar Lawrence and Capulet are represented as individuals with lives wider than the events of the narrative, and just as Benvolio is given an existence of his own, so the references to the nurse's husband, to Susan, to Lucentio, to Rosaline, to Friar John's "bare-footed brother," and the indications of Mercutio's and Paris' family relationships, as well as the brief appearances of an apothecary and of Friar John himself—all evoke a life wider than that of this particular story. If such an impression were purposeful, Shakespeare's characteristic widening of the scope of his dramas resulted, in this instance, in something more than the reconciliation of the Capulets and Montagues as the drama closes (V, iii, 291 ff.). Establishing a view of the play-world for the eyes of different characters seems to have been extended so that that world itself exists within a larger one, to which characters refer, and from which other characters briefly move into the sequence of events being dramatized.

This technique may be construed as an extension, appropriate to this play, of the use of the *narratio* or the *descriptio* in such a speech as that given to Hubert when he reported that he saw

> . . . a smith stand with his hammer, thus,
> The whilst his iron did on the anvil cool,
> With open mouth swallowing a tailor's news;
> Who, with his shears and measure in his hand,
> Standing on slippers, which his nimble haste
> Had falsely thrust upon contrary feet,
> Told of a many thousand warlike French
> That were embattailed and rank'd in Kent.
> Another lean unwash'd artificer
> Cuts off his tale and talks of Arthur's death.
>
> (*King John,* IV, ii, 193-202)

Similarly, in *Richard II* the multitude hailing Henry and throwing dust on Richard exist on the border of the events being dramatized. So do the many nameless persons who with "hearts harder than steel" flocked to Bolingbroke; and from that border appear the commons with a "suit" and the nameless groom.

In *Romeo and Juliet,* however, the divergence between the tragic story and its border of extended existence approaches the divergence between a malevolent fate and actions meant "all for the best." This is not true for Shakespeare's use of the *narratio* and the *descriptio* in the dramas that have been examined here, nor is it true for what has just been noticed in *Richard II*. In that drama, the protagonist's preoccupation with his own majesty and his neglect of those who fill up this border about his story constitute his sin in governing. Like all members of a commonwealth, those figures should be animated by the king's beneficent and vigorous action. They cannot be animated by the mere fact of kingship's divine office. With the exception of the groom, the relationship between the central figure of *Richard II* and those in the extended play-world is essentially centrifugal; it is what one might expect in view of current political thought. In contrast, once the main play-world of *Romeo and Juliet* is seen as existing within a larger one, the movement between them is essentially centripetal. This agrees with the way in which an adverse fate operates through man's best wishes; and thus the impression of human life beyond and behind the confines of the narrative seems to be Shakespeare's perceptive corollary to the tragic irony of his story.[69] Even as that corollary seems to represent his tendency to widen the scope of his dramas, so it is compatible with his tendency to give value to human beings and their knowledge and actions.

To complete the picture here sketched of Shakespeare's artistry through the years 1595-96, *The Tragedy of Richard the Second* must also be considered. Especially interesting is the total design of the drama, some minor features of its artistry, and the portrayals of both Richard and Bolingbroke.

As far as the narrative is concerned, *Richard II* shows the usual features of a five-act structure, especially when one's attention is directed toward the story of Bolingbroke, whose rise is concomitant with Richard's fall. From such a point of view, there is a clear narrative focal point for each act. That for the first act is Bolingbroke's exile. That for the second, his return. The third act focuses upon the meeting of Bolingbroke and Richard at Flint Castle and Richard's visual descent (III, iii). The fourth act focuses upon Richard's deposition. Its ending, however, inaugurates a "new encounter," that is, a plot against Henry in behalf of Richard. This "breaks out" and is concluded in the fifth act. In that last act, a new movement against Richard is also dramatized (i.e., his assassination by Exton).[70] Thus the fifth act bifurcates, but both developments lead to the final picture of Bolingbroke regnant. The relationship between this narrative development and the way in which a large number of Elizabethan plays were worked out in accordance with protasis (I and II), epitasis (III and IV), and catastrophe (V) is obvious.

Especially interesting, moreover, is the way in which the second act establishes the grounds of the argument and then indicates that Richard's fall is imminent by a choric scene that will be elaborated more fully later. Upon Richard's exit after Gaunt's death, Shakespeare brings to his audience's attention the Earl of Northumberland, Lord Ross, and Lord

Willoughby. Their dialogue on the ills of the realm ends with news of Bolingbroke's return in opposition to Richard and in redress of grievous wrongs (II, i, 224 ff.). A countermovement censuring Henry is established almost immediately but is qualified by the debate-like process of the scene (e.g., II, iii, 83-112, 140-47, 152-57; 113-39, 148-51). It is then followed by a short scene anticipating Richard's downfall (II, iv). This last episode ends the second act; and after the meeting at Flint Castle has been dramatized, a longer choric scene ends the third act.

The preceding structural outline, however, is quite inadequate for representing Richard's story, even though the portrayals of Bolingbroke and Richard are interlocked. The first two points of interest in Henry's story (I, iii; II, iii) are balanced by Richard's departure from England and his return (II, i; III, ii). As a result, the narrative focal points of what might be called the protasis (as far as Bolingbroke is concerned) are blurred by the focal points that center upon Richard and that are related to the dominant but varying emotions Shakespeare pretty clearly would arouse by his developing portrayal of this English ruler.

From this last point of view, *Richard II* shows three emotional developments: an anti-Richard one (I, i, through II, i), an equivocal one (III, ii, through IV), and a pro-Richard one (V). The first emotional focal point occurs with the dramatization of Gaunt's death and Richard's departure from England (II, i). This lowest point of Richard's appeal is used to introduce Bolingbroke's return. Upon Richard's return (III, ii), the scenes develop in accordance with Salisbury's forecast (II, iv), with minor elements of pathos in the first two acts, and with qualified censure of Bolingbroke that extends into the third act (e.g., III, i, 31-34). Upon these bases, the equivocality of the episode at Flint Castle is developed. Therein Lancastrian interpretations of history alternate with Richardian or Yorkist ones and both emphases are fused for a completely Janus-like effect in the unique ending that shows Richard's descent to the "base court" (III, iii). This partial shift of emotion from an earlier antipathy for Richard is then underlined explicitly in the garden scene:

> *Gard.*   Hold thy peace.
> He that has suffer'd this disordered spring
> Hath now himself met with the fall of leaf.

                                                    (III, iv, 40-49)

The precarious balance so achieved is magnified in the deposition scene, wherein reproval of Richard and Bolingbroke and sympathy for Richard are fused for an appreciable period of time.[71] So far, however, the tragic nature of Richard's downfall has not received an unqualified emphasis. Accordingly, when the first scene of the fifth act dramatizes the parting of Richard and his queen, Shakespeare begins to concentrate upon the pathos inherent in this picture of a fallen ruler. Act II, scene i, consequently, shows the culmination of an anti-Richard emphasis. Act V, scene i, marks a point when pathos for Richard will be emphasized in one process of the final development. Between those points of different emphasis, Shakespeare develops a transitional fusion of criticism and pity.

The total development of *Richard II,* consequently, shows a basic pattern similar to that apparent in Marlowe's *Edward II.*[72] In the earlier plays about Henry VI, that structural movement was obscured by the multiplicity of incidents and of characters involved in Henry's fall and by the use of other structural motifs—by, in brief, the cyclical nature of Shakespeare's artistry. In *King John,* pathos was never focused for any extended period of time upon the ruler, even when he had been poisoned; and thus the total development of that play did not show a pattern of censure, fall from power, and pathos. It is this emotional development of *Richard II,* however, that probably was inescapable in the theater.

Once more, a basic precision is apparent, even in this combination of structural movements. Act II, scene iv, and Act III, scene i, for example, indicate respectively the future process of the drama as far as Richard and Bolingbroke are concerned. The immediate approach to deposition is separated from the deposition proper by a choric scene focusing upon Richard (the gardeners' scene, III, iv, some 107 lines). Also between the scene at Flint Castle and the deposition proper is a grouping of characters focusing upon Bolingbroke (the challenging nobles, IV, i, 1-106). This last situation repeats a process that had started the drama; and in the fifth act, with Henry instead of Richard as the ruler, another uncle advises a course of action "as a judge" rather than "like a father." This also reflects a situation in the first act after the challenging of nobles had been stopped. The last two repetitive developments, of course, are now connected with Aumerle, and thus with another rebellion against a ruler. This minor narrative movement begun as the fourth act closes is also developed precisely and effects a purposeful ambiguity. Although it demonstrates Henry's adherence to his word and to the kingly virtue of mercy, this development interrupts the pathetic scenes centering upon Richard; thus its display of a constant and merciful king is marred by the murder of that king's opponent. Already minor situations in the large emotional pattern of censure, fall from power, and pathos demand attention; but the precise development of that emotional pattern and its fusion with an equally precise narrative one illustrate the controlled complexity of Shakespeare's art—which is, nevertheless, basically simple.

Before turning to some minor features of Shakespeare's artistry in *Richard II,* one should note that Aumerle's scene with Henry follows that ruler's reference to his "unthrifty son" (V, iii, 1). Similarly, Henry's vow to go to the Holy Land appears at the end of this drama and at the beginning of *1 Henry IV.* In *Richard II,* both developments look forward to the dramatization of more English history. In spite of the many differences, one is reminded of the endings of the three plays about Henry VI. For that matter, rebellion quelled at the end of *Richard II,* in the first and second parts of *Henry IV,* and at the beginning of *Henry V* seems to indicate a cyclical pattern of revolt. Although that pattern would be more apparent to playwright and actor than to any one audience, this balanced appearance of revolt in four plays seems to be congruent with the fact that when Shakespeare refers specifically to an incident he had dramatized in *Richard II,* he also specifies the doctrine of recurrence in history (*2 Henry IV,* III, i, 45-93). In brief, even though a cyclical technique is abandoned in *Richard II,* as it had been in *Richard III,* a cyclical concept seems to have been in Shakespeare's mind and to have emerged specifically *ca.* 1598.

When one turns to a more detailed examination of *Richard II,* it is interesting to notice how Shakespeare prepares his audience for his first emotional focal point. Even his representation of quarreling nobles lays a groundwork for the anti-Richard emphasis in the first scene of the second act. As the play begins, Henry's charge that Mowbray traitorously spent money belonging to the king's soldiers, that he has plotted treason for eighteen years, and that he murdered Gloucester is denied by that duke, who in turn calls Bolingbroke a traitor. This beginning might seem to be a tangential one; but by the scene separating those that are devoted to combat, Shakespeare tips the scales in Bolingbroke's favor and against Richard. The debate-like process of this second scene builds upon the familiarity of recognizable types—the passionate, wronged woman (the Duchess of Gloucester) and the loyal nobleman (John of Gaunt, Duke of Lancaster). Emotion versus a restraining reason was constant in the Elizabethan theater; and both the emotion and the restraint that are represented here presumably would create a theatrical appeal for the figure demonstrating a vigorous and understandable grief and for the one showing an intellectualized, loyal patience. By the lines given to the Duchess of Gloucester, Shakespeare turns against Richard the force of rhetorical bravura, of the bonds of family, and of a desolate grief (I, ii, 9-36, 58-74). Similarly, although Gaunt's rejoinders elaborate Richard's doctrine of divine right—

which had appeared briefly in a few of the king's earlier speeches (I, i, 174-96)[73]—they also imply that this ruler is guilty of the death of Thomas of Woodstock, Duke of Gloucester:

> Alas the part I had in Woodstock's blood
> Doth more solicit me than your exclaims
> To stir against the butchers of his life!
> But since correction lieth in those hands
> *Which made the fault* that we cannot correct,
> Put we our quarrel to the will of Heaven;
> Who, when they see the hours ripe on earth,
> Will rain hot vengeance on offenders' heads.
>
> (ll.1-8)
>
> God's is the quarrel; for God's substitute,
> His deputy anointed in His sight,
> *Hath caused his death;* the which if wrongfully,
> Let Heaven revenge; for I may never lift
> An angry arm against His minister.
>
> (ll. 37-41)

As a result, the Richard of the latter part of *Woodstock* is reflected even in a divine-rightist's refutation of passionate speeches that emphasize a guilty Richard and the need for vengeance.[74] In contrast, the Duchess' wrathful sorrow may find some satisfaction in Bolingbroke's "spear" (I, ii, 47).

Upon the Lancastrian emphases in this dialogue between Gaunt and his sister-in-law, Shakespeare then develops his second representation of the conflict between Bolingbroke and Mowbray. In it and in the scene that follows, three developments, each resulting from the previous one, are of particular interest. In the first place, Richard's stopping the combat may well have aroused conflicting emotions. On the one hand, it would run counter to any belief in the validity of trial by combat, as expressed, for example, by Sir Thomas Smith in his treatise on the Elizabethan state.[75] That belief, of course, was embodied also in the office of Elizabeth's Champion;[76] and although the exercise of that office had become essentially an occasion for pageantry, its reason for existence drew upon the concept that the God of Battles could determine the truth. Of this, an audience might have been reminded by the participants' invocation of God. Trial by combat might also seem to accord with the current acceptance of war and bloodshed as a remedy for unwholesome peace,[77] and certainly battle and warfare were theatrical signs of heroic endeavor. In brief, Richard's action may have run athwart conceptual emotions that could validate the whetted appetites of a vulgar audience for bloody spectacle. On the other hand, Richard's action might seem to demonstrate a kingly dominance, and it is represented as being taken on good advice to avoid the shedding of English blood. Reaction to Richard in this situation, consequently, may well have been ambivalent.[78]

When Shakespeare dramatizes the outcome of Richard's action, however, he again weights his theatrical scales on Bolingbroke's side; for the conclusion of the scene clearly is meant to be emotional. With its emphasis upon old Gaunt's sorrow and upon the mutual love between father and son, with Gaunt's lyrical consolation of Bolingbroke, who is leaving the "jewels" he loves, and with Bolingbroke's own expression of his suffering under "Fell Sorrow's tooth" (I, iii, 67-77, 255-57, 302), what might seem to a modern to be Hereford's blatant patriotism in all probability constituted, for chauvinistic Elizabethans, a patriotic fortitude in adversity. Upon such a note, the pathos of parting closes:

> Then, England's ground, farewell; sweet soil, adieu;
> My mother, and my nurse, that bears me yet!
> Where'er I wander, boast of this I can,
> Though banish'd, yet a trueborn Englishman.[79]
>
> (ll. 306-9)

From such a development, Shakespeare then shows how he can capitalize upon the effect of placing a character in disjunction with the dominant, immediate context of a play-world. After the portrayal of a patriotic though cast-down Hereford, the next speech that an audience would hear refers to a "high Hereford" and is given to Richard (I, iv, 2). Bolingbroke so far has been portrayed as "high" only in his conviction of the justness of his cause and in his anger at Gloucester's murder (e.g., I, i, 109)—an attitude substantiated by the second scene in the drama. The "sky-aspiring and ambitious thoughts, / With rival hating envy" (I, iii, 130-31), which Richard believed had "set on" the combatants, have existed only within the context of challenge and counterchallenge and within the context of the Duchess of Gloucester's anti-Richard lines. When the combatants were cast down from such emotional heights and banished, "Fell Sorrow's tooth" was emphasized and focused upon Gaunt and his son. Immediately after such a development, consequently, Richard's reference to a "high Hereford" finds no theatrically valid focal point. Indeed, it runs counter to the context just developed. The emotions of a "store of parting tears," which Richard requested Aumerle to describe, had just been represented in the love, the consolation, and the fortitude of Gaunt and his patriotic son. Now a reference to those emotions serves only to specify Aumerle's hostility to Bolingbroke and to introduce Richard's description of Hereford's "wooing" the common people.

Other things being equal, this description could be construed as showing a censurable, even a villainous, ambition. Yet within the walls of a theater, the spectators have viewed the drama up to this point only, and other things are far from equal. Richard's present attitude is the antithesis of that which the playwright apparently attempted to create by both pathos and patriotism. Thus Shakespeare seems to have placed Richard in purposeful disjunction with an immediate emphasis that in all probability aroused an audience's sympathy; and in such circumstances it seems a fair assumption that Richard's description of Bolingbroke received, and was meant to receive, a qualified reception.[80] That assumption is substantiated, indeed, by the development that follows the description. Immediately thereafter, Shakespeare introduces the Richard of the early part of *Woodstock,* the ruler who supports "too great a court," who farms his "royal realm" and uses "blank charters" to force from his subjects "large sums of gold" (I, iv, 42-52). It is this Richard and his followers who avidly receive the news of Gaunt's sudden mortal sickness; and in such an unfavorable context, Richard's Irish expedition also is introduced:

> Now put it, God, in the physician's mind
> To help him [Gaunt] to his grave immediately!
> The lining of his coffers shall make coats
> To deck our soldiers for these Irish wars.
> Come, gentlemen, let's all go visit him,
> Pray God we may make haste, and come too late!
>
> (ll. 59-64)

These invocations of God, which are underlined by the "Amen" that follows, also give an anti-Richard turn to the verbal process in this play that would make Richard "God's substitute, / His deputy anointed in His sight." There also is bitter irony in Richard's reference to Gaunt—the figure who has expressed unequivocally the doctrine of obedience that might be a major corollary of the theory of divine right.

As a consequence, by these developments after Richard's description of Bolingbroke, this ruler is also placed in disjunction with some of the Elizabethans' strong emotions about a prince's duty and his conduct;[81] and thus the ending of the scene intensifies the effect of Richard's reference to "high Hereford" at its beginning.[82] Richard's attitude is also contrary to the patriotism and the pathos that will be created immediately by the portrayal of Gaunt on his deathbed. In a very real sense, then, Richard at the end of the first act is placed in disjunction not only with

Elizabethan public emotions about ruling conduct but also with the emotions that are developed in this drama immediately before and immediately after the present scene.

Obviously, Shakespeare is not only moving toward his anti-Richard focal point but also establishing some of the basic antitheses upon which he will develop later variations. Even as Hereford is criticized for winning the love of the people—a love that Richard has lost—Shakespeare anticipates later developments; and his unique portrayal of a ruler who would view the world only through his own predispositions begins to emerge. In the future course of the drama, this aspect of Richard's portrayal will accord with his calling for a mirror after his deposition and seeing, as he might look backward, not Gaunt's "tenement or pelting farm" with a state of law that is "bondslave to the law" and not the gardeners' land of weeds, or a "disordered spring," but primarily the form of fallen majesty. The sureness of an artistry that would so bind the ending of the first act with one aspect of the fourth act needs no comment.[83]

At the moment, as has just been noted, the appealing patriotism of a dying Gaunt intensifies the unsympathetic aspects of Richard's portrayal. In the scene beginning the second act, Shakespeare also utilizes other public emotions. Dislike of a tyrannical anger, the Elizabethan's belief that a ruler should heed good advice, that he should act for the good of the whole, that the English commonwealth was a society of free men not bondslaves, that dying words should be heeded, that loyal counselors should be rewarded, and so on, are all used against Richard. England has been violated by an unstaid, youthful ruler interested only in flattery, "lascivious metres," Italian fashions, and new vanities. To such a one all "wholesome counsel" comes in vain (ll. 1-30). He is unconcerned over the state of his kingdom and the death of an old, loyal, counseling kinsman, whose own estate he also violates. Indeed, the basic nature of any commonwealth is prophaned by this ruler, now *iratus* (ll. 115-23, 139-40). He is one who has failed to differentiate, as Shakespeare's learned contemporaries never did, between a commonwealth and a "living together" of landlord and bondslaves.[84] As a result,

> This blessed plot, this earth, this realm, this England
>
> . . . .
>
> Is now leas'd out, I die pronouncing it,
> Like to a tenement or pelting farm.
>
> (ll. 50-60)

One of the excellent rhetorical developments given Gaunt ends with lines that, even as they pun, point out that Richard is "Landlord of

England," not king; that his "state of law is bondslave to the law" (ll. 113-14). Richard's rule, in other words, is what Le Roy would call a "masterly" one, that is, one unconcerned with equity.[85] Accordingly, in this scene, Richard is, at the best, a "most degenerate" king (l. 262). These devolepments, within a strong appeal to patriotism, might be expected to arouse any Elizabethan audience's feelings against Richard, not simply upon intellectual grounds, but upon emotional ones as well. The widespread belief that a king must heed and follow good advice is rooted here in the fact that that advice is developed from and with the pathos of a dying Gaunt, who for his pains receives only anger from his ruler.

In addition, a verbal and conceptual process about family relationships and their connection with commonwealths and with the English state reaches a culmination here. With a cohesive artistry as striking as anything in *King John,* it stretches back to the first scene in the drama. At that time, *blood* was used for the most part in its literal sense, in accordance with the conflict being dramatized (e.g., I, i, 152-57); but *blood* in the sense of family bonds also had appeared in the dialogue (e.g., ll. 104-8, 115-21). In the following scene, the merged meanings of *blood* were elaborated by the images of a vial of blood and the root and branch of blood—a process in which the meaning of the word as it might signify descent was italicized:

> Edward's seven sons, whereof thyself [Gaunt] art one,
> Were as seven vials of his sacred blood,
> Or seven fair branches springing from one root.
> Some of those seven are dried by nature's course,
> Some of those branches by the Destinies cut;
> But Thomas, my dear lord, my life, my Gloucester,
> One vial full of Edward's sacred blood,
> One flourishing branch of his most royal root,
> Is crack'd, and all the precious liquor spilt,
> Is hack'd down, and all his summer leaves are faded,
> By Envy's hand and Murder's bloody axe.
> Ah, Gaunt, his blood was thine! That bed, that womb,
> That mettle, that self-mould, that fashion'd thee
> Made him a man; and though thou liv'st and breath'st,
> Yet art thou slain in him. Thou dost consent
> In some large measure to thy father's death,
> In that thou seest thy wretched brother die,
> Who was the model of thy father's life.
>
> (I, ii, 11-28)

The family frequently was conceived of as giving rise to states; and Hooker, for example, would base some of his arguments upon the idea that one's ancestors were alive in an individual.[86] Since the verbal process connected with *blood* is kept alive by giving to Richard lines that draw upon images of conflict and upon *blood* in the sense of a kingdom's blood and "kindred's blood" (e.g., I, iii, 123-43), Gaunt in his last illness quite appropriately elaborates upon the excellence of Richard's ancestors—an excellence that contrasts with this ruler's actions. The idea is repeated by York; and York will insist that Richard denies his blood and invalidates the principle of descent when he breaks the law of primogeniture, the "fair sequence and succession" whereby he himself rules, the "charters and the customary rights" of Time itself (II, i, 51-56, 104-6, 171-83, 189-208).[87]

At the same time, concepts that gave validity and heroic proportions to successful warfare become increasingly explicit in the stage's criticism of Richard. Those concepts move from Gaunt's mouth, to York's, to Northumberland's, to Ross's (II, i, 50-56, 171-81, 252-55, 259-61); and thereby an audience would learn that Richard is not known for Christian and chivalric deeds as far from England as the sepulcher of "blessed Mary's son"; that he never had raged like a lion in war, even though he has not been a lamb in peace; that he has yielded upon base compromise what his noble ancestors achieved with blows; and that he has wasted more in peace, despite "burdenous taxation," than they had spent in conquest.[88]

Even details in this scene substantiate what has been indicated. Some of them also look forward to the subsequent development of the drama. When Gaunt ends his speech of moving patriotism with the thought that "England, that was wont to conquer others / Hath made a shameful conquest of itself" (ll. 65-66), the meaning *England* may have as "the ruler of England" is not entirely absent, in spite of the impersonal *itself*. Earlier in the speech, Gaunt had elaborated the figure of England as an island bulwark—a figure that Mildmay, for example, had used in one of his speeches to Elizabeth's House of Commons, presumably because of its effective appeal.[89] But Gaunt's England had also been a "royal throne of kings" and a "teeming womb of royal kings" renowned for their deeds throughout the world. With such kings, Richard is being contrasted. That he as *England* has made a "shameful conquest" of himself might well be implicit thereby. The implication, at any rate, will be specified later when Richard, the landlord, is said to be "possess'd now to depose" himself (l. 108). By this statement, Gaunt exactly, though briefly, adumbrates the scene at Flint Castle and the scene of Richard's deposition. Some of the lines given York also indicate the future course of the drama. When he argues that Richard violates the very principle by which he reigns, York specifies a basic argument whereby the Lancastrian movement to the scene at Flint Castle will be justified (II, i, 195-99, iii, 122-24). When he refuses to "be by the while" as Gaunt's estate is seized, the lines are also choric ones:

> What will ensue hereof, there's none can tell;
> But by bad courses may be understood
> That their events can never fall out good.
>
> (ll. 212-14)

A conventional situation thereby arises. As in *Edward II, James IV, Woodstock,* or *2 Henry VI,* it could draw force from one of the oldest developments in the morality. Not only is a virtuous figure here removed from the ruler by death but another good graybeard leaves him. Quite conventionally, an enumeration of the ills of the realm then follows. Upon flatterers' information this ruler "prosecutes" nobles severely, acting even against their lives, their children, and their heirs (ll. 238-45). Other noblemen have been fined for ancient quarrels (ll. 247-48). The commons have been robbed "with grievous taxes," and daily such new exactions as blanks and benevolences have been devised (ll. 246-47, 249-50). The realm is "in farm" to the Earl of Wiltshire (l. 256). Wars have not wasted the revenue, for Richard has not warred (ll. 252-55). Yet he has money for his Irish expedition only by his robbery of the banished Bolingbroke (l. 261). The hearts of all are "quite lost" (ll. 247, 248). "Reproach and dissolution" hang over Richard (l. 258). Only at Ravenspurgh can be found the means for making "high majesty" look like itself again.

By his seizure of the initiative and by the fact that he is the only speaking lord who is named (l. 274), Northumberland must have been meant to emerge as the central figure in this dialogue on the ills of the realm. From this situation, there will develop easily his portrayal as the unbending messenger at Flint Castle (III, iii, 72-73), the driving accuser of the mirror episode (IV, i, 222-27, 269, 271), and the figure who is the immediate cause of separating Richard and his queen (V, i). Northumberland will receive, progressively and theatrically, much of the antipathy redounding from the pathos of falling and fallen Richard. But as this dialogue on the ills of the realm can build only upon what has preceded—whereby, for example, not even the names of the other lords would be known to an audience—this enumeration of the ills of the realm would underline Shakespeare's anti-Richard emphasis. Upon these dramatic grounds, as well as by tradition and by its immediate development, the dialogue seems to have been designed for a choric effect, regardless of what might grow out of it.

A variation from the preceding pattern is effected, however, when York reappears as lord governor of Richard's England. Yet overtones of the morality probably did not desert the drama entirely. York would seem representative of all those who would be loyal to the ruler on the throne, who were aware of the wrongs done to Bolingbroke and of the public wrongs done by Richard, but who were unable to remedy the woes of a "declining land" because of Richard's malfeasance. From a "neuter" position (II, iii, 159), York moves with his rising nephew. In the third act, he remains on stage with Bolingbroke after Northumberland has left to see to the execution of the parasites (III, i, 36). Then he critically, silently, and at last with concurrence, accompanies his rising nephew, but sorrows and weeps for his falling one (III, iii, 16-17, 68-71, 202-3; IV, i, 107-12, 177-80).

By the preceding considerations alone, one perceives a firm approach to the artistry of Acts III and IV. In addition, one should note that in Bolingbroke's two scenes before the return of Richard, Shakespeare both condemns and defends his rising figure's actions in debate-like dialogue (II, iii, 83-112, 113-39, 140-47, 148-51; III, i, 1-30, 31-34). The development anticipates the alternating emphases, comparable to Marlowe's, that are used in the scene at Flint Castle and in the depositon scene. Moreover, just as Richard will be the principal speaker of lines creating pathos for Richard, so Bolingbroke is now the principal speaker of lines defending Bolingbroke.

The first two acts have provided another sort of groundwork for what is to follow when Richard will reappear and sorrow will be associated with him. In the first act, contexts of bloodshed and grief had alternated. The revenging sorrow of the Duchess of Gloucester (I, ii) had reappeared as the pathetic and patriotic grief of Gaunt and Bolingbroke (I, iii, 208 ff.). In the second act, the sorrowful admonitions of Gaunt (II, i, 1-138) reappeared but were transformed into the "tide of woes" "rushing on this woeful land at once" (II, ii, 98-99). At that time, the queen was grieving for her absent husband;[90] but when Bolingbroke's return had been dramatized, woe and sorrow came to rest upon the falling ruler. Thereby Shakespeare inaugurates a poetic process that will effect his major variation in the portrayal of Richard.

Into an England suffering from Richard's actions, Bolingbroke came as a deliverer, and even as a child of destiny, according to some Lancastrian historians.[91] In contrast with such an emphasis, Shakespeare concentrates upon Richard's woe and uses his lyrical lamentations to illustrate his regal inadequacy, even as Richard insists upon his divine right to kingship. Consider, for example, the following speeches, the first two by Richard, the third by Carlyle:

> Not all the water in the rough rude sea
> Can wash the balm off from an anointed king;
> The breath of worldly men cannot depose
> The deputy elected by the Lord.
> For every man that Bolingbroke hath press'd
> To lift shrewd steel against our golden crown,
> God for his Richard hath in heavenly pay
> A glorious angel; then, if angels fight,
> Weak men must fall, for Heaven still guards the right.
>
> (III, ii, 54-62)

> For God's sake, let us sit upon the ground
> And tell sad stories of the death of kings:
> How some have been depos'd; some slain in war;
> Some haunted by the ghosts they have depos'd;
> Some poison'd by their wives; some sleeping kill'd;
> All murdered: for within the hollow crown
> That rounds the mortal temples of a king
> Keeps Death his court, and there the antic sits,
> Scoffing his state and grinning at his pomp,
> Allowing him a breath, a little scene,
> To monarchize, be fear'd, and kill with looks,
> Infusing him with self and vain conceit,
> As if this flesh which walls about our life
> Were brass impregnable; and humour'd thus
> Comes at the last and with a little pin
> Bores through his castle wall, and—farewell king!
> Cover your heads, and mock not flesh and blood
> With solemn reverence. Throw away respect,
> Tradition, form, and ceremonious duty;
> For you have but mistook me all this while.
> I live with bread like you, feel want,
> Taste grief, need friends: subjected thus,
> How can you say to me I am a king?
>
> (ll. 155-77)

> My lord, wise men ne'er sit and wail their woes,
> But presently prevent the ways to wail.
> To fear the foe, since fear oppresseth strength,
> Gives in your weakness strength unto your foe,
> And so your follies fight against yourself.

> Fear, and be slain; no worse can come to fight;
> And fight and die is death destroying death. . . .

(ll. 178-84)

Here as elsewhere, Richard's concept of rulership is personalized and concentrated in divine ordination and coronation. Beneficent, vigorous action and the consent of the ruled, that is, his subjects' love, are, and have been, neglected. Here as elsewhere, Richard is opposed by regal attributes that he lacks; and the present manifestation of this is apparent in Carlyle's speech. An excellent ruler should not suffer "the frute of any profitable counsaile for want of timely taking to be lost"; never by "retiring back"—or perhaps by discharging the power he has (III, ii, 211-18)—would an excellent ruler "encourage injuries."[92]

Paradoxically, however, by his lyrical lamentations, as well as by his intermittent vigor, Richard is given a theatrical and tragic appeal that persists throughout the remainder of the drama. Similarly, although Richard's constant and increasing search for Renaissance correspondences might give to his portrayal its impression of self-intoxicated vacillation, yet for Elizabethans it could also give to that portrayal an impression of intellectuality, the appeal of which could draw upon a liking for the simplified scheme of a world-order.[93]

At the same time, when Shakespeare dramatizes Richard's sorrow, overtones from the morality again may have been perceptible to Elizabethans. As has been noted, the conventional application of the cardinal virtues to the duties of kingship, when harmonized with the concept of fortitude (sometimes called "magnificence") and represented in narrative form, could show how sycophants intruded during prosperity and how the way to despair opened during adversity.[94] Granted that Richard's grief is not preceded by an increasingly dark descent into vice, yet Richard's despondency is shown in part by a lyrical evocation of "antic" Death. The vascillating hopelessness of this ruler then continues until he descends to a "base court," where he starts what Gaunt had foreseen of Richard's malfeasance and what will become the visual destruction of his kingship. In such a light, Shakespeare's portrayal of Richard during the third act may well have had overtones of familiarity for an age that was conscious of the doctrine of fortitude and that of despair and was interested in matters *de regimine principum*. If so, the effect presumably would be one of censurable sadness, buttressed by concepts about the way in which "Sorrow and grief of heart" could make one "speak fondly, like a frantic man" (III, iii, 184-86).[95]

This complex and qualifying artistry is apparent in the entire development of the scene at Flint Castle. At that time, as has been noted, Shakespeare in general alternates Lancastrian with Richardian or Yorkist interpretations of history (e.g., III, iii, 31-67, 104-20, in contrast with ll. 68-103, 133-41). He then fuses those contraries in the descent of a Phaëthon-like Richard. The dominant emotion of such an ending would again be conducive to a feeling of sorrow and pathos. Such an intent is indicated, for example, by Shakespeare's representation of a weeping York (l. 202). This artistry is then continued and amplified when Richard appears in the deposition, or parliament, scene. Among other considerations, the incident with the mirror fuses aspects of truth and prudence with aspects of pride and vainglory, while Richard's Christ images move awry upon the course of the action.

Although Richard, when chastened, is not restored to a sun-like magnificence that will banish flatterers and truly "make beholders wink," he is restored figuratively and dramatically during the last act. His lyrical lines about the compassion some will feel upon hearing of "the deposing of a rightful king" (V, i, 40-50) accord with the pathos of his parting from his queen. York's description of "poor," "gentle" Richard and the pathetic interlude with the nameless groom continue that thought and emotion (V, ii, 22-38, v, 67-97). In his last scene, with a double-edged irony, Richard abandons patience (l. 104) and emerges perceptive of self both in poetic soliloquy and vigorous action. His perception of his former false magnificence—an element of truth in the episode with the mirror—is underlined in his soliloquy (V, v, 45-49). By his vigorous action in fighting his attackers, Richard finally becomes, in the words of his murderer, "As full of valour as of royal blood" (l. 114). Here as elsewhere in the drama, by the contradictions that he has established and merged, Shakespeare creates the impression of Richard's growth and individuality.

In the last act, of course, there also appears Richard's constant, though intermittent, censure of Henry, who now is called not simply "proud" but "jauncing" (V, v, 59, 88-89, 94). Those words intensify York's description of Bolingbroke, a description that had been balanced with that of Richard (V, ii, 7-21). From that criticism and from Richard's valor, as Shakespeare concentrates upon the pathos in Richard's fall, there might arise an anti-Henry emphasis as strong as the anti-Richard one in the first scene of the second act. The portrayal of Bolingbroke, consequently, demands attention also.

Many critics have compared Henry's overt honesty at the end of the drama and in *1 Henry IV* with his hypocrisy as he rises in *Richard II*. Those remarks, however, say nothing about the way in which such an effect might have been achieved for Elizabethans as they watched *Richard II* only. More to the point, perhaps, would be a consideration of the fact that the rise of Bolingbroke varies noticeably from comparable developments in Shakespeare's earlier artistry or from Marlowe's representation of the rise of Mortimer. Martial heroism, ambitious machinations, a theatrically appealing titanism, and chivalric attributes appear as essentially successive or episodic emphases in the portrayal of York. Marlowe's portrayal of Mortimer moves from that of an angry nobleman opposing a regal vice to that of a Machiavel staining a king's nuptial bed. Like the characterization of Richard, the portrayal of his opponent is more restrained and intellectual than is Marlowe's comparable characterization; and since that opponent is also Richard's "heir," the portrayal is much more consistently ambivalent than are those of York and Mortimer. Until the last act, the Lancastrian emphases in the drama, Richard's malfeasance and vacillation, the use to which Northumberland is put, and Shakespeare's intellectualized restraint keep the pathos in the characterization of Richard from redounding noticeably against Henry.

As has been noted, it is easy to gloss the description of Bolingbroke's wooing the people by referring to the way in which that action might be an external sign of a vicious political ambition. Witness the description of the hated Guise; and even for "ignorant" theater-goers, who might acquire some of their knowledge by seeing Marlowe's plays, Guise probably was linked inextricably with the massacre of Protestants on St. Bartholomew's Day: ". . . among his other qualities [he] had one most proper to his purposes, and that was a kind of facility, gentlenesse, and popularitie, the inseparable companions of ambition. To the end to ouersway the mightie of the realm, hee stooped to the inferiors: from one end of the street to an other he wolde go with cap in hand, saluting either with heade, hande, or word euen the meanest."[96] Such a description is certainly paralleled by Richard's lines about Henry:

> Ourself and Bushy, Bagot here and Green
> Observ'd his courtship to the common people;
> How he did seem to dive into their hearts
> With humble and familiar courtesy,
> What reverence he did throw away on slaves,
> Wooing poor craftsmen with the craft of smiles
> And patient underbearing of his fortune,
> As 'twere to banish their affects with him.
> Off goes his bonnet to an oyster-wench;
> A brace of draymen bid God speed him well
> And had the tribute of his supple knee,
> With "Thanks, my countrymen, my loving friends,"

As were our England in reversion his,
And he our subjects' next degree in hope.[97]

(I, iv, 23-36)

It would be equally pertinent, however, to use another conventional idea as a gloss, not for the preceding speech about one who has just been banished, but for its speaker. At this point in the drama, Richard appears with his sycophants and with his plan to farm the realm. Thus Sidney, for example, notes that "most Princes *(seduced by flatterie* to builde upon false ground of government*) make themselves (as it were) another thing from the people;* and so *count it gain what they can get from them....*"[98] As a preceding discussion has indicated, at this time the entire development of the drama is running against Richard. In conjunction with the idea that there must be some rapport between ruler and ruled, the immediately preceding consideration probably lead to a qualified reception of the description, especially since the subsequent speeches elaborate the idea in the third phrase quoted above. In the immediately following scene, moreover, the unscrupulous seizure of subjects' goods and the fact that this ruler is surrounded by flatterers are emphasized by Gaunt and York and dramatized by Richard's seizure of Gaunt's estate.

At the moment that an audience would hear the preceding description, then, Shakespeare pretty clearly seems to have created a situation capable of having unfavorable emphases in the portrayal of both his rising and falling figures; but if the drama is to be criticized as drama, any impression of hypocrisy on Bolingbroke's part would be submerged in the movement of the play toward its anti-Richard focal point.

For that matter, throughout most of the drama, through at least the time that an audience would hear of the "commons' suit" (IV, i, 222 ff.), Richard's grievous sin has been to lose the hearts of the vast majority of his subjects, both noble and common—a sin of which Elizabeth and her father were never guilty. By Richard's actions, the governed certainly could not perceive their ruler's "unenvious love"; and hence one would not expect to find this governor "secure in the midst of secure citizens."[99] In contrast to their "hard hearts" as far as Richard is concerned, the commons' adherence to Bolingbroke and their joy in him is constant, however it be represented by others. At the time of Richard's description, moreover, Henry had just shown a patriotic fortitude in adversity.

In view of the last consideration, an earlier detail that may have gone almost unnoticed in the theater needs some attention. It too seems equivocal; and if so, it also would substantiate Shakespeare's purposeful ambiguity. After Henry had been given vigorous speeches about combat, and even as he spoke of exile, Shakespeare gave him lines about the power of kings:

> How long a time lies in one little word!
> Four lagging winters and four wanton springs
> End in a word: such is the breath of kings.
>
> (I, iii, 213-15)

A brief impression of rebelliousness may seem the obvious result. Also possible, however, and equally momentary, might be a different impression, one related not so much to rebelliousness as to a heroic appreciation of a ruler's magnificence and power, even though its expression lacks the intensity and the Eastern locale given it when an impulse characteristic of the *fortunati* would lead Tamburlaine to his first acquisition of "empire."[100]

Although the pathos of parting between Bolingbroke and Gaunt immediately becomes dominant, the preceding lines are, at least, equivocal. On the one hand, they may substantiate Richard's description, with its implication of Bolingbroke's ambition and hence of his potential rebelliousness. On the other hand, they may have given a faint heroic overtone to this patriotic exile's speeches. Indeed, a later speech can make the equivocal impression of the preceding lines congruent with a Lancastrian interpretation of history that represented Henry as a child of destiny:

> *York.* Take not, good cousin, further than you should,
> Lest you mistake the heavens are o'er our heads.
> *Boling.* I know it, uncle, and oppose not myself
> Against their will.
>
> (III, iii, 16-19)

To such a figure, who says he is acting in accordance with the favor of the heavens, even as Pontano's *fortunati* did, "both young and old" have flocked. To follow him "White-beards have arm'd their thin and hairless scalps," and

> ... boys, with women's voices,
> Strive to speak big, and clap their female joints
> In stiff unwieldy arms. ...
>
> (III, ii, 112-15)

Elements of the heroic certainly play about this portrayal.

Also in contrast to Richard, but in accordance with a vigorous acceptance in prosperity, as well as in adversity, of what the heavens or fortune offers, Bolingbroke suffers not "the frute of any profitable counsaile for want of timely taking to be lost." Witness the lines with which he moves into a situation likely to result in battle:

> Come, lords, away,
> To fight with Glendower and his complices.
> A while to work, and after holiday.[101]

> (III, i, 43-44)

Bolingbroke is also represented as doing what Richard should have done:

> The weeds which his [Richard's] broad-spreading
>   leaves did shelter,
> That seem'd in eating him to hold him up,
> Are pluck'd up root and all by Bolingbroke,
> I mean the Earl of Wiltshire, Bushy, and Green.

> (III, iv, 50-53)

Given no heroic titanism, but given a brief disclaimer of a flattering speech and made to participate in open debate (II, iii, 19-20, 85 ff.), the portrayal of returned Bolingbroke, upon these grounds alone, would vary markedly for an Elizabethan audience from the portrayal of Richard Duke of York. In Bolingbroke, moreover, is embodied the concept of the consent of the governed and of a country's need for vigorous action that also shows a ruling mercy and a chivalric regard for honor (V, iii, 23 ff.; vi, 28-29).

The fact that Shakespeare never gives a soliloquy to Bolingbroke is especially important. By the usual "rules" of Elizabethan drama, an audience never knows whether Henry's motives are other than those expressed by himself in dialogue. At the same time, through other characters an audience hears contradictory interpretations of his actions. It is hard to see how a purposeful ambiguity could be more clearly indicated as the author's intent; and this ambiguity differs from the "silent" hypocrisy of the usual Elizabethan character. Shakespeare's artistry in this respect anticipates that of Daniel, when he wrote a drama in which the undisclosed motives of great historical figures would be interpreted differently by different persons and by different classes.[102] From the second through the fourth acts, it is in York's censure and in his admonitions, countered immediately by Henry's lines, and it is in the tangential world of Richard's references to an ambitious and a "high" Hereford that the silent hypocrisy of a modern character might be said to exist. But because Henry never speaks in soliloquy, in more than one scene he is a "silent" prince (IV, i, 290).

In other words, if the fate of Richard II and the rise of Henry IV as represented by Shakespeare through the fourth act were used for an Elizabethan debate, the doctrine of obedience, in all probability, would be included in that exercise. There might also be included the doctrine that a mutual love should exist between ruler and ruled and that a king must exercise a beneficent vigor. Both considerations would make this drama a historical and political mirror *de regimine principum,* and some of the debaters might be reminded of that fact by the mirror episode itself. In addition, and as a consequence of the need for a beneficent vigor—a need that would specify Richard's political sin or error—there also might be included in this debate some consideration of the grievous state of Richard's kingdom. One of the points that Sir Thomas Smith would bring to bear upon the question of the hazardous resistance to a ruler was a consideration of the ills then present. Smith's other point to be considered in connection with this perilous crux in political thought was the motives of the doers.[103] But in this instance, there is no soliloquy upon which to rely; there are only some striking contradictions. Because of this fact, then, one can conceive of an Elizabethan being especially interested in *Richard II* as the drama moves into the fifth act. The story of opposition to Bolingbroke has just been promised; and thus an audience of spectators, and not of debaters, might expect his characterization to be rounded out with a representational method capable of effecting one of the successive emphases in the portrayal of York, or apparent in the portrayal of other rising figures.

The drama continues, however, upon its unique way. At first, Shakespeare seems to counter the increasing pathos of a fallen Richard by representing Henry in a new and unquestionably favorable light. This has been noted briefly. The actions of Henry in answer to the Duchess of York's cry for pardon give him the merciful attribute of a Christian prince, who pardons "as God shall pardon" him (V, iii, 111-31, 135). In a religious age with barbarous legal punishments, but with a literature that frequently emphasized the need for mercy,[104] this development would be based upon strong emotions. To a lesser degree, the "hero's" regard for "High sparks of honour," apparent in Henry's merciful judgement of Carlyle, could also be a sympathetic emphasis (V, vi, 24-29).

On the other hand, after Richard *has* been given a soliloquy,[105] Shakespeare effects a glaring qualification of Bolingbroke's mercy, first extended to Aumerle and then to Carlyle. In representing this situation, Shakespeare also draws upon a dramatic process whereby other individuals act for Henry. York had introduced Richard to his deposition. Northumberland, the executioner of the favorites, the messenger who did not bend a knee to Richard, had appeared as Richard's insistent "Fiend" and then as Bolingbroke's messenger to send Richard to Pomfret and hasten the queen's departure for France (IV, i, 270; V, i, 51-54). Both are now supplanted by a murderer, acting, he says, on Henry's words: "Have I no friend will rid me of this living fear?" (V, iv, 2). Words spoken twice while the new ruler "wishtly look'd" at Exton (l. 7).

Shakespeare certainly could have represented this situation as an incident illustrating the "curse of kings" (*King John,* IV, ii, 208-14); but he lets those reported words stand unexplained, except for the bare statement that Henry wished Richard dead, hates the murderer, and loves the murdered (V, vi, 39-40). This is neither hypocritical nor unqualified, but an equivocal effect is nevertheless achieved. In the first place, a striking juxtaposition of antithetical emphases has been curtailed in length when repeated. Bolingbroke has shown mercy (V, iii, 23-146); he has been connected with murder (V, iv, v); he has shown mercy (V, vi, 19-29); he has been connected with murder (V, vi, 30-52). In addition to such a process, which reminds one of the ending of *1 Henry VI,* a conventional representational method comes into play. In accordance with frequent Elizabethan practice, a speech by the person of highest degree on the stage here ends a tragedy. As a result, Henry's lines represent the final expression in this drama of woe and of indignation at that woe. Through indignation, Exton is banished. With woe, Henry recognizes his own guilt and vows to weep after Richard's "untimely bier" and voyage to the Holy Land. When a coffin is carried off stage, this drama, like Marlowe's *Edward II,* closes with a pageantic exit, here led, however, not by the son and heir, but by the opponent and "heir" of a former English ruler. One may call this "heir" an honest hypocrite; but in doing so, one may overlook too easily an artistry that effected a purposefully qualified, ambiguous portrayal. Even in his fifth act, Shakespeare works with antithetical emphases that he now resolves equivocally by a conventional representational method. As a result, he also fuses, quite unconventionally, opposition, indignation, woe, and pageantry. The final sorrow of this drama is embodied in a ruler whose "soul is full of woe / That blood should sprinkle" him "to make him grow."

As has been pointed out elsewhere, in *Richard II,* especially, the ideal of order yields to the problem of order and to the historical fact that the gravest disorder occurs when a ruler does not act like a king, when he forgets his duty and the love that should exist between ruler and ruled. It is as if *Jack Straw* were fused with *Woodstock,* as the events of history are changed and a preceptual dilemma dramatized—a dilemma that, among other considerations, involves balancing the woe of a present land with a woe to come. This artistry makes *Richard II* a problem drama as purposeful as any of Shakespeare's "problem comedies."[106] In brief, Shakespeare does what Marlowe avoided when he turned from Kent's soliloquy to portray a vicious Isabella and Mortimer.

Upon a narrative movement reflecting academic precepts about five-act structure and upon an emotional pattern showing a censurable ruler, his fall from power, the pathos of his death, and the concomitant rise of his opponent, Shakespeare fuses conflicting political and historical emphases for the focal points of his epitasis. Upon those episodes—that is, upon the scenes at Flint Castle and in Parliament—he also brings to bear the struggle, woe, and despair of the preceding play-world; and by his last stroke in the portrayal of Bolingbroke, Shakespeare produces a final, ironic sorrow. Above all, Shakespeare utilizes fully his lyrical power in creating Richard. By it, as well as by the almost complete absence of soliloquies, Shakespeare produces an impression that the best historians of his age also created. The individuality of great persons is portrayed clearly, and upon the confines of their actions an equivocal world emerges from the censures, the follies, the sins, and the unexpressed motives of men.[107] With its ambiguity arising from a perilous crux in Elizabethan political thought, this drama interprets history for Shakespeare's contemporaries. In doing so, it also interprets its age as it tells a story on the universal theme of one king's death and the creation of another.

Richard II is of value in itself. It was also of value to Shakespeare. Upon the basis of Bolingbroke's portrayal as it has been described, Shakespeare will develop his later picture of Henry IV in the two plays of that name. When in *1 Henry IV,* a Yorkist statement of silent hypocrisy is given to Henry, the development of the scene qualifies it.[108] Conversely, when Henry shows an explicit concern for religion, he also shows an awareness of the political soundness of a foreign expedition.[109] Similarly, this king's awareness of a ruler's perpetual "watch" reflects a commonplace about the actions of good princes; but leads into Henry's preoccupation with Richard and "his eye brimful of tears."[110] As in the characterization of Richard, so it is here. Henry is an individual who does not fit into a scheme of simple ethical dichotomies. In *Richard II,* at least, his ultimate motivation is unknown and is capable of being interpreted in a variety of ways. Some ten years after writing *Richard II,* moverover, Shakespeare would repeat its basic emotional pattern in writing *Lear,* condense the initial development, and give a deepened pathos to his portrayal of a ruler separated from power—a pathos based less upon concepts and emotions about kingship than upon man's feeling for the communion of existence and the ultimate viciousness that results when charity is absent. Obviously any progress toward this end was also of the greatest value.

VIII

Conclusion

IN THE PRECEDING chapters, Shakespeare's technique and his artistic intent in writing his early plays have been examined in the light of the probable expectations of contemporary theater-goers and their possible familiarity with current concepts, current representational methods, and current features of the Elizabethan scene. Folk merriment and Elizabethan mirth illumine both the form and the intent of scenes in the drama; and no playwright utilized this background, and the probable expectations arising from it, more skillfully than did Shakespeare. Even *Love's Labour's Lost,* the most Lylyesque of his plays, constantly strikes notes that could have been comically familiar to uneducated Elizabethans who attended a theater infrequently. The same is true of *A Midsummer Night's Dream,* and Shakespeare's portrayal of Thurio and the introduction of Faulconbridge show a similarly sure comic touch. As one might expect, Shakespeare and his fellow dramatists also worked with comic motifs and techniques already established upon the stage, and some of the most mature comedy in Falstaff's scenes continues the early practice of Shakespeare, especially when he creates a nonderisive, free laughter. As is apparent also in the scenes devoted to Cade and his rebellion, Shakespeare's use of conventionally comic motifs and representational methods demonstrates a true originality.

Some four to seven structural movements that usually were associated with certain serious types of character also illumine Shakespeare's method and purpose in writing his early plays. When analyzed in accordance with their basic structural movement, dramas by Kyd, Marlowe, Greene, and others provide a background for examining Shakespeare's artistry in his early tragedies and histories and for considering, among other things, the structure of his plays written earlier than 1596. In this respect, all but one of Marlowe's dramas have been considered in greater or less detail. Their spectacular artistry is unique. Like the majority of the non-Shakespearian plays here analyzed, they also reveal an artistic conscientiousness comparable to what one finds in Shakespeare's work, even though Marlowe is not as facile or as intellectually perceptive as Shakespeare. This last fact is especially apparent when one compares *Edward II* with *Richard II* or when one examines carefully some of the features of the Henry VI trilogy.

Although it develops in accordance with the structural movement found also in *The Spanish Tragedy, Titus Andronicus* is closer to the dramatic tradition that displayed the vice and to episodic features of the current theatrical scene than is Kyd's play. A case can be made out, however, for the startling, episodic effects of Aaron's role being harmonious with constant features of Shakespeare's artistry in this early tragedy. At the same time, aspects of its sophisticated brutality build upon what might be calculated to appeal to those aware of the current academic tradition. With a comparable intent, perhaps, Shakespeare utilizes an academically derived structure in *The Comedy of Errors* and *The Two Gentlement of Verona*. In the first of these dramas, his control of a nonclassical multiplicity is especially firm, even though the laughter and the amusement, for the most part, are classically derived. In the second, his use of courtly motifs reflects the Elizabethans' belief in the validity of a gentleman's discipline. An attitude and an awareness that were probably familiar to a vulgar audience underlies each of the comic tones, and the succession of those tones accords with the thematic resolution of the play.

Shakespeare's integration of the comic with other contexts and his control of his comedy by an over-all precision are apparent likewise in his earliest history plays, which are developed in a cyclical manner reminiscent of the earlier mysteries. In the second and the third parts of *Henry VI* especially, Shakespeare seems more concerned with climactic scenes of theatrical effectiveness than with five-act structure, Tudor doctrine, or theories of kingship. Like some of his contemporaries, he also modifies the conventional pattern of moralities that dramatized the conflict between virtues and vices. As these historical dramas build upon dramatic forms that in previous generations had had the greatest vitality, the course of the entire tetralogy shows an objective intent that would portray the way in which the annals of England illustrate the vicissitudes of states, especially when a Christian beneficence and a forceful vigor are not embodied in a single ruler. Of particular interest is the ambivalence produced by the episodic, qualifying, and interlocked portrayals of York and Henry. Of almost equal interest is the portrayal of Richard III. In the characterization of that Machiavel and tyrant, Shakespeare develops a rhetorical virtuosity that builds upon concepts about Richard which probably were familiar to his educated contemporaries. Merging the terrifying and the risible more convincingly than had either Kyd or Marlowe, Shakespeare also sustains his movement to the catastrophe by an ironic development having tragic potentialities.

Although some of the appurtenances of the stage villain as he might be represented in serious, political milieus are reflected in the boisterous circumstances of *The Taming of the Shrew,* Shakespeare's laughter at techniques and motifs that he and his contemporaries also developed seriously appears most noticeably in *Love's Labour's Lost* and *A Midsummer Night's Dream.* Both dramas show a constant, critical detachment: the first, in its interpretation of the rhetorical ideal; the second, in its comic interpretation of antithetical attitudes about love and marriage. *Love's Labour's Lost* validates a witty virtuosity even as it mocks aberrations of wit, including its own departure from the norm of comedy. It has so close a grip upon the Elizabethans' concern with wit and rhetoric, however, that it probably must remain a sixteenth-century drama. In contrast, the dominant laughter of *A Midsummer Night's Dream* makes this play valid for any age, as it illustrates the fact that "reason and love keep little company." In these comedies, Shakespeare also laughs at a partially Neo-Platonic aspect of love but reflects a similar concept when he looks seriously at his laughter. In all of his dramas, his precise control is noticeable; and in *A Midsummer Night's Dream* features of his earlier artistry seem to underlie his basic structural intent. This is especially true as regards his tendency to write patterned sequences and to develop initial and final emphases wider than those of the complication proper.

Shakespeare's architectonic neatness is again apparent in the development of the three remaining dramas that have been considered here. The rhetorical process of *King John* is singularly interesting, as similarities are extended into the varying situations that recreate John's story in the light of Elizabethan fears. In this play, with its many final ironies, the clash of irreconcilables receives a cohesive dramatic expression. Perhaps most revealing of Shakespeare's increasing maturity as a dramatist is the fact that in *Romeo and Juliet* the characteristic widening of the scope of his dramas produces a world that rounds out the border of the story as an adverse fate works through the characters' unawareness of the play-world and through their likely Elizabethan reactions. Similarly mature is the display in *Richard II* of Shakespeare's strength, shown not simply by his lyrical vigor but also by his intellectualized restraint. Through his original use of a structural movement also used by Marlowe, Shakespeare constantly keeps alive the political and dramatic contraries that make this tragedy an Elizabethan problem play.

Many other features of Shakespeare's technique, as it illumines his intent, as it compares or contrasts with the practice of his contemporaries, or as it builds upon his own practice, have been examined. But a study that consists almost entirely of analyses of dramas is not conducive to conclusions. What has been written will be convincing only as the preceding pages are read in their context. From them, it is hoped that the reader will have gained an increasing appreciation of how Shakespeare utilized and transformed concepts and methods thoroughly conventional to his theater and his age, and how his early dramas, as well as some by his contemporaries, can be studied with profit by anyone interested in the form and substance of a new and a great secular drama.

Notes

CHAPTER I

1. Throughout this study the point of view about "continuous copy" is that expressed by E. K. Chambers, *William Shakespeare* (Oxford, 1930) I, 150-53, 225-35. As some of the subsequent discussions will indicate, however, I do not always agree with his comments about the individual plays. Not infrequently the charge that one shows timidity in relying upon the folio text is negated by a careful examination of that text. See, for example, David Galloway, " 'I am dying, Egypt, dying': Folio Repetitions and Editors," *N & Q*, CCIII (1958), 330-35. See also below, p. 41 n. 126, for examples of what are sometimes called actors "gags"; yet it must be granted that acting authors like Robert Wilson and Shakespeare might give their principal comedians such lines.

2. See Elmer Edgar Stoll, "Symbolism in Shakespeare," *MLR*, XLII (1947), 9-23, in which this statement by the poet Abercrombie is quoted (p. 11).

3. The concept that God was English is a case in point. For its appearance in Elizabeth I's Parliaments, see J. E. Neale, *Elizabeth I and her Parliaments, 1584-1601* (N.Y., 1958), 169-70, 193, 200. Note, too, the anti-papal spirit of celebrations of Elizabeth's Accession Day. Roy C. Strong, "The Accession Day of Queen Elizabeth I," *Journal of the Warburg and Courtauld Institute*, XXI (1958), 86-103.

4. See, e.g., Freda L. Townsend, *Apologie for 'Bartholomew Fayre'* (N.Y., 1947), 91-97. A characteristic attitude is that expressed by Giraldi Cinthio: "The writer should use great diligence that the parts of his work fit together like the parts of the body, as we said above. And in putting together the bony frame he will seek to fill in the spaces and make the members equal in size, and this can be done by inserting at suitable and requisite places loves, hates, lamentations, laughter, sports, serious things, beauties, descriptions of places, temples, and persons, fables both invented by the author himself and taken from the ancients, voyages, wanderings, monsters, unforeseen events, deaths, funerals, mournings, recognitions, things terrible and pitiable, weddings, births, victories, triumphs, single combats, jousts, tournaments, catalogues, laws, and other matters. . . ." For there is nothing in heaven and earth "which cannot with varied ornaments adorn the whole body of his composition and bring it not merely to a beautiful but to a lovely figure, for such things give to all the parts their due measure and fit ornament in such proportion that there emerges a body well regulated and composed. . . ." *On the Composition of Romances* (1549), tr. A. H. Gilbert, *Literary Criticism, Plato to Dryden* (N.Y., 1940), pp. 264-65. See also Tasso's discussion of the fact that "variety is especially pleasing to our times" and the comments on Ariosto. Gilbert, *Lit. Crit.*, pp. 500-1, 495 ff. Note, too, B. Sprague Allen, *Tides in English Taste* (Cambridge, Mass., 1937), I, 17-18. From another point of view, explicitly applicable to the playwright Robert Wilson, see the Latin letter from one Thomas Bayly to one Thomas Bawdewine, thanking him for a tragedy presented at Sheffield on St. George's day and requesting him to pro-

cure another play "short, novel, pleasing, attractive, charming, witty, full of buffoonery, rascality and wrangling, and replete with hangings, banditries, and panderings of every kind." Joseph Hunter, *Hallamshire: The History and Topography of the Parish of Sheffield in the County of York,* ed. A. Gatty (London, 1869), p. 8.

5. This constitutes one of the major points in Jonson's "Grex" that precedes *Every Man out of his Humour,* e.g., ll. 247 ff. *Ben Jonson,* ed. C. H. Herford and Percy Simpson, III (Oxford, 1927). This is the edition used for all subsequent references to Jonson's works.

6. George R. Kernodle, *From Art to Theatre: Form and Convention in the Renaissance* (Chicago, 1944), p. 7.

7. Although the interest of such persons may seem impossible to assess, yet one should always allow for the knowledge that can be acquired aurally. Thus one of Sir Christopher Hatton's arguments against the Puritan Bill and Book in 1586-87 was that the set prayers of the Anglican Book allowed the illiterate to learn that which might comfort them out of church. J. E. Neale, *Eliz. & Parl., 1584-1601,* p. 159. Similarly one would expect the effect of the formalized *dispositio* in Aphthonian rhetoric to become familiar and expected. See also Wolfgang Clemen, *English Tragedy before Shakespeare: The Development of Dramatic Speech,* tr. T. S. Dorsch (London, 1960), *passim.* In this connection also, the probability of formalized acting is pertinent. See Alfred Harbage, "Elizabethan Acting," *PMLA,* LIV (1939), 685-708; A. G. H. Bachrach, "The Great Chain of Acting," *Neophilologus,* XXXIII (1949), 160-72. For different points of view, see e.g., Marvin Rosenberg, "Elizabethan Actors: Men or Marionettes," *PMLA,* LXIX (1954), 915-27; Leonard Goldstein, "On the Transition from Formal to Naturalistic Acting in the Elizabethan and Post-Elizabethan Theatre," *Bull. N.Y. Public Library,* LXII (1958), 330-49.

8. *The Works of Francis Bacon,* ed. James Spedding, Robert Leslie Ellis, and Douglas Denon Heath (London, 1858), IV, 457; V, 23-24. The basic point in the following discussion has been elaborated by many critics upon many occasions. For the sake of brevity, however, I use a comparison with what Ernst Cassirer calls "mythical thought." *The Philosophy of Symbolic Forms. Volume Two: Mythical Thought* (New Haven, 1955), pp. 34-36. What is written in this paragraph is, perhaps, but another way of saying that Elizabethan drama is explicit.

9. The ramifications of this last consideration are many—and not simply as they underlie any parody about the number of Lady Macbeth's children. A Renaissance censor's zeal, his conscious or unconscious appreciation of the phenomenon about which Bacon wrote, and his failure to differentiate between oratory before a mob and drama within a theater could cause trouble for both playwright and acting company. Of course, one would not expect a censor to be interested in a dramatist's artistry; but a failure to distinguish between what probably was meant to be speculative or argumentative and what probably was meant to be dramatically compelling can cause trouble even for the modern critic. I have discussed aspects of this consideration in *The Problem of Order: Elizabethan Political Commonplaces and an Example of Shakespeare's Art* (Chapel Hill, 1962), pp. 121-200.

10. See, for example, Glynne W. G. Wickham, *Early English Stages, 1300 to 1660,* I (London, 1959), 51-111.

11. See, for example, Walther Ebisch and Levin L. Schücking, *A Shakespeare Bibliography* (Oxford, 1931), pp. 112-17, and their *Supplement for the Years 1930-35* (Oxford, 1937), pp. 37-39. The two chapters immediately following are devoted in part to this consideration. As the discussions there develop, particularly in Chapter III, a scholarly precision in differentiations between character types has sometimes been avoided purposefully. I believe, however, that critics who have been concerned with detailed classifications will find that the total picture sketched there, in view of its somewhat different purpose, does no injustice to

their studies. See, e.g., W. A. Armstrong, "The Influence of Seneca and Machiavelli on the Elizabethan Tyrant," *RES,* XXIV (1948), 19-35, and below pp. 65-67 (in this respect, however, also note Chapter IV, below); or Bernard Spivak, *Shakespeare and the Allegory of Evil* (N.Y., 1958), pp. 147-50, 170, and below p. 7 n. 3 (in this respect, too, see subsequent remarks on the general nature of the conflict morality plays, e.g., p. 62 n. 1 below).

12. In this respect, see David Klein, "Did Shakespeare Produce His Own Plays," *MLR,* LVII (1962), 556-60.

13. A point of view worth establishing at the start of this essay is that imagery exists only within the narrative movement of a play and only within the over-all emotional development of a drama. Although, in general, one finds little to quarrel with in recent studies of imagery in Renaissance drama, such as Edward B. Partridge's *The Broken Compass: A Study of the Major Comedies of Ben Jonson* (London, 1958), in other studies the image is sometimes overly exalted, and critics seem to write as if the word or phrase caused the dramatic form of the play, instead of being one means to an end—instead of being, figuratively speaking, a *visibilia* of an immediate purpose. Even in Partridge's study, for example, one wishes that the reader had been told something about Elizabethan and Jacobean pronunciation and that certain passages of Jonson's plays had been considered not simply in a discussion of the theme of bestiality but also from the point of view of their theatrical hilarity. See, e.g., *Bartholomew Fair,* II, v, 161-90. As regards the meaning of Shakespeare's images, a thoroughly sound approach is that of John Erskine Hankins, *Shakespeare's Derived Imagery* (Lawrence, Kansas, 1953).

14. *The London Times Literary Supplement,* Jan. 6, 1945, p. 7.

CHAPTER II

1. See, e.g., George Whetstone, "Epistle Dedicatory," *Promos and Cassandra* (1578), in *Elizabethan Critical Essays,* ed. G. Gregory Smith (Oxford, 1904), I, 59-60; William Cartwright's second poem "Upon the report of the printing of the Dramaticall Poems of Master *John Fletcher," Comedies and Tragedies Written by Francis Beaumont and John Fletcher* (London, 1647), sig. d2v.

2. Jonson's humor in this respect is commented upon too infrequently. Although Mitis has objected that the argument of comedy should show "crosse wooing" with a "clowne" as a serving-man, he later objects also to Sordido's "purpos'd violence" as "more then the nature of *Comœdia* will in any sort admit." *EMO,* III, vi, 191-200; viii, 80-85. Just as he had been silenced by an authoritative definition of comedy (III, vi, 202-12), so he is silenced by a citation of Plautus' *Cistellaria,* wherein Alcesimarchus is said to appear with "a drawne sword ready to kill himselfe" and is "e'ne fixing his brest vpon it" (III, viii, 86-94). The truly learned Cordatus, however, does not mention the explicitly feigned nature of this action by Alcesimarchus, any more than he mentions the native tradition noted below. An authoritative definition and a classical citation are alone sufficient for the insipid objector. An entirely different attitude, as well as an entirely different point of reference, is shown by Sidney, who may have found some early plays indecorous but who, like Jonson, was willing to accept a "true" tragicomedy. *Complete Works,* ed. Albert Feuillerat, III (Cambridge, 1923), 39-40, 22.

3. Northrup Frye, "Characterization in Shakespearian Comedy," *SQ,* IV (1953), 271-77. What is written in these paragraphs would also be applicable to the two servant types in "elegiac comedy," or in the *Geta* tradition, and applicable also to any differentiation between "sot," "badin," and different types of the "vice." See, e.g., Karl Young, *The Drama of the Medieval Church* (Oxford, 1933), I, 7-9, and B. J. Whiting, "Diccon's French Cousin," *SP,* XLII (1945), 31-40. Such distinctions, of course, are valid and necessary, but primarily for purposes other than that of this essay. It is interesting, indeed, that Cotgrave's definition of

badin ("A notable coxcombe, an Asse in graine; also a foole, or Vice in a play," Whiting, p. 34) indicates how easily such types merged in actual playwriting. See also Francis Hugh Mares, "The Origin of the Figure Called 'the Vice' in Tudor Drama," *HLQ,* XXII (1958-59), 11-29; and above pp. 5-6 n. 11.

4. See, for example, Madeleine Doran, *Endeavors of Art* (Madison, 1954), pp. 217-18 and *passim.* The quotations are from Thomas Wilson, *Arte of Rhetorique,* ed. G. H. Mair (Oxford, 1909), p. 179.

5. *The Works of Robert Armin, Actor,* ed. Alexander B. Grosart, Occasional Issues of Unique . . . Books, XIV (privately printed, 1880), 1-59; John Redford, *Wit and Science,* Malone Soc., 1951, e.g., ll. 460 ff.; Armin, *Works,* pp. 81-83, 87-88; Louis B. Wright, "Madmen as Vaudeville Performers on the Elizabethan Stage," *JEGP,* XXX (1930), 48-54; and for the connection between the subplot, which involves types of madness, and the main plot of *The Changeling,* see Karl L. Holzknecht, "The Dramatic Structure of *The Changeling,*" *Renaissance Papers: A Selection of Papers Presented to the Renaissance Meeting in the Southeastern States,* 1954, pp. 77-87.

6. See Enid Welsford, *The Fool* (London, 1935) and Robert H. Goldsmith, *Wise Fools in Shakespeare* (East Lansing, 1955).

7. Such a background has been considered in part by C. L. Barber, *Shakespeare's Festive Comedy* (Princeton, N.J., 1959), e.g., pp. 1-6. The remainder of the present chapter, however, both in content and in method, varies appreciably from this interesting discussion.

8. Charles Read Baskervill, *The Elizabethan Jig* (Chicago, 1929), pp. 6, 35.

9. Henry Chettle, *Kind-hartes Dream, 1592,* Bodley Head Quartos (N.Y., 1923), pp. 15-23; Charles Butler, *The Principles of Musik* (London, 1636), pp. 130-31. Note, too, John Northbrooke, *A Treatise against Dicing, Dancing, Plays, and Interludes,* Shakesp. Soc., No. 14, pp. 150-51, 176-77; Philip Stubbes, *Anatomy of the Abuses in England, 1583,* ed. F. J. Furnivall, New Shakesp. Soc., Series 6, No. 6, II, 156; and Thomas Lodge, *Wits Miserie and the Worlds Madness, 1596* (Hunterian Club, 1879), p. 84. With a witty *double entendre* Lodge would remind the reader of the fate of "LEWIS Archbishop of Magdenburghe," who "in treading his lauoltos and corrantos with his mistresse, in trying the horsetrick broke his necke. . . ." See below, pp. 15-16 and n. 38, 39-40.

10. *A Dialogue Full of Pithe and Pleasure,* p. 6, col. b, in *The Works in Verse and Prose of Nicholas Breton,* ed. Alexander B. Grosart (Edinburgh, 1879).

11. P. 84.

12. W. Barclay Squire and J. H. Fuller-Maitland, *Catches, Rounds, Two-Part and Three-Part Songs . . . by Henry Purcell,* Purcell Soc., XXII, pp. iii, xxv; e.g., Nos. III, L.

13. Charles Read Baskervill, *English Elements in Jonson's Early Comedy,* Univ. of Texas Studies in English, I (Austin, 1911), pp. 174-75, 176-77; *The Paston Letters,* ed. James Gairdner (Westminister, 1904), III, 89 (April 16, 1473).

14. *Social England Illustrated, An English Garner* (N.Y., 1903), p. 400.

15. *The Dramatic Records of Sir Henry Herbert,* ed. Joseph Quincy Adams, Cornell Studies in English, III (New Haven, 1917), pp. 132-33, 134.

16. *The First and Second Parts of King Edward the Fourth: A Facsimile Reprint of the First Edition 1599. . .* (Philadelphia, 1922), sigs. L4v-M1.

17. In 1537, for example, strict orders were given to prohibit May-games; one in particular, in which Husbandry went out of the book to criticize gentlemen, had become "seditious." In 1543, the authorities stated that it was lawful to set forth songs, plays, and interludes to rebuke vice and foster virtue as long as they did not meddle with interpretations of Scripture contrary to what was authorized; and a royal proclamation of 1549, as well as subsequent orders and the earlier one of 1537, indicate that the authorities were concerned with interludes, song-drama, *ballade-débat,* the singing of relatively simple satiric motifs, or mumming. *Letters and Papers, Foreign and Domestic of the Reign of Henry VIII,* XII, Pt. I (London, 1890), 557; see also p. 585. E. K. Chambers, *The Medieval Stage* (Oxford,

1903) II, 220. Baskervill, *Eliz. Jig*, pp. 43-56, especially Guzman's description of mumming at Hinchinbrook, which was directed at Bonner (1564). In the reign of Mary, on April 30, 1556, as a result of "seditious" plays and interludes in the "north parts" by some six or seven persons calling themselves Sir Francis Lake's men, public officers were ordered by the Privy Council not to allow "any playes, enterludes, songes, or any such like pastimes . . . under any color or pretense." In the next year, when the authorities were searching for several players in London and Canterbury, one at least was connected with a "Sacke full of Newes," which by its title indicates satiric intent and, in its context, probably a religious one. John Strype, *Ecclesiastical Memorials* (Oxford, 1822), III, Pt. 2, 413-14; *Acts of the Privy Council in the Reign of Queen Mary, 1556-1558*, Second Series (London, 1893) IV, 102, 110, 119, 168-69. In the reign of Elizabeth, the writing of books, farces, and songs prejudicial to other princes, apparently Catholic and Spanish ones, is complained of; and the general nature of this material is indicated also by a reference to certain anti-Catholic plays usually given "daily" in taverns and by a similar reference to an order forbidding "in the future the performance in the hostels and taverns" of certain "plays and games on holidays." *Calendar of Letters and State Papers, Spanish, 1558-1567* (London, 1892), p. 247; *Calendar of State Papers and Manuscripts, Venetian, 1558-1580* (London, 1890), pp. 27, 65, 71, 80-81; see also pp. 11, 53. References to "sedition" and "abuse" may be, of course, quite inaccurate. What was traditionally innocuous could be viewed with alarm by a propagandist who had his own row to hoe, and what was meant to have only a general social pertinence might be construed as an attack upon specific persons or as dangerous criticism of some event. As part of a plan to popularize Henry's break with Rome, a writer would object to the circumvention of the Sheriff of Nottingham in Robin Hood plays. It showed disrespect for the law. But declaring the abomination of the Bishop of Rome and his adherents in "Playes, songes and books" was to be allowed. *Letters and Papers, Foreign and Domestic of the Reign of Henry VIII*, XVII (London, 1900), 707. At other times, although libel or "sedition" would be noted when resentment was aroused, it might also be noted when it seemed wise to be on the lookout for any sign of an attempt to inflame the unruly multitude. C. J. Sisson, *Lost Plays of Shakespeare's Age* (Cambridge, 1936), pp. 162-77; *Acts of the Privy Council of England, 1591-1592*, New Series, XXII (London, 1901), 549 (June 23, 1592). At any rate, the propagandist's or satirist's variations might be expected to build upon what was traditional and familiar in folk merriment. The "Overthrow of the Abbyes, A Tale of Robin Hoode" is based on the material of May-games; but in it one shepherd tells another a story in which Robin Hood symbolizes a bishop. *Ballads from Manuscripts*, ed. Frederick J. Furnivall (Ballad Society, 1868-72), I, 295-98. Similarly, when the London stage would cudgel Martin Marprelate, it did so in a manner that caused individuals to think of current mirth. See below, p. 22.

18. *Ben Jonson*, VIII, 656. The verse translation is Brome's; *Ben Jonson*, XI, 360, ll. 21-23.

19. As it is indicated by the 1584 record of an Oxfordshire investigation into the singing of a libellous song, even formulae seem to have been circulated whereby individuals' names might be fitted into "balettis" and, perhaps, in Falstaff's words, "sung to filthy tunes." Baskervill, *Eliz. Jig*, pp, 66-67, citing *Bagford Ballads*, I, xviii-xix. For jigs in praise of a person, see, for example, *The Works of Thomas Nashe*, ed. Ronald B. McKerrow (London, 1958), I, 296 ("light foote" jigs).

20. This consideration has been advanced, from a different point of view, by C. J. Sisson, *Le Goût Publique et le Théâtre Elisabéthain* (Dijon, 1922).

21. Susanne K. Langer, *Feeling and Form* (New York, 1953), p. 331.

22. Vigorous antics and dancing, as well as acrobatics, were always on the outskirts, at least, of theatrical performances. See below, pp. 39-40, and Baskervill, *Eliz. Jig*, p. 46 and *passim*. In the Low Countries in 1586, Kemp pleased

Leicester and the Prince Elector by his "leaping into a dtich," R. C. Bald, "Leicester's Men in the Low Countries," *RES,* XIX (1943), 396. And a dozen years later, enthusiasm for Kemp's jigs was so great that it drew the fire of satirists. In 1592, the tumbling antics of "Nick" of Strange's men probably enlivened the second part of *The Seven Deadly Sins;* and a Nick's acrobatics entertained the court as late as December of 1601. E. K. Chambers, *The Elizabethan Stage* (Oxford, 1923), II, 347; *Henslowe Papers,* ed. W. W. Greg (London, 1907), p. 61, 1. 41; *Henslowe's Diary,* ed. W. W. Greg (London, 1904), I, fol. 95v, ll. 11-14. Nor might comic vigor be shown only by "leapinge" and dancing. If we are to believe a contemporary critic, the comedian Greene at the Red Bull in the years 1610-12 was noted for his "*Scylla*-barking, *stentor*-throated bellowings" and was still engaged in antics comparable to those associated with earlier actors or noted with distaste by solemn critics of the stage and others. Edwin Nungezer, *A Dictionary of Actors,* Cornell Studies in English, XIII (1929), 164 (the citation from *This Worlds Folly*). Those watching a performance of *John a Kent and John a Cumber* (*ca.* 1590-94) would see and hear a crew of clowns, a Moor, and a Maid Marian present an oration to visiting lords, rouse a bride and bridegroom on their wedding day, and perform a morris dance. *John a Kent,* Malone Soc., 1923, ll. 335-88, with ll. 1364-66, 554-645, 1354-88, 1443. Notice, too, the four singing and dancing "antiques," ll. 780-845.

23. I am quite aware that some editors of *The Taming of the Shrew* have considered "Soto" to be evidence either of a late insertion (cf. Fletcher's character of that name in *The Woman Pleased,* 1620) or of an earlier play belonging to the company performing Shakespeare's drama. But surely the obvious interpretation of the name—that it is akin to *sot* (fool, dolt, blockhead)—is correct. For the convenience of the reader, the text used for Shakespeare's plays, unless otherwise indicated, is *The Complete Plays and Poems of William Shakespeare,* ed. William Allan Neilson and Charles Jarvis Hill (New York, 1942). I have seen no need, however, to reproduce such insertions as "[*Aside*]."

24. For Sincklo, or Sincler, and his probable appearance, see Nungezer, *Dict. Actors,* p. 326 (the reference to Gaw's study); for the Farmer's Eldest Son and comparable figures, see Baskervill, *Eliz. Jig,* pp. 155, 192-93, 247-334.

25. *The Works of Sir David Lindsay of the Mount,* ed. Douglas Hamer, Scottish Text Soc., Ser. 3, No. 2, II, 1. 141 S-D, ll. 142-75, 208-37.

26. For a fuller discussion, see Baskervill, *Eliz. Jig,* e.g., pp. 189, 25-26, 29-30, 247-49, 253.

27. *Cobbler's Prophecy, 1594,* Malone Soc., 1914, ll. 1018-22.

28. Malone Soc., 1910, ll. 781-811. See also *Wit and Science,* Malone Soc., 1951, ll. 1032-39, 224-28, 1125-27; *Marriage of Wit and Wisdom,* ed. J. O. Halliwell, Shakesp. Soc., No. 31, pp. 59 ff. (scene x); *Nice Wanton,* in *Old English Plays, Dodsley,* ed. W. Carew Hazlitt (London, 1874) II, 168-73; *Three Ladies of London,* in *Old English Plays, Dodsley,* VI, 260-62.

29. Baskervill, *Eliz. Jig,* p. 355; see also pp. 249, 253, 256; and, e.g., for the dancing of Jack-o-Lent, p. 23.

30. Baskervill, *Eliz. Jig,* p. 250.

31. *Chief Pre-Shakespearean Dramas,* ed. Joseph Quincy Adams (N.Y., 1924), pp. 357 ff, ll. 265-87, 356, 378, 330-42, 555, 438-39, and 566-69.

32. Baskervill, *Eliz. Jig,* pp. 104-5, especially when discussing the contents of *Tarltons Newes out of Purgatorie.*

33. *Skialetheia,* sigs. D5r-v; see also, e.g., John Marston, *The Scourge of Villanie, 1599,* Bodley Head Quartos (New York, 1925), p. 106 (Satire X) and *The Roxburghe Ballads,* with notes by William Chappell (Ballad Soc., 1869-71), I, 59, ll. 115-16.

34. Baskervill, *MP,* XXIV, 423-28; see also Willard Farnham, "The Contending Lovers," *PMLA,* XXXV (1920), 247-323.

35. Spenser Soc., No. 38, p. 4.

36. The ballad was entered in the Stationers' Register on Sept. 4, 1564;

for a fuller discussion, with references to similar ballads, see Baskervill, *Eliz. Jig,* pp. 263-66. The convention of the ridiculous old wooer is reflected also in Sidney's portrayal of Basilius: e.g., "the prettie kind of dotage" he might have grown into had he continued writing verse; his sonnet on the appropriateness of age and love, which "being done, he looked verie curiously upon himselfe, sometimes fetching a little skippe, as if he had said, his strength had not yet forsaken him"; his reaction after being reproved by Zelmane, when he "was so appalled, that his legges bowed under him; his eyes lookt as though he would gladly hide himself; and his old blood going to his hart, a generall shaking all over his bodie possessed him." *Complete Works,* ed. Albert Feuillerat (Cambridge, 1912), I, 151, 149, 254.

37. Ed. R. Warwick Bond, *Early Plays from the Italian* (Oxford, 1911).

38. For lists of ballads involving a girl with varying degrees of innocence, see Baskervill, *Eliz. Jig,* pp. 205-7. See also Chaucer's treatment of Malyne, that young female with "kamus nose" and "buttokes brode," as it involves, e.g., a mock aube. R. E. Kaske, "An Aube in the *Reeve's Tale,*" *ELH,* XXVI (1959), p. 300. For Beatrice's song, see Baskervill, *Eliz. Jig,* p. 205 n. 4.

39. In the *Arcadia,* of course, one might also cite Sidney's description of Miso, in spite of its sophisticated veneer about decorum: "so handsome a belldame, that shee was counted a Witche, onely for her face, and her splay foote, neyther inwardly nor owtewardly, was there any good thing in her, but, that shee observed *Decorum;* having in a wretched body a froward mynde, neither was there any humour, in wch her husband and shee coulde ever agree, but in disagreeing. . . ." *Complete Works,* IV, 27.

40. For roistering females, see Baskervill, *Eliz. Jig,* p. 138 n. 3, citing, i.a., ballads on Meg of Westminster, entered August 27, 1590 and March 14, 1595. Although Mary Ambree might be represented as a valiant virago at "the siege of the Citty of Gaunt," see also Charles L. Felver, "Robert Armin's Fragment of a Bawdy Ballad of 'Mary Ambree,' " *N & Q,* CCV (1960), 14-16. For Armin, see, Nungezer, *Dict. Actors.*

41. See Baskervill, *Eliz. Jig,* pp. 19-21, citing, e.g., Dunbar's "Brash of Wooing"; *Roxburghe Ballads,* IX, 600, 846; *Bagford Ballads,* I, 519; and see his citation, pp. 21, 81-82, of situations in *The Bugbears* (I, iii), in *Promos and Cassandra,* etc.

42. Ed. R. B. McKerrow (Stratford-upon-Avon, 1922), p. 58; and, for Elderton's ballad, the occurrence of the refrain in *Horestes* and in C. Robinson's *Handful of Pleasant Delights,* pp. 91-92, see also Baskervill's discussion of the passage, *Eliz. Jig,* p. 101.

43. See Baskervill, *Eliz. Jig,* pp. 209, 237 n. 2.

44. See Baskervill, *Eliz. Jig,* p. 237 n. 2, and below pp. 18 n. 50, 41 n. 124. *Locrine,* in *The Shakespeare Apocrypha,* ed. C. F. Tucker Brooke (Oxford, 1929), pp. 42-43 (I, ii).

45. See James M. Osborn, "Benedick's Song in 'Much Ado,' " *TLS,* Nov. 7, 1958.

46. For this quotation, as well as the one immediately following, see Baskervill, *Eliz. Jig,* pp. 68-71, where one will also find a list of pertinent ballads, etc. See also Margaret Galway, "Flyting in Shakespeare's Comedies," *SAB,* X (1935), 183-91.

47. See Baskervill, *Eliz. Jig,* p. 24, as well as *A Transcript of the Registers of the Company of Stationers of London, 1554-1640,* ed. Edward Arber, I (London, 1875), 269 ("T purfoote"), 294 ("J alde," "Cowell"), 311 ("hudson"), 315 ("hackforth"), 328 ("shyngleton"), 388 ("greffeth"), etc.

48. Barber, *Shakespeare's Festive Comedy,* pp. 6-7; *RRD,* Malone Soc., 1934, ll. 515-21, 2011-23; *NW,* p. 170.

49. Robert Lemon, *Catalogue of a Collection of Printed Broadsides in the Possession of the Society of Antiquaries* (London, 1866), pp. 29-32.

50. See T. W. Craik, "The True Source of John Heywood's 'Johan Johan,' "

MLR, XLV (1950), 289-65; and W. Elton, *TLS*, Feb. 24, 1950, p. 128. Lyndsay, *Works*, II, "Proclamation," ll. 59-100. Ingeland, *Disobedient Child*, in *Old English Drama, Dodsley*, ed. W. Carew Hazlitt (London, 1874), II, 303-6; note also 295-99. *Cambises*, in *Chief Pre-Shakespearean Dramas*, ed. J. Q. Adams, ll. 126-292. *The Famous Victories of Henry the Fifth*, Shakespeare Quarto Facsimiles, No. 39, scene x, ll. 1-38. *Locrine*, IV, ii, 21-56. See also Baskervill, *Eliz. Jig*, pp. 127, 302-7.

51. *Cobbler's Prophecy*, e.g., ll. 91-115, 118-19, 1346-48. *Selimus*, Malone Soc., 1908, ll. 1877-1907 (scene xx), and its song on the shrew.

52. Baskervill, *Eliz. Jig*, e.g., pp. 138, 202-3; 64-65, 170-71, 322; 82-83, 90-91, 190 (the jig "betwene Jenkin the Collier and Nancie"), 287 (the "Blackman"); 266 (i.e., Pickleherring the miller), 276-81.

53. P. 42.

54. Sisson, *Lost Plays*, pp. 104, 80-124.

55. Baskervill, *Eliz. Jig*, pp. 170, 201, 226, 244, 332; and, e.g., the mock dedication of Nashe's *An Almond for a Parrot*, in *Works*, ed. McKerrow, III, 341.

56. Baskervill, *Eliz. Jig*, pp. 234-38 (especially p. 235), 286, 444-49.

57. See, e.g., the note about three memorable incidents: "[1] how Tarlton played the God Luz with a flitch of bacon at his back, and [2] how the Queen bade them take away the knave for making her to laugh so excessively, as he fought against her little dog, Perrico de Faldes, with his sword and long staff, and bade the Queen take off her mastie; and [3] what my Lord Sussex and Tarlton said to one another. The three things that make a woman lovely." *Calendar of State Papers, Domestic Series, 1581-90* (London, 1865), p, 541. Here apparently was successful burlesque, some mock bravery and cowardice, and some extemporizing, perhaps in a generally satiric manner, although Baskervill believes that the last sentence refers to "a court-of-love debate." *Eliz. Jig*, p. 98. For the nature of Tarlton's acting, as well as his verses and his literary work, see M. C. Bradbrook, *The Rise of the Common Player* (Cambridge, Mass., 1962), pp. 163-77. Miss Bradbrook points out that Tarlton's art "represented the first stage of separating clowning from the traditional folk sports which in style and subject it still recalled" (p. 164).

58. Especially when Ralph insists on his prophet's role: e.g., ll. 236-44, 393-98. See also *Selimus*, ll. 1944-47; and Derricke, continuing his pose in *Famous Victories*, e.g., ii, 54-62.

59. P. 253.

60. Malone Soc., 1927.

61. Above, p. 11 n. 17, 14-15; below, pp. 21-22.

62. Pp. 251, 257, 324.

63. E.g., ll. 1409-48.

64. See his account of his valorous deeds (ll. 198-206, 285-95), his false pride in being "homely clad" (ll. 274-84), his lust (ll. 296-97). In contrast with the other characters mentioned here, however, Soldier is treated sympathetically; though there are base soldiers, the excellent one is truly noble (e.g., ll. 435-48), even though he may be censured for bluntness by those whom he attacks (e.g., ll. 373-74, 386).

65. E.g., ll. 228-32, 408-14.

66. *Three Ladies of London*, p. 254; Revesby Play, ll. 333-37.

67. For details, and for references to plays as well, see Baskervill, *Eliz. Jig*, pp. 200-1, 239, 297-98, and the text of Jig no. 14 (1586); Chambers, *Eliz. Stage*, II, 179 n. 5.

68. See, e.g., Baskervill, *Eliz. Jig*, pp. 58 n. 1, 100, 101 n. 1, 318-19 (citing, i.a., *Roxburghe Ballads*, VII, 268-72; see also 272-78); and Ralph's mock prophecy, *Cobler's Prophecy*, ll. 800-13.

69. Especially prevalent, Baskervill suggests, during Christmas pastimes when "the spirit of parody and burlesque ruled." *Eliz. Jig*, p. 62. For the details immediately following (the Colchester minstrel, Roy and Barlow, the 1557 notice),

see pp. 48-49. For Fenton (A forme of christian pollicie gathered out of French), see p. 60.

70. Tell-Trothes New-yeares Gift, ed. F. J. Furnivall, New Shakesp. Soc., Ser. 6, No. 2, See also Transcript Stationers' Register, I, 270 ("Tom Tell Truth," July 22, 1565). For Tarltons Jests, see below, pp. 27-28. That Tarlton's forte was comic and satiric song, see Baskervill, Eliz. Jig, pp. 101 ff. For a connection between the news motif and the ship of fools, see, e.g., Hyckescorner, in Old English Plays, Dodsley, ed. W. Carew Hazlitt (London, 1874), I, 161-65, 169, 185; also C. H. Herford, Studies in the Literary Relations of England and Germany in the Sixteenth Century (Cambridge, 1886), pp. 370-72. See also the variation in Cobbler's Prophecy, ll. 608-84.

71. Baskervill, Eliz. Jig, pp. 22-23, 46-47.

72. The Works of George Peele, ed. A. H. Bullen (London, 1888), I.

73. The Complete Works of Thomas Nashe, ed. Alexander B. Grosart, I (London, 1883), 166, 175-76; Works, ed. McKerrow, I, 92, 100. The first quotations are from Martins Months Mind, a tract probably not by Nashe. The Jack-o-Lent reported by Machyn probably was executed, and his testament may have been delivered; see the titles noted by Baskervill (Eliz. Jig, pp. 46-47): ". . . then cam the dullo and a sawden, and then [a priest?] shreyffyng Jake-of-lent on horssbake, and a do[ctor] ys fezyssyon, and then Jake-of-lent['s] wyff brow[ght him] ys fessyssyons and bad save ys lyff, and he shuld [give him] a thowsand li for ys labur; and then cam the carte with the wyrth hangyd with cloth of gold, and full of ban[ners] and mynsterels plahyng and syngyng. . . ." The Diary of Henry Machyn, ed. John Gough Nichols, Camden Soc., XLII (1847-48), p. 33.

74. See, e.g., John Leon Lievsay, "Newgate Penitents: Further Aspects of Elizabethan Pamphlet Sensationalism," Huntington Libr. Quar., VII (1943), 47-69. For Tarlton's use of a burlesque testament, see, e.g., Tarltons Jests and News out of Purgatory, Shakesp. Soc., No. 20, pp. 35-36.

75. Tarlton, e.g., was remembered for his extempore verses. See, e.g., James Orchard Halliwell, Tarltons Jests, p. xviii ff.; Nashe, Works, ed. McKerrow, I, 188; Lyly's statement that "These tinkers termes, and barbers iestes first Tarleton on the stage, / Then Martin in his bookes of lies, hath put in euery page," Complete Works, ed. R. Warwick Bond (Oxford, 1902) III, 426. After a play, "as Tarltons use was," everyone might "throw up his theame," Tarltons Jests, p. 28; cf. also p. 27: ". . . it was his custome to sing extempore of theames given him," and Transcript Stationer's Register, II, 526 (Aug. 2, 1589): "A sorowfull newe sonnette, Intituled Tarltons Recantacon vppon this theame gyven him by a gentleman at the Bel[le] savage without Ludgate (nowe or ells never) beinge the laste theame he songe." See also Chettle, Kind-hartes Dream p. 44; Letter-Book of Gabriel Harvey, ed. E. J. L. Scott, Camden Soc., New Series XXXIII (1884), p. 67. According to Stow, Robert Wilson also was noted for a "quicke delicate refined extemporall wit." Annales, or A Generall Chronicle of England (London, 1631), p. 698, col. a.

76. The italics are mine.

77. See Baskervill, Eliz. Jig, pp. 49-50, 70-71, 166-69, 174-79, 202-3, and the "Dialogues," passim. For forms, ideas, and attitudes in plays of the Heywood circle, see Pearl Hogrefe, The Sir Thomas More Circle (Urbana, Ill., 1959), 274-75, 289-97, 306-9, 337, 278-88, etc.

78. Transcript Stationers' Register, II, 360 (Sept. 18, 1579); see also Cobbler's Prophecy, e.g., ll. 348-92, and Baskervill, Eliz. Jig, pp. 166-69, 176-79, as well as Velvet Breeches, Cloth Breeches, Ruffling Richard, Margery Sweete, Mannerly Margery (Greenes News).

79. Countryman is censured especially for his grasping cruelty, Courtier for his debts, Scholar for his slanderous attacks, etc. The quotation that follows is from the 1594 text, with but one variation: its line numbered "323" is here divided after a rime, and thus fourteen lines are balanced against the fourteen beginning with "Then."

80. The Fool's prophecy in *Lear* (III, ii, 80-95) indicates the vitality of this motif. It also provides the basic framing device for the *Cobbler's Prophecy;* and therein the satirically mocking, rather than the riddling, prophecy verges into the area of the wise, relatively extended aside that effects social or religious satire (e.g., ll. 122-95). For the notation that neither the "Book of Prophecy" and the man who kept it nor he who played husbandry had been apprehended, see *Letters and Papers, Foreign and Domestic, Henry VIII,* XII, Pt. 1, 585. Husbandry had criticized gentlemen (above, p. 11 n. 17).

81. For a discussion of Nashe's play, see Barber, *Shakespeare's Festive Comedy,* p. 58-86.

82. As edited by C. F. Tucker Brooke and Nathaniel Burton Paradise, *English Drama 1580-1642* (N.Y., 1933). When not otherwise specified, the numbering of act, scene, and line is that of the plays in this anthology. Note also the comedian's interpolations during the game of cards (III, ii, 126 ff.) and see, e.g., the lost play *Game of Cards* (1582), presumably a belated morality. Chambers, *Eliz. Stage,* IV, 158; see also I, 268; II, 37; IV, 99; and Wilson's lines in *The Three Ladies of London,* pp. 258, 265 (Fraud, the "clubbish knave"; Usury, the "hard-hearted knave"; Simony, the "diamon' dainty knave"; Dissimulation, the "spiteful knave of spades").

83. *Three Ladies of London,* pp. 253, 288, 313, 327-28, etc. See e.g., *Cobbler's Prophecy,* ll. 129, 169, 171, 237, 243-44, 247, etc.; ll. 685-94, 874-78, 901-05, 930 ff. Although Simplicity's "mistakings" appear constantly, there is less emphasis upon them at any one time than is true for Ignorance in *Wit and Science,* Moros in *The Longer Thou Livest,* Newfangle in *Like Will to Like,* or Mouse in *Mucedorus.* In view of Wilson's concern with social satire, this seems understandable. Yet pointed wisdom is constantly apparent in roles for the principal comedian. Aside from the examples that follow, note such remarks, even in the role of Derricke, as that found in scene iv of *The Famous Victories,* ll. 57-59.

84. As it has been noted above, the technique of Simplicity's role in *The Three Ladies* is quite similar to that of Ralph's in the *Cobbler's Prophecy:* see, e.g., Simplicity's comments on Dissimulation ("Semblation") or on Simony, pp. 311-12, 259-60, 327. See also the earlier comments here about the *Cobbler's Prophecy.* The choric function of the principal comedian, however, is so well known as almost to preclude comment; see, e.g., Lysander Cushman, *The Devil and the Vice in English Dramatic Literature before Shakespeare,* Studien zur Englischen Philologie, VI (Halle, 1900), pp. 138-44.

85. Scene ii, 124-30, 156-59; 22-25, 35-39, 93-95.

86. This effect was noted, i.a., by writers on logic and rhetoric; see Sister Miriam Joseph, *Shakespeare's Use of the Arts of Language* (N.Y., 1947), pp. 368 ff.

87. In this respect, a notation of November 12, 1589 seems pertinent: players of "comon playes and enterludes" are said to have taken "uppon them to handle in their plaies certen matters of Divinytie and of State unfitt to be suffred." *Acts of the Privy Council,* New Series XVIII (London, 1899), 214-16. In addition to what has been noted already, see Lyly's *Pappe with an Hatchet* for references to Martin and to Elderton ballads that will be "better than those of Bonner, or the ierks for a Iesuit." The first "begins, come tit me come tat me, come throw a halter at me." *Works,* III, 398. On February 13, 1581, there was licensed a "Ballad Intituled A gentle Jyrke for the Jesuit." *Transcript Stationers' Register,* II, 388. "Come tit me," emanating from Elderton and an ale-house, may be meant, therefore, as a parody of this earlier production. For the continuity of this satire, see Baskervill, *Eliz. Jig,* pp. 43, 47, 55-66.

88. Chambers, *Eliz. Stage,* I, 294. See also *Cobbler's Prophecy,* ll. 641-50, 1222-25; *Three Ladies of London,* pp. 271-72, 287-88.

89. *Henslowe's Diary,* I, 13 (7, l. 14); II, 152. See, e.g., *Polychronicon Ranulphi Higden Monachi Cestrensis,* ed. C. Babington, J. R. Lumby, Rolls Series, No. 41, VI, 330-35. On the popularity of Higden, I, x1-x1v; C. L. Kings-

ford, *English Historical Literature in the Fifteenth Century* (Oxford, 1913), pp. 137-39, 23-24, 32-37, 279. On other names of the female pope, see J. J. I. von Döllinger, *Fables Respecting the Popes of the Middle Ages,* tr. Alfred Plummer (London, 1871), p. 37.

90. *1 TR,* Shakespeare Quarto Facsimiles, No. 40, scene xi, with prose interspersed.

91. *AYLI,* III, iii, 64 ff. For "A Ballet of O swete Olyuer Leaue me not behind the" (Aug. 6, 1584), as well as an answer two weeks later, see Baskervill, *Eliz. Jig,* pp. 181-82. For a medley in MS Harl. 7578 (". . . then came peres of pelton / Jenken and dawey / Sad olywer / abyde abyde / and I wil bere / yow company") and for similar references in the works of Nashe, Dekker, Jonson, etc., see *Eliz. Jig,* pp. 182-83. For burlesques of laments in ballads, in other nondramatic literature, and in plays, see p. 181 n. 3, as well as *12th N,* II, iii, 110-12; and above, p. 16 n. 38, for Chaucer's mock aube.

92. In the *pastourelle* tradition, there might be represented the way in which an aristocratic character condescendingly woos a shepherdess. Such a one, when interrupted or denied, can depart "without chagrin, confiding to the reader, even like Thibaut de Navarre, *n'oi cure de tel gent!"* Helen Estabrook Sandison, *The "Chanson d'Aventure,"* Bryn Mawr College Monographs, XII, pp. 15-16. For rival wooing and a comic show of boldness in matter reminiscent of Adam de la Halle's *Robin and Marion,* which had passed into English tradition, sometimes with farcical overtones, see above p. 19 n. 56.

93. For Robin Goodfellow in Christmas games of England, see Baskervill, *Eliz. Jig,* pp. 22, 62, 92; and Baldwin Maxwell, "Wily Beguilded," *SP,* XIX (1922), 231-32 (citing Jonson, Heywood, and others). *Tarltons Jests,* p. 49; *Transcript Stationers' Register,* II, 559.

94. Robin's epistle, after that of the Cobbler, in *The Cobbler of Canterburie. Tarltons Jests,* p. 110. Robin's appearence as a "lob of spirits" (*MND,* II, i, 16), if "lob" is to be taken literally, may have been similar to the possibly grotesque-like appearance of Tarlton himself. Bradbrook, *Rise of the Common Player,* p. 166. If so, it would not be discordant with Milton's "lubber fiend" of "hairy strength" ("L'Allegro," ll. 110, 112). In *Wily Beguiled* (1596-1606, though based, perhaps, on an earlier play) Robin Goodfellow is a clownish, sometimes lubberly, goblin, a "Calue-skin companion" (l. 313), an inhabitant of ale-houses and associated with Cobbler and Shoemaker (ll. 483, 1640-71), one who plays the "Bugbeare" and frightens all (ll. 478-80), especially by putting on his "flashing red nose" and his "Christmas Calues skin" (ll. 116-17, 1254-58), one who would perpetrate "the art of Knauerie" (ll. 2239-43 and *passim*) and who thereby is connected with social satire (ll. 723-34, 2021-75), even as he is beaten. Malone Soc., 1912. His is the role assumed by the Devil's assistant in *Grim the Collier* (1600), wherein he is dressed "in a suit of leather, close to his body; his face and hands coloured russet-colour, with a flail." *Old English Plays, Dodsley,* ed. W. Carew Hazlitt (London, 1874), VIII, 442 (IV, i). To Jonson he is "Puck-hairy"; the "hine" of Maudlin, the witch; as well as the witch's devil; he also may "daunce about the Forrest" and "firke it like a Goblin." *The Sad Shepherd,* "The Persons of the Play," "The Argument of the third Act," and III, i, 1-19. Cf. the German *pickle-härin,* i.e., a figure with a hairy or leafy dress. In *The Devil is an Ass,* I, i, 18, Jonson utilizes both the idea of Robin Goodfellow's pranks and that of playing "round Robbin," i.e., playing the incubus, a suggestion found elsewhere, e.g., in Harsnet's *Popish Imposture* (1603). *Ben Jonson,* X, 220, and G. L. Kittredge, "The Friar's Lantern and Friar Rush," *PMLA,* XV (1900), 415-41; cf. also *Wily Beguiled,* ll. 723-34. See also Baskervill, *Eliz. Jig,* p. 148; James Orchard Halliwell, *Illustrations of Shakespeare's Fairy Myth,* Shakesp. Soc., No. 26 (London, 1845), pp. 120-80; K. M. Briggs, *The Anatomy of Puck: An Examination of Fairy Beliefs among Shakespeare's Contemporaries and Successors* (London, 1959), p. 79.

95. See, e.g., Daniel C. Boughner, *The Braggart in Renaissance Comedy*

(Minneapolis, 1954), pp. 91 and n. 8, 94-99, 178, etc.; "Vice, Braggart, and Falstaff," *Anglia,* LXXII (1954-55), 35-61.

96. See P. W. Long, "The Purport of Lyly's *Endimion,*" *PMLA,* XXIV (1909), 164-84; Bernard F. Huppé, "Allegory of Love in Lyly's Courtly Comedies," *ELH,* XIV (1947), 102-7. It is difficult, however, to see Semele as Honor.

97. Jonson, *Every Man out of his Humour,* V, ii (1601 Quarto).

98. Baskervill, *English Elements, passim.*

99. E.g., Alfred von Martin, *Sociologie der Renaissance* (Frankfurt am Main, 1949), *passim.*

100. *Anatomy of Abuses,* I, 55-56, 58-59.

101. See below, pp. 63-65.

102. In the following pages, I use the word *dizzard* for characters creating such an impression. For the use in seasonal games of the leader or presenter and his foil the jester, see, e.g., Charles Read Baskervill, "Conventional Features of Medwall's *Fulgens and Lucres,*" *MP,* XXIV (1926-27), 435-38; and above, pp. 24-26. In the paragraphs that follow an inconsistency will be noted in the spelling of *Berowne,* for I use in the text of this study the quarto and folio spelling. The italics in the following lines are mine.

103. Chambers, *William Shakespeare,* II, 332.

104. See, e.g., Doran, *Endeavors of Art,* pp. 310-22.

105. For a comic comparison between a clock and a woman's tongue, see, e.g., *A Looking-Glass for London and England . . . 1594,* Malone Soc., 1932, ll. 708-10.

106. O. J. Campbell, e.g., relates the comic figures in this play to the *commedia dell' arte* and believes that the drama is modelled upon the Progresses of Elizabeth. *Studies in Shakespeare, Milton, and Donne,* Univ. of Michigan Publications in Language and Literature, I (1925), 3-45. I believe that the appropriate background is a good deal wider; see also Boughner, *The Braggart,* pp. 70-99, 178, and also "The Braggart in Italian Renaissance Comedy," *PMLA,* LVIII (1943), 42-107. For the song referred to, see *The Alleyn Papers,* ed. J. Payne Collier, Shakesp. Soc., No. 18 (1845), pp. 29-30; and above, p. 17, as well as references to the Spaniard, p. 21. See also Baskervill, *Eliz. Jig,* pp. 209, 237, 261, 281 (citing, i.a., "Good luck at last: or, The Art of Scorning discovered"). See also *Ralph Roister Doister,* III, iii, wherein a mock requiem for the dead ridicules the braggart's pose of dying for love.

107. See above, p. 22 n. 75, and Bradbrook, *Rise of the Common Player,* pp. 166-67.

108. V, i, 134-36; and see Lyndsay, *Works,* II, "Proclamation," ll. 160-75.

109. Eric John Dobson, *English Pronunciation, 1500-1700* (Oxford, 1957), I, 398; Helge Kökeritz, *Shakespeare's Pronunciation* (New Haven, 1953), pp. 222-25.

110. E. W. Talbert, "The Purpose and Technique of Jonson's *Poetaster,*" *SP,* XLII (1945), 238-39.

111. Boughner, *The Braggart,* pp. 11-12, 15-16, 16-17, etc.

112. For the ballad and for French brawls, see *Love's Labour's Lost,* ed. Richard Davis, Arden Shakespeare (Cambridge, Mass., 1951), pp. 66-67, 46; and above, p. 13 n. 22. For the hobbyhorse, see Baskervill, *Eliz. Jig,* p. 356, and E. K. Chambers, *The English Folk Play* (Oxford, 1933).

113. Baskervill, *Eliz. Jig,* pp. 267, 273, 311-12, 322-25; Bond, *Early Plays from the Italian,* pp. xxix-xxx.

114. Above, p. 23, and, e.g., ll. 118, 222-25, 350-70.

115. The following examples will, perhaps, suffice. The use of dialect and malapropisms stretches from the role of Mak, for example, (Towneley "Second Shepherds Play") to that of People (*Respublica,* 1553) or to the use of rural speech in both the *Trial of Treasure* (pr. 1567) and W. Wager's *Enough is as Good as a Feast* (1559-69). Some characteristic corruptions of names are "Flebishiten" for Physician (*Enough is as Good,* Tudor Facsimiles, sig. F3v); "brother Snappes" for Sapience (*Trial of Treasure,* Tudor Facsimiles, sig. C2); "Diricke Quintine" for Discipline, "Pinenuttree" for Piety; "Arse out of fashion"

for Exercitation (*The Longer Thou Livest,* Tudor Facsimiles, sig. B4v). For song and dance, see *Trial of Treasure, passim,* and the examples that follow in the text. The similarity between social satire in medieval drama and in the medieval sermon has been amply illustrated by Gerald Robert Owst, *Literature and the Pulpit in Medieval England* (Cambridge, 1933), pp. 210-547. Although one must question Owst's point of view as regards derivations, note the proud, angry, and boastful Herods and Caiaphases; the Towneley Pilate, dicing with the Romans and trying to wangle the prize by tricks and flattery; the Pilate of the *Ludus Coventriae* and his wife, going to bed quite tipsy. John Skelton's *Magnyfycence* (1515-23) and David Lyndsay's *Satire of the Three Estates* (1540-44) are replete with social satire; and elsewhere Sin, for example, installs All for Money as magistrate (T. Lupton, *All for Money,* 1559-77). Reflections of the *caballarius gloriosus* and of related comic types can be seen in Watkin (Digby *Innocents*), Pride (Henry Medwall, *Nature,* 1490-1501), Hyckescorner (*Hyckescorner,* 1513-16, but selling in 1582), Sensual Appetite (John Rastell, *Nature of the Four Elements, ca.* 1517), Courtly Abusion (*Magnyfycence*), Youth (*Youth,* 1523-29), Nicholas Newfangle (Ulpian Fulwell, *Like Will to Like,* 1562-68), etc. See Boughner, *Anglia,* LXXII, 35-61. Ribaldry, obscenity, and low life might also be mentioned here: e.g., Cain in the Towneley "Killing of Abel," the jests of the accusers in the Towneley "Trial of Joseph and Mary," many lines in *Mankind,* Hyckescorner and Imagination in Newgate together (*Hyckescorner*). See also Taverner in Rastell's *Nature of the Four Elements,* Idleness in *The Marriage of Wit and Wisdom* (1570-79), and such names as Hance the drunkard, Tom Tosspot, Ralph Roister, Cuthbert Cutpurse, Pierce Pickpurse in *Like Will to Like.* The medieval jests about shrewish wives, for example, and the portrayals of Noah's wife in drama are so well known that their mention seems supererogatory. See also Joseph's lines addressed to an audience on how men must please their wives or suffer much "dis-ease," in the Coventry "Weaver's Play" (ed. Hardin Craig, E.E.T.S., E.S., 87), ll. 463-70. Then there is the disarrayed young lover, threatening but sore afraid, in "The Woman Taken in Adultery" of the *Ludus Coventriae;* and for the overheard confession, etc., see the motifs in *Recueil de Farces Françaises Inédites du XVᵉ Siècle,* ed. Gustave Cohen (Cambridge, Mass, 1949). There one finds marital and extra-marital goings-on with lovers escaping in chests and sacks and with other twists on jealous husbands and shrewish or unfaithful wives, who are aided by clerks or by supposed watchers who fail to whistle. Therein such dupers are duped as a lecherous monk, three disguised lovers, and the sharper fooled by the fool. One finds debates by "estates" and professions; pastoral themes, such as the delights of the country; imaginary exploits in imaginary lands; and mutual complaints of husbands and wives. There also appear confessions in which the mock priest hears of his wife's or his daughter's immorality and confessions or absolutions that exist more nearly for their own sake, as of the bigot or the braggart. Complaints both religious and secular occur as do the motifs of news from purgatory and a crying of wares. A mountebank-doctor appears, and a fantastic Latin is used during the course of teaching the arts to three Parisian ladies. Song and dance appear frequently, and there is a constant emphasis upon bawdry, with some pieces relying almost solely on gross words and phrases, unless they embody such an action as Xantippe is said to have perpetrated on Socrates.

116. *Mary Magdalene,* ed. F. J. Furnivall, E.E.T.S., E.S., 70, ll. 1178-1209, as well as the entire scene; *Mankind,* ed. F. J. Furnivall and A. W. Pollard, E.E.T.S., E.S., 91, ll. 659 ff. Note also, e.g., Mak's goodnight prayer, "Manus tuas commendo / Poncio Pilato" (Towneley, "Second Shepherds," ll. 266-67), Pharoah's "Hefe uppe youre hartis ay to Mahowmnde" (York, "Exodus," ll. 401-02, and the *sursum corda* of the Mass), or the parody on methods of instruction effected through the figure of Ignorance (John Redford, *Wit and Science,* ll. 460-561).

117. See, e.g., George Fenwick Jones, " 'Christis Kirk,' 'Peblis to the Play,' and the German Peasant Brawl," *PMLA,* LXVIII (1953), 1101-25. Sensual

Appetite in *The Four Elements* (*ca.* 1517) "syngyth this song *and* dan[c]yth with all And euermore maketh countenaunce accordying To the mater *and* all the other aunswer lyke wyse." The vice in *Like Will to Like* (1562-68) cries, "And now will I dance, and now will I prance." And from Jonson as late as *The Devil is an Ass* (1616), one hears of the vice of the old school, who is entertaining at a sheriff's dinner and might at the end "Skip with a rime o' the Table" and "take his *Almaine*-leape into a custard." *Nature of the Four Elements*, Tudor Facsimile Texts, sig. E6; *Like Will to Like*, in *Old English Plays*, Dodsley, ed. W. Carew Hazlitt (London, 1874), III, 332 (see also the other song and dance therein, including an "evil-favoured" one); *Devil is an Ass*, I, i, 95-99.

118. Sigs. civ-c2; and note, e.g., William Keith's "Ballet declaringe the fal of the whore of babylon intytuled Tye thy mare tom boye wt other," wherein the Catholic church was represented as an unmanageable horse. J. Payne Collier, *Bibliographical and Critical Account of the Rarest Books in the English Language* (New York, 1866), II, 196-200. For further details and for other examples similar to Keith's ballad, see Baskervill, *Eliz. Jig*, p. 46.

119. Above, pp. 5-6, 8; see also Robert Withington, "The Ancestry of the Vice," *Speculum*, VII (1932), 525-29. For the "roarer," see Boughner, *The Braggart*, pp. 161-62, 165-66, 177, etc. For the relationship between the hungry knave and a particular actor, see Baldwin Maxwell, *Studies in Beaumont, Fletcher, and Massinger* (Chapel Hill, 1939), pp. 74-83.

120. E.g., *Cambises*, ll. 971-93; *Locrine*, IV, ii; *Selimus*, ll. 1908 ff. See also *Looking Glass*, ll. 2237-2311, 1325-26, 1909-68, and scenes iii, vii.

121. Even when one allows for the fact that the servant breaks into verse. *The Wounds of Civil War . . . 1594*, Malone Soc., 1910, ll. 1750-1805; *Looking Glass*, ll. 370-78, 385-99, 629-43; and, e.g., scene iii *passim*. See also the rude riming of Strumbo, *Locrine*, II, iii, 55-58, 67-75, as well as ll. 82-88.

122. E.g., *Cambises*, ll. 126-302; *Soliman and Perseda*, in *Old English Plays*, Dodsley, V, 266-76, 278-80, 292-95, 311-14, 342-47, 363-64, etc.; *Locrine*, II, v, 94; *Famous Victories*, xvii, xiii, xix, 16-21. For the resolution of cowardice into wisdom, see below, p. 47 n. 141.

123. E.g., *Locrine*, II, ii, 42-91; *Famous Victories*, x; *Cambises*, ll. 126 ff.

124. *Locrine*, I, ii; III, iii; IV, ii, 21-54. *Looking Glass*, ll. 1293-1359, wherein Adam's master, the Smith, becomes a wittol through the clown's chop-logic and physical strength; in this respect, see also ll. 258-75, 1706-27.

125. E.g., *Looking Glass*, iii, vii; *Famous Victories*, ii, xvi; *Locrine*, II, ii, 1-36, III, iii; *Cambises*, ll. 813-42. E.g., *Looking Glass*, ll. 205, 1352-54, 1880-93; *Locrine*, I, ii, 45-50, II, iv, 19 ff., and above, pp. 19-20, 30-31.

126. Especially when the principal comedian enters: e.g., *Selimus*, ll. 1878-79; *Cobbler's Prophecy*, ll. 607-8; *Famous Victories*, ii, 27, 31; vii, 1-5; xix, 1-3; *Cambises*, ll. 126, 742-44, 1133. Here, too, might be mentioned the laughter resulting from a reference to the stage, to the play, or to the audience: e.g., "O no bodie tell her I am vnder the stoole," *Cobbler's Prophecy*, l. 76; "Here is the right picture of that fellow that sits in the corner," "You think I am going to market to buy roast meat, do you not? I thought so; but you are deceived...," "But yonder is a fellow that gapes to bite me, or else to eat that which I sing," "Now, sirrah, hast eaten up my song? and ye have, ye shall eat no more today, / For everybody may see your belly is grown bigger with eating up our play. / He has fill'd his belly, but I am never a whit the better, / Therefore I'll go seek some victuals; and 'member, for eating up my song you shall be my debtor," *Three Ladies*, pp. 288, 310, 327-28. See also *Locrine*, IV, ii, 21-22; *Selimus*, ll. 1879-83; *Cambises*, ll. 953-64. This particular trick has been commented upon already. Above, p. 3 n. 1; that it can be used in an effective and sophisticated manner, see below, pp. 249-50.

127. *The True Tragedy of Richard the Third, 1594*, Malone Soc., 1929, ll. 580-84; see above, p. 39 n. 115 (Taverner, etc.).

128. See T. M. Parrott, "Mak and Archie Armstrong," *MLN*, LIX (1944),

297-304; R. C. Cosby, "The Mak Story and Its Folklore Analogues," *Speculum,* XX (1945), 310-17.

129. See also Homer A. Watts, "The Dramatic Unity of the 'Secunda Pastorum'" *Essays and Studies in Honor of Carleton Brown* (N.Y., 1940), pp. 158-66. The author, of course, is not concerned with the variation in laughter here being considered. Nor is Miss Ola Elizabeth Winslow, although similar situations are indicated in her *Low Comedy as a Structural Element in English Drama* (Menasha, Wis., 1926), e.g., pp. 41-43, 69 *(Horestes),* 77-82.

130. E.g., *Works,* I, 432-34, 22, 87, 178-79.

131. *H V,* III, i, 1; ii, 1. In this respect, see also, e.g., the institution of the Boy Bishop: "... on Saint *Nicholas* night commonly the Scholars of the Countrey make them a Bishop, who like a foolish boy, goeth about blessing and preaching with so childish termes, as maketh the people laugh at his foolish counterfaite speeches." George Puttenham, *Arte of English Poesie,* ed. Gladys Doidge Willcock and Alice Walker (Cambridge, 1936), p. 273. See Chambers, *Medieval Stage,* I, 274-371; II, 56-57; Young, *Drama Medieval Church,* I, 104-11; II, 99-100. What seems pertinent is the spirit of hilarity, rather than the attitude implicit in the remark that familiarity breeds contempt, especially among the poorly paid and the poorly educated. Note also the contrast between what is considered here and what is noted, however briefly, in George Kitchin, *A Survey of Burlesque and Parody in English* (Edinburgh, 1931), pp. 1-67.

132. Such a technique is akin to the motif of escaping punishment by means of a jest, as, e.g., in the tales of the sixth day in Boccaccio's *Decameron, etc.* Note how the motif is handled by E. E. Stoll, *Shakespeare Studies* (N.Y., 1927), pp. 447-50.

133. Or he may appear as an uninspired chorus; for from the point of view of the spectator, speeches that anticipate or even comment mockingly upon a stage situation lose any vicious or moralistic tone and approach the nature of a simple chorus, soliloquy, or aside, the more the play, or the emphasis of an individual scene, lacks a driving didactic purpose. L1. 634-41, 676-77 vs. ll. 126-306, 754-842. Notice also the choric lines, 602-20; especially 610-12, 732-53, 938-50, 1133-58, etc.

134. See Whiting, *SP,* LXII, 31-40.

135. For Tattle, see *The Staple of News,* "The first Intermeane after the first Act," ll. 23-28. Also pertinent for the general consideration just mentioned is what has been written above, pp. 36-39, etc. See also Withington, *Speculum,* VII, 525-29; and his "Braggart, Devil, and Vice: A Note on the Development of Comic Figures in the Early English Drama," *Speculum,* XI, (1936), 124-29; Boughner, *Anglia,* LXXII, 35-61; Mares, *Huntington Libr. Quar.,* XXII, 11-29.

136. The rigidity that Bergson speaks of in his analysis of laughter is certainly applicable to the stage situation, though not, momentarily, to Bottom; for in this play-world the incompatibility of reason and love is generally pertinent, and Titania has fallen into an obviously anticipated situation.

137. *Poetaster,* "Prologue," after "The third sounding," l. 14.

138. Elsewhere I have urged that only by a careful consideration of the dramatic order of *Poetaster* can Jonson's purpose be understood, although he is concerned usually with developing derisive contexts. Thus in the banquet scene (IV, v), within the larger bounds of what Jonson takes for historical fact, and aside from laughter at his butts (Albius, Crispinus, Tucca, Chloe), a different comic emphasis is effected by laughter connected with the witty comments suited to the nature of the mythological masquing and directed by the witty participants at themselves in disguise and, hence, at the incongruity between their immediate god-like appearances and the lowly position of poets. Ironically, when Caesar interrupts the banquet, obviously unaware of this aspect of the scene, he remains adamant in banishing Ovid, in spite of the pleas of Meccœnas and Horace (IV, vi, 60-61). Thus a perception of such a variation in laughter illumines the purpose of the play, as well as Jonson's technique in dramatizing the difficult situation of

banishing a poet while defending poetry. Aside from the fact that this variation in laughter speaks for itself, any other interpretation of the play so far advanced removes Jonson, i.a., from the side of Mecœnas and Horace, and ignores the majority of Jonson's lines. *SP,* XLII, 241-47.

139. *Ben Jonson,* IX, 732.

140. See also Ralph Nash, "The Comic Intent of *Volpone,*" *SP,* XLIV (1947), 26-40.

141. Moreover, as it has been noted, when a comic figure is given valid comments on a situation in which he has been, or in which he is, involved, he approaches, at least momentarily, the position of a witty derider, but a witty derider of himself as well as of others (see, e.g., *1 H IV,* II, ii, 36-37, 49-50, 52; *Cobbler's Prophecy,* ll. 460-70; *Selimus,* ll. 1958-61; etc.). Thereby he does not persist in a ridiculous pose, like the braggart, or remain constant in the attitude whereby he was, or might be, the object of derision. This is also true when the comedian is given longer speeches that provide extra-dramatic moments of soliloquy, which may be chorus-like or simply revealing of character. In such lines there also can be found "gleeks" embodying general or specific notes of satire on the actual world or on the stage-world; and if effectively written, such speeches can also dispel a past context of derision and aid in dispelling a future one. In crude form, without a gleek, the admitted comic fright of Ambidexter, followed by his account of how he laughed at himself, could have produced such an effect, had the context of the previous scene been anything other than that of slap-stick farce. In those scenes, by the very nature of the case, there would not be applicable the derision of society appropriate to the pretentious (*Cambises,* ll. 293-302). Similarly, Strumbo's constant antic accompaniment of the serious action, as well as his low degree, makes it doubtful that much in the nature of derision was ever pointed in his direction, and certainly not when he insists that he is dead and cannot speak, or even when as a vocal "corpse," he runs away at the cry of thieves (*Locrine,* II, v, 70-73, 94-95, 97-98, 114-16). More to the point is the speech of Basilisco, hungry for honor, as Strumbo never is, with its obvious attempt at a true wit and a comic didacticism on the theme of *ubi sunt* (*Solimon & Perseda,* pp. 363-64). Although Basilisco's wit does not dominate his pretensions to conventionally recognized aspects of character—i.e., the gifts of nature and benefits of study—with the last turn of his speech, Basilisco's chorus-like anticipation of events moves away from a persistence in a pose of bravery:

> Faith, he can doe little that cannot speake,
> And he can doe lesse that cannot runne away.
> Then sith man's life is as a glasse, and a phillip
>   may cracke it,
> Mine is no more, and a bullet may pearce it:
> Therefore I will play least in sight.

Shakespeare, undoubtedly, knew both the first and the third stage-situations here referred to (*1 H IV,* II, iv, 426; *K J,* I, i, 244); and without regard for his doubtful authorship of *Locrine,* like the regular theater-goer, he probably knew that play as well. There is, however, no need to pin-point scenes. Any enlarged chorus-like gleek approaches the nature of the soliloquy, and both types of speech when given to a comic figure would normally bring speaker and audience together, and by that tend to dissipate any derision in the laughter that may have been pointed at the speaker by preceding contexts. Notice, for example, the beginning of two extra-dramatic speeches in Shakespeare's later artistry, wherein swaggering roarer and exquisite, who have also been given attributes of the braggart and who have been revealed, summarize the stage situation (*H V,* V, i, 85-90; *AWEW,* IV, iii, 366-67), plan to act on the basis of what they have referred to (*H V,* V, i, 90-94; *AWEW,* IV, iii, 367-76), and confide in the audience as they turn to current roguery, described with riming gleeks on the evils of the times. Since both speeches end scenes, these comic characters and the Elizabethan audience (finally, in the first instance, and temporarily, in the second) probably rested in a familiar, relatively sympathetic and nonderisive relationship quite comparable to that conventionally associated with the commenting, mischief-making vice.

142. In general, the usual attitude in Renaissance criticism seems to have been comparable to Piccolomini's treatment of comedy as it could be developed from Aristotle's incidental remarks in the *Poetics*. Florindo V. Cerreta, "Alessandro Piccolomini's Commentary on the *Poetics* of Aristotle," *Studies in the Renaissance,* IV (1957), 163-65. See, however, Lane Cooper, *An Aristotelian Theory of Comedy* (N.Y., 1922), pp. 5-6, 76-80, 82-98, etc.

143. E.g., J. W. Fortescue, "The Army: Military Service and Equipment," *Shakespeare's England* (Oxford, 1916), I, 113-15; Paul A. Jorgensen, *Shakespeare's Military World* (Berkeley, Cal., 1956), pp. 25-26.

144. E.g., Stoll, *Shakespeare Studies,* pp. 411-24, 427-41.

145. D. C. Boughner's discussion of Falstaff is an illuminating one. He sees in the portrayal a merging of court jester, braggart, tavern-reveller, military peculator, and "Elizabethan funny man." "Traditional Elements in Falstaff," *JEGP,* XLIII (1944), 417-28; *The Braggart,* pp. 152-53, etc.

146. The italics, of course, are mine.

147. The correctness of "made" has been discussed recently by Henry Hitch Adams, "Falstaff's Instinct," *SQ,* V (1954), 208-9. Adams does not note, however, the homophonic pronunciation of *made* and *mad* (F3). Both words seem to have had doublet forms in early Modern English. Dobson refers incidentally to the possible shortening of the vowel in *made. English Pronunciation,* II, 625 n. 1. Indeed, there seems little doubt that there was such a form (e.g., the spelling "mad" for *made,* NED: *Genesis* and *Exodus, ca.* 1250; *Cursor Mundi, ca.* 1300; *Alexander, ca.* 1400-1450; Pecock, 1449; also *madde, ymad,* etc.; cf. also EDD *med*-spellings). Kökeritz refers to a form of *mad* with long *a* and cites puns on *made-maid-mad,* as well as the rime in Sonnet 129, ll. 7-9. *Shakespeare's Pronunciation,* p. 164. The origin of the doublet form of *mad* is fairly clear. "Normal form"—OE (*ge*)*mædd* > ME *mad* > e Mod. E, Mod. E *mad* (mæd). "Doublet form, with long vowel"—OE (*ge*)*mǣd* > eME *mad(e/es),* i.e., inflected forms > ME *mād(e/es)* > eModE *mād* (me̞:d). E.g., Ferdinand Holthausen, *Altenglisches Etymologisches Wörterbuch* (Heidelberg, 1932-34); Samuel Moore, *Historical Outlines of English Sounds and Inflections,* rev. Albert H. Marckwardt (Ann Arbor, 1957), p. 67; Henry Cecil Wyld, *Studies in English Rhymes from Surrey to Pope* (London, 1923), pp. 99-100. The origin of the doublet form of *made* could be explained by following Karl Luick's hypothesis, whereby syncope and vocalization before open-syllable lengthening could give the short vowel form of *made,* which could come into Shakespeare's English from *mbăde,* a form wherein the quality of the vowel was probably not of full length and hence capable, in some instances, of becoming (mæd). "Sprachkörper und Sprachfunktion," *Engl. Studien,* LVI (1922), 199-201, 462. See the objection of Hermann M. Flasdieck that such an hypothesis would lead only to the short vowel form; hence he would begin the process of change after open-syllable lengthening. "Zu ME. *Made," Engl. Studien,* LVII (1923), 139-41. I am indebted to Dr. Fred C. Robinson for much of the preceding information.

148. The Ciceronian *habitus:* i.e., manner of life; education; instructors in the liberal arts and the art of living; associates; occupation, trade, or profession; the management of one's private fortune; domestic habits. *De Inventione,* tr. H. M. Hubbell, Loeb Classical Library (Cambridge, Mass., 1949), pp. 72-73 (I, xxv).

149. This last consideration is obvious. For the debate technique in drama, see above, p. 34 n. 104; also p. 23.

150. I.e., the vast corpus of treatises *de regimine principum.*

151. See above, pp. 23, 25, 41. As it also has been noted, what is written here comes close to a portion of Stoll's criticism of Falstaff wherein the old motif of a culprit escaping punishment by a joke is referred to, after the author has

argued that Shakespeare embodied in Falstaff conventional aspects of the braggart. Shakespeare's technique, however, even in terms of the theatrically familiar, is a good deal more complex than Stoll would demonstrate in view of his immediate purpose. See also Boughner's studies cited above, pp. 28 n. 95, 39 n. 115. Not simply are the theatrically obvious bases of braggart and tavern reveller, plus witty companion of a prince, fused and elaborated in accordance with ideas that appear in the scene; and not simply does the wit of the principal comedian move from his would-be duping through the mock interview (and in that movement remain constant in a logical irrefragibility that turns laughter back on the invention which, when incompletely applied, would point laughter). In addition, that duping and its development is made to grow out of two relatively extended bits of burlesque and mimicry. The first, the Gadshill episode, (itself congruent with current accounts, actual or fictionalized, of roguery on the London road) had been carefully developed so that its mock bravery and miming were not left solely to the impromptu antics of a comedian. See Charles Hughes, "Land Travel," *Shakespeare's England*, I, 207-8. Such a scene, then, has its own mock repetition acted out in a tavern with the realistic properties of a targe, a hacked sword, pierced clothing, and bloody associates. Thus even as the duper is duping, his actions probably would be associated by a contemporary audience with laughing revelry, rather than with a derisible braggart; with Tarltonian merriment and its Elizabethan milieu both on stage and off, rather than with derisible figures of a relatively sophisticated literature. With a logical, comic continuation of a duping invention, a third situation of mimicry and revelling then occurs—a situation, which although anticipatory, is pointed constantly backward at the material out of which it arose. In other words, Shakespeare's comic dramaturgy here is unique essentially because of its magnificent fullness and its harmonious, truly original development of a comic mélange, including a comic atypicality, which was embedded in the current stage tradition and apparently close to the merriment of Elizabethan life. It is also interesting to note that, with allowance for this basic element of comic familiarity, what Bergson calls the attempt of comedy to produce an internal harmony and consistency is certainly applicable to this comic process. In this instance, moreover, both reality and stage-reality come into play, for this comic consistency accords with Elizabethan merriment and also partakes of the serious ceremonial side of Elizabethan life, which, like any social ceremony "always includes a latent comic element . . . only waiting for an opportunity to burst into full view." Henri Bergson, *Laughter: An Essay on the Meaning of the Comic*, tr. Cloudeslye Brereton and Fred Rothwell (N.Y., 1911), pp. 44-45; see also pp. 180-90.

152. E.g., above, pp. 10-12.

153. *Respublica*, ed. Leonard A. Magnus, E.E.T.S., E.S. (1905), ll. 1904-8; cf. *Looking Glass*, ll. 2237-311, and Cushman, *Devil and Vice*, pp. 116-17, 120 (*King Johan, Appius and Virginia, Nice Wanton, Trial of Treasure, The Tide Tarrieth No Man*); also below, pp. 129-30.

154. Above, p. 22; see also p. 9. Note, too, the entrance of Newgyse with a rope about his neck well before the days of Tarlton. *Mankind*, in *Chief Pre-Shakespearian Dramas*, ed. Adams, ll. 605-17. The comic in the role of scapegoat has been commented upon occasionally, especially when such a "role" is extended from the mock execution in a dance-like *ludus* to hangings, to the constant beating of comic figures, and even to a figure being carried off by a demon or by the devil (e.g., *Friar Bacon*, xv). Regardless of origins, however, one certainly should not let interpretations of Elizabethan comedy or comic scenes become too straight-faced. Notice, moreover, the way in which the last situation parallels vi, 174-76; ix, 160-64.

155. III, v; vi, 17-120.

156. *Ben Jonson*, IX, 455-57. Also see above, p. 7 n. 2.

157. Above, p. 22 and n. 73.

158. Interesting, too, is Sidney's account of Chremes. He was hated by the

country people for his villainy and niggardliness; and when he was sentenced to be hanged by the King of Iberia, neither the death of his daughter nor his own shameful end were "so much in his mowth as he was ledde to execution, as the losse of his goods, and burning of his house: which often, with more laughter than teares of the hearers, he made pittiful exclamations upon." *Works,* I, 274-77.

159. See Talbert, *Problem of Order,* pp. 45-46, 224 n. 6.

160. Barber, it seems to me, pushes the effect of Cade's first scene too far when he speaks of Cade's "anarchy by clowning." To him, Shakespeare represents "a popular rising *throughout as a saturnalia.*" (The italics are mine.) An abhorrence of "communality" has already been noted, and see also Brents Stirling, "Shakespeare's Mob Scenes: A Reinterpretation," *Huntington Libr. Quar.,* VIII (1944-45), 213-40; *The Populace in Shakespeare* (N.Y., 1949), e.g., pp. 190-91.

161. Note, e.g., the pun on *sallet* and the chance for comic miming as the actor eats.

162. Above, p. 41 n. 127.

Chapter III

1. See, e.g., Doran, *Endeavors of Art,* pp. 303-5. One should note, however, that in comparison with those moralities wherein the central figure succumbs to vice, the development spoken of here would be especially noticeable in plays like Bale's *King Johan* and the anonymous *Respublica.* These dramas, of course, as well as morality plays like the *Castle of Perseverance* and *Mankind,* develop the motif of the conflict between virtues and vices. Since they usually end with a final redemptive struggle or situation, they might be considered comedy rather than tragedy. See, e.g., Chambers, *Medieval Stag,* II, 209-11, 70 n. 2; Young, *Drama Medieval Church,* I, 6-7; Hardin Craig, *English Religious Drama of the Middle Ages* (Oxford, 1955), 348-51. For an outstanding exception, see *The Conflict of Conscience* and, e.g., Lily B. Campbell, "Dr. Faustus: A Case of Conscience," *PMLA,* LXVII (1952), 219-39. For a much fuller treatment of what follows immediately, see Fredson T. Bowers, *Elizabethan Revenge Tragedy, 1587-1642* (Princeton, 1940); see also above, pp. 5-6; Doran, *Endeavors of Art,* pp. 306-8; C. L. Barber, *The Idea of Honour in the English Drama, 1591-1700,* Gothenburg Studies in English, VI (1957).

2. "Desire, Joy, Fear, Grief" are the basic perturbations of Pierre de la Primaudaye's *The French Academie,* the great Protestant and Platonizing encyclopedia of the late sixteenth century. For variations in the enumeration of these four primary passions, see Rolf Soellner, "The Four Primary Passions: A Renaissance Theory Reflected in the Works of Shakespeare," *SP,* LV (1958), 549-67. See also A. H. Gilbert, "Seneca and the Criticism of Elizabethan Tragedy," *PQ,* XIII (1934), 370-81.

3. E.g., Wilson's *Arte of Rhetorique,* ed. Mair, p. 32.

4. On the relationship between springs of conduct applicable to a private vice and virtue and to a public vice and virtue that depends essentially upon the complex of rule, see below, pp. 90-92, 89 n. 56.

5. See below, pp. 72 ff.

6. Above, p. 62 n. 2.

7. See above, p. 6 n. 11, and Edward Stockton Meyer, *Machiavelli and the Elizabethan Drama.* Litterarhistorische Forshungen, I (Weimar, 1897); also Marlowe's *Jew of Malta,* "Prologue."

8. See especially Armstrong, *RES,* XXIV, 19-35, and above, p. 6 n. 11.

9. Talbert, *Problem of Order,* pp. 29-30.

10. Talbert, *Problem of Order,* p. 22.

11. *The Civil War,* tr. J. D. Duff, Loeb Classical Library (N.Y., 1928), p. 473 (viii, 489-95). L. 490 might read *acies,* instead of *arces;* "whole armyes fall, swayed by those nyce respects," *Ben Jonson,* VIII, 423.

12. *Ioannis Saresberiensis Episcopi Carnotensis Policratici,* ed. Clemens C. I. Webb (Oxford, 1909), I, 237-66; II, 1-11, 23-24, 345-58 (IV, 2-8; VI, 1-2, 9; VIII, 17). Note also John Dickinson, "The Medieval Conception of Kingship and Some of its Limitations in the 'Policraticus' of John of Salisbury," *Speculum,* I (1926), 308-37; and below pp. 89-90, 95, 98-99.

13. Notice, e.g., the "Conclusion" of *Selimus:*

> Thus haue we brought victorious Selimus
> Vnto the Crowne of great Arabia:
> Next shall you see him with trinmphant [*sic*] sword,
> Diuiding kingdomes into equall shares,
> And giue them to their warlike followers.
> If this first part Gentles, do like you well,
> The second part, shall greater murthers tell.

14. For the horrifying death of Herod, see, e.g., the Benediktbeuern Christmas Play. Young, *Drama Medieval Church,* II, 194-96. See also Warren E. Tomlinson, *Der Herodes-charakter im englischen Drama,* Palaestra, CXCV (Leipzig, 1934), to which, however, some distinctions of more recent scholarship should be applied. A definitive treatment of *de casibus* tragedy is, of course, Willard Farnham, *The Medieval Heritage of Elizabethan Tragedy* (Berkeley, Cal., 1956). Note, too, the sudden death of Cambises "by sodain chaunce" (l. 1160) and the stage direction *"Heere let him quake and stir."* Whether or not the force of Fortune is argued out of the universe by a Petrarchan philosophy or an Augustinian insistence upon a superior retribution for sin depends upon the individual play. For *Cambises,* see, e.g., ll. 1155-58; and, in spite of its conclusion, for *Selimus,* see ll. 2134-71.

15. Gilbert, *Lit. Cit.,* pp. 255-59.

16. For a concise discussion of this double-conflict pattern in early moralities, a pattern that may become triple or even quadruple, see Robert Lee Ramsey's introduction to his edition of Skelton's *Magnyfycence,* E.E.T.S., E.S., 98 (1906), pp. cxlix-clvi.

17. This statement, like the others in this portion of the chapter, will be elaborated by subsequent discussions of individual plays; e.g., below, pp. 95 ff.

18. See the portrayals of Anjou and Navarre, below, pp. 88-89, 100 and Strong, *Jour. Warburg and Courtauld Inst.,* XXI (1958), 86-103.

19. See below, p. 70 n. 26, on the miracle play. The dramatization of the deeds of valiant knights was academically tempered in Hughes's *The Misfortunes of Arthur* (1588), but the "scenicall strutting" in such plays as *Common Conditions* (1576, SR.) and *Sir Clyomon and Sir Clamydes* (1570-83) is obvious. This type of drama seemed contemptible to Ben Jonson (*Discoveries,* ll. 772-79) and risible to Francis Beaumont *(Knight of the Burning Pestle).* Those plays are purely melodramatic; and in spite of the heroes' ultimate fortune, the total impression, heightened by such an ending as that in *Sir Clyomon,* is one of a hopefully sensational, meandering mélange. *Sir Clyomon and Sir Clamydes,* however, may have been in the repertory of the Queen's Men; and it may even have been carried to the continent, in one version or another, as late as 1626. John Green's performance of *The King of Denmark and the King of Sweden* at Dresden in that year may represent not a version of this early play but a version of Dekker's *King of Swethland* (written before 1632 and entered in the Stationers' Register in 1660). The confusion about the meaning of the title given to Green's play, however, as well as the seventeenth-century dates just mentioned, substantiates the validity of Beaumont's satire of an audience's taste for dramas of this type. See Chambers, *Eliz. Stage,* II, 286; III, 304; IV, 6. Both Sir Clyomon and Sir Clamydes, for example, are in love with the fair daughter of a king; enchantments are performed by such an individual as Bryan Sans Foy; giants are killed; a heroine is kidnapped; a lady disguises as a page and then as a shepherd boy; the characters Rumour, Knowledge, and Providence appear; the last allegorical figure is let down from

Heaven and pulled up again after stopping a suicide by one of the ladies who has mistaken the headless corpse of her enemy for that of her loved one; the final combat between the two knights is held before Alexander the Great. Characteristically enough, in view of what has been written about comic figures, a folk hero may also appear with conventional figures of folk merriment to play out a romance of low degree developed with a nationalistic appeal (e.g., George-a-Greene).

20. Jakob Burckhardt, *The Civilization of the Renaissance in Italy,* tr. S. G. C. Middlemore (London, 1921), e.g., pp. 145-53, 398, 454-55. See also Katherine Everett Gilbert and Helmut Kuhn, *A History of Esthetics* (N.Y., 1939), pp. 170-75.

21. See, e.g., Hardin Craig, "The Shackling of Accidents," *PQ*, XIX (1940), 16-17. The expression of this titanism, embodied in the Hercules story, for example, can also range from the villainy of a Selimus and a Richard III to the driving emotionalism of a Bussy d'Ambois and of other heroes in Chapman's dramas.

22. For possible errors in the interpretation of plays, resulting from a failure to recognize this fact sufficiently, see below, p. 121 n. 105.

23. Apparent, e.g., in the concern of Elizabeth and her counselors when the "honor" of Alençon or of the aging Leicester was involved. Conyers Read, *Mr. Secretary Walsingham and the Policy of Queen Elizabeth* (Oxford, 1925), e.g., II, 97-100, 108 n. 3; III, 131-38; *Mr. Secretary Cecil and Queen Elizabeth* (N.Y., 1955), pp. 332-33; *Lord Burghley and Queen Elizabeth* (London, 1960), pp. 392-93 and *passim.* See below, p. 74 nn. 34, 35; Talbert, *Problem of Order,* pp. 224 n. 6, 229 n. 33.

24. In spite of the possible corruption of the text of *The Famous Victories,* for example, one can see some concern for structure in the successive blocks of material emphasizing the figurative rise of Hal. Thus the career of the prince is dramatized from the lowest point of his relative degeneracy; and his rise is marked by three major situations. There is Hal as profligate (in the Gadshill episode, at the court of law, in conversation about future topsy-turvy degrees of valiancy); there is Hal as penitent (both in a father-son relationship and a ruler-heir one); there is Hal as a valiant king (both at home, in the brief law-king relationship, and abroad, where the successful wooer of historical tradition rounds out his rise). Here too should be noted briefly the variation effected by the rising figure who appears as a malcontent and who rightfully gains or regains what is his. Although, as a type, he is too late for the period of particular concern here, some of the malcontent's theatrical *visibilia* are described in the dramatic surroundings of a Christmas festivity during the winter of 1594-95: "*Item,* that no knight . . . shall take upon him the Person of a Male-content, in going with a more private Retinue than appertaineth to his Degree, and using but certain special, obscure Company, and commending none but Men disgraced, and out of Office; and smiling at good News, as if he knew something that were not true, and making odd Notes of his Highness's Reign, and former Governments; or saying, that his Highness's Sports were well sorted with a Play of Errors; and such like pretty Speeches of Jest, to the end that he may safely utter his Malice against His Excellency's Happiness. . . ." *Gesta Grayorum, 1688,* Malone Soc., 1914, p. 31. For the differentiation that Shakespeare effects between the rising Faulconbridge and a Machiavel, see, above, pp. 32-33 and especially below pp. 262-63.

25. See, e.g., Farnham, *Med. Heritage of Eliz. Drama,* pp. 86-88, 365-67, 389, and *passim.*

26. This would be true especially if there were noticeable repetitions or repetitive processes involved in the essentially successive dramatizations of one figure's fall and another's rise. The mystery cycles, with their repetitive representation of theological *types,* moved through and coalesced a large period of time until the climactic manifestation of God-made-man was dramatized. In some of the mystery cycles, moreover, as in that at York, the Ascension received a repetitive

representation in the Assumption of the Virgin Mary, etc. In the miracle play, with its repetitive conflict between different manifestations of vice and a blessed virtue, one can hardly fail to see a linear multiplicity; and just as the Eustace legend, for example, is strikingly comparable to the material of secular romance, so the similiarity is obvious between the repetitive structural movement of this type of drama and that of the hero play especially. See John M. Manly, "The Miracle Play in Medieval England," *Essays by Divers Hands,* Trans. of the Royal Soc. of Lit. of the United Kingdom, New Series VII (1927), 133-53.

27. This has been elaborated especially by T. W. Baldwin, *Shakspere's Five-Act Structure* (Urbana, 1947). I am not concerned here primarily with the divisions by act which vary in accordance with different discussions of the nature of the three parts of a play but with the dramatic *practice* shown in the plays analyzed, e.g., in Chapter XXI of Baldwin's study. It is because of this practice that one can overlook, I believe, objections to Baldwin's study based upon the statements of some Renaissance critics. See also W. W. Greg, *Dramatic Documents from Elizabethan Playhouses* (Oxford, 1931), II, 80-81; and, e.g., E. A. J. Honigmann's review of Wilfred T. Jewkes's *Act Division in Elizabethan and Jacobean Plays, 1583-1616,* in *RES,* XI (1960), 322-23; or Rudolf Stamm's review of Georg Heuser's *Die aktlose Dramaturgie William Shakespeares,* in *English Studies,* XLIII (1962), 510-12.

28. Jonson, *Bartholomew Fair,* "The Induction," ll. 106-12.

29. Philip Edwards in his edition of *The Spanish Tragedy,* Revels Plays (London, 1959) dates the drama *ca.* 1590. In contrast to T. W. Baldwin (dating the play 1584), F. S. Boas (1585-87) and F. Carrère (the first half of 1588), Edwards discards, e.g., the allusion to the play in Nashe's preface to *Menaphon.* See, however, F. Carrère, *Le Théâtre de Thomas Kyd* (Toulouse, 1951), pp. 133-45.

30. E.g., J. W. Cunliffe, *The Influence of Seneca on Elizabethan Tragedy* (London, 1893), pp. 58, 127; and Cunliffe's introduction to *Early English Classical Tragedies* (Oxford, 1912), pp. xciii-iv.

31. See William H. Wiatt, "The Dramatic Function of the Alexandro-Villuppo Episode in *The Spanish Tragedy,*" *N & Q,* CCIII (1958), 327-29, and below p. 77 n. 38.

32. As edited by Brooke and Paradise, above, p. 25 n. 82. When one omits the "Induction" and the choruses, as well as the additions, these "units" run as follows: I, i through II, v; III, i through III, xiv; IV, i through IV, iv. In the first two choruses (at the end of Act I and Act II), Andrea's discontent increases, underlining, i.a., the tangential nature of the beginning of this play; while in the third chorus, which precedes the effective plot of Hieronimo's, one finds the refrain "Awake, Revenge." The fourth chorus, of course, closes the drama.

33. E.g., I, iv, 64-72.

34. For the general treatment of this and comparable situations, see Bowers, *Eliz. Revenge Trag.,* pp. 280-84. Although the attitude expressed in the quotation is apparent in Seneca's two Hercules plays, in his *Medea, Agamemnon,* and *Phaedra,* as well as in his *Thyestes* (wherein it is linked with ambition), to many of Kyd's contemporaries it probably would seem to be embodied most obviously in the Italian *novelle,* wherein it appeared in connection with all sorts of intrigues and crimes of passion. See, e.g., Mary Augusta Scott, *Elizabethan Translations from the Italian* (N.Y., 1916), especially Chapters I and IV. Nor would it be incongruent with the touchy "honor" of Elizabethans of relatively high degree and with the way in which elections to the House of Commons, for example, might give vent to county feuds. J. E. Neale, *The Elizabethan House of Commons* (New Haven, 1950), pp. 63-67, 71-74, 91-92, etc. Cf. also the Lambert-Serlsby matter in Greene's *Friar Bacon,* x, 1-89; xiii, 38-74.

35. E.g., III, vi, 1-10; xii, 82-100, a situation congruent with I, ii, 96-100, 123 ff.. 165-74; see also III, xiii, 51-55; xiv, 61-63.

36. See F. S. Boas's argument that the additions interrupt the pattern of action in the play written by Kyd. *Works of Thomas Kyd* (Oxford, 1955), p. lxxxviii.

For a recent examination of the effect of those additions, see Charles K. Cannon, "The Relationship of the Additions of *The Spanish Tragedy* to the Original Play," *Studies in English Literature*, II (1962), 229-39.

37. E.g., I, iii, 15, 28-30; II, iii, 43; II, v, 111-12; III, i, 8-11; x, 102-3; etc.; as well as the *sententiæ* in Hieronimo's soliloquy just mentioned.

38. Like the majority of the plays in the repertory of Queen Elizabeth's Men, for example, *The Spanish Tragedy* shows, not the development, but only the possibility of a well-worked-out complex of ideas. The point can be illustrated by considering the Portuguese line of action. The public force of a concern over Bel-Imperia's marriage to the Portuguese prince leads simply to the situation whereby Hieronymo is frustrated at court (III, xii, 25-26, 31-55, 101-4) and to the milieu of the final situation. The scenes involving the aspiring Portuguese villain Villuppo are at best a dramatic embroidery, whereby villainy is mixed with the thoughts of a defeated ruler. Although, as it has been indicated, some of the lines in those scenes (I, iii; III, i) might well serve as chorus lines for the main action, they are too scattered, and too far from the dramatization of appropriate matter in the main plot to give them much, if any, choric force in the world of the theater. Equally loose, though in a different manner, are ideas about rule. Statements about the justness and largess of a pious ruler, about false ambition and about the grief resulting from Fortune's foot on a rolling stone, as well as *sententiæ* about kings who "would be fear'd, yet fear to be belov'd," are only incidental to particular scenes and even to particular speeches. One, consequently, may wish to qualify somewhat the conclusions of Wiatt, *N & Q*, CCIII, 327-29. Note also the paragraph which follows.

39. III, x.

40. See above, pp. 63-64.

41. III, xiv, 115 ff.; IV, i.

42. This belief is mentioned constantly by editors; for an enlargement upon it, see Arthur Melville Clark, *Thomas Heywood* (Oxford, 1931), pp. 287-98. The reader of this last discussion, however, can supply alternate explanations of the lines Clark comments upon; see below, pp. 82-86.

43. Particularly does this seem true when clear signs of later rewriting and any consequent textual disruption are conspicuous by their absence. Here, as elsewhere, there seems little need to comment upon the telescoping of time in Elizabethan drama—as when Barabas has completely regained his wealth (II, iii, 7-11). The convention is well known.

44. Such a belief, however, may have been less fanatical in England than elsewhere. E.g., C. J. Sisson, "A Colony of Jews in Shakespeare's London," *Essays and Studies by Members of the English Assoc.*, XXIII (1937), 38-51. It also should be noted that the actions of Barabas exist in a play-world for which Elizabethans might well have no strong predilections. In general, it is a world of Turk versus Spaniard (e.g., II, ii; I, i, 94-96); and the Christianity of the island is represented by such anti-Catholic lines as

> And yet I know the prayers of those nuns
> And holy friars, having money for their pains,
> Are wondrous.—and indeed do no man good . . .
>
> (II, iii, 82-84)
>
> *Abig.* And witness that I die a Christian.
> 2 *Fri.* Ay, and a virgin too; that grieves me most.
>
> (III, vi, 40-41)

45. See C. F. Tucker Brooke, "The Prototype of Marlowe's Jew of Malta," *TLS*, June 8, 1922, p. 380.

46. See also above, pp. 63-65. In this respect the conventional attitude of villainous isolation also accords with a favorite text against the covetous man: e.g., "Therefore god by his prophet denownceth wo unto suche riche carles, saying, Wo

be unto you that ioine house to house, and lande to land, even unto the very
boundes of the place. Do you thinke to dwell alone upon the earthe?" Thomas
Wilson, *A Discourse upon Usury,* with an historical introduction by R. H. Tawney
(London, 1925), p. 221.

47. The concept of an animate, and hence an unnatural, wealth occurs most
frequently, perhaps, in attacks upon usury, for the usurer was said to live by
usury "as the husbandman doth by his husbandry," making money breed money.
Such a process of thought lent itself very naturally to a figurative development.
Usury was "a thinge so monstrous in nature, as if thorns should beare figges, or
stones shoulde brynge foorthe livelye creatures"; by it, money would increase itself
"as a woman dothe, that bringethe foorthe a childe." Wilson, *Discourse,* pp. 272,
286-87; see also pp. 258, 355, and, of course, *The Merchant of Venice,* I, iii. 62-99.
Barabas' imagistic development *per se*—that is, with no application to usury—also
accords with St. Ambrose's statement about using money to wage battle. Wilson,
Discourse, pp. 219, 256-57.

48. In which Acts III and IV show the performance of villainous plots, with
the incompleteness of that of the poisoned flowers being dramatized at the beginning of Act V and leading into that of the feigned death, the appearance of the
Turks, and the doubled reversal of Barabas' fortune.

49. See Paul H. Kocher, "Contemporary Pamphlet Backgrounds for Marlowe's
The Massacre at Paris," *MLQ,* VIII (1947), 151-73, 309-18. The probability
of his statement that the portrayal of the Guise was not necessarily designed as
that of a Machiavel, but developed in accordance with some current pamphlet,
seems to be established. Yet the result on the Elizabethan stage would certainly
accord with Marlowe's linking of Machiavelli with the Guise in the prologue
to *The Jew of Malta,* ll. 1-4. In *The Massacre,* see such references to the Guise,
and such lines given him, as i, 52-54; ii, 107-8 (his "intellectual" traps); ii, 40-42,
48-59 (his villainous isolation); ii, 96-106 (his preference for raw power and fear);
ii, 64-69 (his hypocrisy); xvi, 55-58, 67-74 (his ambitious and insolent force); iv,
49-50; vi, 28-36; xvi, 59-62 (his villainous "wittiness"); ii, 34-36, 38-39, 43-47
(some Machiavellianisms). *The Massacre at Paris,* ed. H. S. Bennett, *The Works
and Life of Christopher Marlowe,* gen. ed. R. H. Chase, III (N.Y., 1931).

50. For the way in which Caesar might be related sometimes to the tyrant and
the Machiavel, see William Blisset, "Lucan's Caesar and the Elizabethan Villain,"
SP LIII (1956), 553-75.

51. For the ease with which even the Holy League's interpretation of current
events in France could accord with unfavorable aspects of the portrayal of Henry
III, see, e.g., *The Paris of Henry of Navarre as Seen by Pierre de l'Estoile,*
tr. and ed. Nancy Lyman Roelker (Cambridge, Mass., 1958), pp. 54, 64-65, 66-67,
105-6, etc.

52. E.g., *Cambises,* ll. 554 ff.

53. See especially his words to Navarre and his message to Elizabeth (xxi, 66-
71; 97-113). Interestingly enough, scenes xi and xviii frame six scenes that alternate between events connected with Guise and Henry and events connected
with Navarre. Scenes xii and xiv are concerned with the affair between the royal
favorite Mugeron and the Duchess of Guise; scene xvi shows the death of that
favorite "in despite of" Henry, the king's seizure of the initiative, and the flight to
Blois. The other three scenes (xiii, xv, xvii) show Navarre progressively triumphant
and about to join forces with Henry. After scene xvii, the relatively long scene
numbered xviii makes this second part of the drama counterbalance the first. Note
also the implicit reference to Fortune's Wheel (xviii, 14-16) and Guise's
"titanism," comparable to Mortimer's, but linked specifically with Cæsar once
more (xviii, 67-87).

54. E.g., above, p. 66; and since minions frequently were linked with flattery,
below, pp. 92-93, 95, 98, as well as p. 89 n. 56.

55. *Pride of Life,* ll. 143-78, 263-302, etc. *Quellen des Weltlichen Dramas in
England vor Shakespeare,* ed. Alois Brandl, Quellen und Forschungen zur Sprach-

und Culturgeschichte der Germanischer Völker, LXXX (1898). *Magnyfycence,*
ll. 240-395, 1375-1540, 1756-1802, 1875-2063, etc.

56. There can be no doubt that it is necessary to distinguish between private
and public vice if one is to understand fully the historical dramas of the period.
The point has been emphasized by Lily B. Campbell, *Shakespeare's "Histories":
Mirrors of Elizabethan Policy* (San Marino, 1947), pp. 8-116; Irving Ribner,
"The Tudor History Play: An Essay in Definition," *PMLA*, LXIX (1954), 591-
609, *The English History Play in the Age of Shakespeare* (Princeton, 1957), pp.
3-30. As it will be pointed out, such a differentiation appears explicitly in Marlowe's *Edward II*, even though it does not remain valid in that play-world. Yet
such a consideration should not obscure the fact that writers portraying princes
would also draw upon current concepts about the basic perturbations of mankind.
That the ruler must be able to rule himself before he can rule others was a basic
precept. See, e.g., Talbert, *Problem of Order*, pp. 28-29, 225-26. Thereby the
door might be opened for making applicable to rule all sorts of precepts connected
with the cardinal sins, just as Shakespeare, for example, has Northumberland apply
two of the basic perturbations to Richard II in describing that king's actions and
words. Talbert, *Problem of Order*, p. 175. Conversely Elizabethan tragedies are
not devoid of public, i.e., politic, meanings, although Freudian interpretations
quite naturally overlook this fact. By the very nature of Hamlet's or Othello's or
Lear's or Macbeth's story, such meanings appear in the dramas. See also, e.g.,
Gilbert, *PQ*, XIII, 370-81. In brief, regardless of the narrative being dramatized,
the historically minded critic can ignore neither the private nor the public virtues
and vices. See, e.g., Jonson's closing *sententia*, "A vertuous *Court* a world to vertue
draws," *Cynthia's Revels*, V, xi, 173; the basic concept of Jonson's masques (E.
W. Talbert, "The Interpretation of Jonson's Courtly Spectacles," *PMLA*, LXI
(1946), 454-73; W. Todd Furniss, "Ben Jonson's Masques," *Three Studies in the
Renaissance*, Yale Studies in English, 138 (1958), pp. 89-179); Baldwin's words
noted below, p. 92 n. 65; or L. C. Knights, *Shakespeare's Politics With Some
Reflections on the Nature of Tradition* (Oxford, 1958), wherein the author argues
that the political is inseparable from the moral and the ethical since all turn
upon a practical awareness of the "cooperation and mutuality" essential for the
existence of a commonweal. Thus, e.g., the humanists' concern to oppose tyranny
and help create just rule might lead to an attack upon medieval romance. Robert
P. Adams, "Bold Bawdry and Open Manslaughter," *Huntington Libr. Quar.*, XXIII
(1959), 33-48.

57. E.g., *Cyropaedia*, VII, 5. 72-85; Allan H. Gilbert, *Machiavelli's 'Prince'
and Its Forerunners* (Durham, N.C., 1938), pp. 107-8, 179-85, 186-87, etc., and,
e.g., Talbert, *The Problem of Order*, pp. 80-85, 112-15, 65-67, 68 and 207 n. 27,
29. For a tradition that develops the four cardinal virtues, relates them to the
neo-stoic doctrine of fortitude and to magnificence (frequently made synonymous
with magnanimity), and is applicable to an early sixteenth-century morality, see
William Oliver Harris, "Theme and Structure in Skelton's *Magnyfycence*"
(Ph.D. diss., Univ. of N.C., 1947), especially his Chapter V. As one might expect,
in this tradition fortitude-magnificence was applied especially to princes. Aside
from classical treatises (e.g., Cicero's *De Officiis*) and sixteenth-century English
works (e.g., Elyot's *Governour*), such compilations as the following contributed
to this process of thought: St. Thomas Aquinas, *Summa Theologica* (e.g., II-II, Q.
123, A4, Resp., Dom. tr. XII, 200; Q. 128 and Resp., Dom. tr. XII, 245; Q. 129,
Dom. tr. XII, 249; Q. 134, A1, Reply Obj. 2, Dom. tr. XII, 294; Q. 134, A2, Resp.,
Dom. tr. XII, 296); the *Moralium Dogma Philosophorum;* Giraldus Cambrensis,
De Principis Instructione Liber; Brunetto Latini, *Li Livres dou Tresor;* Vincent of
Beauvais, *Speculum Doctrinale;* St. Ambrose, *De Officiis Ministrorum* (e.g., *PL,*
XVI, 82); St. Augustine, *De Diversis Quaestionibus LXXXIII* (e.g., *PL*, XL, 21);
Macrobius, *Commentary on the Dream of Scipio* (e.g., tr. W. H. Stahl, 1. 8. 7-8,
12); Julianus Pomerius, *De Vita Contemplativa.*

58. The survival of this play in a scribe's manuscript, which seems to be a

prompt copy for some provincial performance during the 1630's, has caused it to be dated sometimes very late in the last decade of the sixteenth century. As others have pointed out, however, there are good reasons to place it in the very early 1590's, particularly since it shows characteristics of "the semi-Senecan" school. However it be dated, this play certainly shows that what is being considered here impressed itself upon the mind of a very poor playwright. *Edmond Ironside or War Hath Made All Friends,* Malone Soc., 1927, pp. i-ix, x-xi. For the reference to Herod, see, e.g., Young, *Drama Medieval Church,* II, 75-101, etc., i.e., the pompous greetings addressed to Herod. Although such lines accord with the ostentation of Herod's court, they also accord with the point in question.

59. *Edmond Ironside,* ll. 278-331, 461-563; *Looking Glass,* ll. 1060-1150; *The Scottish History of James the Fourth,* 1598, Malone Soc., 1921, ll. 409-555; *Woodstock, A Moral History,* ed. A. P. Rossiter (London, 1946), I, ii, 57-132.

60. The garbled nature of the surviving text involves, i.a., a consideration of the authenticity of the "Collier leaf"; see, e.g., *The Massacre at Paris,* Malone Soc., 1928, pp. xi-xvi. In view of what has just been pointed out, note also the intrusion of a cutpurse (xi, 27-37).

61. I.e., the *Siege of London* (1580-94) and the *Tanner of Denmark* (Tamworth ?, 1592). Chambers, *Eliz. Stage,* II, 122, 146; IV, 10. Alfred Harbage, *Annals of English Drama* (Philadelphia, 1940), p. 64. In Heywood's play, for example, the ill consequences for the state of Edward IV's wantonness, soothed by "spaniels of the Court," is emphasized by the Duchess of York as the play begins (sigs. A2-A3); but soon Heywood's sentimentality takes over.

62. *The Shakespeare Apocrypha,* ed. C. F. Tucker Brooke (Oxford, 1929), II, ii, 94. For comparable costuming and action in morality plays, see T. W. Craik, *The Tudor Interlude: Stage, Costume, and Acting* (Leicester, 1958), pp. 58, 73-92, 102-3, etc.

63. See also, e.g., II, ii, 109-10, 118-20, 161-63.

64. For a brief indication of the sources, see *Shakespeare Apocrypha,* pp. xx-xxi.

65. Although he is concerned especially with the public virtue Justice, Baldwin, e.g., in his "Dedication" of *The Mirror* notes that "the goodnes or badnes of any realme lyeth in the goodnes or badnes of the rulers" (p. 64). Note also the constant refrain that the purpose of *The Mirror* is "to diswade from vices and exalte vertue" (p. 110), and even "to diswade all men from all Sinnes and vices" (p. 267). *The Mirror for Magistrates,* ed. Lily B. Campbell (Cambridge, 1938).

66. The first *novella* of the third decade in the *Hecatommithi.*

67. After seeing, e.g., that only another murder will serve his turn (l. 2073).

68. For an identification of Ateukin with John Damian, see Waldo F. McNeir, "Ateukin in Greene's *James IV,*" *MLN,* LXII (1947), 376-81.

69. Purveyance, i.e., the levy providing victuals and carts to convey them for the royal household, and the rapacity of purveyors were attacked frequently. Burghley was aware both of the dissatisfaction and of the problem involved and favored "composition," i.e., establishing for the merchants and farmers liable to this levy, a specific quantity of victuals at a set price. By 1580, fifteen counties were under this arrangement. By the end of the century, after the parliamentary pressure of 1589, nearly every shire had "compounded." Read, *Lord Burghley,* pp. 84, 441, 527.

70. In the preface to his edition of *Woodstock,* Rossiter, arguing for the influence of *2 H VI* and minimizing that of *Edward II,* summarizes other discussions of the relationship between the three plays. Pp. 53-71.

71. The same is true for the appearances of Isabella in the first two acts. Sorrowful at being banished from Edward's side, she persuades Mortimer to allay the quarrel between king and nobles. In a scene with a tableau-like effect, her sorrow is called to the audience's attention (I, iv, 187-88). When the situation is repeated (II, iv), she gives the nobles information that effects the capture of Gaveston, though Marlowe still represents the relationship between the queen and Mortimer

as being innocent. Although Edward's suspicions would misconstrue the situation (ll. 53-56), Isabella's first soliloquy begins "Heavens can witness I love none but you [Edward]" (l. 15); and although in her second soliloquy she expresses a willingness to live with "sweet Mortimer" "for ever," she resolves to importune Edward once more "with prayers." By this last development, however, Marlowe adumbrates his final emphasis in representing his Isabella-Mortimer relationship. So constant is the repetitive nature of Marlowe's artistry that it is apparent also in minor situations lacking the theatrical appreciableness of those indicated here. For example, although the stage situation of II, ii, 138-99 is developed obviously and purposefully, yet even as a scenic arrangement, it had been anticipated during an earlier speech by Mortimer (I, iv, 416-18).

72. Of the plays here considered, this is seen, for example, in *Edmond Ironside, James IV, Woodstock;* and it is reflected in Marlowe's *Massacre.* For a public expression of this conventional association, see Talbert, *Problem of Order,* pp. 80-81.

73. See also, of course, I, i, 50-72.

74. See Marlowe's subsequent lines about young Spencer, the "putrefying vine," III, ii, 163-64, as well as, for example, I, ii, 26.

75. E.g., Chambers, *Eliz. Stage,* IV, 26; Craik, *Tudor Interlude,* pp. 110-18; *Eliz. Stage,* III, 496-97; cf. also *The Seven Days of the Week,* etc., and above, p. 67 n. 16.

76. I.e., a total lack of power upon the Continent; loss of control over the seas about England; success against the English in Ireland; a successful invasion from Scotland. To appreciate such a picture one needs but to glance at the fears expressed in Commons and by Elizabeth's councilors *ca.* 1571-87. Neale, *Eliz. and Parl., passim.* To all this, Marlowe adds disaffection among nobles and commons and an "unloving" ruler. See Talbert, *Problem of Order,* pp. 14-15, 22-23, 86-88 (as regards a "loving" ruler).

77. Notice, e.g., how Kent has been used. His first speech censured strongly the Barons' pride that made them "brave the king unto his face," and he had counseled Edward to "revenge it, and let their heads / Preach upon poles, for trespass of their tongues" (I, i, 107-8). But then Kent objected to the excessive titles Edward was heaping upon Gaveston: "Brother, the least of these may well suffice / For one of greater birth than Gaveston" (ll. 158-59). This was no braving of a ruler but sound admonitory advice. Edward received it, however, as he had received the nobles' objections to the recall of Gaveston—with headstrong irritation, if not anger. Indeed, Kent's admonition led only to other excessive favors and grants of authority for Edward's minion (ll. 160-70). Thus Kent, who already had avoided the Elizabethan's possible censure of one who resisted a ruler, was placed in a position to speak lines that would express acceptably any feeling of protest at what was happening. It is Kent who objects to laying violent hands upon a bishop (ll. 189-90). He heeds Edward's previous command that he say nothing derogatory of Gaveston, but he again admonishes his half-brother and points to a reaction about complaints to Rome that accords with the way in which an audience might well have felt both hostile and derisive in such circumstances, but—in view of the bull against Elizabeth and the force of Spain—fearful as well. In the remainder of the first act, Kent is silent when Gaveston scorns the absent noblemen (I, iii); and later, when he is on stage with the king, the barons, and Gaveston, he once more insists on the duty that the lords owe their ruler (I, iv, 22). All the more theatrically forceful, therefore, is his subsequent break with Edward, for by speech and action Kent has been represented as the good counselor and loyal nobleman. Even in the scene of his banishment, he reproves Mortimer's threatening manner (II, ii, 146); and since he has been used to channel an audience's reaction in his previous admonitions, he can carry the audience with him when what has been anticipated occurs—and anticipated not simply by Kent's counsel against favoritism but by the larger situation underlying the struggle between king and nobles, a struggle that had carried with it the distinct probability that public evils would result from the ruler's preoccupying

wantonness. In Act II, scene ii, consequently, before he gives Kent anything more than one line, Marlowe develops the situation about ransoming the elder Mortimer so that an audience would hear at length of the grievous ills in the commonwealth. Then the play develops so that a loyal counselor is confronted not simply with the most perilous of choices but has his choice made for him by his ruler. In such a manner, Kent leaves Edward and sides with the barons for the "realm's behoof" (II, iii, 3).

78. The opening lines of II, ii, for example, show a perilous disregard of affairs in France as Edward's "mind runs on his minion" and on the "stately triumphs" associated with that figure (ll. 1-14). Such an unsympathetic emphasis is then partially reversed when the barons' descriptions of their devices in the forthcoming ceremony apparently show their "rancorous minds" in spite of the previous "reconcilement." At least Edward so interprets the devices: they are "private libelling" against Gaveston and Kent (ll. 15-35). The queen's statement that the king should be content, since all love him (l. 36) leads, however, to Edward's threatening interpretation of the devices (ll. 37-46), and thereby Marlowe shifts in the direction of an anti-Edward emphasis once more and develops it by repeating Edward's excessive regard for Gaveston (ll. 47-64). The subsequent insults to Gaveston, which take the form of salutations by the nobles with the titles previously heaped upon him (ll. 65-68), repeat the immediately preceding movement begun with the descriptions of the devices. This time, though, it is Kent who points out the derision that must have been meant to accompany those lines (l. 69), and Edward's brief expressions of anger follow immediately, while the queen sorrows that "these begin to jar" (ll. 69-72). Briefly, emphases relatively anti-Edward (ll. 1-14, 37-64) alternate with relatively anti-noble ones (ll. 15-35, 65-72), while Isabella now appears as the sorrowful, but ineffective, pacifier (ll. 36, 72). The wounding of Gaveston, commented upon above, then follows.

79. In this respect, one might also note that, as indicated above, during the first act it was a Roman bishop who had been deprived of his power.

80. E.g., III, i, 32-33, 43-45; iii, 21-23; IV, vi, 80-81.

81. This, of course, is the converse of favoring a flattering minion; for a fuller gloss, see Talbert, *Problem of Order,* pp. 80-81, 84-85, 87-88, 114.

82. That *scourge* implied a censurable, tyrannical ruler, see *NED,* 3. For the relationship between *virtue* and an amoral *virtù,* see below, pp. 115-16, and Talbert, *Problem of Order,* p. 94 n. 10.

83. The very form of the complaint testifies to such a purpose. Although admonition is constant in such a compilation as *The Mirror for Magistrates,* see, e.g., pp. 112, 212-13:

> Beholde my hap, see how the sely route
> Do gase vpon me, and eche to other saye:
> Se where he lieth for whome none late might route,
> Loe howe the power, the pride, and riche aray
> Of myghty rulers lightly fade away.
> The Kyng whyche erst kept all the realme in doute,
> The veryest rascall now dare checke and lowte:
> What mould be Kynges made of, but carayn clay?
> Beholde his woundes, howe blew they be about,
> Whyche whyle he lived, thought never to decay.

> What harte is than so hard, but wyl for pitye blede,
> To heare so cruell lucke so cleare a life succede?
> To see a silly soule with woe and sorowe souste,
> A king deprived, in prison pente, to death with daggars douste.

> Would god the way of birth had brought me to my beere,
> Than had I never felt the chaunge of Fortunes cheere.

Would god the grave had gript me in her gredy woumbe,
Whan crowne in cradle made me king, with oyle of holy thoumbe.

Would god the rufull toumbe had bene my royall trone,
So should no kingly charge have made me make my mone:
O that my soule had flownen to heaven with the joy,
When one sort cryed: God save the king, another, *Vive le roy.*

Or *Parts Added to The Mirror for Magistrates by John Higgins and Thomas Blenerhasset,* ed. Lily B. Campbell (Cambridge, 1946), pp. 145, 443:

If any wofull wight haue cause, to waile her woe:
Or griefes are past do pricke vs Princes tel our fal:
My selfe likewise must needes constrained eke do so,
And show my like misfortunes and mishaps withal.

You mourning Muses al, where ever you remayne,
Assist my sobbing soule this drierye tale to tell:
You furious Furies fearce of *Lymbo Lake* belowe,
Helpe to vnlade my brest of all the bale it beares:
And you who felte the falle from honors high renowne,
From graues you grizie ghosts send forth, to help me mourn.

Drayton, as it might be expected, would also work both censure of Mortimer and pathos for Edward into his treatment of that king's death. (e.g., *Mortimeriados,* ll. 2038-44). *The Works of Michael Drayton,* ed. J. William Hebel, I (Oxford, 1931). For the dramatic tradition in back of this development, see Robert Y. Turner, "Pathos and the *Gorboduc* Tradition, 1560-1590," *Huntington Libr. Quar., XXV* (1962), 97-120.

84. The context of the quotation from Seneca is as follows. After Atreus has placed a crown on Thyestes' head, the chorus speaks, ending with this thought: "No lot endureth long; pain and pleasure, each in turn, give place; more quickly, pleasure. Lowest with highest the fickle hour exchanges. He who wears crown on brow, before whom trembling nations bend the knee, at whose nod the Medes lay down their arms, and the Indians of the nearer sun, and the Dahae who hurl their horse upon the Parthians,—he with anxious hand holds the sceptre, and both foresees and fears fickle chance and shifting time that change all things. O you, to whom the ruler of sea and land has given unbounded right o'er life and death, abate your inflated swelling pride; all that a lesser subject fears from you, 'gainst you a greater lord shall threaten; all power is subject to a weightier power. *Whom the rising sun hath seen high in pride, him the setting sun hath seen laid low.* Let none be over-confident when fortune smiles; let none despair of better things when fortune fails. Clotho blends weal and woe, lets no lot stand, keeps every fate a-turning. No one has found the gods so kind that he may promise to-morrow to himself. God keeps all mortal things in swift wheel turning." *Seneca's Tragedies,* tr. Frank Justus Miller, Loeb Classical Library (N.Y., 1929), II, 141-43.

85. The kinship between such lines and the death lament is obvious.

86. It seems unnecessary to note, in anything more than the briefest detail, that Mortimer is now given theatrical signs of the vicious, rising Machiavel. Although the first of his soliloquies here (V, iv, 1-21) does not show the mockery characteristic of more effective portrayals of the type, both it and his subsequent soliloquy (V, iv, 48-72) emphasize his vicious cleverness, hypocrisy, and reliance upon force and fear. The first, moreover, wherein his cleverness in not punctuating his order is pointed out (V, iv, 5-16), begins with lines that also indicate the emphasis in this last movement of the play as well as the pattern of rise and fall:

The king must die, or Mortimer goes down;
The commons now begin to pity him.

(ll. 1-2)

The second, after a strong, villainous repetition of ideas in Gaveston's earlier soliloquies—for now the context of the action is entirely that of a vicious public ambition (ll. 48-57)—moves to a satirical, mocking description of such "a bashful puritan" as Mortimer himself and expresses his willing acceptance of being feared (ll. 58-64). The last lines (e.g., l. 69) also express a contempt for Fortune, which fittingly precedes a fall from her wheel.

87. Line 96 of the quotation refers to earlier situations at the end of the fourth act and the beginning of the fifth, when the Prince and Kent are aligned in their regard for defeated Edward. Mortimer's seizure of the young prince as he calls to Kent for help (V, ii, 111) continues this alignment, as does the fact that Edmund's execution on Mortimer's order creates a wise fear in young Edward's mind (V, iv, 108-9). As a result, England's new ruler turns to "the council-chamber" (V, vi, 20-21) to seek the "aid and succour of his peers," and thereby the villainous are punished and the political unity of the play-world finally established.

88. See Talbert, *Problem of Order,* e.g., pp. 50-51, 60 and n. 120.

89. Navarre's Protestant rise is linked clearly with God's will and with His immediacy in the affairs of men (*Massacre,* e.g., ll. 845-56, 951-54, 963-64, 1577-82). At the same time, Navarre is given such heroic attributes as welcoming battle (ll. 877, 891-92), effecting "terrour of" a "happy victory" (l. 956), and rising to dominate the play-world.

90. For emphases within a repetitive pattern, as in *Edward III,* which are effected by concentrating on particular battles, see below, p. 116.

91. E.g., *Selimus,* or the early portions of the portrayal of Rasni and Remilia in the *Looking Glass;* see also Talbert, *Problem of Order,* pp. 22, 77 n. 38, and, e.g., Louis Wann, "The Oriental in Elizabethan Drama," *MP,* XII (1915), 423-47.

92. *Aristotles Politiques or Discovrses of Government, translated out of Greek . . . by Loys Le Roy* (London, 1598). The quotations will be found in the commentary on I, ii: "What is a Citie: and that it consisteth by nature: and that man is naturally a sociable and ciuill creature," pp. 13-14. For Le Roy's reputation, see, e.g., Talbert, *Problem of Order,* pp. 23, 21 n. 2.

93. Le Roy, *Arist. Polit.,* pp. 25-26.

94. That Marlowe was acquainted with a number of accounts of Tamburlaine's career is indicated by the signs of indebtedness in his two Tamburlaine plays. See, e.g., *Tamburlaine the Great,* ed. Una Ellis-Fermor (N.Y., 1930), pp. 17-48. Marlowe may have read a considerable body of Eastern history, or he may have had access to Richard Knolles's specialized library, or even to Knolles's manuscript, from which there was to result *A Generall Historie of the Turkes* (London, 1603). Hugh G. Dick, "*Tamburlaine* Sources Once More," *SP,* XLVI (1949), 154-66. That his sources were multiple is an established fact, unless the last alternative is true; and even then, the material of the manuscript would have been drawn from a variety of sources. At any rate, there can be little doubt that Marlowe was familiar with information that he chose not to dramatize. He probably knew that the real Tamburlaine was not born a shepherd, that he was, in a sense, reasserting his rights, that he succeeded not simply by military prowess but by statesmanship, and that he was a man of no mean intellect. As has been indicated earlier, one would expect Tamburlaine's career to be represented as successful; but it is revealing that Marlowe chose to emphasize Tamburlaine's rise from a shepherd and a raiding "thief" to a world emperor and that, in doing this, Marlowe linked his hero's invincibility with the stars and then emphasized the intense will of his heroically rising figure.

95. The relationship between Pontano's theory and Marlowe's plays was pointed out by D. C. Allen, who notes, i.a., that "fortune" is referred to in the Tamburlaine plays twenty-nine times, in contrast with *Dido* (6 times), *Faustus* (2), *Edward II* (8), *The Jew of Malta* (6), and *The Massacre* (1). "Renaissance Remedies for Fortune: Marlowe and the *Fortunati,*" *SP,* XXXVIII (1941), 188-97.

96. In such contexts, the emphasis upon a worldly crown is obviously outside of any such villainous and envious frame of reference as that found in *Selimus* or, e.g., in the *Cobbler's Prophecy,* wherein Ennius speaks as follows:

Suppose he [the ruler] haue beene kinde, liberall, and free,
Why I confesse it, but its my desire,
To be as able to bestow as hee,
And till I can my hart consumes in fire.
O soueraigne glory, chiefest earthly good,
A Crown! to which who would not wade through blood.

(ll. 722-27)

Similarly, in the context established by Tamburlaine, Caesar is one of the *fortunati* (III, iii, 152), not a world tyrant (above, p. 87 n. 50).

97. See, e.g., above, p. 68, or Talbert, *Problem of Order,* p. 94 n. 10.

98. Even the horoscope of Mycetes, for example, agrees with his ridiculous portrayal. Johnstone Parr, "The Horoscope of Mycetes in Marlowe's *Tamburlaine,*" *PQ,* XXV (1946), 371-77.

99. See above p. 66.

100. A study of the rhetoric of the play seems to confirm this point. Donald Peet, "The Rhetoric of *Tamburlaine,*" *ELH,* XXVI (1959), p. 146. See also Charles Brooks, "*Tamburlaine* and Attitudes toward Women," *ELH,* XXIV (1957), 1-11.

101. In other words, both Zerocrate's lament and Anippe's speech are a reminder (negative in one instance and positive in the other) that Tamburlaine is one of the *fortunati.*

102. See, e.g., Greville's signing the warrant for the torture of Edmund Peacham, a clergyman who had written a "seditious" sermon. James Spedding, *The Life and Times of Francis Bacon* (Boston, 1878), II, 48-50 (Jan. 18, 1614-15).

103. Le Roy makes such a statement in his *La Vicissitudine o Mutabile Varietta delle Cose nell' Universo,* as cited by Allen, *SP,* XXVIII, 194.

104. E.g., the "course of crowns," IV, iv, 122 S-D, and such lines as the following (in which the italics are mine):

Deserve these titles I endow you with
By valour and by magnanimity.
Your births shall be no blemish to your fame,
For *virtue* is the fount whence honour springs,
And they are worthy she investeth kings.

(ll. 143-47)

See also the context of Le Roy's reference to Tamburlaine, above, p. 111.

105. A failure to achieve Marlowe's dominant poetical aura can be seen in Greene's "heroic" *Alphonsus King of Aragon,* which is a good example of a dramatist forcing his genius. Although a failure to perceive the theatrical force of Marlowe's aura may not necessarily be seen in Greene's comment about "daring God out of heauen with the Atheist *Tamburlan*" (*Perimedes,* "To the Gentlemen Readers"), it may be seen, perhaps, in modern criticism, which would make "answers" to Marlowe out of some of the heroic and Turkish dramas mentioned above, plays that fail to achieve the constant poetic power of Marlowe's artistry. See, e.g., Irving Ribner, "Greene's Attack on Marlowe: Some Light on *Alphonsus* and *Selimus,*" *SP,* LII (1955), 162-71. Similarly, although Marlowe's reflection of contemporary science is sure, it seems essentially wrong to force the Tamburlaine plays into anything approaching an anti-ambition framework; e.g., Johnstone Parr, *Tamburlaine's Malady and Other Essays on Astrology in Elizabethan Drama* (University, Ala., 1953), p. 11. As a reviewer has argued about another study that would make *1* and *2 Tamburlaine* "one of the most grandly moral spectacles in

the whole realm of English drama," one does not solve much "by confusing drama with morality." Moody Prior, *MP,* XL (1942-43), 290.

106. Catherine has not been mentioned in the discussion of Marlowe's *Massacre.* Suffice it to say that she and Guise are fellow conspirators. For incestuous Remilia, see also such lines of hers as "For were a Godesse fairer than am I, / I'le scale the heauens to pull her from the place" (*Looking Glass,* ll. 508-9).

107. *Edward III,* V, i, 39-46.

108. E.g., III, ii, 56-62; V, ii, 344-73.

109. For such a description of Iarbus, see the account under "Dido" in Thomas Cooper, *Thesaurus Linguæ Romanæ et Britannicæ* (London, 1584, etc.).

110. After scene xiii, 86-90, Faustus' earlier line, "My heart's so hard'ned I cannot repent" (vi, 18), becomes true. Notice the tense, e.g., of xiv, 89-91 (QQ 1616, 1631), on which see *Marlowe's 'Doctor Faustus' 1604-1616: Parallel Texts,* ed. W. W. Greg (Oxford, 1950), p. 390. For an analysis emphasizing the thought in the lines just quoted, see Clifford Davidson, "Doctor Faustus of Wittenberg," *SP,* LIX (1962), 514-23. I believe that what I have pointed out should supplement, and sometimes qualify, this discussion. The repentance motif, of course, appears in many other plays, wherein it usually is valid, e.g., *The Looking Glass, Friar Bacon, Knack to Know a Knave, James IV,* as well as its possible appearance in *Woodstock.* Most of these dramas are Queen's or Strange's plays. The Queen's plays also show in some form or another, e.g., the fairly constant appearance of the motif of patient Griselda or Constance.

111. Above, p. 95 n. 70.

112. Rossiter's edition (above, p. 90 n. 59) is used throughout. For the conventional frame of reference apparent in these quotations, see, e.g., Talbert, *Problem of Order,* p. 80.

113. Rossiter, *Woodstock,* pp. 24-26.

114. I, i, 1-26.

115. In this respect, see also IV, i, 138-49 (cancelled in the MS).

116. In other words, the tension of the play in this respect is between Gloucester's virtue and the immediate developments of the drama, rather than between Gloucester's loyalty and his opposition to a rule that violates the very nature of a commonwealth. Although an effectively ironic scene may result, the play-world does not show the intellectual and emotional tension apparent, for example, in Marlowe's portrayal of Kent. It approaches such a situation in depicting Woodstock's loyalty to the throne and his sympathy for the commons; yet except for his last scene, in each instance the representation of Gloucester's difficulty is brief. At first, Richard's "wanton humour" is "not deadly yet, it may be cured" (I, i, 144-48). Then Woodstock believes that the commons must be pacified and a parliament held to examine the favorites' deeds and that if

> ... by fair means we can win no favour
> Nor make King Richard leave their companies,
> We'll thus resolve, for our dear country's good
> To right her wrongs, or for it spend our blood.
>
> (I, iii, 260-63)

Otherwise, Gloucester in general enunciates the doctrine of nonresistance. Although he is sympathetic with the "rebels," nobles and commons must not strike back though they are struck (III, ii, 85-113). As a consequence, when Woodstock sees a topical significance in the masquing device of some unknown "courtly gentlemen" (IV, ii, 136-51), he grants that "So many wild boars root and spoil our land / That England almost is destroyed by them" but he refers to those grievous ills as God's punishment for subjects' sins. Richard is "our king: and God's great deputy"; and if those gentlemen wish Gloucester to second them in "any rash attempt" against Richard's "state," Woodstock avows that

> Afore my God, I'll ne'er consent unto it.
> I ever yet was just and true to him,
> And so will still remain: what's now amiss
> Our sins have caused . . . [*sic*] and we must
> bide heaven's will.
> I speak my heart: I am Plain Thomas still.

The courtly gentlemen, however, are the disguised Richard and his favorites bent upon capturing Gloucester; and thus his loyalty, and even aspects of divine-right-ist thought, are being used to portray Virtue and Vice and to underline the excellence of the Duke. Similarly, just before his murder, Woodstock will not attempt to escape, nor yet to entreat Richard, but only to admonish him (V, i, 183-92, 147-52, 155-66). But at the same time, the author has turned to the tradition of the *visio.* Both the ghosts of the Black Prince and of Edward III have reaffirmed the dominant emphasis of the drama. The Black Prince attempts to waken Woodstock and avert "King Richard's ire" that will cause Gloucester's blood to be upon the head of the Prince's "wanton son." Edward III goes further. Himself awakened by the wrongs done Gloucester, Edward speaks to the Duke of "Richard of Bordeaux, my accursed grandchild" (l. 86). Richard is "a landlord to my kingly titles". Crown revenue is rented out; the Englishmen who died for Edward in conquering France and who watched his triumphant return are now being racked; and thus Edward exhorts the Duke:

> Haste thee to England, close and speedily!
> Thy brothers York and Gaunt are up in arms,
> Go join them: prevent thy further harms.
>
> (ll. 90-101)

As a result, if by the fifth act any abhorrence of revolt had not been exorcised by the portrayals of Virtue and Vice, it would not have been the author's fault. In this instance, he obviously is using both patriotism and an admiration for heroism to complete his design. On the essential nature of a commonwealth, see, e.g., Talbert, *Problem of Order,* pp. 14-15, 22, 86-88, and *passim.* The most recent editor of *Woodstock* suggests that the disappearance of Richard at the end (i.e., as far as the incomplete MS goes) may be because the author wished to avoid thereby a "direct encounter with Divine Right." This assumes, i.a., an ending that focuses upon Tresilian and Nimble. Rossiter, *Woodstock,* pp. 30, 238.

117. The author's use of conventional comic devices is masterful. Even in the omnipresent device of mistaking words, Master Ignorance is limited and repeats an otherwise meaningless "pestiferous" (III, iii, 7, 33, 99, 145, 151, 205, 219, 243, 264). With comic irony, the device is extended to the frightened "rich chubs," who speak of the "Black" charters that are to be signed (ll. 75, 76). Corrected in their ignorance, these rustics then sign the blanks, since no one could think it any harm to set his mark to nothing (III, iii, 115-18). When they are seized as "privy whisperers," there appears the old, but still effective, joke connected with an execution:

> *All.* Now out alas, we shall all to hanging, sure!
> *Nimb.* Hanging? Nay that's the least on't, ye shall tell
> me that a twelvemonth hence else.
>
> (ll. 146-48)

Even more appropriately, with a blissful, unintentional reverse upon the reverse English of the "libellous" songs, Master Ignorance considers their refrains to be "most shameful treason, for ye said 'God bless my lord Tresilian' " (ll. 155-207). The final situation of whistling treason is then explained by Nimble's fool logic (ll. 234-40); and the searching questions of Master Ignorance—"who did set you a-work? or who was the cause of your whistling? or did any man say to you,

'Go whistle'?"—bring an answer as comically appropriate as the earlier "shameful treason": "The truth is, sir, I had lost two calves out of my pasture, and being in search of them, from the top of the hill I might spy you two at th' bottom here, and took ye for my calves sir ... " (ll. 250-53). The scene ends with the whistler condemned to "limbo" by these representatives of authority. There, with another comic turn, he will be "quartered and then hanged"; for his crime is great in making "a pitiful fellow of a Bailey too!" (ll. 256-60). Similarly, the plan to punish the schoolmaster reflects the fact that such a figure was liable to Elizabethan laughter (IV, iii, 93-97); and for a burlesque of lawyers' Latin, see, I, ii, 123-28; V, vi, 27-35.

118. E.g., Talbert, *Problem of Order,* pp. 37, 57-58, 108-9.

119. The scene, of course, leads directly into the dramatization of how Richard actually let out his realm to lease (IV, i). Although an audience probably would not know that the author utilizes one of the articles brought against Richard at his deposition, their reaction to the scene—when for £7,000 a month Richard delivers his kingdom into the hands of the flattering, wanton four—undoubtedly would come close to being what lines marked for deletion indicate, namely, that Richard by "the meanest subject" will "be censured strangely" when it is told how his "great father toiled his royal person / Spending his blood to purchase towns in France," but how Richard to ease his "wanton youth" became "a landlord to this warlike realm" and rented out his

> ... kingdom like a pelting farm
> That erst was held, as fair as Babylon,
> The maiden conqueress to all the world.
>
> (IV, i, 141-49)

120. It is also interesting to note that Nimble's armour is reminiscent of Ambidexter's accouterment (V, ii, 5, 46; *Cambises,* ll. 126-302).

121. The preceding sentences are based especially upon Act II, scene ii. As has been noted earlier, Woodstock also shows a humorous wittiness (I, iii, 59-65, 88-98). By contrast, Tresilian's "wit" is vicious and accords with the fact that this character is rising villainously in the body politic by his crooked law (e.g., I, ii, 45-50, 57-70), that he represents a sycophantic avariciousness (e.g., IV, i, 1-16), and that he sometimes speaks in a vice-like, gleeking manner (e.g., I, ii, 29-38).

122. E.g., John Neville Figgis, *The Divine Right of Kings* (Cambridge, 1922), pp. 104-5. The text used for *Jack Straw* is *The Life and Death of Iacke Straw,* London, 1593, Tudor Facsimile Ed., 56.

123. W. W. Greg is probably right when he argues that the play was not performed and the manuscript not "finally revised for presentation." *The Book of Sir Thomas More,* Malone Soc., 1911, pp. xiii-xvi. See also pp. xvi-xix. He is also undoubtedly right in his criticism of the text of this play as given in *Shakespeare Apocrypha;* but since quoting from Greg's text would, at times, make the reading of quotations quite difficult, I again use C. F. Tucker Brooke's edition. Italics are mine. The presentation of the course of the drama in *Shakespeare Apocrypha,* indeed, is probably a good representation of what the play might have been like if it were performed. For the problem connected with Hand D (i.e., Shakespeare's hand), see R. C. Bald, *"The Booke of Sir Thomas More* and Its Problems," *Shakespeare Survey,* II (1949), 44-65.

124. This riot, if it were performed, would fall into the broad category of historical civil discord, found, e.g., in *Edward II, Woodstock, Jack Straw,* perhaps the lost *Siege of London,* and Shakespeare's *2 H VI.* When one considers only the plays so far discussed, the variation is great. In *Sir Thomas More,* the unruly multitude is controlled by the protagonist's good name and effective rhetoric. Although More's dominant idea agrees with that in the official *Sermon on Obedience,* he does not emphasize the necessity for degree but rather the necessity for serving divine law, since the majesty of kingly rule derives from

God and since the law of the Golden Rule is basic to all law. These were political commonplaces used by all sorts of propagandists (Talbert, *Problem of Order,* pp. 4-5, 9, 13 n. 17, 15, 22-23, 70 ff., etc.). From proof that peaceful obedience is necessary even to hear and be heard (II, iv, e.g., 62-79) and from a moving *descriptio* of the ends of the rioters, More develops the point that the mob is in arms against God himself (II, iv, 119) and that since the king derives his majesty from God, they should seek mercy from the king (ll. 121-35). The idea is an effective variation upon the concept that a ruler should approximate God's unenvious love. With telling instances, the speech and the scene move to the conclusion voiced by this mob bent on "the removing of strangers": "Fayth, a saies trewe: letts do as we may be doon by" (l. 163). A brief successful exhortation to yield follows, and the action is completed in the next scene. Through the sheriff's haste, Lincoln is not saved by the king's pardon, which has been begged by More, now Lord High Chancellor (III, i, 138-52). A unit-like beginning roughly comparable to what is printed as the first two acts is the result.

125. For his fortitude, see e.g., IV, iii, 90-95. See also the "Later Draft of IV, v, 68 ff.," *Shakespeare Apocrypha,* pp. 419-20.

126. About 690 lines are devoted to More's merry jests, which had been anticipated in the Suresbie incident (I, ii; hence some 207 additional lines). The incidents of Faulkner and Erasmus (III, ii; some 322 lines) follows More's final rise in the body politic, as does the improvising of More at the play-within-the-play (IV, i; some 368 lines), the two situations being joined by twenty-three lines of transition (III, iii).

127. E. R. Curtius, *European Literature and the Latin Middle Ages,* tr. Willard R. Trask (New York, 1953), pp. 425-28.

128. It is noticeable that More's grounds for disobeying the king are never explicitly described as an adherence to Catholicism. The statement that "His [More's] minde will alter, and the bishops too: / Errour in learned heads hath much to doo" (IV, ii, 117-18) is not used, for example, to elucidate the "Errour." Like the relatively few lines that hold out the possibility of More's escaping death, it leads only to brief incidents wherein, to the joy of his loved ones, More apparently agrees to the king's command (IV, v, 158-69; V, iii, 90-99). In brief, the play emphasizes only the first part of the sentence that begins the concluding speech (V, iv, 135-36). It is also strikingly noticeable that the grounds of obedience in the first portion of the drama are never developed in the latter part, for More does not resist his fall.

129. This is frequently true for Elizabethan tragedy. See, e.g., Farnham, *Medieval Heritage,* pp. 37-61 and *passim.*

130. This qualifies somewhat one of the points that Greg makes in his edition of the drama (p. xiii); but see also, e.g., Sisson, *Lost Plays,* pp. 110-14.

CHAPTER IV

1. See also above, pp. 5-6.

2. Above, pp. 71-72. For the pen and ink drawing, see the note immediately following. For a private performance of *TA* in January of 1596, see Gustav Ungerer, "An Unrecorded Elizabethan Performance of *Titus Andronicus,*" *Shakespeare Survey,* XIV (1961), 102-9.

3. A literal interpretation of Jonson's words in 1614 (i.e., at the first performance of *Bartholomew Fair*) to the effect that *The Spanish Tragedy* and *TA* ("Andronicus") had been on the stage "these fiue and twentie, or thirtie yeeres" would place these plays between 1584 and 1589. In view of the congruence between Jonson's words and other circumstances connected with the dating of Kyd's play, it is difficult to dismiss Jonson's testimony about the date of *TA.* See, i.a., T. W. Baldwin, "The Chronology of Thomas Kyd's Plays," *MLN,* XL (1925), 343-48; "Thomas Kyd's Early Company Connections," *PQ,* VI (1927), 311-13. One may, of course, consider Henslowe's "tit(t)us and vespacia" and his "tit(t)us"

to be the same play; but because of a reference to Shakespeare's play in *A Knack to Know a Knave,* performed by Strange's company as "new" on June 10, 1592 (*HD,* I, fol. 8, 1.6), one wonders if there might not be a differentiation between a "new" "tit(t)us and vespacia" (*HD,* I, fol. 7v, 1.2, April 11, 1592) and a play, not new, but called simply "tit(t)us," also performed by Strange's company (*HD,* I, fol. 8, 11. 26, 33, 42, January of 1593). The version of *Titus* belonging to Sussex's men could, then, have been referred to in January 1593-94 as a "new" "tit(t)us and ondronic(o)us," "ondronicous" (*HD,* I, fol. 8v, 1. 30). Henslowe, of course, does abbreviate titles, but this time, perhaps, quite meaningfully: i.e., a new *Titus and Vespasian* (see also the *Destruction of Jerusalem;* or a drama now in two parts, perhaps); an older *Titus* (and hence referred to in a "new" play, *A Knack to Know a Knave*); and a different, or a "new," version of *Titus.*

In view of the natural connection between Titus, Vespasian, and the destruction of Jerusalem, this may be crediting Henslowe with too much care, however; if so, one can predicate of him the same "natural" error that one can predicate of the composer of the derivitive German version of *Titus;* and one still has a *Titus* earlier than *A Knack to Know a Knave.* In the German version Titus' son, Lucius, is named Vespasianus, and in this respect, at any rate, one should hesitate to argue, on the basis of this German Vespasianus, that the *Titus* referred to in *A Knack* was revised throughout (cf. *HD,* II, 155). Thus I follow the usual dating of Shakespeare's play; and this note would not be necessary, perhaps, were it not for some features of T. W. Baldwin's *On the Literary Genetics of Shakspere's Plays, 1592-94* (Urbana, 1959), pp. 402 ff. This recent study, as far as I can see, does not attempt to invalidate the usual dating of Shakespeare's plays, except perhaps for *Titus* and *Romeo and Juliet,* and only then as the arguments lead to hypotheses not dissimilar to some of J. Dover Wilson's. Yet for *Titus* it seems especially perilous to ignore (1) the strong Kydian tradition in the late 1580's and early '90's, (2) the echoes of Marlowe's *Jew of Malta* (ca. 1589-90), and (3) some major features of *Titus* called to one's attention by H. T. Price, "The Authorship of 'Titus Andronicus,'" *JEGP,* XLII (1943), 55-81. Needless to say, the "comprehensive" method of illustrating seems to explain adequately the 1594-95 pen and ink drawing. See John Munroe, "Titus Andronicus," *TLS,* June 10, 1949, p. 385, which comments upon J. Dover Wilson, "'Titus Andronicus' upon the Stage in 1595," *Shakespeare Survey,* I, (1948), 17-22, Plate I. See also the letters by J. Dover Wilson, John Munroe, and A. G. Perrett, *TLS,* June 24, July 1, 1949, pp. 413, 429. For the problems connected with the first scene of *Titus,* the four lines at the end of the play which first appear in Q2, the folio stage-directions, and the "fly scene," see the notes immediately following; W. W. Greg, *The Editorial Problem in Shakespeare* (Oxford, 1942), pp. 117-20, 176-77; H. T. Price, "The First Quarto of *Titus Andronicus,*" *English Institute Essays, 1947* (N.Y., 1948), pp. 137-39.

4. Above, p. 5 n. 10; below, e.g., p. 165 and the opening of *2 H VI.*

5. Price, *Eng. Inst. Essays, 1947,* pp. 137-38, speaks of a "glaring blunder" after line 35. There the following three and a half lines occur: "and at this day / To the Monument of that Andronicy / Done sacrifice of expiation / And slaine the Noblest prisoner of the Gothes." Such lines do accord, however, with that portion of the subsequent S-D which reads that Tamora enters *"and her two sons Demetrius and Chrion."* Thus it is just possible that lines 96-140 might have been omitted, though the compositor of Q1 ignored any marginal line of deletion. There are grounds for believing, however, that the Alarbus incident, instead of being cut, was added in the course of composition, as was the Mutius incident. Munroe, *TLS,* June 10, 1949, p. 385, as well as Perrett, *TLS,* July 1, 1949, p. 429.

6. See also, e.g., W. T. Hastings, "The Hardboiled Shakespeare," *SAB,* XVII (1942), 114-25.

7. The first two have been mentioned already: i.e., the reference, at least, to Alarbus' limbs and entrails with, probably, a display of bloody swords (I, i, 141

ff.) and the killing of Mutius (I, i, 291-93, 341-90). Two others appear in each of the next two acts: that which centers about the pit (II, iii, 116 ff.), that which shows the mutilated Lavinia (II, iv), that which shows the cutting off of Titus' hand (III, i, 185 ff), and that which shows two heads and a hand (III, i, 235 ff). As is indicated in the remainder of the present paragraph, one might continue with a seventh (IV, ii), an eighth (V, ii), and the final ninth (V, iii).

8. E.g., "the whole evil stream of mutual destruction," (*Thyestes*, l. 236); the crimes of Thyestes (ll. 220-35); and such lines as 195-97, 288-89.

9. Below, p. 138.

10. Below, pp. 139-41.

11. Below, pp. 139-41.

12. That is, when the plague had not as yet broken up the large number of actors who had been grouped about the Theater, Curtain, and Rose. Chambers, *Eliz. Stage*, II, 119-20, 129.

13. The phrase is from *Sejanus*, "To the Readers," l. 20, and refers, e.g., to the *sententiæ* of Roman rhetoricians. See above, p. 62, and Leo Kirschbaum, "Jonson, Seneca, and *Mortimer*," *Studies in Honor of John Wilcox* (Detroit, 1958), pp. 9-22.

14. Robert Kilburn Root, *Classical Mythology in Shakespeare* (New York, 1903), 15-17. In opposition to Root's interpretation of this fact, however, see Price, *JEGP*, XLII, 55-81. Note, too, how W. H. Clemen indicates that the use of mythology here shows "the desire of displaying *knowledge*." *The Development of Shakespeare's Imagery* (Cambridge, Mass., 1951), p. 26.

15. It has been argued that Ovid, more than Seneca or the epic poets, is the model for Shakespeare's characterization and style. As in Ovid, e.g., the protagonist is so worked upon by passion that he "ultimately transcends the normal limits of humanity"; and Ovid would be conducive to the rhetoric of "admiration." Eugene M. Waith, "The Metamorphosis of Violence in *Titus Andronicus*," *Shakespeare Survey*, X (1957), 39-49. In this respect, for the influence, which is sometimes very questionable, of *Tamburlaine* upon *Titus*, see Horst Oppel, "*Titus Andronicus*": *Studien zu dramengeschichtlichen Stellung von Shakespeares früher Tragödie*, Schriftenreihe der deutschen Shakespeare-Gesellschaft, Neue Folge 9 (Heidelberg, 1961), pp. 52 ff. See also R. A. Law, "The Roman Background of *Titus Andronicus*," *SP*, XL (1943), 145-53.

16. E.g., T. W. Baldwin, *Shakspere's Small Latine and Lesse Greeke* (Urbana, Ill., 1944), II, 417-19. See also James G. McManaway, "Writing in Sand in *Titus Andronicus*," *RES*, IX (1958), 172-73.

17. Above, p. 86; and note especially *TA*, V, i, 136 and *J of M*, IV, i, 156 ff.

18. Baldwin, *Shakspere's Small Latine*, II, 338-40 (the *descriptio*); *Aphthonii Sophistae Progymnasmata Partim à Rodolpho Agricola, partim à Ioanne Maria Catanaeo latinitate donata: cum luculentis et utilibis in eadem Scholijs Reinhardi Lorichij Hadamarij* (Lvgduni, 1555), pp. 331-35, 342-45; Donald Lemen Clark, *John Milton at St. Paul's* (N.Y., 1948), pp. 245-48. Many critics have commented on the relationship of the first passage to *Venus and Adonis* and of the second to *Thyestes* (ll. 650-56, 666-73, 675-79). For the place of Lorich's Aphthonius and Seneca's tragedies in the grammar-school curriculum, see, e.g., Baldwin, *Shakspere's Small Latine*, II, 288-90, 560.

19. I.e., the "tears" of ll. 6, 14; the "waxing tide," "brinish bowels," or "fountain" of ll. 95, 97, 123; and the development of other figures, as, e.g., earth and a "youthful April," "the honey-dew," the "meadows yet not dry" (ll. 16, 18, 112, 125); etc.

20. *Sp. T*, IV, iv, 193 S-D, and *TA*, "Or shall we bite our tongues, and in dumb shows / Pass the remainder of our hateful days" (ll. 131-32). The thought to be dramatized after Aaron's entrance is "Or shall we cut away our hands" (l. 130).

21. E.g.,

When heaven doth weep, doth not the earth o'erflow?
If the winds rage, doth not the sea wax mad,
Threat'ning the welkin with his big-swoln face?
And wilt thou have a reason for this coil?
I am the sea; hark, how her sighs do blow!
She is the weeping welkin, I the earth;
Then must my sea be moved with her sighs;
Then must my earth with her continual tears
Become a deluge, overflow'd and drown'd. . . .

(ll. 222-30)

22. This point is well made by Clemen, *Shakespeare's Imagery,* pp. 21-26, and ff. One might include here, rather than in connection with the authorship of the play, R. F. Hill, "The Composition of *Titus Andronicus," Shakespeare Survey,* X (1957), 60-70.

23. *The Devil is an Ass,* I, i, 79-88. See Cushman, *Devil and Vice, passim;* and *Ben Jonson,* X, 219-23. Nicholas Brooke argues for the influence of Marlowe on Aaron: "Marlowe as Provocative Agent in Shakespeare's Early Plays," *Shakespeare Survey,* XIV (1961), 35-37.

24. See above, pp. 77-78.

25. Above, pp. 54-55.

26. See also II, i, 24, and for Titus' lines about Rome, III, i, 1-11, 53-56, 73, 80, 168, 290-91, 301.

27. Like the first act, the fifth is organized very obviously, falling in this instance into a triple grouping, both by animated scenes and by causal relationship. This widened scope of the play also accords with the fact that although it may turn in such a direction, *TA* does not develop completely a situation, characteristic of revenge tragedies, wherein the duty to revenge is in conflict with a society that, in some way or another, deprives the injured one of justice. This is true, i.a., because of Titus' initial action against Tamora and because of the slight emphasis upon revenge as a binding duty. Perhaps because of this consideration and because of the beginning and ending emphases, Price writes that this drama "is a political play," with Rome for its hero (*JEGP,* XLII, 72-73). See also Walther F. Schirmer, "Shakespeare und die Rhetorik," *Shakespeare Jahrbuch,* LXXI (1935), 11-31 (especially his comments on the political group of characters, pp. 15 ff.). Price's statement may be true upon reflection, and certainly it is apposite as it appears in a discussion of Shakespeare's authorship; but during most of the drama, the emphasis is elsewhere, and the basic structural movement of this series of horrors is that of the revenge tragedy.

28. Although the judgment conclusions of the Corpus Christi cycles are not wider than the scope of the drama in the sense that the cycle emphasizes the good news manifested through Christ, those conclusions do show the applicability, immediate to all, of what has been dramatized. In such moralities as *Pride of Life* and *The Castle of Perseverance,* the concluding merciful developments are obviously wider than the scope of the struggle proper.

29. The plot is that of Plautus' *Menæchmi,* with one scene in particular (III, i) derived from his *Amphitruo.* Neither Plautus nor Terence, of course, shows the multiplicity within unity which has been noted above (p. 4); yet, in general, Terence's plots are somewhat more complicated than those by Plautus in that they may be said to bifurcate. Whereas the interest of Plautus' comedies will be focused upon the establishment of identity, or upon gulling of a father, a pimp, or a cowardly lover for approval of marriage or for the winning of money or a courtesan, in Terence one finds two pairs of lovers, two fathers gulled, and the son and wily slave doubled. In contrast with Elizabethan practice, however, although the affairs of one Terentian pair may provide the comic situation necessary to sustain the slightly more serious action involving the other pair, each line of action is constantly necessary to the unfolding of the other.

30. The thought that Ephesus is a town of "cozenage," sorcerers, and witch-craft is utilized skillfully. Thus, for example, "goblins, owls, and sprites" are referred to after the second confusion. They must be obeyed or they will suck one's breath or pinch one black and blue. Dromio of Syracuse asks if he is trans-formed and Antipholus asks whether he is asleep or awake, "mad or well-advised" (II, ii, 190-99, 214-18). The thought is repeated after the next confusion centering about the Syracusans (III, ii, 161), and it both introduces and follows the next mistaking of those individuals (IV, iii, 10-11, 42-44), ending with Antipholus' comment that both he and Dromio are "distract" and wandering "in illusions": "Some blessed power deliver us from hence!" Reversed after the encounter that follows, it becomes a conviction on the courtesan's part that Antipholus (to her, of Ephesus) is "mad" (ll. 82 ff.), and it thereby signals the particular form that the epitatical sequence takes as the fourth act closes. It reappears in that reversed form in the catastrophe, when Adriana calls on all to witness how her husband "is borne about invisible" (V, i, 186-87); and it ends each of the first three at-tempts by the Duke to determine the truth (V, i, 270, 281, 329). The appearance of the twins together is then interpreted in a manner that is more specifically classical and mythological than the earlier references to sorcerers, witches, and madness: "One of these men is Genius to the other; / And so of these. Which is the natural man, / And which the spirit? Who deciphers them?" (V, i, 332-34). For these lines, a commentary might have been drawn from *Natalis Comitis Mythologiae, sive Explicationis Fabvlarum, Libri Decem* (IV, iii), a subsidiary school text popular since its publication in 1551. For a fuller treatment of some aspects of this feature of the play, see Baldwin, *Shakspere's 5-Act Structure,* pp. 671-90.

31. Baldwin, *Shakspere's 5-Act Structure,* pp. 701-15.

32. T. W. Baldwin, *William Shakespeare Adapts a Hanging* (Princeton, 1931), *passim.*

33. The first "five o'clock" is pointed toward a reunion between Antipholus of Syracuse and the first merchant (I, ii, 26) and is immediately connected with advancing time only by being turned to the focal point of Acts I and II—"Within this hour it will be dinner time" (l. 11). Thus the first of the many subsequent confusions is developed when Dromio of Ephesus denies knowledge of any money given to him and calls the wrong master to dinner (ll. 41-94). The next comparable references, "Soon at supper-time" (III, ii, 179) and "five o'clock" (IV, i, 10), are lost in Angelo's refusing his money "now," only to do an immediate about-face over the chain (III, ii, 181–IV, i, 13)—a situation that provides a forward movement within the epitasis. Such a movement becomes linked with the madness that stands, in turn, as the focal point of this part of the play (e.g., IV, iii, 82-96; iv, 8 ff.). Again, in its immediate development, this general ticking of the clock is subordinate to the confusion of one Antipholus with the other and to the im-mediately following confusion over a ship or a rope (IV, i, 22-108). The next striking of the hour is turned to word-play with its homophonic "hour"—"whore" and arresting sergeants (IV, ii, 51-62). Then the departure of "the bark Expedi-tion" "tonight" becomes meaningful to the right master (IV, iii, 34-42), but only when puns on arresting officers have become meaningless (ll. 13 ff.). Both references again are subordinate to the developing hustle and immediate confusion that brings Pinch and supernumeraries on stage to bind the madman. I omit only the references to "two o'clock" and to the probability that Antipholus has "gone to dinner" with "some merchant" (II, i, 1-5), for they concern what has been dramatized; and although they lead into the debate-like dialogue between Adriana and Luciana, that dialogue in turn leads into a report of previous action.

34. In developing the confusions, Shakespeare uses, in general a false-true-false process, comparable to that in *Amphitruo,* instead of the true-false-true sequence in *Menæchmi.* Baldwin, *Shakspere's 5-Act Structure,* p. 694.

35. There is the start begun by using Luciana and Angelo to confirm the ac-counts by Adriana and Antipholus of Syracuse; there is that begun by turning to

Dromio of Ephesus and the courtesan; and that begun by Ægeon's incorrect recognition of Antipholus. Each ends with a speech by the duke (ll. 269-74, 280-81, 326-29).

36. Although it is not entirely fair, since Shakespeare, i.a., uses the confusion drawn from *Amphitruo,* a comparison of this development with that in *Menæchmi* italicizes the controlled complexity of *C of E.* In *Menæchmi,* after an explanatory prologue about one set of twins and the place of action has been given, the drama centers about Menæchmus (Antipholus of Ephesus). It is disturbed by his quarrelling with his wife (Adriana) and his connection with Erotium (Courtezan). Only in the second act, consequently, is there a mistaking of identity; and then the situation centers only about Menæchmus Sosicles (Antipholus of Syracuse) as he encounters Cylindras and Erotium. The third act also dramatizes a mistaking of Menæchmus Sosicles—this time by the parasite Peniculus, who had appeared in the first act. Only with the fourth act is the other Menæchmus (Antipholus of Ephesus) mistaken for his twin. The error is first made by his wife—to whom Peniculus has carried his tale—and then by Erotium. In the fifth act, the number of major confusions is increased. There is a confusion centering upon Menæchmus Sosicles. By Menæchmus' father-in-law, by Menæchmus Sosicles' feigned madness, and by the Doctor, it is joined to a second confusion that centers upon the other Menæchmus and upon Messenio (Dromio of Syracuse). Through Messenio, there is then developed the final confusion. It involves Menæchmus Sosicles again, but only briefly, since the other Menæchmus is thrown out of Erotium's house and the twins come fact to face. Separated by act, Plautus' six confusions, of relative simplicity, center on Menæchmus Sosicles (II)—Menæchmus Sosicles (III)—Menæchmus (IV)—Menæchmus Sosicles, Menæchmus, Menæchmus Sosicles (V). Also illustrative of a sixteenth-century multiplicity are the scenes centering upon Shakespeare's Adriana and Luciana (II, i; IV, ii). Although those situations do not turn from the development of the forward movement, they are more tangential to the development of the narrative than is the comparable conversation between Plautus' wife and her father. Similarly, the scenes involving Shakespeare's Balthazar, Angelo, First Merchant, and Second Merchant are much fuller than those involving Plautus' Cylindrus and Peniculus; and the Elizabethan circumstance in the lines given to, or concerned with, Pinch (IV, iv, 55-116; V, i, 168-77, 237-48) contrast with the relatively unadorned appearance of Plautus' doctor (V, iv, v). An embroidery that tends to become tangential is apparent also in Dromio of Ephesus' miming speech (II, i, 58-74) and in Shakespeare's word-play when it becomes extended dialogue involving the figure who is momentarily the chief comic (e.g., II, iii, 39-110). See also below, pp. 146-48.

37. E.g., II, ii, 156 ff.; IV, iv, 71-94; V, i, 22 ff.; V, i, 212-64.

38. *Kemps Nine Days Wonder: Performed in a Daunce,* ed. Alexander Dyce, Camden Soc. 11 (London, 1840), e.g., pp. 6 (l. 3), 10 (l. 10), 11 (l. 10), 13 (l. 4), 18 (l. 21), 19 (ll. 3, 27), 21 (ll. 11, 14-16), 22, (ll. 6-7, 17-18, 21, 27-29). *Diary of John Manningham,* ed. John Bruce, Camden Soc., 99 (London, 1868), e.g., pp. 14 (last line), 16 (ll. 3-5), 17 (ll. 6-9), 36 (ll. 11-13), etc.

39. II, i, 62-71.

40. See especially II, ii. As J. M. Purcell points out, at this point in the drama, Dromio of Syracuse is using proverbs frequently. "Comedy of Errors, II, ii, 57," *N & Q,* CCV (1958), 180 (citing, i.a., Morris Palmer Tilley, *A Dictionary of the Proverbs in England in the Sixteenth and Seventeenth Centuries* [Ann Arbor, 1950]).

41. E.g., above, p. 39 n. 115, and especially *Mankind.*

42. E.g., above, p. 16.

43. Above, p. 13, and the following lines: "They brought one Pinch, a hungry lean-fac'd villain, / A mere anatomy, a mountebank, / A threadbare juggler and a fortune-teller, / A needy, hollow-ey'd, sharp-looking wretch, / A living dead man" (V, i, 238-41).

44. E.g., the chatter of women and the songs of *Ralph Roister Doister,* I, iii; also I, iii, 1-124; II, iii, 37-88; III, iii, 49ff. *Gammer Gurton's Needle,* II, "songe" and "The Fyrst Sceane"; III, iii, 1-50; IV, ii, 1-28; and Diccon *passim* (above, p. 44).

45. For a study of the themes, see Harold Brooks, "Themes and Structure in *The Comedy of Errors,*" *Early Shakespeare,* Stratford-upon-Avon Studies 3 (N.Y., 1961), 55-71.

46. Bernard F. Huppé, for example, emphasizes certain themes in Lyly's comedies. "Allegory of Love in Lyly's Court Comedies," *ELH,* XIV (1947), 93-113. Because of that study, *Endymion* is referred to here; *Midas* is referred to because of its topicality; and *Alexander and Campaspe* because of its treatment of Alexander's recognition of virtue as true gentility (e.g., I, i, 85-91, 118-29) and because of the conflict therein between nobility and love (e.g., I, i, 1-82; V, iv, 191 ff.).

47. E.g., Medwall's *Fulgens and Lucres,* Rastell's *Of Gentleness and Nobility;* and the emphasis upon current discipline in Redford's *Wyt and Science,* in *The Marriage of Wit and Science, Marriage between Wit and Wisdom, Nice Wanton, Disobedient Child, Misogonus,* etc.

48. Geoffrey Bullough, *Narrative and Dramatic Sources of Shakespeare,* I (London, 1957), 203-11. A singularly revealing study, though my emphasis varies somewhat from the author's, is Ralph M. Sargent's "Sir Thomas Elyot and the Integrity of *The Two Gentlemen of Verona,*" *PMLA,* LXV (1950), 1166-80.

49. E.g., Hazelton Spencer, *The Art and Life of William Shakespeare* (N.Y., 1940), p. 141.

50. Sidney's portrayal of Tydeus and Telenos as it contrasts with that of Pyrocles and Musidorus might be instanced as a case in point. Although the former are "men of such prowesse, as not to know feare in themselves, and yet to teach it others that should deal with them," they could be described as thoroughly "setled in their valure" if they had "learned to make friendship *a child and not the father* of Vertue." See Talbert, *Problem of Order,* p. 112; and the footnote immediately following. The italics are mine.

51. See Sargent, *PMLA,* LXV, 1166-80; Lyly, *Works,* I, 187-88; Ruth Kelso, *The Doctrine of the English Gentleman in the Sixteenth Century,* Univ. Illinois Studies in Language and Literature, XIV, Nos. 1-2 (Urbana, 1929), 130-48 and *passim;* Talbert, *Problem of Order,* pp. 108, 111-14, etc.

52. Acts I and II develop toward the situation from which the banishment of Valentine (III, i) arises. Joined with Thurio's wooing and the reappearance of Julia, the consequences of that action constitute Acts III and IV, which end with Julia's soliloquy. With the escape of Eglamour and Silvia (IV, iii, V, i), the play moves to its final situation.

53. Cf., e.g., Spenser's "Prosopopoia: Or Mother Hubberd's Tale," ll. 717-93.

54. E.g., Sargent, *PMLA,* LXV, 1166-80; and, e.g., the *peroratio* of Sidney's *Defence of Poesie:* "But if . . . you bee borne so neare the dull-making *Cataract of Nilus,* that you cannot heare the Planet-like Musicke of *Poetrie . . .* though I will not wish unto you the Asses eares of *Midas . . .* yet thus much Curse I must send you in behalf of all *Poets,* that while you live, you live in love, and never get favour for lacking skill of a Sonet. . . ."

55. (London, 1584), sig. ¶. 5 v.

56. Interpretations of the myth of Phaëthon might make its moral applicable to princes. DeWitt T. Starnes and Ernest William Talbert, *Classical Myth and Legend in Renaissance Dictionaries* (Chapel Hill, 1955), pp. 117-20. As regards the thematic development of this play, however, it should be noted that its emphasis contrasts with that of *As You Like It.* A recognition of the force of a sound discipline upon good parts is constant; yet like the glancing pastoral theme given Valentine or the theological echoes in the explanation of Proteus' redemption (V, iv, 1-3; iv, 79-81, 110-15), it does not dominate the narrative being dramatized

until a transvestite heroine and a sylvan encounter break out "to make good the *Conclusion.*" Valentine's, Proteus', and Julia's discourses on the power of love, for example, show no partially Neo-Platonic developments comparable to those that Lyly elaborated in *Endymion;* nor do they refer to such heroic deeds as those described by Sidney, in which might be seen "the admirable power and noble effects of Love" that make one aspire to "the heavenly Poles" and thereby bring forth "the noblest deeds, that the children of the Earth can boast of." *2 G V,* II, iv, 128-42; vi, 6-43; vii, 15-38; P. W. Long, "The Purport of Lyly's *Endimion,*" *PMLA,* XXIV (1909), 164-84; "Lyly's *Endimion:* An Addendum," *MP,* VIII (1910-11), 599-606; Huppé, *ELH,* XIV, 102-7; Sidney, *Works,* I, 191-92. Even when the catastrophe is being developed, Valentine's willingness to renounce Sylvia is utilized to cause Julia's theatrical swoon, and not to glance even briefly in the direction of "my friend and I are one; / Sweet flattery! then she loves but me alone" (Sonnet 42, 13-14). In other words, the ideas utilized in this drama, though they may animate its beginning and determine its ending, are otherwise congruent reminders of a character's virtue or worthlessness, as romantic love animates the action. Shakespeare's purpose is thematic only as the balances between a true and false friend in love are utilized in dramatizing a courtly story and then drawn upon for the wide concluding emphasis of the duke's lines after the transvestite motif has been resolved by a melodramatic faint. In *As You Like It,* the serious treatment and the mockery of romantic love provide the substance for most of the drama, in which the pastoral ideal also receives a similar treatment (e.g., II, i, 1-17, v, 1-8, 40-47; II, v, 52-59 and III, ii, 11-22). See, e.g., C. L. Barber, "The Use of Comedy in *As You Like It,*" *PQ,* XXI (1942), 353-67.

57. The transvestite motif may well have been derived from Jorge de Monte-mayor's *Diana;* for the additional rival wooer, see above, pp. 31-32.

58. For an appropriate background and for scenes in other plays, see Baskervill, *Eliz. Jig,* pp. 98-99; Louis B. Wright, "Animal Actors on the English Stage before 1642," *PMLA,* XLII (1927), 656-69; to the examples enumerated therein may be added the horse of *Woodstock,* above, p. 125.

59. Baskervill, *Eliz. Jig,* e.g., pp. 86-87, 244, 314.

60. The first comic scene, for example, centers about Speed and involves references to relatively serious situations. References to the departure of Valentine begins the dialogue (I, i, 70-75); and the report of Julia's reception of Proteus' letter, to be dramatized further in Act I, scene ii, is a topic from which the majority of the lines are developed (ll. 99-155). Between the two topics, from word-play with *ship-sheep,* Shakespeare develops the comic logic in the conclusion that Speed is a sheep (ll. 76-98); and thus the first part of the report about Julia is drawn from the comic's punning on "mutton," with its bawdy overtones (ll. 99-110) and with resulting puns (ll. 111-16). The second part of the report about Julia involves exaggerated action and word-play with "noddy" (117-32); the third centers about the comic's conventional begging of *trinkgelt* (136-55), a topic anticipated by lines that stood as a culmination of the first part and a transition to the second part of the dialogue concerning this heroine (ll. 111-16). After the topic of Valentine's departure from Verona has occurred, the sequence, con-sequently, falls into four parts; and it seems indicative of Shakespeare's careful artistry that each division ends in a manner that reflects other conventional devices or jests. "Such another proof will make me cry 'baa'" (l. 97-98) seems a faint reflection of the comic's cries, which if not derived from the older entrances of devils, may well be in the tradition embracing them. "From a pound to a pin? Fold it over and over. / 'Tis threefold too little for carrying a letter to your lover" (ll. 115-16) is a summation of the preceding dialogue in "rough" meter, sometimes characteristic of both an earlier vice's comments and Tarleton's improvisations. "Beshrew me but you have a quick wit" (l. 132) indicates a dramatic tradition embracing not simply Lyly's pages but the *Geta* of the medieval Vitalis as well; and, the proverbial jest, "He that is born to be hanged shall never be drowned," was apparently so well known that it could be implicit in the lines:

> Go, go, be gone, to save your ship from wreck,
> Which cannot perish having thee aboard,
> Being destin'd to a drier death on shore.
>
> (ll. 156-58)

With its emphasis on word-play, this first comic sequence seems a good deal closer to Shakespeare's elaboration of his classical source in *The Comedy of Errors* than do the succeeding ones, although it is basically an antic development of the love motif and balances the similar scene (II, i) concerning Valentine, Sylvia, and a letter.

In contrast, Launce's first miming dialogue (II, iii, 1-35) is a comic parallel, also in no way derisive, of the sorrowful parting between Proteus and Julia "without a word" (II, ii, 16):

> My mother weeping, my father wailing, my sister crying, our maid howling, our cat wringing her hands. . . .

Only Crab, Launce's dog, brought upon the stage for the first time, did not "shed one tear" (II, iii, 6-10). Beginning with the old trick of mistaking words—a trick that will appear in all of Launce's scenes and be specified as his "old vice still" (III, i, 283-4)—this account is followed by Launce's miming of that sad event. It is then that the actor must have used both of his shoes, his hat, and a staff—to which comedians talked in such plays as *Edward I* (xviii) and *The Life and Death of Jack Straw* (above, p. 128). With bawdiness and scurrility (ll. 15-20, 30-32), this miming speech then turns into dialogue with Panthino; and as Launce's weeping sorrow stretches almost to the end of the conversation (l. 60), there is punning on *tide-tied,* joined by surprising action (l. 51) to the old joke of *tongues* and *tales-tails.* The scene then ends with what looks like some brief comic bravery, developed from *call* meaning both "summon" and "name" (ll. 61-63). Here as later, particularly in Act III, scene i, word-play has moved from an emphasis on word *qua* word to a representation of comic misunderstanding resulting from the particular preoccupations of the individuals concerned. Most obviously, this sequence also anticipates Shakespeare's development of a similar parallel scene after the reunion of the masters at Milan. Then the servants greet one another; and Launce, face to face with Speed, becomes the unquestionable chief comedian (II, v). At that time, the conventional habitat of the ale-house is mentioned at the beginning and the end of the scene with a jest of comic logic for each of its appearances (ll. 3-11, 56-63). Between these jokes, the servants comment upon their masters' love; and from lines fed him by Speed, Launce develops bawdy jests about an "understanding" staff and a hot *lover-lubber* who can burn himself.

61. *Works,* I, 290-91, 295-99.

62. Above, pp. 15-17.

63. V, ii; iv, 132-35.

64. Henry Chettle, *Kind-Hartes Dreame,* Bodley Head Quartos, 1923, p. 6 ("To the Gentlemen Readers").

65. Irony provides one of Shakespeare's varying comic tones. The first instance of a scene so developed with striking obviousness centers about Proteus' deception of his father and the fact that he thereby falls in with his parent's plan to send him to Milan (I, iii). In a different manner, the irony is increased during the conclusion to the second act. Valentine, who first spoke against love, now speaks with "braggardism" in praise of his mistress (II, iv, 164). Furthermore, just as his praise of his friend had been inherently ironic, so his praise of Sylvia is represented as being, perhaps, one of the reasons for Proteus' possible love of this woman loved by his friend (II, iv, 196-98). Even more obvious in its irony is the fact that Shakespeare places Julia's praise of Proteus and her plans to be with him immediately after the soliloquy in which Proteus confirms his forswearing (II, vi, vii) and immediately before the scene wherein Valentine, again

with dramatic irony, is trapped by the duke through Proteus' unfaithfulness (III, i, 1-169). When the scheme is afoot to supplant Thurio for Valentine in Sylvia's affections, the irony in Proteus' reference to Valentine as his "friend" (III, ii, 37, 41) is of a different, villainous sort, as Launce remarks (III, i, 261-63). It is soon supplanted, however, by a lighter dramatic irony as Julia witnesses and comments on the serenading episode (IV, ii) and becomes Proteus' emissary to Sylvia (IV, iv, 113-83)—with appropriate extradramatic moments (ll. 95-112, 184-210). Such a note of comic dramatic irony culminates in the old trick of overhearing villainy (V, iv, 1-60), and the play thereby moves to its conclusion. As a result, excluding the scenes with the outlaws and with Eglamour, the only relatively serious ones that do not show some irony are the opening scene and the scene of parting "without a word" between Julia and Proteus (II, ii). This last scene, however, is followed immediately by a comic parallel scene. Certainly Shakespeare's concern with an Elizabethan's likely amusement *qua* amusement seems obvious from such considerations alone.

Other matter not connected with the principal comedians shows some brief "witty" dialogue of high degree; and in accordance with what has just been noted, this dialogue is also paralleled on a lower level and developed, in part, as derision pointed at Thurio. In this respect, some interesting, possibly cohesive, details are noteworthy. The early punning upon musical terms (I, ii, 80-97), later becomes obviously ironic (IV, ii, 55-72). An entire early scene consistent with the comic jest about the affirmative meaning of a maid's "no" (I, ii, e.g., ll. 34 ff.) is briefly utilized by Valentine in the love discipline he imparts to a feigning duke later in the play (III, i, 93-101). And particularly in Act II, scene iv (1-121), witty dialogue, ridicule of Thurio, and love rhetoric are handled with a neat balance that shows skill in effecting diverse comic tones.

66. The dating of Shakespeare's play is intricately connected with its relationship to *A Shrew* and the question of Shakespeare's collaboration with another in writing *The Shrew*. I follow, in general, the line of argument advanced by Raymond A. Houk. He sees only two strata in Shakespeare's play and derives *A Shrew* from an earlier, perhaps unfinished, version of the play which may well have been written by Shakespeare. "The Integrity of Shakespeare's *The Taming of the Shrew*," *JEGP* XXXIX (1940), 222-29; "The Evolution of *The Taming of the Shrew*," *PMLA*, LVII (1942), 1009-38; "Strata in *The Taming of the Shrew*," *SP*, XXXIX (1942), 291-302; "Shakespeare's *Shrew* and Greene's *Orlando*," *PMLA*, LXII (1947), 657-71; "*Doctor Faustus* and *A Shrew*," *PMLA*, LXII (1947), 950-57. Although I am aware of recent attempts to reopen this question of the relationship between *A Shrew* and *The Shrew,* neither all of the facts adduced by Houk nor their relationship to his total argument has as yet been met (e.g., John W. Schroeder, "*The Taming of A Shrew* and *The Taming of The Shrew*," *JEGP,* LVII (1958), 424-43). Especially important is the theatrical situation in 1593 as it can be related to Pembroke's men. After touring the provinces during the plague, they were back in London by September 28, when they were mentioned by Henslowe as being forced to pawn their wardrobe. Then, presumably, at least four of their plays came into the booksellers' hands. In addition to *A Shrew,* those dramas are *Edward II* (pb., 1593), *Titus Andronicus* (pb., 1594, perhaps through or with Sussex's men), *The True Tragedy of Richard Duke of York* (pb., 1595, i.e., the bad quarto of *3 H* VI). Here, too, should be included, in all probability, *The First Part of the Contention of York and Lancaster* (pb., 1594, i.e., the bad quarto of *2 H VI*). With those plays in the repertory of Pembroke's men, there may well have been *Doctor Faustus. Marlowe's 'Doctor Faustus,' 1604-1616,* ed. W. W. Greg (Oxford, 1950), pp. 60-62. In the circumstances of provincial performance and a lack of funds, and in view of the large group of actors connected with an earlier amalgamated company, it seems eminently logical that this repertory would include three bad quartos, or two bad quartos and a play based on portions of what would be Shakespeare's *The Shrew* and pieced out with lines showing the popularity of *Tamburlaine* and a knowledge of another

drama in the repertory (i.e., *Faustus*). For the derivative patchwork in *A Shrew*, see, e.g., *The Taming of a Shrew*, ed. F. S. Boas (London, 1908), pp. xxx-xxxii. For the relationship in language between these texts and Shakespeare's *2 H VI*, *3 H VI*, and *The Shrew*, see, e.g., Alfred Hart, *Stolne and Surreptitious Copies* (Melbourne, 1942), pp. 439-40 and *passim*. See also below, p. 161 n. 1.

67. I paraphrase Ben Jonson: "Stay, and see his last *Act*, his *Catastrophe*, how hee will perplexe that, or spring some fresh cheat, to entertaine the *Spectators*, with a convenient delight, till some unexpected, and new encounter breake out to rectifie all, and make good the *Conclusion.*" *The Magnetic Lady*, "Chorus," after Act IV, ll. 27-31. See also Baldwin, *Shakspere's 5-Act Structure*, pp. 314-15.

68. See the comments on *Sir Thomas More*, above, p. 130; and Houk's argument in the articles noted above, p. 157 n. 66. Although *The Shrew* is sometimes dated as late as *ca*. 1596, Chambers, e.g., who sees more than one hand in the play, would date it *ca*. 1594. *William Shakespeare*, I, 324, 326-27. See also Tommy Ruth Waldo and T. W. Herbert, "Musical Terms in *The Taming of the Shrew*: Evidence of Single Authorship," *SQ*, X (1959), 185-99.

69. Aphthonius, *Progymnasmata*, p. 176.

70. This also may have been derived from *Supposes*. George Gascoigne, *Supposes and Jocasta*, ed. John W. Cunliffe (Boston, 1906), e.g., IV, iv-viii.

71. Above, p. 73; *The Shrew*, I, i, 47 ff. (with Sly and his associates also watching); I, ii, 141-63; IV, ii, 1-43; V, i (the characters within and above, the characters below, and the watching Petruchio and Kate).

72. E.g., *Supposes*. I, ii (Balia); II, iii-iv (Dulipo).

73. In *A Shrew*, the characters of the Induction speak occasionally throughout the drama, and that line of action is completed in an epilogue. Nearly every editor mentions possible explanations for Sly's disappearance in *The Shrew*.

CHAPTER V

1. The preceding statements may seem to ignore a considerable body of scholarship devoted to strata in the dramas about Henry VI and to the relationship between *2* and *3 H VI* on the one hand and, on the other, *The First Part of the Contention betwixt the two famous Houses of Yorke and Lancaster* (pb. 1594) and *The true Tragedie of Richard Duke of Yorke* (pb. 1595). In spite of Charles Tyler Prouty's *'The Contention' and Shakespeare's '2 Henry VI': A Comparative Study* (New Haven, 1954), the theory still prevails that the latter plays are bad quartos of *2* and *3 H VI*. This is because of such evidence as that presented by Hart, *Stolne Copies*, p. 440 and *passim*. External evidence (Henslowe's *Diary*, Nashe's *Pierce Penilesse*, and Greenes *Groats-Worth of Wit*) points to the composition of the trilogy by early 1592. Whether those plays originally were given the form they now have or whether they have such a form as the result of Shakespeare's work with earlier dramas, it is certainly possible that a structural conception other than one that would be applicable to a single play alone may have constituted a formative element in their composition. Although he did not apply his statement to Shakespeare's dramas and although he emphasized "formlessness" and a national spirit, John W. Cunliffe wrote many years ago that the "character of the earliest surviving history plays in the vernacular suggests that the impulse to their composition was not academic but popular, and their models not classical tragedy, at first or second hand, but miracle plays, the methods of which" were applied to "national history, as had been done in France more than a century before." *CHEL*, V, 92. Quite recently, e.g., Ribner referred in passing to such an idea when he was writing about the Henry VI plays; and Baldwin, while emphasizing their five-act structure, asserted that Shakespeare was responsible for the structural form of these dramas and that they were written chronologically. Ribner, *Hist. Play*, p. 100; Baldwin, *Genetics of Shakspere's Early Plays*, e.g., pp. 340, 348 (his comment on the protasis of *1 H VI*), 381, 390. As is

well known, E. M. W. Tillyard in his *Shakespeare's History Plays* (N.Y., 1946) emphasizes the Tudor myth and aspects of political thought compatible with the doctrine of obedience, while Lily B. Campbell in her *Shakespeare's "Histories": Mirrors of Elizabethan Policy* (San Marino, Cal., 1947) sees in the dramas reflections of specific situations resulting from "Elizabethan policy," although she leaves the Henry VI dramas for a separate study. Of the revisionists' theories, that by J. Dover Wilson in his edition of the dramas (Cambridge Ed., 1952) is perhaps most characteristic: e.g., (1) Greene was the "plotter" of all three in collaboration with Peele and Nashe; (2) *2* and *3 H VI* were written in 1591-92 for Pembroke's men, with Shakespeare later being called upon to revise them; (3) *1 H VI* was written after *2* and *3 H VI* as a result of their success and of the topical bearing that Essex's Normandy expedition of 1591-92 might have; (4) after the amalgamated Admiral-Strange group of actors "broke" with Greene, Shakespeare "shaped" the unfinished "book" of *1 H VI* for production, perhaps in collaboration with Nashe; for Shakespeare already had been the revisor of *2* and *3 H VI,* and through him, this company acquired "rights" for *1 H VI.* For an argument that Margaret's role shows signs of indebtedness to the old *Leir*—an argument that proceeds in accordance with one aspect of this complicated theory—see Thomas H. McNeal, "Margaret of Anjou: Romantic Princess and Troubled Queen," *SQ,* IX (1952), 1-10. Note, however, the cogency of such criticism as that by Leo Kirschbaum, "The Authorship of *1 Henry VI,*" *PMLA,* LXVII (1952), 809-22. As the following pages will indicate, moreover, the artistry of the three plays shows a progressive capability. For a summary and a brief criticism of Andrew S. Cairncross' argument concerning the text of *2 H VI* (Arden Ed., 1957) see the review by George Walton Williams, *MLR,* LIII, (1958), 236-37.

2. None of those histories show the dramatic rhetoric nor the panoramic scope of these three Shakespearian plays.

3. For details, see James Munro, "Some Matters Shakespearian—III," *TLS,* Oct. 11, 1947, p. 528.

4. E.g., E. K. Chambers, *William Shakespeare,* I, 289-93.

5. *Pierce Penilesse, His Svpplication to the Divell,* Bodley Head Quartos, 1924, p. 87.

6. John Munro, *TLS,* Oct 11, 1947, p. 528.

7. See, e.g., Read, *Sec. Walsingham,* I, 224, and the passage quoted from the admiral's advice that lumps Elizabeth and the King of Spain together as enemies to "the safety and maintenance of this [the French] crown." See also *3 H VI,* IV, i, 36-46. The quotation is from Ponet's *A Shorte Treatise of politike pouuer,* p. 22, facsimile ed. in Winthrop S. Hudson, *John Ponet* (Chicago, 1942).

8. Talbert, *Problem of Order,* pp. 129 ff.

9. Pp. 86-89.

10. Aphthonius, *Progym.,* p. 284. For characteristic forms of the death lament and its use in metrical romances as well as in Elizabethan drama, see Velma Bourgeois Richmond, "The Development of the Rhetorical Death Lament from the Late Middle Ages to Marlowe" (Ph.D. diss., Univ. of N.C., 1959).

11. Here as elsewhere, of course, quantity is recognized as being far from an infallible criterion for indicating emphasis, but it can be corroborative of other features of an author's artistry; and other things being equal, it does roughly indicate playing time—with allowance being made here for the greater time probably given to the stage action centering about Orleans in the second sequence than to the skirmishes and similar matter in the first three scenes.

12. Above, p. 110, as well as Tamburlaine's sensing of success. In connection with the Black Prince's heroism, the heroic Edward III also seems to show something akin to the folk-hero's misunderstood cleverness (III, v, 10-18). The author modifies this, however, by giving to the king a fortitude that was meant, perhaps, to heighten what suspense there was in the prince's encounter with "a world of odds" (ll. 19-63).

13. Including tumult off stage and three skirmishings (III, i, 75, 85 S-D, 92, 103).

14. Act IV, scene ii, with a pageantic opening, utilizes again both upper and lower stages and posits the immediate perilous situation. The two succeeding scenes, which balance one another, increase that peril. Act IV, scene v, by the new figure of John Talbot, complicates emotionally the narrative development; and scene vi shows Talbot's rescue of his son, with a subsequent development that emphasizes this mixture of paternal and filial love with heroism. The final scene (vii) ends with both of the Talbots dead. In this Bourdeaux sequence, consequently, there once more appears a rescuing Talbot, the death of an heroic English warrior, etc.; and the conclusion intensifies the difference between the endings of the Orleans and the Rouen sequences.

15. I.e., York having Joan "fast" (V, iii, 30); Suffolk with Margaret *"in his hand,"* "Be what thou wist, thou art my prisoner" (V, iii, S-D and l. 45).

16. *The First Part of the Contention betwixt the two famous Houses of Yorke and Lancaster, with the death of the good Duke Humphrey: And the banishment and death of the Duke of* Suffolke, *and the Tragicall end of the proud Cardinall of* Winchester, *with the notable Rebellion of* Iacke Cade: And the Duke of Yorkes first claime vnto the Crowne.

17. For some relationships between stage effect and doctrine, see Stephen Joseph Laut, S. J., "Drama Illustrating Dogma: A Study of the York Cycle" (Ph.D. diss., Univ. of N.C., 1960). Note, i.a., the mature Isaac lying bound on the ground (ll. 277-78, 283-84) and the stretching of Christ on the cross, which has been laid on the ground (e.g., ll. 39-40, 75-76). *York Plays,* ed. Lucy Toulmin Smith (Oxford, 1885), pp. 63-64, 350-56.

18. E.g., the patterned technique of the plays of the prophets and of the harrowing of Hell, or the similar technique constantly apparent in the Chester cycle as it reflects, or continues, the patterns of many Latin dramas of the medieval church (the deluge play, excluding the comic development centered about Noah's wife). See also Laut, "Drama Illustrating Dogma."

19. Chambers, *Med. Stage,* II, 113.

20. See, e.g., Alfred Harbage, *Annals of English Drama, 975-1700* (Philadelphia, 1940), under 1585. Note also, e.g., *1, 2 Tamburlaine* (1587-88); *1, 2 Troublesome Reign* (1588); *1, 2 Tamar Cham* (1592, 96); *1, 2 Caesar and Pompey* (1594, 95); *1, 2 Godfrey of Boulogne* (1590, 94).

21. E.g., *Abraham and Lot* (1580-94), *Hester and Ahasuerus* (1580-94), *David and Bethsabe* (1581-94), *History of Job* (1586-93), or *Looking Glass for London and England* (1587-91), with its Jonah matter and lines from the Bible.

22. E.g., Chambers, *Med. Stage,* II, 130; the prologues of the Norwich Grocers' Play (*The Non-Cycle Mystery Plays,* ed. Osborn Waterhouse, E.E.T.S., E.S., 104, pp. 11-12); the prologue of the Digby massacre, ll. 25-32 (*The Digby Plays,* ed. F. J. Furnivall, E.E.T.S., E.S., 70, p. 2); or the speech by Contemplatio before the King Herod play in *Ludus Coventriae,* ll. 9-20 (ed. K. S. Block, E.E.T.S., E.S., 120, p. 271).

23. Above, p. 90 n. 58.

24. Talbert, *Problem of Order,* pp. 28-29, 80-81, 104-5, 110-11, etc.

25. *Arcadia,* I, 185. See also Talbert, *Problem of Order,* pp. 38, 59-60, 109-10, 144 n. 33, etc.

26. Talbert, *Problem of Order,* pp. 26, 29-30, 34-36, 61-62, 115-16, etc.

27. Above, pp. 126, 177-78 n. 25.

28. The garden scene shows an alignment of three to one for York. Although Somerset's outburst of anger at that alignment is answered in kind, it nevertheless breaks his promise to "Yield the other in the right opinion" (II, iv, 60-61, 42). Within the bounds of a great one's honor, the emphasis also favors Plantagenet (e.g., II, iv, 80-103); and although the closing speeches prophecy a bloody sequel to this quarrel, that thought again had been inaugurated by Somerset (e.g., ll. 50, 61).

29. In accordance with the earlier appearance of skirmishing (I, iii), the scales are weighted further on the side of Gloucester, and hence indirectly for York but against Somerset. It is Gloucester and the king who attempt to stop the riotous outbreak, but asides by Winchester and Somerset upset the union on the stage both before and after Plantagenet has been restored to his title.

30. An audience already would have been reminded of the opening of the drama, for some of Lucy's lines had referred to that situation (IV, iii, 47-52).

31. Only his opponent speaks of York's ambition: "York set him on to fight and die in shame, / That, Talbot dead, great York might bear the name" (IV, iv, 8-9). As it will be pointed out, those lines occur, however, as Somerset is denying the dominant emphasis of both sequence and play; and they are overridden immediately by Lucy's censure and by the focal point of interest in Talbot's death—nor is the thought ever repeated. Somerset then disappears from this play-world, while an audience watches and hears York during the capture of Joan.

32. One should also remember that although Lucy's soliloquy about the "vulture of sedition" had followed his dialogue with York, it also had introduced the Somerset scene, just as Exeter's presage of some ill event had introduced the entire sequence.

33. I.e., as York might be said to stand between excellent heroism and an honor that leads to the vulture of sedition.

34. Nearly all editions of Marlowe's *Faustus* or Greene's *Friar Bacon* refer to the popularity of theatrical supernaturalism.

35. For classical derivations of a traditional relationship between braggart and prostitute, see Boughner, *Ren. Braggart,* pp. 7, 11, 15-16 and *passim;* for a traditional relationship between clown, frequently cowardly, and shrew or ugly wench, see above, pp. 16, 29-30, 37-38.

36. Above, p. 41.

37. This contrasts with the earlier derision of Winchester, a brief development based on the fact that a portion of his jurisdiction in Elizabethan times was noted for its stews (I, iii, 35-56).

38. For the scenes Act III, scene iii through Act IV, scene i, see the second paragraph following.

39. In addition to what has been noticed above, p. 100 n. 75, allegorical inductions seem to have been somewhat popular, especially during the 1580's and early '90's; cf. *Gismond of Salerne* (1566, 68), *Rare Triumphs of Love and Fortune* (1582), *The Spanish Tragedy* (1584-89), *Dido, Queen of Carthage* (1587-93), *Misfortunes of Arthur* (1588), *Solimon and Perseda* (1589-92), *Woman in the Moon* (1590-95), *The Tragedy of Caesar and Pompey* (1592-96), *Two Lamentable Tragedies* (1594-98), *Histriomastix* (1599, based perhaps on a play *ca.* 1589), *Old Fortunatus* (1599, with *Fortunatus,* 1580-96). See also *James IV* (1590-91).

40. Above, pp. 63 ff.

41. See Talbert, *Problem of Order,* pp. 14-15, 22-23, and *passim.*

42. See, e.g., *Castle of Perseverance,* ll. 566 ff., 2649 ff; *Mankind,* ll. 598 ff.; and even more appropriate, the establishment of the alliterative vices at court after Fancy's success in *Magnyfycence,* ll. 251 ff., e.g., ll. 639-88.

43. In *A Looking Glass, James IV, Edward II, Edmond Ironside,* and *Woodstock,* a favorite appears with individuals of low degree, as in four of the five plays he hires followers. See above, p. 90. Just as Gaveston already has been exiled because of his favored position, so Suffolk always has been of high birth; and perhaps as a result, in the dramas by Marlowe and Shakespeare little or nothing, respectively, is made of any comic hiring. In both instances, however, the favorite's contempt for the poor multitude and his use of the situation for his own advantage is apparent.

44. E.g., see above, p. 178 and n. 25; the phrase, of course, is used ironically by Sidney, *Works,* I, 278.

45. In three of the non-Shakespearian plays just noted, this appearance of a favorite with those of low degree occurs in the morality-like process of Right

struggling with Wrong for the control of a kingdom. The exceptions are *A Looking Glass* and *Edmond Ironside;* yet in these plays, too, the public consequences of the triumph of Wrong are apparent, even though they do not show the morality pattern noted above, pp. 107, 145-48, 154-57, 187-89.

46. Although it usually was given to the ruler, an insistence upon absolutism was part of the dramatization of similar situations in *James IV, Edward II,* and *Woodstock.* Above, pp. 92-93, 98-99, 103, 124. See also, pp. 87-88, and for a conventional association between absolutism and tyranny, Talbert, *Problem of Order,* pp. 27-30, 94-95, etc.

47. As many critics have noted, the double conflict pattern of the struggle between Vice(s) and Virtue(s) is itself doubled in *The Castle of Perseverance,* with the fourth "struggle" being supplanted by the debates between Body and Soul and the Four Daughters of God. For morality-like elaborations of a cycle, see, e.g., the Norwich Grocers' play.

48. See, e.g., Sister Mary Philippa Coogan, *An Interpretation of the Moral Play Mankind* (Washington, 1947), pp. 53, 59-71. Therein a similar situation in *Magnyfycence* is also discussed.

49. Talbert, *Problem of Order,* pp. 18-20, 30-31, 50-53, 59.

50. See, for example, the title of the quarto, above, p. 174 n. 16.

51. Above, pp. 56-60.

52. Warwick appears with "many Commons" at III, ii, 122; Salisbury speaks for them at III, ii, 242. Although in both incidents there is an indication of noise before their entrance (ll. 122 S-D, 239), they apparently are well disciplined.

53. Note the repetition of the Suffolk-serpent figure from, e.g., Henry's speech (l. 47) and the reference to Henry's "death."

54. Neale, *Eliz. & Parl., 1584-1601,* e.g., pp. 296-97.

55. This point has been made in regard to censorship; Talbert, *Problem of Order,* p. 225 n. 13.

56. See especially III, ii, 380-412.

57. In this respect, some of the information noted by Ruth L. Anderson, "Excessive Goodness as a Tragic Fault," *SAB,* XIX (1944), 85-95, might be used to gloss Henry's piety. See also Hugh Dickinson, "Shakespeare's Henry Yea-and-Nay," *Drama Critique,* IV (1961), 68-72.

58. There should be little need to comment upon the laws against witchcraft and against meddling in the supernatural, especially when it might be construed as having a political purpose.

59. See above, pp. 103-5, and below, pp. 313-14, as well as Talbert, *Problem of Order,* pp. 162-66, 184-87.

60. E.g., see Camden's comment on Essex's "genealogy," Campbell, *Shakespeare's "Histories,"* pp. 180-81.

61. See, e.g., Talbert, *Problem of Order,* pp. 114-15, 87-88.

62. See, e.g., Sidney, *Works,* I, 194, 392, 186-87.

63. For "titanism" see Craig, *PQ,* XIX (1940), 1-19, and above, pp. 68-69, 105, 108.

64. The phrase "Repairs him with occasion" is also congruent with the emphasis here upon the vigorous rise of one who grasps opportunity; see below, p. 273 n. 17.

65. For citations of Aristotle, Plato, Plutarch, Montaigne, Machiavelli, Bacon, etc., see Anderson, *SAB,* XIX (1944), 85-95.

66. See, e.g., the preceding discussion of Margaret's lines (III, i, 223-34; V, ii, 72). Human equivocality, as it is described here, need not, of course, be divorced from the operation of an impersonal Fortune; and to represent the existence of Fortune in conjunction with an emphasis upon character was not at all uncommon. Farnham, *Medieval Heritage, passim.* But for my emphasis here upon character, rather than upon Fortune, Fate, prophecies, or Nemesis, see below, pp. 219 and n. 72, 234 and 103.

67. By *habitus* and *natura,* I refer to the Ciceronian "places" of character: *habitus* being a stable condition of mind or body acquired by training or practice;

natura being such things as family connections, inborn physical or emotional or intellectual endowments. *Affectio* would be an unstable condition, resulting from desire, joy, fear, etc. *Studium* would be an assiduous application of the mind to some body of knowledge. *Consilium,* the reason for doing or not doing a thing. These places were aids in categorizing persons and might be used, e.g., in the *confirmatio* of an oration. Other places were *nomen,* name; *victus,* manner of life; *fortuna,* circumstances of life. With *consilium,* as they related to the judicial oration, were *facta,* things done; *casus,* things befalling; *orationes,* things said. See Doran, *End. of Art,* p. 219 n. 5.

68. As regards the fluctuating fortunes of these houses, critics frequently comment upon Warwick's role; but just as noticeable in the theatre, if not more so, would be the way in which the changes of allegiance given to the Yorkist Clarence accord with the course of events. Granted that Warwick's alliance with the Lancastrians (III, iii) adumbrates the major narrative development of Act IV, yet Clarence's first change of allegiance (IV, i) solidifies that adumbration, just as his second change (V, i) solidifies the adumbration of future action at the end of Act IV (scenes vii, viii). These changes agree, moreover, with the thought inherent in the sight of three joined suns (i.e., also "sons," II, i). Then, too, the capture of Edward results as much from the circumstances of his camp as from the power of Warwick. Furthermore, Warwick's change of allegiance does not appear as the third act begins, whereas the representation of dominant attributes of character does—a representation that leads into a development not completed until after Warwick's death and a representation, as far as Edward is concerned, that causes Warwick's alliance with the Lancastrians. These considerations, of course, have no bearing upon the theatrical effect of Warwick's death nor upon the way in which Shakespeare merges the conception of Warwick the king-maker with his structural movement that progresses to the death of Henry.

69. E.g., above, pp. 204 n. 61, 205 n. 62.

70. *1 Tamburlaine,* II, iv.

71. For current interpretations of the myth of Phaëthon, see Talbert, *Problem of Order,* pp. 169-71; and for the political precept referred to immediately below, pp. 38, 59-60, 109-10, 115 (Euarchus), etc.

72. One might see in this development a situation slightly comparable to what one finds in some Greek tragedy, wherein the immediate ambiguity of "right" in human conduct is submerged by the course of nemesis, in this instance, by the ultimate cause of the conflict as it can be traced to Richard II's disposition. As has been indicated in the first chapter, however, for the play in the theatre—and hence, in part at least, as an Elizabethan playwright must have conceived of it—one's attention should be focused upon the immediate impetus of the play-world established by what is called explicitly to an audience's attention. Upon reflection, Henry's references to God and Fortune might be resolved in a number of ways, not the least important of which would be to draw upon the concept of a Christian patience that does not in any way mitigate the omnipotence of God. See, e.g., Comes, *Myth.,* III. vi. Yet one may well ask about the time available in the theater for reflection.

73. Although neither figure embodies the complete fortitude of a Christian ruler, their actions in adversity might well seem to reflect aspects of this far-flung concept. See above, p. 89 n. 57, especially the tradition indicated by the citations of St. Ambrose and Julianus Pomerius, on the one hand, and, on the other, that indicated by citations of Macrobius and Cicero (e.g., *De Officiis,* 1. 18. 61, and, to a degree, 1. 23. 80, as it might relate to the vicissitudes of war).

74. With this movement from physical to emotional endowments, there then appears a statement of his plan and an enumeration of the actions in which he is proficient, actions that make his purpose feasible. The *natura* of Richard, no less than of Edward, can thus be said to be a *consilium* for action and, in Richard's case, an attribute basic to the discipline and exercise of his "wit" (e.g., playing

"the orator as well as Nestor"). Thus his *habitus,* and by implication his *studium* as well, might also be said to be determined by his *natura;* and his *nomen* has already been played upon briefly. See II, vi, 103-9.

75. III, iii, 145-61. Note in addition Lewis's question, "Is Edward your true king? for I were loath / To link with him that were not lawful chosen" (ll. 114-15).

76. It is tempting to relate this also to *natura* (i.e., sex, race, country, and especially family connections), but even though "honor" might be a convincing theatrical attribute in view of the way in which the highborn seem to have been aware of it (above, pp. 69 n. 23, 126, etc.), by 1590 it probably should be considered a conventional representational method, both generic and ready-made, by current thought and literary practice, for use in any particular play-world. It thereby varies, both in manner and nature, from the character emphasis in III, i and ii, wherein Shakespeare developed the dominant and causative traits of three individuals.

77. See the last two or three lines of each of the eight scenes. In each instance, except for IV, v, the reference is to an immediate action that must be done quickly.

78. The need for fortitude was implicit in Lewis' advice to Margaret. She should not yield her neck "to fortune's yoke" but let her "dauntless mind / Still ride in triumph over all mischance" (III, iii, 16-18). The idea of the rise and fall of the mighty, implicit in Warwick's soliloquy (III, iii, 262-63), becomes "Fortune's malice" when Edward specifies what has overthrown his state (IV, iii, 46). That ruler's mind, however, "exceeds the compass of her [Fortune's] wheel" (l. 47), and his fortitude abides "what fates impose" (ll. 58-59). Henry also will refer to Fortune's "spite" (IV, vi, 19), accepting it as his lot, during a scene in which subsequent speeches emphasize the fortune of Warwick, to whom "the heavens" in his "nativity" "Adjudg'd an olive branch and laurel crown, / As likely to be blest in peace and war" (ll. 33-35). See above, p. 219 n. 72, and the note immediately following.

79. Quite noticeable, for example, would be the irony of the scene wherein Henry once more appears as a ruler; for an audience knows of Edward's escape (IV, v, vi). From it will grow neither an olive branch nor a laurel crown for Warwick (IV, vi, 34). Similarly, in the next scene in which Henry appears (IV, viii), just after he has enunciated the Christian excellence of his rule (ll. 38-50), he is captured by the Yorkists. In addition, note how the keeper briefly plays with Henry's word "content" (III, i, 66-67)—a development balanced by the watchman's realistic and comic comments on Edward's martial "honour" (IV, iii, 12-19). But in Acts III and IV, ironic niceties probably were less noticeable in the theater than were the swift vagaries of Fortune, regardless of how she manifested herself.

80. With Edward's return from France, the idea appears that "fearless minds" climb "soonest unto crowns" (IV, vii, 62). Following the pageantic setting of the entrance to York, (IV, vii), and during the even more pageantic entrance to Coventry (V, i), Edward is given the hero's sensing of success immediately before Clarence's final switch of allegiance (V, i, 70-71); and Edward's heroic resolution is obvious as he marches to Tewkesbury (V, iii, 18-24). Agreeing with these more specific manifestations of heroism are the fearless speeches of both Edward and Warwick (IV, i, 75-78; v, 15-17; vii, 1-15; and, e.g., IV, ii, 6-11, 18-29).

81. See especially the episodes in which Henry appears.

82. The phrase is Sir Thomas Smith's when he is discussing the question of whether the danger of disruption be greater or less than the danger of not resisting an evil rule. *De Republica Anglorum,* ed. L. Alston, with a preface by F. W. Maitland (Cambridge, 1906), p. 13.

83. E.g., *3 H VI,* IV, vi, viii.

84. IV, i, 66-87.

85. For an analysis of this play, indicating how it is constructed around a series of choric and didactic set pieces (Clarence's dream, the laments of Anne,

the curses of Margaret, Buckingham's farewell, Richard's early monologues balancing Richmond's final speeches, the symmetrical pageantry of Bosworth field), see Wolfgang Clemen, *Kommentar zu Shakespeares Richard III: Interpretation eines Dramas* (Göttingen, 1957). See also below, p. 234 and n. 104. The primary sources, of course, are Hall and Holinshed, but see also J. Dover Wilson, "The Composition of the Clarence Scenes in 'Richard III,'" *MLR*, LIII (1958), 211-14. One, of course, must always allow for Wilson's persistent theory of "continuous copy."

86. See below, pp. 226, 232-34.

87. Rivers, Grey, and Vaughan, as well as Hastings, are killed in Act III, but dramatic emphasis falls on the last death. Even the short scene that shows the other characters on the way to execution ends with a reference to Hastings. Similarly, Buckingham's final scene (V, i) is obviously subordinate to Richard's. Although in the fourth act the murder of the princes is not performed on stage, notice the beginning of IV, i (ll. 1-28); the lamentation of IV, iv; and the appearances of Tyrrel, which surround the memorable "Rougemont-jack passage." For this last scene and the constant explanation based on "political grounds," see Greg, *Edit. Problem*, pp. xxxvi, 77-88 (especially p. 80 n. 1).

88. See, e.g., Baldwin, *Shakspere's 5-Act Structure*, p. 323 (Latomus, etc.), as well as Ben Jonson's theory and practice. With Jonson, the end of the fourth act usually shows a false resolution.

89. IV, i, 39-47, 92; the previous counteractions are the retreat to sanctuary and the opposition of the princes (II, iv, 16 ff; III, i, 1-153).

90. Note also that Margaret's vituperative *ubi sunt* lines (IV, iv, 92 ff.) repeat a minor development in the earlier histories and that her joy about being able to smile in France at "English woes" (l. 115) indicates how Shakespeare would apparently keep her outside of an Elizabethan's unqualified sympathy.

91. Above, pp. 67 n. 16, 92. As regards the unification of *R III*, there seems little need to posit Shakespeare's indebtedness to any one author. Not as frequently as formerly do critics refer in this respect to Marlowe's concentration on a single figure.

92. In this respect, he expresses a conventional Elizabethan attitude. Jorgensen, *Shakespeare's Military World*, pp. 170-97, and, e.g., the soldier in the *Cobbler's Prophecy*, above, p. 20 n. 64.

93. Above, pp. 7 n. 3, 44; also Cushman, *Devil & Vice, passim*.

94. E.g., *Magnyfycence* and *Respublica*.

95. A confirmation of one of the consequences of this premise, for example, is dramatized in accordance with the way in which its development has been rooted in features of a conventional love rhetoric and love psychology (ll. 175-81, 132, 150 ff.). Thereby an impression was probably created that such a sophistic approach had actually won the argument—as the new development of stichomythia would indicate (ll. 193-201)—before its success was confirmed by the giving of a ring. Moreover, in Richard's request that the funeral of "noble" Henry be left to him so that he may "wet" the grave with his "repentant tears," there appears a dramatic confirmation of the "truth" of Richard's correlative premise—i.e., of his being "penitent" (l. 221)—a consequence theatrically denied, of course, by the brief dialogue after Anne's exit and by the long subsequent soliloquy.

96. Above, p. 78.

97. Generalities of this sort are always dangerous, but one should remember that although one would not expect sympathy among those watching the execution of Lopez, one does find that the spectators laughed greatly when he, a Jew, swore to his innocence by Christ. G. B. Harrison, *An Elizabethan Journal . . . 1591-1594* (London, 1928), p. 304.

98. E.g., above, pp. 66-67.

99. See especially George B. Churchill, *Richard the Third up to Shakespeare* (Berlin, 1900), *passim* (e.g., pp. 541-42, the treatment of the burial of the princes as found in Holinshed or the treatment of Anne).

100. Richard Rainolde, *The Foundacion of Rhetoricke*, with introduction by Francis R. Johnson, Scholars Facsimiles and Reprints (N.Y., 1945), sigs Dl-2. See also Wilson's *Arte of Rhetorique*, ed. Mair, p. 179, as well as *3 H VI*, I, ii; III, ii, 188; and the *ingenium excellens* that Fabyan, More, Hall, and Holinshed also give Richard.

101. Its popularity is attested, i.a., by the immortal joke involving a citizen's wife (Manningham, *Diary*, p. 39), although the authenticity of this portion of the manuscript has been questioned.

102. As a preparation for this rhetorical aspect of an epitatical complexity, Elizabeth also has been characterized as "witty" (e.g., *3 H VI*, III, ii, 33; *R III*, III, i, 154-56, and the earlier lines, 132-35). This full debate, like the shorter one with Anne, also builds upon not only the villain's conventional pose of honesty but also the Machiavel's virtuosity in words which is especially effective with women, as well as his witty stamina in argument (e.g., above, p. 78, and Marlowe's *Jew*, I, ii, 37-154).

103. In this respect, any argument seems unfortunate that would substantiate early "genetics" for *Romeo and Juliet* by emphasizing the appearance in these history plays of fate or of a universe controlled by God's punishment of sin (Baldwin, *Genetics of Shakspere's Plays*, pp. 503-4). Shakespeare's giving weight to human action can not be overlooked in *Romeo and Juliet*, and it is apparent in all of the plays so far examined. In *R III*, for example, this is partially expressed by the scrivener. Richard's palpable evil would make "all come to naught / When such ill dealing must be seen in thought" (III, vi, 10-14). Although the fears of the citizens may be described as "a divine instinct" that makes "men's minds mistrust / Ensuing danger" (II, iii, 42-43), the third citizen's "leave it all to God" (l. 45) is a thoroughly inadequate expression of the "right" impetus of the play. Similarly, when being "heav'd a-high, to be hurl'd down below" is equated with "the course of justice" (IV, iv, 86, 105), the emphasis falls upon being "well skill'd in curses." Even the extension of the ego, apparent in all mythical thinking, can become operative only by a course of human action:

> Forbear to sleep the night, and fast the day;
> Compare dead happiness with living woe;
> Think that thy babes were sweeter than they were
> And he that slew them fouler than he is.
> Bett'ring thy loss makes the bad causer worse;
> Revolving this will teach thee how to curse.
>
> (ll. 118-23)

104. In some respects, the rhetorical process of this play shows a continual use of what had appeared much less frequently in *3 H VI:* e.g., dividing a formal oration among different speakers (*3 H VI*, I, ii, 8-35) and using stichomythia for an antiphonal effect (*3 H VI*, I, i, 206-10; II, v, 103-13) or for emphasizing the parry and thrust of debate (*3 H VI*, III, i, 59-62, 72-75). For a fuller consideration of this aspect of the drama, see Louis Edgar Dollarhide, "Shakespeare's *Richard III* and Renaissance Rhetoric," (Ph.D. diss., Univ of N.C., 1954). Shakespeare seems to have appreciated the fact—more clearly perhaps than any other tragedian writing for the popular stage before Jonson—that the dominance of a viciously plotting riser who will receive a retributive fall could be merged with the age's interest in the formal rhetoric that permeated the academic curriculum.

CHAPTER VI

1. Here as elsewhere I follow the consensus in dating the plays. As regards *LLL*, one cannot dismiss easily the total argument provided by Rupert Taylor, *The Date of 'Love's Labour's Lost'* (N.Y., 1932). Even if one sees at least two strata in this play, the form in which it has survived probably represents Shake-

speare's final reworking of his drama, the verbal ingenuity of which argues strongly for not placing it before *2GV*. For that ingenuity, see below, as well as Gladys D. Willcock, *Shakespeare as a Critic of Language*, Shakesp. Assoc. Papers, 18 (London, 1934). An explanation of what used to be considered a clear sign of Shakespeare's revision of his "earlier" play is indicated, however, by Greg, *Edit. Problem*, p. 127. I also believe it more important to appreciate the comic course of the drama than to be concerned with reflections of a "school of night." As regards *MND*, only recently have students had their attention called to the possibility that its "genetics" is after that of *The Merry Wives*. Baldwin, *Genetics of Shakspere's Plays*, pp. 478-80, 465-66. Yet such an argument, involving properties that may have been used for a number of years, seems especially hazardous; and no one has ever seen the earlier *Jealous Comedy*. Similarly, I place greater weight upon the nature of a play than upon any "actor pattern" that might seem to emerge therefrom. See the references in *MND* to the inclement weather of the mid 1590's, below, p. 251 n. 41.

2. Chambers, *Shakespeare*, II, 332.

3. Franciscus Patricius Senensis, *De Regno et Regis Institutione* (9. 19), trans. Gilbert, *Machiavelli's 'Prince'*, p. 230.

4. If a king "be helped forwarde with the instructions, bringinge up, and art of the Courtier, whom these Lords have facioned so wise and good, he shall be moste wise, moste continent, moste temperate, moste manlye, and moste juste, full of liberalitie, majestie, holynesse, and mercye: finallye he shall be moste glorious and moste deerlye beloved both to Godde and manne: throughe whose grace he shall atteine unto that heroicall and noble vertue, that shall make him passe the boundes of the nature of manne, and shall rather be called a Demy God, then a manne mortall." *The Book of the Courtier from the Italian of Count Baldassare Castiglione Done into English by Sir Thomas Hoby*, ed. Walter Raleigh, Tudor Translations (London, 1900), pp. 313-14. James's first clause states that ". . . Hee can not bee thought worthie to rule & command others, that cannot rule and dantone his owne proper affections & vnreasonable appetites. . . ." *The Basilicon Doron of King James VI*, ed. James Craigie, Scottish Text Soc., Series 3, No. 6, p. 24.

5. Peter de la Primaudaye, *The French Academie* (London, 1618). The translation of the first part had appeared in 1586, and in its dedication to Henry III, the author, for example, quoted Plato to the effect that "Commonwealths begin then to be happy, when kings exercise Philosophy, and Philosophers reign."

6. *Book of the Courtier*, pp. 340 ff. For the reference to Basilius and for similar ideas, see above, pp. 204, 216.

7. That is, he mocks those young ("green") geese who have just mocked him.

8. Here, as elsewhere, details of Shakespeare's pronunciation can be found in their appropriate place in Kökeritz, *Shakespeare's Pronunciation;* cf. pp. 167, 201-2.

9. Baldwin, *Shakspere's Small Latine*, II, 312. As it has been indicated in an earlier chapter, Armado's language is one of his major pretensions to the "body of compliment." As in the portrayal of Holofernes, this emphasis fills out a typical pattern. Above, pp. 28-31; Daniel C. Boughner, "Don Armado and the *Commedia Dell' Arte*," *SP*, XXXVII (1940), 201-24.

10. As J. Le Gay Brereton remarks, such a reading "should certainly be retained for its intended suggestion of the entanglements of sin." *Writings on Elizabethan Drama* (Melbourne Univ. Press, 1948), p. 91.

11. See above, pp. 38-39 (Armado, Holofernes, Nathaniel).

12. Above, pp. 15-17, 21.

13. For allusions to a ballad on the subject, see *LLL*, ed. Richard Davis, Arden Ed. (Cambridge, Mass., 1951), pp. 66-67 (IV, i, 66-67).

14. The development spoken about would be perfectly natural, regardless of the "parts" of a play; see, e.g., Laut, "Drama Illustrating Dogma," pp. 40-41.

15. E.g., Baskervill, *Eliz. Jig*, pp. 304-06.

16. E.g., V, ii, 563. See also V, i, 39-44.

17. See the dialogue between Berowne and Katherine (II, i, 114-28).

18. Ll. 120-21, 123-28, 186-93.

19. Riming of longer lines reappears with punning on *sheep-ships* and with word-play on *pasture-lips*. This involves the theatrically obvious refusal of a kiss (II, i, 221-22) and anticipates the ladies' mocking of "grim" Boyet as "an old love-monger" and "Cupid's grandfather" (ll. 254-55). Moreover, Boyet's word-play (ll. 237-41, 247) leads directly into another bit of brief comic riming that terminates with exits—a situation that had appeared in connection with Berowne (ll. 192-93), Dumain (ll. 194-95), Longaville (ll. 207-8), and Berowne again (ll. 213-14):

> *Mar.* He is Cupid's grandfather, and learns news of
> him.
> *Kath.* Then was Venus like her mother, for her father
> is but grim.
> *Boyet.* Do you hear, my mad wenches?
> *Ros.*   No.
> *Boyet.*   What then, do you see?
> *Mar.* Ay, our way to be gone.
> *Boyet.*   You are too hard for me.
>
>   (II, i, 255-58)

20. For the brawl, see above, pp. 39-40 and n. 117; for the French brawl, see *LLL,* ed. Davis, p. 46.

21. Above, p. 40 and n. 118.

22. E.g., above, p. 22 n. 75. For guesses at the topical meaning of the sequence, see *LLL,* ed. Davis, pp. xxix-xliv; Anthony G. Petti, "The Fox, the Ape, the Humble-Bee, and the Goose," *Neophilologus,* XLIV (1960), 208-15.

23. The punning and the witty development that was started as this scene opened had concerned ladies' shooting at the deer, had involved the forester's presence, and had been enlarged by references to a woman's fairness so that it reflected the language of sonneteering. From an initial pun on *mounting-*"mountain" (IV, i, 4, cf. also ll. 1-2), the position of the princess for the "fairest shoot" had carried meanings faintly implicit in her being a politic suitor to the king, but quite unmistakably appropriate to her being the fair wooed one, the sonneteers' conventional wounder of hearts. As a consequence, the place where she "must stand and play the murderer in" (l. 8) becomes the "fairest shoot" (l. 10). *Fair-*"best" with *fair-*"beautiful" can then be played with (ll. 11-23) for some generalized witty satire that continues the riming and includes lines that echo conventional sonneteering devices and the variable meanings inherent in *deer* and *hart:* e.g.,

> As I for praise alone now seek to spill
> The poor deer's blood, that my heart means
> no ill.
>
>   (ll. 34-35)

Boyet's speech then applies those punning implications to "curst wives," an application reinforced by lines given the princess before Costard's entrance with the wrong letter:

> *Boyet.* Do not curst wives hold that self-sovereignity
> Only for praise' sake, when they strive to be
> Lords o'er their lords?
> *Prin.* Only for praise; and praise we may afford
> To any lady that subdues a lord.
>
>   (ll. 36-40)

After this letter has been read and commented upon, the scene returns to the witty punning connected with deer-shooting. With Costard on stage, however, the movement from a courtly wit to a lower level is intensified. It had been started by Boyet's lines just quoted; and with the reappearance of the word *shooter* (i.e., "suitor" also) and with the suitor-like rhetoric of Boyet (ll. 110-11), phrases like "putting off," "putting on," "hitting lower," and striking "at the brow" appear, as do references to deer's horns and cuckold's horns (ll. 112-20). The dialogue becomes increasingly bawdy as the lines of a ballad are recalled which pointed out that if one like Boyet could not "hit it," a younger could. For details about this ballad, see *LLL*, ed. Davis, p. 73. With the inevitable appearance of *marks* and *prick* (ll. 132-34), Costard joins in the mirth with quips called even bawdier (l. 139) as Boyet is "put down."

24. Kökeritz, *Shakespeare's Pronunciation*, pp. 112-13, discussing the suggestion of A. L. Rowse.

25. There is also a comic irony in "sweetly varied" epithets, for schoolboys were expected to be facile in synonyms not simply in their translation of Latin but also from their acquisition of "copy." In the two sequences that follow, Dull is again used to ridicule Holofernes and Nathaniel. Just as the uneducated ear of one who is confident that he knows his bucks may have seemed comically dear to both learned and unlearned, so too, perhaps, was Dull's insistence that the answer to his riddle holds in the exchange from "collusion" to "pollusion"; for the moon *never* is more than a month old (ll. 35-48). And that insistence, as far as the pricket is concerned at least, establishes Dull's point, just as Holofernes' "extemporal epitaph" in a rum-ram-ruf vein (ll. 58-63) continues the alliterative manner of Dull's assertion (ll. 49-50). The epitaph develops into obvious but intricate word-play, akin to that in both naïve and sophisticated riddles. It also leads to Dull's punning, which is derisive of flattering Nathaniel and the prideful Holofernes (ll. 65-66), to whom Shakespeare gives overtones of the lecherous clown (ll. 77-78, 81-82). A comparable process then appears briefly when Costard solves with common sense Holofernes' word-play of *pers-on* and *pierc'd* (ll. 85-90).

26. See, e.g., Baldwin, *Shakspere's Small Latine*, II, 402-16.

27. Holofernes' Latinized pedantry also illustrates another aspect of Tudor concern over vocabulary and pronunciation: i.e., *dout, doubt; det, debt; cauf, calf; hauf, half; abhominable, abhominable* (V, i, 18-28); and that concern obviously exists here within a context of ridicule. For details, see *LLL*, ed. Davis, pp. 120-21. The deriding wit of Moth is directed especially at Holofernes on the bases of the horn-book in "petty-school" education and a jesting reference to *wit-old* (*wittol*) and cockold (V, i, 47-73). Again Costard, who now displays a bigger word than any in "the almsbasket of words," gleefully points to the wit of Moth (ll. 74-83). As these characters turn to the entertainment of the princess, Shakespeare gives to Dull a comment that emphasizes the meaninglessness of those scraps that the curate, the schoolmaster, and the fantastic have stolen from a "great feast of languages":

> *Hol. Via*, goodman Dull! thou has spoken no word
> all this while.
> *Dull.* Nor understood none neither, sir.
>
> (ll. 156-58)

28. A final grouping of French characters serves as an introduction to this wooing, and quite suitably it too is called witty sport. "A set of wit well play'd" (l. 29) between Katherine and Rosaline is developed from the lovers' verses, specifically from the king's sealing his letter "on Cupid's name" (l. 9). After Rosaline mocks her fairness as part of her mockery of Berowne's lines (ll. 32-41), she triumphs in a second wit encounter by a description of Katherine's amber hair and pock-marked face. Boyet enters "stabbed with laughter" (l. 80) to deliver a laughing description of a laughing preparation for the Muscovite disguising (e.g., ll. 81-118); and after the music of masquing is played, "mock for

mock" is effected (l. 140). In this process of the lovers' wooing, dialogue sequences of roughly equal length involving the four pairs of lovers (ll. 158-264, 337-483) alternate with two shorter sequences, also of comparable length, wherein the men and the women are not paired with one another (ll. 120-57, 265-307). Although Boyet is twice mocked by Berowne (ll. 315-338, 463-67), mockery of the lovers is constant.

29. If for *LLL* one wished to develop an analogy with the dance, the language of its wit might be called its gesture, which, after focusing upon the ridiculous, increases in tempo until Mercade's entrance. For this last character's name, see *LLL*, ed. Davis, p. 185 (V, ii, 705).

30. That psychology has been expressed already (IV, iii, 299-365); but see the reference to Greg, above, p. 235 n. 1. The concept expressed in the first six lines appears, of course, in ll. 309 ff.

31. *Works,* I, 266-68.

32. See T. W. Baldwin, *Shakspere's Love's Labour's Won* (Carbondale, Ill., 1957), as well as its review by R. C. Bald, *MP,* LV (1958), 276-79.

33. Edmund Spenser, "An Hymne in Honour of Love," ll. 193-96.

34. Even Barber, I believe, moves too far in this direction, though he does affirm what is emphasized here. *Shakespeare's Festive Comedy,* pp. 107-9, 111-13 (cf. 116-18), 97. Emphasis upon conduct seems to me to be constantly subordinate to an emphasis on the artistry of speech and writing. In contrast, see Bassanio's action and words in the casket plot as it illumines the concept of an ideal lover. For a brief, but contrary, interpretation of the drama, see, e.g., Derek Traversi, *William Shakespeare: The Early Comedies* (London, 1960), pp. 29-39; see also Cyrus Hoy, "*Love's Labour's Lost* and the Nature of Comedy," *SQ,* XIII (1962), 31-40.

35. It is noticeable that the earlier description of Longaville's wit (II, i, 40-51), rather than that of Berowne's (II, i, 66-76), is more compatible with Rosaline's present description. Instead of substantiating J. Dover Wilson's theory of continuous copy, and aside from the considerations to be advanced, this might well be construed as agreeing with Rosaline's shrewishness, which had been emphasized in the last grouping of the French ladies (V. ii, 46; see also ll. 60-68).

36. Above, pp. 46-47, 54-60.

37. Above, p. 41 n. 126.

38. IV, i, 42-50; V, ii, 43-45. V, ii, 834, 846.

39. In this sense also, one might note how Berowne embodies Shakespeare's balance between the critical and the creative faculties of his language. For different interpretations of the conclusion of the drama, however, see, e.g., W. Schrickx, *Shakespeare's Early Contemporaries: The Background of the Harvey-Nashe Polemic and 'Love's Labour's Lost'* (Antwerp, 1956); S. K. Heninger, Jr., "Chapman's 'Hymnus in Noctem,' 376-377 and Shakespeare's *Love's Labour's Lost,* IV, iii, 346-347," *Explicator,* XVI (1958), 49. Such interpretations, I believe, ignore the points made here, as well as those indicated above, pp. 247-48.

40. Even though Shakespeare's laughter may seem strained to such an age as the twentieth century—which separates wit and rhetoric and, even more definitely, logic and rhetoric—both the learned and the unlearned have always been willing to laugh at the logical twists that a fertile brain can find in language's defiance of logic. Lyly, who drew his euphuism from academic rhetoric, relied upon the vitality of that rhetoric to animate the patterned cadences of his style; but in *LLL,* what is patterned is treated with laughter, and when it is exaggerated, it is made derisible. From the point of view of an Elizabethan audience, moreover, no sophisticated nicety had to be acquired to find amusement, e.g., in the twists given to Berowne's final virtuosity and effected by the last appearance of Armado. The same is true for the scatalogical situation that had undone Nathaniel (see Brereton, *Writings on Eliz. Drama,* pp. 89-90); for the punning on *elder;* for the mockery of Holofernes' face; for the word-play with *ass* in *Judas,* which had baited the schoolmaster successfully; and for the rowdy challenge that had put down Armado.

From such a point of view also, the ending of the play accords both with its beginning and its middle, in which sophisticated and vulgar mirth have been fused. For a Chaucerian echo underlying the ending, see Robert K. Presson, "The Conclusion of 'Love's Labour's Lost,' " *N & Q,* CCV (1960), 17-18.

41. Nearly every editor of the play notes the indication of its date. The bad weather of II, i, 88-117 is related to the wind-storms and torrential rains from March through September of 1594. The excessive cold and dearth continued in 1595, and there was some unusually bad weather as late as August to November of 1596.

42. Whether or not *MND* was designed originally for the celebration of some nobleman's wedding at which Elizabeth was present and whether or not alternate endings resulted, the last act, after Theseus and Hippolyta have commented upon what has preceded, shows in its fullest form a neat balance similar to what appears elsewhere in the drama: the introduction to the play-within-the-play (V, i, 28-107); its performance with spectators' comments (ll. 108-377); the masque-like balance after the reappearance of Puck (ll. 378-445, including a song). In its entire development, then, this entertainment at court approaches more nearly the actual nature of such entertainments than it would if one of the "alternate" endings were omitted. The comparable ending of *LLL,* before the appearance of Mercade, also approaches closely this sort of "reality"; and just as the princess' lines about the forthcoming Pageant of the Worthies (*LLL,* V, ii, 516-21) need not imply a gracious ruler's presence in any audience save that provided by the stage, so need not Theseus' lines (*MND,* V, i, 89-105). Without noting this last consideration, Barber also refers to the genre of the court masque in this respect. *Shakespeare's Festive Comedy,* pp. 331-32. Somewhat surprisingly, however, he does not consider the noisy, farcical nature of this play.

43. The reference to an "imperial" chastity "throned by the west" occurs at II, i, 148-68. The graciousness of Theseus (V, i, 90-105) might seem to be a realistic reference to such difficulties in royal entertainments as that implied by Elizabeth's remark that she had been told Mr. Aglionby would be afraid of her. John Nichols, *The Progresses and Public Processions of Queen Elizabeth* (London, 1832), I, 311-16. Note also the rude mechanicals' presentation of a lion, what may have been an occurrence at the Scottish court (I, ii, 76-80), Flute's desire to be a wandering knight, and the total theatrical scene.

44. Although there is a certain congruence between this development and that of protasis (I, II) and epitasis (III, IV), especially since the first use of the love-juice at the end of Act II anticipates the confusion of Acts III and IV, yet the fully developed framing action and the fact that it points conceptually to what is dramatized elsewhere seem to arise from features of Shakespeare's earlier artistry *(TA, C of E, 2GV).* The neat balance and precision of individual scenes can be illustrated by two examples. In the first scene of the drama, two passages of stichomythia in which Hermia takes part (ll. 136-40, 194-201) produce a perceptible balance. In the first situation, her single lines have the effect of asides to Lysander's speech, while in the second they inaugurate answering lines from Helena. In both instances, however, they are related to a relatively long speech by another character, and in both instances the subsequent development turns to the plan of escape from Athens. As a result, that portion of the opening scene that concerns Hermia and Lysander has its own introduction (ll. 20-45), its development (ll. 46-127), and its temporary conclusion (ll. 128-55). Its forward movement is then indicated; and as this is done, the second passage of stichomythia appears, to be resolved by a repetition of the lovers' plan and by Helena's soliloquy. After a comic contrast has been effected by introducing the rude mechanicals (I, ii), a balanced process is also apparent in Act II, scene i. Two quarreling sequences (ll. 60-145, 188-244) alternate with three dialogues in which Robin Goodfellow is a participant. The first dialogue introduces this folk figure and reports the quarrel that is first dramatized. The second and the third posit parallel solutions to the two quarreling sequences. In relation to Act I, scene i,

this scene, which also completes the introduction of Shakespeare's major characters, shows situations that are the reverse of the first scene: rulers quarrel, a
youth and a maid quarrel, and a ruler would further the course of true love.

45. This development begins with two repetitive sequences (II, ii, 1-34, 35-83).
In the first, song is followed by conjuration in four-foot verse; in the second, a
wittily developed lovers' dialogue is followed by four-foot verse and conjuration.
As the second leads to the first farcical situation, so the first leads to the comic
parallelism involving Bottom. In the development that follows, moreover, Act
III, scene i, shows a process similar to one in Act IV, scene i. The first portion of
Act III, scene i, showing Bottom and his crew in the forest, effects a shift to the
locale anticipated at the close of Act I, scene ii. It is resolved into the dramatization of Titania's confusion, the report of which carries over to the first forty lines
of Act III, scene ii. Similarly, the awakening scene (IV, i) begins with a repetitive
continuation of the Bottom-Titania situation (ll. 1-48); and it is resolved into a
double conclusion, the last aspect of which extends through the forty-six lines of
Act IV, scene ii.

46. Hermann Reich, "Der Man mit der Eselskopf," *Shakespeare Jahrbuch*, XL
(1904), 108-28. For the possibility that Shakespeare was indebted for the ass's
head to the 1592 translation of *The History of the Damnable Life and Deserved
Death of Dr. John Faustus*, see Robert R. Reed, Jr., "Nick Bottom, Dr. Faustus,
and the Ass's Head," *N & Q*, CCIV (1959), 252-54. Calling the low comic an ass
was, of course, thoroughly conventional (e.g., *Famous Victories*, 1. 68; *Three
Ladies of London*, p. 324).

47. E.g., Barber, *Shakespeare's Festive Comedy*, pp. 123-24.

48. A very "open" page is produced also by an unusually large box. Charlton
Hinman, "Cast-off Copy for the First Folio of Shakespeare," *SQ*, VI (1955),
259-73 (cf. pp. 264-65).

49. See, e.g., Greg, *Dramatic Documents*, I, 302, 210 n. 2.

50. The citation is noted, e.g., by George Lyman Kittredge, *A Midsummer
Night's Dream* (N.Y., 1939), p. 132.

51. This accords, i.a., with Lysander's insistence that reason leads him to
Helena and that he had no judgement when he swore to Hermia (II, ii, 115-22;
III, ii, 134); and thus the love rhetoric of foresworn lovers (e.g., II, ii, 103-22; III,
ii, 58-61, 122-44, 186-88; see also ll. 208-15) also effects cohesion within the almost
mechanical development of the play.

52. See above, pp. 45-46.

53. E.g., above, pp. 19-20.

54. E.g., above, pp. 20, 40 n. 119, 246.

55. For the late performance of at least the first of these dramas, and an
appropriate background, see Chambers, *Eliz. Stage*, II, 286; III, 39-41: IV, 6-7.

56. *RRD*, III, iv, 36-70, cf., e.g., Clarence Griffin Child's edition (N.Y., 1912),
p. 31.

57. See, however, above, p. 254 n. 42

58. E.g., Baskervill, *Eliz. Jig*, pp. 22, 62; *MND*, II, i, 16; above, p. 28 n. 94.

59. Kenneth Muir, "Pyramus and Thisbe: A Study in Shakespeare's Method,"
SQ, V (1954), 141-53; Bullough, *Narr. and Dram. Sources*, I, 375.

60. *Progymn.*, pp. 31-35. Ovid, of course, contains more than a hint of
burlesque: e.g., *Met.*, IV, 121-24 (*Progymn.*, p. 33).

61. Also the device of the love-juice, like the major narrative of *2GV*, just
may have been derived from *Diana Enamorada*. E.g., Bullough, *Narr. and Dram.
Sources*, I, 372.

62. See below, p. 286 n. 45 (*The Knight of the Burning Pestle*).

63. Frank Kermode, "The Mature Comedies," *Early Shakespeare*, p. 219; see
also, p. 220.

64. "He that is but of a meane conceit, hath a pleasant and plausible narration,
concerning the famous exploites of renowned Heroes, set forth in most sweete
and delightsome verse, to feede his rurall humor. They, whose capacities is such, as

that they can reach somewhat further then the external discourse and history, shall finde a morall sence included therein, extolling vertue, condemning vice, euery way profitable for the institution of a practicall and commonwealth man. The rest, that are better borne and of a more noble spirit, shall meete with hidden mysteries of naturall, astrologicall, or diuine and metaphysicall philosophie, to entertaine their heauenly speculation." *The Third part of the Countesse of Pembrokes Yueychurch: Entituled, Amintas Dale* (London, 1592), sig. B2r.

CHAPTER VII

1. For a detailed comparison of Shakespeare's drama with this earlier one, see F. Liebermann, "Shakespeare als Bearbeiter des *King John,"* *Archiv,* CXLII (1921), 177-202; CXLIII (1922), 17-46, 190-203. See also Hart, *Stolne and Surr. Copies,* pp. 439-40. For criticism of E. A. J. Honigmann's attempt to reverse the dating and indebtedness (*King John,* Arden Ed. [Cambridge, Mass., 1954]), see the review by T. M. Parrott, *JEGP,* LV (1956), 297-305, and Robert Adger Law, "On the Date of *King John,"* *SP,* LIV (1957), 119-27.

2. As regards the soliloquy, the traveler as a favorite object of ridicule hardly needs to be glossed. See, e.g., Hyckscorner in the play of that name and Donne's "Satyre IIII," ll. 17-154. Although the subsequent development of this speech specifies Faulconbridge's "mounting spirit," his intent to rise and "to deliver / Sweet, sweet, sweet poison for the age's tooth," the lines are resolved by the thoroughly honest thought that this poison will "strew" his rising footsteps. He "will not practice to deceive," but he will learn such poison "to avoid deceit" (I, i, 205-16). See above, pp. 32-33. Throughout the early portion of the play, moreover, this figure's gleeking humor takes the form of blunt "madcap" lines.

3. E.g., Robert Fabyan, *The New Chronicles of England and France,* ed. Henry Ellis (London, 1811), pp. 300-4 (e.g., the "fayned taylys"), 309-10; *Holinshed's Chronicles* (London, 1807), II, 204-5, 216, 220-22, 230-31, etc.; the woodcut of Richard tearing the heart out of a lion in Rastell's *The Pastime of People* (reprod. *King John,* ed. J. Dover Wilson [Cambridge, 1954]); the metrical romance *Richard Coer de Lyon,* surviving in at least seven MSS (John Edwin Wells, *A Manual of the Writings in Middle English, 1050-1400* [New Haven, 1926], pp. 150-53); the early seventeenth century *The Famous History of George, Lord Fauconbridge Bastard Son to Richard Cordelion* (*STC* 10709); etc.

4. This feature of the role may well underlie the criticism that would make Faulconbridge the hero of the drama. For a refutation of that point of view on grounds other than those advanced here, see Honigmann, *KJ,* pp. lxxi-ii. For a different point of view, emphasizing the Bastard's "disparate functions," see Julia C. van de Water, "The Bastard in *King John,"* *SQ,* XI (1960), 137-46. This article also objects to making Faulconbridge the hero of the play; but since his "disparate functions" accord with Shakespeare's immediate emphases, they do not invalidate the constant nature of the role.

5. William Warner, *The Second part of Albions England* (London, 1589), pp. 104-10; e.g., "Thus Lyons-hart (his courage got that surname) lastlie sped, / To whom King John, in courage not inferior to the other, / Succeeded: but in life and death more tragicke than his brother" (p. 105). The sentence from Holinshed continues "and wanted nothing but faithfull subiects to haue assisted him in reuenging such wrongs as were doone and offered by the French King and others." The summary begins by noting that John "hath beene little beholden to the writers of that time in which he liued; for scarselie can they afoord him a good word, except when the trueth inforceth them to come out with it as it were against their willes." *Chronicles,* II, 339.

6. See, e.g., Honigmann, *KJ,* pp. xxviii-xxxi, following Campbell, *Shakespeare's "Histories,"* pp. 142 ff., from which the present quotation is taken (p. 137).

7. The opening paragraphs of Camden's history, a work finished and published

in James's reign, point out that Elizabeth held the throne by right of descent, by specific law, by the polity of the realm, and by the will of the ruled. Both Houses of Parliament, "vna voce & vna mente," "vno ore," declare the other daughter of Henry VIII, "Elizabetham veram legitimamque regni hæredem ex successionis lege anni XXXV. Henrici VIII." When Elizabeth was so proclaimed the people were joyous, "nec alterum vnquam Principem populus proniore & constantiore mente & amore, maiore observantia, lætiori applausu, & votis repetitis, quoties in publicum prodiret, toto vitæ decursu, vnquam prosecutus est." *Annales Rerum Anglicarvm, et Hibernicarvm, Regnante Elizabetha* (London, 1615), pp. 17-18.

8. Below, p. 390 n. 37.

9. A similar basis in analyzing the play is used by William H. Matchett, "Richard's Divided Heritage in *King John*," *Essays in Criticism,* XII (1962), 231-53. Matchett is elaborating and confirming James Calderwood, "Commodity and Honour in *King John*," *Univ. of Toronto Quar.,* XXIX (1960), 341-56. Matchett's emphasis is thrown, once more, upon the bastard, whose kneeling to the youthful prince at the end of the drama is a sign that he "renounces his recently established 'right' to the throne and thus ensures his already suffering country against civil war." This interpretation admittedly deals with speeches as "understatements" and with what is not explicit in the "key scenes."

10. Above, p. 201.

11. E.g., II, i, 141-46.

12. The relationships here noted are given a curious, but characteristic, twist by J. Dover Wilson, *King John,* pp. liii-iv. Kyd's lines express a variation upon the conventional difference between the producer and the user of a commodity, and they need not refer in any way to Richard and Lymoges.

13. See below, p. 309 n. 89.

14. The idea of service is apparent in such phrases as "painfully with much expedient march" (l. 223), "To save unscratch'd your city's threat'ned cheeks" (l. 225), "Forwearied in this action of swift speed" (l. 233).

15. In this respect, Shakespeare's skill in utilizing Faulconbridge is again noticeable; for his interpolations blur the seriousness of John's right witnessed by many English hearts, even as they also mock the French:

> *K. John.* Doth not the crown of England prove the King?
> And if not that, I bring you witnesses,
> Twice fifteen thousand hearts of England's breed,—
> *Bast.* Bastards, and else.
> *K. John.* To verify our title with their lives.
> *K. Phi.* As many and as well-born bloods as those—
> *Bast.* Some bastards too.
> *K. Phi.* Stand in his face to contradict his claim.
>
> (II, i, 273-80)

16. Above, p. 228 n. 92, and Jorgensen, *Shakespeare's Military World,* pp. 176-78.

17. See, e.g., Howard R. Patch, *The Goddess Fortuna in Medieval Literature* (Cambridge, Mass., 1927), pp. 115-17.

18. Although the bastard's mocking verse, for example, mars the concord of this resolution, it anticipates a later anti-Lewis emphasis (II, i, 504-9). In the immediate scene, moreover, his mockery of love-rhetoric accords with his mockery of the citizen-orator's proficiency; and Philip uses, in an abated context, images that are similar to the earlier martial ones and that testify, even by a figurative identification of rhetoric and conflict, to the age's belief in the validity of the trained, spoken word (ll. 455-67). This identification also expresses a conventional attitude that might be manifested, for example, in the disputation, especially when it became a formal and required academic exercise.

19. The suggestion that this soliloquy had a topical significance in view of Henry IV's conversion to Catholicism in the summer of 1593 ("Paris vaut bien une messe") and that it, consequently, may be a later addition should not ignore its firm connection with the anticipatory developments noted above and hence with the varying emphases of the preceding stage-world (e.g., even the movement from enraged kings to "mad" kings). See, of course, Wilson, *KJ,* pp. lv-lviii, who quotes Elizabeth's message to Henry IV in which she informed him that she could "in no wise allow or think it good before God that for any worldly respect or cunning persuasion he should yield to change his conscience and opinion in religion from the truth wherein he was brought up from his youth, and for the defense whereof he hath continued many years in arms."

20. The folio heads the present Act III, scene i, "Actus Secundus" and the subsequent entrance of King John *et al.* (after III, i, 74) "Actus Tertius, Scaena prima." Obviously III, i, 1-74, is meant to dramatize what is mentioned at II, i, 540-50. Constance's line "Here is my throne, bid kings come bow to it" is a denial, consistent with Constance's portrayal here, of John's order "Call the Lady Constance; / Some speedy messenger bid her repair / To our solemnity" (II, i, 553-55). Such an *enjambement* is both logical and natural. See also the situation in *E II,* I, iv, 187-88. For the term *enjambement* applied to dramatic texts, especially when the situation is not skillful, see Greg, *Marlowe's 'Doctor Faustus',* pp. 20-21. For a theory that copy different from that used for Acts I-III was used by the folio printer for Acts IV-V, see Greg, *Edit. Problem,* p. 143 n. 1. This theory might seem to accord with the fact that from the beginning of Act IV "the construction, which up to this point has been leisurely, is speeded up, the source being more compressed"; but the return of haste to this play-world, as discussed below, and the particular form that it takes in the John-Arthur relationship, might well produce, with artistic integrity and with no regard for the nature of copy, an effect quite different from that of the rhetorical emphases in the scenes just considered.

21. Clemen, *Development of Shakespeare's Imagery,* p. 86 n. 1, calls attention to this fact. Without qualifying his main point, one should note, however, that he ignores the meaning of *blood* as "passion" and hence, e.g., the applicability of this imagistic development to the bastard's line about the "rich blood" of kings' being "set on fire" (II, i, 351), John's heat in successful battle, (III, i, 340-47; III, ii), and John's subsequent villainy (III, iii). As the previous discussion and the following pages indicate, one should also note imagistic developments in the second act that are related to "mouthing" and especially to heat and haste.

22. One cannot fail to note the varied circumstances in which a sun that "stays in his course" next appears (e.g., V, v, 1-4, and below, p. 283). Similarly, the Platonic overtones in Constance's speech to Arthur (III, i, 43-54) are varied later when Hubert's appearance is in question; below, p. 282.

23. In the commodity soliloquy, with a literally breath-taking satire, the bastard's comments run from remarks about the princes John and Philip (ll. 562-66), to censure of the world (ll. 566-80), to censure of King Philip (ll. 581-86).

24. In view of the way in which the process of this drama is comparable to that of the citizen's oration, one should expect John's repetition, in a different context, of an idea in Pandulph's greeting ("you anointed deputies of heaven," "the free breath of a sacred king," ll. 136, 148). Note too, e.g., John's repetition of the word *usurp* in the last line just quoted.

25. Curiously enough, Calderwood neglects this, *Univ. of Toronto Quar.* XXIX, 341-56.

26. As has been indicated, it is doubtful that these emotions provide a key to the author's basic and total intent. Later John inaugurates a villainous plot and Arthur appears, even more strongly than before, as a pathetic and tragically innocent figure. Much more likely is Shakespeare's use, here and elsewhere, of contemporary feelings to heighten an immediate situation.

27. *R II,* III, iii, 61-67; Talbert, *Problem of Order,* pp. 165-66, and *passim.*

28. See Lily Bess Campbell, *Shakespeare's Tragic Heroes: Slaves of Passion* (N.Y., 1952), pp. 79-83 and *passim*.

29. In this respect, it is also interesting to note that in the rush surviving from successful battle, the bastard had been dispatched to "shake the bags / Of hoarding abbots" and to "set at liberty" "imprisoned angels" (III, iii, 7-9). As a consequence, when he answered, "Bell, book, and candle shall not drive me back, / When gold and silver becks me to come on" (ll. 12-13), the earlier commodity vein was again linked, although in a different manner, with Catholicism.

30. In spite of its interest, the French scene following John's victory must be treated only in passing (III, iv). With the appearance of Constance, Shakespeare intensifies and varies developments already established in this play and at the same time merges at least three representational concepts: that of grief and consolation; that of plot, franticness, and counterplot; and that of the rise and fall of princes. The display of frantic Constance's grief includes an evocation of Death—a "carrion monster" of "sound rottenness" (ll. 25-36). As this happens, a theatrical process, already noted in part, is intensified. It began with Constance (III, i, 1 ff.); included Blanche, whirled "asunder" by the two armies that held her "hands" (III, i, 326-36); and now ends with Constance, as it culminates in a rhetorical elaboration of madness. Later in the scene, moreover, youthful blood and greenness are again predicated of a sorrowful prince (ll. 125, 145; cf. II, i, 472-73). This situation, focused upon Constance's loosened hair (III, iv, 61-75), probably was contrived to produce a grim pathos akin to that produced when other frantic females lamented a deed that provided the motivation for a counterplot. Since, however, the "canker sorrow" and another personified Grief (ll. 82, 92-98) are dominant here, the balancing emotion, instead of being revenge, is one of consolation; and since Philip and Pandulph are unable to console Constance, Pandulph is left to console Lewis. This consolation inaugurates the plan to invade England. It thereby starts, in effect, an action that counters the vicious plot against Constance's son, even as it agrees with moral philosophy and a recognized rhetorical method. (See also *3 H VI*, II, i, 45 ff.). In the cardinal's speeches conventional maxims of state result in his balancing a "misplac'd John" against an "infant Arthur" as they both are placed upon the "slipp'ry" rise and fall of princes:

> John hath seiz'd Arthur; and it cannot be
> That, whiles warm life plays in that infant's veins,
> The misplac'd John should entertain an hour,
> One minute, nay, one quiet breath of rest.
> *A sceptre snatch'd with an unruly hand*
> *Must be as boisterously maintain'd as gain'd;*
> And he that stands upon a slipp'ry place
> Makes nice of no vile hold to stay him up.
> *That John may stand, then Arthur needs must fall:*
> So be it; for it cannot be but so.
>
> (ll. 131-40)

With a repetition of this maxim (ll. 147-48), Pandulph forecasts a breach between John and his people. This will be aided by the mythical thinking of the era (ll. 153-59). Thereby Lewis may rise. The skillful, and truly original, ingenuity that works in such a manner with conventional concepts and representational methods is obvious.

31. The ironies inherent in this speech and in its context, as well as in John's granting the nobles what they wish (IV, ii, 1-68), look forward to the concentrated ironies that will follow.

32. Although Miss Campbell refers in this respect to Elizabeth and Davison after the execution of Mary, Queen of Scots, (*Shakespeare's "Histories,"* pp. 160-64), in addition to what has been pointed out, notice the way in which Ponet, for example, focused his censure less upon Mary Tudor than upon those surrounding

her; and notice, too, a conventional process of thought that emphasized the fallibility of a ruler (Talbert, *Problem of Order,* pp. 76-78, 27-29). In a later age, Pym was determined to keep a list of Charles's errors before Parliament, lest the punishment of his advisors and favorites might seem to remedy the evil.

33. In this respect, the brief return of a delaying imagistic development in speeches to John, as well as the appearance of Peter of Pomfret, may have heightened, by the irritation of delay, an audience's perception of the need for haste, specified in the lines just cited. See, e.g., ll. 141-52 and especially ll. 185-202. Even more important is the fact that Shakespeare indicates how ill tidings rush upon John. The process of John's thought from "They [the nobles] burn in indignation. I repent. / There is no sure foundation set on blood ..." (ll. 103-4) is interrupted by news about the arrival of French forces on English soil. The king's reaction to that leads to news of Eleanor's death and to John's lines that accord with his being "made giddy / With these ill tidings" (ll. 131-32): "With-hold thy speed, dreadful occasion! / O, make a league with me, till I have pleas'd / My discontented peers! What! mother dead! / How wildly then walks my estate in France" (ll. 125-28). When John returns to "My mother dead" (l. 181), he again is interrupted, this time by the re-entrance of Hubert. Were it not for the delaying imagery, and especially the appearance of repentence, the scenic process would be strikingly similar to that in *R III,* IV, iv, 432 ff.

34. See also E. C. Pettet, "Hot Irons and Fever: A Note on Some of the Imagery of *King John,*" *Essays in Criticism,* IV (1954), 128-44, and Tillyard, *Shakespeare's Histories,* pp. 221-22.

35. As it was pointed out at the beginning of this discussion, Faulconbridge's portrayal proceeds upon a relatively straight-forward premise. The same is true for that of Arthur. It shows no signs of an unfavorable development that incidents in Holinshed might have provided. In view of his earlier homage to John, for example, this young duke's demands upon the king could have been displayed with an unwarranted pride discordant with an English, anti-papal victory. *Holinshed's Chronicles,* II, 285 and 279, 280. Conversely, Arthur could have been given lines showing a regal vigor that an audience apparently found appealing in youthful figures (e.g., the young princes in *3 H VI* and *R III*). Instead, Arthur moves con-sistently toward a pathetic end; and the tragedy of his precipitancy is expressed by Faulconbridge, loyal to King John.

36. Thereby a variation in a Cecropia figure (the mother of Amphialus in Sidney's *Arcadia*) is also produced and contrasts with that effected in the figure of Eleanor. Eleanor, in turn, varies from such a female Machiavel as Marlowe's Catherine primarily because of Shakespeare's qualified portrayal of John, especially the vigorous, anti-papal John.

37. Shakespeare's last act, indeed, is close to the spirit of John's appearance in the *Mirror for Magistrates* early in the seventeeth century. In Richard Niccols' 1610 additions, John is whitewashed almost completely. A corollary of this is the emphasis upon his being a "haplesse King": "deep waves of woe" bring con-fusion to John's state and crown; "mischiefe on mischiefe fals t'encrease" his woes; etc. *Mirror for Magistrates,* ed. Joseph Haslewood (London, 1815), II. 2, 700, 703 (stanza 9), 706 (stanza 24); see also stanzas 33-35. In a number of sixteenth-century narratives in the *Mirror,* there is a concentration upon the events of a fall and its total effect, or its immediate applicability, rather than upon the character of the protagonist. See, e.g., Richard S. Sylvester, "Cavendish's *Life of Wolsey:* The Artistry of a Tudor Biographer," *SP,* LVII (1960), 44-54; and note such marginal glosses in Grafton as "Troubles & vexations encrease vpon king John," "This king was in great perplexitie," "The miserable estate of king John," "A presumptuous clergy," "King John in great perplexitie." *Grafton's Chronicle* (London, 1809), I, 232, 236, 241, 243. It is just this feature of the play which is called to one's attention by the continuous tableau-like effects, by the rhetoric and imagery of the drama, as well as by the return of haste to the play-world during the fourth act and the final portrayal of a dark indigest. The sharp variation

between excellence and villainy that one sees earlier in the portrayal of John also agrees with other sixteenth-century concepts of this ruler. A favorably interpreted John was the John of militant Protestants; a vicious John was the John of annals written by his monkish adversaries (see Holinshed's comment, above, p. 265 n. 5) or the John of Robin Hood legends, especially those concerned with the downfall and death of Robert, Earl of Huntington, or *1* and *2 Robin Hood,* as Chettle and Munday would phrase it in 1598. See Ruth Wallerstein, *King John in Fact and Fiction* (Philadelphia, 1917). Shakespeare's solution to this divergence is again noticeably apt, even when one allows for his dependence upon *The Troublesome Reign.*

38. A clear indication of the purposeful and all-embracing irony in *T & C* is afforded by the way in which Shakespeare combines the greatest variety of current emphases in the theater from about 1598 to about 1602. William Wesley Main, "The Dramatic Context of Shakespeare's *Troilus and Cressida*" (Ph.D. diss., Univ. of N. C., 1954). Although his emphasis is quite different from the present one, see M. M. Reese, *The Cease of Majesty: A Study of Shakespeare's History Plays* (London, 1961), pp. 280-81: *King John* is "the most cynical and disillusioned of the histories"; it is "a dark picture," in which issues "of right and wrong are debated fully, and every time [?] the wrong prevails."

39. The initial premise of a powerful possession, qualified by its secret "wrong," versus a powerless "right," qualified by its foreign support, becomes a possession buttressed by Rome versus a foreign invasion. Thus I cannot agree entirely with Adrien Bonjour, "The Road to Swinstead Abbey: A Study of the Sense and Structure of *King John,*" *ELH* XVIII (1951), 253-74.

40. That the final play-world of *Gorbuduc* was meant to have a strong and immediate admonitory force is a commonplace of literary history—one that has been emphasized recently by Neale's study of Elizabeth's Parliaments.

41. The Elizabethans' enthusiasm for their ruler was grounded upon fact and hence was noted by Camden, e.g., as well as by Hooker (Talbert, *Problem of Order,* pp, 63-64, also pp. 86-88). The rhetoric of R. Norton, consequently, would have substance for at least some of the readers of his translation of Camden (1630). See, e.g., his comparison between Henry IV and Elizabeth, especially apt in view of suggestions noted above (pp. 275 n. 19, 278 n. 26), or the following passage: *"But aboue all may the Reader obserue (to the glory of our good God) his admirable blessings vppon this our Land, vnder the profession of the Gospell, and the happy gouernment of Queene* Elizabeth *our late glorious Soueraigne of renowned Memory; Of whom though much be spoken to her Honour in this History; yet because it may perhaps be not vnpleasing to many to heare her prayses againe and againe Recorded, whom in their hearts they somuch Honored, giue me leaue,* (gentle Reader,) *euen me the meanest of many thousands that admired her vertues while shee liued, and honour her Memory being dead, to present vnto thee these few Collections out of worthy Authors, in expression of my zeale and duty rather then any ability or sufficiency to relate her worthy prayses, or set forth those singular vertues that shone so illustriously in her royall Brest, making her glorious fame to be spread ouer the whole World, and her dayes to be renowned to all succeeding ages, dayes not to be passed ouer slightly without one touch vpon that string which so long time sounded so sweetly in our eares, without one sigh now after almost thirty yeares breathed forth in her sacred Memory. For what true English man doth not still retaine deeply imprinted in his remembrance, and with his best faculties acknowledge the happinesse of her times? whrein [sic] euen Forraine Princes and Nations abroad as well as her owne People and Subiects at home, were Blessed with the Fruites of her* Halcyon *Dayes: whom the World admired for her eminent Vertues, her owne Subiects attended with their deuout prayers, and God assisted with his Heauenly blessings, preseruing her euen to Miracle against all open Practises and Hostilities of her enemies abroad, and priuy Conspiracies of Traterous subiects at Home, so often and so dangerously plotted, and attempted, that (as shee sayd her selfe in Parliament,) shee rather maruayled*

that shee was, then mused that shee should not be, were it not that Gods Holy hand protected her beyond expectations." *The Historie of the Life and Reigne of the most Renowmed and Victorious Princesse Elizabeth, Late Queene of England* (London, 1630), "To the Reader," sigs. Alv-A2, Blv.

42. The Spaniards' return was expected in the early 1590's, although there was alarming news in 1595-97 especially; e.g., Harrison, *Eliz. Journ.*, II, 39-40, 82, 94, 147-48, 219, 221, etc.

43. See Bertrand Evans, "The Brevity of Friar Lawrence," *PMLA, LXV* (1950), 841-65.

44. In Act I, scene v, for example, seventeen lines of bustling comedy (except for Potpan) lead into a jovial, crowded stage; some thirty lines of a gallant love are interrupted by some thirty-nine of anger; and the entire process closes in a double ending, one for Romeo (ll. 113-29) and one for Juliet (ll. 130-46). Yet all is so integrated into the progress of the play (e.g., the wooing that surrounds anger and thus results in a paradoxical outburst of lyric quietness) that what might be only precision becomes dramatically convincing. Note, too, the repetition of servant comedy (I, i and I, v; I, iii and I, v); the two processes in the scene of Romeo's being controlled by the friar (III, iii, 1-78, 78-175) and in Juliet's being "controlled" by Lord and Lady Capulet (III, v, 65-126, 127-96); Mercutio's first and second scenes with their comparable sequels (I, iv, I, v, and II, i, II, ii); the two balcony scenes (II, ii; III, v 43-64); Romeo's premonitions (I, iv, 106-13; V, i, 1-11); the threatened suicides (III, iii, 107-108; IV, i, 50 ff.); the bustle of the ball and of the planned marriage (I, v, 1-42; IV, iv) etc. See also R. A. Law, "Shakespeare's Changes of his Source Material in *Romeo and Juliet,*" Univ. of Texas *Studies in English,* 1929, pp. 95-96.

Consistently a rapid movement of events is emphasized, especially from noon Monday to early Wednesday (e.g., II, iv, 200; v, 1-11; III, i, 1-4; IV, i, 90; IV, ii, 35-47). The friar's "two and forty hours" is then terminated in Act V, i.e., in the night of Thursday-Friday. Nearly every critic notes this variation from Shakespeare's source, a variation that agrees with the weight given to an adverse fate.

45. See Franklin M. Dickey, *Not Wisely But Too Well: Shakespeare's Love Tragedies* (San Marino, Cal., 1957). Note also some of the information given by Robert P. Miller, "The Myth of Mar's Hot Minion in *Venus and Adonis,*" *ELH,* XXVI (1959), 470-81. One can not, of course, avoid the fact that Friar Lawrence censures Romeo's love and that critics frequently refer to him as a chorus for the love action comparable to Prince Escalus as a chorus for the feud. The constant conflict between youth and age in matters of romance does not explain adequately this feature of the drama. Youthful and witty Mercutio also criticizes Romeo's love. Although he does this in a manner greatly different from that of the friar, the lines of both characters are theatrically inescapable. Similar to what is noted frequently about Friar Lawrence's role is a dominant feature of Mercutio's. His association with revelry and masquing (I, iv), his constant wit and mockery, his magnificently bawdy attitude that "this drivelling love is like a great natural, that runs lolling up and down to hide his bauble in a hole" (II, iv, 95-97) undoubtedly would give his role overtones corresponding to those normally attributed to a disard of high degree, "Neither-Loving-nor-Loved." If other things were equal, or if Mercutio's role were taken out of the dramatic contexts of this play, it might well seem to provide mocking notes potentially chorus-like in nature. Certainly some of his lines, like the speech just quoted, would accord easily with a similar but serious attitude given Friar Lawrence (II, ii).

The attitudes of Friar Lawrence and Mercutio about romantic love were familiar to Elizabethans; for love might be conceived of as being a dangerous passion, the heat and haste of which should be controlled, or it might be considered effeminate and enervating. Equally pertinent is the fact that betrothal and marriage for Elizabethans was a family matter of both social and financial concern. In this respect, the youth of hero and heroine, emphasized when the play begins, could stress the consideration that they should not neglect "the authority and advice of parents." Granted that playwrigths might represent, in passing or in detail, the theme of the miseries of enforced marriage, and granted that an attitude sympathetic with the parents, rather than with the lovers, would be made hilariously ridiculous by the commenting citizens who are brought on stage in *The Knight of the Burning Pestle,* yet parental dominance was rooted in everyday fact. The author of Shakespeare's principle source was well aware of the way in which Romeo and Juliet might be criticized by "the wiser sort." In his preface, Brooke describes his hero and heroine as "unfortunate lovers," *"thralling* themselves to *unhonest desire, neglecting the authoritie and advice of parents and frendes,* conferring their principall counsels with dronken gossyppes and superstitious friers (the naturally fitte instrumentes of *unchastitie*) attemptyng all adventures of peryll for thattaynyng of *their wished lust . . .* abusyng the honorable name of lawefull mariage to *cloke the shame of stolne contractes,* finallye, by *all meanes of unhonest lyfe,* hastyng to most unhappye deathe." Bullough, *Narr. and Dram. Sources,* I, 284-85.

As indicated above, some of the lines in *R & J* may seem consistent with the preceding attitudes. Not only do Friar Lawrence's lines in his first dialogue with Romeo seem to reflect such a process of thought (e.g., II, iii, 65-84, 93-94), but a cry by Romeo himself (III, i, 118-20) agrees with Mercutio's attitude (I, iv, 42 [Q1 reading]; II, iv, 11-18, 92-97; III, i, 76). "Fearful" Romeo's grief at banishment (III, iii, 12-70), which is demonstrated in part by his attempt to stab himself (ll. 105 ff.), may also seem to correspond with such a point of view, one that allowed Sidney, for example, to develop some oratorically censorious speeches about a young hero's "inclination to love." This point of view Shakespeare also had expressed in Valentine's initial speeches to Proteus:

> And writers say, as the most forward bud
> Is eaten by the canker ere it blow,
> Even so by love the young and tender wit
> Is turn'd to folly, blasting in the bud,
> Losing his verdure even in the prime
> And all the fair effects of future hopes.
>
> (*2GV,* I, i, 45-50)

With Valentine, it will be remembered, even Proteus had concurred momentarily.

> Thou, Julia, thou hast metamorphos'd me,
> Made me neglect my studies, lose my time,
> War with good counsel, set the world at naught;
> Made wit with musing weak, heart sick with thought.
>
> (ll. 66-69)

As the following discussion indicates, however, such a combination of attitudes about love and marriage is not the whole story; and in the world of the theater, as in the wider world of nondramatic literature, it is a good deal less than half. Paul N. Siegel, e.g., notes how Shakespeare transforms the "frivolously inconsistent attitude toward passionate love of the other novelle adaptations into a complexly unified attitude." "In *Romeo and Juliet* the ideas of the religion of love and those of Christianity in part work together and in part pull in opposite directions, creating a tension which is relieved only with the transcendence of love at the very end." *"Romeo and Juliet* and the Literature of Romantic Love," Columbia Univ. Seminar in the Renaissance, Jan. 6, 1959, reported in *The Shakespeare Newsletter,* IX (1959), 19. With such a statement I certainly agree, although I de-emphasize the tension within this complex of romantic Christian love and note instead the way in which Shakespeare avoids any diametric opposition within his dominant emphasis.

46. As the subsequent discussion indicates, the speech is almost choric in its applicability to Romeo and Juliet:

> Ay me! for aught that I could ever read,
> Could ever hear by tale or history,
> The course of true love never did run smooth;
> But, either it was different in blood,
>
> . . . .
>
> Or else misgraffed in respect of years,
>
> . . . .
>
> Or else it stood upon the choice of friends,
>
> . . . .
>
> Or, if there were a sympathy in choice,
> War, death, or sickness did lay siege to it,
> Making it momentany as a sound,
> Swift as a shadow, short as any dream,
> Brief as the lightning in the collied night,
> That, in a spleen, unfolds both heaven and earth,
> And *ere a man hath power to say "Behold!"*
> *The jaws of darkness do devour it up:*
> *So quick bright things come to confusion*

(I, i, 132-49)

This is specially true for the italicized lines.

47. E.g., "Black and portentious must this humour prove / Unless good counsel may the cause remove" (ll. 147-48). Romeo is to himself "secret" and "close," and if Montague could "but learn from whence his sorrows grow," he would "as willingly give cure as know" (ll. 153-61).

48. Excluding, of course, the meanings associated with conscience (e.g., Hankins, *Shakespeare's Derived Imagery*, pp. 53-75).

49. That attitude, of course, was associated frequently with the eye-love psychology of the era. See, e.g., *Vives and the Renaissance Education of Women*, ed. Foster Watson (London, 1902), pp. 84-89, 94-102; or the famous passage about the difference between an old and a young lover in Hoby's translation of *The Courtier*, wherein the function of the eye and the spirits "that twinkle out" of it are noted. Although "it may be granted the Courtier, while he is young, to love sensuallye," when he is in "riper yeres," he should be "heedful that he beeguyle not him self, to be led willfullye into the wretchednesse, that in yonge men deserveth more to be pitied then blamed. . . . Therefore when an amiable countenance of a beautiful woman commeth in his sight . . . as soone as he is a ware that his eyes snatch that image and carie it to the hart, and that the soule beeginneth to beehoulde it with pleasure, and feeleth within her self the influence that stirreth her and by litle and litle setteth her in heate, and that those livelye spirites, that twinkle out throughe the eyes, put continually freshe nourishment to the fire: he ought in this beginninge to seeke a speedye remedye and to raise up reason, and with her, to fence the fortresse of his hart, and to shutt in such wise the passages against sense and appetites, that they maye entre neyther with force nor subtill practise" (pp. 352-53; Bk. IV). Benvolio's counsel is homeopathic.

50. This point is also made, though with a slightly different emphasis, by Leo Kirschbaum, *Character and Characterization in Shakespeare* (Detroit, 1962), pp. 111-18.

51. In this respect, Romeo's love is not discordant with the reasonableness of a *senex* restraining Tybalt, the angry, youthful advocate of the family feud.

52. Jonson's gloss on "From out of *Chaos*" reads as follows: "So is he [Love] faind by *Orpheus*, to haue appear'd first of all the *Gods*: awakened by *Clotho*: and is therefore call'd *Phanes*, both by him and *Lactantius*." Lilius Gregorius Gyraldus notes under "Cvpido" that "*Phanes* etiam dictus est Amor, quod ex Chao primus apparuerit, quod Orpheus et Lactantius ajunt," and under "Parcae" he notes that according to Fulgentius, "*Clotho enim Graece* evocatio *Latine dicitur. . . .*" *Opera*

Omnia (Lvgdvni Batavorum, 1696), cols. 409, B; 207, B (*De Deis Gentium,* XIII, VI). See also Starnes and Talbert, *Classical Myth,* pp. 357-58.

53. When Romeo first spoke of love, his use of *oxymoron* built upon the previous brawl so that love was a "brawling love," a "loving hate"; but it was also "anything, of nothing first create" (I, i, 182-83). Thus with a brief, but frank, acceptance of antitheses—but with no reflection of any academic differentiation between "nothing" and "chaos"—Shakespeare expresses a thought akin to the mythological commonplace just noted. Obviously such a phrase would be subordinate to the high comic process being developed; but as a straw in the wind, it implies an acceptance of the universal beneficence of love; thus, in its way, the detail is indicative of Shakespeare's basic, sympathetic attitude.

54. III, ii, 1-31.

55. The ending of the scene also makes the first speech of the friar's applicable to the feud; thereby that speech agrees likewise with the Prologue's line about extremities and with the later union of the lovers and their extremities. By specifying the merged opposites of life, by noting the opposed "kings" in man—grace and "rude will"—and by pointing out that "where the worser is predominate, / Full soon the canker death eats up that plant" (ll. 27-30), the speech is choric for the entire drama as it destroys what would turn the "households' rancour to pure love." See also the following discussion of Romeo's desperate scene, wherein "rude will" is conquered, and of Juliet's comparable scene.

56. I.e., II, iv, 35-37.

57. Above, pp. 215, 280 n. 30; below, p. 295 n. 60; as well as R. Soellner, "Shakespeare and the 'Consolatio,'" *N & Q,* CXCIX (1954), 108-09. Soellner points out the reflection here of a consolation by Erasmus.

58. Note especially the first line, "Wilt thou be gone? it is not yet near day." Here *aube* is meant to refer to any "dawn-song"; cf. German *tageliet,* Provençal *alba,* French *aube* or *aubade.*

59. In passing, it is also interesting to note that the action at night throughout the play and the "hot" day of the feud are also contraries. In the night scenes, however, the conventional beneficence of light has been joined with the beauty of the nocturnal lovers.

60. See above pp. 192, 89 n. 57. For the relationship between fortitude and despair, wanhope, and "mischief," see *Magnyfycence* and the passages cited by Coogan, *Interpretation of 'Mankind',* pp. 59-71, as well as *Mundus et Infans,* ll. 804-10, 854-61 (*Specimens of the Pre-Shaksperean Drama,* ed. John Matthews Manly [Boston, 1897], I, 380, 381); *Mankind,* ll. 298-99, 792 ff.; *Magnyfycence,* ll. 150-54, 2130-34, 2284-2324, etc. Note also, e.g., the contrast between magnanimity (which entails choosing the hard life) and the evil that can result from sloth, when the devil or his agents put one "in wanhope and purchaseþ his deeþ and sleeþ hym...." *The Book of the Vices and Virtues,* ed. W. Nelson Francis, E.E.T.S. 217, pp. 29, 164-66. Cf. Romeo's line, "Well, Juliet, I will lie with thee to-night. / Let's see for means. O mischief, thou art swift / To enter in the thoughts of desperate men" (V, i, 34-36). Also interesting in this respect is the possible reflection of the Mercy-Priest relationship, discussed by Sister Coogan.

61. The fearsome and macabre development is also kept alive after Juliet's scenes by, e.g., the description and appearance of the apothecary (V, i, 37-86), wherein it is interesting to note how any spirit of censure and of admonition is turned toward gold, the "worse poison to men's souls" (ll. 80-82).

62. Romeo's lyrical delay after the death of Paris may have aroused another emotion that we who always have been aware of the tragic ending are liable to forget. The story of Romeo and Juliet was well known, and its tragic ending, foretold by the Prologue, is by this time artistically irrevocable; yet even as Romeo kisses Juliet, an audience accustomed to a lesser art, which could be exceedingly melodramatic, may have had their emotions stretched further by a feeling that at any moment the operation of an adverse fate might be stopped. The appearance of the watch could cause an entanglement, and Friar Lawrence has left

for the tomb with a complete and saving explanation; whereas the words of the Prologue are some two hours away. One wonders if Peter's last scene (IV, v, 96-150) should be mentioned in this respect, rather than being dismissed simply as a bow to the taste of the "vulgar." Even for a courtly audience, Richard Edwards had introduced a comic interlude, with beatings and the folk figure of Grim the Collier, to precede the final suspense of the fortunate ending of *Damon and Pithias* (ll. 909-1374). Since this conclusion is that of a "tragical comedy," so the interlude is a good deal longer than that given to Peter, whose lines, nevertheless, might have been conceived of as contributing to a hope for a fortunate ending. Although the opening of the next scene (V, i, 1-11) contributes to a tragic irony, it shows an exuberance that is momentarily compatible with the dominant emphasis of the first portion of the drama.

63. E.g., above, p. 285 n. 43.

64. II, i.

65. Baskervill, *Eliz. Jig,* pp. 326-30 and *passim.*

66. E.g., Doran, *Endeavors of Art,* pp. 78, 158, 220-21.

67. E.g., I, v, 32-42; I, ii, 1-13; I, iii, 14, 69-73.

68. See above, pp. 62 n. 2, 279 n. 28, 286 n. 45; and, e.g., Primaudaye, *French Academie,* pp. 455, 409-10.

69. That tragic poets constantly represent the irony of fate working through individuals who unwittingly bring about their own greatest sorrow is so much of a comonplace that it almost precludes glossing. For a drama close to Shakespeare's, however, see Marlowe's *Dido, Queen of Carthage* (published, 1594). Therein Iarbus, for example, promises the Trojans protection, brings them to Dido (I, ii), and supplies Æneas with the means to leave Carthage (V, i, 71-74). His actions thereby lead to the death of the queen he loves.

70. See, e.g., Jonson's words, even though he is writing about a comedy: "Stay, and see his last *Act,* his *Catastrophe,* how hee will perplexe that, or spring some fresh cheat, to entertaine the *Spectators,* with a convenient delight, till some unexpected, and new encounter breake out to rectifie all, and make good the *Conclusion." Ben Jonson,* VI, 578.

71. At least three traditions confronted the sixteenth-century historian of Richard's reign. In general, fifteenth-century Lancastrian chroniclers represented Richard as an incompetent ruler, sometimes even a tyrant, indulging in corrupt rule for personal advantage. Bolingbroke they represented as a just nobleman, the publicly acknowledged heir of Richard, the savior of England, and sometimes the beneficent child of Destiny. Yorkist chroniclers were, in general, more interested in blackening Henry than in exculpating Richard. As a consequence, although they may portray Richard as the victim of an unscrupulous politician, they tacitly admit the corruption of Richard's government. French chroniclers especially looked upon Richard as a martyr king and upon Bolingbroke as a shrewd politician. For details, see Richard Jerome Geehern, "Fifteenth and Early Sixteenth Century Interpretations of the Character and Career of King Henry IV" (Ph.D. diss., Univ. of N.C., 1952); Louisa DeSausurre Duls, "The Complex Picture of Richard II Inherited by Sixteenth-Century Writers from Fourteenth- and Fifteenth-Century Chronicle Sources" (Ph.D. diss., Univ. of N.C., 1962). In the following pages, I use "Lancastrian" to indicate attitudes favorable to Henry. "Yorkist" indicates attitudes unfavorable to Henry; "Richardian," attitudes compatible with the concept of Richard the martyr king. For the usefulness of this terminology and for a detailed analysis of the scene at Flint Castle and of Richard's deposition, see Talbert, *Problem of Order,* pp. 158-200.

72. Above, pp. 67-68, 95 ff. A point of view that I believe questionable in some respects, but that need not be incompatible with what is written here, is expressed by Brooke, *Shakespeare Survey,* XIV (1961), 40-41.

73. That is, as Richard's lines reflect both a simplified scale of being with its corresponding planes (e.g., I, i, 174) and the fact of regal birth (e.g., l. 196); see also l. 118.

74. For Shakespeare's familiarity with *Woodstock,* see *The Life and Death of King Richard the Second,* ed. Matthew W. Black, New Variorum Edition (Philadelphia, 1955), pp. 473-77 (especially Rossiter); see also Brereton, *Writings on Eliz. Drama,* pp. 100-1.

75. Smith believes it unfortunate that judgement by battle, never favored by the Pope and the clergy, is "at this present not much used," though it has never been abolished. *De Rep. Angl.,* pp. 64-65, 113-14.

76. E.g., above, p. 68 n. 18.

77. Jorgensen, *Shakespeare's Military World,* pp. 176-97.

78. Kirschbaum makes the point that even the development of the first scene in the drama has overtones unfavorable for Richard. *Character and Characterization,* pp. 139-43. See, e.g., I, i, 158-59 (Richard's alignment with Mowbray).

79. As part of this development, and from faint beginnings in a speech by Richard, Shakespeare has moved the appeal of stage patriotism to these Lancastrian figures; thus Richard's concern that his "kingdom's earth shall not be soil'd" with the "dear blood" that it "hath fostered" nor her "civil wounds" "plough'd up with neighbour's sword" (I, iii, 125-38) emerges with the naïve force of Hereford's lines just quoted.

80. This description of Bolingbroke is discussed in some detail below, pp. 315-16.

81. Talbert, *Problem of Order,* e.g., pp. 14-15, 16, 22-23, 28, 84-85, 87.

82. Only if the lapse of narrative time (I, iv, 2) accorded with an actual interval of stage time would the appreciableness of this disjunction be diminished; and of such an interval in performance between Act I, scene iii, and Act I, scene iv, there is no indication.

83. For a fuller discussion of this aspect of the deposition scene, see Talbert, *Problem of Order,* pp. 182-94. It is also pertinent to note that this technique of placing Richard in disjunction with a dominant context is anticipated as far back as the first scene in the drama. When trial by combat is viewed in the light of those emotional concepts that could give it validity, Richard's limitation of that great hazard to phlebotomy (I, i, 152-59) corresponds with what is elaborated and intensified as the first act ends and Shakespeare moves into his focal point of anti-Richardian emotions.

84. In addition to what has been noted in these pages, see, e.g., Smith's statement that no commonwealth exists when a large number of people are living relatively permanently under the rule of one person but living as bondmen. The ruler of such a community is "to be accompted onely as one that hath under him an infinite number of slaves or bondmen among whom there is no right, law, or common wealth compact, but onely the will of the Lorde and seignior." The ancient Greeks would not consider such a society to be any type of public rule or "policy." *De Rep. Angl.,* pp. 20-21. Moreover, a violation of magnificence or fortitude in prosperity might be represented by an acceptance of surface values and by a reliance upon flattery. This concept is dramatized clearly in Skelton's *Magnyfycence,* ll. 637-88, 710-44, 1629-1802. For some of the other aspects of Gaunt's speech, see Kenneth Muir, "Shakespeare among the Commonplaces," *RES,* X (1959), 283-86.

85. *Aristotles Politiqves,* pp. 24-30, 57-58.

86. Talbert, *Problem of Order,* p. 214 n. 93.

87. Although they are used in a context emphasizing primogeniture, the words about Time's charters and his customary rights, since they are connected with matters of property, also remind one of the Commons' concern for their "charters" and "customary rights" and their power over men's estates—matter that must have been known to the London populace at least. As the 1590's progressed, such emotions showed themselves increasingly in a concern for the economic welfare of England; e.g., Neale, *Eliz. & Parl., 1584-1601,* pp. 325-94. The congruence between this speech, consequently, and later lines about Richard's having lost the hearts of the commons may have been strikingly firm.

88. In addition, because of York's lines about Richard's interest only in

vanities, Richard's Irish war would brush elbows with Renaissance concepts about
a true and a false magnificence.

89. Neale, *Eliz. & Parl., 1584-1601,* p. 168. See also, e.g., the 1522 pageant
representing the "Ile of englonde," Robert Withington, *English Pageantry,*
(Cambridge, Mass., 1918), I, 177; *KJ,* II, i, 23-29; Muir, *RES,* X, 286-88. In this
respect, one should also note how the progress of the play to Act II, scene i, would
be substantiated further by the fact that the first line in the play is addressed to
Gaunt and that he is on stage almost continuously. He is absent only during six
lines of an introductory dialogue (I, iii, 1-6) and during a scene of sixty-five lines,
in which the last eleven are devoted to him (I, iv). The way in which his portrayal
would accord with concepts of a good subaltern ruler is obvious, even in some of
its details. Thus, e.g., to educated Elizabethans, his courtly punning (II, i, 72-83)
may have seemed to agree with the doctrine of "words of silk," even though they
introduce vigorous censure that understandably violates the precept *laudendo
præcipere.*

90. The neatness of this last scene and its relationship to the immediate development of the play is worth considering. Censure of Richard is at first absent when
the queen speaks of her sorrow in being separated from her husband and when
Bushy would console her (ll. 1-40). But after the queen's grief has increased with
mention of Bolingbroke and of the flight of powerful lords from Richard, criticism
of a ruler who has lost the hearts of both nobles and commons appears again (ll.
84-85, 88-89). To it is added Richard's guilty connection with the murder of
Gloucester (l. 102). Quite understandably, then, an audience already has been
reminded of Woodstock's duchess (ll. 90-97), the report of whose death adds an
additional woe to the scene. In addition, by bringing Bushy, Bagot, and Green on
the stage and by dramatizing their desertion of York (ll. 123-48), Shakespeare
not only returns to an earlier criticism of Richard but also substantiates choric
lines within the scene. In this last respect, one is struck by the way in which
Shakespeare ironically utilizes the tradition embodied in such a chapter heading as
"How to Tell a Flatterer from a Friend":

> Now comes the sick hour that his [Richard's] surfeit made;
> Now shall he try his friends that flattered him.
>
> (ll. 84-85)

In this manner, the scene looks forward to the capture and execution of two of
the "caterpillars" (II, iii, 163-67; III, i); and in this manner, the appropriateness
of that vehicle is substantiated. Such a development, of course, builds upon York's
and Gaunt's earlier references to Richard's flatterers and stretches back to one of
Richard's earliest speeches (I, i, 25). Moreover, when the queen refers to flattery
in censuring all who would console her (ll. 67-72), there is an anticipation of the
intensified recurrence of that thought at the close of the scene in which Richard
next appears (III, ii, 215-16).

The total effect of references to Bolingbroke in Act II, scene ii, also anticipates
the "neuter" position that York will take at first; and by alternating Lancastrian
and Yorkist emphases in those references, Shakespeare also anticipates his
technique in the scene at Flint Castle. With the appearance of Green, mention of
Hereford varies from the way in which he had been referred to in the immediately preceding scene. Then he was the restorer of England's "high majesty."
Now he is "banished Bolingbroke," repealing himself "with uplifted arms" (ll.
49-51). Immediately thereafter, he is a leader of "traitors." Finally, in accordance
with the sorrowful anticipations of this scene, he is the "dismal heir" of the queen's
sorrow (l. 63). This relatively neutral vehicle precedes a return to criticism of
Richard, which is followed by the representative dilemma of York and the flight
of the favorites.

91. Above, p. 301 n. 71.

92. The quotations refer to Sidney's Basilius. Applicable to Richard also,

especially as regards the state in which he left England under York, would be the concept expressed by Sidney when he wrote that Euarchus was "none of them who thinke all things done, for which they have once geven direction. . . ." *Works*, II, 150.

93. Talbert, *Problem of Order*, pp. 3-20.

94. Above, pp. 89 n. 57, 192, 295 n. 60. Although the ideas that Michael Quinn considers are not always those emphasized in the present discussion, see " 'The King is not Himself': The Personal Tragedy of Richard II," *SP*, LVI (1959), 169-86. The relationship between patience, a concept that Quinn emphasizes, and fortitude is obvious, for patience and perseverance were two attributes conventionally associated with fortitude in adversity.

95. These lines about Richard, which are spoken by Northumberland, can be glossed, e.g., by passages from Peter de la Primaudaye's *French Academie*, pp. 455, 409-10. Inasmuch as they occur in the second book, they had been available in English translation since 1594. The affections or passions of the soul, of which sorrow is one, are said to arise from the soul's irascible power and to draw with them attendant perturbations, grounded not on reason but following the unreliable dictates of "Fantasie," which is "a sodaine and tumultuous judgement." As a result, man's soul might be filled "with endlesse trouble and disquietnes"; for "fancie beeing very turbulent and skittish" draws "to it selfe confusedly some shew and apparence of opinion and judgement, whereby it deemeth that which is offered vnto it to be either good or bad," but "deemeth" incorrectly or un-substantially. It is the cause "that we liue in the middest of maruelious troubles in respect of our affections of feare, of desire, of sorrow, of ioye, and that one while we weepe, and sodainly wee laugh againe."

96. Cited by Kocher, *MLQ*, VIII, 311; from *An Excellent Discourse upon the now present estate of France* (London, 1592).

97. For the probable source of these lines, see *R II*, Variorum Ed., pp. 87, 91. Everard Guilpin's *Skialetheia* ("Satira Prima," ll. 57-70) certainly indicates that the educated might recognize the potentially Machiavellian nature of such a person. In the light of Guilpin's lines, one probably should read the poem cited by Brereton in his identification of Bolingbroke and Essex, although the anony-mous author may have had his eye also upon these lines by Shakespeare. *Writings on Eliz. Drama*, pp. 102-4. See, nevertheless, Talbert, *Problem of Order*, pp. 128-29, as well as the dramatic context of this passage, above, pp. 305-7.

98. *Works*, I, 187.

99. Talbert, *Problem of Order*, pp. 15, 84.

100. Above, pp. 114-15.

101. For the cheerfulness in this approach to battle, even though it is restrained, see the immediately preceding note.

102. I.e., *Philotas;* for which, see Talbert, *Problem of Order*, pp. 130-44.

103. Talbert, *Problem of Order*, pp. 40-41.

104. This is usually noted, e.g., by critics writing about *Measure for Measure* or *The Merchant of Venice*. See also the ending of *The Comedy of Errors*.

105. V, v, 1-66. Although the length of some of Richard's lyrical speeches may give them the effect of soliloquies, they are represented as being heard by others (e.g., III, ii, 27, 33, 82, 178; iii, 170-71).

106. The phrase was used by William Witherle Lawrence, *Shakespeare's Problem Comedies* (New York, 1931). In his portrayal of York's dilemma, Shakespeare also develops what can not be found in the portrayal of Woodstock (above, p. 125 n. 116). For a different interpretation of this ambiguity, see Max Lüthi, *Shakespeares Dramen* (Berlin, 1957), pp. 327-36. The author is concerned with the concept of Shakespeare, the "great Baroque artist."

107. In this respect it is interesting to note a passage from Hooker, which is related to his concept of necessity: "But such is the lot of all that deal in Publick Affairs, whether of Church or Commonwealth, that which men list to surmise of their doings, be it good or evil, they must beforehand, patiently arm their minds

to endure. Wherefore to let go private surmises, whereby the thing it self is not made, either better or worse; if just and allowable Reasons might lead them to do as they did, then are all censures frustrate." *The Works of That Learned and Judicious Divine Mr. Richard Hooker, in Eight Books of Ecclesiastical Polity* (London, 1676), p. 183 (IV. xiv). Such a consideration might seem valid for this reported or implied world of *R II,* including even Northumberland's mention of "policy" (V, i, 84). See also Richard's line, "I am sworn brother, sweet, / To grim Necessity; and he and I / Will keep a league till death" (V, ii, 20-22).

108. As I have noted elsewhere, in *1 H IV,* III, ii, a false identification of Hal and Richard and a false accusation that Hal is likely to be subservient to Hotspur lead to the vigorous denial that Henry desires, that the audience expects, and that specifies the form of Hal's reformation, as well as the nature of the catastrophe. In other words, even when a Yorkist statement of an ambitious "humility" is given to Henry, it is qualified by his attempt to force Hal to speak out and by the impetus of the drama. In *2 H IV,* when a tormented cry for forgiveness is given Henry, it is followed immediately by Hal's acceptance of a "plain and right" succession (IV, v, 90-225).

109. *1 H IV,* I, i, 1-27.

110. *2 H IV,* III, i. When Henry V appears on the eve of Agincourt, however, Shakespeare unequivocally emphasizes the perpetual watch of the good ruler and his Christian religion. This is apparent in incident, in Henry V's conversation with others, and in his soliloquies (*H V,* IV, i). One might expect this; for the embodiment in Henry V of kingly requisites that Shakespeare otherwise has separated in his histories agrees with the pageantic funeral that had inaugurated the earlier history plays. In the light of such a meaningful progression, one is reminded again of Hooker's words, though one need not refer to the necessity about which he is writing: "If we leave Nature, and look into Art, the Work-man hath in his Heart a Purpose, he carrieth in mind the whole Form which his Work should have; there wanteth him not Skill and Desire to bring his labour to the best effect. . . ." *Laws,* p. 198 (V, ix).

Index

This index cites the first reference to a work by a modern writer or editor; there the details of the publication may be found. A play or a nondramatic work is listed under the name of its author, when known.